BOOKS BY
JACQUES BARZUN

THE FRENCH RACE

RACE: A STUDY IN MODERN SUPERSTITION

OF HUMAN FREEDOM

DARWIN, MARX, WAGNER

ROMANTICISM AND THE MODERN EGO

TEACHER IN AMERICA

BERLIOZ AND THE ROMANTIC CENTURY

BERLIOZ

and the

Romantic Century

VOLUME II

Berlioz in 1867

". . . gazing with weariness, with compassion,
with dignity, on the alien world.

— RALPH WOOD

BERLIOZ
and the
Romantic Century

JACQUES BARZUN

VOLUME TWO

AN ATLANTIC MONTHLY PRESS BOOK
LITTLE, BROWN AND COMPANY · BOSTON
1950

For permission to quote from Laurence McKinney's *People of Note,* the
author acknowledges obligation to E. P. Dutton and Co., Inc. Copyright, 1940,
Laurence McKinney; from B. H. Haggin's *Music in the Nation,* to William
Sloane Associates, Inc.; from Matthew Josephson's *Victor Hugo* to the
Doubleday Company; from Nicolas Slonimsky's *Music Since 1900,* Frederick
Dorian's *History of Music in Performance, The Musorgsky Reader,* and from
Harold Bauer: His Book to W. W. Norton; from Paul Rosenfeld's *Musical
Portraits* to Harcourt, Brace and Company; from Thomas Craven's *Men of
Art* to Simon and Schuster, Inc.; from Cecil Gray's *History of Music* and
André Gide's *Journal* to Alfred A. Knopf; and from John Rewald's *History
of Impressionism* to the Museum of Modern Art.

For supplying certain of the illustrations, the author is indebted to Miss
Ruth Forbes, Mr. Bernard Van Dieren, Jr., Mr. Cecil Hopkinson, the Joseph
Muller Collection of the New York Public Library, the Culver Service
Collection, J. M. Dent and Sons, and the Theodore Presser Company, pub-
lishers of *The Etude.*

ATLANTIC–LITTLE, BROWN BOOKS
ARE PUBLISHED BY
LITTLE, BROWN AND COMPANY
IN ASSOCIATION WITH
THE ATLANTIC MONTHLY PRESS

*Published simultaneously
in Canada by McClelland and Stewart Limited*

PRINTED IN THE UNITED STATES OF AMERICA

Contents

Illustrations

INTERCHAPTER

20. Memoirs of Art and Life

> Let Berlioz, like Cellini, give us some day the faithful story of the vicissitudes in his life, and we shall be painfully surprised to see how such a great intellect and such a noble heart aroused in others so many low passions. We shall not want to believe that instead of sympathy, help, or at least impartiality, he encountered among many of his kind only opposition, injustice or dull indifference.
>
> — LISZT

THE YEARS during which Berlioz, feeling equally uprooted whether abroad or at home, produced *Tristia* and the *Te Deum,* were also the years in which he composed the bulk of his *Memoirs.* Begun in London, as we saw, in 1848, the rough draft lacked only three chapters and a Postscript by the time of Berlioz' second visit in 1851. By 1855 he considered the work finished and, at Liszt's instigation, thought of having a translation into German privately made.[1] It is therefore appropriate as well as convenient to discuss the text as if completed at this point, and to take the opportunity of summarizing the character of the author as we see him in this self-portrait and elsewhere.

The word "composed" and the conception of the *Memoirs* as a work terminable halfway through life accurately describe this unique document which, like Berlioz' other productions, grew by accretion and revision and fulfilled a long-matured purpose intimately connected with his conception of the artist.

The Preface speaks in the usual way of correcting prevalent biographical errors and of friendly urgings that Berlioz should fill out the personal sketches included in his *Voyage Musical* of 1844. But the statement of the main purpose is sandwiched between these two: "This backward glance will further enable me to supply some exact notions of the difficulties which in our time beset the career of a composer and to offer my col-

---

[1] *207,* II, 21. The project was given up a month later. (*Ibid.,* 24-5.)

leagues some useful information." [2] Berlioz specifically disavows the purpose of writing confessions. "I shall say only what I choose to say." [3] Given his purpose, this was to consist chiefly of "what, in the course of my arduous and eventful life, will seem to me likely to interest the friends of art." [4]

The materials he had at hand were abundant: first, the long descriptive "letters," nominally addressed to friends and colleagues, which he had sent back to the *Débats* from his two trips through Central Europe; then the account of his trip to Russia, which that newspaper had not managed to print before the 1848 revolution broke out. Together these make up somewhat less than half the *Memoirs*. Still of musical import, but closer in style to the travelogue, are the chapters on Berlioz' Italian journey, now recast from their two previous appearances in 1835 and 1844. When this is added up, with the Postscript — also on musical matters — thrown in, the *Memoirs* appear in their true proportions — that is, as a didactic work more than half given over to objective matters of musical fact, organization, and technical opinion. [5]

And yet, by the effect of varied tone and narrative pace, the whole has most often been read purely as a personal story, as autobiography, though the tale is neither complete nor continuous. Berlioz was probably not aware of the fact, but he fashioned the account of his life out of recurring themes and representative moments, much like one of his dramatic symphonies. The first twelve chapters may be considered the thematic catalogue, which includes as chief subjects his devotion to music and to his father, his passion for Estelle and for Virgil, his love of travel and of nature. In this delightful "first movement," moreover, the pattern which his artistic life developed is set before us: Berlioz creates music spontaneously and easily, though in the teeth of outward difficulty — local indifference and parental opposition at first, later academic, financial, and social obstacles. The next section — chapters thirteen to twenty — recount his mature awakening to love and literature (Shakespeare and Goethe; Harriet and Camille) at the same time as Weber and Beethoven enlarge his musical horizons beyond Gluck.

We are then ready for the Italian journey, which strengthens his musical convictions and stiffens his character: Berlioz is now full fledged as man

[2] *Mem.*, I, i.
[3] *Mem.*, I, ii.
[4] *Mem.*, I, i.
[5] In Adam Carse's volumes on the history of the orchestra — the latest being dated 1948 — one may see how this portion of the *Memoirs* continues to have scholarly value; it is in fact a primary source unique in scope and authority.

and artist. Seven more chapters record Berlioz' individual output amid the artistic flowering of the 1830's. Berlioz is married and producing, in both senses, the first six of his great scores. Under the pressure of personal and practical discomfiture at home, the idea of the mission abroad now comes to a head. A very brief transition indicates the change in his marital condition, telescoping the two painful years which it actually occupied. At this, the mid-point of the *Memoirs*, Berlioz closes the first, formative half of his life by summarizing ahead of time the significance of the German venture: "Though it was an arduous exploration, it was at least musical . . . and I enjoyed the privilege of living in a sympathetic atmosphere, out of reach of the intrigues, meanness, and platitudes of Paris." [6]

The three hundred pages that follow take us — with an occasional interweaving of comments later in date than the narrated facts — to the end of 1848. These comments are all of that very year, and so is the account of Dr. Berlioz' death and of Hector's revisiting the mountain haunts where he first saw Estelle. In other words, the fifty-eighth chapter is the true end of the drama, which closes — like a musical work — with a recapitulation of the principal themes. The rest is a kind of epilogue as in a folk tale, giving cursory news of what happened to the chief characters and enunciating the moral of the pilgrim's progress.

Berlioz knew he had truly finished at the point just indicated, for he begins the final portion with these words: "I am eager to have done with these *Memoirs* . . . when I have written the few more pages I mean to write, I shall have said enough, I hope, to give a nearly complete idea of the main events of my life, and of the cycle of feeling, work, and grief within which I am destined to turn until — until I no longer turn at all. The road still before me, however long it may be imagined, must surely resemble that which I have already traveled." [7]

There can be no question, then, that Berlioz adapted to the composition of his *Memoirs* his characteristic method of sampling and condensation. He never set his hand to any material without giving it artistic form, visible in both the detail and the structure, and this form was always a species of drama.[8] This explains why so many other artists have found these *Memoirs* speaking to them more directly and powerfully than any comparable work; it explains also why historians whose bent and business are more literal have been correspondingly disconcerted. They take the work as

---

[6] *Mem.*, I, 359.

[7] *Mem.*, II, 332.

[8] He says in 1865: "I have ever since then [1848] constantly revised the style and the narrative movement." (*Est.*, 12.)

they would a diplomat's day-to-day record and find it inaccurate and incomplete. They judge by tenable standards indeed, but which happen not to apply. Like Berlioz' music, his *Memoirs* do not unfold their fullness and justness immediately, nor ever to the casual or unimaginative observer; but whoever delves deeper than the outward "story" finds both truth and wisdom. "The *Memoirs*," wrote Henley in a milieu that largely agreed with him,[9] "are invaluable as a personal record of the works and ways of musicians in the Paris of the Romantic revival. Berlioz is revealed in them for one of the race of giants." And regarding Berlioz' conception of autobiography, he adds: "One feels that for one thing he was too complete an artist to be merely literal and exact; that for another he saw and felt things for himself, as Milton did before him . . . ; and for a third that from his own point of view he was right, and there is an end of it." [10]

More recently, Mr. W. H. Auden has remarked that he places this autobiography in the same class with Rousseau's and Saint Augustine's. As for the numerous musicians who have been inspirited by reading Berlioz' odyssey, they range from Debussy to Peter Warlock, and their views may be summed up in the statement made by the late Ernest Schelling that many times in his student days it was the recollection of Berlioz' struggle with adversity that kept him going.[11] The writer's chief purpose, one concludes, has been fully accomplished.

Still, the objection of critics who read the book for historical detail must not be dismissed without a hearing, however tedious for the convinced admirers. Time was when under the double assault of Messrs. Hippeau and Boschot Berlioz was made out to be a sort of congenital liar.[12] Nowadays, the prevalent opinion is that Berlioz is truthful but that his account of the truth is "exaggerated." [13] It is generously implied that Berlioz being

[9] *E.g.*, Wilde's appreciation of Berlioz as self-revealer (*1137*, 92) and Shaw's friendship for Henley based on a "common liking for the work of Mozart and Berlioz." (*1207*, 88.)

[10] *679*, 127 and 129.

[11] Mr. Auden's remark was made to me in 1947; Debussy's and Warlock's comments are in *975* and *958*; Ernest Schelling's was spoken whenever he played Berlioz at his Saturday morning concerts in Carnegie Hall. The hostile Richard Aldrich acknowledged in 1928 that Berlioz' *Memoirs* have been "for a couple of generations . . . a source of edification, entertainment, and knowledge." (*316*.)

[12] Francis Thompson seems to have been deceived by this charge, which he reiterated with the addition of a most uncharitable religious animus. (*688*, 23.)

[13] *E.g.*, Mr. John Burk in *1294*, *passim*.

of "the wild, romantic temperament" or of "the wild, artistic temperament," must not be subjected to the same standards as other writers. This principle is part true, part false. Berlioz must be judged exactly like everybody else insofar as he was doing the same kind of work or making the same claim to credence. He must be judged according to his own standard when he does something unique or when he uses the classical device of dramatizing incidents: his dialogues have just the same function and value as the speeches in Thucydides.

In any event, to judge the *Memoirs* by one's sense of probability is to commit the very fault imputed to the author. We shall later report an attested fact which, had Berlioz himself told it, would have been sure to make him suspect of invention and thus "confirmed" the disbelief commonly felt in the face of the unusual.[14] Where no verification is possible, the true critic must judge, not by his private notions of likelihood, but on the basis of Berlioz' character as revealed in his scores, his letters, and in his criticism of music, which for this purpose includes nearly four hundred pages of these very *Memoirs*. Now throughout this body of documents we find Berlioz a man of cool judgment, unswayed by vulgar prejudice; a writer who takes pains to ascertain the truth and has the skill to convey it; finally a moral being who eagerly records his obligations and gives intellectual credit regardless of personal likes and dislikes. The psychological likelihood is that such a man would be too proud to earn a cheap and transitory renown by misrepresentation.

What then have been the grounds for calling the *Memoirs* unreliable or even "exaggerated"? The commonest ground is the result of the critic's applying the measure of his own emotions to those of Berlioz and dismissing the overplus as verbalism: the critic cannot imagine anyone's feeling so passionate about Shakespeare; the critic is never moved so deeply nor so physically by music; nor has he experienced such amazing personal triumphs by comparable displays of genius and will — hence Berlioz exaggerates.[15] This, of course, may be a natural way of dealing with a document but it is not a critical way; if truth is our object we must enlarge our capacities to the scope of our subject's instead of securing our comfort

---

[14] See below, Chapter 28, *ad fin.*

[15] Shaw makes a parallel observation about Shakespeare's always seeming "hyperbolical . . . to people who cannot conceive so vividly as he. . . ." Berlioz' description of the effect of music upon him uses to excess the composer's knowledge of physiological changes during emotional stress. Shaw says: "Shakespeare conceived and expressed all his emotions with a vehemence that sometimes carried him into ludicrous extravagance." (*1125*, 123 and 124.)

by reducing his to ours. For the act of seeing life as the writer saw it is the aim of all addiction to literature as well as the special justification of the autobiographer.[16]

Even this is not enough. In order to be critical, we must decide in any one instance what it is we are dealing with, for Berlioz' spirit has wings and requires agility to follow: he modulates as swiftly in prose as in music. Thus the *Memoirs* contain a number of amusing but unimportant incidents which fall under the heading of "good stories." They are a kind of spice or leaven, and Berlioz set much less store on their significance than on their function. Aware of their fictional atmosphere, he himself warns us in a footnote to one of them that he has added an apocryphal detail; [17] and it may well be this excess of conscience on the narrator's part, combined with his pleasure in telling such stories on himself, that sows unworthy suspicions in readers accustomed to more solemn self-portraits.[18]

Finally, one must keep in mind the relativity of the observer's eye and the changing perspective of memory itself. To take an extreme case, Berlioz' childhood did not seem to his parents *nor to himself as a child* what he made it out to be in looking back from his London exile, in 1848. In a certain sense, then, Berlioz is not giving us the historical truth. But to say this is to misunderstand the nature of autobiography altogether. What we want from man observing himself is what he remembers, in the way he remembers it — not the census-taker's view of the outward facts.

As a corollary, it follows that the same childhood looks different to the same man at different times: this is part of the law of adaptation for conscious beings. So when Berlioz came to his Italian journey which was already in print, he recast, omitted or added small points — in short, worked upon the text like an artist to make it fit his present view of the case as well as the new context for which he intended it. When the biographer juxtaposes

---

[16] Unfortunately the only extensive treatment of the Autobiography as a genre is extremely shallow — incredibly so in its passing references to Berlioz. (*1060*, 279, 325, 393.) In the works of better critics one finds only casual insights into the form. The best of these, as regards Berlioz, are in the article by C. F. Kenyon (*681*).

[17] *Mem.*, I, 229 *n.* 2.

[18] It should be noted how often Berlioz disclaims an ability which he elsewhere gives evidence of possessing — for example, a knowledge of foreign tongues. Besides Latin, he was a fluent reader of Italian and English, and he spoke all three with various degrees of facility. He knew English well enough to point out errors to his translators (*127*) and though he said he did not feel poetical beauties in English as he did in the romance languages, his choice of quotations argues an accurate ear for verse, even in German (*95*, 104).

two or three of these versions he naturally finds discrepancies, but he is
naïve if he thinks that these imply fabrication or a careless view of truth.[19]
He should on the contrary be grateful that he has these various sources for
his imaginative reconstruction of a life.[20] In other words, it argues a deficient view of life coupled with a bigoted faith in the art of writing, to
suppose that words on paper transfix reality. They merely transcribe it
and, short of black-and-white inconsistency, more than one transcription
is true.

What the comparison of Berlioz' drafts shows is that as he grew older,
verbal exuberance gave way to more decisive summaries of what the past
had meant. Where he added, we have ample evidence that his memory was
excellent and behaved reliably except in regard to dates.[21] Again and
again the *Memoirs* relate events in words almost identical with those of a
letter written ten or fifteen years before, of which he had no copy: the
bearing of the fact had stamped itself on his mind once for all. But here
the critic is on the edge of another pitfall, if he erects letters into an in-
fallible test. It is by no means axiomatic that a letter is the best source of
fact because it is written hot upon the event. A letter is written *to* someone, and personal relations affect, not the writer's truthfulness, but his
emphasis. It is obvious that about the same concert Berlioz would write
differently to his father and to a confrere in journalism. Neither account
need disprove the other; nor does the omission of a detail at the time justify
the belief that it was subsequently invented. Saint Augustine's *Confessions*
do not tally with the facts he gave in certain little-known dialogues written earlier. Does this make him a liar? Gibbon gives two distinct accounts
of the moment when he was first inspired to write his great work. Does

[19] The coeditor of the German edition, Charles Malherbe, published in 1905
an early autobiographical sketch of Berlioz, which d'Ortigue had used for his
book. In comparing this with Berlioz' later *Memoirs* he finds one discrepancy
among others which he takes as a sign of the writer's whimsicality. It is the
statement that in youth Berlioz heard the quartets of Haydn: Berlioz later
changed this to "the quartets of Pleyel." An intelligent editor would have
pondered this instead of carping, and would have found that in the early 1800's
the quartets of Pleyel were often passed off as being Haydn's, the former
being the latter's pupil. Berlioz undoubtedly discovered the true authorship
and changed the name without any fuss. Thus it is that many details which
make Boschot call the *Memoirs* "*fantaisistes*" are in fact corrections unob-
trusively made. It is worth recalling that Boschot relied heavily on Malherbe,
whom he acknowledges as a virtual collaborator. (*267, 516.*)

[20] Dr. Johnson: "Thus it is that characters are written: we know somewhat
and imagine the rest. . . . It is ridiculous to oppose judgment to imagination."
(*Lives of the Poets: 1183*, I, 230.)

[21] His familiar letters show that he was often uncertain as to the day, month,
year and (once) century.

that mean somebody else is the author? He may well have had the idea twice and entirely failed to remember one occasion when he described the second. Memory is capricious and all utterance incomplete.

The biographer must therefore give up his favorite paper game which looks so scientific: "Since A says this on the authority of B, who could not have known it because X (as we learn from his diary) was still away, A must have invented the whole thing." Verbal triangulation of this sort is entertaining but almost always futile.[22] A hundred possibilities undercut the If-then argument; from a negative nothing positive can be inferred, and from discrepancies nothing but the complexity of things imperfectly known.[23]

This complexity is indeed one cause of the autobiographer's failure of memory. In a life as full of plans, concerts, people, journeys and occupations as his own, Berlioz inevitably confused a quantity of details.[24] As T. S. Wotton put it, if Berlioz' report were more exact it might justly be suspect as to the time of its composition, for the same reason that persons giving evidence at law are chargeable with collusion if they tell identical stories. The only deliberate confusion in the *Memoirs* is, as we noted, the one covering the years of Berlioz' break with his wife. He had warned the reader in the Preface — possibly with this passage in mind — that he would tell only what he chose, and he may have felt in addition that those years offered nothing "representative": the painful interlude would be a *longueur* equally painful to read. The one important musical fact of these years, namely his part in the revival of *Der Freischütz*, he intercalated between the two German trips. This would be a serious chronological misdeed only if the doings of an institution like the Paris Opera were not

[22] This is true even when official documents are involved. If we believed the papers signed by the kindly Horace Vernet as director of the Academy in Rome, we would suppose Berlioz had never left it. Similarly the dates on receipts for official payments often follow bureaucratic convenience rather than the calendar — whence the confused financial history of the *Requiem*. Our favorite phrase, "Off the record," shows how much faith we ought to place in the accuracy of the record.

[23] An excellent example relating to Berlioz is that offered by two studies of the original manuscript of the Rákóczy March and cognate documents (574 and 572). In one the author ascribes to Liszt's score the idea and much of the development of the Berlioz version; in the other it is shown, by a still wider survey, but most definitively by a look at the two pieces, that the compositions were wholly independent of each other.

[24] Winston Churchill has told how in going over documents he was astonished to find that the part he had taken in great events had left no trace on his memory. "One impression effaced another." (*The World Crisis: The Aftermath*, Preface.)

matters of public record, and if Berlioz did not constantly group events topically rather than by sequence of times.[25]

Finally, every autobiography needs interpreting with respect to local intent and the language of the period. Even a factual blunder may unconsciously make a sound point, as when that excellent historian Henry Adams complains that his education at Harvard, finished in 1858, gave him no inkling that Karl Marx existed or had written *Capital*.[26] Elsewhere Adams also misstates the facts about his first hearing Wagner. No autobiography is free from such blemishes. The point is not, How many such slips does it contain? but, Is the underlying meaning important and the intention true? By the same token, outmoded phraseology must be "translated" in order to keep the meaning intended. Both Berlioz and Mark Twain, for example, assert that they burnt manuscripts later found intact. Obviously, in an age of open fireplaces, "burn" means discard, put aside; and occasionally, as happened to Berlioz' *Rob Roy* overture, a real burning is defeated by a second copy in other hands.[27]

A critical view of Berlioz' *Memoirs* must consequently differ from the pseudocritical view which cross-examines the author as if he were testifying in a criminal case. The work of Boschot, the leading representative of that view, does not itself emerge very creditably from such an investigation, and yet his pretensions and his duty required just the kind of meticulous care he finds wanting in the *Memoirs*.[28] Judged by appropriate standards, Berlioz' autobiography is in fact thoroughly candid, sober, and truthful.[29] One major chronological inversion, two or three untestable anecdotes, and a number of small errors do not impair its fundamental reliability. Berlioz put himself in evidence to the best of his high introspective ability. It would have been strange indeed if the dramatist whose music

[25] Thus in the very next chapter he takes up his drudgery as reviewer and skips a space of six months in 1843–4, although it witnessed the appearance of his *Treatise*, of the *Voyage Musical* and of the *Roman Carnival* overture. His reticence was thus not always on personal grounds, but for concision.

[26] *369, 60:* Marx did not publish *Capital* until 1867 and remained obscure for more than a decade after that date, but we see what Adams means — that he received no modern teachings in political economy.

[27] Tovey, misled by Boschot on this point, rashly generalizes: "In Berlioz' vocabulary, 'burnt' means carefully preserved." (*590, 74.*) It is over such trifles as these that an artist's reputation for truthfulness — if not sincerity in his art — can be ruined.

[28] For an assessment of Boschot's own performance in reporting facts, see Supplement 2.

[29] Hanslick incidentally confirms the accuracy of Berlioz' report about young Germany's enthusiasm for his music: "Berlioz did not in any way exaggerate." (*351, 383.*)

shows such a genius for strong veracity had been unable to reveal himself in words with comparable force and precision.

It remains to see what kind of man he exhibits, and to supplement his sketch with others. For contrary to the usual belief, we should expect that a man's autobiography will show him to worse advantage than he really was. As Montaigne says: "All things considered, one never speaks of one-self without loss: one's self-accusations are always believed, one's self-praise disbelieved." [30] What Berlioz most vividly brought to light of his heart and soul was the passionate, impetuous, and daring element, not only because he knew the demonic to be intimately connected with artistic genius, but also because the active part of oneself is best adapted to por-trayal. A man cannot easily record his own patience and quiet sagacity: they must be inferred. In the same way, Berlioz set down instances of his extreme sensitiveness, impressionableness and susceptibility to despair, for those, too, are necessary ingredients of artistic ability. But it is clear that extreme sensitiveness and great impetuosity, besides being at loggerheads, would separately make a man ineffectual and unstable if both were not controlled by a strong will guided by a lucid mind. So that whereas the heedless peruser of the *Memoirs* is struck only by Berlioz' passion, or only by his attacks of spleen, or only by his headlong pace in action, the alert reader soon begins to notice rather the dynamic equilibrium that Berlioz achieves out of all these stresses and thrusts.

This was a truth about himself to which he could not do justice in writing because, reared in an age that admired the Napoleonic virtues, he did not think it necessary to show how they differed from a maniac's be-havior.[31] Besides, he had a proud dislike of explaining or justifying him-self.[32] Though the *Memoirs* may sound as if he held back very little, they really reveal the intimate depths only indirectly. What we see plain in the foreground is the artist and man of action, for by the time the book came into being Berlioz was a public figure whose personality and past history were already widely known — or misknown. On the one hand, journalism had for twenty years broadcast his "characteristics," and had dealt with his

[30] Book III, Ch. 8 (*1268*, IV, 32)

[31] But it is necessary now, when we prefer the artist silent, cool and cucum-brous, and mistake the former ideal: a British broadcast of 1935 allegedly based on the life of Berlioz was as completely mad as the French film of 1947. (H. W. Farren in *154; 250.*)

[32] Note his regret at having given his reasons for the structure of the *Damnation of Faust,* and the edge of impatience in his Preface to the second edition of *Romeo and Juliet.* (*Mem.,* II, 261 and *Min. Sc.*)

marriage to another public figure almost (but not quite) as Hollywood gossip deals with such things; [33] and on the other, he had long since learned to conceal his native shyness behind the façade — the mask which Nietzsche says every great spirit needs in order to breathe freely. By giving away the part of himself that had already been publicly seized on, and even perpetuating some of its legendary features, he could like Paganini live a private inner life known only to himself and his friends.

This intimate self is not difficult to know from the *Memoirs* if one first gives up the silly modern notion that character follows regular formulas in which certain human attributes are compatible and others not.[34] Berlioz had what Sainte-Beuve says is the definition of Distinction: "A certain natural pride or reserve mingled with simplicity." He was accordingly modest, naïve, naturally gay, outgoing, and full of spontaneous humor, at the same time as he was conscious of his superiority, shy, and inclined to pessimism. Different circumstances brought out in Berlioz one or another aspect of these traits, but there was no contradiction among them, however unusual the intensity of each. Take the humorous self-depreciatory tone with which the *Memoirs* open and which establishes what might be called the key of his egotism:

I was born on the 11th of December, 1803 at La Côte St. André, a very small town of France, situated . . . between Vienne, Grenoble, and Lyon. During the months preceding my birth my mother never dreamt, as Virgil's did, that she was about to bring forth a laurel branch. However painful to my self-esteem, I must also confess that she did not fancy either — like Alexander's mother Olympias — that she carried within her breast a fiery brand. Strange, I admit, but true. I saw the light of day quite simply, unheralded by any of the customary signs that usher in those destined for glory. Can it be that our age lacks poetry? [35]

No doubt a perfectly humble man would not raise, even ironically, the question of greatness. But Berlioz genuinely feels at once the simplicity of his birth, like the insignificance of his birthplace, and the premises of his greatness. He goes on to give a charming, unaffected account of his

[33] The Camille Moke episode, as involving another public person, was similarly public property before the appearance of the *Memoirs*. (*497, 306.*)

[34] See above Chapter 14. Either everyone is "a bundle of contradictions" or no one is: the phrase has no meaning unless one supposes an abstract cause behind a man's actions, which is then "contradicted" by other actions. But this only proves the observer to have made a false induction, and to have forgotten that all acts come from mixed motives. If a man *reasons* about his motives we may then attack his principles as contradictory, for he is attempting to generalize and perhaps doing as poor a job of it as the outsider.

[35] *Mem.*, I, 1.

family, the countryside, his teachers and his love of music; but in this
first paragraph he has forecast his stature and as it were established his
authority by intimating the species to which he belongs. For Berlioz sets
out to tell us what happens to artists and it is his *kind* that he speaks of
when he refers to Virgil, Gluck, Weber, or Shakespeare. So a statesman
might say that he is and has remained a man of the people.

Nor does Berlioz imply that the circle of the elect was closed after his
entry into the world: his book is full of grateful acknowledgments of
friendship, addressed to a host of composers, performers, patrons, and
amateurs of all the arts. It is indeed Berlioz' immense capacity for friendship, raised by him into a cult, which is the final proof of his genuineness.
He made friends readily and kept them long; which does not mean that
everyone found him equally lovable or accessible.[36] Within a week of
meeting the musician George Hainl, they were addressing each other by
their first names, and fifteen years later Berlioz was successfully helping
his friend become conductor at the Opera. But young Gounod, whom
Berlioz also aided and who deemed his elder a "noble, generous and loyal
character" [37] nevertheless always felt uncomfortable in his presence.[38] A
conversation that Gounod had with another of Berlioz' younger friends,
Saint-Saëns, throws light upon the point: " 'What elegance in Berlioz!'
said Gounod to me one day. The remark is profound. Berlioz' elegance
does not appear at first sight . . . it lies hidden in the web, one might
even say in the very flesh of his work; for it is latent in his prodigious
character . . . which is comparable to no other." [39]

Saint-Saëns goes on to speak of Gounod's superficial elegance concealing a more vulgar soul, in both music and life, and the contrast affords a
clue to the younger man's discomfort. There was something chilling and
unintentionally censuring in Berlioz' glance when he withheld his trust,
just as there was something scorching in his attack against abuses of faith
or intellectual principle. The *Memoirs* simply pursue and codify the daring candor of the *feuilletons*, which diplomacy rarely subdued. It was a
daring candor because Berlioz was too intelligent not to foresee the con-

---

[36] Ignaz Moscheles, who met Berlioz in 1839, was surprised to find him cold
and "not outgoing" (*978*, II, 40). Schumann also had expected "a more fiery
personality," though his fiancée, Clara Wieck, who saw Berlioz first, had mentioned that the young genius was silent and modest. (*298*, 203 and *307*, 248.)
All these artists, who should have known better, assumed that Berlioz would
be continuously intense, like *some* of the movements in his symphonies. At the
same time, he understood cordiality and showed it without regard to rank
or other privilege: an excellent account of a stranger's "Visit to Berlioz" is
given in *184*.

[37] *L.I.*, Pref. v.   [38] *362*, 140.   [39] *386*, 85.

sequences, yet went ahead — a reasoned courage which in turn amazed the more artful Saint-Saëns.[40]

This transformation of natural impulse and justness of vision into a superiority conscious of itself (the "elegance," "distinction" or "nobility" of the aristocrat)[41] made habitual the reserve which Wagner among others seems to have resented. He himself resembled far more the type of the expansive, uncontrolled artist, and his close friend Praeger who observed him and Berlioz together remarks: "Berlioz was of an excitable temperament, too, but could repress it. Not so Wagner. He presented a striking contrast to the polished, refined Frenchman, whose speech was almost classic through his careful selection of words." [42]

We have another sketch of Berlioz in society from the pen of Guizot, who adds a physical touch or two applicable to these same years. Guizot is writing to his daughter in 1862 about a soiree at Legouvé's. Gounod, Gustave Doré, Gautier, and Ritter (of whom we shall hear more) were present: "A moment later I saw next to me a gentleman of spare frame, with a tousled head of hair, a piercing eye, and a spirited and quite noble countenance. Legouvé approached him and said, 'My dear Berlioz' — we were introduced. He turned out to be a true enthusiast, not at all talkative, until the moment when his enthusiasm grips him, and then he becomes full and eloquent: a striking contrast with the skeptical and sensual writer Théophile Gautier." [43]

Later Guizot said to his host: "I have met many illustrious artists at your house, but none has impressed me like M. Berlioz. *There* is an original being!" [44] Legouvé, who had known Berlioz for twenty years, concurs in the epithet and shows that its fitness did not depend on a first impression but survived intimacy and the revelation of other facets of character: "He was an extraordinary mixture of enthusiasm and sarcasm; his mind always gave forth the unexpected. His conversation kept you in suspense by the very unevenness of its flow.[45] Sometimes he would be silent for a

---

[40] *1005*, 252–3. Compare Mozart's effect on his contemporaries, also due to his awareness of great powers: " — a man of superior talent (which I cannot deny myself to be, without blasphemy)." *1026*, 286.

[41] Both Ferdinand Hiller and Eduard Hanslick used similar phrases — "a true and upright nature," "in the full sense of the word a man of honor" — to describe Berlioz, whom they knew under the most varied and trying circumstances. (*352*, 555 and *351*, 377.)

[42] *990*, 261.

[43] *194a*, 384.

[44] *362* (1903) 170.

[45] Confirmed by all observers, from his sister Nanci in 1824 to his latest acquaintances.

long while, looking darkly at the ground and seeming to plumb I know not what abysses. Then an awakening, sudden and dazzling. He was then a geyser of witty, humorous, touching words, with bursts of homeric laughter and the gaiety of a child." [46]

In most accounts — including the present one — the details of Berlioz' "arduous career" allow the part of laughter very little room. It is not easy to say: "Here he laughed." Yet his letters show how natural humor was to him and how much he relied on its healing power. He writes to his sister, for example: "When we meet we shall laugh a great deal"; and again, in alluding to convivial gatherings with other artists, he speaks of "that good homeric laughter which sweeps away all cobwebs." [47] His *feuilletons*, like the *Memoirs*, are full of anecdotes, exaggerations, and fantasies worthy of Cervantes; and it is these that have sown suspicion in the minds of the literal. Unable or unwilling to interpret the gambols of an active mind, they charge "exaggeration" as a crime prima facie — though it is only "the habit of vivid expression which all would emulate if they could." [48] Legouvé points out that it was the very spontaneity of Berlioz' similitudes that made them devastating as criticism, for they appeared like unpremeditated expressions of truth, and his own pleasure in them was so free from contrived meanness that it won a friend or made an enemy depending on the character of the victim. [49]

This exuberant gaiety was not always childlike. Berlioz had a strong Rabelaisian streak in him, that is to say, a vein of grossness intellectualized, [50] which may have something to do with the background of medical studies common to him and Rabelais. Like him and many other great masters of reality, Berlioz also had the unconventional command of words that delights in puns. His conversation and his columns were liberally sprinkled with them and this caused the usual offense to staid minds, who scorn what they call the lowest form of humor without perhaps being themselves capable of a higher. The fact that Molière was one of Berlioz' favorite authors sufficiently shows that the punster also appreciated high comedy, yet without spurning the intermediate kind, for Berlioz quotes Bottom the Weaver — which may well be the sole example of a French reader's taking pleasure in the humor of Shakespeare.

[46] *362* (1903) 170.

[47] Respectively *M.C.*, 111 and *Grot.*, 261 and 284. See also *Corresp.*, 199.

[48] Havergal Brian: *324*, 209.

[49] Heller adds that one could answer back with the utmost freedom and, pursuing the banter, strengthen the affection. (*282*, 148 *n.*)

[50] *E.g.*, *385*, 497. The notion of Rabelais as a wallower more full of *joie de vivre* than of wit misreads both his book and his portrait.

Legouvé, in the remarks given earlier, spoke of the "touching" expressions to be found in Berlioz' conversation. That the musician could convey an unsentimental, masculine tenderness is evident enough in every one of his works, but the man might easily have suppressed its verbal counterpart. In point of fact, Berlioz may be said to have sought every opportunity for the gentler feelings, and to have been a fighter by necessity rather than choice. He asks, in a semi-autobiographical fiction, "Is it not a cruel thing to preserve energy only for the purpose of hatred?"[51] The phrase has a peculiar force when one considers the revulsion Berlioz felt against cruelty, and the characteristic use he makes of the word itself. We have seen his expostulation about the laws that allowed his dying sister to suffer needlessly. He likewise developed an almost obsessional anger against the hunting and mistreatment of animals.[52] And unlike many sensitive people he was very much alive to others' feelings in situations involving mental cruelty. Thus he speaks of Beethoven's having had the "naïve cruelty" to make his famous rejoinder to Paer;[53] and he himself while taking unworthy comfort in the downfall of *Tannhäuser* had the awareness to say that he was "cruelly avenged."[54]

Revenge was in truth entirely alien to Berlioz' temperament, despite the provocations which he felt he had endured and the virtuoso pleasure he took in verbalizing his angry scorn. He never imputes motives. As appeared in the Duponchel affair, he maintained in the event his courteous composure, and only posthumously revealed his awareness of the trickery. Again, when the eccentric Jullien who had blithely swindled him returned to Paris for some new enterprise, Berlioz obtained the bankrupt's release from the judgment that hindered his business plans. The beneficiary could scarcely believe this and embraced Berlioz in the courtroom.[55]

What is more, a comparison of Berlioz' autobiography with his critical

[51] *Soirées* (12th) *Eves.*, 144.

[52] He apparently gave up hunting birds after a single trial, and at the end of his life risked some valued friendships by remonstrating about the way "gentlemen" finished off wounded birds with their boots. (*362*, 139 and *Corresp.*, 341; see also his remarks on bull-baiting, fashionable in the Paris of 1835, *L.I.*, 161.)

[53] *Soirées* (2nd Epilogue) *Eves.*, 315. Beethoven had supposedly heard Paer's *Leonora* and meeting the composer said: "I like the subject of your opera; I think I must set it to music." The anecdote is now deemed apocryphal.

[54] See below, Chapter 24. Legouvé states as a general proposition: "All his sardonic wit disappeared the moment he feared it would hurt someone, even an obscure person." (*362*, 140.)

[55] *Mem.*, II, 370. About Liszt and other friends, Berlioz repeatedly declares his appreciation of kindness as a virtue which is "very rare among intellectuals." (*Corresp.*, 198; *M.E.*, 210; *S.W.*, 142.)

writings shows that no taunts or backbiting — such as Cherubini and Rossini were guilty of towards him — affected his attitude toward their music. And when in the *Memoirs* he apostrophizes the "asses," "toads," and "worms" who stood in his way, he keeps their incognito. Like Milton, and in much the same words, he is fighting the Philistines, not degrading himself to personalities.[56]

One is of course free to wish that Berlioz' magnanimity had induced him to forbear even from such shooting over the heads of the mob. But then we would have had a different Berlioz, much less virile and verbal, and possibly less attractive in other ways, for it was Berlioz' tenacious memory of his wrongs which prompted him also to remember and proclaim his benefactors. The reader of the *Memoirs* must have an equally good memory and recall that side by side with the thunder and damnation *contra gentiles*, there are passages differently pitched: "I believe I have already made the remark, but it will bear repetition, that if I have encountered many a scoundrel and many a cheat in my life, I have been extraordinarily lucky in finding the opposite. *Few artists have found as many kind hearts and as much generous devotion as I.*" [Italics added] [57] This passage comes at the end of a detailed account of the loans offered by several friends and two mere acquaintances to enable Berlioz to go to Russia and recoup his fortunes. He goes on: "Dear and kindly men, who have doubtless forgotten your openhanded behavior, allow me to remind you of it and to give you heartfelt thanks. It is with inward joy that I think of my obligation to you." [58] In a word, Berlioz was vindictive on paper, and by the same token explicit in his gratitude. But he was grateful in deed as well, for he repaid debts of money no less than help and favors.[59]

A similar union of traits explains, though it may not excuse the fault of not suffering fools gladly, which entailed for him the feeling of being isolated and misunderstood. Like Shaw in our own day, Berlioz was only at ease in the company of the spiritually great. It was not merely that his views on art and life were of uncommon breadth, but that on a hundred matters of daily opinion he saw through cant, and felt without effort the

---

[56] See Milton's second sonnet on his detractors, who are likened to "owls and cuckoos, asses, apes and dogs."

[57] *Mem.*, II, 265.

[58] *Ibid.*

[59] See below, Chapter 27. Legouvé sums up: "He always remembered a kindness . . . [and] wrote of it in his *Memoirs* in letters of gold, giving us in gratitude a full repayment, just as if he had not reimbursed us as well." (*362*, 139.)

liberality of thought which others obtain only by self-discipline in the teeth of convention.[60] When Berlioz was young, he covered up this sense of being different by assuming a pose, for the ebullience of youth would not let him stifle his words. Self-control came later and made him the cool, reserved person we have seen. But to the end the desire remained to give himself wholly and absolutely to a worthy friend or mistress. His assurances of love and loyalty to Ferrand, Liszt, Vigny, J. W. Davison, and many others; his devotion to Adèle and his successive love affairs (which Stendhal would have called "crystallizations," that is to say, projections) all betokened the predominantly outgoing character of his libido. Nothing perhaps distinguishes his generation from ours more thoroughly than this difference between men whose outlook upon the world was primarily loving, affectionate, erotic, and men of equal gifts perhaps but whose whole being seems defensively tight, emotionally blocked, and in every way full of mistrust.

When in the latter third of his life, Berlioz' lot became still harder to bear, despite financial ease and showered honors, the *Memoirs* briefly record the mood of embittered complaint; and coming last this portion is apt to color our recollection of the rest: we like happy endings.[61] But in not concealing this appropriate last act of the tragedy, Berlioz was true to his plan of making the autobiography a compendium for artists. In modern society it seems natural or at least inevitable that creative talents should end in some form of neglect, which cannot help being bitter. As Redon remarked on reading the *Memoirs*, Berlioz was one of those "meek deep minds who out of love and in good faith seek the foundations of things," and are therefore "doomed whatever they may wish to do, to live in bitterness only." [62]

But there was more in Berlioz' testament for artists than a demonstration

[60] *E.g.*, on the question of nationality in the arts, he says bluntly: "Patriotism, fetichism, moronism!" (*Mem.*, II, 261), and on the repulsiveness of *mariages de convenances:* "When I see such stupid compliance and insolent parental requirements, such disgusting cruelty crushing out fine passions . . . I should like to be able to put all reasonable people, virtuous heroines, and far-sighted fathers into a sack with a hundred thousand pounds of good sense and throw them into the sea. . . ." (*Grot.*, 76.)

[61] Wagner felt offended by the book — which refers to him twice in terms of praise — and took it as a sign of French decadence. (*947*, 399.) He at once began dictating to Cosima his own (much less reliable) memoirs. Somewhat later, Verdi also expressed distaste for what he took to be Berlioz' unrelieved bitterness, making at the same time a sally against the Wagnerians. (*967*, 140.) We may gauge from these acts of revulsion against seeing greatness in misery the general, almost neurotic relief felt by artists at Wagner's worldly success.

[62] *1275*, 214 (1876).

of the vanity of things. There was the sense of active persecution, which also seems the normal lot of all but a few artists in old age.[63] Not that Berlioz believed for a moment in any conscious conspiracy — the unconscious is enough, and he could document the unreasonable obstacles placed in his path, the lies, deceptions, and cabals, and above all the intangible resistance of the entire social milieu to what he and his "gods" had sought to do. Almost to the very end, he felt unused creative powers which could have found expression if the making of a work had not also entailed a public bout.[64] He occupied, in short, the position of Melville, Turner, Henry James, or Delacroix, and he expressed about it feelings rather less soured than those of Henry Adams or Thomas Hardy.

So far from being clouded, his judgment in those trying circumstances produced what is perhaps the soundest of all the opinions ever given on his music: "The prevailing qualities of my music are passionate expressiveness, inner fire, rhythmic drive, and unexpectedness. When I say passionate expressiveness, I mean an expressiveness bent on embodying the intimate purport of a subject, even though the subject be the opposite of passion, as in the rendering of soft and tender feelings or of deep calm." [65]

With the same precision, neither boastful nor humble, he vindicates the melodic essence of his work, supplying while he does so the basic reason for public incomprehension of his scores: "I have always taken care to lavish melody upon my compositions . . . one can dispute the worth of these melodies, their fineness, originality, or charm: it is not for me to assess them. But to deny their existence is, I maintain, bad faith or incompetence. Only, these melodies being often of very large dimensions . . . or again, being combined with other secondary melodies . . . or else so different from the funny little snippets called melodies by the musical groundlings . . . the latter are not willing to give the same name to both kinds." [66]

The clear knowledge of what he had and had not done could breed satisfaction without complacency, and the attentive reader of the *Memoirs* will be struck by Berlioz' real modesty, that is, freedom from any atti-

---

[63] Beethoven had, for similar reasons, a touch of persecution mania — as did Leibniz and Newton — in what seems to us quite tolerable circumstances; but we are not proper judges of the special sort of frustration that vents itself thus.

[64] The common notion that Berlioz' genius was abundant and inventive only up to middle age rests on general ignorance of the later works and the documents of the closing decades. (See below Chapter 23 and 25 *n.1.*) More, this error overlooks the friction between Berlioz' artistic mission and contemporary culture.

[65] *Mem.*, II, 361.

[66] *Ibid.*

tudinizing with regard to his achievements.[67] Whether he dashes off a piece
in one night or succeeds only slowly and painfully, he tells us with equal
readiness. He acknowledges numerous criticisms which he took from
competent sources and was thankful for, and only complains that other
objectors did not specify their grounds so that he could make use of the
hint.[68] Artist's vanity weighs on him so lightly that he can cite persons
whom he loves and esteems — Mendelssohn and Ingres being the chief
examples — who openly dislike his work without thereby forfeiting his
love or his admiration. And as Berlioz adds line upon line to his portrait
of the artist as musician, he does it without simpering or loftiness, ever-
ready to sacrifice the façade of author's dignity to the sharp strokes of a
dramatic rendering.

This is not incompatible with his laying stress on what has been called
the heroism of his career and openly resenting the lack of encouragement,
recognition, praise, or what you will that it should have received. He re-
sents this personally and corporately — for his art and for himself.[69] Considering all the ovations, medals, laurel wreaths, and warm lifelong friendships which his musical activity brought him, one may think he was
greedy of a commodity which is at best rare. Yet he was neither unmindful
of these tokens nor mistaken in his estimate of their insufficiency. Most of
them he had to earn by repeated superhuman feats, and he was not reconciled — as the public so readily is — to the fact that the creator never ends
his period of probation, is seldom granted adequate technical means, and
must wrest each new triumph in the teeth of an opposition not even decent
enough to put its ideas in order. Berlioz, arguing as it were for his class
interests, was quite right not to be reconciled, but instead to project in
memoirs the figure of the embattled artist, to serve as a warning and an
encouragement to the young.

[67] Just as a comparison in modesty, one may instance Rimsky-Korsakov's
treatise on orchestration, in which all the examples come from the author's
works. In Berlioz' *Treatise*, there are but eleven quotations from his scores
out of sixty-six.

[68] *Mem.*, I, 342. Stephen Heller suggested a number of changes in the *Romeo
and Juliet* symphony which Berlioz made use of, but when Heller kept urging
that he suppress the entire last movement of the *Fantastique*, Berlioz stopped
him with a: "Be quiet! You do not know what you are talking about!" (*282*,
141.) From d'Ortigue, Liszt, Chorley, Pauline Viardot, and Legouvé he gratefully took such criticisms as served his purpose.

[69] His notion of musical co-operation such as he rarely found comes out in
a phrase describing Carvalho — "a man . . . devoted to an idea once he has
adopted it." (*A Trav.*, 238.) As for Berlioz' own family, it appears that only
his brother-in-law Suat spoke of his career in other terms than those of material success. (*91*, 459.)

If he loses a certain formal dignity in airing this grievance, it must be put down not to vindictiveness but to vindication; and if the egotistical element in the claim seems excessive, it must be measured not by guesswork but by documents. Berlioz' "very real heroism," as Katharine Boult has suggested, "comes out only in his letters, and then quite unconsciously." [70] Which is only another way of saying that in the *Memoirs* he made conscious what his letters tell us he had actually experienced. The battle was real and long drawn out. "Yes, he met the shocks of fortune well and they were many and rude." So says Ernest Newman, speaking as an experienced biographer.[71] Earlier, Flaubert had said that when one knew Berlioz' life, one no longer had the right to complain of one's own.[72]

Berlioz' vicissitudes moreover brought with them what they are supposed to bring, but rarely do, a refining and strengthening of all the qualities. "If we want a summary contrast of the later and the earlier Berlioz," Mr. Newman goes on, "we have only to compare the ebullient letters of his youth with the letters written to the Princess Sayn-Wittgenstein between 1852 and 1867. The very style is altered; the later letters read easily and beautifully, without any of those abrupt distortions and exaggerations that pull us up with a shock in the earlier ones. When he has to castigate, he does it like a gentleman, with a rapier, not a bludgeon. And how perfectly does he maintain the essential dignity of the artist against this well-meaning but inquisitive and slightly vulgar aristocrat; with what fine breeding, what exquisite use of the iron hand within the velvet glove, does he repel her interferences with matters that concern only himself . . . !" [73]

Taking a hint from those writers who contend that a man's truest likeness is that which he carves line by line upon his own countenance,[74] Mr. Newman, still speaking of Berlioz, advises us to "Look at him in his later portraits, with that fine intellectual mouth, full of a strength that is not contradicted but reinforced by the ironic humour that plays over it." [75] The familiar photograph of 1863 with the hand on the temple brings out those features and shows Berlioz in a characteristic attitude. It

---

[70] *63*, viii.

[71] *374*, 62.

[72] *192*, V, 363.

[73] *374*, 62.

[74] Hazlitt: "The face, for the most part, tells what we have thought and felt — the rest is nothing." (*1256*, 429.) And elsewhere: "A man's look is the work of years; it is stamped on his countenance by the events of his whole life . . ."

[75] *374*, 62.

was thus that he sat with his intimates, speaking or silent, drinking innumerable cups of tea, but not smoking, and abhorring the thought of card games or other substitutes for conversation.[76] Outdoors, one would note the springy step of the thin straight figure with the remarkable head, the step of one who had once been a tireless cross-country walker and who, like Beethoven, would still occasionally sing or talk to himself on the street as if on a solitary hike.[77]

In all these circumstances one would find Berlioz rather different from the enthusiast who impressed Guizot or the aristocrat who intimidated Gounod; that is, one would see the man under the aspect of a relaxed will. The *Memoirs*, by their very purposiveness, give to this facet of the social man rather less attention than is due,[78] which may account in part for the legend of the volcanic creature perpetually in eruption. But the truest view can only be that which keeps in mind the many-sidedness of a being who comes as close as anyone in his century to Montaigne's definition of the ideal man, *ondoyant et divers*, though without the serpentine suggestion this has acquired. Indeed, Berlioz resembles Montaigne himself in his capacity for self-revelation tempered by the preference that the essayist expresses for "giving himself meagerly and proudly" to those about him, and even "assisting the injurious imputations that fortune strews upon me, because I shirk self-justification, excuses, and interpretings, deeming it an attainder against my good conscience to plead on its behalf." [79]

At the same time, Berlioz was at once too generous and too much a master of expression to keep the delicacy of his feelings forever hidden from his friends in the manner now approved as proper self-control. Fearing to be thought sentimental, men no longer tell each other of their regard except perhaps posthumously, and the very word effusion is become a reproach. Not so with the generation of Berlioz and Liszt, to whom the former writes in July 1853: "You write me letters twelve pages long dealing with me and my affairs, and I am naïve enough to answer you *on the same subject*. Yet it is nothing more than naïveté, mixed with a slight fear of treading indiscreetly upon matters that you do not want to broach. Please be assured, my dear Liszt, that no one — no one, do you hear? — is more concerned than I about whatever touches you, and no one will be

[76] *1388* (1903) 267; *388*, 6; *Grot.*, 170; *Mem.*, I, 229 *n.*; *A Trav.*, 90.

[77] *1385*, Oct. 2, 1907; *813*, 346.

[78] Though it is by no means unrepresented: see the Italian chapters.

[79] *1268*, IV, 192. Berlioz never replied to any public attack, save that of having manhandled the music of Palestrina and Weber; and never condescended to defend his esthetic. See below, Chapter 22.

happier than I at the settling of the difficulties that still mar the tranquillity of your existence." [80]

The diametrical extremes of an ambit so wide as to include reticence and effusion may be called directness and discipline, candor and acute self-knowledge, or in Nietzschean terms Dionysus and Apollo. Ascribing the fullest stretch of these powers to Berlioz is no conjecture. Eyewitnesses of different ranks and grades have alike recorded the "evident *finesse* and cultivation" and the "dose of simple grandeur" which to the very last shone in Berlioz' "admirable face, the only one perhaps which ever possessed in equal degree two qualities that clash — subtlety and greatness." [81] Yet the same consensus establishes the unity and wholeness of this extraordinary character: "Just as Nature sometimes imparts to objects vibrations of so rapid a frequency that nothing can deflect them, so it seems as if [it] took pleasure in creating certain men whose life trajectory presents the same inflexibility. Berlioz never resorted to craftiness, never met obstacles circuitously: all appearances to the contrary notwithstanding." [82] If John Jay Chapman is right in saying that history remembers only types, we may borrow from his classification the type which he names after the ancient hero, Hector the Pure, and make it stand for the artist type embodied and glorified by his namesake Hector Berlioz.[83] For wherever one strikes Berlioz he rings true, and because he steadily braved what the people of his time called reasonable, he turns out to be one of the sanest men of his century.[84]

We now know enough about Berlioz to go beyond his "case" and judge through him the lot of the artist in the nineteenth century as well as the healthy relation of art to life in the creator. It is a popular belief nowadays that the artist is simply an ordinary man who has learned his trade and works at it hard. In reaction against the sentimental imitators of Romanti-

[80] *M.C.*, 95. The allusion is to the tangled question of the Princess's papal divorce then pending and the fate of her property, still held by her husband.

[81] Respectively: Griepenkerl (*440* and *479*, 75), Bouyer (*414*, Dec. 7, 1903), Pontmartin (*498*, 60). See moreover Saint-Saëns, *passim.*

[82] Grenier: *1385*, Nov. 29, 1903. Compare a scholarly judgment of Rabelais: "Very likely nothing in Rabelais is put on, nothing affected, neither wisdom nor folly. We have here a really enigmatic nature, a singular temperament, a unique genius, at once exuberant and controlled, bizarre and full of sense, overflowing and judicious, endowed with prodigious faculties, with remarkable elevation of thought, and fits of gaiety that nothing can stop." (*1273*, xxxviii.)

[83] *1065*, 74.

[84] Wilde: "Anybody can be reasonable, but to be sane is not common." (*1136*, 172.)

cism who assumed the outward pose of inspired poets, the fact of inspiration — and almost of poetry — has been denied, even by artists. Their pride
has found a new lodging, it seems, in being industrious and even industrial, since some affect a belief in the propriety of judging their worth in
money. We have a false notion of democracy to thank for this, besides the
artist's secret hope of becoming naturalized in modern society on the
footing of an expert — like the man of science. From this comes the pedantry, the wry self-explanation, the sinking of high individuality, to conform with the imagined level of the common man. By these contraries one
can gauge the extent of the shift in feeling and manners during the last
seventy-five years. And conversely, by conjuring up the opposite of what
we know at first hand we can, without implying any adverse judgment
upon modern artists and their work, recapture the nineteenth-century
vision of the artist as hero.

Though calling Berlioz aristocratic, and his twentieth century counterpart democratic, is culturally speaking a precise statement, it does not of
course mean that the modern artist is either a man of the people or conspicuously a good fellow. Rather it means that whereas Berlioz considered
himself one of a company of equals set apart from the rest of mankind by
natural gifts, the democratic artist tends to emerge alone (or not at all),
and if fortunate, to rule in his sphere like a dictator. Notice how our
demagogic age, with its facilities for turning on or off the faucet of fame,
singles out one painter, one musician, one novelist as supreme; and how
certain governments, also based on this form of the One and the Many,
follow suit by setting up a tzar over the remaining artists, who are themselves "co-ordinated" and coercible to a degree inconceivable a century
ago. Quite logically, the requisite for this sort of pre-eminence is craftsmanship, but craftsmanship uncomplicated by a venturesome spirit. The
nineteenth-century valuation of originality has been replaced by an osten-
tatious love of tradition and a series of "returns" to this or that past master.
Again, though experimentation has been abundant, it has been abundantly
explained, technical talk being a form of respect to the inescapable though
anonymous "democracy." The artist is in fact less and less of a skirmishing
knight, master of the *gai saber*, and more and more of a teacher in resi-
dence or a solemnly deliberate "social worker."

At bottom, of course, the human impulses both then and now remain
constant, but the forms they assume differ and may obscure the kinship.
Thus we must not impute it to Berlioz as if it were pure choice that instead of being an academic he carried on his teaching mission as a free
lance; that he took his respect for musical tradition so for granted as never

to boast of it;[85] that he stressed novelty without discoursing on it and admired technique more for its results than as the insigne of the expert. He did not need to play the humble, plain fellow, for the social necessity had not arisen. His true modesty was shown in his immense capacity for admiring great work,[86] just as his open bid for praise, power, and fame arose from a belief in the worthiness of a desire ancestrally associated with the noble mind.

If he complained to excess of the reviewer's hackwork which many a modern would be only too thankful to have, it was because he felt it to be constricting his talents and wasting the divine energies. He might have been soothed to learn that talents and energies were mere fictions which his successors would no longer contend with; but there is the possibility that they only think inspiration mythical because the inner channel by which it comes has been cut off. It takes a very special freedom of the intellect to be at once as critical as Berlioz, and as convinced of the beauty of his own best work.[87] Again, the power that enabled him to separate and dramatize for others' edification the artist self within the man seems very different from the shuffling affectations, absurd maxims and awkward bravado of our contemporaries, who are no less — yet very differently — unhappy. The difference is that which marks off self-awareness from self-consciousness,[88] and one test of the difference seems to lie in two kinds of sensitiveness to criticism — the modern betraying a lack of moral stamina and a secret identification of the whole self with the fate of any trifling piece of art. Berlioz, to be sure, had no patience with those who told him that he did not understand Shakespeare or that he had mutilated Goethe, but to those who offered particular criticisms he willingly paid heed.

---

[85] Montaux: "I have heard certain anecdotes . . . which constitute a kind of tradition . . . bearing witness to Berlioz' characteristic respect for his art and the ready welcome he gave to any information — however humble the source — that might add to his technical equipment." (*588*, 1890, 270.)

[86] *Effective* admiration, of course: Berlioz did not defend or play only the dead, but Spontini, Mendelssohn, and Liszt as well; and his correspondence with lesser lights steadily conveys encouragement.

[87] From Beethoven through Wagner this attitude forms an unbroken tradition. It is during the last quarter of the nineteenth century that the convention of despising one's work begins, parallel with the factory worker's feeling for his truly contemptible "work": Ruskin's prediction has come true.

[88] I tried to depict our uncomfortable view of ourselves in Chapter VII of *Romanticism and the Modern Ego*. A reviewer, otherwise very kindly, asked with some sharpness whether I was so different from those I chose for illustration. The fact is of course that I could not possibly know much worth telling about this state of mind if I did not observe it within me, a cultural self superimposed on the others.

When compared with many a contemporary of ours, who feel that whatever comes from his hand is sacred, Berlioz appears almost unassuming; and when compared with the many who are made ill by censure, he seems clothed in the hide of a buffalo.

But the surest guarantee of his being at one not only with himself but with the artistic mythos of his time is that the "cycle of feeling, work, and grief" in which he revolved never impaired the independence of his creative powers. He could suffer illness, worry, despair, and misprized love and still reproduce in sound the infinite variety of imaginable moods that lay beyond those which at the moment enslaved him. The joyful or serene prayers of the *Te Deum* were written when he thought his life broken — and said so in the *Memoirs;* and the youthful charm of light melancholy that pervades *Beatrice and Benedict* is the fruit of a time when Berlioz was solitary, ill, aged, and in gloom.

For us the "lesson of Berlioz" brings home a twofold historic paradox. It appears in the first place that the twentieth-century artist, although he would cuddle closer to the social structure, is actually doing more violence to himself than the former *"desdichado"* who seemed rebellious only because he truly embodied tradition and was carrying it forward against the perennial standpatters.[89] Put another way, it looks as if the democratic, populist culture now in vogue were less attuned to the permanent impulses of the artist's nature than the former heroic and aristocratic fighting style.[90] And in the second place, it seems as if the doomed and disappointed figures (nineteenth-century style) from Berlioz to Henry James had in reality come out as victors. Certainly as one casts up the account of victories and defeats in Berlioz' career, the successes predominate: France insulted and finally neglected him, but he created the French school; he roused Central Europe from its Italian and operatic slumbers and made the return to its national tradition easier and more fruitful; in five visits to England he gave its audiences something else to meditate than Handel and Mendelssohn, and in time there arose an English school; just as in Russia, after his two trips and a multitude of contacts, Tchaikovsky and the Russian Five found their true goal. It was not that Berlioz produced all this by himself in the way of gathering disciples and imitators; on the contrary he made few or none. His success, as will appear, lay deep and was the longer hidden. But even before his time of harvest, one must say of him what Carlyle said of

[89] See Nerval's sonnet *El Desdichado,* which emphasizes the ancestral view of the dedicated as accursed.

[90] For a subtle analysis of this mystery, see Lionel Trilling's answer to a questionnaire in *Partisan Review* for August 1948.

Mirabeau — that he was "not victorious but unvanquished while life is left him."[91]

To show that Berlioz, working in the heroic tradition, was a hero in his life and work is not to say that he was a saint. He was, as W. J. Turner put it in quaint old-fashioned words, "a great man."[92] And like all men, great or small, he had defects of character, which are most often the excess or mistiming of qualities. Berlioz' quickness of mind became irritable impatience; his tenacious will became overinsistence to the point of self-defeat — as in his marriage to Harriet; his imagination and the saving grace of naïveté could generate illusion and false trust in men, followed by disillusion and momentary despair;[93] his critical sense and native gaiety could overwhelm blockheads out of proportion to their sins, just as his reserve could seem haughty. The passion for art, nature, and human goodness could overstimulate the verbal powers and produce bathos, especially in early days. But to call these specks, as a recent biographer has done, "innumerable vices," or to say that Berlioz was his own worst enemy, or a trial to his friends, is to put oneself unwarrantably in their place without knowing either them or him. Everybody is his own worst enemy: the phrase is merely one way of distinguishing a human character from a starfish. As against these amateur judges, it is a conclusive test that Berlioz earned the respect of the three choosiest men in his century, men who were not his friends and had no reason to belie their knowledge or firsthand impressions — Sainte-Beuve, Guizot, and Wagner.[94]

[91] *French Revolution*, II, 169.

[92] *309*, 280.

[93] He had himself anatomized the causes of illusion in a letter of his twenty-second year (*A.R.*, 31) but to understand a phenomenon is not to have the power of invariably averting it. When Berlioz was in London in 1848, he apparently deceived himself as to the possibilities of a permanent post in England (*213*, 7) and at other times, like Wordsworth or Goethe, he was forced to cultivate illusion in order to create: a work of art is so radically *un*necessary to the outer world that the maker must forget this knowledge by an effort of will in order to keep going. This pragmatic use of illusion is self-justifying, and we are familiar with it in the lives of artists generally. But to judge it more accurately we should study the illusions of politicians, businessmen, housewives, gamblers, and scientists. We should then have a comparative criterion for "reality" and we might find that our common division of mankind into artists (or thinkers) and practical men is baseless.

[94] In his obituary note, written shortly before his own death, Sainte-Beuve speaks as of an admitted fact of Berlioz' "noble intellect" (*1212*, XII, 152). Guizot's comments we have read above. As for Wagner, who feared and loved and hated and admired Berlioz by turns, he conceded while living, Berlioz' "enormous musical intelligence," artistic integrity, and breadth of character.

Yet as in the lives of heroes in classical tragedy, there is amid the many events of Berlioz' admirably concentrated life of action one flaw, one mistake which deserves mingled censure and compassion: the culpable neglect of his son during the first years of the domestic crisis. Berlioz, it is true, was harassed and disappointed, he was planning his first German tour and he was also enmeshed in his new love for Marie. But knowing Harriet's deficiencies of all kinds — linguistic, managerial, and moral — and what is more, knowing what his own father had meant to him in a troubled childhood, he had no excuse. What he should have done — since we must put Shaw's query to any biographer who criticizes — is hard to say, since Harriet was devoted to the child and would not part from him.[95] But *that* something should have been done, Berlioz' belated anxiety and efforts sufficiently prove. His conscience troubled him, as we can see in many a letter from 1852 onward: "The poor dear child," he writes to Adèle, "has not the slightest notion of economy. . . . But I beg you never to reproach him on that score. His profession [apprentice seaman] is not of the jolliest and when he is on shore and I have money, I don't want him to feel deprived. And then we are such good companions that more than half the time, when he gives me fantastic accounts I burst out laughing as if I were in on the joke. And indeed I am, on much more than half of it. . . ."[96]

Berlioz knew that by his own act of neglect he had made Louis indolent, ill-educated, spendthrift, and perpetually unhappy, and that this could not be undone. From the time that he recognized this, Berlioz had scarcely any peace of mind about him. He loved him with all the added weight of regret for what he had withheld, and the misery of their relations until the end seems almost more than any sentient being should have been asked to bear. Their long separations coming at a time when death was taking Berlioz' friends and relatives contributed to that final mood of isolation in which the Postscript to the *Memoirs* is written. It ends in resignation but not in hope, after sounding again the theme of unavailing love for the original Estelle, as in the closing bars of the first movement of the *Fantastique*.

The theme of love miscast and yet always treasured and linked with

---

After Berlioz' death he would brook no caviling at the man he had himself attacked. See below, "Berlioz and Wagner" in Subchapter 24.

[95] Her single letter to her son which has been preserved (and printed) is heart-rending in its semiliterate and untranslatable French, but it seems to confirm her pathetic inadequacy to cope with the situation in which she was placed. (*M.E.*, 154–5.)

[96] *M.C.*, 44–5.

the creative powers,[97] that is to say, never rejected as a delusion or an infirmity, cannot help striking the modern reader who has a smattering of Freud at command and who is accustomed to would-be analytic studies of artists. Berlioz was obviously aware that his passion and his genius were akin, though as Mr. Josephson has pointed out in his fine work on Victor Hugo, these modern discoveries were often matters of course to the Romantic poets. What Berlioz cannot have known so simply and directly was the nature of the psychic wound inflicted on him by his mother. All his life he sought the love she had denied and was no doubt torn between desire for the gentleness which she lacked and attachment to the imperious character which she exhibited. Above all, his father had supplied him with a model of what love-with-intelligence could be — it is an artist's desideratum in any case — hence Berlioz pursued the will-o'-the-wisp of a woman who should be musical yet educated, gentle yet passionate, feminine yet somehow like his mother.[98] While commiserating with him in his endless quest, one can only consider him fortunate in not having suffered worse warping of the emotions than he did, or met with worse misadventures. Best of all, he did not lose his capacity to love before life itself.[99]

The price he paid was to experience bouts of his dread "isolation," which we may translate as the child's sense of being bereft. In the grown boy and man, it took the form of feeling that "life escaped him," that he could only catch shreds of his own existence, which may have unconsciously spurred him to fashion works in which life is caught, pinned down, held forever. But hence also, at times of intense composing which brought elation, he experienced moments of inexplicable anxiety [100] —

[97] Twice while composing the *Requiem* he dreamt of Estelle's little garden at Meylan (*Mem.*, I, 308 *n.*) and his other scores are dotted with tunes associated in his mind, not with actual love affairs, but with the anticipation or recollection of love. Near the end of the *Memoirs* he asks, "Which of these two powers, love or music, lifts man to the greatest heights? It is a difficult question, yet it seems one might say this: Love can give no idea of music, whereas music can give an idea of love. But why separate the two? They are the two wings of the soul." (*Mem.*, II, 422.)

[98] And hence, for this last characteristic, the projection on Estelle.

[99] The purity or idealism or whatever one may want to call the quality of his feeling for Estelle in his and her old age, was by no means sentimental or "literary." Berlioz visited the elderly woman in her distress, took an interest in her children, and with his usual practicality left her an annuity which eased her last days. (*158* and *282*, 492–3.)

[100] E.g., to Adolphe Samuel shortly after beginning *Les Troyens:* "I am ill, apprehensive, quivering, but nevertheless still working." (Nov. 22, 1856: *93*, June 29, 1879; also *91*, 460.)

further proof, if needed, that his music was "the imagination of love in sound." Or rather, that was its genesis. As an object, his music was many things which we have not yet done exploring. But having just reviewed his life as man and artist through the prism of the *Memoirs*, we may say of him with even greater certainty what Keats said of Shakespeare: "He led a life of allegory and his works are the comment on it." [101]

[101] *198, 305.*

21. *Victorian London:* Evenings with the Orchestra

May 9, 1851
to July 9, 1853

Music is good to the melancholy, bad to those who mourn, and neither good nor bad to the deaf.

—Spinoza

BERLIOZ paid his second visit to England in the spring of 1851, officially for the purpose of judging musical instruments at the Great Exhibition. But he hoped at the same time to be able to recoup the debacle in which he had been involved three years before by Jullien's mismanagement. By good fortune he soon found among his English acquaintances the almost ideal backer. T. Frederick Beale, the barrister-musician who was a partner in the publishing house of Cramer and Company, had faith in Berlioz as man and artist and the confidence was returned: "I am dealing with a business man of a rare kind — honest, intelligent, charming, and rich." The plan was to establish a new concert society.[1]

Beale put Berlioz on salary from the moment of his arrival (£600 a year) which not only relieved the composer of a good deal of journalism, but also helped him out as official delegate, for France was acting in the most niggardly fashion towards its representatives. It paid their expenses while in London, but not the cost of going there and returning, and it set a limit to their stay regardless of the duties undertaken. Berlioz, who liked to see things through, stayed last of all the French committee "in order to see justice done. . . . France comes out ahead beyond any possible comparison: Erard, Sax, and Vuillaume. The rest is more or less in the class of penny whistles and pots and pans." [2]

Together with Sterndale Bennett, Thalberg, George Smart and six others, Berlioz had to examine and listen to all the instruments from piccolos to organs, submitted by the makers of five nations. Even the

---

[1] *M.E.*, 350. Another guarantor of the enterprise was Thomas Brassey, the famous navigator and chronicler of ships.

[2] *Corresp.*, 181.

composer's worst enemy might consider that he suffered on this occasion more than was his due. "It splits your head to hear these hundreds of wretched machines, each more out of tune than the next, three or four excepted." [3] But for once trade and art happened to combine their claims upon his trained ear. As a practiced flute player, he was especially interested in Böhm's latest designs and could assert that in comparison with the product of twenty years' experimentation, the old eight-hole wooden flute still in use when Berlioz began was "only fit to be played at a fair." [4] These, of course, were his casual pronouncements. The final report he wrote for his "Section" was as precise and dignified as any chancery could wish. [5]

The contrast in the quality of the wind instruments aptly symbolizes the kind of progress which the entire Exhibition — the largest and richest yet assembled — was to illustrate. The Prince Consort had had difficulty in obtaining consent to his "extravagant" plans, but their practical success won over the envious and the timid. Coming so soon after the troubles of 1848–1849, the gathering was feared by Continental rulers who saw themselves being conveniently massacred under one roof. In England, some had forecast hooliganism on a large scale as a result of letting "the people" out of their hovels. To the contrary, the most impressive feature of the show was the respect, good nature, and self-discipline of the huge crowds. It was estimated that at one time one hundred thousand persons milled about in the nineteen acres of Hyde Park covered by the Crystal Palace. This structure, by the way, although we tend to associate it with garishness, was in fact the fulfillment of fifteen years of new thought in architecture and the first piece of genuine industrial building in glass and metal. [6] It was the first of the many exhibition buildings out of which came the Eiffel Tower and the Galerie des Machines, themselves forerunners of twentieth-century architecture in steel, glass, and concrete. We may thus date the beginning of the combined mass age and machine age from 1851. So new was it to the human imagination that Berlioz had to explain

[3] *M.E.*, 329.

[4] *753*, 159. By 1851 many players still hung on to the old-fashioned inadequate wood winds because the new and better ones required a different fingering, which they were loath to learn. Berlioz predicted that the Böhm system would soon prevail. (*69*, 7.)

[5] *69*. See also a first report in *1386*, Dec. 30, 1851, reprinted with minor changes in *Grot.*, 45–58.

[6] As early as 1837 (in *Contrasts*) Welby Pugin had enunciated the principles of functionalism in architecture, urged respect for new materials, and preached innovation as against archeology. And in 1845, William Vose Pickett (in *A New System*) had proposed metal construction and prefabricated parts.

to Adèle how unlikely it was that he could find his uncle Félix Marmion by chance in the crowded enclosure. The two men's letters had miscarried and though both were in London for some time, they failed to meet.[7]

But despite Tennyson's call —

> Uplift a thousand voices full and sweet
> In this wide hall with earth's invention stored

no music in keeping with the age graced the Exhibition itself. Modern painting, too, was represented elsewhere, in Litchfield House, St. James's Square, to which Delacroix sent his "Moorish Cavalry Charge." Berlioz had to content himself with drawing up a plan for a possible concert which would represent European composers and performers while furnishing the visitors with four opportunities to hear a program of monumental music ranging from Handel and Bortniansky to Rossini and Berlioz' own *Te Deum*.[8]

The only monumental music available in London was the concert of charity children at St. Paul's to which reference was made earlier. This "musical impression" moved Berlioz and some of his colleagues to tears, while it furnished a practical demonstration of his views on this type of mass art. "There," as he wrote to d'Ortigue, "is the realization of a part of my dream, and the proof that the power of musical masses is absolutely unknown, on the Continent at least. . . ."[9] Berlioz wrote "a part of my dream" without underlining *a part*, but we should stress again what he took as a matter of course, namely that untrained voices singing in unison and without a proportionate orchestra afforded only the beginnings of a monumental music. The composer of the *Te Deum* did not dwell on this because he also knew that d'Ortigue was a devotee of plain song, and therefore resistant on doctrinal grounds to Berlioz' vision.

Those whose resistance rests on the less rational ground of micromania may note that in the very same moment Berlioz was equally open to the diametrically opposite style: a Frenchman named Rousselot had organized in London a Beethoven Quartet Society, of which Berlioz' friend Heinrich Ernst was first violin. Berlioz lodged in the same house with

[7] *M.E.*, 330.

[8] The detailed plan was found in Berlioz' papers and printed in *86*, 418–20. It exemplifies his grasp of all practical necessities, from the timing and housing of rehearsals to the financial provisions for the performers' travel allowances and the entrepreneur's profit. The site he chose within the Palace for placing his 1500 musicians and building the organ was the East Gallery, United States Section.

[9] *Corresp.*, 180.

him and was invited to sit in on the rehearsals. At times when Berlioz had
to write his article for the *Débats*, he would keep the doors open between
rooms, even though this stopped all writing. "Enter, ye sublime melodies!
. . . Where, where can Beethoven have found these thousands of phrases,
all so poetically characteristic and all different? What unexpected turns!
But what's this, what's this? — a prima donna is beginning an aria! John,
shut the door." [10]

Besides the less-known Beethoven, the London offering just then gave
Berlioz a chance to hear *The Marriage of Figaro* and, still rarer, *The
Magic Flute* — ". . . those wonderful pages, in which Mozart has used the
style which might be called antique-religious . . . Beauty reigns throughout — expression, melody, harmony, rhythm, instrumentation and modulation. Never before Mozart had anyone approached such perfection in the
genre, and I fear no one will approach it again after him. It would be
folly to attempt it. . . . What is most to be admired is the sovereign
majesty, the commanding calm of Sarastro, to whom everything in the
Temple of Isis gives obedience . . . ; nothing equals this grandeur, serenity, strength, and sweetness combined. . . . He sings . . . and the mysterious echoes of the place seem to answer him . . . The earth and its sad
passions are forgotten. He himself, as he sings, falls into sublime ecstasies.
. . . We are on the threshold of the infinite." [11]

These impressions Berlioz could gather in spite of the indignities practiced upon the score by Michael Costa, director of Covent Garden and
himself a "composer." Ill-rehearsed in ten days and sung mostly in the
rowdy Italian manner, Mozart's work was further defaced by "trombonization" — "a three-part continuo with bass-drum and attached-cymbal
obligato . . . The bovine instrument couches on Mozart's delicate orchestration as aptly as would a trowelful of mortar on a painting by
Raphael. . . ." [12] Critical honesty made Berlioz utter this just complaint,
although self-interest would have indicated a discreet silence, for Costa
was a great power in London music. Like a second Habeneck he was in
charge both of the opera and of the chief orchestra, the Philharmonic.
It was enough to be defying him in action, the plan of Berlioz' backers
being to set up a New Philharmonic and to impose on Covent Garden
Benvenuto Cellini or any new work for the stage that Berlioz might write.
Accordingly, though Berlioz went back to Paris in August and reported
on the Exhibition, he had leased an apartment in London for 1852.

[10] *Soirées* (21st) *Eves.*, 236–7.
[11] *1386*, Aug. 12, 1851.
[12] *Ibid.*

Benvenuto was in the air because Liszt wanted to produce it at Weimar. Berlioz was touched and a look at the score acted like a tonic. "It will be a great pleasure for me to see this poor brainchild revive, or rather, be born under your direction. I have sent the score to my copyist who is repairing it and making a few necessary changes." [13] These changes ultimately amounted to the thorough revising of the dramatic plan — three acts instead of two with only two changes of scene; a swifter denouement; [14] and the removal at once of verbal irrelevancies and of some concessions demanded by singers and managers in 1838. [15] "What ravages those opera people forced me to make then . . ! ; it's devilish lively, and I shall never again find such a shower of young ideas." [16] This was to Morel later; previously he had written to Liszt: "However childish my joy may seem, I shan't pretend otherwise with you. Yes, I am full of joy at the thought of having the work presented to an unprejudiced public, and presented by you. I have just looked it over carefully after 13 years of oblivion, and I swear I'll never again find such verve and Cellinian impetuosity, nor such a variety of ideas. But this only makes it the harder to perform: theatre people, singers especially, are so devoid of *humor*. But I count on you to Pygmalionize all those statues." [17]

By February 1852, Liszt had been working at the opera for four months and the *première* was set for the sixteenth. He invited Berlioz to come and stay with him and the Princess Wittgenstein at the spacious Villa Altenburg.[18] Berlioz tactfully declined: "You can guess that Marie, who has never heard *Benvenuto*, wants to join me . . . so don't press us, but be

---

[13] *M.E.*, 333–4.

[14] He added a wonderful recitative in which Cellini, pointing to the glowing Perseus, reads out the Latin inscription upon it: "*Si quis te laeserit, ego tuus ultor ero.*" (If anyone harms thee, I shall be thy avenger.)

[15] The work of revision, in which Liszt made helpful suggestions, may be followed in the correspondence between the two (*207*, I, 187 ff. and *M.C.*, parallel dates). It might be added that "concessions" were still demanded by singers in 1852, and Weingartner points out how one air may be restored to its intended charm and purity by being sung a little slower than it is marked. (*911*, 73.)

[16] *Corresp.*, 184.

[17] *M.E.*, 336.

[18] An excellent description of it is given by Mr. Sitwell (*1011*, 159–61). The largest of the four music rooms, decorated with medallions of Berlioz and Wagner and the death mask of Beethoven, ultimately contained the great piano-organ built by Alexandre. About this construction Berlioz busied himself on Liszt's behalf from 1852 to 1854. The instrument, combining features of the two keyboard machines in its name, possessed three manuals, sixteen registers, and one pedal. Berlioz was concerned that not only its sound but its shape be beautiful.

good enough to reserve a small suite for us at the Hotel de Russie or elsewhere . . . My arrangements with Beale," added Berlioz, "are now concluded and I have to be back in Paris by the 24th at latest." [19]

Berlioz never left Paris. Before the scheduled opening, *Benvenuto* had
to be postponed. Liszt explained that Beck, the tenor, and a small group of
his "followers" were sabotaging the work and spreading the rumor that it
would ruin the voices of the participants. "It surprised me greatly," replied the hardened Berlioz, "that some such thing had not yet occurred
. . . The worst thing about this tenor is that his ill-will goes with a lack
of capacity, and that his crowd . . . may form a cabal on the first night.
But I shall say nothing to discourage you further. I am behind you in
exact proportion to your own noble persistence. Act as if I were not
involved . . . If the tenor spoils his role, perhaps the audience will notice
it; besides, if the rest comes through I'll be more than content. . . .

"Farewell. No need to recommend Joachim to me: I know him of old
and esteem him highly.[20] I leave [for London] in a few hours. The Paris
papers must have told you the facts about the New Philharmonic Society.
It has devilishly stirred up London and I shall have on my neck, as soon
as I arrive, all of old England in a fury. Anderson, Costa and the rest are
the angriest. But if Beale lets me have the *needful amount of rehearsing*
I snap my fingers at their opposition. Farewell, dear Liszt . . . write to
me in London — *the truth* as always: I have faith only in you. . . ." [21]

The six months that Berlioz spent in Paris between the Exhibition and
his return to London had seen a change in the government. In December
1851 Louis-Napoleon had by his first *coup d'état* made himself Prince-
President for life and virtual dictator. The Second Republic was certainly
overthrown by force, for quantities of resisters were arrested, shot, or
exiled, but the change could not be called a revolution and many liberals
took it with resignation or indifference. As the philosophical Doudan
put it: "If I had been asked to guess last year who would go to the left
and who to the right in this last affair, I should have guessed mostly
wrong." [22]

[19] *M.E.*, 341–2.
[20] Joseph Joachim (1831–1907) had played before Berlioz in Leipzig and
Vienna, and had been engaged by him as soloist for the concerts of the Paris
Philharmonic in 1850.
[21] *M.E.*, 348–9.
[22] *188*, III, 284. The *coup d'état* was "announced" by placards posted before
six in the morning: everything had been done in the night — the arrest and
replacement of Republican officers in charge of the Paris troops, the detention
of Assembly members, including Cavaignac, Thiers, and the Secretary of War.

On his side, Berlioz noticed that the rise and fall of regimes brought no alteration in the state of music. Meyerbeer held the stage at the Opera: when *Le Prophète* was off, *Les Huguenots* was on. The Opéra-Comique, always happy-go-lucky, assimilated anything whatever. " 'For the belly, everything counts' as Sancho Panza used to say. That doughty squire would have been such an intrepid follower of comic operas! . . . Of Gluck and Mozart this breed will never know anything. It thinks *Don Giovanni* was written by Musard because the latter unquestionably wrote quadrilles on themes from the opera." [23]

Within that half year a few concerts had taken place at which Berlioz was performed, not under his baton. With him gone, his Paris Philharmonic disintegrated completely. It had played the work of a gifted young man, Ernest Reyer, who had put up fifteen hundred francs for the performance, but it could not be mustered when Berlioz received a later offer of two concerts. This was still before the *coup d'état* and public attention, expecting it, was focused upon the form this would take. People turned out in order to gape at Louis Napoleon, who was courting popularity at horse races and official balls. He was in fact wearing down opposition by repeated false alarms. Fatalism was being encouraged, and the result, predictable for the nation as a whole, seemed for many individuals scarcely a matter of choice: even Doudan, echoing the statesmen of the former government, felt a calm helplessness: "For me who have always lived under freedom of thought, speech and press, I shall find things hard to get used to . . . one has the impression of living in another planet, where all is silence and cold dry wind. Deep minds say it is the prerequisite of order. I couldn't contradict them if I would." [24]

Berlioz, being neither in politics nor close to it, remained as unmoved as Delacroix by acts that would once have aroused his indignation — for instance the treatment of Hugo and other intellectuals. But such is the effect of what we nowadays call times of crisis. The power to respond is blunted by overuse. Hugo had made more than one bid for political power

---

Soldiers were posted at all government offices, newspapers, and printing plants. The placards further announced that a plebiscite would be held to ratify the seizure of power in the name of the sacred revolution of 1789 and in the cause of peace and order.

A brief insurrection on December 4 was quelled, some thousand being shot. A list of proscribed men, including Victor Hugo, Thiers, and Laboulaye, was published. Many others fled or were sent outside the borders or shot without formality. The plebiscite ratified the act of the Prince-President, whom Pius IX at once recognized.

[23] *Soirées* (Second Epilogue) *Eves.*, 334.
[24] *188*, III, 284.

Berlioz in 1850, by Courbet

"Except perhaps in his portrait of Berlioz, I do
not know of any likeness . . . by Courbet in
which there is a particle of inner life."

— JACQUES-EMILE BLANCHE

and his party was now in flight: he must take the consequences. Both Delacroix and Berlioz hoped that a stable government would favor their respective arts, more dependent than literature on official favor. If the Prince-President held views similar to his uncle's, and if the regime were proud and decorative, it might provide occasions for grand ceilings and *Te Deums*.[25] What Péguy said of Victor Hugo's Bonapartism certainly applies to the other two members of the artistic trinity: "*Le vrai Napoléon, c'est le Napoléon où l'on rythme.*"[26]

Even so, it may be deemed fortunate that it was not Berlioz' *Te Deum* that was chosen in January 1852 to celebrate the brummagem pomp of the nascent Second Empire. Berlioz was in fact suspect to the new regime. He belonged to the house of Bertin, whose Orleanist opposition continued *in petto;* he had played for the Republic and been protected from its rigors by the Director of Fine Arts, Louis Blanc's brother Charles. He was, above all, an independent mind, whom official theaterdom and the "sound" people could not overawe. In a word, he was *persona non grata* — again just like Delacroix[27] — to the dubious new authorities. For this was not a Napoleonic regime but rather the first modern dictatorship — demagogic in tone, bourgeois in manners, anti-intellectual in both capacities. What Louis Philippe had been to monarchy, Louis Napoleon was to Empire, a Philistine half-breed in the pay of expanding industry and finance.

Before leaving for his London engagement, Berlioz conducted two concerts for Heinrich Ernst, and since no music of his own was played, he could publish an account of them. They were great successes which somewhat redeemed the dead level of ordinary music, even if it was the violin of Ernst and the piano of Leopold von Meyer that drew the crowd. Anywhere else, thought Berlioz, "the beautiful is not the ugly but the dull . . . The public does not even like what is bad. . . . We artists live in a state of death. . . ."[28] This could not be the view of a government which like its predecessors found the Opera a good instrument of rule: patronage, women, a means to celebrate glory and to show off stability. Berlioz, with reckless honesty, wrote a *feuilleton* on behalf of his fellow musicians who, he said, had such just grievances that on an official occasion they

[25] *181*, III, iii; *M.C., passim.*
[26] (*1271*, 89.) A paraphrase on Molière's line resolving the servant's doubt when he is faced with two masters who look exactly alike: "The true Amphitryon is the one where I dine." Péguy's notion is that Hugo found the genuine Napoleon to be the one he could turn into rhythm — *i.e.,* poetry.
[27] *181*, III, 269 and *passim.*
[28] *1386*, Jan. 27, 1852; *Corresp.,* 183.

made audible murmurings and the Prince-President found it expedient to withdraw. By an oversight, the article passed despite the censor and came out in the *Débats* as the sole outburst of criticism in a muzzled press.[29] Berlioz was swamped with visits and letters of congratulation. The working half of the Opera now loved him, the other half cursed, while Louis Napoleon's shady entourage put him down among those to keep a watchful eye on.

Urged by his advisers, Berlioz wrote the Prince's private secretary a letter to show that his published remarks signified neither defiance nor blackmail. His attitude toward the Prince for "pulling France out of the morass . . . could be summed up as one of grateful admiration."[30] The letter was sincere; it was necessary and yet impossible to make convincing, therefore useless and — what is worse — unbecoming for a man in the position that Berlioz should have occupied. He derived no benefit from it, for one has to be of the chameleon blood to profit from acts of submission, and it was plain that future acts of independence would occur. This was all the more likely that after the suppression of political news, Bertin counted on Berlioz for extended treatment of whatever subjects were in the air. The canny editor and opposition leader was even loath to let Berlioz go to London.[31]

By the spring of 1852, Beale and his partners had launched the New Philharmonic and subscriptions were coming in. The rate was two guineas for six concerts; artists were entitled to half price. Exeter Hall was chosen, despite Berlioz' strong feeling that it was too large for musical and practical results. The investment of over £2000 had persuaded his backers that they needed box-office returns in proportion. "I have an excellent orchestra," wrote Berlioz to Adèle, "and a choice chorus, so that everything goes as it should. Only the soloists defy all efforts to animate them; they sing like marble monuments. . . ."[32] Berlioz and Marie had a small but comfortable place on Old Cavendish Street and the composer, who read Dickens and took in matinees, became more of a Londoner than ever. He liked the green squares and parks, and took walks into the country, finding delight in the "luxuriant vegetation not to be matched anywhere on the Continent."[33]

As on earlier visits, he received many invitations "of which the British are very lavish" to clubs and private houses, and like all persons whose character combines reserve with lively feelings, he found quite congenial the formal — even stiff — manners of Victorian intellectuals and men of

[29] *1386*, Feb. 3, 1852.   [31] *M.E.*, 349.   [33] *M.E.*, 330.
[30] *M.E.*, 346.   [32] *M.E.*, 350.

business. For Adèle's peace of mind he had to refute French superstitions about English brutality. "Your opinions about cockfighting and other such things you'll allow me not to answer seriously . . . They are ideas which date back to the Empire." [34] Berlioz felt especially welcome at the house of Harriet Grote, wife of the historian, whose salon brought together statesmen and artists of all nationalities. His contacts with the musical and theatrical worlds were of the most cordial and he had the respect of all the critics without exception.

Before the first concert, due March 24, Berlioz heard good news of *Benvenuto* at Weimar. "My dear, good and wonderful friend," he wrote in reply to Liszt, "I am overjoyed . . . to have this new proof of your friendship for me. I embrace you with all my heart and say 'Thank you' without making phrases. . . . Don't forget to transmit my gratitude to the artists of the Weimar theatre for the talent and the work they have put into seconding your efforts, and you can add some words of excuse for the difficulties which my score entails. Tell them that in performing as they have done such whimsical and impetuous music, they have given the greatest proof of musicianship that anyone could ask of artists today." [35]

Berlioz also wrote a well-turned letter in answer to Princess Carolyne's congratulations and, at her suggestion, another to the Grand Duchess of Weimar. They prove again that when the deed involved no compromise with truth or self-respect he could be as worldly as a courtier and a sincere artist still. To the Paris newspapers he merely communicated a part of Liszt's victory bulletin: "Hail the Master-Goldsmiths! . . . *Benvenuto Cellini*, which was performed here yesterday, revealed its full stature as a work of art. . . . I thank Berlioz most heartily for the noble pleasure that the attentive study of his score has given me. It is one of the most powerful works I know, at once gorgeous filigree work and living sculpture of true originality." [36]

This vindication of his musical drama must have strengthened in Berlioz the retrospective mood which had accompanied the revision of the score, for we find him revolving the idea of a complete edition of his works, including the *Treatise on Orchestration*.[37] He had begun going over his printed scores, tabulating errors, replacing older instruments,[38] and making

---

[34] *M.E.*, 351. An unconscious sign that to Berlioz, living on the verge of the second, *the* Empire meant the days of his childhood — 1804–1815.

[35] *M.E.*, 352–3.

[36] *1398*, Apr. 4, 1852.

[37] Letters to Liszt: *207*, I, 219; II, 68–9.

[38] Notably the substitution of a tuba for one of the ophicleides.

other corrections based on recent rehearing. On the flyleaf of one copy we find a significant note: "Twenty-five works at an average of 10 francs each would make 250 francs the set. I should like the complete works to be sent to the Chapel or Philharmonic Societies of Brunswick, Hanover, Carlsruhe, Berlin, Vienna, Weimar, Munich, Bremen, Hamburg, Dresden, Leipzig, Amsterdam, London, and St. Petersburg." [39]

This task occupied only leisure moments during several years, for republication under one imprint was beset with difficulties. For the time being, Berlioz could only draw up a list of all the available items, with a description of each and the name of its publisher. The catalogue, issued by Brandus, was preceded by a note summing up Berlioz' "mission" and suggesting its technical significance; [40] bearing the date 1852, it argues the author's awareness of the form and meaning of his career.

The first six concerts of the New Philharmonic were a series of triumphs — a demonstration that Berlioz' mission was anything but mistimed or misplaced in England. While Liszt was conducting the second night of *Benvenuto*, Berlioz was presenting the "Jupiter" symphony, Beethoven's triple concerto, Weber's *Oberon* overture, Rossini's *William Tell* overture and the first four parts of the *Romeo and Juliet* symphony — all of which the audience and the press received with enthusiasm. It was, according to the *Musical World* "the commencement of a new epoch" in English orchestral music. [41]

At the second concert, the *pièce de résistance*, garnished with solos and trifles, was Beethoven's Fifth. For the third, besides repeating on request the excerpts from *Romeo*, Berlioz had determined to force down large fragments of Spontini's *La Vestale* against a British prejudice of twenty-five years' standing. He meant to commemorate the composer's recent death and would brook no opposition. All by himself he incarnated the Spontini tradition, the last phase of the reformed opera style based upon the works of Gluck and Mozart. On the afternoon of the concert, Berlioz received an oblong package with a letter from Spontini's widow: ". . . Allow me to offer you the conductor's baton with which my dear husband

[39] Reverse of flyleaf of *Harold en Italie* (Schlesinger) Bibl. Nat. (Rés. Vm 7·521.) Just above, he notes: "Griepenkerl [at Brunswick] already has *King Lear, Waverley*, and the *Fantastique*."

[40] *251* and see below motto of next Subchapter. The series of *Oeuvres* (not *Op.*), numbered from one to twenty-five, disregards their order of composition and puts the Treatise as *Oeuvre 10*. (See Supplement 5.) This classification was reproduced, with additions, as advertisement pages at the end of Berlioz' next two volumes of prose.

[41] Quoted in *1391* (1903) 522.

used to direct the works of Gluck and Mozart as well as his own. How could it be better used than by your able hand. . . . Tonight, as you conduct *La Vestale*, it will remind you . . . of him who loved you so much and so greatly admired your works. . . ." [42]

At this same concert, by a coincidence easily explained, Mme. Pleyel — the former Camille Moke — played the *Concertstück* of Weber: she now had connections with the *other* firm of French piano manufacturers, Erard, and Erard was Spontini's brother-in-law. He had escorted to London his sister and the "queen of pianists," who at the final concert was also to play one of Liszt's great pieces. [43] There was in fact a duel of virtuosos between Camille Pleyel and Liszt's pupil Wilhelmine Clauss, whom Berlioz thought highly of. In her anxiety over this championship bout, Camille complained to the trustees that Berlioz had accompanied her badly in the Weber. No one else had noticed it, and she lacked the wit to see that although Berlioz might at one time have shot or strangled her, at no time would he commit a crime against Weber.

For the fourth concert, Berlioz produced Beethoven's Ninth, which had been mangled once by Costa and had remained for most listeners "a sort of disagreeable acrostic." [44] Under Berlioz' baton, and with the plentiful rehearsals which he called for, Beethoven was vindicated, even though George Grove, hearing it for the first time "could make very little of it." [45] The work was greeted with storms of applause, the conductor being recalled six times at the end. Clara Novello, Martha Williams, Sims Reeves and Berlioz' favorite bass, Staudigl, sang the solo parts. Berlioz felt that the symphony had sounded even more impressive than at the Conservatoire. In the chorus, the sopranos and altos were remarkable. "One has no conception in Paris of these Englishwomen's voices, still less of the musicianship of choristers who in three sessions learn *by heart* the most complicated scores." [46] The orchestra was a picked international group and as before it had "sung like a quartet."

---

[42] *1391* (1903) 522.

[43] This program and plans for later ones sufficiently refute Mr. Sitwell's groundless supposition (*1011*, 166) that if Berlioz had been in charge at Weimar, his direction would have been "more selfish" than that of Liszt — meaning presumably more self-centered. Berlioz was "in charge" all over Europe and one does not have to *suppose* anything about his devotion to other music than his own. That he did not admire Liszt's later works is a critical question, not one of character.

[44] *M.E.*, 365.

[45] *1391* (1903) 522. This did not prevent Grove from subsequently maintaining that Berlioz did not understand Beethoven so well as he.

[46] *M.E.*, 365. There had been seven full rehearsals besides the sectional ones.

Berlioz' passion for Beethoven was just then enhanced — if that were possible — by the appearance of a large work on the master from the pen of Berlioz' Russian friend Wilhelm von Lenz.[47] It was the fruit of twenty years' research and the first attempt at a scholarly presentment of Beethoven (both biographical and critical) in opposition to the grudging or hostile opinion still prevailing in many quarters. Berlioz reviewed the two-volume work in great detail and found time as well to compose out of his own published essays, short stories and fictional critiques the entertaining volume entitled *Evenings with the Orchestra.*[48]

England's favorites, Handel and Mendelssohn, occupied the fifth program, together with Berlioz' *Francs-Juges* overture. At the sixth and last, the Ninth Symphony was repeated by request, and two parts of the *Damnation of Faust* were performed for the first time. Enthusiasm again rose to a high pitch. Berlioz took bow after bow amid the shouting crowd, a wreath was tossed on the stage, and the press was all but unanimous in praise. The "but" was Chorley of the *Athenaeum*, a born operagoer who deplored all the "new" music since Mozart as delirious and unintelligible.[49]

Berlioz had found his London "twelve hundred" and perhaps more. Unfortunately, the cost of doing things right had exceeded the returns, and the backers of the New Philharmonic had a deficit to face. This fact seems to have served the ends of Henry Wylde, one of the founding members, whose ambition was to conduct and play his own works.[50] In any case, the Committee did not engage Berlioz again for 1853. The nonmusical members, no doubt thinking of the profits of dance bands and promenade concerts, did not know what is accepted today in every large center, that an orchestra must have trustees ready to foot the bill. Berlioz' adequate rehearsals were certainly expensive, and Wylde was probably most economical in this regard.[51] But today, we have gone further in skimping, by

[47] *Beethoven et ses trois styles,* St. Petersburg, 1852, 2 vols.

[48] *Les Soirées de l'Orchestre.* See below, next Subchapter.

[49] His *Thirty Years' Musical Recollections* published in 2 vols. in 1862 are none the less informative about the middle decades of nineteenth-century music.

[50] Wylde (1822–1890) was a pianist and organist, as well as professor of harmony at the Royal Academy of Music. Berlioz had a low opinion of his ability as a conductor; the New Philharmonic played his *Paradise Lost* and other cantatas in 1853 and 1854.

[51] It should be noted that in 1853 the directors followed Berlioz' original advice and moved to a smaller hall, but then Wylde did not draw like Berlioz and they still had a deficit; whereupon they renounced their capitalism and advertised that any profit would be turned over to charity. (742, 180.)

virtually excluding from the regular repertory works that require soloists and choruses. For Western civilization is not primarily a musical civilization; rather, if we judge by its expenditures for things other than subsistence, it is a gum-chewing, liquorish, smoking, and moviegoing civilization. One need not feel any snobbish disdain of these pleasures in order to note that their evident priority denies us the right to boast of the meager alms which go to our few orchestras.

After the glory and deep satisfaction of the London season, it was dismal to return to Paris and its predictable routines and drudgeries. To these was added the grimness of Berlioz' private situation. Harriet was "quite well, that is to say, just the same," attended day and night by two reliable nurses. While Berlioz was in London, young Louis, who was back from his cruise, had suddenly decided to give up the sea. Fearing opposition, perhaps, he expressed his wish with impudence and also intimated that he was losing his mind. This brought down a remonstrance from Berlioz together with a one-hundred-franc note, necessitated by the boy's spendthrift ways. Louis was in Paris when his father returned, and the boy's indolent, pointless existence was a double burden, spiritual and financial. He was finally persuaded to continue in the merchant marine. He re-embarked in August. To augment his resources Berlioz was ready to sell Les Jacques, but there were no acceptable offers.

Unlike the unattached epicurean Stendhal, tracing in the dust with his cane the words "I'm going to be fifty," Berlioz at the same age was not in the mood to deplore missed opportunities of romance. Those he had taken were costing him his very blood in worry and effort. His hair was almost all gray and his nervous energy so depleted that he left rehearsals in the condition of "a wet rat" and spent intervening days in bed. "I cannot work during the night too," he wrote to Hiller, "for I find I have to have sleep . . . Even if I had to be guillotined at nine in the morning, I should all the same want to sleep till eleven." [52] But wit was only temporary relief and the therapy of grumbling has its limits. His season over, he must once again drag the reviewer's chain and ball for a living. At ten francs a column, he had to write from four to six columns a week about "pot-pourris of waltzes and galops . . . platitudes, turpitudes, things that are no-things . . ." [53] An offer, it is true, had come from the United States

[52] *Corresp.*, 190.
[53] *Mem.*, II, 158. It is remarkable how lively these articles are, in spite of their worthless points of departure. Berlioz moreover kept a reporter's eye on musical Europe, threw in brief notices of technical books, and missed no chance to teach esthetic lessons.

to conduct a series of concerts, but he awaited better terms. "If ever I accept . . . it will be solely in the hope of being able on my return to give up this job of music critic which is my shame and my despair. If you knew what I have had to hear since I came back from London, and what they want me to praise that I will not praise. . . ." [54]

The paradox of this job, "not of critic but of article clerk [*articlier*]" was that Berlioz' satiric dramatization of it was bringing him reputation, even popularity. Though the publisher of the *Voyage Musical* declined the *Evenings with the Orchestra*, another snapped it up and sold an edition very rapidly. Berlioz might well have feared the effect of becoming known in a double capacity, for his literature was obviously closer than his music to the standard of consumers' goods. Yet given a fit occasion, his music was not forgotten. In the fall of 1852, Baron Taylor was asked to carry out those provisions of the will of another connoisseur, Baron de Trémont, which concerned the five "artists' unions." [55] He suggested that Berlioz' *Requiem* be given in honor of the little old man who had been so generous a patron of the arts. This accordingly was done at St. Eustache on October 22.[56] The best singers and players of Paris took part as simple choristers or second desks under Berlioz' lead, and the audience was equally choice. The reviews were highly laudatory and the question arose whether the composer's *Te Deum*, as yet unheard, would be chosen for a coming official fête.

Louis-Napoleon was touring France and selling the idea — as our elegant modernism has it — of Empire. More accurately, he had bought all the politicians with munificent salaries, and he was now seducing the peasants by proffering the gold brick of peace with empire. The rest of Europe could afford to see these moves with greater serenity than they had felt at the struggles of the Republic. Central Europe was quiet, its chief excitement being the sale at auction of Germany's fleet, first formed in 1848. No one as yet could foresee the consequence of Bismarck's being sent as Prussian envoy to the Federal Diet and securing Austria's adherence to the Zollverein.

It was to this becalmed Germany, purged of politics and once more

---

[54] *M.C.*, 6.

[55] Between these two barons, the guilds of French writers, artists, and musicians were founded, nurtured, endowed, and given opportunities to come before the public in their professional capacities. This type of patron was even then dying out. Wagner was perhaps the last artist who succeeded (in the late seventies) with their aid.

[56] This was the performance which electrified young Saint-Saëns and which he was still thinking of and writing about nearly seventy years later. (*385, 406.*)

steeped in culture, that Liszt bade Berlioz and Marie to Weimar for a "Berlioz Week" beginning November 17, 1852. On the first night, *Benvenuto Cellini* won a still warmer reception than it had eight months before. The next two days were given to rehearsals for his own concert, at which young composers and virtuosos — friends of Berlioz or pupils of Liszt, such as Hans von Bülow, Klindworth, and Pruckner — were happy to play the lesser percussion instruments. On the twentieth an ovation greeted *Romeo and Juliet* and the first two parts of the *Damnation of Faust;* after which the Grand Duke conferred the Order of the Falcon on the composer-conductor. A second performance of *Cellini* followed a ducal dinner, and was itself topped by a banquet and ball in Berlioz' honor. He was accompanied to his train at a late hour by a shouting band of ecstatic admirers.

More important than official and friendly tribute was the winning over of the young. Bülow was a devotee from the first, calling himself fortunate to see Berlioz at work and proclaiming that the latter's mission was giving European music fresh vigor and a new start in the right direction. *Benvenuto,* he felt, restored the style of singers and orchestra to a "correct dramatic expression" which had been lost in Germany since the time of Gluck and Weber owing to the popularity of "French and Italian trash." [57] For public enlightenment, Bülow wrote a series of articles on *Benvenuto Cellini* calling its author "the hero of our modern music" and the "immediate and most energetic successor of Beethoven." The "grandiose work," *Cellini,* deserved study for its "numberless beauties." [58]

Liszt, who knew how much he owed artistically to Berlioz' genius and spiritually to his friendship, was repaying his debt in a princely manner, which Berlioz appreciated to the full. "Our ill-wishers," he wrote to the Princess, "seek for the *motive* [of Liszt's actions] and that they will never understand." [59] What Berlioz could not know was that Liszt's different and unobligated fondness for Wagner was causing him some embarrassment. For Wagner, without knowing the music of either *Cellini* or the *Damnation,* was casting doubt on Liszt's judgment of them by offering his own: "The poem of *Benvenuto Cellini* is bad, and the composer has been put into the unnatural position of having to fill with purely musical inventions the lacunae which only the poet can fill. Berlioz will never be

[57] Letter to his father, Jan. 21, 1853 (*171,* I, 412–3).

[58] From two separate essays, published serially in Leipzig and in Weimar; reprinted in *548,* I, 63 ff. and II, 12, 94, 189 and 234 (Notes). Compare Griepenkerl's pamphlet to the same effect, published in Brunswick a decade before. (*440.*)

[59] *M.E.,* 354; see also *M.C.,* 3.

able to rescue his unfortunate *Cellini*, but tell me which is worth more —
Benvenuto or Berlioz? Let the first go and save the second. It's horrible
for me to watch these efforts at resurrection. Let Berlioz write a new
opera . . . for only one thing can save him, and that is drama. . . . Believe me, I love Berlioz despite the capricious distrust that keeps him distant from me. He does not know me but I know him. If I expect something from any composer, it is from Berlioz, but not if he follows the line
that has led him to the platitudes of his *Faust* symphony." [60]

This letter, written by one who asserted that "he knew Berlioz" although he had neither heard the two works he attacked, nor could have
studied them since both were still unpublished (moreover mistaking the
Damnation for a symphony),[61] shows merely that Wagner sensed the purport of Berlioz' dramatic method and rebelled against it a priori. The remark about "gaps that only the poet can fill," and the belief that "Berlioz
can only be saved by drama," reveal Wagner's conception of opera and
his essentially literary bent, diametrically opposed to Berlioz' "purely
musical inventions." Possibly Liszt had described to Wagner how Berlioz
treated the Carnival scene in *Benvenuto* and this went against the grain
of the other's genius; so much so that he thought of becoming Berlioz'
librettist. Himself still uncertain whether his genius drove him to play-
writing or to music, he admired Berlioz enough to want to propose to
him a drama on *Wieland the Smith*.[62]

As for the objection that Wagner put forth when Liszt revived *Benvenuto* we do not hear of it when a similar effort went into *Lohengrin* or
Tannhäuser, nor is there any hint of "capricious distrust" when Berlioz reprinted, with a warm introduction, Liszt's eulogy on this last-named opera.
The triangular situation — half friendship, half enmity — must have been
very trying to Liszt, for he knew that Wagner had launched a major
attack on Berlioz in a massive work entitled *Opera and Drama*, which had
not yet been translated or excerpted, but which sooner or later would be
brought to his older friend's notice. Meanwhile the author of these am-

[60] *239*, I, 177.
[61] Ernest Newman was the first to show the impossibility of Wagner's knowing what he was talking about, as well as the efforts of later Wagnerians to
cover up the blunder by garbling texts. (*374*, 305 ff.) Wagner's onslaught upon
an unknown work must rank with two other deeds of the same sort —
Dryden's attack on *Gorboduc* and Arthur Bingham Walkley's on Shaw's
Saint Joan.
[62] *239*, I, 178. Liszt took Wagner severely to task about *Cellini*, and Wagner
apologized twice, pleading that Liszt "must have misunderstood." (*Ibid.*, 181
and 182.)

bivalent gestures resented the fact that Berlioz, their victim, was keeping his distance.

In France a second plebiscite had been held and doctored in order to make an indubitable emperor out of a Prince-President. The success of Berlioz' *Evenings* coinciding with this development, there was a bare chance that the Imperial chapel would be entrusted to him. He even sketched a project for adjoining to the Chapel an up-to-date school of music, but the post went to Auber who was already Director of the Conservatoire as well as on the list of prospective Senators at thirty thousand a year. Auber was seventy and had never achieved anything like the success of his *Masaniello* a quarter century before, but he was a tireless courtier and Lothario, endearing qualities to a ruler of the same cloth. The official beginning of this Second-Empire style of life was promulgated on the anniversary of Austerlitz, the Bonapartes' lucky day, December 2.

The new year 1853 opened for Berlioz with continued praise of his *Evenings*. His enemies themselves granted that he had the "wittiest, most imaginative, most ingenious and poetic mind." [63] His manner, it was said, recalled that of Diderot. In the same month, too, his English friends succeeded in having *Cellini* accepted at Covent Garden over Costa's opposition. The libretto had to be translated into Italian, and Berlioz made further musical revisions, the fruit of two hearings at Weimar and of suggestions from Liszt. He also corrected proofs of an Italian edition of the *Requiem*. Little else occupied his real mind. After long bargaining he yielded to Richault the rights to the *Damnation:* what proved to be twenty years later a fortune for this publisher was exchanged under pressure of necessity for a few hundreds. Berlioz' financial position was exactly what it had always been: respectable but strained. Louis had returned, and while taking a scientific course at Le Havre, had to be supported there. This was the period to which Berlioz refers in one of the most moving episodes of the *Memoirs* — that of the symphony that he voluntarily suppressed.[64]

Berlioz had by now three completed scores in his portfolio, for besides the *Te Deum*, he had finished the *Corsair* overture (out of the former "Tower of Nice")[65] and had expanded his "Shepherds' Farewell to the

---

[63] *1383*, quoted in *269*, 304.

[64] *Mem.*, II, 349–50. The fact, incidentally, is vouched for by Legouvé. (*362*, May 30, 1903.)

[65] The history of this delightful overture is worth recalling in brief, for it clinches our contention that Berlioz used events or literary titles purely as "association items" in the presentation of his works, the music remaining quite

Holy Family" into what is now the second part of *The Infant Christ,*
namely "The Flight into Egypt." But it was not the existence of these unplayed works that contributed to the suppression of the (fifth) symphony
in A. Rather, it was the moral exhaustion induced by a sense of having to
run in order to keep abreast of the same point. In one way, Berlioz' career
was enormously successful. His music, his training of performers, his
ideas, were impregnating Europe and germinating in hundreds of minds.
And he had brought this about by main strength, without help from
patron or angel. But the facilities which his achievement should have
brought him were still withheld, and the feat of endurance by which he
pursued the even tenor of his mission was beginning to tell on his physique.

After a bout of his old ailment — sore throat and fever now invariably
accompanied by nervous gastritis — his energy and morale recovered. His
articles once more sang the praises of work. "Keep going, ignore small

---

independent and nonprogrammatic. At Nice in 1831, Berlioz sketched the
work, having by then pondered the impressions of his first sea voyage. But he
probably did not finish the scoring. A second trip to the same city thirteen
years later renewed his interest in the material and he brought back the overture of the "The Tower of Nice," so called from the ruined tower, two hundred feet above the sea, where he perched and wrote. (*Soirées* (16th) *Eves.,*
190.) Played once in January 1845, the score did not please him and he set it
aside for revision. This took place, as we just saw, in London in 1851–1852,
at which time he renamed the overture *Le corsaire rouge.* Why so? The reason
appears when we know that this is the translated title of James Fenimore
Cooper's *The Red Rover* — not the meaningless "Red Corsair," as critics have
imagined in their determination to fasten Byron's plot upon Berlioz' music.
Now Cooper, who had been one of Berlioz' favorite authors, died in 1851 and
it is probable that Berlioz reread the sea tale as he was recasting his "Tower of
Nice." In Cooper's story a tower or mill on a rocky coast plays an important
role, which suggests a further link with Berlioz' *caption* for the overture, the
themes and form of which had long been set with no reference to the novel.
On thinking over this title chosen out of commemorative interest, Berlioz
struck out the adjective, no doubt realizing that it would seem puzzling to
those who knew nothing of Cooper, or who, knowing the book, might begin
to scan the music for the depiction of events. He left it, then, as *The Corsair*
— a mere label suggestive of the sea and conveniently personifying the jaunty
first theme. For the composer, the name connoted all his associated experiences
— the actual corsair who had sailed with him to Genoa, Byron's poem, Cooper's
novel, the two sojourns in Nice, and the great storm he had encountered on
his first crossing. But here again, one can verify the unliteralness of Berlioz'
musical mind: in a letter written shortly after the storm he says: "The wind
played a regular concert in the bare rigging . . . like an orchestra of piccolos."
(*Corresp.,* 78.) Yet no imitation of wind occurs in the overture; no piccolos
are used; the only suggestion of the sea is in the strings' graceful chromatic
arabesques, followed by syncopated chords, which open the piece and recur
twice more in the most formal and decorative fashion.

hurdles and small men, small emotions and all smallnesses in the world. What is done is done; that is the great challenge: *to do something.*" [66] This valor, coinciding with the return of spring, went into tasks of musical upkeep: correcting the parts for the London *Benvenuto;* preparing a manuscript of the *King Lear* overture for Liszt, who wanted to make a piano reduction and play it; [67] and dealing with Edouard Bénazet, the manager of the casino at Baden-Baden, who wanted good music and proposed to put on some or all of the *Damnation.* At last on May ninth, the *Benvenuto* rehearsals having begun, Berlioz left for his fourth London journey.

Covent Garden was then almost exclusively an Italian theater. It appealed to a public of dilettanti who came for the singers and who considered vocal feats the *raison d'être* of all opera. The singers in turn freely embroidered their parts, each acting to the gallery while the orchestra played a very modest second fiddle. Berlioz was in the enemy's house. Costa knew it, but he behaved in the most friendly and courteous manner. The score of *Benvenuto,* requiring an exact balance between *bel canto* and orchestral precision, and so highly organized for ensemble effects, could easily succumb to individualist tactics in the normal opera style. Though all but Tamberlick (Cellini) found their parts unusual, they took their cue from Costa and gave Berlioz their best co-operation. The rehearsals were arduous but satisfactory. Costa had also agreed to Berlioz' giving a concert at the *Old* Philharmonic. Berlioz was therefore rehearsing (for May thirtieth) a program consisting of the *Harold* symphony, the *Roman Carnival* overture and the *"Repos de la Sainte Famille"* from his *Flight into Egypt.* His good friend Sainton played the viola in *Harold* and did it so superbly as to win great applause despite the competition of a prolonged thunderstorm.

Three and a half weeks later, *Benvenuto Cellini* met with disaster. It was hissed practically from the beginning, despite the presence of the Queen and Prince Consort. The innocuous *Roman Carnival* overture was hissed even while playing, though as in Paris earlier, the *Benvenuto* overture proper was asked for twice. Berlioz did not repeat it, deeming it too long. The whole occasion partook of madness. Two or three of the songs were encored; at other times the hissing began before the singers opened their mouths. At his entrance and at the end, Berlioz was enthusiastically called

[66] *269,* 312. Compare Rude's motto, given in Michaud: "The great thing for an artist is to *do.*"

[67] Though usually reported as lost, it actually was written (see *207,* I, 237 and *M.C.,* 73) and Raabe lists it as being in the Liszt Museum at Weimar (*994a,* II, 272).

for and applauded. He of course declined to appear at the final curtain.[68]
Victoria and her Prince held their ground to the very last. The cabal of
the dilettanti was provable by the fact of preparatory meetings and their
behavior during the performance,[69] but a good many independent critics
opposed the score by reason — as usual — of evil features which it did not
contain. By an oversight, Costa had not asked the reviewers to the dress
rehearsal and they heard only the tumultuous *première*. Berlioz withdrew
the opera the next day.

The most curious result of the occasion was Chorley's candid revelation of the real trouble: "It will surprise those who only recollect *Benvenuto Cellini* by its performance, on going through the published music,
to find how considerable is the amount of real idea existing in it. — In no
other of its writer's works is the melody so abundant or so natural." After
telling how he had had his ears opened at the Weimar performance,
"the excitement of which was remarkable — almost amounting to a contagion not to be resisted — " Chorley reverts to "the beauties" of a
work that made him "almost forget the partisanship which belonged
to it." [70]

Two days after the London fall, two hundred and twenty singers and
players gathered and sent delegates to Berlioz to express their indignation
at the treatment his work had received. They spontaneously offered their
services for a testimonial concert of his own works at his own time. Independently of this, a subscription was taken up among musicians and publishers, and the sum of £200 was presented by Beale to the composer as
a token of good will. Berlioz declined the gift, and shortly thereafter the
proposed concert as well: "My dear Mr. Smythson," he wrote to the
chorus master, "The concert for which the artists of Covent Garden so
generously promised their aid cannot take place. I am none the less deeply
touched by the kindness shown me by these artists on this occasion. Please
thank them on my behalf and tell them I feel more happy and proud at
this proof of their friendship than if I had given the most splendid con-

---

[68] In accordance with custom, a supper party had been arranged for the cast,
the composer, and his friends. Berlioz appeared punctually, and so did J. W.
Davison, but the rest stayed away, out of misplaced embarrassment. The two
friends, showing signs of emotion at first, stayed to enjoy each other's company at one end of the glittering banquet table. (*340*, *655*.)

[69] The *Morning Post* wrote: "The work . . . was hissed with a determination which the major portion of the audience failed to overpower. . . . The
conduct of a certain number . . . looked extremely suspicious. The sibilations
were delivered with a simultaneousness, precision and perfection of ensemble
which savored strongly of collusion. . . ." (*1391*, *1903*, *654*.)

[70] *938*, II, 200–2.

cert in the ordinary way. Let me say, too, how grateful I am for the pains you took in rehearsing *Benvenuto Cellini*." [71]

On the same day Berlioz also wrote his thanks to Costa and less formally to Sainton, who being permanently settled in London as teacher and performer, was Berlioz' spokesman to the profession: "I am leaving on Saturday and have so much to do tomorrow that I cannot possibly accept your kind invitation. Do excuse me . . . I am also writing to Beale to thank the members of the committee — of whom you are one — for their delightful idea of publishing an English edition of my *Faust*. Nothing could be more delicately kind-hearted and artistically thoughtful." [72]

In these notes, as in those that Berlioz dispatched to intimates in France, there is no hint of bitterness or self-pity. If Berlioz felt either, he was too great a gentleman to let it contaminate his expressions of gratitude to friends, or of civility to enemies who, like Costa, had behaved honorably and helpfully.[73] Just as he had kept quite cool while conducting his work through the racket — hissers had even been posted in the wings — so now he was unshaken and indeed prophetic as to the inherent virtues of the work: "*Between ourselves*, I am sure that a real future is in store for this score (in Germany first and later in France). . . . Whatever may be its present fate . . . it is to my mind a new sort of music, of unconquerable vitality." [74]

A trivial detail, mentioned by the editor of these farewell letters from London, adds a stroke to the portrait of Berlioz as a man: "To Smythson . . . , Berlioz writes in a scrupulously legible hand, which it is amusing to compare with the rapid scrawl of his note written on the same day to his compatriot Sainton." [75] The sense of fitness, which is the true basis of order, no more deserted him in adversity than the sense of obligation whenever the bond of art linked him to another human being.

[71] *1380*, Aug. 10, 1935.

[72] *88*.

[73] He later had reason to think that Costa had only kept up an outward courtesy and was all the while privy to the cabal.

[74] *M.C.*, 81. This prophecy was fulfilled from 1879 on. At a revival in 1883, the pianist-composer Marie Jaëll, wrote to a Paris critic: "Indeed, it may be hard to believe in Paris that one of the greatest masterpieces of French dramatic music has been left buried for forty years. It is easier to deem it not worth reviving. But [when it is revived] how many other glories will fade! . . . For it will live as long as French music itself; no one will write another *Cellini*: it is more Gallic than anything Gallic that has been written. There is in it Rabelais and Voltaire . . . this dazzling effervescence of mind and wit . . . no one has captured like Berlioz, and it will be his undying glory." (*283*, 275.)

[75] Richard Capell, *1380*, Aug. 10, 1935.

Berlioz Colleague and Conductor

> Today the progress brought about by these
> . . . works in the ways of vocal and instru-
> mental performance is very widespread; the
> author has conducted them in most of the
> capitals of Europe, where his teachings have
> taken root: the old habits have been broken.
> — BERLIOZ' draft of a prospectus
>   for a Complete Edition of his
>   works (1852)

If in his *Memoirs* Berlioz may be said to moralize from his own life
about the duties of the musical artist, in the *Evenings with the Orchestra*
he dramatizes the same lesson in the mood of comic satire; that is, he illustrates his *métier* and the humor of it by facts of observation and of record, and by fiction of his own contriving. The scheme of the book is well
known: the imaginary narrator spends his evenings with the members of
an orchestra while they play in the opera pit of "a civilized town." [1] When
a bad work is being performed, good talk or the reading of a good book
indemnifies the instrumentists. We come to know some ten or twelve by
name, point of view, and physical traits, chief among them being Corsino,
first violin as well as composer, who often serves as Berlioz' mouthpiece.
All converse on an equal footing until one of the group improvises or
reads aloud the piece that Berlioz wishes to reprint from among his articles.
When an operatic masterpiece is being played — which Berlioz is careful
to name — they attend to their parts and there is no soiree.

The wit and artistic fervor of the book are equalled only by the excellence of the prose and the author's virtuosity in modulating from subject
to subject.[2] As for the felicity of the satire, it may be sampled by quoting
its underlying "myth": since "even in an ordinary opera" the absence of
the leading orchestral parts would be noticed, the performers take turns,

[1] *Les Soirées de l'Orchestre* has been translated into English (see *Eves.*)
but so clumsily and with so many blunders ("Key of G" for "G clef" and so
on) that it ought to be done over. The title then to be preferred would be
that used in the text above, for evenings *in* the orchestra suggests the paying
holder of an orchestra *seat*, whereas Berlioz' narrator spends his evenings *with*
the orchestra as one spends time with friends: the players, as Berlioz says,
form a club and hold soirees for their own and the reader's entertainment.

[2] Ernest Newman: ". . . the mere jointing and mortaring of the articles is
the work of a consummate literary artist. . . . The feeling for fitness and
proportion is as admirable as the design itself is original." (*Eves.*, xix.)

Berlioz conducting, by Doré (1850)

"Around 1876, this caricature was still being reproduced . . . on wallpaper. . . . At my grandfather's, it showed up in the billiard room, and it reappeared — regularly, obsessively — in my childhood dreams."

— ADOLPHE BOSCHOT

and "it follows that when the conversations and literary studies languish on the one hand, they revive on the other, and the fine talkers on the left take up their talk when those on the right take up their instruments." On one occasion, therefore, after a particularly dull opera, the conductor was moved to admonish his orchestral intelligentsia: "Silence, gentlemen, the performance is over!" [3]

In this volume also we have the biographies of Spontini, Méhul, and Paganini; the major essays on the state of music in France and England, on the monumental style, and on Euphonia; the account of the Beethoven celebration at Bonn and of Lenz's biography of the master; together with half a dozen humorous extravaganzas and innumerable observations on the life of art, some of which have supplied the most pregnant quotations in these chapters. As the English editor of the *Evenings* remarks, considering Berlioz' irritation at having to write constantly about nonentities or abuses, "all the greater must our admiration be for the artistic detachment that enabled him . . . to stand at a distance from the cause of his sufferings and see them objectively as subjects for the art of letters, to universalize them, and to sprinkle them with the salt of an irony that has kept them fresh. . . . He has really left little more to be said on such sempiternal topics as tenors, professors, coteries, claques, Philistines, opera houses, and the curious belief of the English that there is something vastly more creditable in playing an orchestral work or putting on an opera badly after two rehearsals than there would be in doing it well after ten." [4]

"Doing it well after ten" was of course the goal Berlioz set himself when he turned from critic and theorist to practicing conductor, and he achieved it most conspicuously during the very London season when he composed the *Evenings*. "Berlioz as a conductor," wrote a critic at the end of that year, "must be placed in the first rank of orchestral generals." [5] The term "general" is as appropriate as the profession was in fact novel, for until complex scores employing large orchestras became usual, such generalship was unnecessary and unknown.

There were conductors before Berlioz and Wagner, it is true, and all alike met somehow the problems of keeping time and accompanying singers and soloists, but the demands of the earlier music and especially of its public were far less exacting. The intricacies of conducting grew with the "polyphonization" of the instrumental band. Stamitz about 1750 introduced nuances into ensemble playing and amazed Mozart by the Mann-

[3] *Soirées* (Prologue and 10th) *Eves.*, 2 and 126.
[4] *Eves.*, xx-xxi.
[5] *742*, 181.

heim piano and forte. But the leader was still seated and playing the cembalo. Mozart himself directed in this fashion his last opera, *The Magic Flute*, on September 30, 1791 [6] — the cembalist's aide also directing, sometimes with an audible whack of a long stick upon the floor.[7] This was still the general practice in Haydn's time, though after the turn of the century the violinist-leader, waving his bow, became prominent. Among that class, Spohr and Habeneck cut loose from their music desks and stood up facing their men.[8] Spohr surprised the Londoners in 1820 by using a baton, as Habeneck was to do regularly until his death in 1849, although he still conducted most often from a first-violin part with cues (so-called *violon-conducteur*) instead of a full score. After Weber and with Berlioz the conductor *sui generis*, trained and known for his specialization, is an established fact.[9]

It is obvious, however, that this second period of transition spanned by the lives of Berlioz and Liszt, called for a subsidiary gift — that of initiating hundreds of orchestral players and operatic singers into the difficulties of what was for them a new art.[10] It was new because it marked the last step in the gradual change from music considered as a canvas for ad libbing melodic ornaments, nuances, instrumentation, and sometimes harmony, to music as a text fully noted in advance and presumably enforced by the composer's representative, the conductor. The transformation might be likened to the rise of chemistry from empiricism to a science with standard symbols and formulas, a progress which covered the same half century. This training in musical exactitude was part of Berlioz' mission, to which, as we have seen and shall see, he gave unremitting attention, both in writing and by direct action. Whether he had to show the tenor trombone how to play the pedal notes in the *Requiem* or taught singers that they must never change their parts but sometimes change their style, he forced into many a musical head a new conception of what art means. His engraved scores, moreover, were the first to contain hints and directions for the conductors themselves, based on his practical discovery of their deficiencies.

[6] *219*, III, 1436 *n.* 2.

[7] See Rousseau's *Dictionnaire* under *Baton* and *Battre la Mesure*. In the *Soirées* (13th) Berlioz records in story form a belated manifestation of this noisy habit. The transgressor is no less a person than Habeneck.

[8] See Spohr's *Autobiography*, II, 81.

[9] Spontini was famous as a conductor of his own operas and of a very limited repertory which he had learned with considerable pains. For a chronology of conducting technique, see *705*, 339–42.

[10] A. E. Keeton: "[Berlioz] not only taught his followers how to write for an orchestra, but he showed them besides how to play upon it." (*358, 939*.)

It was the want of competent leaders that drove Berlioz to become one of the world's great conductors. As a young man he had led the second performance of his Mass and somewhat later had agreed to lead an amateur orchestra.[11] But unlike Wagner, who was drawn to music because seeing Weber, he too wanted "to stand there and direct," [12] Berlioz at the time of composing his first overtures and symphonies was content to entrust their performance to Habeneck or Girard. Unfortunately Girard was a bungler who liked to alter the orchestration, even in Beethoven, and Habeneck could not be counted on to take the right tempi or to conduct throughout.[13] In self-defense Berlioz had to learn the art by himself; there was not even a textbook on the subject, let alone a course. Berlioz in fact was to write the first manual, *L'Art du Chef d'Orchestre* in 1855, reprinting it afterwards as the final chapter of his *Treatise on Orchestration.*[14]

His decision to take up conducting (made in December 1834) is significantly paralleled by Mendelssohn's acceptance of the leader's post at the Gewandhaus in Leipzig: both men went into action toward the end of 1835, only a few years before Otto Nicolaï — the third of the "new" conductors — assumed command at Vienna. Of the three, Berlioz was to travel the most widely, and it was with justice therefore that in the words quoted at the head of this section he took credit for fifteen years' orchestra leading and training throughout Europe: his discipline had broken and replaced "the old habits."

The new habits may seem to us simple and obvious, but even now, for all our exaggerated worship and ruinous subsidy of the man on the podium, they are far from universally understood or enforced.[15] Were Berlioz to come back to life, he would have to start afresh, though with a far more agile and responsive personnel. He would strive to enforce the three demands that he considered fundamental: fidelity, precision, strict tempi. He warred incessantly against alterers or arrangers, whether the mutilation was done to show off a voice, to "correct" a new composer or modernize an old, or to secure ease and convenience for the performer.[16] This

---

[11] *Grot.*, 20.

[12] *1091*, 9, 20–1.

[13] *386*, 10–1 and *300*, 114.

[14] Gassner's *Dirigent and Ripienist* (1844) is not in any way comparable. For Berlioz' essay, see *42*, *43*, and *46* through *50*. The quotations from it will hereafter be taken from the second ed. of *40* and marked *Tr.*

[15] Is it possible that our worship is akin to Wagner's "not to be king or kaiser, but to stand there and direct"? In most discussions of conducting the spell of power seems to overshadow the conscientious application of knowledge.

[16] If one should think Berlioz' account of the prima donna who "resigns herself to sing a masterpiece" and "covers it with embroidery" to be an

is to say that Berlioz would altogether oppose the twentieth-century notion of coauthorship in virtue of which every conductor in his vanity
offers the public a "new reading" of the classics, patented as "*my* Fifth
Symphony," even if this makes Beethoven's music unrecognizable.[17]

After fidelity, which implies intelligent study and an unquestioning
subdual of self to the composer's intention, the other requisites of precision
and strict time are specified for the very reason that the printed score is
at best approximate: it is this which makes music "the most exacting of
all the arts," and conducting the highest kind of fiduciary trust: "Of all
creative artists, the composer is almost the only one who depends on a
host of intermediaries between the public and himself; intermediaries who,
being intelligent or stupid, faithful or hostile, active or inert . . . can
help glorify his work or disfigure, libel, and even utterly destroy it." No
audience hearing a new score can see through a bad performance and discern "the ravages committed by the conductor." [18] The final responsibility
rests squarely upon him, for which reason he must be given full and absolute powers.[19] In order to exercise them justly, he must know his business,
which begins with time beating and ends with establishing "an invisible
bond" between himself and his players so that he may communicate to
them "the vital radiation of musicianship." [20] Only then will the performing mass display both ensemble and verve, sureness and fire. In short, Berlioz' philosophy of conducting reflects again the Romanticist interplay of
reason and impulse, neither usurping the other's rights.[21]

---

exaggeration (*Grot.* 127), consult the tenor Roger's own recollections of the
same Baden seasons directed by Berlioz, where the singers of Mozart or Weber
begin by saying: "MY aria in the first act is too long, I shall cut it"; and "I
do well in the little phrase in A during the quartet." (*1001*, 8.) Singers were
not the only menace. "When a new ballet succeeds, the opera is docked,
shaved, whittled, and exterminated, were it even a masterpiece consecrated
by public acclaim." (*Grot.*, 209.)

[17] See *1391* (1931) 21. It is scarcely a joke of prewar days that in Germany
Beethoven was termed "the ideal *Furtwaengler-komponist.*"

[18] *Tr.*, 299.

[19] Berlioz repeatedly uses the analogy of the ship's captain, and wittily
strengthens it by describing the mishap which overtook a lugger that was
commanded by a clarinet player. Berlioz was fully aware of the dangers and
disagreeableness of despotism, but he quotes the opening scene of Shakespeare's
Tempest to show that since the first mate risks as much as the duke, the noble-
man had better keep hands off and go below. "Even so," adds Berlioz, "it is
still a gruelling task to manage successfully an enterprise like the Baden Festival, so numerous are the small obstacles and so detrimental may the slightest
of them prove to the perfection of the whole." (*Grot.*, 102 ff., 123–4.)

[20] *Tr.*, 300. See also *Soirées* (16th) *Eves.*, 191.

[21] The historian of Music in Performance expresses surprise at this combination of opposites, apparently adopting the current view of the mind as a

To apply this principle in detail requires the seemingly overelaborate instructions that Berlioz imparts and explains at every opportunity: the clear and regular beat in various rhythms, the anticipatory cue for attack under different conditions of distance or instrumentation, the variable placing of the several groups of performers, the handling of special rhythmic and other combinations, the rehearsing by sections, the determination of tempi and nuances, and the enforcement of the written note, as to pitch, range, tone-quality, and dynamics. Little wonder that "the conductor's talent is as specialized as that of the violinist," though in Berlioz' day the statement still sounded paradoxical: the mere title of musician was thought to imply all the necessary acquirements for conducting any "musical hostilities." [22] From Berlioz' injunctions it is easy to discover what improvement he and his peers managed to bring about and what inertia from without resisted their efforts: "The indifference of most directors of musical institutions, their instinctive aversion towards whatever disturbs old habits . . . their parsimony as regards any genuinely musical expense, and the complete ignorance of the principles of our art among almost all those entrusted with its destiny." [23]

The rare instinct for what is fit and needful Berlioz possessed in an extreme degree.[24] Thus he not only deprecates any noise made with the baton ("it is worse than a poor device, it is a barbarism"), he also wishes the orchestra to tune up before they appear, and to make the least amount of racket compatible with leaving and returning to their seats. To prevent the deplorable lag between chorus and orchestra or any players remote from one another, he advocated the use, first of synchronized assistant conductors, and later of the "electric metronome," which he had built to his specifications. When he found that the click of the key which he

---

single-phase engine: "If, in the beginning, we called the interpreter Berlioz a typical French romanticist expressing power and fantastic emotionalism, we must enlarge this picture by emphasizing the other equally important trend of his interpretation — rigid objectivity, purity. Such duality, it is sure, makes for a strange yet fascinating combination." (*713*, 249.)

[22] *Soirées* (Second Epilogue; Prologue) Eves., 313 and 1. On a later page, Berlioz has to explain how Beethoven could be a poor conductor and none the less a "marvelous composer."

[23] *Tr.*, 309.

[24] "He took endless trouble to get everything right. I remember his asking Silas and me to come and see him in King Street, St. James's, just to try over the passage for the little cymbals. [In the *Queen Mab* scherzo] . . . Everyone was intensely enthusiastic and anxious to please Berlioz, who was a wonderful conductor. . . . It was generally admitted that no such orchestral performance had ever before been heard in England." (Wilhelm Ganz, *Memories of a Musician*, pp. 61–2.)

man in action. This discrepancy is due to the different circumstances of rehearsing and of performing. For the public view, Berlioz adopted very sober gestures. He warned the beginner against drawing the visual attention of the audience to himself: it inevitably detracts from the music.[38] But in rehearsal, and especially in Germany, where Berlioz could not speak the language, he gesticulated and pantomimed very broadly until he had conveyed his wishes and magnetized his players.[39] The net effect as it struck an English critic was "great decision and energy."[40] And again, "his beating was emphatic and intelligible, and the mass of instrumentalists followed the slightest indication of his baton, the minutest shade of expression which he desired to obtain, with marvellous accuracy."[41]

In the great test of Beethoven's Ninth, Berlioz outdid himself: "The time of the *allegro* was indicated to a nicety, and amidst all its extraordinary combinations, its exciting crescendos and overwhelming climaxes, the majesty which is the prevalent characteristic of the movement was never lost sight of. The *scherzo* was equally well-timed, and the *trio*, for the first time in our remembrance, played as fast as it should be . . . the audience . . . , charmed by its originality and the admirable decision with which it was executed, burst into an absolute uproar of cheers at its conclusion."[42]

The English obviously agreed with the Russians, Central Europeans, and French about Berlioz' justified pre-eminence as a leader. When both Berlioz and Wagner were in London together, and had later become widely known elsewhere, it was difficult to resist making comparisons. "I much prefer Berlioz to Richard Wagner as a conductor of Beethoven," wrote Cui. "Despite all his excellent qualities, Wagner often shows affectation, and introduces rallentendos of doubtful sentimentality."[43] And judging Berlioz in the performance of his own works, he exclaims: "What simplicity of manner, what sobriety and at the same time precision in his gestures! Of all the conductors we have seen in St. Petersburg, Berlioz is certainly the greatest."[44]

---

[38] *Tr.*, 301. Mozart in 1777: "Herr Stein sees and hears that I am more of a player than Beecke, that without grimaces of any kind I play so expressively . . . that I always remain strictly in time." (*219*, II, 497.)

[39] This is no doubt what Anton Seidl describes at second hand from Cosima Wagner. (*512*, 237.)

[40] Desmond Ryan: (*Musical World*, Dec. 11, 1847; *340*, 444).

[41] J. W. Davison (on Feb. 12, 1848; quoted in *340*, 446).

[42] *340*, 523.

[43] *345*, 252–3.

[44] *345*, 253.

This contrast is in a sense unfair to Wagner, who enjoyed performing but lacked both Berlioz' craftsmanlike interest in preparatory work, and his real capacity for winning over his men.[45] "Not a little of the unusual excellence of this performance is due to the highly favorable impression which M. Berlioz has known how to produce among the members of his orchestra by his polished and courteous manners. No conductor that ever entered an orchestra was more affable in his demeanor or more gentlemanly in his conduct. M. Berlioz respects and loves his orchestra. . . ."[46] But not even musicianship, magnetism, and respect for players wholly accounted for Berlioz' success. One more element contributed to it, an element which at first sight may seem extra-musical but which is as much a *sine qua non* as the rest: like a general he studied the ground and disposed his forces to the best advantage. Though his knowledge of acoustics was wholly empirical it was none the less exact; he knew most halls in Europe, tried to minimize their defects, and invariably saw to it that the ignorant or careless blocking of one performing group by another was remedied. He often directed not only instrumentists but also carpenters; his scores specify alternative dispositions, if the best are unpracticable; and his books are filled with remarks upon auditorium construction and with pleas for *smaller* opera houses and concert halls.[47] In short, being a creator as well as an interpreter, Berlioz conceived of orchestral music as a plastic ordering of sound within a space, and took pains to control or adjust all means toward that end.

This attention to the invisible design made by sounds naturally went with the conscious ability to diversify the substance of dramatic music — the styles and effects he chose for diverse occasions — and this leads naturally to a consideration of the proper performing of his works.[48] It is clear that if one of his monumental scores, such as the *Requiem* or *Te*

[45] Hueffer tells us of Wagner's impatience at rehearsals: Wagner "storms, hisses and stamps his foot." (727, 70.) "The truth is," Hueffer continues, "that Wagner's strength did not lie in keeping great masses together by a firm beat, or in helping an orchestra over the difficulties of . . . new and intricate music. But when these difficulties were overcome he would make them do things which a humdrum conductor would never think of." (*Ibid.,* 73.)

[46] *340,* 446. Berlioz was grateful besides: see, among a quantity of similar letters, the one he addressed in December 1853 to the Leipzig Singakademie. (*147* and *M.C.,* 139.)

[47] *A Trav.,* 94 ff., 212, 272-3; *Grot.,* 119, 214-5; *Mem., passim; Soirées* (10th) *Eves.,* 116.

[48] "Bach always knew exactly the effect that large-scale works would produce in a given hall." (Forkel, quoted in *943,* 308.)

Deum, is to be played, it must be done as nearly as possible under the conditions for which he designed it. When the *Te Deum* was given for the first and last time under Berlioz himself, the role which he assigned to mass and space in this antiphonal composition was evident. "Let one imagine," said Escudier, "nine hundred musicians, players and singers, the ones grouped in the midst of the nave in serried ranks, the others on benches rising in tiers above the altar, and Berlioz at the center, plunging his eagle glance into the army of performers whom he seemed to hold at the end of his marshal's baton — it was a spectacle that defies description." [49]

What the critic saw was the bulk; what Berlioz had conceived was the solemn dialogue between orchestra and organ from opposite ends of the church, while a double chorus stood in that same relation to a third. In this drama, the conductor's beat must throughout be seen or relayed for perfect concert. It follows that when at the inauguration of Carnegie Hall on May 5, 1891, the same work was given with all the performers jammed at one end of a nonreligious edifice, with inadequate risers causing mutual muffling, the music suffered a serious distortion. The critic of the *New York Times* noticed it, adding with unwitting sarcasm: "It stood the test well." [50]

Similar care must go into the production of the *Requiem*, so that the *Tuba mirum* occurs *in time* as well as in space. The four brass choirs are not placed at the corners of the orchestral mass in order to represent the geographical position of the angels, but to vary for each hearer the point of origin of sound: it yields an effect in dynamics which is as legitimately musical as the placing of a little piece of wood upon the strings of a violin. We can appreciate the value of space even better now than in 1837, since most of us have become inured to music coming out of a box. The pleasant surprise of a "live" concert largely comes from our sense of the multiple starting points of what we hear. Berlioz' directions for placing the instruments, among themselves and in relation to the audience, thus embody not only his suggestions for efficiency but also his idea of music as the production and *modification* of sound. Since he employed a variety of means, most of them simple, and not at all arbitrary despite their unfamiliarity, the first rule of performance for his works is to follow his instructions in the spirit of his own teachings — fidelity, precision, and strict tempi.

[49] *1383*, May 6, 1855.
[50] *N. Y. Times*, May 6, 1891. Tchaikovsky, who was present, records none the less his pleasure at the final movements. (*Diaries: 1020*, 311.)

The result of fidelity, as more than one hardened conductor or critic has testified, is invariably rewarding and sometimes astonishing.[51] This does not mean that Berlioz' specifications as to numbers need be fulfilled at all times. He was the first to scale them down when necessary;[52] but his proportions should be kept, and the question asked, whether with the forces at hand the musical ideas can be realized. It is an amazing fact that people who would be quite put out if the salt and pepper were missing from the table begrudge to artists the basic ingredients they call for. Critics automatically assume that Berlioz is asking for more than he needs but the wise conductor will have faith in Berlioz' technical intelligence. If instead he is imbued with the prefabricated view of Berlioz as a wild and fiery particle, he will suppose himself able to edit what he considers flighty or superfluous; the result will be unsatisfactory, and he will ascribe his own limitations to the music itself. As Saint-Saëns has said of the *Hamlet* March, most conductors cannot imagine ahead of time the moving grandeur of the piece. The only thing to do then is to observe the fundamental law of musical performance: "When in doubt, play what's written."[53]

It should be more of a commonplace than it is that we do not know the piece — any piece — until we have heard it done right. Much of the ostensibly firsthand objections to Berlioz as an artist come from unsuspected travesty. In the Enchantment scene of the *Damnation of Faust*, for instance, the three calls of Margarita's name are marked respectively *piano*, *mezzo forte*, and *dolcissimo* — which is why most tenors in performance and on the records, bellow the girl's name fortissimo throughout and

[51] Pierné: "Nothing [in his scores] is pointless. The most insignificant details — or so they would seem — have a purpose which is revealed when actually played." (*1305*, 2548.) When Sir Thomas Beecham gave the *Symphonie Fantastique* "just so," with four harps for the Waltz and exact intonation for the woodwinds, the critic called it "magnificent . . . an event which will be talked of for days to come." (*1380*, Feb. 24, 1933.) See also Mr. Percy Scholes "conversion" to the same symphony when well-played: "Then for the first time I saw something great in it." (*526*, 31.)

[52] For example, he gave the *Requiem* at Baden in 1861 with only three pairs of kettledrums instead of eight, partly because he could not find the full complement and partly because the hall was a tenth as large as the Church of the Invalides and much more resonant. (*A Trav.*, 288.) Conductors of good will should emulate Toscanini and read the essays and letters of the composer whose works, for whatever reason, they produce under altered conditions.

[53] This of course means what Berlioz wrote, not what the editors of the German, so-called complete, edition substituted for his text. In this same *Hamlet* March, for example, they omit the injunction to muffle the drums, which changes the effect of 48 bars out of 118. For a list of other alterations and omissions, see below Supplement 5.

"prove" to the uninformed listener the vulgarity of the composer's taste.[54]

The law-abiding conductor will, needless to say, give especial attention to tempi. With few exceptions, the works of Berlioz bear metronome marks, and within movements Berlioz is careful to indicate the relation between the bars of a fast tempo to a preceding slow one or vice versa. He was concerned with this from his very first published score of 1828, and it is a fact provable by ear that the failure to observe these relations in the music of Berlioz undermines the architecture of the whole work. One's impulse may be to retort that it must be very strange music which is so fragile, but a moment's thought shows on the contrary that it must be an uncommonly godlike art which is diffused through every element of the organism.[55] No one thinks of saying that it is a poor melody which cannot stand being sung out of tune, or a weak quartet which won't come through despite lack of ensemble: music is above all an art of adjustment, and Berlioz' times, nuances and phrasing are as important as his instrumentation, "spacing," and intonation. One cannot have it both ways, saying on the one hand that his art relies on crude effects and on the other that his demand for precision is a kind of finickiness not needed for sturdy fellows like Mozart or Debussy.

Mr. Bernard Haggin gives a perfect demonstration of these truths which merits being quoted at length. The current recording of *Harold in Italy*,[56] says Mr. Haggin, "has enabled me to document my dissatisfaction with the performance when I heard it in Carnegie Hall last November. The work did not have the effect I remembered and expected . . . its sections fell apart into detached episodes instead of cohering in a unified utterance. And I can see now that the performance is the product of a man with an ear for sonority but no feeling for pace. . . .

"In the third movement Berlioz gives a metronome number for the *Allegro assai* of the introductory section and another metronome number for the *Allegretto* of the serenade, to implement his direction that the dotted quarter-note of the *Allegretto* shall equal the dotted half-note of the *Allegro assai*, — or in other words that one measure of the *Allegretto* shall take the time of two measures of the *Allegro assai*. But Koussevitzky

---

[54] Again, in the introduction to the *King Lear* overture, the nuances for the drum (*Min. Sc.*, pp. 12–16) are unmistakably clear, as is the instruction to use sponge-headed sticks. If the timpanist lets himself go, a passage of delicate contrasts turns into an air raid.

[55] Bela Bartók, in his later scores, stipulates the total playing time in minutes and seconds. In a movement composed of differently paced sections this still leaves the apportionment of time to the conductor.

[56] See *1436*.

slows down the *Allegretto*, altering its relation to the *Allegro assai* and changing what Berlioz intended as a fairly animated serenade into a rather lugubrious lament. Later . . . Berlioz further integrates the two by continuing the sharply rhythmed accompaniment-figure of the *Allegro assai* into the half-as-fast *Allegretto* as a background for the serenade. Clearly, the accompaniment-figure must continue unaltered in speed and character, and *Berlioz' directions for the two tempos must be obeyed literally* [italics added]; but Koussevitzky again slows down the *Allegretto* and with it the accompaniment-figure. . . ." Mr. Haggin then shows how the work is further disjointed: "There is another example of this involving two movements: when the viola solo of the introduction of the first movement recurs in the course of the second movement it should move at the same pace — as it does if one takes Berlioz' tempos for the movements; but with Koussevitzky's altered tempos it comes out enormously slower in the second movement." [57] Finally, Mr. Haggin criticizes the disregard of Berlioz' opposite nuances (*pp*'s against *ff*'s) which creates some of the noise on the recording — all of these details being of course not surface ornaments open to free choice but being in a literal sense the molecules out of which the music is made.

Mr. Koussevitzky is certainly not the only conductor of Berlioz who has been hoist with his own *ritard*, nor the only one whose attempt to give a "reading" has made great music tedious or irritating.[58] But all the characteristics of the man and artist in Berlioz point to the fact that his music must not be played by physical or intellectual anarchists. It is true of all good performance that "the musicianship is harder than the notes," but whatever may be argued about style in the older masters who did not specify nuances is patently false with respect to Berlioz who did. The nature of his melody, harmony, and rhythm is inherently expressive and dramatic; no further "expression" therefore has to be troweled on the contours molded by his hand. More important still, no preconceived idea of program or illustrative effect must enter into the performer's head. The most instinctively musical leaders, from Mottl to Toscanini, have always given the best renderings of Berlioz. But they were also men of intelli-

---

[57] *1393* (1945) 426.
[58] The modern menace is the conductor who automatically exaggerates, stuns the hearers with speed in moments of vigor and lulls them to sleep in the contemplative. One recording of the *Fantastique*, made some ten years ago *and which won a prize*, races through the March with the half note equaling 85 and going up to 100 (instead of 72); then languishes through the adagio with the dotted quarter equaling 72 instead of Berlioz' 84. One reviewer, noticing the drag, remarked on Berlioz' "sentimentality."

gence, whose musicianship did not stop short of the head, where sound stimulates the imagination to perceive all the internal links which make music independent and self-propelling. This is undoubtedly what Toscanini means when, in rehearsing the *Romeo and Juliet* symphony, he raps impatiently and shouts "T'ink!"

To sum up, the best conductors for Berlioz are those who, like the late Felix Weingartner, are known for their "neoclassic rigidity." [59] This is not the "icy stiffness" Berlioz deplored, but the rigorous self-possession he required and exhibited in his own directing. Among the living, Toscanini is the great exemplar of this style, with Erich Kleiber a close second. Such a leader must in addition have a liking for the music, especially if he undertakes to do one of the big unfamiliar works for which he has no standard of comparison. [60] For these — the operas above all — there must obtain what Chesterton's uncle called "positively Nubian" [61] conditions, that is, perfect, utopian — and yet so simple: rehearsals by sections [62] and in sufficient numbers; trained performers willing to be led; unified direction emanating from a mind conscious of the need to make every detail subserve one end (this merely defines the artist) [63]; and finally an adequate supply of the sinews of war, to be disbursed for "genuinely musical expenses."

Otherwise it is better to refrain altogether from the enterprise. [64] The suggestion of war is apposite throughout. If the leader in the Berlioz tradition is a general, he must prepare for victory from the start, for the nature of his performance is such that he can neither change his mind during the action nor explain away disaster afterwards. Real war, of course, has this advantage over all other undertakings of civilized man that nearly everyone engaged in it understands its object. In this respect artistic en-

---

[59] *504*, 184.

[60] One wonders how Leopold Auer managed the *Requiem* in St. Petersburg, while confessing himself unable to understand what he was conducting. (*925*, 52–61, 253.)

[61] After a shoe polish which contained exactly the ingredients specified on the bottle. See Chesterton's admirable *Autobiography*.

[62] "Only in this way can modern music be done right." Berlioz to Lecourt, April 19, 1840. (*86*, 581.)

[63] Mottl who triumphantly revived *Benvenuto Cellini* in the 1880's declared that it was harder to direct than *Die Meistersinger*, and Weingartner has related at length his difficulties with the score in Berlin. Once they are mastered everything seems easy and applause rewards the participants. The *Damnation of Faust*, which is now almost hackneyed in France, occupied Colonne a whole winter before he risked a public audition (1877).

[64] "To present [the symphony] after one rehearsal, according to the London habit, would be complete murder." Berlioz to Osborne, Feb. 23, 1859 (*224*, 104).

deavor is at the bottom of the scale, and hence requires the founding and maintaining of a tradition. None knew this better than Berlioz. "The idea can be written down, the form may be outlined, but the feeling for performance cannot be fixed; it is intangible; for it is genius, soul, the living flame, which when it dies leaves behind it a darkness all the more profound that its brilliance has been more dazzling. And this is why not only the works of the great virtuosi inventors lose more or less in not being played by their author, but why also those of original and expressive composers retain only a part of their power when the author does not direct their performance." [65] Berlioz, speaking at the outset of Paganini, is obviously led on to think of himself. When he wrote these lines he had barely started his own tradition; when he reprinted them in the *Soirées* in 1852, he still had ahead of him fifteen years of work to the same end.

[65] *Soirées* (16th) *Eves.*, 191.

22. *Religious History:* L'Enfance du Christ

July 10, 1853 to
February 3, 1855

Perhaps he thought of God only when he
wrote *L'Enfance du Christ*, that tender masterpiece. And, who knows? perhaps also
God in his goodness took it for a prayer.
— BARBEY D'AUREVILLY

THE TWO YEARS measured by Berlioz' fourth and fifth visits to London
(July 1853 to June 1855) represent the harvest time of his career. He had
sown in Paris for a quarter century, in Central Europe for almost fifteen,
in England for seven; and everywhere recognition, honors, and spontaneous devotion were his to reap. He was still alone and overworked, still
attacked, but the active musical minority sided with him and some of the
old irreconcilables — Fétis, Moscheles, Adolphe Adam — were beginning
to act reconciled. As composer, organizer, man of letters, and man of
the world Berlioz was in demand. The financial reward was slight but
with the small income from his inheritance and the trickle of royalties, he
enjoyed a fair livelihood. He could occasionally buy his freedom from
journalism for a seaside vacation, and he repeatedly received more musical
offers than he could accept.

These coming rewards Berlioz had no means of foreseeing. Returning
from the London failure of *Benvenuto*, he had the prospect of going
the next month to conduct at Baden-Baden and the immediate task of
proofreading three unpublished scores — the *Damnation*, the *Te Deum*,
and the *Flight into Egypt*. Fatigue put him in two minds: "After [these
publications] the Lord knows what I shall decide to do. I am torn between the love of art and disgust, between lassitude about the known and
eagerness for the unknown, between obstinate tenacity and Reason which
cries 'impossible!' " [1] Seeing too well around his own position and observing that Liszt's recent effort on behalf of the new music exposed his friend
to the same intrigues and insults, Berlioz voiced an ironic doubt: "Could
it be that we are simply imbeciles, possibly even impudent rogues, with
our private pretensions?"

[1] To Liszt, *M.C.*, 93.

He then modulates to a touchy subject that Liszt had brought up: "I am as convinced as you are that it will not be hard for me to mesh gears with Wagner, if he will only put a little oil in the wheels. As for the words to which you refer, I have never read them and hold no grudge on their account. I myself have too often fired into the marching throng to be anything like surprised at getting broadsides in return." [2] The allusion was to Wagner's ambivalent attack in *Opera and Drama* two years before. As for the meshing of gears, it did not take place for another two years, Wagner being still an exile in Switzerland, and Berlioz in the interim shuttling back and forth between Paris and Germany.

The reason for Berlioz' engagement at Baden was the presence there of Edouard Bénazet as holder of the gambling concession. He was an adroit entrepreneur who had studied a little at the Conservatoire, mingled with artistic and diplomatic society, and who now undertook to make the Baden waters an unusually chic resort by providing a season of artistic notables matching the high society. The great lounge known as "the Conversation" was made into a concert hall, and there on August 11, 1853 some three hundred listeners indoors (and twice as many outdoors) heard Parts I and II of the *Damnation of Faust*.[3] Though this was not the dreamed-of public of Euphonia, Berlioz' task was made very agreeable by Bénazet's closing of the gaming tables for the day. The "King" — as the impresario was called — had also provided at his expense additional instrumentists from Carlsruhe. To rehearse them, Berlioz covered the twenty-five miles by train. He and his men were hospitably cared for by the croupier-Maecenas, who thenceforth offered Berlioz a yearly opportunity to direct.

From Baden Berlioz went to Frankfort-am-Main, gave two concerts, and with the local music societies projected a Shakespeare evening at which he might hear the appropriate numbers of his *Tristia*. Back in Paris, two *feuilletons* "leaped at his throat," but he shook them off to prepare for Hanover where the young blind King especially delighted in Berlioz' music. Brunswick and Leipzig also put in bids for the composer's presence. At Detmold, without his help, the reigning family of Lippe was preparing an audition of *Romeo and Juliet* entire. The Prince would sing Friar Laurence and the young Princesses joined the chorus. About this time, too, an offer came from England which sounded so attractive

[2] *M.C.*, 94.
[3] The uniqueness of the new Baden is frequently described in the belles-lettres of the period. See the Goncourt brothers' *Charles Demailly*, Turgenev's *Smoke*, and such memoirs as Sir Horace Rumbold's *Recollections of a Diplomatist*, London, 1903, 2 vols. (I, 216 ff.).

that Berlioz became suspicious and asked for a deposited guarantee lest he fall into the hands of another Jullien. "They agree to everything, which frightens me." [4] In Paris, the opening of Meyerbeer's new opera was being coddled by a new device — the press conference — and Berlioz had to attend the solemn gathering at the Café de Paris. As he was leaving for Germany, it mattered little to him that the Institute, just then stimulated by death to take fresh thought, omitted Berlioz from its list and elected Reber.

Ample compensation was in store at Brunswick where Berlioz' two concerts created a lasting commotion. He was played by the Park band, serenaded, given a silver-gilt baton, smothered in laurel, and hugged on the streets by perfect strangers. The musicians' fund was named after him, and the orchestra, which had the reputation of being "tough," followed his lead to his extreme satisfaction. [5] In two rehearsals he had "broken the muscle-bound rhythms" which he feared for his works. [6] Not losing sight of the future, moreover, he had asked Joachim to play the viola in *Harold*, "one of my main motives for giving *Faust*," being, as he wrote to the virtuoso, "that you should hear that score complete." For Joachim was "a superb talent," young, and ambitious of fame as a composer. [7]

Griepenkerl, the critic and theorist, followed Berlioz to Hanover and began to arrange for a Leipzig concert. The Hanoverian rulers had heard *Cellini* hissed in London, and their subjects had been rather cool on Berlioz' first appearance ten years before, but this time warmth was universal. Diamond-studded gifts were added to the wreaths and plaudits. The King was beside himself with joy. "I cannot see you conduct, but I can sense how you do it." [8] Most touching of all, the orchestra voted not to take its usual fees and to turn them over to the composer-conductor. Berlioz accepted, on condition that it should never happen again. Goethe's (and Beethoven's) Bettina von Arnim, aged seventy-two, came out on purpose, not to *see* Berlioz, as she said, but to *look* at him.

The next step was north to Bremen for a single concert, then diagonally across Germany to Leipzig, the citadel to be stormed again and again. Liszt came, accompanied by the faithful: Peter Cornelius, Richard Pohl,

---

[4] *M.C.*, 110 and 113.

[5] *1406* (1853) 344.

[6] *M.C.*, 120.

[7] *M.C.*, 115. It is worth stressing the fact that nearly every one of Berlioz' partisans and performers, young or old, was a composer or intended to become one. Their later careers or the modest fame as creators which we now assign to them was not a part of the situation as it appeared then.

[8] *M.C.*, 129: King George V, though young, had been blind for fifteen years.

Klindworth, Remenyi, Pruckner, Raff, Joachim, and others. Before the concert, the *Kapellmeister*, Ferdinand David, gave a soiree at which Liszt played piano arrangements of Berlioz, including a comic fantasia by Bülow on two motives from *Benvenuto*. The concert the next day was an unqualified success, and a second ten days later brought excitement and banqueting to effervescence.

The press was divided as before, but the reminiscent critics could report Berlioz' visible advance in public esteem. "He has convinced us," said one interpreter, "that he possesses not only a musician's spirit and an artist's mind, but a heart also. He likes to express . . . the most tender and ethereal feelings. . . . Each voice in his orchestra is an animate thing. . . . His music is truly polyphonic, and those who deny its organic unity are in error. . . . For a long while Shakespeare's *Hamlet* was held to be obscure, inorganic, full of enigmas and contradictions. One day Goethe found its meaning and the marvelous work became clear and intelligible: just so with Berlioz. . . ."[9]

Otto Jahn, the great Mozart scholar, continued to jeer at all modern music ("there is no other God but Berlioz and Liszt is his prophet"), condemned its lack of melody and roughness of texture and, arraigning its supposed program, went on to criticize Berlioz' Roman Carnival because it did not match *his* conception of the occasion.[10] The term "modern music" had been used by Berlioz himself in an interview given to J. C. Lobe and published in the *Fliegende Blätter für Musik*.[11] Feeling as he did about systems and pedantry and knowing history, Berlioz naturally refused to limit the scope of either music or modern music. He pointed out that a commentary on the present state of the art would fill a volume (he had just published one and had written enough for three more) and that the issuing of manifestos went against his principles: "I have not the slightest ambition to *represent* anybody, nor to be deputy, senator, or consul. . . . Besides, if I had such a wish, it seems to me I need not do anything more in order to earn the approval of my fellow-practitioners . . . than to imitate Coriolanus . . . and bare my breast to show the wounds received in defending our territory.

"As for my own confession of faith, is it not . . . in my works . . . in what I have done and what I have not done? What music is today, you know as well as I do; what it will be, neither you nor I can tell. . . . Music

[9] *1406* (1853) 393–4.
[10] Originally published in *Grenzboten* (1853) 481 ff. Reprinted in *450*, 109–10 and 111.
[11] *1382*, V, 296–300 (in French and German); French original in *Ménestrel*, Feb. 22, 1885, reprinted with two slight errors in *M.C.*, 130–4.

is the most poetic, the most powerful, the most alive of all the arts; it should be the freest, though it is not yet so. Hence our artistic travails, obscure devotion, weariness, and despair. . . ."

Berlioz then recurs to the symbol of Perseus whom he had chosen for his opera on the theme of art, and develops a parable whose luxuriant imagery merely veils its precision: "Modern music, music proper (and not the courtesan one meets everywhere under that name) is like the antique Andromeda, divinely naked and beautiful, whose burning glances break into many-colored rays by shining through her tears. Chained to a rock on the edge of a boundless sea . . . she awaits the conquering Perseus who will break her chains and destroy the Chimaera named Routine. . . . I believe that by now the monster is getting old: his motions are not so energetic as of yore . . . his heavy paws slip on the edge of Andromeda's rock.[12] And when the devoted lover of the sublime captive . . . has restored her to Greece, at the risk of seeing his passion repaid with cold indifference, it will be vain for neighboring satyrs to laugh at his ardor and cry: 'Leave her in chains! How do you know that once freed she will be yours? In bondage she is easier to possess . . .' The loving lover wants not to wrest but to receive. He will save Andromeda chastely, and would . . . even give her wings to augment her liberty.[13]

"This," concludes Berlioz, "is the only confession of faith I can make, and I make it solely to prove to you that I have a faith. Many have none, and unfortunately I have one, which I have too long proclaimed from the housetops, in pious obedience to the gospel." [14]

In other words, Berlioz declined to bind himself or anyone else by a program, and to assume the role of leader of a school. His faith was clear from his deeds and parables, and strong without the buttressing of a cosmic philosophy. He knew the danger of so much self-reliance: "It is not true that 'faith is the only salvation.' On the contrary, faith is the only perdition, and by faith I shall be damned." [15] This was prophetic. Berlioz had not read "the lines" by Wagner which Liszt referred to,

---

[12] This same myth was one to which Browning recurred in a comparable way. See W. C. De Vane, *A Browning Handbook*, 305.

[13] *M.C.*, 132-3. The modern musicologist Constantin Photiadès has written an admirable study of "Berlioz et Andromède" (*493*), in which he details the fitness and lasting value of Berlioz' allegory.

[14] *M.C.*, 133-4. One thinks of Shaw, who said "I am nothing if not explanatory," but who never discourses upon his technical skill, so that like Berlioz he has been called by shallow minds "no artist": Mr. Eric Bentley has ably shown the playwright's mastery of craft in his *Bernard Shaw* (1947).

[15] *M.C.*, 134.

and which later served the doctrinaires as a systematic weapon against Berlioz' "lack of a scientific esthetics."[16] But Berlioz chose the right part for him, and now that Wagner's theorizing appears in all its inconsistency, Berlioz' decision to stand on his accomplishment rather than on a platform appears also as sound judgment. How could he, arguing for freedom, be a party to boxing up his art within a creed? Nor, believing as he did in the integrity of the individual artist, could he claim the liberation and renovation of music for himself alone. He knew what he had done but as he said in explaining to Adèle his successes in Germany, "it is *Time* which has moved ahead . . . and the great number of young artists newly established in Hanover. . . ."[17]

Berlioz' meditations on artistic faith were not remote from those other feelings which from his twelfth year had linked in his mind music and religion. Lately, the gentle and intimate aspects of that association of ideas had borne fruit in the little score of *The Flight into Egypt*, which he heard for the first time entire on November 30, 1853. Everywhere the final section entitled "*Le Repos de la Sainte Famille*" had been so well liked that he was thinking of enlarging the work by means of a sequel — *The Holy Family in Egypt;* and since his two nieces, the daughters of Adèle, were especially devout and especially desirous of seeing their names on a score, he promised them the dedication.[18]

The decision to proceed with the work occurred just when Berlioz met Brahms, whose favorite within the Berlioz repertoire turned out to be this very score.[19] Then aged twenty, Brahms and his first works made a strong impression on Berlioz: "I am grateful to you," he tells Joachim, "for making known to me this shy young composer who is bent on writing modern music. He will have much to endure . . ."[20] Meanwhile in Weimar, an-

---

[16] *337, 138; 504, 6;* and elsewhere.

[17] *M.C.,* 135. The supposition that he was unaware or unreflective in his endeavor is refuted by many casual remarks, of which perhaps the most striking is his annotation on the proof sheets of a stupid article submitted to him in 1860 by the editor of a biographical dictionary. Berlioz writes: "My 'eccentricities' have today been taken up throughout Europe and seem perfectly normal." (*60, 615.*)

[18] *M.C.,* 137.

[19] Brahms to Clara Schumann: "I have often heard it and it has always enchanted me. I really like it best of all Berlioz' works." (*231,* I, *53.*)

[20] *M.C.,* 142. Berlioz heard the Scherzo, op. 4 and the adagio of the Sonata, op. 5. Brahms tells Joachim: "On Sunday I even went to see Brendel in spite of the . . . Leipzigers . . . Berlioz praised me with such great warmth and cordiality that the others humbly followed suit." (*965, 39.*)

other young musician, Peter Cornelius, who called himself

> A pale and candid Lisztian
> To his last breath and tone;
> A Berlioz-Wagner-Weimar-Christian,
> And yet Cornelius-like in mind and bone . . .[21]

was hard at work supplying or revising the German for several Berlioz scores, and spurred on by his study of his chosen masters was beginning to compose his own delightful comic opera, *The Barber of Bagdad*. Admittedly reminiscent of *Benvenuto Cellini*,[22] but revealing a distinct personality as well, this gay opera, in which a modern critic finds "beautifully polished workmanship and something more — a dash of real genius," [23] was later to provide a test of Weimar's toleration for the new music: Liszt produced the work; it fell and he resigned.

But this was still five years away. As yet Cornelius came before the public only as a disciple, though a vigorous one. It was Cornelius who in an article published in Berlin in mid-January 1854, launched the slogan of the "three B's" — the *original* three B's: "On the heights where Bach and Beethoven already dwell, there will the third great B first find recognition. For if I mistake not, the specific polyphonic musician in Berlioz controls the poet in such a way as to create within the symphony a dramatic form fit for his variegated expression. . . . Allow me then in concluding to sound a small fanfare for my favorite modern master, for the proud and daring hero, Hector, for the many-voiced composer and many-sided writer Berlioz, who is also one of the great humorists of our nineteenth century . . . three cheers, now: 'Bach! Beethoven! Berlioz!' " [24]

When this apotheosis took place, the subject of it had been back in Paris for only a fortnight. The change of occupation should have brought rest from the rehearsals, the correcting and shipping of parts, and what Matthew Arnold used to call the battle for life with headwaiters. But it had brought no relief because there were as many letters and errands to do as on tour, more proofs to correct, and rehearsals to boot. Seghers of

---

[21] From his autobiography, quoted in *354, 366*: "*Blassen Lisztianer, Bis zum letzten Ton und Hauch; Berlioz-Wagner-Weimarianer, Einen Cornelianer auch.*"

[22] Cornelius to Liszt, Oct. 12, 1855 (*207*, II, 50).

[23] Gerald Abraham, *692*, 210. Mr. Sitwell in his book on Liszt calls the work (which he incidentally misnames the "*Caliph* of Bagdad") a "harmless opera" by a "pupil" (*1011*, 226). Can he have heard the one production of it in modern times, with Liszt's overture as *hors d'oeuvre* — or is his remark just music criticism?

[24] *354*, 366–71. Later the slogan of the three B's was, with a number of other things, turned to different uses by Hans von Bülow. See below, Subchapter 24.

the *Sainte Cécile* society wished to perform *The Flight into Egypt,* and being a feeble conductor, he had to be helped. At the same time the battle for life took the form of an unexpected lawsuit. A Polish count was suing the Opera on grounds which must have delighted Berlioz: the count had bought a ticket which said *"Freischütz"* and had been given only a cut and patched version. The lawyer for the defense, however, tried to exculpate the Opera by throwing the blame upon Berlioz, who twelve years before had supervised the mounting of the work and had composed recitatives. The press, with its professional short memory and love of dogfights, represented Berlioz as guilty and receiving his deserts at last.

This confusion of the facts due to the Opera's legal smoke screen caused Berlioz a great deal of worry, fury, and real harm.[25] Though he at once wrote letters to the Paris newspapers and to his German friends, the mischief had been done.[26] Angry letters came from music students, and newspapers throughout Europe copied from one another the garbled facts. "This stupid business," wrote Berlioz to David at Leipzig, "vexes and outrages me as you can readily understand: I have spent fifteen years of my life as critic combating correctors, arrangers, and mutilators. When *Freischütz* was put on at the Opera, I prevented its being shorn of a single note; I managed to have it performed in full, and now I am accused of having cut it up myself, though the cuts were made during my absence from the country, without my being notified, and by a Director with whom I am not on speaking terms. . . . It is revolting by its absurdity and injustice." [27]

On top of this annoyance, whose repercussions were not soon over, the owner and director of the *Débats,* Armand Bertin, suddenly died. Berlioz mourned him as a friend who had stanchly supported him throughout their association. His death might mean Berlioz' removal from his entrenched position, for Louise Bertin had given up music and her brother Edouard — a childhood friend of Delacroix's — was a landscape painter. Without a Bertin to head it, the newspaper would be sold, possibly to the government. Fortunately Edouard gave up painting and Berlioz kept his post. Among his duties immediately after this scare, was to give an ac-

[25] As late as 1931, a German scholar maintained that there was "no pressing occasion" for Berlioz' orchestrating Weber's *Invitation to the Dance.* The same writer, who had published a biography of Berlioz fourteen years before, seemed to be moved by nationalist fervor into forgetting the facts. (*971,* 265; and see *357* and *286.*)

[26] See the autograph dated Jan. 7, 1854, which begins: "Sir: Apparently you read the slanders but you do not read the rebuttals." (*140.*)

[27] *M.C.,* 153. This was the second and last time that Berlioz replied to any accusation. See above the similar charge of disfiguring Palestrina, Chapter 15.

count of that "world-shaking event" — so said the *Gazette Musicale* — the opening of *L'Etoile du Nord* at the Opéra-Comique. With this score (known also as *La Stella del Nord*) Meyerbeer's monopoly of Paris theaters was complete. Louis Napoleon and Eugénie his new Empress led the applause, and Berlioz had to praise the show. But he took much of it back in a daring last paragraph which conveyed what he thought of the patent formula for producing this kind of work.[28]

Meanwhile at the concert of *Sainte Cécile*, Berlioz' *Flight into Egypt* had been warmly received and he was composing the remainder. "The Arrival at Sais," much longer than the first part, was finished by January 1854. This in turn called for an opening section to balance it. Musical ideas came in abundance, and the present first part, "Herod's Dream," was ultimately the longest. But the organizing of the whole had to wait, for the proofs of the massive *Damnation of Faust* were still being run off and the time of the engagements in Germany was approaching. Suddenly, Harriet took a turn for the worse. Summoned, Berlioz flew to Montmartre, but she lingered on. On Friday March third, just after he had again left, she died.

Louis had been spending four days with us and had gone back to Calais the previous Wednesday. Fortunately she saw him again. . . . I had to take care of everything myself — registry office, cemetery — I am in misery today. Her condition was dreadful. Paralysis was complicated by erisypelas and she had difficulty in breathing. She had become a formless mass of flesh — and beside her that radiant portrait which I had given her last year, where she looks as she was, with her great inspired eyes. Nothing left. My friends have stood by me. A large number, with Baron Taylor leading, followed her to the cemetery. . . .

And the dazzling sun, the panorama of the plain of Saint-Denis — I couldn't follow. I stayed in the garden. I had gone through too much the previous day while going to find the Pastor. By a barbarous chance, as so often happens, my cab had to go past the Odéon where I saw her for the first time 27 years ago, when she had at her feet the intellectual elite of Paris [29]. . . . The Odéon, where I suffered so much — we could neither live together nor leave each other, and we have endured this torture for ten years past. We each suffered so much at the other's hands. I have just come from her grave. She rests on the side of the hill, facing north, towards England, to which she never wanted to return.

I wrote to poor Louis yesterday. I shall write to him again. How horrible life is. Everything comes back to me . . . her great qualities, her cruel demands, her injustice, and then her genius and her woes. . . . She

[28] *1386*, Feb. 24, 1854.

[29] Sainte-Beuve recalling those days after Berlioz' death wrote: "Miss Smithson was then ravishing all our hearts." (*1212*, XII, 152.)

made me understand Shakespeare and true dramatic art. She suffered penury with me; she never hesitated when we had to risk our savings for a musical undertaking. Yet contrariwise, she always opposed my leaving Paris. . . . If I had not taken decisive steps I should still be virtually unknown in Europe. And her jealousy, *without cause*, which ended by altering my whole life. . . .

I have no taste for anything. I care about music and the rest about as much as ——. I have kept her hair. I am here alone in the large living room next to her empty bedroom. The garden has buds. Oh! to forget, to forget! . . . We all live so long — and now here is Louis so tall, he is no longer like that dear child I used to see running down these garden paths. I see here his daguerrotype portrait at the age of 12. It seems to me I have lost *that* child, and the big one whom I kissed six days ago does not console me for the loss of the other.

Don't be surprised if I sound strange. What a deadly faculty to remember the past. Is it the reason why I have so cruelly succeeded in arousing similar impressions in some of my works? Yet everybody says we must be glad she is no longer suffering. It was a dreadful life; but I have nothing but praise for the three women who tended her. Farewell, dear sister. . . . Take care how you write to me; your letter can help me bear up or break my resistance further. Farewell. Fortunately there is Time which keeps moving and crushing, which kills everything, sorrows and all.[30]

Harriet's passing was signalized in the press by articles written to honor her relation to Berlioz and recall her earlier glory. Alexandre Dumas had a kind word, Gautier praised her, and Jules Janin wrote a fine evocation, quoting at the close the litany from Juliet's Funeral March in Berlioz' symphony, "Strew on her flowers . . ." Liszt wrote a consoling letter assuring Berlioz: "She inspired you, you loved her and sang your love of her, her mission was fulfilled." [31]

Adèle, to whom Berlioz kept pouring out his overfull heart, was her usual loving self. "Dear, admirable sister: You are right to say that I should feel thankful at having been near. I cannot face the thought of her dying all solitary. . . . I go to the cemetery every morning; it hurts me less than if I kept away." Then since the province-bred little sister, surmising perhaps that her brother would legalize his relation to Marie, asked

---

[30] *M.C.*, 163–6. This remarkably Proustian letter repays study in all its details.
[31] *Mem.*, II, 340. A modern biographer of Vigny, Professor Arnold Whitridge, remarks on this that "romantic egotism could go no further." (*1231*, 194.) This seems to misconstrue Liszt's intention as well as to contradict itself; if Liszt is taken as the Romantic here, what he says is that individual life is not for self alone, but to inspire others and serve a higher end — such as art; wherefore the grieving composer may take comfort in the thought that his beloved did not live in vain. Isn't it the critic's view which is egotistical on behalf of the dead woman?

a practical question, he replies: "Yes, of course there was a marriage contract. I have just reread it. How can it be of use to Louis? Against whom? Not against me, I suppose. We were married under the law of community property, with the following conditions: I was not held accountable for her debts prior to our marriage, though I acknowledged them and they have been paid long since. . . . The survivor is entitled to property worth a thousand francs from the estate. I shall take nothing; I give everything to Louis absolutely. . . . I tell you all this without precisely grasping the point you raise in your letter. . . . Unfortunately, Louis is still such a child that I am forced to give him but little at a time and myself to buy some of the things he needs." [32]

Louis had in fact been for six months a midshipman on the cutter *Le Corse*. He had passed his examinations well, was earning forty francs a month and had sworn off prodigality. Having interested Admiral Cécille in the boy's career, Berlioz had reports that those in charge of the young officer-in-training spoke well of him. Berlioz was beginning to believe that the man was emerging from the child when a new source of worry assailed him. The year 1854 began with preparations for war against Russia and Louis Berlioz was in line to see active duty.

Meanwhile the legal settlement took longer and was more complicated than Berlioz at first imagined, the boy being a minor and the estate subject to registration. Adèle's lawyer-husband finally straightened everything out. As for Louis, we can imagine him working out in his customary solitude his difficult emotional problems. In the only extant letter from him, we see how close was the temperamental kinship between father and son, the exact counterpart of the resemblance between Berlioz and *his* father: "Since my poor mother's death," he writes to his Aunt Adèle, "I have several times meant to write to you, but the shattering memories that I would then have aroused held me back. My poor mother! What a sad life she has had! No, one cannot regret life on her behalf; now that she sleeps in her grave she does not suffer. I have always lived far from her. While still a child, I left for Rouen and then saw her only at long intervals, so in the short times I had with her I had to hide my desolate heart under a laughing face. Sometimes my courage failed me and I would leave abruptly, so that some people thought me a bad son. . . . She had to die far from me. I couldn't follow her to her grave, any more than I was to walk her on my arm or see her on the stage. It is all over. I have only my father left, my poor kind father. I can't love him more than before, for I love him as he does me and only God sees the depth of the

[32] *M.C.*, 170–1.

friendship between us. I have caused him grief sometimes but I am very young, dear aunt, and young people go through terrible times. Since the loss of my mother I feel new strength and I want to use it to spare every kind of grief to him who is dearest to me in all the world. God willing, he will be proud of his son. I can't speak of the day when he will have to quit this earth, because, as I have felt since I reached the age of reason, that day will be my last. The thread of my life is but the continuation of his. When it is cut, both lives are at an end. . . ." [33]

Louis then modulates in true Berlioz fashion to news of his ship and touching remarks about his young cousins. He wanted to go and spend some time with Adèle who had invited him. Berlioz supplied the money but war orders prevented.

The return engagement at Hanover came for Berlioz as a release from brooding, and in the two concerts (one at Brunswick) he even surpassed his earlier performance.[34] One of his objectives this time was Dresden, where Karl Lipinski as of yore, and the newly arrived Bülow, desired to have Berlioz appointed Music Director. Not liking what he had first seen of the Saxon court, Berlioz had been reluctant to go, but he yielded now and strove to make a perfect showing. On April 22, the *Damnation of Faust* was received with acclamations. At the dinner following the concert, a Royal minister significantly attended. The press was favorable except for the ubiquitous old guard who repudiated Beethoven's later works and accepted only some of those in the "second manner." Mozart was the god with whose unconscious aid Berlioz was damned, and when the words "pure" and "classic" failed, the charge was that Berlioz lacked inspiration and "ciphered with notes." [35]

Other criticisms were more alarming because still farther off the point. Berlioz was French, and this in many quarters was becoming a serious handicap. Since the failure of the Frankfort Parliament and the quasi-national "humiliation of Olmütz," patriotism had grown touchy and some persons let Berlioz feel it directly.[36] He spoke no German (though he

---

[33] *M.C.*, 173–5.

[34] Joachim: "Truly I never heard the woodwinds sound with so much sweetness and nobility as at this last concert . . . the vehemence of his invention, the breadth of his melody, the sonorous spell of his works have really enheartened me . . . You know, besides, the power of his personality." (*207*, I, 329.)

[35] *M.C.*, 197, 201.

[36] As early as 1844 a German expatriate writing a Paris Letter in the Frankfort *Didaskalia* (No. 129) spoke of Berlioz' first tour as "the invasion of a musical Napoleon" and more in that strain. (Quoted in *674*, 28 *n.*)

could at need write out his programs in that language)[37] and therefore used French, English, or Italian while rehearsing. Once, too, a piece of irony had miscarried: when advance news of the Dresden directorship had leaked out in Paris, Berlioz had denied it in a squib saying he would leave his beloved Paris only to direct for the Queen of the Hovas in Madagascar. Whereas this was a dig at the Parisians, a German journalist took it as an insult to the German musical princes. Such stupidity was unanswerable.

Nor was this all. Berlioz was playing his *Faust*, composed on what had become since Goethe's death a national poem.[38] Critics objected to the disfigurement of the lines and the plot. Berlioz had to explain in a Foreword to the score just then in press that the German text was "a translation of a translation," while the whole was a reworking of the legend. Berlioz always resented having to explain himself and "prove to people that you do not mean to dry up the Caspian Sea."[39] But expostulation did not help. He was accused of having "libelled Mephisto" by making him deceive Faust. "For you must know," Berlioz wrote to Griepenkerl "that Mephisto is a virtuous and honest devil whose word is as good as his bond."[40] Further, Berlioz was made out to be another of those immoral Frenchmen for having written in the students' Latin chorus that they went by moonlight *quaerentes puellas per urbem* — "seeking girls through the town." German students, Berlioz was informed, had never done such a thing. "I had to read this with my own eyes to believe it."[41]

Though Berlioz had to give four concerts instead of two, the Dresden offer did not materialize, whether because of national feeling, or because it would have meant victory for the conspiring modernists — Liszt, Bülow, Cornelius, and Lipinski (with Wagner in the offing) or again be-

---

[37] Schloesser: *388*, 7. His testimony is corroborated by the surviving autograph of a program for the Leipzig concert of Dec. 10, 1853. (*127.*)

[38] It was by no means so in Goethe's old age. See his conversations with Eckermann, Jan. 10, 1825 and Mar. 14, 1830.

[39] *Min. Sc.*, "Avant Propos." Berlioz could have pointed out that in order to compose the finale of the Ninth, Beethoven had mangled Schiller's "Ode to Joy."

[40] *M.C.*, 201. Later he added, "Thus I am convicted of having slandered the spirit of evil and mendacity, and have been proved worse than a demon, not worthy of the Devil." (*Mem.*, II, 288 *n.*)

[41] *M.C.*, 201. The Moscow censors likewise objected (*Mem.*, II, 288). Earlier, it had been Victor Hugo's words to *Sara la Baigneuse* which had cast odium on the composer, because the poet speaks of the bather's beautiful neck and bare foot. In England, to this day, genteelism covers up the realities of the Faust legend in such phrases as: "Marguerite sings her ballad and is presently at home to Faust."! (*558*, 646.)

cause of Marie Recio's indiscreet remarks about Wagner's latest attack on Berlioz. For fragments of *Opera and Drama* were being reprinted and discussed, and the old guard enjoyed seeing one of the innovators manhandle the other in print. Though Berlioz was willing to follow Liszt's advice and "grease the wheels," it was clear that Wagner was pouring sand. Marie, lacking equally in tact and self-respect, could not refrain from drawing indignant comparisons between Berlioz' reprinting in the *Débats* Liszt's praise of *Tannhäuser* and Wagner's deliberate assault in his book. Bülow then took a hand, with just as little judgment as the annoying woman. He urged Liszt to caution Berlioz that Dresden was still faithful to Wagner, not seeing that a word of caution to Wagner was also necessary if the moderns were to show a united front.

Berlioz, who after all had not thrust himself in but had been invited, tried to keep aloof and remained grateful throughout for the hearty welcome he had received. "There are rascals in Germany as elsewhere," he concluded, "but one must confess that there is in that country much more cordiality and a deeper feeling for art than in the rest of Europe. I have been treated with understanding, respect, and affection, which touches me to the bottom of my heart. Moreover . . . it is only owing to this dear country that I keep alive." [42]

During the next three months (May through July 1854) Berlioz finished his delicate triptych on a sacred theme, *The Infant Christ*. He dated the manuscript of this quiet "page out of a missal" on the twenty-fourth anniversary of the day when he won the Rome Prize, the opening day of the July Revolution raging outside. Louis Philippe seemed far away. Already the Louis Napoleon who had protested that "the Empire means peace" had turned into a swashbuckler at war with Russia; and a third Louis — Berlioz' cherished son — grown into a naval officer, was caught in the foolish enterprise. It was already known that the French army was dying of disease in the Danube delta and that to prepare a landing in the Crimea a diversion must be made in the Baltic. Louis Berlioz, on board of the *Phlegeton*, was part of this diversion. The father bade him farewell and concealed his apprehension under encouraging words, but letters to Adèle and others show his real thoughts: "I look for a letter from him every day. He wrote to me that the *Phlegeton* is assigned to carrying despatches only. . . . Even so, at night I get terrible spasms of the heart. . . . The vessel, they tell me, will not be in the battle but I don't believe it." [43]

[42] *M.C.*, 205.   [43] *M.C.*, 209, 212.

He was right. In August the ship took part in the bombardment of Bomarsund. "I have been in torment these last few days. . . . He tells me nothing of his impressions but I can imagine what the poor child who has never even seen a skirmish must have felt in the midst of that hell which is called a naval battle. I had gone to spend a week . . . at the seashore . . . when a local paper mentioned the ship. I came back to Paris as soon as I could for news. . . .

"What intoxicating air I breathed a week ago, stretched out of the cliffs of St. Valéry, with the calm sea softly swishing three hundred feet below my green bank. What marvellous sunsets, what peace on those heights and what purity in that layer of the atmosphere! Only such passionate interviews with nature as these can make me forget for an instant the griefs of outraged love or art. But these very same sights quickly kindle them again more burning than before: all is interlinked." [44]

Before leaving for the country, Berlioz had once more been a candidate for the Institute, making the necessary calls on people who he knew would not elect him. They chose Clapisson.[45] "Having begun, I am bound to persevere. The place is worth 1500 francs [a year], which means a good deal. I don't speak of the honor, which is a fiction when you consider who belongs and has always belonged to the Academy. I have tried only twice. Hugo knocked on their door five times, Vigny four; Delacroix after six tries has not been admitted yet; Balzac never did get in. . . ." [46]

By the sea, recovering from Paris and the Institute and suppressing dark thoughts, Berlioz wrote two more chapters of the *Memoirs*. The text itself records the strain the writer was under. At the mention of Louis, Berlioz breaks out with his buried imaginings about a fight at sea: "These enormous guns which he has to *serve;* these red-hot cannon balls, these congreve flares, this hail of shrapnel, fire, the hold filling up, exploding steam! I shall lose my mind. I cannot write." [47] Louis was reported safe. The diversion was over. He would return to France and set out again for the Crimea. During the interim, Berlioz took the opportunity of going to La Côte for a family reunion. The familiar sights stirred memory again, and Berlioz resumed the abandoned chapter, which he

[44] *M.C.,* 226–9.

[45] Antoine Louis Clapisson (1808–1866), a violinist and opera composer whose *Gibby la cornemuse* was at that time his chief claim to renown. He collected musical instruments and taught harmony at the Conservatoire. Offenbach wrote an indignant squib in *L'Artiste*, expressing his admiration for Berlioz' genius and learning, which the Institute had passed over for the sake of an entertainer. (*1388*, Dec. 6, 1903.)

[46] *M.C.,* 227–8.

[47] *Mem.,* II, 307.

dated on his return to Paris, October 18, 1854. On November 1, Louis landed at Cherbourg. "The fullest joy of the soul is mine. Louis is here. . . . I wrote to him at Cherbourg the news that you may already know — that I have remarried. He replied to me with affection and good sense." [48]

The day after he had brought up his *Memoirs* to cover the time of Harriet Smithson's death, Berlioz ratified his liaison of fourteen years' standing, and Mlle. Recio became Mme. Berlioz. It was done, as he said, without ostentation or concealment. "My situation," he wrote to Louis, "is more fitting thus, being more regular. I make no doubt that if you harbor in your mind any painful memories or unfriendly feelings for Mlle. Recio, you will conceal them utterly out of affection for me." [49] Louis proved not only affectionate but self-possessed and quite a man of the world. He was beginning to seem so even to others. Not long since, he had called on Liszt's daughters Cosima and Blandine, who were visiting Paris, and they reported that he impressed them as an entertaining young blood.[50]

Simultaneously with these events, the score of the *Damnation* appeared and attracted notice. It was almost a curiosity in a world occupied with war and fed on Meyerbeer's cumulative successes. The spirit of innovation had become as outmoded as the liberties that Napoleon III had extinguished. "In the thirties and forties," said *La France Musicale*, "fresh blood revivified art; men were in the grip of a fever, but also of a faith . . . It was then Hector Berlioz appeared, an eagle-eyed pioneer. Today the arts languish; we have lost that inward energy which keeps the soul aloft in the realms of poetry." [51]

It could not be denied that Berlioz had maintained his course through those realms in spite of all discouragements and against all likelihood. He was even then preparing for the thankless capital two great musical events — first the performance of *The Infant Christ* ("I expect to lose some eight or nine hundred francs by it")[52] and second, the use in connection with the Great Exhibition of 1855 of his no less great *Te Deum*. The man seemed indestructible and his music took after him: even before these new musical projects, and independently of any move on Berlioz' part, the manager of Covent Garden had put *Benvenuto Cellini* on the list of operas for the coming season. This act of reparation did not take place, but why announce a work so recently and thoroughly hissed, unless there were qualms stirring in the commercial conscience? The truth is that the exhibition years were like moral holidays taken from business life, and

[48] *M.C.*, 244.
[49] *Corresp.*, 217.
[50] *947*, 39.
[51] *269*, 310–1.
[52] *M.C.*, 251.

not only for Berlioz but for Delacroix and Courbet, 1855 marked a sudden glorification after the long struggle against hostile neglect.[53]

The first of Berlioz' concerts was set for the day preceding his fifty-first birthday, December 10, 1854. He invited some of his old intimates of the 1830's now in seclusion, such as the invalid Heine and the retired Alfred de Vigny, to whom Berlioz wistfully addressed "farewell, dear invisible poet." [54] Contrary to his forecast, the concert proved a financial as well as an artistic success. Repeated on Christmas eve, the work netted its author eleven hundred francs and was immediately asked for by the charitable foundation known as The Infant Jesus for a benefit in January.[55] The *première* was, according to Cosima Liszt, the most important event of the season. "The whole hall was stirred to the depths. . . . In a word, Berlioz' work achieved a gigantic success." [56] This was perfectly true and the press (saving only Scudo) was unanimous in praise. Heine apologized to Berlioz for having questioned his melodic gift seventeen years earlier in speaking of the *Requiem*. The Empire's official newspaper said: "Berlioz has garnered in one day the fruit of many years of struggle and patient labor." [57]

All this the composer took with a grain of salt. "The good people of Paris say that I have changed my manner, that I have reformed. I needn't tell you that I have only changed my subject. . . ." [58] The reception of his new brainchild, he told Liszt's Princess, "is insulting to its elder brothers"; [59] and to Liszt himself: "So be it — I have become a good little

---

[53] "I am on probation to have it settled whether I am painter or dauber . . . [and] it will be just 30 years next year that I am in the dock." (Delacroix in 1851.) In 1855 he writes: ". . . if I do any more painting I shall only follow my instinct, which used to pass for a kind of madness and now finds admirers." (*181*, III, 86 and 265.) Delacroix's able editor sums up the situation, precisely parallel to that of Berlioz: "In 1855, after three quarters of his life had elapsed, and thirty years of painting had insured his growth, Delacroix had the opportunity to cast a backward glance . . . and to present his work. . . . The attempt succeeded admirably: he was consecrated as a great painter. . . . He won his victory, but at a price. He had defeated his adversaries but not disarmed them. He was to remain . . . as isolated as before." (*Ibid.*, iv-v.)

[54] *339*, 864.

[55] Berlioz' title *L'Enfance du Christ* is here translated as *The Infant Christ* because this correctly describes the subject of the words and music. The more usual and literal *Childhood of Christ* is a misnomer in English and sounds rather like a report by a group of progressive educators.

[56] *947*, 40. At this concert, dramatically enough, the two girls met their mother again after a separation due to Liszt's estrangement from her. (*Ibid.*, 42.)

[57] *Moniteur Officiel*, Dec. 17, 1854.

[58] *M.C.*, 259–60.

[59] *M.C.*, 260.

boy, human, clear, melodic. I am at last writing music like everybody else. We are all agreed on that score." The favor he now met with in his compatriot's eyes came to him on three counts, which they took care to specify for his information — as composer, as conductor, and as poet. For the words of the trilogy were entirely his, and though he was still diffident about his versifying, the approval it received as literature encouraged him in the planning of his next two works.

At the third hearing, Berlioz substituted for the Haydn symphony and Mendelssohn trio which framed his oratorio, a piece of occasional music that he had written earlier on the foolish words of a Captain Lafont. Entitled *Le Dix Décembre*, it celebrated the Empire, and Berlioz later renamed it *L'Impériale* or *Emperor* cantata. As music, it shows what technique can do to supply breadth of style when this does not arise from genuine feeling: it yields an artificial pearl. Berlioz seems to have valued the work chiefly for one orchestral "find," [60] and for the help it might give in getting the court to authorize the *Te Deum*.

The year 1854 closed with undertones of worry beneath the artistic satisfactions. Berlioz had grippe, Marie was suffering from hives, Louis was halfway to the Black Sea, at Malta, and then not heard from. Nevertheless the German concerts had to be prepared. On top of this, a dispiriting contretemps spoiled a London victory which might have matched that in Paris: two weeks after Berlioz had accepted a moderately good engagement to conduct two concerts of the New Philharmonic, he heard from Sainton that Costa had resigned from the Old and that his post was for Berlioz to take. It amounted to a recognition of Berlioz' pre-eminence over all living conductors, and carried with it honor, money, and opportunity for acclimating the moderns in England, as earlier Beethoven and Mendelssohn had been entrenched by this very society. Berlioz tried to obtain an honorable release from Dr. Wylde who, thinking himself Berlioz' rival, took care not to grant it. The Old Philharmonic, also disappointed, turned to Spohr and failing him, to Richard Wagner.[61]

At Hanover early in February 1855, *The Infant Christ* brought Berlioz further acclaim and the Order of the Guelfs. At Weimar a second "Ber-

[60] The unison of the double chorus, supported by the trombones and declaiming the main theme, which chords on the woodwind punctuate. Above, a tremolo on the strings, and below the snare and kettle drums beat irregularly as in military salutes. Incidentally, the theme of this particular pomp and circumstance comes from the *Sardanapalus* of 1827 where it ushered in the King of Kings. (See *606*.)

[61] In a recent book on *The Orchestra in England*, by an excellent scholar who rightly values Berlioz, this transaction in several steps is inexplicably reduced to one. (*742*, 182.) See likewise *699*, 198–9.

lioz Week" presented the same work. But after the "pious" new score, Berlioz had Liszt put on the "impious" *Lélio*, much cut down as to word- age and excellently performed as to music; or to speak more accurately, the Episode in an Artist's Life was given in full – first the *Symphonie Fantas- tique*, then its vocal and pantomimic sequel – in which Liszt played the piano part as well as that of the Chinese gong.[62] The public was somewhat taken aback by the speechifying but was charmed by the music; it liked even better the pieces with which it was now quite familiar: *Romeo*, the "Chorus of Master Goldsmiths" from *Cellini*, the "Concert of Sylphs" from the *Damnation*, and the orchestral song *La Captive*. Liszt played his E-flat concerto, "dazzling with verve and power," said Berlioz, "as always." [63]

So full of verve, indeed, that he and his acolytes gave Berlioz the great- est triumph of his career. It was the high point of his harvesting season: Liszt was still his alter ego; Lauchert painted him; Cornelius was ready to exchange "any opera" for *La Captive;* and at the banquet of Weimar's notables, the poet Hoffmann von Fallersleben improvised a Latin toast which Raff at once set to music and the guests sang: Berlioz was called *Hospes Germanorum*, was told he had fulfilled their desire, and was bidden to remain "*amicus Neo-Wimarorum.*" [64]

At the same time, a more lasting effusion of feeling was taking effect at the Altenburg. Liszt and the Princess in their long intimate talks with Berlioz filled him with the zest to undertake a large new work on the subject he had dreamed of since youth – the *Aeneid*. *L'Enfance* had strengthened his belief that he could deal with the antique otherwise than in the narcotic manner of the Opera, and it had shown him that his best librettist was himself. At the height of his worries about Louis, while brooding by the sea, he discovered that his "passion for music, or rather for all art, takes on inordinate proportions. I feel within myself powers that are stronger than ever, and that are only impeded by material ob- stacles." [65] Only his practical sense of these barriers made his lust for

[62] It can be surmised that Berlioz' desire to play this composite work in full was connected with the retrospective emotions aroused by Harriet's recent death. As for the change of terminology from *mélologue* to *monodrama*, it is more than probable that it is due to Berlioz' knowledge of Tennyson's recently published *Maud, a Monodrama*.

[63] *86*, 424. A titled lady is reported to have said: "Weimar is a remarkable city. In one concert Liszt plays and Berlioz conducts. Where will you find anything so wonderful and rare?" (*353*, 162.)

[64] *353*, 166–8 and *86*, 424–5. In a letter to his hosts, Berlioz spoke of these "unforgettable" moments, and doubtless enclosed the paraphrase of Virgil (in manuscript at Harvard) which speaks of "Father Hoffmann" [von Faller- sleben] as having led the plaudits. (*140*.)

[65] *M.C.*, 229.

creation seem to him inordinate. It was therefore a blessing that Liszt and the Princess, moving in the freedom of luxury, should impart to Berlioz a little of their sense of power. The result was that composing words and music for his Virgilian subject occupied him for the next three years, filled though these were with English, German, and Parisian concerts, besides the usual load of private cares.

Berlioz' Religion of Art

> I have often asked myself what could be
> the purpose of the mystification called Life:
> it is to know what is beautiful; it is to love.
> Those who do not love and do not know
> are the ones who are trapped by the mysti-
> fication; and as for the rest of us we are
> entitled to flout the great mystifier.
> — BERLIOZ to Princess Sayn-
> Wittgenstein (1859)

The success of *The Infant Christ* should not have surprised anyone. But the causes were mixed, some superficial and some profound. The superficial ones were that Berlioz' German reputation had rebounded, that his undeviating persistence at home compelled admiration, and that the *visible* simplicity of his present musical apparatus looked to the heedless as if the composer had reformed. We know that there had been movements as simple and as quiet in the *Requiem*, in *Harold*, or in the *Damnation*, but the presence of many performers, however silent, betokened "noise," through the eyes, to the majority who have ears and do not hear.

A deeper cause of success was the fact that for the first time since Berlioz had begun composing, the bulk of his listeners were truly familiar with the dramatic situations for his music. The actors in the Christian drama, whether taken as legend or as gospel history, formed part of common knowledge. When the tenor Battaille sang "*Le Repos de la Sainte Famille*" everyone was *attendri* because the setting was easily grasped and the spiritual gesture informing the music had the simple appeal of childhood itself. This had obviously not been true of the "artist" in the *Fantastique*, the "wanderer" in *Harold*, the "philosopher" in *Faust*. The widely varied moods through which these figures passed came too quickly and were too special for the common hearer to catch his breath. As for the Requiem service that everyone supposedly knew, it had apparently not occurred to anyone but Berlioz to take it seriously, to conjure up on that occasion a Day of Judgment, to fear, tremble, pray, hope, and be contrite. In short *L'Enfance* spoke of the intimate, familial side of religion and everyone understood.

They moreover understood — for the same reason — that there were in Berlioz' music no events to follow, nor pictures to see, but successive states of mind to undergo in obedience to the character of the musical sections. The genesis of the work tells us again that "character" in Berlioz' art came first: shortly after finishing the *Te Deum*, during a social evening made dull for him by everyone else's playing cards, he began to sketch a four-part andantino for organ. His old friend and fellow guest, Pierre Duc, prodded him to write instead a parlor piece for his album, but "a certain character of primitive, pastoral mysticism" in the melody led Berlioz to invent an occasion for it: he imagined the shepherds bidding farewell to Jesus on the eve of the Holy Family's flight into Egypt. He wrote appropriate words and then thought of a further embellishment:

"Now," he told Duc, "I am going to put your name to this. I want to compromise you."

"That's absurd! Everybody knows that I know nothing about writing music."

"That is indeed a brand-new reason for not composing, but wait! Since vanity prevents your adopting my piece, I am going to make up a name out of yours. I shall call the author Pierre Ducré, whom I hereby appoint music master of the Sainte-Chapelle in Paris during the seventeenth century. My manuscript thus acquires enormous archeological value."[1]

The remaining parts of the *Flight into Egypt* were soon added and in 1850 the little work was performed, still under the name of Ducré. All but one of the critics fell into the trap, although the original "Farewell" contains a characteristic Berliozian modulation which gives away the hoax.[2] Berlioz shortly published the work under his own name, though keeping the caption "Attributed to Pierre Ducré, imaginary chapel master." How the other two parts grew around this core has been told in the preceding account of the years since 1850 but it is interesting to note that more than a year after that date Berlioz was not exclusively thinking

[1] *Grot.*, 170–1.
[2] (*1383*, Nov. 17, 1850.) Berlioz says that one has to be "as ignorant as a fish" to believe the date 1679 which he assigned to the piece. (*M.C.*, 149.)

of the Infant Christ but was toying with another subject similarly bound up with popular and primitive religious feeling. "Tell M. Arnaud," he writes to d'Ortigue, "that I shall be most happy to set to music a series of his poems on Joan of Arc, if I too hear a voice from above. But let him write short stanzas . . . The thing should be fashioned like a popular legend, very simple yet fine, in a quantity of songs or sections." [3]

Thus throughout its avatars *The Infant Christ* stands for a definite musical mood pre-existing in Berlioz and ready to attach itself to a suitable dramatic subject. In Paris and Rome before 1831 he had worked at a "March and Chorus of Magi" and kindred pieces,[4] but this strain of "rustic mysticism" had no place in either the *Requiem* or *Te Deum*. It must find another outlet and no more appropriate occasion for it can be imagined than the one Berlioz chose: we may be glad that the voice from above did not lead him to substitute Joan of Arc and to accept the verses of another poet.

The first part of *The Infant Christ*, entitled "Herod's Dream," begins with a recital in the antique manner which introduces in thirty bars the subject of the drama: Jesus had just been born, the powerful trembled, and the humble took heart. Herod in his fear was planning the massacre of the innocents. The quiet woodwind accompaniment, dramatized for a short space with a tremolo in the upper strings, modulates sharply and expressively through seven keys, from F minor to C major. It ends *dolce* as it began, and without further words, the "scene" shifts to a street in Jerusalem which Roman soldiers patrol. A delicate march, built on a series of interlinked motives, establishes a mood of nocturnal mystery. In the middle it comes to an abrupt stop during which two centurions hold a brief dialogue. The march themes begin again but break down, after which a long decrescendo gives us, in inverted order, the mysterious opening. It is indeed, as Artur Schnabel has said, a very strange piece of music.[5] At once atmospheric and formally unique, it requires considerable familiarity in the hearer to perceive all its artistry — notably in the subtle *pseudo* repetition of the decrescendo.

The next section, Herod's vigil, was for Berlioz the most interesting of

[3] *Corresp.*, 181. The Abbé Arnaud was Canon at Poitiers.
[4] A chorus of angels celebrating Christmas; a choral prayer for sunshine in the native Italian style; a psalmody for voices accompanied by seven wind instruments, on words by Thomas Moore, "for those whose soul is sick unto death." (*Corresp.*, 91–2.) None of these pieces has survived as such.
[5] *309*, 270. Cosima, who heard it at the *première*, wrote home: "The march with which the first part opens is indeed a fascinating thing and produced an extraordinary effect." (*947*, 40.)

the score. Built on a single one-bar theme, in the manner that Wagner was to make his own by systematizing it, the scene speaks of Herod's sleepless fears. An introductory recitative ends on a Dorian cadence and leads to Herod's air written in the Phrygian mode of plain song, with "somber harmonies" that the composer described to Bülow.[6] Not only was Berlioz interested in the technical problems raised by his scheme, but one may also find in the words he gave the King a partial identification between himself and Herod as ruler:

> *O misère des rois!*
> *Régner et ne pas vivre,*
> *A tous donner des lois,*
> *Et désirer de suivre*
> *Le chevrier au fond des bois.*

"To reign and not live, enacting laws for all, yet wish to follow the goatherd to the woods" states precisely the conflict in Berlioz between mission and desire.

A passage of twelve bars, held by the strings, flutes, and horns, and agitated by a simple clarinet figure, comes after Herod's plaint and yields perhaps the only expression in music of tormented insomnia. Throughout, the means employed are extremely simple, yet never monotonous and infallibly suggestive. The reprise of Herod's air comes almost as a relief from the tension created, but the evocation of the sylvan retreat does not last, and the scene ends on a repeat of the disquieting mixolydian scale.[7] This brooding reverie does not in fact conclude: it is dramatically interrupted by the centurion Polydorus who with the single phrase "My Lord!" startles his master and introduces the augurs who are to foretell his future. By a wonderful conception, replacing any protracted dialogue, the augurs engage in a cabalistic dance upon a rhythm of three beats in a bar followed by a bar of four, so that each pair of bars equals a measure of seven beats.[8] The instrumentation continues simple yet the movement, with its vocal introduction and coda, is one of the composer's most highly packed and subtly organized.[9] The closing dialogue between the dervishes and Herod precipitates the King's decision. He verbally and musically *anticipates* the massacre of the children, and the whole Palace scene ends on a grave orchestral decrescendo which after a long chromatic scale and pianissimo strokes in the basses, settles on the dominant of C major, in which the reciter's initial narrative ended.

[6] *Corresp.*, 212.

[7] Or, rather, its modern "synonym."

[8] Already used by Berlioz in *Benvenuto;* see Subchapter 11.

[9] Cosima: "Extraordinarily fine and wonderful. . . ." (*947*, 40.)

There is a measured pause of seven bars (which the conductor must beat)[10] and we are in the stable at Bethlehem. The Virgin is singing to her son as she feeds the lambs. The strings chiefly accompany her, the double basses giving only a few pizzicatos, and three woodwinds an occasional touch of cool color. Soon Joseph's voice joins in the tender melody, at the end of which the angels afar off utter a warning and bid the family flee into Egypt.

The second part, named after the flight, opens with a short overture in fugue style and in the hypodorian mode.[11] This charming piece of chamber music makes at first a strange impression with its quaint scale (F sharp minor with E natural), its subdued dynamics seldom straying from piano and pianissimo, and its agile transformations of two related motives, one of which is to be heard again when the narrator begins his famous recital of the Holy Family's rest in the desert oasis. Before we reach this, the shepherds sing their farewell to the voyagers — the kernel of the full-blown score. Their chant is rustic and naïve and idyllic. Then to isolate, as it were, the coming narrative of the Holy Family's rest in the desert — the high point of the emotional and musical sublime — the orchestra broaches the several themes of the tenor's long *melopeia*.[12] It is as fine an example of *chant récitatif* as Berlioz produced, developed from the four-bar germ first heard in the fugue[13] into a forty-five-bar continuous melody.[14]

The "Arrival at Sais" forms the third panel of the triptych. The narrator sings again, on another motive taken from the "Flight" fugue, the hardships that the Virgin and Child endured before they reached Sais. After this comes Joseph's moving appeal for hospitality and the rebuffs they meet on all sides until a family of Ishmaelites take them in. An extended movement, using recitative, four-part chorus, and orchestra alone, dramatizes the reception, of which compassion and gratitude and the sense of human and divine destiny form the emotional substance. A sublime modulation underlines the close of Joseph's answer to his host: "Her name is Mary, mine Joseph, and the child we call Jesus." As for the choral ensemble which concludes by predicting a quiet and happy future for the

[10] Throughout the score the pauses between sections are marked in bars — silence is measured.

[11] Performed for the first time in New York by Hans Lange and the Philharmonic Chamber Orchestra on Feb. 3, 1936. On records, *1427*.

[12] An excellent record of this was made by Jean Planel. (*1432*.)

[13] *Min. Sc.*, 109 bb. 10–3. It is shorn of triplets and reduced to three bars when first stated in the *Repos*. (*Ibid.*, p. 125 bb. 1–3.)

[14] See Charles Maclean: *394, 157*.

child, it rises to that same "Biblical grandeur" which another critic also found in the finale of *Romeo and Juliet*.[15]

For the pilgrims' entertainment the Ishmaelite children play the trio for two flutes and harp which inspired Bizet in *L'Arlésienne*, and which, thanks to recordings, is almost as well known as the *Repos*.[16] The melodic and rhythmical charm of this interlude shows again that the finely chiseled chamber-music style was as fully at Berlioz' command as the monumental. The Ishmaelite paterfamilias has the last word and sends the weary travelers to rest, while a small chorus, taking up the theme of his recitative, sings a benediction that ends very quietly as the rescued pair utter four simple words of thanks. A few bars of the string quartet bring us to the concluding narration by the tenor, as compactly modulated as the opening one. It tells how after having been saved by an unbeliever, Jesus was to fulfill the prophecy and sacrifice himself for the salvation of man.

To frame the story properly required a further touch, a slightly heavier line. Therefore after another measured pause, the narrator's unaccompanied voice begins a prayer, "O my soul, for thee what is yet left to do? but to shatter thy pride at sight of this mystery." The sopranos repeat the phrase, and the remaining voices then conclude *a cappella*, answered by a seraphic *Amen* afar off.[17]

No one can doubt that in the poem and the music both, Berlioz found for his "mystery play" accents at once tender and sublime, and one can agree with the militant Christian Barbey d'Aurevilly that the score is fit to be considered a prayer. But to what Deity? The same poet-composer had been equally moving when he rendered Faust's pantheism, and in his own person from earliest days he had expressed the Voltairian agnosticism inherited from his father the physician. He continued to consider himself an unbeliever, saying so without affectation on the first page of his *Memoirs*, and uttering casual witticisms about the traditional omnipotent God.[18] Yet he continued to affirm his "sympathy" with the forms and beliefs of his church, and a survey of his career shows him repeatedly drawn to religious subjects. The number of religious passages in his secu-

[15] D'Ortigue: *1386*, Dec. 20, 1854; see also Subchapter 12.

[16] *1433*.

[17] Each part ends with a single word sung in this manner — the first "Hosanna," the second "Halleluia," and the last "Amen."

[18] "My dear Pohl," Berlioz scribbled at Baden in 1861, "Liszt told me that you would like to have a triangle: here is one from Sax's which has just served in the *Harold* first movement. Its shape is in the image of God, like all triangles, but more than other triangles, and more than God in particular, you will find it plays true. Yours H. B." (Facsimile in *296*, opp. 276.)

lar works is moreover astonishingly large; so that if one should ask, "What is the prevailing mood of Berlioz' music?" the answer might reasonably be: "the religious" — only the term would have to be understood in its fullest variety.

It is quite consistent, then, that Berlioz should write often and vehemently about the nature and problems of sacred music,[19] and not surprising that his religious works moved even the orthodox when they were musical as well. After the *première* of *The Infant Christ*, the same Abbé Arnaud who wanted Berlioz to set his poems on Joan of Arc wrote to say that the composer had "transformed the concert hall into a temple" and that one could not "overpraise the artist who, after having so faithfully portrayed the stormiest passions of the heart, could now turn to the . . . sublime gospels and rise to such heights in religious contemplation." [20]

One can only conclude that despite his antitheistic sallies, Berlioz was intrinsically a religious man. Once again he occupies in music the position held in painting by Delacroix, who, though a spiritual descendant of Voltaire, an unbeliever and probably an atheist, was the greatest — perhaps the only — religious painter of the nineteenth century.[21]

The contradiction between heretical *thought* and religious *feeling* is a fact of the century. Its cause, whenever we probe it, attaches less to the men as individuals than to them as products of a culture in which theology and secular knowledge were at war. Berlioz was entirely aware of this disharmony, which compelled him — like Péguy later — to think of religion chiefly as a force "which brings out the original fire, which presses the inner spring." [22] In the confessional mood of a letter contemporary with the finishing of *The Infant Christ*, Berlioz contrasts his position with that of his old companion d'Ortigue — the lifelong follower of the early Lamennais (another man of faith and music) as well as a proponent of strict views forbidding expression in religious music: "Yes, my good and dear d'Ortigue, you are right. . . . Forgive me for having let you read

[19] See above (Chapter 19) quotations from his early article of 1829 (*1377*, Apr. 11, 1829, 54–5). Other statements include the review of d'Ortigue's book (*A Trav.*, 258 ff.), the digression in the *Treatise* (art. Organ), passages in the *Memoirs* (Ch. 39) and the *Soirées* (16th and 18th), as well as innumerable letters wholly or partly devoted to the subject.

[20] *M.C.*, 272. It will be remembered that another priest had expressed similar views after the first performance of the *Requiem*. (*L.I.*, 179.)

[21] *181*, iii–iv. Delacroix writes in 1858: ". . . I do not believe in that little being called soul which is generously ascribed to us" (*Journal*, May 24) yet the period was for him one of abundant production on religious themes; only two days later he writes of the *Christ in the Tomb* which he is meditating. (*182*, III, 195–6.)

[22] *1272*, 115 and 117.

my thoughts so easily. Though I knew they might pain you, I found it impossible to hold back the words. It is perfectly natural that your religious beliefs should lead you to parallel beliefs in your artistic theories. I should have reflected on this and kept quiet. When it is a question of my own works being criticized, the habit of battle makes me stand it as I should, that is to say silently and even resignedly. But as soon as criticism hits at my idols — for it is clear that I am a fanatic — my blood boils so . . . that its disturbance must look like anger and be an offense to my interlocutor.

"As you say, I love the beautiful and the true, but I cherish another love that is far more vast and impassioned: I have the love of love. So that when some idea tends to rob the object of my affection of the qualities that make me love it — . . . then something in me breaks down and I cry out like a child whose toy someone has spoiled. My analogy is literal: it is childish of me. I truly feel this and make every effort to overcome it. Anyhow, you punished me like a Christian in returning good for evil, for your letter has made me happy. Let me take your hand and thank you. . . ." [23]

It may be added that when d'Ortigue heard Berlioz' new score he found it touching in a truly devotional way, despite the discrepancy between Berlioz' views and his own.[24] But it is likely that he took the religious words in Berlioz' letter as metaphors, whereas it is incumbent upon the uncommitted reader to take them as a precise statement of belief. When Berlioz speaks of his "idols," when he calls himself a fanatic, when — as in the Foreword to his *Faust* — he protests against the charge of defacing masterpieces because that would mean repudiating "the religion of my entire life," he is using expressions that come as close to the object of a real worship as do those same expressions when applied by others to the Creator. It is in fact proper to make Berlioz' meaning pivot on that word and say that his religion is the worship of creation, in its double aspect of nature and art. But while eighteenth-century philosophy and nineteenth-century science tended to remove conscious spirit from behind the works of nature, they could not destroy in Berlioz the conviction that the creators of art were conscious, divine, and indeed born to suffering like the Man-God.

Their humanity makes them less perfect recipients of adoration, less fulfilling for the worshiper — which may be why Berlioz called them

[23] *Corresp.*, 202–3.
[24] *1386*, Jan. 3 and Dec. 20, 1854. See also d'Ortigue's *La Musique à l'Eglise* pp. 196–212.

idols and himself a fanatic. But for them he none the less performed the usual religious rites: he sacrificed for them, defended them, and preached their gospel. If one includes the poets, especially Virgil and Shakespeare, his idols formed a pantheon with whom to commune and to whom to withdraw for inspiration and solace. It has been thought queer that he freely admitted "worshiping" Shakespeare and called him "God" and "Father." [25] Rather, any modern philosopher of religion would see in this that Berlioz thoroughly understood the role of God the Father — all-knowing, creative, and worthy of adoration.

In so doing Berlioz was not displaying a singular choice. Romanticism, with its roots in Spinoza who was among the first intellectualist interpreters of religious feeling, makes Divinity of the divine in man; Blake complains of the creeds which have "forgot that all deities reside in the human breast"; [26] Wordsworth speaking of poets declares

> Such men are truly from the Deity
> For they are powers; [27]

and Hazlitt concludes about artists, just like Berlioz, "The living are merely candidates for popular applause; the dead are a religion or they are nothing." [28] Another "atheist" of this peculiar brand — Shelley — revered Tasso as a god in this same special sense, such spiritual ancestor worship being of course classical and Christian in the historical meaning of these terms. When Berlioz inscribed his *Troyens* score: "Divo Virgilio," he was in the tradition of Lucretius or Cicero, who call Epicurus or Plato *deus;* and he was no less at one with Dante, who follows the whole Middle Ages in considering Virgil a divine messenger.[29] In our day, Shaw supplies the inclusive formula when he asserts that the great dead form the Communion of Saints referred to in the Creed.

Berlioz further agrees with Shaw as to the bearing of Shakespeare's work, though they differ as to its value. Berlioz put the poet at the head of the divine company because for him the plays expressed the world-weary faith, at once secular and transcendental, which was Berlioz' own — a naturalistic pessimism that does not exclude morality and love. The *Memoirs* use as a motto Macbeth's description of life as "a tale told by an idiot," but the final volume of musical essays, *A Travers Chants*, bal-

---

[25] *Encyclopaedia Britannica*, 11th ed., art. "Berlioz."
[26] *Marriage of Heaven and Hell.*
[27] *Prelude*, XIV, 112.
[28] "Trifles Light as Air" (1829).
[29] Compare Victor Hugo: "*Dans Virgile parfois, dieu tout près d'être un ange . . .*" (*Les voix intérieures*, XVIII, Mar. 21, 1837.)

ances the Virgilian epigraph *"Hostis habet muros"* — the enemy holds the walls — with the Shakespearean *"Love's Labour's Lost."* In other words, Man as the repository of spirit continues to risk his soul in the teeth of nature's indifference. He is obligated to do so by being spirit, and this is the meaning of Berlioz' statement about the mystifier and the mystified (quoted at the head of this section) just as it is the meaning of the musical parable about Andromeda quoted earlier.[30] No wonder then that *Hamlet* was for Berlioz the complete commentary on the life of action and *Lear* the complete commentary on the life of the affections. In neither can a visible providence be found ("we are to the gods as flies to wanton boys") yet morality is not in doubt; it is maintained by the true characters in spite — not because of — the course of human affairs; and it is the Christian morality of love.

This is only one side of Berlioz' religion. Adoration, the casting away of self, and justification by works, are individual manifestations of faith. But the love thus sublimated can also unite men, and Berlioz in his candor never fails to recognize it. On the Romanticist principle that whatever belongs to the beautiful becomes the character of God, Berlioz wanted Liszt, d'Ortigue, and the strangers in the stalls next to him to share his worship and thus give universal worth not only to objects of beauty, but to the truths those objects symbolize. Seeing that this was impossible, that absolute, universal beauty did not exist, Berlioz perforce remained a skeptic, but no less of a "fanatic," and no less hopeful of establishing human bonds through a common passion for art: a coreligionist is a friend.[31]

A "humanism" of this kind, taking the place of a revealed religion, is often deemed dangerous on the ground that it exalts man and makes him proud of his puny works — justifies him in his own eyes. This argument is in reality a false generalization, which pivots hastily from "men" to "Man." Men of the same belief do not all act alike. Berlioz shows by his life that the religion of art can be one of humility, striving, and unforgetful serving of spirit. Examples of self-conceit in other humanists prove nothing about the creed when rightly held — one might as easily point

---

[30] See also Berlioz' philosophic fantasia on the earth's thinking and "the poem of the world" in relation to the meaning of life — "which would drive one insane if one went too deeply into it." (*Grot.*, 93–4 and 151.)

[31] This began early (see *Mem.*, I, 80 ff.) and lasted late. In 1846 a stranger to Berlioz named Martin d'Anger wrote an article on church music. Berlioz' letter agreeing with him concludes: "Permit me to shake your hand and sign myself — if not your friend, for I have not the honor of knowing you — at least your devoted servant." (*M.E.*, 147–8.)

to certain orthodox believers who act as if they held a power of attorney from their God to lord it over other mortals. In short, the *quality* of a belief must always enter into our judgment of its validity.

Unquestionably, Berlioz' attitude entails a conflict — which he was aware of — in both the personal and the universal realms of his faith: neither art nor nature supplies a restful unity, a resolution of desire in supernal peace.[32] On the contrary, ceaseless effort is needed to defend consciousness, spirit, and beauty. The faithful must struggle for the good as they see it — a moral pragmatism that William James dramatized when he spoke of an "unfinished" God who needs our help to preserve or extend his beneficent sway.[33] This is clearly a form of the traditional heresy, known as Manichaeanism, which dominates western culture and which says that Evil exists — the devil is a real enemy. With this spur to action, to which Berlioz was more than responsive, it might be thought that pantheism would conflict. It is assumed that a pantheist, finding God in all things, must conclude that whatever is is right. The opposite is true, for nature is not mechanical but animate, which is the sign of creation; not hostile but unmoved, which is the principle of majesty. Hence comes its power to yield solace, to deliver a revelation, and by its ample fertility to teach individual resignation. Here Berlioz is at one with Rousseau, Goethe, and Meredith.

If the resignation tends to sadness, pessimism, or even despair, we may correctly ascribe this to the secular knowledge which excludes a hereafter from the humanist's vision of the cosmos: no eternal rightness or compensating bliss answers to his desire for order and justice. But we must also remember that on the same high plane of acute awareness, many a dogmatic believer has suffered kindred pangs, and done so to the end of life in spite of the consoling certitudes conventionally imputed to old establishments — Cardinal Newman is but one notable instance. In judging the Romantic religion of art it behooves us to ponder these parallels, giving up the drawing-room courtesy by which the liberal mind usually concedes that only organized religion is genuine. The true statement of the case is that only genuine believers possess a genuine religion, and one test

[32] See again the closing lines of *Nature immense* (Subchapter 17) and the numerous denials of absolute beauty.

[33] It should be noted, however, that Berlioz' militancy always strove to stop short of intolerance. As a youth in Rome he had teased Mendelssohn about religion but he regretted and apologized for it, as he did later to d'Ortigue. It is characteristic that in the *Damnation of Faust* he has a note saying that when given before a devout audience the parody *Amen* fugue should be omitted.

of that genuineness is their humility before their gods and willingness to sacrifice in their service.

To sum up, the very element of life implies will, and it is will that links nature on the one hand to moral choice, and on the other to art. The will to create — or procreate — is spirit asserting that its forms shall not perish; art is consciousness scratching its mark upon matter; love of fame is love of continuity, of survival, and all these require energy, which desires form and attains worth. His dominant trait as a man, energy, is for Berlioz one of the tests of art — only notice in his music the vigor of most of his opening phrases. Even tenderness must be strong, masculine, never languorous or mawkish, and love must be supreme awareness, not (as in Wagner) Nirvana or death. For life to Berlioz means vertebrate existence, brain and sinew. Here he is at one with Stendhal, Balzac, and Nietzsche, all of whom find the essence of beauty in the excitement of the will and the enhancement of being. Art, as Nietzsche says over and over again, is the great seducer and stimulus to life.

The circle of Berlioz' religious affirmations is thus continuous despite the tension within. It is complete as a circle, but something less than a system because he drew only the corollaries that he felt need for. Unlike the orthodox or the conservative philosophers of his day, he nowhere found evidence of an encompassing absolute spirit. Their arguments said that such a Being *had* to exist in order to justify the chaos of experience, no less than to explain the order of nature or the genius of Beethoven. As a dramatic artist Berlioz could not accept this convenient but anti-dramatic totality. He was a pluralist, and working moreover in a great epoch of science. Reading and observation told him that the abstraction of an Absolute conformed neither with natural fact nor with moral justice. This is why in his copy of *Paul et Virginie* — an early classic of natural philosophy — he wrote "This book would make one an atheist were one not so already." [34]

"Atheist" here does not mean materialist; Berlioz did not yield to the lure of full negation. Writing in 1854 of his "passionate interviews" with nature, and mentioning Shakespeare and Beethoven as "perhaps the two greatest landscape artists who ever existed," he adds: "But I feel myself

[34] *285, 325.* On the same point take at random a competent but independent witness: "At the present time," writes Prince Chlodwig Hohenlohe in July 1853, "we see the conviction growing more and more that knowledge and faith must be completely separated. . . . The school of natural science declares war on transcendentalism and banishes the transcendental to the sphere of [mere] belief." (*1176,* I, 72.)

tugged at in the opposite direction by the analytic mania which the — so to speak — chemical philosophy of our time breeds in the brain." [35] When therefore Barbey d'Aurevilly calls Berlioz "an artist with the anger of a Samson, whose wrath did not disarm for a single day . . . a man without faith, living in evil days and who like other artists of his time knew only Beauty as his sole God . . ." [36] the words "faith" and "evil days" must be read in the light of history. The evil days were even worse than Barbey implies. For by 1850 the scientific vitalism of the Romantic Era, by which poets, philosophers and scientists shared a common ground of faith and action, was superseded by a narrow and pseudoscientific positivism that quickly enticed the greater number. It was cocksure, oversimple, enterprising: it was Realism.[37] "People," Berlioz tells us, "no longer say, 'What do I know?' like Montaigne, but 'What's the use?' I myself am obsessed by plans for vast and daring works; I am about to begin and I stop. Why undertake such a work, I ask myself, and feel growing within me a frightening enthusiasm for it, . . . only to have it fall into the hands of children or of boors . . . ? The English talk of erecting to Shakespeare's memory a statue 400 feet high and *they have not a single theatre* where he is worthily put on." [38]

He was revolted equally by the barbaric trust in progress ("no need to prove to me that dreadful reality; I know perfectly well that next year peaches will be as big as melons")[39] and by its counterpart, the shabby spiritualism of the table-turning kind which he immortally ridiculed in his "Beethoven and the Mediums." [40] The picture with which the new and handsome magazine *L'Illustration* characterized the year 1853 showed all Europe levitating furniture for want of truer mysteries. Berlioz could rightly say: "The mightiest products of the human spirit have at this day neither hearth nor home." [41]

It was an impossible choice which nothing since has alleviated: religious men must either cling to the letter of an ancient creed, venerable and beautiful but narrowed by conflict — and thus give the lie not merely to

---

[35] *M.C.*, 230.

[36] *1047*, 48. See Odilon Redon's estimate of Berlioz' position: above, Chapter 20.

[37] See my essay *Darwin, Marx, Wagner*, Boston 1941.

[38] *M.C.*, 230. He correctly ascribes the projected statuary to "a belated gesture of national vanity; a true feeling of admiration is [among the English] neither general nor genuine." *Ibid.*

[39] *M.C.*, 266.

[40] *A Trav.*, 86 ff. and see below, Chapter 25.

[41] *M.C.*, 230. Balzac had predicted that unbelief would make men not more scientific but more credulous.

science and philosophy but to the more complex and generous view of man elaborated through the centuries; or else, unable to "believe" in this sense, pass for skeptics and atheists and suffer being likened to the brutish multitude of Podsnaps. Even the willing submitters felt that religious feeling had to be hoarded and poured into set forms lest it dissolve without ever coloring the secular stream. D'Ortigue was one of these, and the reason Berlioz could not take refuge with him in an automatic kind of otherworldliness was the price he would have had to pay: binding his perceptions and constricting his energies. In ages when faith inspires great theologies, religion is not exclusively sublime and solitary, it is also humorous, workaday, exuberant — vulgar in the human sense we descry on the cathedrals. Religious art then depicts the plowman digging and also Aristotle writing.[42] Of such a religion, we may suppose, Berlioz could have been a devout adherent: it would have satisfied his many-sided nature as well as used him, for such a religion would not be an activity apart but an accompaniment of all activities, and because of this readier to accept expressiveness in art.

More, an uncontested and truly catholic religion tends to solve the problem of audience, by letting everyone participate in ritual for *his* reasons instead of as a connoisseur. This is why in Euphonia (and later in Bayreuth) the "great work" takes the guise of a religious festival. Berlioz steadily felt that the question of religious music was central. In the letter to Martin d'Anger already quoted he says: "I admire . . . your coolness in discussing a problem the very statement of which always puts me in a fever, and which is so vital for art that one may say it involves the whole of it." [43] Berlioz means the artist's right to be expressive in church as well as elsewhere. He claims this right in order to keep art in touch with life, and claims it on grounds of simple logic and intellectual freedom.[44] But he also has in mind the capacity of art to minister to mankind, by distributing as it were the balm of religion throughout the emotions and purging the soul in the way of tragedy. Berlioz tells of going on an excursion to the plain of Enghien and being moved to mixed medita-

[42] Chartres, north porch, right-hand bay. Jubal is there too, playing the lyre.
[43] *M.E.*, 146.
[44] If lack of expression and impersonality form the merit of sacred music for the orthodox, Berlioz argues, then it should seem that "a statue reciting the liturgical words impassively on a single note" would be the logical fulfilment of the ideal. (*A Trav.*, 262.) Elsewhere he argues *ad personam:* "They want religious music to have no melody, no harmony, no rhythm, no expression, no instrumentation, and no clear tonality because as soon as all this will be proved unnecessary, they will have all the requisite qualities for being excellent composers of religious music." (*S.W.*, 15.)

tions by the sight of people, youth, cornfields, the sound of birds, and distant church bells. He finally reaches the church at vesper time. A poor organist is playing Berlioz' favorite psalmody, *In exitu Israel de Aegypto:*

The persistence of this melancholy psalmody in the minor mode, returning ever the same in each stanza, ends by lulling your harmonic pains and inducing reverie. This time the daydream turns to art. One imagines how fine it would be to have this church to oneself so that music could make its home there and display its gentlest charms, a home where it could blissfully sing its hymns, idylls, and poems of love, where it could pray, meditate, call up the past, weep and smile, and keep its virginal pride from being profaned by the herd, and live forever pure and angelic for herself and her few friends. Now the organist plays a little dance tune from an old operatic ballet and the contrast with the antique psalmody of the choir irritates you so much that you go out.[45]

As he often did about other matters, Berlioz argues about religious art in dialectical fashion. Against one group he argues the folly of a disembodied, expressionless piety; and against the rest of the orthodox, he argues the unworthiness of a worldly-timid compromise with current taste — the taste not of common men but of the miseducated herd. His temperamental aversion from sensuality, which is one of the stumbling blocks to the ready appreciation of his music, puts him once more in a "third position" equidistant from the extremes: "It is the unhappy truth that music is understood by only a limited number of cultivated minds, and that it acts on the uncultivated entirely through its sensual side. Whence the monstrous doctrines . . . and still more monstrous corruptions that the frivolous or gross tastes of the multitude have brought into its use. One must combat the latter and cultivate the former, but this double task can be properly done only with the aid of abundant examples, irresistibly beautiful and striking." [46]

The kind of example he meant, uniting expressiveness and intimations of the supernatural, he found in Mozart and Beethoven. In *The Magic Flute* was the antique religious style that Berlioz himself attains in *The Infant Christ*. The modern (or naturalistic) religious style occurs in some of Beethoven's adagios (by no means exclusively the symphonic): "There, no earthly passions, no hymns to joy, love, or glory; no childlike songs, soft speeches, comic or sarcastic sallies, no more of those terrible outbursts of fury and hatred that escape him in the throes of his secret sufferings; not even the savage indignation of the heart: he is no longer one of us, he has forgotten us and left our atmosphere. Calm and solitary, he

[45] *Soirées* (18th) *Eves.*, 205. Compare Shaw's "On Going to Church."
[46] *M.E.*, 147.

floats in the ether like an eagle of the Andes soaring at a height below which other creatures have already found death. His gaze cleaves the spaces, he flies toward all the suns, singing infinite nature." [47]

With regard to Berlioz' sacred music as a whole one can only repeat and extend Barbey's judgment about *L'Enfance du Christ:* the varied scores on religious subjects are so many prayers, or as the title of one of them suggests, so many religious meditations. They are to be judged as we would judge any similar testimonials of faith. We do not really know what the cathedral builders individually believed; we cannot be sure of Bach's or Handel's orthodoxy — even Dante's is in doubt; and when we have biographical knowledge of an artist's piety, as we have about Mendelssohn's or César Franck's, we usually remain in doubt about the quality or depth of it. This we must infer — that is, try to read in their music. [48] In Beethoven's fugues and masses the most diverse hearers have found symbols of their own innermost convictions, not knowing or not caring whether the composer was Catholic, Protestant, or agnostic. Music, in short, remains exact but unliteral.

Conversely, we weigh Berlioz' religious utterances in music with the aid of his essays and letters. From the very beginning, under the influence of the liturgy which set him to composing, and later under that of Gluck's Greek tragedies, Berlioz seized every opportunity to elevate his dramatic subjects by inserting religious scenes, or by treating human passions in a religious mood. After discarding his *Passage of the Red Sea*, he filled his prize cantatas with hymns and sacred songs; his earliest performed work was a Mass. In his first two symphonies (including *Lélio*) he considered several movements religious; out of his first dozen songs, two were on sacred subjects; and one, the "Meditation" on Moore's poem, shows how deep was Berlioz' natural piety at an age when he may superficially have seemed wild and rebellious. [49]

Significantly it is only in this mood that Berlioz shows the slightest tendency to repeat himself: the close of this *Meditation*, of the *Agnus*

---

[47] "On the Trios and Sonatas of Beethoven" (*A Trav.*, 64–5).

[48] *E.g.*, Vincent d'Indy writing of certain passages in César Franck's *Redemption* and *Beatitudes:* "The poor dear master cudgels his brains to express an evil and a moral ugliness which the simple beauty of his own character precluded his being able to conceive." (*945, 125.*)

[49] "The *Méditation religieuse* is one of Berlioz' finest pages, triumphant in its issue, profound in its inspiration, and most dramatic in its working out. The thing lives through passages of terror, of doubt, and of hesitation, until finally it emerges into the wonderful beauty of the simplest of melodies, 'Weep then, sad heart' . . ." (*597*) This London critique of 1903 applies to the orchestrated version included in *Tristia*.

Dei, and of the *Faust* finale depicting Gretchen in Heaven have a certain resemblance, as if the pacified heart were one. But this expresses only a single attitude among the many comprised in the religious life. If the epilogue "O my soul" in *The Infant Christ* is a prayer in the contrite mood, the *Hostias* of the *Requiem* is another in the heroic and sacrificial; and in the Easter Chorus of the *Damnation* a whole people prays in thanksgiving. Berlioz' relatively slight output in Rome was, as we saw, largely religious [50] and it is fair to deduce that the impressions he was gathering found place in the ensuing secular works. All of them, including *Benvenuto*, number one or more religious scenes, and the "Judgment Day" oratorio and Funeral Symphony which he then planned furnished later great works with inspiration ranging from religious grief to prayers of thanksgiving and strains of divine pomp.[51]

For the central mystery of the religion to which he was born, he recaptured the stained-glass simplicity and perfection that inform *The Infant Christ;* and in the work next to be dealt with — a tragedy on an antique theme pondered since early youth — his mind naturally recurred to the "hymns of gratitude, exultation and faith" which his century and the land of his birth had seemingly no use for.[52]

[50] In addition to the list given above one should note that the *religioso* close of the first movement of the *Symphonie Fantastique* was written at that time. Perhaps it is not farfetched to suppose that Berlioz' having faced death by drowning *twice* since he left France helped turn his thoughts toward religious subjects.

[51] Even the cantata celebrating the Northern Railway has a grave *religioso* passage for the basses. (*Ger. ed.*, XIV, 50 ff.) In the specifically sacred *Requiem* and *Te Deum* the proportion that such moments bear to those of terror and punishment are roughly three to one, a figure which, when taken with the rest of the moods at Berlioz' command, reduces his exploration of the terrible to a far from prevailing tendency. See Wotton's "Berlioz the Blood-Curdler." (*534.*)

[52] Quoted from a letter to Liszt, who in 1853 was urging Berlioz to compose a *Missa Solemnis*. Berlioz replied that it was futile to think of producing in France such prayers and hymns as he enumerated, whereas "a *Requiem* mass has at least a powerful and tireless patron — Death." (*M.C.*, 56.)

23. *Virgilian Music Drama:* Les Troyens

> . . . thou that singest
> Ilion's lofty temples robed in fire,
> Ilion falling, Rome arising,
> Wars and filial faith and Dido's pyre

February 1855
to April 7, 1858

> Landscape-lover, lord of language
> Thou majestic in thy sadness . . .
> I salute thee,
> I that loved thee since my day began.
> — TENNYSON on the nineteenth
> centenary of Virgil's death

BERLIOZ' latent desire to compose a new work of large dimensions based on Virgil, the oldest of his "idols," had been kindled by long conversations with Liszt and Princess Sayn-Wittgenstein during the second "Berlioz Week" at Weimar in February 1855. This new task, at once literary and musical, was to occupy him for three years, during which he kept the Princess informed of his progress in a series of letters that also record interruptions by concerts, journeys, and ill-health. But it may be noted in passing that the mood of *The Infant Christ* had not vanished all at once. Naïve religiousness produced another flower, the *Children's Morning Prayer*, on a text by Lamartine, which Berlioz scored for two-part female chorus and which has been likened for touching simplicity to some of Herrick's verses.[1] This afterglow of inspiration shows that Berlioz could probably have continued, at any point in his career, the production of music in any given style that had found favor. The determination with which after each major score he turns his back upon success and seeks out a new field to till is an index of his stature and explains why he remained, for his own time and for a good while after, a musicians' musician.

Home from Weimar, Berlioz suffered the usual letdown, with aggravating circumstances. The "intestinal inflammation," which was diagnosed

---

[1] *310*, 130. Its only performance that I know of in recent times was given by the late Hubert Farren and his string orchestra in Coventry (England) on October 18, 1934. An enthusiastic Berliozian and a conscientious conductor, Mr. Farren met death fighting incendiary bombs during the blitz.

only later, now occurred as a regular symptom added to his old ones of sore throat, fever, and headache. It seems likely that Berlioz never had a disease properly so-called his whole life long. His nervous system when strained produced functional disorders, which in time became localized lesions and finally killed him. Until then a congenial musical task would "cure" his most violent pains, so that he may be said to have died a professional death rather than a casual or self-indulgent one.

A week in bed partly restored him for his concerts in Brussels, where he met again Adolphe Samuel, a young composer of thirty who greatly admired the French master and soon became one of his confidants.[2] Meanwhile Belgian rehearsals proved trying. "Whatever does not come down on the first beat makes them lose their heads. . . . They made me suffer like Hurons."[3] Only the final concert satisfied the conductor, but at all of them the music was new — or rather, the public was, and its response correspondingly uncertain. Fétis, as we know, had revised his views a second time and thus regained his original position of somewhat alarmed admiration for Berlioz. At dinner he found Berlioz "a man of wit and great intelligence, both general and musical . . . unfortunately the richness of his imagination does not come up to his acquired technical skill."[4]

More wholehearted was Edgar Quinet, Michelet's friend and fellow historian, whom Napoleon III had exiled: "I had the other day the great joy of receiving a visit from Berlioz, whom I did not know and whom I have always admired in the teeth of public opinion. I love and admire this artist who follows the Muse without flattering the public . . . disinterested and disdainful of easy success. Berlioz himself attracts me as much as his music: his will power, his energy, his pride are as fine as any of his symphonies. What a fine work is the life of a true artist! He had my admiration, he leaves with my friendship. Moreover, we didn't only converse. I twice heard his oratorio *The Infant Christ,* which contains songs that Raphael might have created."[5]

On his return to Paris Berlioz was greeted by the first performance of the *Corsair* overture which he had recast in London and dedicated to his

---

[2] Also a music critic and long a professor of harmony at the Brussels Conservatory, Samuel became head of the musical institutions of Ghent.

[3] *Corresp.*, 224.

[4] Fétis had the naïveté to write this fumbling judgment to Liszt. (*207*, II, 17.) It was then that Fétis composed his article on Berlioz for the biographical dictionary he was revising. (*344*, I, 362–5.)

[5] *228*, I, 217–8 (Apr. 5, 1855). Just before these concerts there was another meeting of music and literature: George Eliot and Lewes, returning from Berlin, "sat at the same table with the composer Berlioz" — no doubt at the hotel. (*1232*, 109.)

friend J. W. Davison. The next musical move was the preparation of the *Te Deum* and other concerts in connection with the Great Exhibition. Berlioz as usual did all the organizing, from finding the advance capital and the instrumentists to supervising the publicity and the building of stands.[6] "The expenses alone come to 7000 francs. It's enough to give you the shivers." [7] Doubtless recalling the setback of the *Damnation* and hating the very thought of debt, Berlioz formed a virtual partnership to divide the risk. The profits were allocated in advance: the Church would receive fifty per cent, the district commissioner of the poor twenty per cent, and himself thirty per cent. Despite the share allotted to the Church for its trouble and to the poor for theirs, the Archbishop at the last minute threatened to stop the enterprise. By an adroit use of the press, Berlioz coped with this impediment; but in between errands and rehearsals he had to lie down, feverish and writhing in pain.

On April 28, 1855 the public dress rehearsal of the *Te Deum* took place at St. Eustache. The critics were lifted out of their usual apathy, and their enthusiasm insured the financial success of the public hearing two days later. The church was full to overflowing and everything went without a hitch.[8] It was after this occasion that Berlioz wrote to Liszt the letter quoted earlier about the Babylonian work which was own brother to the *Requiem*.[9] The former director of the Opera, Roqueplan, who had treated Berlioz so shabbily, came forward with many others and warmly congratulated him. "The end of the world is near," [10] was Berlioz' dry comment to Princess Carolyne. And to Liszt, in saying farewell, "I am taking to my bed."

His stay in bed must have been short because in early May he was calling at the Ministries for authorization to give subsequent Exhibition concerts. Of the seven that were planned, he was put in charge of three, in-

[6] At precisely the same time, Delacroix was going through the same drudgery in order to collect for the Exhibition a retrospective and representative display of his life's work. One must read in his Correspondence (III, 242 ff.) the exasperating difficulties put in his way by every bureaucrat and underling in the land.

[7] *207*, II, 11.

[8] Berlioz was delighted with the perfect ensemble despite the physical remoteness of the organ at the other end of the church. It was kept in time with the aid of the electric metronome and a second conductor. What proved more difficult, indeed impossible, was to *tune* organ and orchestra, for the organ, though recently built, was a quarter-tone below concert pitch, and the wind instruments could neither transpose nor lengthen their tubes to meet it. (*A Trav.*, 298.)

[9] See above, motto of Subchapter 19.

[10] *S.W.*, 10.

cluding the first. Yet pain and fatigue still plagued him and we find him giving Liszt explicit instructions for publishing the *Memoirs* if he should die suddenly. "Forgive me for writing to you in this testamentary tone." [11] Before the beginning of the London season to which he was committed, he had proofs to correct, piano reductions to oversee (young Saint-Saëns was doing *Lélio*),[12] and the usual *feuilletons*.

In London with his wife by June 9, Berlioz had the weaker of the two orchestral societies to conduct in two concerts. His first included Mozart's *Magic Flute* overture and G Minor Symphony, fragments of *Romeo*, and the *Templar* overture by a young composer named Henry Leslie. Richard Wagner, of whose presence in London Berlioz heard from Liszt, was in the audience. He had been badly handled by the press for his conducting of the other orchestra, but was reported calm in spirit and sure of "dominating the musical world in 50 years." [13] This first concert of Berlioz aroused the subscribers so mightily that their cheers, according to a witness, made the walls of Exeter Hall vibrate.[14] And the loyalty of the old-timers was such that protests were received at the omission of the choral parts of *Romeo* — an omission due solely to the lack of the right voices.

The second concert on July fourth featured *Harold in Italy* (viola solo by Ernst), the *première* of Henselt's piano concerto in F minor,[15] and a scene from Meyerbeer's *Prophète*. The composer was in England to aid in the mounting of *Stella del Nord*, for which Queen Victoria lingered late in the capital. Berlioz moreover conducted a benefit at which, after Rossini's *Stabat Mater*, no less than eight prima donnas of both sexes sang fashionable airs. Ernst played little pieces on the violin and the success was complete. On the next day Berlioz would leave England for the last time.

[11] *207*, II, 21.

[12] Saint-Saëns also did parts of the *Damnation of Faust*. A list of the musicians who worked in this way on Berlioz' scores would suggest a parallel to young painters copying old masters. Besides Liszt and Bülow, it would include Czerny, Thalberg, Pixis, Benedict, Ritter, Balakirev, Cornelius, Chabrier, and many lesser lights.

[13] *Corresp.*, 229.

[14] *340*, 715.

[15] This time Berlioz did not encounter his former fiancée at the keyboard, though Mme. Pleyel was still on tour in the British Isles and under Jullien's management. Earlier in the year De Quincey had written from Edinburgh to his daughter: ". . . on two separate days of next week Julien (or is it Jullien) gives concerts. . . . Will you come? . . . There is always a great crowding at these concerts which (as you know) wear a vulgar, snobbish character but always offer the attractions of a severely selected and severely trained orchestra and *partially* good music. And on this particular occasion there is the *extra* . . . attraction of Mme. Pleyell, the celestial pianofortist. Heaven nor earth has yet heard her equal." (*1204*, II, 97–8.)

Before his departure, however, he and Wagner had had their first and only long, uninterrupted conversation. It was at the house of Berlioz' friend Sainton that the two spent an evening together informally, and came as near knowing each other as it was granted them to do. Their previous meetings had been brief interludes in the midst of action, and the well-meant efforts of Liszt, Bülow, and others had only resulted in developing as much difference as kinship between them. It is usually difficult to make one's friends become mutual as well as common friends, and with men who have ideas at stake it may be fatal. Besides, just as Davison (who disliked Wagner's music and conducting) was not slow to represent to Berlioz how violently Wagner attacked him in print,[16] so there were those in Germany who stirred up Wagner to a comparable though unmotivated resentment. Since, finally, the willingness to forget attacks that Berlioz had expressed to Liszt was not encouraged by Marie (she took her husband's magnanimity for laxness in self-defense) it might have been expected that the evening at Sainton's would be, at best, stiff.

It turned out precisely the opposite. Immediately after, Wagner was writing to Liszt:

One real gain I bring back from England — the cordial and genuine friendship which I feel for Berlioz and which we have mutually declared. I heard a concert of the New Philharmonic under his direction and was, it is true, little edified by his performance of Mozart's G Minor symphony, while the very imperfect execution of his *Romeo and Juliet* symphony made me pity him.[17]

A few days later, we two were the only guests at Sainton's table. He was lively, and the progress I have made in French while in London permitted me to discuss with him for five hours all the problems of art, philosophy, and life in a most fascinating conversation. In that manner I gained a deep sympathy for my new friend; he appeared to me quite different from what he had before.[18] We discovered that we were in reality fellow sufferers, and I thought that upon the whole I was happier than Berlioz.

After my last concert he and the other friends I have in London called on me; his wife also came. We remained together until 3 o'clock in the morning and took leave with the warmest embraces.[19]

[16] Davison was about to reprint parts of Wagner's *Opera and Drama* in *The Musical World*, as it were to show up Wagner's errors and incite Berlioz to battle.

[17] It is not clear whether Wagner means that the performance was incomplete, which it was, or inadequate, which it was not, except in the Scherzo. After hearing the Adagio, Toussaint Bennet (the father of the pianistic prodigy Theodore Ritter) came to admit for the first time that an orchestra could be more variously expressive than a piano. (*Corresp.*, 230.)

[18] It was three years since Wagner had said of Berlioz, again to Liszt: "He does not know me, but I know him."   [19] *239*, II, 82.

On his side Berlioz had written to Liszt:

We spoke a great deal about you with Wagner recently, and you may imagine with how much affection, since, on my word of honor, I believe he loves you as I do. He will no doubt tell you of his stay in London and of all he has had to endure from prejudiced hostility. He is superb in his ardor and stoutness of heart, and I confess that even his violence pleases me. It seems fate itself is at work to keep me from hearing his latest compositions. . . . If it is true that we both have asperities [of character] those asperities dovetail into each other thus: [20]

What Berlioz, with a tactfulness Wagner did not emulate, refrained from telling Liszt was that he had not enjoyed his new friend's conducting "in a free style, the way Klindworth plays the piano . . . *sempre tempo rubato*," nor that just before leaving, he had at last been shown the very words of Wagner's attack.[21]

Liszt rejoiced. "I am delighted," he told Wagner, "at the news of your friendship with Berlioz. Of all contemporary composers he is the one with whom you can talk in the simplest, openest, and most interesting manner. Take him for all in all, he is a splendid, honest, tremendous fellow." [22]

The impression, already quoted, of an actual witness to the second meeting in London,[23] was also the impression of the public at large with regard to the two musicians' conducting: polish and precision as against impetuosity and self will. "Wagner, embittered by his long struggle against poverty, depreciation, and failure, . . . [was] in a very unfit condition to make friends, even if he had been the most genial of men. He appears to have set everyone by the ears. . . .[24] Berlioz, on the other hand, resembled Mendelssohn in the charm of his manner and the desire to be affable. It was by a mere chance that . . . he did not settle in England,

---

[20] *207*, II, 30–1.

[21] Berlioz reports this to Ritter in a light vein: ". . . we went to drink punch with Wagner after his concert, he renews his expressions of friendship, embraces me passionately, saying he had entertained many prejudices about me; he weeps and stamps his foot and hardly has he left when *The Musical World* publishes the passage in his book where he slates me in the most amusing and witty fashion, Davison roaring with delight as he translates it for me — the world's a stage, as Shakespeare and Cervantes have said." (*113*.)

[22] *239*, II, 84–5.

[23] Praeger. See above Chapter 20.

[24] Among others, George Eliot, who received Wagner at her house, had to deal with his tactless remarks about her other guests.

or at least make it to a large extent his home." [25] Certainly his English friends, admirers, and backers formed an ever enlarging group and seemed a more compact and active following than any he had met. The British tradition of Handelian oratorio favored an understanding of Berlioz' dramatic forms. During his stay he had arranged for an English publication of *The Infant Christ*, and had signed a contract with Novello for a revised edition of the *Treatise on Orchestration*, to which the author agreed to add his essay on "The Art of Conducting." The trip as a whole had been morally and materially profitable.

Awaiting him at home was a mass of arrears. The *Te Deum*, *L'Enfance*, and *Lélio* were coming out together. "I do nothing but read proof from morning till night." [26] Since the *Te Deum* was being published by subscription, Berlioz must also write letters to possible buyers. *Benvenuto Cellini*, widely called for in Germany, was being engraved at Brunswick. On top of this, Berlioz was again on the jury for musical instruments at the Paris Exhibition. It was "enough to kill off a ressuscitated man." [27] The heat was unusually great; Louis, who had been quite ill in a naval hospital at St. Mandrier, was recovering slowly; and there were already premonitions of the next war.

Nevertheless, the *Treatise* was revised and issued and four works, one of them in two distinct editions, were published and distributed. In September, declining Wagner's invitation to visit him in Zurich, Berlioz wrote: "So you are melting the glaciers as you work upon your *Nibelungen*. It must be splendid to compose in the presence of Nature. That is another delight I am deprived of: beautiful scenery, high peaks, and the grand aspects of the sea absorb me entirely instead of prompting thought. At such times I can only feel and not express. I can only draw the moon by looking at its reflection in a well.

"I should like to be able to send you the scores you so kindly ask for. Unfortunately my publishers no longer give me any [of the earlier ones]. But there are two, in fact three — the *Te Deum*, *The Infant Christ* and *Lélio* (a lyric monodrama) which will come out in a few weeks and these at least I can send you. I have your *Lohengrin;* if you could let me have your *Tannhäuser*, it would give me much pleasure." [28]

The next month the Exhibition would close and rehearsals must begin for Berlioz' three concerts. This was "a furnace in which to broil alive," for although the conductor expected to be worn out by the usual ubiqui-

[25] *340*, 717.
[26] *Corresp.*, 230.
[27] *207*, II, 35.
[28] *Corresp.*, 226–7.

tous chores, he now found himself faced with an Imperial Committee that interfered at each step and "co-operated" destructively. Like the Quaker housewife, Berlioz had only strength enough to do things by himself. "Yesterday," he writes to the Princess on November 6, 1855, "I began my rehearsals, my struggle with the architects, the copyists, and so on. I have nine days to go, baton in hand from nine to four. . . . The whole of Paris wants to sing, blow, and scrape, and one has to tune all these voices, instruments, and pretensions." [29]

For good measure he sandwiched in a few errands for his correspondent and her lover, seeing to the shipping of saxophones and claiming of unpaid royalties. Liszt had composed two symphonic poems which Berlioz wanted to know more about in order to publicize their existence, and Liszt again had finished a long essay on the *Harold* symphony, with sidelights on *Benvenuto* and Berlioz' method in general. He now wished Berlioz to have the essay published in Paris. [30]

The first concert began at noon on November 15 — prize-giving day — in the presence of Napoleon, Eugénie, Prince Jerome and the Duke of Cambridge. After the parade, Berlioz began his *Emperor* cantata, now or never appropriate, and moreover quite short. But the Emperor himself interrupted it by getting up and fingering his speech. The remainder of the concert — works by other composers — was similarly hashed up, but the performers cheered the conductor in spite of protocol. The next day, with no officials but an immense audience, the whole program, from Beethoven and Berlioz to Handel, Gluck, Meyerbeer and Rossini, was acclaimed. He had massed his cohorts on and around the Imperial platform, which was the correct acoustic spot, and the effect lived up to his design. [31] In the *Te Deum* March for the Trooping of the Colors and the *Apothéose* there were two hundred drums.

But this was nothing to the armies corralled on succeeding days by other conductors: Gounod led sixteen hundred singers one day and forty-five hundred later on. Berlioz gave his program with his smaller, better balanced and better trained forces a second time and received most of the notices. They were hardly musical judgments, but Berlioz was used to that. His irritation, as the year ended, was spent on Liszt's behalf; for after a

---

[29] *S.W.*, 11–13. He chose twelve hundred.

[30] It never was, being too long and too serious a eulogy. A short version had appeared in five numbers of the *Neue Zeitschrift* (1854) and the full text is now only available in German translation (Liszt's *Ges. Schrift.*, IV, 319–405). Originally the essay was only to be the first of a series, making up a volume on Berlioz, part biographical, part critical.

[31] So did the receipts. Berlioz' share was 8000 francs.

concert in Berlin where his friend had played his own setting of the thirteenth Psalm, the critics had served up their old arguments against expressive music on religious subjects. "So the Berlin Ph.D's are riding their Rosinante to tilt at the religious paradox again! Materialist music — dramatic — passionate — worldly! They want the Christian to pray as a statue would if it could . . .

"And these same heavyweights who find modern music wrong in being thus expressive . . . make no objection whatever to the nonsense contained in the innumerable [operas] with which Europe is flooded. . . . In short, Raphael and Michelangelo committed a crime against religion in painting when they used color; they should have used only black and white, and even so their Madonnas have faces that are too expressive and meaningful. . . . The Gotha concert will definitely take place on February 6. I have another at Liège on January 29, and one here in Paris on the 23rd. I'll send you a list of the ladies who are killed or injured." [32]

At the Gotha concert Berlioz received two hundred thalers, a cross from the Grand Duke, and a visit from Liszt who was unwell. Together they went to Weimar, where the pianist, now a Perfect Wagnerite, hoped to make Berlioz a convert by playing him large portions of the operas at the keyboard. The occasion of Berlioz' stay was really a third "Berlioz Week," beginning with *Benvenuto Cellini*, which proved as successful as before; but Berlioz was made to feel that Liszt had adopted a new idol which he, Berlioz, could not add to his own Olympus. The friendship between the old companions of 1830 was as real and affectionate and serviceable as ever, but a new doctrine — as Liszt explicitly admitted later [33] — was depriving it of artistic significance. Liszt had every right to like and to champion any music he chose, and Berlioz was too great a mind to question that right for an instant. But he could not concede the Wagnerian theory of musical evolution, namely that Wagner's new art superseded that of Weber and Beethoven. [34]

There was something a little crude in Liszt's attempt to make Berlioz agree to this proposition, something a little blind in accepting it himself — what room did it leave for the very works of Berlioz which Liszt continued to conduct and eulogize in print? Moreover, there was as yet not a single work answering to Wagner's description. *Lohengrin* and the origi-

[32] *S.W.*, 15–18. Other projects for the season included Prague, Vienna, and London once more, but these were given up in favor of composing.

[33] *235*, II, 387. Throughout 1855, Liszt had been studying Wagner's prose works.

[34] This same letter of Liszt's states unmistakably that this was the chief point at issue between him and Berlioz. (*Ibid.*, and see below, Subchapter 24.)

nal version of *Tannhäuser* were not "works of art of the future." Berlioz and Liszt thus bogged down in painful and futile debates which by common consent they did not renew.

What made the situation critical for each of them was that the three men involved were producing: Liszt had taken fire orchestrally, Wagner was also approaching the fulfillment of his long preparation, and Berlioz was taking the step by which the dramatic symphony and dramatic legend were adapted to the stage in a music drama of epic style and proportions.[35] For despite the setbacks of illness and concertizing the Virgilian project was taking shape. Letters from his "encouragers" as he called Adolphe Samuel in Brussels, the Baron von Donop at Detmold, Auguste Morel in Marseille, and Liszt's Princess as well, kept him from yielding to the "inert and glacial" atmosphere of Paris. There Prince Jerome was an island of comfort, being desirous of "establishing" this French composer with a European reputation whom Paris maintained only as a critic. But the Emperor, the source of all power and possibility, was unapproachable, perhaps because "he execrates music like ten Turks." [36]

Instead of the signs of quickened life, the spring of 1856 brought home to Berlioz rather the watchful presence of death. Not only did he himself experience unpleasant spells of faintness, but many in his circle were mortally stricken. First, young Fumagalli died, a pupil and friend of Liszt's, aged twenty-eight; then Mlle. Pleyel, Camille's daughter — also a pianist and very like her mother in looks — from galloping consumption at twenty; then Montfort, who had won the Rome Prize the same year as Berlioz. Also Heinrich Heine, who had matched wits with Berlioz for a quarter century, and whom Berlioz had continued to cheer by visits during the last years of the poet's invalidism. Likewise Berlioz' doctor, Amussat, who had once been Hector's teacher at Medical School, and another physician, Vidal, always a stout Berliozian, though attached in a professional capacity to the Opera. "I am always at the cemetery," writes the survivor, "the good Lord is mowing us down. . . ." [37]

Louis was another source of worry. After his illness, the young man wanted to leave the Navy and enter the merchant marine. Berlioz tried to secure dispensations in order to avert loss of rank. In the end, the boy's position had to remain as it was. But the general rise in prices compelled Berlioz to move to a smaller apartment, at 4 rue de Calais, in the Clichy

[35] For this description of the work, see below Tovey and Grout (next Subchapter).
[36] *Corresp.*, 232.
[37] *S.W.*, 20–1.

district. And Caesar's economics, as usual, was affecting things belonging to God: the occasions for serious musical criticism were becoming fewer. The small Salle Herz, built the preceding year, held in its couple of hundred seats all those who cared for genuine music. At the Opera the great attraction was *Le Corsaire*, a ballet by Adolphe Adam, the popularity of which was largely due to the real ship which could be seen in the last act. "Music! That's the last thing anyone thinks of." [38]

At the instigation of a Swiss publisher, Berlioz had just revised all of his *Nuits d'Eté* and completed their orchestration. Fresh music too was stirring within him. "I am gathering my strength," he writes in mid-April, "I have blocked out the main lines of the great dramatic business that the Princess takes so much interest in. It's beginning to take shape, but it is huge and therefore dangerous." This was to Liszt; [39] a month later, he informs the Princess: "Day before yesterday I finished versifying the first act. It will be the longest and it took me ten days to write it — the first ten I have had clear since my return from Weimar. . . . I have been a dozen times on the point of throwing everything into the fire and giving myself over to the contemplative life. But now I am sure not to lack the courage to reach the end. The work has got hold of me. Besides, I reread your letter from time to time to spur myself on. Usually, I feel discouragement at night but come back into the breach in the morning — in the day's youth. Now I can hardly sleep: I think of nothing else and if I had my time wholly free, in two months the mosaic would be finished." [40]

No statement ever described more briefly or more exactly the overcoming of inertia at the beginning of a great work, that psychological dead weight which has nothing to do with the nature of the task, the author's preparation for it, nor even his desire to be at work, but is an emotional resistance due to the disparity between the world of created things and the world of the uncreated. The conception on its way to birth,

> Like the red outline of beginning Adam

is unreal and, as it seems, superfluous — reality being complete without it. In Berlioz, we know, this sense of the folly implied in creation was heightened by his knowledge of practical affairs. Paris under the Second Empire virtually forbade the kind of enterprise he had in hand.

The artistic problem was to form a dramatic sequence of musical scenes from the narrative contained in Books II and IV of the *Aeneid*, that is, the story of the sack of Troy, followed by the landing of the Trojans

[38] *93*, 241.   [39] *207*, II, 69.   [40] *S.W.*, 19.

at Carthage and the tragic love of Dido for Aeneas — a subject which has traditionally attracted dramatic musicians from Monteverdi and the masque composers to Purcell and Piccinni. In keeping with his habit, Berlioz did not want long explanatory passages, nor the usual operatic dialogue (accompanied by gesticulation) which hitches the plot forward.[41] Hence the planning of his "book," not to speak of the lines, was bound to be a very delicate task.

He interrupted it to stand for the Institute: Adolphe Adam had died suddenly. This time the academic musicians put Berlioz at the head of their list and he was elected; but only on the fourth ballot lest popularity should go to his head. In effect, Parisian circles took the event as a revolution — a second was in store for them when Delacroix succeeded to the same honor six months later. The admittance among the officially immortal of these two young men (aged fifty-three and fifty-nine respectively) marked a date in France's recognition of modern art. It was also a triumph for the loyal Horace Vernet.[42] Berlioz was chiefly glad of the fifteen hundred francs a year which helped reduce the number of necessary *feuilletons*, but he also knew how his new title would impress the public and his outlying relatives: "I was sitting on a bayonet, now I am in an armchair."[43]

By this time (mid-June 1856) Berlioz had finished the third act of his drama. During the cab rides to the houses of the members who were to vote for him, "I thought not of what I was going to say . . . but of what I ought to make my characters say."[44] Ten days later the last scene of Act V was in progress. "I grow more impassioned about the subject than I should, and I resist the blandishments that music exerts to have me attend to her. I want to finish everything before I begin the score. Yet last week I could not help composing the Shakespearian duet:

> In such a night as this
> When the sweet wind did gently kiss the trees, etc.[45]

So the music of this litany of love is done. But I shall need another fortnight to file down, carve, polish, correct, twist and untwist the verses

[41] After looking over Adolphe Samuel's opera, *The Two Suitors*, Berlioz had written to him: "What an anti-musical subject! How the dickens did you find so much music to pour into it?" (*93*, 226.)

[42] *91*, 456.

[43] To his uncle Félix Marmion (*269*, 436). Seats in the Academy are traditionally known as armchairs (*fauteuils*).

[44] S.W., 22.

[45] *I.e.*, Berlioz began his score with the music of a love scene, the words of which, as he tells Adèle, he "stole from Shakespeare and Virgilianized." (*91*, 454.)

such as they are. . . . I have still twenty-two confreres to call on and thank. I saw fifteen this morning, and I was obliged to stand the embraces of a number of those who voted against me. . . . Forgive the triviality and coldness of this letter: could it be that already I —— ? No! My Institute uniform has not even been ordered. . . ."[46]

By July, the tentative title *Les Troyens* was adopted. "But that is of no moment," wrote Berlioz in sending the Princess his manuscript, "the question is one of music and you will see what an enormous score this text presupposes."[47] Unlike Wagner, supported by friends and trusting tradesmen in his Swiss retreat, Berlioz could not count on long stretches of free time. No sooner had he been elected to the Institute than he had to sit on the Rome Prize committee, after which he was detailed to study and conduct a Mass by Niedermeyer. This done, he had his regular stint to do for Bénazet at Baden.

From there on August 12 he wrote to the Princess thanking her for comments on his text: "What an excellent analysis! That is what I call entering into the author's intentions! You wanted to cheer me along and I shall not be deluded by your words. You go so far as to credit me with the beauty of Virgil's poetry and praise me for my thefts from Shakespeare! Have no fear: I have the grit to carry on to the end; it was not needful to try and lure me forward with eulogies that I do not deserve — it is beautiful because it is Virgil; it is striking because it is Shakespeare. I know it. I am only an interloper; I have ransacked the gardens of two geniuses, and cut there a swath of flowers to make a couch for music, where God grant she may not perish overcome by the fragrance. . . . As for Dido's scene with her sister . . . it is a simple mirage of love which I have conjured up in order to avoid the invariable *dream* of the classics."[48]

Berlioz then turns to the musical side, saying that when he is once again in Paris he will free himself as much as possible for the strenuous task ahead. "May all Virgil's gods come to my aid, else I am lost." It is at this juncture that he states for the first time in relation to one of his own works his conception of the proper role of music in music drama, and this of course leads him to mention Wagner's contrary view, too reminiscent of eighteenth-century literary theories to suit the man who all his life had worked to make music free and independent:

[46] *S.W.*, 22–3.
[47] *S.W.*, 25.
[48] *S.W.*, 27–9. The "mirage" was later replaced by a different scene.

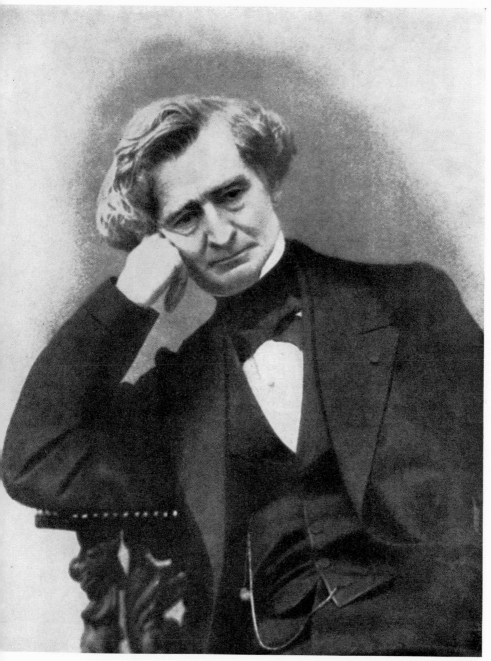

Berlioz in a familiar pose (*c.* 1855)

"I see him now . . . drinking cup after cup of tea . . .
a shock of hair in which he frequently buried his fingers
. . . and a somewhat melancholy expression. . . ."

— ADOLPH SCHLOESSER

The great difficulty [throughout] is to find the musical *form* — that form without which music does not exist, or exists only as the humbled slave of speech. There lies Wagner's crime: he wants to dethrone music and reduce it to expressive *accents*. This is to outdo the system of Gluck (who most fortunately *did not succeed* in following his own impious theory). I am for the kind of music that you yourself call "free". . . . Music is so powerful that in given instances it can conquer alone, and it has a thousand times earned the right to say with Medea:

> "Myself, which is enough."

To want to bring music back to the old recitation of the antique chorus is assuredly the most incredible and, luckily, the most useless folly in the history of art.[49]

To find the way of being expressive and truthful, without ceasing to be a musician; to endow music, rather, with new means of action — that is the problem. . . . Another hurdle in my path is that the feelings to be rendered move me too much. That is bad. One must try to do coolly things that are fiery. This is what held me up for so long in the *Romeo and Juliet* adagio and the finale of Reconciliation. I thought I should never see my way. . . . Time! Time! He is the great master. Unfortunately he behaves like Ugolino, he eats his children. . . .[50]

At Baden, Berlioz had conducted Beethoven, Gluck, and Mozart, together with an excerpt from *The Infant Christ*, but the audience was small, for the August weather was mild enough to make the outdoors pleasant even at midday. Feeling unwell after the confusing interruption of this session, Berlioz returned to Plombières, the French water resort, where he had spent two weeks before going to Baden. He had while there met the Emperor and been invited by him to a soiree at which Vivier the horn player, mimic, and raconteur had entertained a small group.[51] It was clearer than ever that Napoleon III took not the slightest interest in serious music, even when composed by a newborn academician. During his second stay at Plombières Berlioz rested, which means worked at *Les Troyens* while strolling in the woods. He quickly recovered his health, was full of

---

[49] One may discern here the "new" doctrine, more or less based on Wagner's scholarly flirtation with Greek tragedy, that Liszt and the Princess preached to Berlioz at Weimar. However garbled, it conveyed clearly enough to Berlioz the one point on which he differed — the role of music in relation to drama, a role he refused to make subservient, much less obligatory.

[50] *S.W.*, 27–33.

[51] Auguste Vivier (1821–1900), a Corsican virtuoso, one of whose specialties was playing full chords on the horn by singing one note and blowing another which yields a factitious third note (*e.g.*, C with the horn, A above sung, F heard between). This feat would punctuate or illustrate some ludicrous improvised tale. Vivier seems moreover to have been Flaubert's precursor in collecting platitudes and publishing a repertory of them.

gaiety and could dash off amusing *feuilletons* without qualms since he had composed three scenes of his music drama.

By virtue of a neurosis which he seems to have dimly observed, his return to Paris was always gloomy. He necessarily found the old worries and obstacles, and found them as if he were still in the desperate straits of his twenties, when Dr. Berlioz had said "Do or die" and had loaded the option by cutting off funds. In Paris, Berlioz felt, "I seem to hear nothing but the resonance of empty or extinguished souls." His illness returned and was diagnosed on November 14 by Alphonse Robert, the cousin (now famous) with whom he had first come to Paris to study medicine in 1821. But diagnosis seemed no avenue to cure. The prescription was six drops of laudanum in a spoonful of water. "It leaves an inner tremor which is rather disagreeable." [52] Abdominal pain gripped him so hard and so relentlessly that he had to spend whole days in bed, and he came to think that he might not live to finish his work.[53] Nor did he lack mental afflictions. Louis was still making himself a burden by his free spending and his disinclination to go on with any career.

Nevertheless, by January 1857 the first act of *Les Troyens* was virtually completed. In consequence, after fifteen years of straightforward enmity, Berlioz must once again be concerned with an institution he despised: he would soon have a score designed for the stage, and the Opera's was the only large stage available. But while he was rejuvenated by creation [54] the Imperial theater was supersenile: it could not or would not even give *William Tell* entire; and access to the ministerial controls was even more

---

[52] *91*, 461. Compare Mérimée's description of the "ether pearls" given him for a similar purpose, as an antispasmodic. (*218*, II, 154.)

[53] It may be convenient to review the course of Berlioz' health. He started with a sound constitution, of the type called in his day "nervous" or "asthenic." Before the Italian journey, his father and other doctors recommended that he avoid stimulants (tea and coffee), heat, and overwork. When Berlioz was ill it was with sore throat and fever, often as a result of worry and disappointment. By 1845, gastric pains became added symptoms of strain. Gastralgia was then the tautological name for what may have been anything from ulcers to cancer (see Vigny and Delacroix, *passim*). Berlioz found in any case that diet had no effect on his condition, to which no clearer name has since been applied. Posthumous diagnoses by literary doctors have been numerous but they reflect musical superstitions rather than medical science. The best is perhaps Singer's (*881*, 35, 55, 71, 90, 92). Dr. Gould of Philadelphia diagnosed astigmatism (*Biographical Clinics, IV*) as he did for every other nineteenth-century notable; and the rest safely dabble in secondhand psychiatrics. (*E.g., 343*.)

[54] "I am aquiver from head to foot and from heart to brain with impatience, pain, enthusiasm, and superabundance of life . . . I cannot write my score fast enough. It requires a huge, a disastrous amount of time." (To Adèle: *91*, 460.)

remote than in the days of good King Louis-Philippe. Only, Napoleon's manners were better, and he took care to send Berlioz a medal for his part in making the Exhibition of 1855 a success.

Despite the prospect of never hearing his *Troyens* live in sound, Berlioz worked on. Music was pouring out of him for several scenes at one time, out of sequence, the while he steadily furbished up the lines, withdrawing foolish concessions to current taste [55] and nourishing himself on Virgil and Shakespeare. "I am quite transported by some words of old Nestor in Shakespeare's *Troilus and Cressida*. I have just reread this amazing parody of the Iliad, where none the less Shakespeare makes Hector even greater than Homer did. Nestor says that Hector raising his sword aloft to spare the trembling Greeks as he sped through battle in his chariot made him think:

Lo, Jupiter is yonder, dealing life! [56]

What a painting that would make! . . . God in heaven but it's beautiful. . . . I feel my heart will burst when I come across lines like that. . . ." [57]

Each scene would be composed in the rough within a space of two or three days and then instrumented and polished during as many weeks. Being ill gave Berlioz an excuse not to be sociable, though his duties as critic brought on the periodic "calamity" of having to go to the Opera. The Italian Theater meanwhile teased him with hints that they might put on *Benvenuto Cellini*. Was it to purchase his good-will? In the houses of friends where he felt at home, there was always the danger of being involved in artistic discussions which just then Berlioz was not in the mood for. Thus at Mme. Viardot's (Pauline Garcia) he ran into Delacroix, old, nervous, and ailing like himself, and the two masters of Romanticism, differing on pinpoints, would end by annoying each other.[58] Yet when the next Institute vacancy occurred among the painters, Berlioz urged Delacroix's election. It took place on January 10, 1857, at the ninth attempt. So few were left who had understood the message of the century in the thirties and persevered in giving it form! The neoclassical reaction was in full swing, aided by the vague political drift which likened Caesar and

[55] An excellent example of how a great mind can fall lower than a common man of "taste" — and can recover itself — is given in a note to the Princess: "It struck me that Dido's dying allusion to the future supremacy of France in North Africa was a piece of puerile chauvinism and that it was far more decent and dignified to keep Virgil's idea [the prophecy of Hannibal's descent on Rome]." (*S.W.*, 42.)

[56] Act IV, Sc. V, 191.

[57] *S.W.*, 35–6.

[58] *182*, II, 423.

Napoleon the First with the present incumbent. The narcotic playwright
Ponsard was winning a reputation for depth and originality by lectures
proving that Shakespeare lacked artistry. "Noodle!" exclaims Berlioz in
his correspondence, "overripe cucumber!" [59]

Music was still streaming "in floods." He timed the first act and found
it ran one hour and ten minutes. This meant that "all the rest must be as
compact as possible to keep the whole within reasonable proportions." [60]
He would invite certain of his instrumentist friends and have them play
some of the "solos" (*i.e.*, outstanding melodic parts) while he accompanied them sketchily on the piano. "The Opera clarinetist (Leroy) is a
first-rate virtuoso, but cold . . . My piano was a little low, so our two
instruments were not in tune, the virtuoso phrased 'only approximately,'
finding it *very pretty* — which made me devilishly mad. . . . What a torture *approximation* is in musical performance! Yet I think the young man
will end by understanding his solo if I make him study it bar by
bar. . . ." [61] This was the sublime scene without speech in Act I, where
Andromache leading her orphaned son walks past the Trojan women to
pray at the altar and receive Priam's blessing.

Was it a good omen for such conceptions that the Parisians had taken
a sudden liking for Weber, whose *Oberon* was filling the Théâtre
Lyrique? [62] On first being told of the projected production, Berlioz had
echoed Rossini's famous, "What? All of it?" and wound up thinking "Poor
Weber!" But he had lent a hand at the rehearsals, and it now seemed that
"the burghers are actually amazed to find they like this music which, although far from perfectly executed, is nevertheless better done than it
would be at the Opéra-Comique and much better than at the Opera." [63]
The old question whether the public likes what it gets or gets what it likes
could be debated apropos of this musical surprise and Berlioz would have
to make up his mind about it before venturing his *Troyens*. He inclined to
the view that the public was more often corrupted than corrupting.[64]

The love music which fills the fourth act was now complete and instrumented. The pillars of the edifice being in sight, the masses and proportions could be inferred. At a dinner given by Prince Jerome for
Academicians, Berlioz had the pleasure of seeing his dear friend Vigny

[59] *S.W.*, 44.
[60] *S.W.*, 46.
[61] *S.W.*, 47.
[62] Directed by Léon Carvalho (*né* Carvaille) 1825–1897, of whom we shall
hear again.
[63] *S.W.*, 51.
[64] *Mem.*, II, 226; *Soirées* (9th and 10th, *passim*); *93* and *L.I.*, *passim*.

again — for the last time — and of meeting Disraeli.[65] A few weeks later
at the Tuileries, he was presented to the Empress who charmed him by her
classical knowledge (Mérimée had been her tutor) and by her great beauty.
Berlioz spoke to her of his work and was graciously told he might read
his poem to her.[66] Nothing came of this purely imperial promise, but the
idea remained with Berlioz of creating interest in his work by reading the
poem. Moreover the experience of *The Infant Christ* had taught him the
importance of prepared minds. He gave two readings of *Les Troyens* —
at the Bertins' and at his own house — which considerably impressed the
listeners.

This was in March 1857. The next month he conducted a concert for
his favorite protégé, the composer and pianist Theodore Ritter — the son
of Berlioz' friend Bennet. Berlioz admired the young man's musicianship,
he was forming his taste, and he enjoyed in his company something like a
father-and-son relation of the kind that poor Louis could not help denying
him.[67] Ritter showed his gratitude by making the piano reduction of
Romeo and Juliet — the best so far (according to Berlioz) of all the arrangements he so disliked.

Paris was now as full of musicians as of writers and painters.[68] A few

[65] To his nieces, Adèle's daughters, he writes that having five decorations to
wear — two more than any other member of the Institute — his chest "resembles
a hardware store" and makes a noise "like crockery in a high wind." (*91*, 462
and 472.)

[66] "Heavens, but she is beautiful! If I had a Dido like her, my drama would
be ruined: the pit would throw eggs at Aeneas for thinking even one minute of
abandoning her." (*S.W.*, 56.)

[67] The boy was just seventeen. It was of him that Ernest Reyer said: "Berlioz
never took pupils but the two of us consider ourselves his disciples." (*91*, 454.)
One may see the progress of Berlioz' affection for Theodore in the letters,
beginning in April 1855 (*Corresp.*, 224 and 230). For Ritter's talents see *Débats*
(1856) *passim* and note Guizot's statement in 1862 that Ritter was "the great
pianist of the day." (*1944a*, 384.) A few years earlier, Berlioz had written to the
youth:
"My dear, very dear Theodore — Remember January 12, 1856. That is the
day on which you began the study of great dramatic music and its marvels,
the day you approached the sublime conceptions of Gluck. As for me, I shall
never forget that your artistic instinct recognized at once and fervently adored
his genius which was new to you. Yes, you may be assured in spite of all the
half-passionate and half-learned critics that . . . there are two superior deities
in our art: Beethoven and Gluck . . . and though the first is far above the
other as a musician, there is so much of the one in the other that these two
Jupiters make but one god. . . ." (*Corresp.*, 233-4.)

[68] See the first two chapters of Balzac's *Cousin Pons*, published in 1847 but
dating back to 1844, in which the novelist generalizes about these conditions
of musical and artistic life.

years before, Zimmerman, who had retired from the concert platform, told Berlioz, "It is frightful! Everybody plays the piano nowadays, and plays it very well"; to which the composer had replied, "Yes, only the two of us are left who *don't* play." [69] Now one could find as many as eight recitalists all striking their first chord simultaneously before as many audiences. In one of his reviews Berlioz gathers the names of one hundred and sixty-three performers who had just given or were on the point of giving recitals. One hundred and fifty he could arrange in riming couplets: the other thirteen had neither rime nor reason. It would soon be necessary to pass ordinances: "No concerts given here," or "Commit no music on these premises." [70] Paris was as far as ever from Euphonia.

"Nothing," he wrote to Morel on the subject now much in his thoughts, "will keep the public from going to the Opera — whence a complacent carelessness on the part of the management which is beyond belief. . . . You should hear the music that is occasionally played at Court. And now here is the poor King of Prussia who has lost his mind; I do not know whether his brother shares his feeling for art. The small German courts where music is really prized are not very wealthy, and Russia (like England) is monopolized by the Italians. There remains Queen Pomaré, but Tahiti is rather far away." [71] Berlioz had thought of giving the *Damnation of Faust*, "which is unknown in Paris," but he could find neither hall nor singers. Moreover Pasdeloup's expanding orchestra raffled whatever instrumental talents might be momentarily unused.[72] Berlioz could have gone to Sweden, from which an offer came, but he preferred to keep

[69] *M.C.*, 65–6. (April 7, 1853.) Zimmerman died in October of that year.
[70] *1386*, June 2, 1856.
[71] *Corresp.*, 250–1. The allusion is to the extravaganza Berlioz had written, ostensibly as a letter to the Tahitian Queen, after the Exhibition of 1855. It shows his curious knowledge of the South Sea islands and the native terminology, doubtless culled from a favorite book of travels. (Reprinted in *Grot.*, 60–4.) Berlioz also wrote as a *jeu d'esprit* the words and music of a *Salut Matinal* in the "native tongue and music." This four-page autograph was sold in 1884 to a South American collector and has remained untraced since. (*285*, *221 n.*)
[72] Jules Pasdeloup (1819–1887) had been a drummer in Berlioz' Philharmonique and seeing both the merits and the defect of that enterprise, had begun his own by soliciting financial backing. He was thus able to put Seghers's *Sainte-Cécile* out of business and to remain the sole orchestra leader in Paris, despite his very inferior ability. He played chiefly the German classics (until 1870) and defended his interpretations by striking his chest and saying that a man who felt music as deeply as he did could not be wrong. Saint-Saëns ascribes Pasdeloup's success to the blurring acoustics of the Cirque d'Hiver and the lack of competition until Colonne came in the late seventies.

working at his score. One event that gave him pleasure at the end of this season at the Institute was the award of the Rome Prize to a promising youth named Georges Bizet.

It was now midsummer and the Baden concerts loomed. Berlioz and his wife went first to Plombières, and since the Emperor was not among the visitors, the town was quiet, propitious for country rambles and steady composing.[73] After a month, the Festival brought him again into the free-handed, regal atmosphere of Bénazet's realm, where his old friends the musicians of Carlsruhe, and his German admirers — Princess Stephanie of Prussia, the Duchess of Baden, Countess Kalergi, and others — made him feel he had a place in their affections. This time they heard and applauded no less than five of his works, including the *Judex crederis* from the *Te Deum*.

Between early September, when Berlioz returned to Paris and the end of November, the third act was composed, but in a growing musical isolation for its author. The Second Empire's honeymoon with art was over. Like other new regimes it had shown a few years' excited awareness, followed by a relapse which seems to say: "Whew! We've done our duty." [74] Berlioz' old friend d'Ortigue was now almost exclusively interested in his studies of plain song, and shortly Liszt would also appear in Paris as the herald of an orthodox religious withdrawal from the world. Carvalho's Théâtre Lyrique had followed up *Oberon* with *Euryanthe*, which had fallen utterly flat, for reasons Berlioz could understand: "I don't believe that any one ever put on the stage comparable nonsense. It must be difficult to be so stupid. We all agree in praising the music . . ." Yet the failure made Berlioz "sad all over." [75]

This feeling must have been aggravated by the rise of the Wagnerian crusade — an obvious answer to the prevailing platitude of Parisian offerings, but based on the principle of *omne ignotum pro magnifico*. Those who preached the new gospel knew at most the one opera produced in

[73] Delacroix was there too, very ill also, but no record exists of their meeting which, given the size of the town, must have occurred.

[74] Delacroix's biographer: "Within the Institute itself he remained as isolated as before; he was deliberately held at a distance and he suffered from it." (*181*, III, v.) The painter's own words are: "In making me an academician, they did not mean to make me a teacher at the School [Beaux-Arts], for this would spell danger in the eyes of our learned colleagues." (*Ibid.*, 369.) As for Rude, who had died in 1855, he had not even been admitted to the Institute, though encouraged by its members to stand so they could blackball him. (*1127*.)

[75] *Corresp.*, 245.

Weimar — *Tannhäuser* — and unrevised at that. But the converts, who naturally included the best and liveliest minds, were full of doctrine and spoke with confidence of a new score "which would be still more stunning." Even the rumors uttered by Wagner's enemies helped, for they roused men like Gautier, Reyer, and a little later Baudelaire, to defend with indignation the beauty and power of the fragments they knew. Gautier was asking for a "solemn test" of *Tannhäuser* at the Opera. This might prove either good or bad for *Les Troyens*, but the proposal hardly respected the claim to the French public's attention that Berlioz had the right to exercise before anyone else.

This unwitting injustice was at bottom due to cultural politics rather than to musical feeling. To these half-informed devotees, Wagner was the dark horse who stood a better chance than the war-worn Berlioz to vindicate art against Philistinism.[76] Besides, Wagner's campaign literature was more abundant, mysterious, and solemn. He was beginning to acquire the status of a national artist, interpreting the deep Germanic soul to the world — a close parallel to the Italians' conquest of French opera in the eighteenth century. Berlioz had already witnessed a recurrence of Italianism in the 1820's and had next endured Meyerbeer's monopoly. Having suffered a great deal from blind attack, he was by no means unwilling to see justice done to Wagner's works. He himself was eager to hear them. But Wagner's admirers were bent on creating still another monopoly, exclusive and doctrinaire, and on making Berlioz admit that in music as in industry the latest was the best. To the Princess, he replied very philosophically about being pushed against his will (he might have added,

[76] The men of letters took the lead: Nerval published his *Souvenirs de 'Lohengrin,'* Gautier his report of a pilgrimage to Germany where Wagner was the new unknown. Within a few years, groups were formed even in the provinces to discuss the new art *in abstracto.* Baudelaire's letter to Wagner after his first Paris concerts is typical of the mood the *Zeitgeist* induced: "You are not the first man, sir, about whom I have had occasion to be pained and to blush for my country. Finally, indignation prompted me to express my gratitude to you; I said to myself: 'I want to single myself out from all these imbeciles. . . .' You won me over immediately. What I experienced is not to be described but if you are so good as not to laugh, I shall try to put it into words. First, it seemed to me that I already knew this music. Later on, thinking over it, I understood the cause of this mirage: it seemed then that this music was *mine.* . . . To anyone but an intelligent man this would be a profoundly ridiculous remark, especially when said by one who, like me, knows nothing about music. . . . I had begun to write a few meditations on the excerpts from *Tannhäuser* and *Lohengrin* but I saw the impossibility of saying everything. And so I could go on forever . . . From the day I heard you, I tell myself, in bad moments, 'if I could only hear a little Wagner tonight.' There must be others like me. . . ." (Feb. 17, 1860; *1401*, Nov. 1922, 2–4.)

against chronological fact)[77] into the conservative position: ". . . it is so easy to abstain from certain discussions and there are so many other points on which I have the good fortune to agree with you that I hope in future not to be drawn into such sanguinary debates." [78]

The great work went on. "I go at it with a concentrated passion which seems to increase as I satisfy it." But it took a heavy physical toll requiring systematic rest. This did not keep Berlioz from assisting in the establishment of a Beethoven Music School — a private venture begun by the singer Louis Paulin, who tried to put into effect two new ideas: he asked Berlioz to teach Instrumentation; and in the manner of a modern collegiate music department he planned to have the students give a fortnightly concert free to the parents and friends of the school. In the end, Berlioz could not spare the time for the course, but he helped defend the new enterprise against the attacks of the monopolistic Conservatoire.

The question of teaching carried Berlioz back many years, just at a time when his Brussels friend Samuel was complaining of the difficulties inherent in earning a living while doing "one's own work." Berlioz tried to cheer him by matching woes. "You *give* lessons; we *receive* them here, from every Tom, Dick, and Harry. . . . I should have answered you at once, but I was feverishly gripped by an impassioned scene in my fifth act, which I really could not tear myself from. I finished it this morning and I breathe a little easier.

"I wonder what I am about to undergo in the way of burning regrets and vexations when I have completed this huge musical and dramatic construction. The time is near. In two months it will be all done. Where shall I then find the theatrical manager, conductor, and singers that I need? [79] The new opera will lie there like Robinson Crusoe's canoe until the sea comes up to set it afloat — if there is such a thing as the sea for works of this nature. I am beginning to think that the sea is only a dream of shipbuilders." [80]

In January 1858, Berlioz' disease held him bedridden.[81] Liszt, he heard,

---

[77] This fact being that *Lohengrin* and *Tannhäuser*, though new to Paris, were by this time nine and twelve years old respectively. Hence Liszt's symphonic poems and three works of Berlioz were newer and "technologically" more up to date.

[78] *S.W.*, 59–60.

[79] In the French theaters of Berlioz' day the composer was not allowed to conduct his own scores.

[80] *93, 250.*

[81] Six months before he had told Adèle, who also suffered from neuralgia, that he was "really discouraged" by his ailment, "not because it is dangerous but because it torments me." (*91, 749*.)

had again been ill. Meanwhile Wagner had come to Paris and had called. The object of his visit was to find an opening for any one of his operas at some official theater. He and Berlioz agreed to meet again at Emile Ollivier's, the present Minister of Justice, who had just married Liszt's daughter Blandine (Cosima's elder sister) and was thus Wagner's patron in Paris. Berlioz returned Wagner's call, but their London entente was not easily resumed.

Shortly after, Berlioz again read his poem before a cultivated gathering at the house of his fellow-academician, the architect Hittorf.[82] Though the result was not intended, such a reading could only set Berlioz and Wagner as runners in a race to reach the first vacant stage. Prince Jerome, always friendly to Berlioz, declared the Opera hopeless, impregnable.[83] Meanwhile Liszt and his other son-in-law, Hans von Bülow, were doing all they could to take Berlioz into camp by writing him long letters, putting excerpts from his works on their programs in Germany and thus trying to assign him his role as elder statesman in the Wagnerian movement. "The young man," wrote Berlioz to his son about Bülow, "is one of the most fervent disciples of the extravagant school known in Germany as the music of the future. They will not give up their determination that I should be at their head as standard bearer. I say nothing, write nothing, and let them have their way. Sensible people will know what to make of it all." [84]

There is little doubt that if Berlioz had accepted this part of John the Baptist which the younger men thrust upon him, he would not have been cast into the semi-obscurity of his last and immediately posthumous years. But he would also have been purchasing a position at the price of lost integrity. Besides, he was not an elder statesman or titular chief but an originator still, with energy for several bouts to come. Perhaps the young Wagnerians took it as a counteroffensive when Berlioz helped another German musician, Henry Litolff, to give concerts in Paris. The truth is that Berlioz sincerely admired Litolff's music, which was somewhat influenced by his own; and that Litolff, though opposing Wagner, was an old friend of Liszt's. He was also a music publisher in Brunswick who on Berlioz' journeys there had been affable and helpful. Berlioz was paying

[82] Jacques Hittorf[f] (1792–1867) was a good classical scholar and archeologist, who had helped to establish the fact of polychrome architecture among the ancient Greeks (1830).

[83] For the first time in three years, a new work was being put on (Halévy's *Magicienne*) and everybody was buzzing about the great novelty in it, a chess-playing scene — the very epitome of what Berlioz would consider "antimusical." See the score, Act II, p. 121 where on a rising scale "the chess box appears" and pp. 124–32 for the game itself.   [84] *Corresp.*, 258.

a debt of gratitude — and most effectively, since the concerts were very successful.

Toward the end of the same month (February 1858) all but the final scene of the gigantic *Troyens* was finished. Berlioz gave another reading at his house, always noting the effect and the comments of his picked hearers.[85] The day before he wrote to Samuel: "I have worked at the poem with extreme patience and will not have to make major changes. Why should we not have patience? — I was reading yesterday in a Life of Virgil that he took eleven years to write the *Aeneid*, yet so unfinished did it seem to him that as he lay dying he ordered his heirs to burn it. . . .

"I think you will be satisfied with my score. You can easily guess what the scenes of passion, of tenderness, or of nature, whether serene or stormy, must be like; but there are other scenes of which you cannot as yet have any idea . . . It no longer matters to me what happens to the work — if it is produced or not produced. My musical and Virgilian passion has been sated. . . ." Berlioz pushes this philosophic calm to the point where it passes into its opposite: "Farewell, dear friend, Patience and Persever-ence! I may even add, Indifference: what matters anything?" [86] But this skeptical question is itself open to doubt: "You know my Pyrrhonism," he tells the Princess, "I believe in nothing; that is to say I believe that I believe in nothing. Wherefore I believe in something. Just see what words are good for and where logic takes you! Nothing is real but feelings and passions. Another absurdity I am saying! What of pain, and death, and fools . . . and a thousand other too real realities? I wish you would ask Liszt to be good enough to compliment Mme. Milde for me on the way she played *Alceste*. . . ." [87]

Pyrrhonism and Perseverance in Berlioz only *seemed* to cancel each other; as he practiced them they really created fruitful tension while pro-tecting the will with a Stoic's buckler — as in Marcus Aurelius. So we must not misread Berlioz when he stops working and tries to give an ac-count of himself to the Princess. A born letter writer always adapts his epistle to its reader, and Berlioz being particularly adept at this adjust-ment, his letters enable us to infer what hers were like.[88] Full of extra-

---

[85] During the whole year past he had taken advice when it seemed fit: "Legouvé made four important comments whose aptness I perceived and acted upon." (*91*, 467.) At one of these hearings Baron Taylor, onetime manager of the Théâtre Français, said that there was nothing equal to the poem since Quinault's *Armide*, which Gluck had set.

[86] *93*, 250.

[87] *S.W.*, 70.

[88] Two are preserved in *235*, II, 304–7 and *1401*, May 1930.

vagant praise, of prying curiosity, and also of mystical moralizing about duties that he understood quite as well as she — though differently — the Princess acted as a dispenser of rather enervating good will. Berlioz appears much more lively and free in his letters to Liszt, Bennet, Louis or Adèle. These and his *feuilletons* prove that when gastric pain did not pin him to his bed, his energy was unabated. He had been thinking, among other things, of "an exhibition of my whole output in ten concerts" — a project to be undertaken only after the present score was done.

Meanwhile he had innumerable offers — to conduct for five months in New York, Philadelphia, and Boston for twenty thousand dollars; to inaugurate a new concert hall in London; to celebrate a royal wedding in Sweden. He must also busy himself about numerous concerts of his works given without him in Vienna and elsewhere, but which required scores, biographical notices, and injunctions to managers. Early in April 1858 he has so much to attend to that every morning he makes a list of tasks and errands and despite steady going never reaches the end by nightfall.[89] He was enlisting his people for the Baden Festival at which the first four parts of *Romeo* were to be given. He was also planning a direct appeal to the Emperor to bespeak his interest in *Les Troyens*. The letter asking for an audience and stating the motive was respectful without flattery. The tone was not that of a courtier, but of a proud warrior who has served the state and is conscious of his title of nobility; hence when Berlioz showed the draft to the Duc de Morny, illegitimate half brother of the Emperor, the duke found it "rather unsuitable." [90]

Another half-recognized genius, meanwhile, had been compelled to leave Paris after a similarly fruitless attempt. Wagner had found that Ollivier's influence was less than sufficient to swing open the doors of the Opera.[91] Although a member of the legislature, Ollivier and especially his circle, which included his wife's mother, Comtesse d'Agoult, were considered to be in the opposition, virtually republicans. It looked as if to conquer Paris Wagner must begin the slow way, by concerts such as Berlioz had been giving these thirty years past. And even when the combination of political pull and public concerts made the Opera yield to

[89] *91*, 770.
[90] *Mem.*, II, 374. Berlioz did not let the document go to waste. He printed it in full in the *Memoirs* (*Ibid.*, and preceding page). Students of cultural history may like to compare it with the text of Prokoviev's letter of submission to his government, reprinted in the pamphlet *On Soviet Music* (American Russian Institute, Hollywood, 1948). See also *1393*, 1948, 209.
[91] It was not only from Berlioz that the Emperor at this time wanted an "economical opera." (*91*, 767.)

Tannhäuser, it was to be another defeat, a prelude to the blackest days from which, as Bülow said, only the miracle of King Ludwig's intervention saved the composer "at the eleventh hour." [92]

The composer's lot in nineteenth-century Paris was indeed constant despite surface variations. "You wish to know," Berlioz replied about this time to a would-be biographer, "the causes of the opposition I have encountered in Paris for 25 years. There are many . . . [but] the principal one lies in the antagonism between my musical thought and that of the great majority of the Paris public. A host of people are bound to consider me crazy since I hold them to be children or simpletons. Any music which deviates from the little path where the makers of comic operas trot back and forth is necessarily . . . the music of a lunatic. Beethoven's masterpiece, the Ninth symphony, and his colossal piano sonatas, are still for these people the music of a lunatic.

"In the next place I had against me the instructors at the Conservatoire, led by Cherubini and Fétis, whom my heterodoxy in matters of harmony and rhythm had wounded in their self-esteem and shocked in their convictions. . . . One must also add among my opponents the devotees of the sensualist Italian school, whose doctrines I used to attack and whose gods I have blasphemed. . . . Today I am more cautious. I still abhor, as formerly, these works which the crowd proclaims to be masterpieces of dramatic music. . . . Only, I have the strength of mind to say nothing." [93]

Berlioz had before this summed up his career in an unpremeditated epigram when, in a scribbled answer to a German inquiry for his *vita*, he had slipped in: "On my return from Italy I began my Thirty Years' War against the routineers, the professors, and the tone-deaf." [94] In the spring of 1858 this war seemed to have reached its Peace of Westphalia; he wrote the last bar line of *Les Troyens* on April seventh, confident that "Come what may, disappointments or tribulations, nothing can prevent the work from being in existence." [95]

[92] *174,* 186.
[93] *Mem.,* II, 355–6 (dated May 25, 1858).
[94] (*148.*) This sentence was later paraphrased by a critic who wrote of "Berlioz' life-long fight against the public, the parlor song, and the cost of living." (*416,* II.)
[95] *Mem.,* II, 355.

Berlioz, Poet and Dramatist

> Whatever its fate, I am perfectly happy to
> have undertaken and finished it.
>
> The thing is solid and great and, despite
> the apparent complexity of the means, quite
> simple.
> — BERLIOZ to the Princess and the
> Emperor, respectively (1858–
> 1859)

Les Troyens is a monumental score in a different sense from that in
which the adjective has hitherto been used in these pages. That is, the
work is not designed for a great mass of performers nor for a national
ceremony focusing simple emotions. It is monumental in being the longest
of Berlioz' dramatic works, the most varied and grandiose in subject matter, as well as the model of the epic style in music drama.

Though in his letters to friends Berlioz kept referring to his first or third
or fifth act, he was not fashioning an opera as the term was then understood. He hoped indeed that some Opera stage would produce the work.
But actually poem and score carried forward the principle of construction
first shown in *Benvenuto Cellini,* the principle which underlies the *Damnation of Faust,* the Berlioz principle, in short, of choosing musical situations
and linking them by the shortest path of recitative. Between larger sections
there are no links. The hearer must make the mental jump with the composer. For instance near the end of Act IV in *Les Troyens* we hear from
Aeneas that he is bent on leaving Carthage and has told Dido of his decision. The next scene is a brief and vain imploration on Dido's part. The
next shows Dido bidding her sister recall the Trojans. Since we have already witnessed Aeneas's inner conflict, and since we are about to see
Dido's despair and death, there is no need to show or talk about the fleet's
departure: we are interested solely in its effect.

In *Les Troyens* even more than in *Benvenuto,* Berlioz took into account
the spectator's interest in *décor,* pageantry, and impersonation. He needed
no theory to tell him what was composable, and he kept stagecraft in mind
as a test for exclusion — to bar what would be dull or difficult to show, not
to include what people were accustomed to seeing.[1] The result is a number

[1] *E.g.,* his self-searching about the appearance of the shades to Aeneas —
doubtless inspired by the scene in Richard III (*S.W.,* 54). We must remember
that in 35 years' critical attendance at the opera Berlioz had acquired a very

of striking novelties, an effect of pace achieved by concision and variety, and — for those who cannot hear as well as they can see — some puzzling moments. After a modern production in Great Britain, a critic who is rather less than partial to Berlioz raised doubts about the form as presupposing "that acquaintance with the story which was all but universal among educated people of Berlioz' day but is now considerably rarer." [2] This is to flatter Berlioz' contemporaries; the fault if any, lies in Berlioz' assuming, as was his wont, a flexible imagination working on a background of legend.

He had seen this unchanging assumption of his succeed in *The Infant Christ*. But it is equally true that one need not "know the story" in order to follow *Les Troyens*. That Troy fell to the Greeks and that Aeneas abandoned Dido is really all the information one requires — *provided* that operatic habit has not developed in the beholder an unmusical demand for minute particulars of plot. The characteristic involvements of ordinary opera — its absurd wrangling and legal technicalities — are absent from Berlioz' *Troyens*. For this reason, as the same observer admits, *Les Troyens* is "not so difficult to follow as are the changing fortunes of the gold in the *Ring*." [3] This is because *Les Troyens* seeks to impart neither metaphysics nor the details of a legend, but only its psychological and emotional substance: "The great human interest of *Les Troyens* makes it an opera for others besides musicians — contrary again . . . to received opinions." [4] The work fulfills the intention Berlioz expressed to Samuel: "At least I will have shown what I conceive can be done on an antique subject broadly treated." [5]

These facts of conception and construction explain why Berlioz apprehended on music's behalf any return to the "antique recitation of the chorus" in Greek tragedy. He gave no special name to the form by which he meant to improve upon current opera while avoiding the theoretical error of the "artwork of the future." But when seventy years later Stravinsky called his own *Oedipus Rex* an *opera oratorio*, musicology came to recognize the long tradition of those who had sought to liberate dramatic

---

precise knowledge of the stage. Besides, he had more than once helped put on Weber, Gluck, and Spontini.

[2] *659*, 848.

[3] For an example of operatic legalism in the *Ring*, take: "Wotan, while striking Hunding dead with a lightning glance, reflects that he has loyally fulfilled his promise to Fricka, which is told us by means of the leitmotif *The Treaty*, which, it will be remembered, applies to every pact and contract of any kind whatsoever." (*834*, 380.)

[4] *659*, 848.

[5] *93*, 250.

music from tutelage to Continuity in word or action. Before both Stravinsky and Berlioz, Bach and Handel tended to treat oratorio dramatically like opera, or opera discursively like oratorio. Between Berlioz and Stravinsky the great links are Saint-Saëns's *Samson and Delilah*, Pfitzner's *Palestrina*, and Busoni's *Faust*, influenced respectively by *Les Troyens*, *Cellini* and the *Damnation of Faust*.[6]

Berlioz' lifelong striving to fuse the religious, symphonic, and operatic traditions has been amply shown earlier; that he found the suitable flexible form is becoming more and more obvious, even though certain critics may need a kind of "control experiment" to see it. Thus when *L'Enfance du Christ* was adapted to the Brussels stage by Kufferath, a reviewer wrote: "Seeing the success of this brilliant performance, one begins to wonder if it does not contain a new formula for the lyric drama; if, instead of presenting us with works that give the continuous development of a dramatic action — so often with unavoidable *longueurs* — it would not be preferable to show us *a few brief tableaux of concentrated musical essence, more or less connected with each other, as M. Debussy in effect has done in* 'Pelléas and Mélisande.' " [Italics added.][7]

One more witness, this time to the distinctive technique that Berlioz employed in order to give unity to his outwardly discontinuous form, will enable us to follow more critically the contents of *Les Troyens*. Coupling that work with the *Damnation of Faust* after having conducted both, Halm remarks: "Berlioz was also a dramatist in this sense that he knew how to impart to action — here the Trojans' departure — the value of a musical consummation. But I call it his special dramatic gift that the drama comes out of the parts and not out of the plot: the ideal momentum of the whole proceeds from the power of the music, without which the matter of the play does not exist. Berlioz has thus created a genuine music drama, as against a merely sound-matched [*vertönten*] spectacle, or a merely literary play 'set to music.' " [8]

The unity and coherence of *Les Troyens* are to be looked for, then, in the music first and next in the "parts," that is in the consistency of the

[6] Bach, it has been pointed out, differentiates in his *Passions* not only his protagonists but his mobs, and Handel's oratorios stand "on the dividing line between stage and concert room, concert room and consecrated edifice." (796, 867.) It is worth noting that even before the twentieth-century radio versions of Berlioz' *Benvenuto Cellini* and *Les Troyens*, the second part of the latter "opera" had been given as "oratorio" in an arrangement by E. H. Krebiehl (New York, Chickering Hall, Feb. 26, 1887).

[7] 594, 267.

[8] 570, 100.

dramatic roles. Three stand out: Aeneas, who has a share in the whole action, Cassandra who dominates the first drama, and Dido who dominates the second. The hero links the two parts, but the second heroine remains after Aeneas's flight, concluding the epic in an individual tragedy that matches the collective tragedy of Troy's downfall. Thematically — aside from more fugitive recalls — the Trojan March leads the listener through the entire score by its dozen recurrences in varied moods from the tragic to the triumphant.

Owing to the ingrained habits of producers and actors, Berlioz in 1863 had to divide his work into two "operas" — *The Taking of Troy* and *The Trojans at Carthage*. But however "serialized," whether on successive evenings or before and after the interval of dinner, the work is and remains one.[9] The major change of place and the shift of interest from Cassandra to Dido only heighten our sense of the vastness of the action. We are no longer in the theater but witnessing a Mediterranean epic, the two heroines serving to mark a change of place and on two counts averting monotony. Each towers above Aeneas because each chooses death, whereas his fate, though noble, is less than tragic. He can therefore be shown in a kind of secondary role, central but subordinate, and perfect equilibrium results for the ear as well as the mind.

So much for the protagonists, only two of whom Berlioz found ready-fashioned by Virgil: Cassandra is the composer's creation from the merest hint.[10] To turn Books II and IV of the *Aeneid* into a pair of consecutive tragedies and maintain the pathos of a people in exile was no less a feat of creation, and it must be examined in detail for any understanding of Berlioz' art at its maturest.

The first tragedy grows from the conflict between Cassandra's prophetic fears and the indifference of the Trojans. We hear the Trojan crowd singing their relief at the armistice after ten years of war. While they go on to shout rather vulgarly in C major, and superstitiously avoid the spot where Achilles camped ("It's in Virgil . . . but he didn't turn the Trojan people into a bunch of Gascons" [11]), shepherds pipe a plaintive melody. Cassandra utters her premonitions, her doomed love for Coraebus, and the fate of her city. Tragic self-awareness is the mark of her soul. Coraebus enters, tries to reassure her in an andante whose calm melody sings the peace and beauty of their homeland. Then comes a conventional al-

[9] To use two different singers for the same Aeneas — as was done in one production — is an absurdity which stultifies the conception.
[10] *Aeneid*, III, 183–8.
[11] *S.W.*, 30. The Gascons are proverbially considered braggarts.

legro, in which Berlioz chose to use still another modified form of the *idée fixe* of his first symphony.[12] Cassandra begs her lover to flee. He refuses, and they plight their troth resolved to die together.

We next see the Trojans assembled to sacrifice to the gods. The national march and hymn that form the chief leitmotif of the score resounds for the first time, sung by priests and people.[13] The modulations of the choral phrase — C major, C minor, D flat major, A flat major — all within eight measures, impart to it an austerity which is heightened by the steadily consonant harmony of the parts and the timbre of the trombones. After this we have the lively contrast of the cestus fighters' procession, and immediately again the religious mood, now changed from nation to person and from grandeur to sublimity: it is Andromache's scene and Berlioz' invention. Brief phrases by the chorus usher in the speechless pantomime of the mother and son: Hector's widow, holding Astyanax by the hand, both clad in the white mourning of the ancients, lay their offering on the altar; the child is blessed by Priam; she lowers her veil and they walk away. As they accomplish this simple rite, out of the muted orchestra arises that unforgettable, heartrending clarinet melody which Berlioz wanted to hear and rehearse by himself.[14] "This scene," he knew, "will be one of the most difficult. . . ," for it must move the imagination through sound, and the usual operagoer is likely to find it "undramatic" if not disturbing. Not knowing "what to make of it," he concludes that it is a *longueur*. The producer usually forestalls him and cuts it, for Andromache does not appear again, why should she exist at all — a useless super on the payroll? Yet Berlioz' conception, poignantly brief, limns the irrevocable woes of war with greater force and finality than the loudest lament that could be said or sung.

Aeneas breaks in with the news of Laocoön's death. The priest and his two sons have perished in the grip of the serpents for having struck with

[12] Undoubtedly in the belief that *Les Troyens* was to be his last work and as a means of closing the cycle of his melodic thought.

[13] To see how this marching hymn generates the theme of the *Marche Troyenne* proper, compare in the piano score p. 47 bb. 6–7 and p. 109 bb. 8–9. Berlioz arranged the March as a concert piece, of which there is an excellent recording by Weingartner. (*1470*.)

[14] In Lesueur's teachings about ancient Greek music, the significance of "hypocritic pantomime" played a large role, which Berlioz certainly remembered here. Wagner drew his views from elsewhere, so that one historian of the dance was far astray when in speaking of the Wagnerian synthesis he writes: "Some time later Berlioz understood very well the Wagnerian genre of 'hypocritical pantomime' — a strict correspondence between music and the artist's body, where orchestration gives its sound to physical movement." (*1094a*, 262.)

a javelin at the wooden horse, which is now ordered brought in. Cassandra's reiterated warning falls on deaf ears; everyone looks upon the occasion as festive. The people's rejoicing, her terror, the aimless excitement of a crowd, its confusion, and the pomp of a processional now mingle in one of Berlioz' superb crescendos. By dividing his orchestra, distributing smaller groups (horns, tubas, trumpets, harps, and voices) backstage or within the wings, and by coordinating their parts with the remaining voices, strings, woodwinds, and brass in a manner not to be foreseen from the initial fragments, Berlioz creates a uniquely powerful finale.[15] His sense of the simultaneity of life had not deserted him just because his subject was classical: Cassandra bewails, the people glee, the cortege advances, the Trojan March breaks out in triumphal tones, and the very vibration of life seems to enwrap these mutually independent projections of being.[16]

These beings move as well as live, for Berlioz adroitly keeps the improbable horse from holding the stage. While Cassandra continues her declamation, the cortege has steadily crossed over behind her and the crowd, and disappeared to the dwindling strains of the March. The curtain falls on an allegro agitato for orchestra alone, following and reinforcing Cassandra's somber intimation of the presence of death.

The drama then leaps forward straight into the heart of prophecy fulfilled. Aeneas, characteristically asleep while Troy burns, as someone remarked, tosses fitfully to the sounds of distant fighting. *Hostis habet muros:* the Greeks are conquering. Strings and woodwinds quiver and moan and are momentarily topped by trumpet calls. Aeneas's son runs past. Suddenly the shade of Hector appears. Sounds of horns, drums, and pizzicato basses dimly frame the ghost. Aeneas wakes. The dead hero instructs the living to escape and to found a new city on Italian soil. Pantheus enters wounded and reports the storming of the palace, the death of Priam. Other warriors come and rush off again to the fight with the cry of despair: "The hope of the vanquished is to give up hope."

In a cinematic twinkling we are at the temple of Vesta where the Trojan women are praying. Preceded by her "theme" in the strings,

[15] Or rather, he matches, in an entirely different atmosphere the great finale of *Benvenuto.*
[16] Those who know the March only from records, and thus incline to treat it as insignificant, never can feel the same after hearing it in its multiple contexts, of which the one described above is the most compelling. A critic writing of the 1921 Paris revival speaks of the "mysterious depths" of the March, which suggest the feeling that "the music itself has become conscious of tragedy." (*654, 225.*)

Cassandra appears and in a sublime recitative urges the women to die rather than yield. They sing a chorus built on a scale which Berlioz thought peculiarly suited to render desolation.[17] Again subdividing his forces, he manages to express all at once the gloom, cowardice, false hope, and incredulousness of the women, in a masterly ensemble dominated by Cassandra's sudden turns from anger to compassion. As they take the oath of death, "the music seems charged with electricity. It feels as if a thundercloud full of lightning were darkening the scene with an awful shadow." [18] The last moments have brought in Greek chieftains who threaten the women and shout for booty. Cassandra stabs herself and with a Berliozian simplicity of phrase hands her dagger to another: "Take it, pain is naught." The women stab their breasts or leap off the parapet as the dying Cassandra invokes a resurrected Troy by calling "Aeneas! Italy!"

Thus ends the first tragedy.[19] Its sequel takes us to Carthage, the sole musico-dramatic substance to fill the gap being a short orchestral *lamento* comparable to the preludes that have become familiar since Wagner and Verdi. Solemn chords going from D minor to F major introduce a broad violin phrase that suggests the hopeless calm of old grief. It is interrupted by long chromatic scales in the strings. A second phrase, related to the first, but in the minor, reminds us of the theme of Cassandra's love scene, but it is saddened by the grim insistence of the bass. The *lamento* ends in solemn broken accents.[20]

By contrast, our first sight of Carthage is one of gladness. The people are lauding Queen Dido in a chorus which demonstrates again Berlioz' ability to write noble popular chants. It is the seventh anniversary of the pilgrims' landing as exiles from Tyre, and abundance has rewarded their toil. The dialogue between Dido and her people, though it employs the classic form of recitative and air, gives us a grandiose conception of what a nation is; it unfolds the variety within collective feeling, and by means

[17] Especially through the harmonies it engenders: the insistent recurrence of the G − D flat helps to convey the strangeness of disaster.

[18] *428,* 305–6.

[19] It is obviously too short to fill a whole evening, and too well contrived not to seem suspensive and unsatisfactory as a drama by itself. Hence the serializing on successive nights is a fatal mistake, even though to an audience familiar with the entire work the playing of this first part in concert form would be quite acceptable.

[20] When *Les Troyens à Carthage* is given alone, a narrator aided by choral and orchestral effects behind the scenes, recites in a few stanzas the substance of the preceding tragedy. The device shows again the kinship of Berlioz' work with dramatic oratorio, and his variation of his own "prologue" scheme in the dramatic symphony.

of a superb parade of builders, sailors, and farmers, it expresses the dignity of labor. From the lightsome opening through the Tyrian national hymn to Dido's *chant récitatif*, and finally to the rhythmical and melodic inventions of the workers' praise, there is enough musical substance to outfit three ordinary operas.

A charming orchestral prelude of a dozen measures takes us from the nation to the person. Dido, left alone with her sister Anna, confesses to a strange sadness — another form of the *vague des passions* treated in the *Fantastique* first movement.[21] Dido is lovesick ahead of any tangible cause. It is Anna who puts a name to her feelings. They sing together, on a theme introduced a moment earlier, a "song presaging love." The destined object of that love appears almost at once, or rather, the strains of the Trojan March, keyed to sadness, evoke for us the storm-tossed exiles. Dido recalls her own tribulations in a superb monologue with dissonant accompaniment: "Wandering o'er the seas," and gives the newcomers audience. The boy Ascanius begs hospitality and in a few measures sums up the ruin of Ilion. But at this juncture, news comes of an enemy army threatening Carthage from the south. Aeneas, who has so far hung back, discloses himself appareled in rich armor and offers to lead the troops against the invader. Dido accepts and in another of Berlioz' astonishingly rapid musical asides, confesses to her sister a nascent admiration for the warrior. This most conventionally "dramatic" scene ends with a military finale in which Aeneas's farewell to his son strikes a religious note.

For the loves of Dido and Aeneas which form the subject of the next movement, Berlioz followed the same principle as in *Romeo and Juliet*. A purely symphonic interlude entitled "Royal Hunt and Storm" (by now quite familiar to concert audiences) takes the place of duets and declarations.[22] Virgil, of course, had shown the way. Venus causes Dido and her guest to be separated from their retinue by a storm, during which they take shelter in a cave and consummate their union. Berlioz' brief orchestral

[21] It may be worth recalling that Chateaubriand's phrase, which helped Berlioz formulate the inspiration of his first symphony, occurs in the same section of the book as the passage on Dido. (*1243*, II, 265 and 291.) See also I, 199 *n.* for Chateaubriand's discussion of the *Iliad* and *Aeneid* in relation to modern feeling.

[22] Recordings *1465-6*. In a so-called "revised edition" of the piano score, issued by Berlioz' own publisher after his death, this scene is placed *after* the scene by the sea which should follow it. This makes nonsense out of both Virgil and Berlioz, as do most of the arrangements by other hands from 1863 to the present. In the several opera "guides," naturally, these aberrations are followed, so that the nomenclature by acts is by now an intricate mess. (*E.g.*, *1357*.)

piece in two moods attains the acme of perfection and conciseness. It is
built on a pastoral theme for oboe, and any imitation of nature it may suggest comes out of ornaments derived from this theme, or from rhythms
used in the familiar way, to interrupt a slow calm melody by rapid scales
or persistent figures. The beautiful horn calls which emerge toward the
middle and blend at the close with a return to the original theme lead to
"a succession of exquisitely wrought details" which Mr. B. H. Haggin
finds "of a startlingly intense loveliness." [23] They prepare us for Berlioz'
ampler expression, in the next scene, of love acknowledged and satisfied —
Blake's "lineaments of gratified desire."

The music for this second love scene came "in a flood" as soon as Berlioz
had made up his canvas, and it is an unbroken series of masterpieces. [24] We
are in the queen's gardens by the sea, at twilight. The lovers and their
suite are gathered for the royal entertainment but dramatic tension subsists between the principals: how strong and of what sort is the passion
which has united them by accident? A reprise of the Carthaginian hymn
introduces Dido, after which the prevailing mood is established: it is
amorous and redolent of nature in serenity. To please Aeneas there are
games and dances followed by a pantomime of Nubian slaves. The first
and third ballets are extraordinary — the first quite casting Salome's Dance
into the shade for seductiveness, and the third giving the quintessence
(instead of the chemical flavor) of orientalism in music. [25]

[23] *1393*, Aug. 24, 1946. For staging, Berlioz directs that woodland nymphs
and satyrs occupy the time with their classical gambols — or such of them as
may be made public. The principals are seen for a brief moment during the
storm, and the nymphs and fauns utter cries in concert with the orchestra as
the brook swells and branches catch fire.

In proof of his suggestion that the direct heir of Gluck is Berlioz and not
Wagner, Mr. Alfred Einstein has called this Royal Hunt and Storm "the last
descriptive ballet" modeled after Gluck. (*950*, 192–3.) This linkage is not without plausibility, yet it overlooks the significant difference that Berlioz' interlude
is neither meant nor fit to be danced — the ballet music is still to come. Rather,
this single instance shows what Berlioz could do in the way of using fire,
water, caves, and wildlife during an orchestral scene. At the same time, concert
experience shows that this piece of music can stand by itself. As such, it is far
closer to Debussy's *Afternoon of a Faun* than to the ballets of Gluck, with
their repeats for dancing.

[24] The songs of Narbal and Anna with which this part begins were cut after
the *première* and are still usually omitted. Yet both are musically worthy,
and were it not for the impatience of the public to get on with the love story
they might well be retained. Artistically, they provide a certain matter-of-
factness which serves to heighten the enchantment to follow.

[25] It makes use of four contraltos to psalmody a couplet in Arabic during
the dance. In the Royal Hunt, as before in the *Hamlet* March and the *Damna-*

Dido then asks for a "country song," which Iopas sings. She interrupts him and asks Aeneas to continue the story of his wanderings. As Aeneas tells the queen that the chaste Andromache has yielded to Pyrrhus, Dido — herself long faithful to her husband's memory — has a magnificent exclamation showing that her last remorse is gone. This leads to the wonderful quintet of which, as Newman truly says, "a man needs to have lived long and to have suffered much to compass a beauty so wistful and so touched with all the humanities." [26] Night has fallen. The voices of the lovers and their kin have been joined by two others to form the equally celebrated septet, which a small chorus hidden in the darkness echoes softly. Here occurs that miracle of subtle and simple orchestration in which the periodic stroke of the bass drum pianissimo joins with a low F in the strings to punctuate the repeated C's of the flutes, clarinets, and horns — also pianissimo.[27] As the plangent Mediterranean beats upon the shore, the royal pair are left alone for the duet that follows after a charming orchestral modulation,[28] which changes the intensity but not the character of this continuously voluptuous scene. The words of the duet are those that Berlioz "pilfered" and adapted from *The Merchant of Venice* — "In such a night as this . . ." — the idea having no doubt occurred to him because Shakespeare goes on: "In such a night stood Dido with a willow in her hand upon the wild sea banks. . . ."[29]

Musically we are at the high point of the scene and of the drama. These pages stand comparison with any love music ever penned. "Once before," to quote Newman again, "in a wonderful passage . . . in *Romeo and Juliet*, Berlioz had sounded this note of a love so vast that the heart becomes almost still under the pressure of it; but here the note is at once more prolonged and more profound." [30] It is love made to seem infinite

---

tion of *Faust*, Berlioz' fondness for this form of vocal obligato found well-motivated occasions.

[26] *666*, (June 19).

[27] Harmonically, this pedal, as Koechlin has pointed out, is the one used again so effectively by Ravel in his *Habanera*. (*453*, 178.)

[28] From F to G flat major: earlier, the pedal of C (dominant of F) hinted several times of its rise by a semitone to D flat, which now becomes the dominant of the new key.

[29] Act V, Sc. I, 9–11.

[30] *666*, (June 19). Mr. Newman wrote after the 1921 revival in Paris, which was far from perfect. In Gide's *Journal* for that year we find an instructive report from his sound and well-trained judgment: "I remembered my rapture of fifteen years ago, . . . when Delna had the role of Dido in *Les Troyens à Carthage*, of which the first act has become the third in this hybrid performance. All that is left is conventional, dull, tiresome. (I am not speaking

by association with the breadth of the physical universe. The feeling —
and therefore the musical germ — lay buried far back in Berlioz' Italian
days when he had wept over his Virgil and improvised wild chants to his
guitar. Five years later in the thick of the Paris struggle, he could still
relive it as he thought of Liszt's grand passion for the Comtesse d'Agoult
running its course in the selfsame setting.[31] Then for twenty years the
music of that sea and that imagined love lay dormant, at last to come to
life anew, taking the form successively of small black marks on paper, of
dominant pedals, and of the whole apparatus of gut and wood and brass
by which miraculously spirit may speak to spirit.

The sudden clangor of a shield struck twice breaks the spell. In a moon-
beam an apparition in the shape of Mercury recalls Aeneas to his mission
with the name "Italy!" gravely repeated. Still in darkness, we now have
glimpses of the Trojan camp and the ships at anchor. Sentries pass and
repass. A young sailor, homesick for the woods and the folk he has left
behind, sings a song of the lulling sea to which he is destined. "I thought
of you, dear Louis, in composing it." [32] The modal melody, accompanied
by a delicate mixture of strings and woodwinds, might — as Mr. Capell
put it — "be easily taken for Glinka or even Moussorgsky." [33]

The boy falls asleep before he ends his plaint but the orchestra prolongs
the rhythm of the sea. Above it one hears mysterious voices calling "Italy!"
The Trojan captains express superstitious alarm but Aeneas seems not to
heed. Neither do two sentries who, on a three-beat march instrumented
in a way to suggest idle contentment, express their distaste for further
adventure and their satisfaction with the food and the women of Carthage.
This interlude of low comedy offends certain connoisseurs of the grand
style, "as if," said Berlioz, "*Don Giovanni* were not an admirable example
of mixed genres . . . and as if Shakespeare had never written." [34]

From this point forward, the tragic figures hurtle to their fate. Aeneas

---

of the musical text, but of the execution.) A much too large orchestra covers
the insufficient voices. Impossible to feel the slightest emotion. . . ." (*1249*,
II, 267–8.)

[31] To her in 1837 Berlioz unknowingly wrote his *mise en scène* of 1857:
"When you are in Naples and Liszt feels the need of a great emotion . . . let
him some evening climb Mount Pausilippo and from the top of that hill dear
to Virgil, let him listen to the infinite arpeggios of the sea, while the sun . . .
drops slowly behind Cape Miseno, coloring with its last rays the pale olive
trees of Nisida — there is a concert worthy of you and of him . . ." (*A.R.*,
343.)

[32] *Corresp.*, 260.

[33] *658*, 19.

[34] Note in the score, and *L.I.*, 248. Berlioz was also interested in the problem
of musical form which this dialogue presented.

tells in monologue his decision to leave. His noble, somewhat stiff recitative, accompanied in canonic imitation, modulates and turns into a heart-rending andante in which the pain of leaving, and worse, of leave-taking, is unsurpassably rendered. The ensuing allegro di bravura shortly develops into the somber dissonant dialogue which he holds with the shades of Priam, Coraebus, Hector, and Cassandra. The remarkable harmonic expressiveness of this passage was, at the time of composition, absolutely new. The recall of the Trojan March, supported by a chorus of soldiers and sailors, leads after a stirring sequence on "Italy!" to Aeneas's great cry of despair and resolution: "For the death of a hero, I am unfaithful to thee!" [35]

Apprised in her palace of these preparations for flight, Dido appears and after a few breathless questions turns from apprehension to indignation and to anger. Aeneas is weakening, when the distant march theme recalls him to duty. Dido lays her curse upon him as he leaves, and the march soars victoriously.

We next find the queen in the mood of repentance and humiliation. She is begging Anna to delay the Trojans' departure. When it is clear that she cannot change her fate, she orders her funeral pyre, and reaching a new height of unresigned forsakenness, she declaims the tremendous recitative, accompanied by string tremolos and scanned by menacing phrases on the bass clarinet: "I am about to die, engulfed in my infinite grief." She then bids farewell to her city. As the clarinet, now plaintive, follows her voice, the horns at intervals softly toll her doom. Dido weaves into her *Adieu* the earlier love theme, which the violas turn to melancholy. When she has done, the priests of Pluto invoke the gods of the nether world to wreak vengeance on the fugitive Trojans. Dido mounts the pyre and stabs herself with Aeneas's sword. Her people rush forward around her. On the verge of death she is given the power of prophecy. She calls out the name Hannibal, but in the last instant foresees the destruction of Carthage and the glory of Rome. The Trojan March rings out majestic, transfigured by the bright sonority of the harps, and it covers the bitter queen's dying oath of hatred. In a distant haze, while the chorus of priests and people vows eternal enmity to Rome, a vision of the Capitol glows with the word *Roma* on its pediment.

* * *

[35] Both at the beginning and near the end, the major heightens the melancholy of the preceding minor. The scene has been well sung in a recording by M. Georges Thill but the latter portions have been outrageously cut. (*1467*.)

Even if indications in words could approximate musical effect, no summary of so vast an epic could exhaust its contents. If one is among those who do not respond to Berlioz' Euripidean conception of life, one should discard the tragedy entire rather than try to pick and choose salvageable bits. If one does respond, one will perhaps take on trust Sir Donald Tovey's dictum that *Les Troyens* is "one of the most gigantic and convincing masterpieces of music drama." [36] One can then begin to classify one's impressions of its power — from drama to poetry to music — for *Les Troyens* is emphatically one of those works which have to be thoroughly known to be enjoyed throughout; its beauties do not take possession of the mind all at once but require to be re-cognized.[37]

That seasoned critic of music and drama, the late James Agate, recommends that one listen to Berlioz first with one's ear rather than one's mind,[38] but since *Les Troyens* is largely inaccessible to hearers, and since operagoers are accustomed to mastering a "book," they may legitimately put themselves in a receptive mood by seeing Berlioz at his poetic task, that is, conceiving and finding words for human emotions. He started, to be sure, from Virgil, which he knew as few scholars have known it, in the cumulative way of an artist whose own experiences of love, landscape, and sound have encrusted the text from the age of twelve.[39] But apart from the skillful choice and translation of a number of Virgilian lines, Berlioz had to modernize the expression of feeling while retaining the epic quality of distance; [40] and finally he had, for musical reasons, to invent. In the *Taking of Troy* especially, Berlioz' handiwork is extensive: not alone the figure of Cassandra but the prodigious last scene of her expostulation with the Trojan women and invocation of a resurrected *patria* in Italy is a piece of true poetry — of making.

In any art this power to conceive is of course the supreme test. We are

---

[36] *590*, 89.

[37] In a brilliant paragraph on Molière's *Misanthrope,* Courteline has shown how "ineffective" the work is for the casual unprepared listener, and why the very density of the genius embodied in the work repels anyone "who does not know the piece by heart." (*1070,* VIII, 83.)

[38] Quoted in *1374* (1945) 191.

[39] "What a great composer Virgil is, what a melodist and harmonist too!" (*Corresp.,* 215.) Compare De Quincey: "Very few writers of any country have approached to Virgil in the art of *composition,* however low we may be disposed to rank him . . . in the unequal contest with the sublimities of the Christian Literature." (*Letters to a Young Man,* no. IV.)

[40] Grout, who calls *Les Troyens* "the most important French opera of the 19th century," asserts categorically: "here is the unique opera in which the epic has been successfully dramatized. . . . The word 'unique' is used advisedly." (*722,* 319 and 320 and *n.*)

used to judging the various grades of executive ability — how well the artist does any particularly fine or difficult thing — but that he should think of doing other, unheard-of things, this is what separates the Shakespeares and Beethovens from the rest. In Berlioz' *Troyens* the presence of this faculty is everywhere. His Cassandra and Dido rank with the greatest of poetic creations, distinct from all models and from each other in the constant play of mood within passion. Their words modulate as swiftly and aptly as the music, and Berlioz emerges as a dramatic psychologist who equals Mozart and holds his own with every first-rank librettist.

In the broader groupings Berlioz renders with seemingly no effort the antique fact and the modern atmosphere arising from the contrast between outer and inner life. Open the first scene at Troy and read the rapid exposition which in twenty-five lines gives us the background of the war and leads us to expect the monstrous horse.[41] After it comes Cassandra's tragic introspection — twenty lines of slower, nobler rhythm, but skillfully broken. Lastly (some ninety lines) the dialogue between her and Coraebus ranging from prophecy to love, fear of death, and a Nietzschean *amor fati*. In one hundred and thirty-five lines the act is over, two characters have been drawn, and the double conflict of individuals and peoples set in motion against a background of natural beauty. Nor does this pace slacken except for the ceremonial and love scenes of the *Trojans at Carthage*.[42]

---

[41] Here is a prosaic translation:

General Chorus. After ten years within our walls, oh, how good to breathe the pure air of the fields, which the noise of battle no longer disturbs.

Dialoguing Chorus. (Young boys run about.) What wreckage — an arrow head! — Here's a helmet. And here two javelins. See this enormous shield; it would hold up a man on the water. What cowards those Greeks are!

A Soldier. Do you know whose tent was on this spot?

Chorus. No, tell us, whose?

Soldier. Achilles'.

Chorus. Merciful gods!

Soldier. Stay, valiant troop! Achilles is dead. You can see his tomb — there it is. (Three shepherds who stood on it flee in terror.)

Chorus. 'Tis true. Of that murderous fiend Paris freed us. Do you know the wooden horse that the Greeks built before leaving for Aulis? That huge horse in honor of Pallas? In its vast entrails a battalion could stand. Well, they are tearing down the walls and tonight we'll drag it into town. They say the king will look into it. — But where is it now? On the banks of the Scamander. Let's go see it at once. Let's go! Let's go! The horse, the horse!

Exeunt in disorder.

[42] The quietness of these later scenes is only another argument for not dividing the work: we are quite ready for oases of calm in acts III and IV,

Berlioz seemed to think that it was only when he came to compose the *Damnation of Faust* that, being on his travels, he had first ventured to versify for himself.[43] He had apparently forgotten that as early as the *Francs-Juges* opera of 1824–1830 he had substituted for the lazy Ferrand, and that since then he had taken a hand in every one of his major texts, helping Deschamps with *Romeo and Juliet*, writing and rewriting parts of *Benvenuto*, and at last showing himself a really accomplished poet in the "Invocation to Nature" of *Faust*. About the same time he replaced the "unknown tongue" of his chorus of shades in *Lélio* with the eight lines used in the 1855 version;[44] he was writing *L'Enfance du Christ* from beginning to end; and immediately after its performance was starting work on *Les Troyens*.

He appreciated the difficulty of tackling an antique subject in a modern tongue, especially in French, whose poetic diction had but recently reacted against the emptiness of the neoclassical idiom. The dangers were: to fall back into it, like Ponsard, or to overdo the opposite, like any burlesquing parodist. It cannot be said that Berlioz wholly escaped the first evil, of frigid inversions echoed from Racine and Voltaire. With Virgil before him and the military pomp of antiquity to reproduce in verse, Berlioz lacked the freedom that was his in dealing with Faust and with the Jesus story. But for the most part the verbal tension of *Les Troyens* keeps high and steady, the diction is clear and simple, stiff at its worst, never flaccid. And in the garden scenes, the religious episodes, the dialogue of the sentries, and the moments of passion, Berlioz finds accents that are purely his own, phrases that unmistakably show the natural poet. Cassandra's *Tiens! La douleur n'est rien* has already been quoted; many of Dido's and Aeneas's replies deserve to be. For the passage in which Aeneas on his way to war takes leave of his son, Berlioz wrote music at once martial and religious and Aeneas's speech has the same inflections:

> *D'autres t'enseigneront, enfant, l'art d'être heureux,*
> *Je ne t'apprendrai, moi, que la vertu guerrière*
> *Et le respect des dieux. . . .*

---

but if this calm comes at the *beginning* of a drama — which it does when Part II is given by itself — our interest flags and we impute to Berlioz the error of his improvers.

[43] *M.E.*, 151 (to his father).
[44] They begin, Hugo-like, with a touch presaging Baudelaire:

> *Froid de la mort, froid de la tombe,*
> *Bruit éternel des pas du temps,*
> *Noir chaos où l'espoir succombe,*
> *Quand donc finirez vous? Vivants!*

Later, Aeneas's allusion to Dido's grief as *cette douleur indignée* is a marvelous touch,[45] as is the sequence of spectral orders from the heroic dead: *Il faut vivre et partir . . . il faut partir et vaincre . . . il faut vaincre et fonder. . . .*

The last act, Dido's imprecations and grief, is thickly studded with verbal felicities, from *Errante sur tes pas*, which translates the Latin, to *Adieu, fière cité* which shows how the note of nobility combines with the simple and modern: *ma carrière est finie.*[46] Berlioz moreover had a natural turn for the eclogues in short lines, of which the sailor boy's song —

> *Vallon sonore*
> *Où dès l'aurore*
> *Je m'en allais chantant*

is but one example.[47] He always maintained that long lines are fatal to melody — even to his long sweeping melodies — and that the timidity which kept poets from mixing their rhythms or timing their speech made prose acceptable as a text for music, provided the word-cadences were well contrived.[48]

Trusting himself to use this freedom, Berlioz, it might be thought, should have avoided those repetitions of words which are supposed to make opera ridiculous and which many people think Wagner's system eliminates. But here again, Berlioz took the logical and unemphatic course. He avoided *excessive* repetitions, knowing on the one hand that musical development always outruns verbal utterance, and that if choruses are given words to sing they may as well repeat them during the maintenance of the mood; and knowing on the other hand that to repeat, in modera-

[45] *Indignée* does not mean "indignant" but wounded by outrage, "unworthed."

[46] The parallel with La Fontaine's words on the "proud city," from the same Virgilian source, is interesting; see Fable I of Bk. II. As for Dido's declaration that her destiny is done, it is surely an echo of "Othello's occupation's gone."

[47] Besides the pastoral, *O blonde Cérès*, which suggests Hugo, Berlioz was to write another, just as flawless, and which makes one think of Verlaine: it is the *Nuit paisible et sereine! La lune, douce reine . . .* of the nocturne in *Beatrice and Benedict*.

[48] He had himself set prose to music on two occasions. It remained for Alfred Bruneau to do it on a large scale in his operas adapted from Zola. On Berlioz' interest in giving measure and rhythm to words, read his essay in *Grot.*, 217–224. See also: *A.R.*, 142, and *L.I.*, 58, 110, 112–4; his inquiries into elision in Latin verse (*151*), and his concern over the use of the watchword "*Italie!*" — "which sounds so poorly compared to *Italiam* with its accent on the second syllable." (*S.W.*, 28.)

tion, words that are sung is by no means as silly as it seems on paper.[49] Wagner took the course of banning repetition and, as Van Dieren showed, had to sneak it back in by using variants and synonyms.[50] The musician in truth cannot get away from the fact that "I love you" takes but an instant to say, and a love scene at least a few minutes to develop. Art seems to counsel mixing the repetitions and the synonyms to a point just short of satiety.

What does deserve censure is Berlioz' occasional neglect of prosody in choral ensembles. Though he was attentive and even meticulous about such blemishes they are found here and there in some of his great works — notably the *Requiem*, the *Damnation*, and *Les Troyens*.[51] Since the fault was not due to carelessness, it can only be ascribed to an unwillingness to change the musical inflection for the verbal after failing to find an alternative. In other words, when it came to a choice Berlioz preferred musical precision to literary.[52] We have further evidence of this in the questions he put to himself after he had plotted his drama and written out the words of his two heroines' tragic moments. The "psychology," as we should say today, had yet to be worked out in the minute detail that only music can render: "There are accents to be found, pauses to be determined, inflexions to be seized on . . ."[53] And later on, with Dido's final lines before him: "Is it a violent imprecation? Is it a tense concentrated fury? If poor Rachel were not dead I might go and ask her. You are probably thinking that it is much too kind of me to worry in this way about veracious expression — it will be always true enough for the public. To be sure; but what about *us?*"[54]

Nowhere better than in this score, perhaps, can the relation of music to drama be studied, for it subsists here in every conceivable form. At no time was Berlioz more outspoken in his hatred of illustrative music,[55] and if he gave his "Royal Hunt" the title of descriptive symphony, we must

---

[49] Saint-Saëns shared this view and Sternfeld made a similar point about Berlioz' mysterious vocables in the "Pandemonium" of the *Damnation*: they look absurd and sing well. (*580*, 491.)

[50] *901*, 155–8.

[51] *E.g.*, in Part I, the octet and chorus that follows Aeneas's recitative about Laocoön.

[52] He is explicit about this as regards translated texts. (*95*, 104.)

[53] *S.W.*, 26.

[54] To Hans von Bülow, *Corresp.*, 255.

[55] See above, Chapter 7; *A Trav.*, 225 ff.; and *S.W.*, 85 on Haydn's *Creation*, quoted in Subchapter 26.

take the words as a mere aid to operagoers and find elsewhere the formal cause of the piece. In Virgil's fifty lines, a few indications define the atmosphere of the scene — a cave, thunder, shrieking naiads.[56] The occasion of the love-making is the hunt, but this in Virgil comes *before* the storm, and the mention of love is at once followed by an agitated digression on Rumor. The musician has no use for this pattern, not aiming at narration. He simply creates a sylvan atmosphere (string and woodwind melodies, flute ornaments) and limits himself to the musical contrast of slow-fast-slow. In the dynamic middle portion of the intermezzo he joins the "storm" and the "hunt" by means of rhythmic figures and horn and trumpet calls. The sounds themselves dictate their place and connection, and the return to the quiet first theme, in conjunction with the "hunt" call in augmentation, is a musical idea which neither Virgil nor any other *literary* craftsman could tolerate.[57] Berlioz does not even think of paralleling a program by employing a "cave" theme or a motif for watersprites: the fitting of instrumental music to scene or action is purely ideal: their connotations coincide and that is all. Where Berlioz is completely at one with Virgil is in considering the storm not only the cloak but also the symbol of passion.

In dramatic moments that issue in words, Berlioz takes advantage of other devices for making music signify. The chaos of human wills is rendered in the polyphonic downfall of Troy, when the women call on Pluto in a tremendous phrase linked to Cassandra's fanatical cries of "Hector! Priam! King! Father! Lover! I join you!" [58] Elsewhere, subtle differences of rhythm and line serve to distinguish the several trades — builders, sailors, and farmers — who form a continuous cortege. At other times a series of dissonances — sparingly used before and after — helps to make us accept the supernatural commands which compel Aeneas to leave. T. S. Wotton has suggested that the weakness of Aeneas's character, already present in Virgil, is aggravated in *Les Troyens* by Berlioz' lack of sympathy with the inconstant lover. This may be true. One feels that Berlioz in his place would have found a way to set Rome on foot and *return*. Still, in his version Berlioz generally manages to transmute the pious warrior's priggishness into heroism, and through both words and music he keeps before us the epic duty of founding Rome: the birth of a

[56] Book IV, 117–72.

[57] For other examples, see the opening movements of *Le Sacre du Printemps* and *La Mer*.

[58] "Her character combines Sophocles and Shakespeare, and her utterance resounds with Wagnerian passion." (Kurt Mey: *478, 346.*)

people is a greater thing than happiness. We sense this, for instance, in the accompaniment to

> *Spectres inexorables!*
> *Je suis barbare, ingrat; vous l'ordonnez, grands dieux!*
> *Et j'immole Didon en détournant les yeux . . .*

this being at once followed by the stirring rhythm of alert and departure that we have heard before. There is no repetition of effect: the discreet use and perpetual variation of the March theme preserves its dramatic value to the very end. We hear only four measures of it when Dido succeeds in breaking down Aeneas's resolution; she at once exclaims: "You start with joy at this triumphal song" — and gives her soul to hate. Melody again serves a dramatic conception in the ensuing scene where Dido's resolve gives birth to fresh love-music by the simple device of joining to Anna's anxious supplication an allusion to her being beloved.

As for the catastrophe, it has often been called an anticipation of Wagner. Brünnhilde, like Dido, ends her life and grief on a funeral pyre. But no two ways of rendering that quietus could be more different than those of the two composers. Sir Hamilton Harty, who first conducted *Les Troyens* in England, justly remarks that "most of [Dido's] final scene is written in low, indistinct accents, as if she were revolving in her own mind all the circle of her weariness and sorrow and was almost dead to the world and its considerations. Her final words, 'Thus it befits a Queen to go down to the grave' could not be more dejected and spiritless. There is no musical satisfaction here — and yet, regarded from another, and I think a higher, point of view, her end is a thousand times more touching and more noble than Brünnhilde's. . . . *The Trojans* is full of instances of definite and obvious refusal on the part of Berlioz to make a conventionally satisfying musical effect at the expense of real living truth." [59]

It is an open question, of course, what one means by "musically satisfying." Tradition or habit has certainly something to do with one's verdict, as Van Dieren implies when he says that *Les Troyens* shows Berlioz to be "the one composer of his time who could write for the voice without ever sacrificing anything of his dramatic intentions." [60] These judgments have

---

[59] *526*, 17–18.

[60] *526*, 28. Van Dieren makes his choice of traditions clear by adding: "Of this work one might say that he has actually achieved in it all that Wagner tried to do, while leaving undone all that has rightly provoked the severest censure of the Wagnerian manner." (*Ibid.*) An American critic, Mr. Herbert F. Peyser, adds (without approving Berlioz' style): "it is curious, for that matter, how much kinship some of this music has with the *Ring*." (*N. Y. Times*, Jan. 1, 1939.)

value as reminders that there is more than one way of composing music drama. Berlioz chose the nonillustrative, nonsystematized; preferred melody to leitmotives and *chant récitatif* to semispoken declamation; [61] and achieved his effect by intense, discontinuous scenes instead of protracted symphonic movements. "Precisely because Berlioz is of a different kind from Wagner and Meyerbeer, the originality of his style . . . marks a milestone in the history of art . . . and whoever considers himself musically educated should, indeed must, come to know *Les Troyens*." [62]

The Preface to *Les Troyens* bids all future producers perform the work as written. This has never been done. [63] In his lifetime Berlioz had to split the work unevenly in two. Revivals in Carlsruhe and Paris in the nineties, and again in Paris, Odessa, and Berlin in the early twenties, were somewhat more respectful, though cuts were made, scenes inverted, and — an amazing thing for a work deemed too long — music added. Everywhere the *mise en scène* is improved upon by the super-Berlioz on hand. [64] At Manchester a few years later, Sir Hamilton Harty gave the work in concert form, which pleased his well-trained Berlioz following but bewildered the critics up from London. Finally in 1934–1935, Erik Chisholm gave a careful performance at Glasgow — the one that "convinced" Sir Donald Tovey — since which time the work in whole or in part has been repeated in England and, under Sir Thomas Beecham, broadcast from time to time. A recent reviewer says: "I cannot understand why Berlioz' *Les Troyens* has never made itself a place in the operatic repertory." And he goes on to detail the beauties which exist in the score "contrary to public opinion." [65]

To the student of Berlioz, this class of remark is at first amusing, then faintly annoying. Another critic quoted earlier did not see why *Benvenuto Cellini* was neglected; certain Paris critics could not see why Berlioz' symphonies, when Weingartner brought them from Berlin, were not

[61] Romain Rolland: "How much more beautiful, it seems to me, is Berlioz' *chant récitatif*, with its long and sinuous lines, than the Wagnerian declamation which, apart from the moments of climax where it flows in broad and strong phrases, is limited to the quasi-notation of speech inflections that jar unpleasantly with the admirable symphony in the orchestra." (*504*, 40.)

[62] *1357*, 61.

[63] The nearest thing to it was Kufferath's production at the Théâtre de la Monnaie, Brussels, in 1906.

[64] For the Berlin Opera Dr. Julius Kapp made a version ("*frei bearbeitet*") which brings the whole within four hours' playing time. How this was staged may be inferred from Dr. Hugo Leichtentritt's report about the "orchestral music of the nocturnal [*sic*] storm." (*1391*, 1930, 748.)

[65] *The* (London) *Spectator*, July 11, 1947, 45.

oftener on their home programs. In New York, Richard Goldman wonders why the *Funeral* symphony has been left unplayed for so long, and the reception of the *Requiem* recordings drew the same kind of contrite amazement. The gloss on all these experiences is quite simple: Berlioz' music is imperfectly known though much talked about; the sincere critic who formerly ignored or dismissed Berlioz has a sudden revelation; and the revelation is nothing more nor less than a good performance in full.[66]

For the seeker of such a revelation, *Les Troyens* must be accorded a special place in the body of Berlioz' work; for experience shows that its architecture can boast of one feature that has often served listeners as a gateway toward understanding Berlioz' music at large: Tovey's illumination is typical.[67] Given the traditions of opera (including the Wagnerian), it is fair to surmise that *Les Troyens* performs this service by exemplifying Berlioz' conception of music appropriate to a visible drama and at the same time independent of it, self-sufficient. He who hears the work and studies his sensations discovers this special quality and comes to agree that Berlioz' music is neither illustrative, nor literary, nor in want of stage events to throw light on its intention: it is dramatic *in* and *per se* — as these pages have tried to show at every possible juncture of art and technique.[68]

But this is not all. *Les Troyens* makes the observer also aware that when applied to music, the term "dramatic" actually refers to a quality of the texture, rather than to any correspondence with a play, acted or imagined. As the analysis of the "Royal Hunt and Storm" demonstrates, a truly independent music cannot parallel the form of an action — of a drama as we use the word in literature. It is this healthy divergence which allows us to call *Les Troyens* a musical *epic* without thereby contradicting its *dramatic* character. In literature, we rightly think of drama as a close involvement of persons whose motives are unintelligible without words. Hence music can never by itself present a drama: it cannot particularize, nor break up its substance into representations of figures in conflict. The epic, on the contrary, is like music in giving sharp expression to broad

[66] See Mr. Virgil Thomson's provocative discussion of this point. (*521.*)

[67] *E.g.*, Albert Schweitzer, Subchapter 24, and *319, 514*, and *659* among others.

[68] Predicting the future of music drama, the veteran English theorist, Sir Walford Davies hopes that "in 1960, all musicians will have learnt . . . common sense" and eliminated the "rudimentary redundancy of Grand Opera exemplified in simultaneously showing a sword on the stage, speaking about a sword in the Book, and introducing a pre-arranged and labelled Sword motive in the orchestral part. In 1960 this, surely, will long ago have proved simply too insulting to the imagination of the least educated spectator-auditor." (*The Pursuit of Music*, London, 1944, pp. 389–90.)

contrasts: the hero is less a man than a symbol — sometimes a symbol of an entire people; epic situations are typical rather than particular; motives are traditional; action is slow or remote or purposely repetitious; in a word, the import of the work is mythic and (in the active sense) formal, rather than individual. Now every one of these characteristics fits the inherent features of the musical idiom that we have hitherto called dramatic. No wonder *Les Troyens* is at once a culmination and a clue!

Les Troyens in fact compels us to round off our definitions of "program" music and the dramatic symphony by adding to them the important conclusion that all so-called dramatic music (opera, oratorio, tone poems, ballet music and kindred genres) approaches its true end in proportion as it resembles the epic. Or to put it another way, one aspect of the art of music is its power to render the tensions of human experience by handling strictly musical ideas in a style akin to the dramatic, while giving them shapes akin to the epic.

Berlioz was therefore prescient when in his late twenties he called the *Symphonie Fantastique* an Episode and alluded to Greek drama in his program notes: the episode is a portion of the epic, and Greek drama is both more musical and closer to the epic than anything we moderns call drama. Hence when we listen to *Les Troyens* and hear the recall of the *idée fixe* from Berlioz' first symphony, it will stand for us as more than a sign of an artistic cycle accomplished: it will remind us of the fixity in Berlioz' conception of music. On this last *Les Troyens* is innocently didactic through being a work for the stage — an epic story, a great pageant, and the tragic view of life embodied in sound.

24. *Esthetes Abroad:* Wagner, Liszt, and the Princess

April 1858 to
August 1860

At the present moment, only we three fellows really belong together, because only we three are equals, and that is — you — he — and I.

— WAGNER to Liszt about himself and Berlioz

IN THE HALF DOZEN years that Berlioz devoted to composing and polishing his musical epic, he felt that the *rapprochement* between artist and audience which had occurred apropos of *The Infant Christ* was but a momentary gain. His awareness of the originality he had just put into renovating opera from within made him feel at times like a sane man in a lunatic asylum — that is to say, made him occasionally wonder who was crazy. For if Biletta's new work, *Rose de Florence*, was dramatic music then *Les Troyens* was folly. If the really important innovation at the Opera was to stage something by that professional amateur, Prince Poniatowski,[1] then *Les Troyens* lacked the right kind of novelty.

The astonishing thing was that after thirty years of public activity and many genuine victories, Berlioz was still alone in his way of conceiving art. He had been understood, admired, and exploited, but piecemeal; and the mysterious resistance of his music to direct imitation, coming on top of his uncommon power of creating a new style for each work, gave him the appearance of a fitful fragmentary personage who had not formed a "school." Being anything but a recluse, Berlioz gauged his own uniqueness and would not rally to either of the well-labeled parties: neither to the music of the present, which meant Meyerbeer, nor to the music of the future, which meant Wagner. No one really knew what Wagner's future

[1] Joseph Michael Poniatowski, Prince of Monte Rotondo (1816–1873), a nephew of Napoleon's marshal, studied under Ceccherini and made his public debut as a tenor. He produced (and sang in) several operas of his own without ever losing his amateur standing or his diplomatic immunity: he was an envoy from Tuscany; Napoleon III made him a Senator, and the Opera produced his *Pierre de Medicis* in March, 1860.

music was, but his published scores had the great advantage of being quite readable and transcribable on the piano. Liszt could read the poem of Berlioz' *Troyens*, and did so with delight, but he could only trust his friend's genius for the musical richness of the whole.[2] He and his group had only penetrated *Benvenuto, Romeo,* or the *Damnation* in rehearsal and by ear. The path of success seemed to lie in literary argument seconded by piano reductions. In short, by 1859 the modern trend toward digest-and-commentary, kin of propaganda and popular culture, was well under way.

Berlioz felt the tacit condemnation of his artistic creed and understood these new beliefs while still pregnant with a work that contradicted them. His only confidant and possible spokesman in the German camp was the Princess, who for reasons of her own feared Wagner and tried to keep him at a distance from Liszt. But she did not wholly recognize how far Berlioz was being gracious by treating her as his equal and spiritual collaborator.[3] She presumed upon it from time to time, which inevitably led to the crisis of 1860. Ultimately, the relations of the three peers — as Wagner called himself, Liszt, and Berlioz — were rendered hopeless, and the course of public opinion was confused, by the tangle of three proud artists and their three women (Marie and Cosima joining in) upon the treacherous ground of esthetics.

Anyhow in 1859 the smell of war was in the air. The Emperor's New Year message to his Austrian "cousin" held a stern threat which must lead sooner or later to a battlefield. People speculated about time and place in the cheerful old way, for war still seemed to the citizen a thing of flags and chargers and heroes holding bridges singlehanded. Berlioz was virtually alone in his truthful imagining of modern carnage and his preference for other forms of heroism.[4] The contrast only heightened his isolation: every casual or deliberate social force was repressing his real self. He began to have the fits of a Hamlet caught in a time out of joint: "In such moments, the slightest accident produces strange results. Day before yesterday, while talking quietly with friends by my fireside, someone brought in a newspaper in which I saw announced a new biography

[2] See below his ultimate judgment of the score, Chapter 26, *n.* 10.
[3] Thus in May 1858 he writes explaining his reluctance to compromise about the staging of his work: "I want to expose to insult neither Cassandra, nor Dido, nor Aeneas, nor Virgil, nor Shakespeare, nor you, nor me." (*S.W.,* 76.)
[4] Only a few years before a British general, Sir Francis Bond-Head, had assured the public that new explosives rendered war impossible because no troops would advance over ground presumably mined with such engines of death. (Quoted in *At John Murray's,* p. 89.)

of Christopher Columbus. At once the whole life of that great man appears to me in a flash. I see it all in one glance, like a painting, and my heart contracts at the thought of that memorable epic. I fall into a fit of indescribable despair, to the astonishment of those present. The incident was laid to the account of my disease, and I was not going to expose myself to mockery by admitting that the name of Columbus had alone brought on the fit. My trouble is an entanglement of causes and effects in which the wisest physiologists and psychologists would lose their way. . . ." [5]

One of the causes undoubtedly was Berlioz' sense of the decadence around him. The unseemly greed for pleasure that Offenbach expressed like a second Petronius, the pre-deluge philosophy of those in power, turned all Columbus figures to ridicule and made of creative effort a joke. It was time for a Berlioz to decline battle and cease trying to nourish spirit on tainted air. He could not of course help translating his alert forebodings into the music for the Fall of Troy, but to save his integrity — like the later Melville after the American Civil War — Berlioz the artist must withdraw.

The doctors said in fact that he had a general inflammation of the nervous system and that he must "live like an oyster, not think and not feel." [6] Yet he had much to think about. His one chance to have *Les Troyens* decently performed was to obtain an Imperial edict ordering one of the subsidized houses to play it. At the Institute his new colleague, Prince Jerome, continued favorable but the Emperor disliked his cousin, so letters of recommendation brought no result and Berlioz ought rather to avoid his supporter. [7] It was tantalizing, for the previous August at Baden the composer had seen what power and good will could do. "King" Bénazet was a true prince: all the special performers that Berlioz wanted he obtained; the whole group were fed, housed, and courteously

[5] *S.W.*, 76–7.

[6] *S.W.*, 76.

[7] Napoleon Joseph Charles Paul Bonaparte (1822–1891), Prince Jerome, commonly known as Prince Napoleon or else by the nickname of "Plon-Plon," was first cousin to the Emperor Napoleon III. Born the third son of Jerome, youngest brother of Napoleon I, he took his father's name after the death of his elder brother in 1847, and will continue to be called Prince Jerome to avoid confusion. Besides being a discerning patron of the arts, he had a strong grasp of political affairs like his uncle, the first Napoleon, whom he greatly resembled in feature. At the court of Napoleon III, Jerome led the liberal opposition and incurred frequent displeasure for his outspoken criticism of policy. He was none the less heir presumptive, and after 1879 his line furnished the leaders of the Bonapartist party in France.

treated, and moreover *thanked* for their work. Nor did Bénazet lose by it — everyone worked twice as hard. There were eleven rehearsals before the fete, and although the "musical fever" was a strain, Berlioz produced one of the finest concerts of his lifetime — Beethoven, Mozart, Weber, a Litolff piano concerto played by the composer, and four parts of *Romeo and Juliet.* "What a performance!" he wrote jubilantly to Ferrand. "Poor Paganini, who never heard the work I composed for his pleasure!"[8] The next day, the beautiful Countess Kalergi averred she was still in tears from artistic bliss.[9] Berlioz' old colleague Georges Kastner was among the most enthusiastic and, giving up an old grudge, embraced Berlioz and took him and Marie home with him to Strasbourg.

The well-being induced by this real Utopia, this approximation of Euphonia, of course evaporated in Paris, where the Emperor had granted Berlioz an audience (with forty others) and graciously permitted the composer to present the text of *Les Troyens.* Napoleon had "his 25 below zero look,[10] and he took my manuscript with the assurance that he would read it if he had the leisure. The trick was neatly done. It's as old as the hills; I'm sure King Priam did it just this way."[11]

At the turn of the year Berlioz had also published suitably cut portions of his *Memoirs,* beginning with the Festival of 1844 and then going back to the early chapters.[12] He wanted to correct some of the misstatements that had appeared in Mirecourt's little volume three years before, to supply once for all the details that foreign concert managers kept asking him to send, and perhaps also to remind the public of his long apprenticeship and undeviating course. This publication brought him many encouraging letters, including a grateful one from Paganini's son, and the usual batch of strangers' poems asking to be set to music at the composer's early convenience.

The articles also brought him a round sum which he would soon need for Louis's period of study ashore. The "dear Indian" as his father ad-

---

[8] *I.e.,* the *Romeo and Juliet* symphony. (*L.I.,* 207–208.)

[9] A niece of Nesselrode and the mother-in-law of Count Coudenhove, she had one of the most brilliant salons in Baden. She had been a pupil of Chopin's and her love of music was a passion, not an affectation. Gautier's poem, *Symphonie en Blanc Majeur* was written in her honor.

[10] Tocqueville: "The words one addressed to him were like stones thrown down a well; their sound was heard, but one never knew what became of them." (*1223,* 269.)

[11] *207,* II, 177.

[12] *Le Monde Illustré,* Feb. 13, Sept. 25 to Dec. 25, 1859; Jan. 1 to July 23, 1860. It may be pointed out that these fragments included the *Requiem* account, which none of Habeneck's friends nor any other eyewitness called into question.

dressed him, was at the Antipodes and much missed, "If your ship goes to China, shall you receive my letters?" Once again the "dear child, dear Louis, dear lieutenant" seemed in a fair way to success. He was due back in the spring of 1859 and when July came, his ship a month overdue, Berlioz went through agonies. Finally on the nineteenth Louis landed. By that time, luckily, the ridiculous war with Austria was over. Napoleon had learned with his own eyes that shrapnel and cannon balls killed the "poor people" whom he sent to war, and that the sense impressions given off by a battlefield at night differed much from those of the boudoirs to which he was accustomed. But after fifty years' lack of practice the nineteenth century no longer knew how to make a war look efficient while protracting it for full employment. Nevertheless, thanks to Eugénie, Magenta, the glorious battlefield, came to denote everybody's favorite color and dressmakers took heart.

Berlioz had by then begun to make his own vocal score of *Les Troyens.* It would be needed for any rehearsals and he found in the process an opportunity for "scraping and scrubbing into every recess of the score." [13] In the task of rendering his many-voiced orchestration on the piano, he was aided by his friend Pauline Viardot, who was an excellent pianist as well as a great singer. Indeed, this remarkable woman, sister of Malibran and daughter of the famous Garcia,[14] was a personage whose place in the century has not yet been adequately presented. A great actress, a superb voice, a strong intellect, a fascinating woman without petty arts and even without regular or beautiful features, she bewitched all those who came near her. She was for years Turgenev's close friend and collaborator, she deeply impressed men as diverse as Dickens, Tolstoy, and Tchaikovsky, and she inspired in Berlioz the worship which he felt for the great in art and character.[15]

This, and the idea of a new dramatic work which he had been commissioned to write for Baden, constituted Berlioz' real present and only tolerable future. Otherwise his mind dwelt in the incredible past: Paris was changing visibly under the radical planning of Baron Haussmann, which

[13] *91*, 146.
[14] The last surviving member of this great musical family, Mme. Viardot's grandnephew and pupil, died in London in 1946.
[15] She was also a composer of songs and it is sometimes erroneously stated that Berlioz let her "correct the harmony" of his score: the fact is that he took two or three suggestions from her as he had always done from his musical friends, and followed her recommendations for making the piano version fingerable. (*91*, 158–9.) Saint-Saëns gives an eyewitness account. (*308*, Jul. 9, 1905.)

made the old city seem to the man of 1830 "a cemetery dotted with memorial stones — here I met Balzac for the last time; there I walked with Paganini; in another spot I accompanied the Duchesse d'Abrantès, a silly good woman;[16] this is the house where Madame de Girardin lived — a clever woman who thought me a fool; this is the sidewalk where I talked to Adolphe Nourrit;[17] that desolate house yonder is that of poor Rachel;[18] and so on, and so on. So many dead! Why aren't *we* dead?" [19]

Letters from the Princess prodding and preaching a little too much, from Morel discussing the musical situation in Marseille, and from the ailing Ferrand imparting his troubles, gave the sense of a dying and shrinking world to a man who had spent most of his life in the heat of action. Being ill to boot, he went from doctor to doctor, with little faith and much Molière in his mind. Yet he lent himself to their experiments, falling at last into the hands of a certain "Dr. Noir," a Negro of great repute who had "cured" Adolphe Sax of a melanotic growth on the lip. The man, whose real name was J. H. Vries, proved to be only a more imaginative quack than the rest. A large fashionable practice daily waited from four to five hours in his anteroom and he managed to persuade the Faculty of Medicine, represented by Dr. Velpeau, to put a hospital and its free patients at his disposal. Ultimately, Velpeau's report put an end to Dr. Noir's hold on his clientele. They none the less gave him a testimonial dinner. Berlioz had by then ceased going, the few fruitless treatments having wasted too much of his time, but he had given in to the plausible manipulator's request and composed for his projected "tabernacle" a *pièce d'occasion* on a religious-humanitarian theme.[20]

What Berlioz obviously needed was a musical life. He dreamed of music at night and recalling his dream "mentally performed . . . the adagio of Beethoven's B flat symphony [Fourth] just as we did it three years ago at Baden, so that little by little I fell into one of those unearthly ecstasies and wept my eyes out at the sound of that tonal radiance which only angels wear. Believe me, dear friend, the being who wrote such a marvel of inspiration was not a man. Only thus does the archangel

[16] At one time Balzac's mistress.

[17] Doubtless an allusion to the time when Berlioz and Osborne tried to dissuade the young singer from committing suicide after hearing Duprez's brilliant debut. See above, Chapter 10.

[18] Elisa Felix, called Rachel, the tragic actress who had died the previous year, aged 38. Berlioz respected as well as admired her, for she apparently always acknowledged the influence of Harriet Smithson on her own acting. (*396, 359.*)

[19] *S.W.*, 81.

[20] *Ger. ed.*, vol. XIV.

Michael sing, as he dreamily contemplates the spheres . . . And not to have an orchestra at hand that would sing for me that seraphic poem. . . . Down to earth, now! Someone is coming in . . ." [21]

As the next best thing to a seraphic orchestra, Berlioz was planning a concert for Easter Week. Louis, who was expected home before then, had not heard any of his father's music since childhood, and this was an added spur. Meanwhile Paris was going to a new opera by Gounod and not liking it. The subject was *Faust* and Berlioz, though he did not say so, must have noticed that some of its best ideas came, a good deal watered down, from another *Faust* which the Parisians had scarcely listened to. The public's hesitancy about Gounod's score only showed how unpalatable was the music which came from the Berliozian quarter of the artistic world. The work being so far superior to anything that had been put on for years — classic revivals aside — Berlioz did his best to keep it afloat, but other critics had learned nothing and forgotten nothing. Gounod, they felt, lacked melody; he wrote "German" music; and — the jibe was over seventy-five years old — he "put all his effects in the orchestra." [22] Berlioz wrote a stout defense, adroitly quoting fashionable gossip about the work, and pointing out to the true connoisseurs the technical and expressive qualities of the best parts. [23]

The real success of the season was Meyerbeer's new work, *Le Pardon de Ploërmel* (in English *Dinorah*) which furnished in a Breton setting his excellent custom-made article, cut from the best material in stock. It afforded besides the Opera's choicest visual delights, and the press confirmed the public's entranced appreciation. By contrast, Berlioz' mingling of reasoned disapproval with his praise seemed unjust and was imputed to envy. Yet Berlioz as before truly valued Meyerbeer's musical gifts and only deplored their misuse and corruption in the service of an antimusical

[21] *L.I.*, 217.

[22] See Berlioz' vindication of Mozart against this *mot* of Grétry's concerning *Don Giovanni* (*Grot.*, 225).

[23] The essay is in *M.M.*, 285 ff. It contains under the first category of arguments the *reductio* imagined by Berlioz as overheard in the lobby — it also dates for us a change in fashions:

"Yes, I confess I had hoped it would fail."

"But why? Do you dislike M. Gounod?"

"I do."

"Why so?"

"Because he wears such a long beard. Has anyone ever seen a musician so heavily bearded? Do Meyerbeer, Auber or Halévy wear a beard? Are we then living in Russia?"

"True, true, very true — Now that I understand your reasons, why, I myself . . ." (*Ibid.*, 291.)

genre. The reigning form of opera he could at least deride openly: "Shall I speak of the *mise en scène*, of the artificial thunder, the broken bridge, the white goat, the sluice that opens and the cascade of *natural* water? No, No! Go and see for yourself!" [24]

Readers enjoy prize fights between artists at any time, and they relished this satirical note, while continuing to know what they liked and to be puzzled by what Berlioz revered and desired. Hence they gave equal acclaim to the new opera and to Berlioz' new collection of squibs and essays, *Les Grotesques de la Musique*, which soon became a best seller.[25] They liked the narrative skill, and the wit and good humor that predominated over the bitterness of the technical parables ("The right to play in F a symphony written in D").[26] The onslaughts on mediocrity they brushed aside on Swift's principle that a satirist aims at everybody but the reader. Besides, it gave one status to be able to "place" Berlioz, on the evidence of one's eyes, as an *esprit fin et cultivé*, an *écrivain spirituel*, a *grand feuilletoniste*, almost as *grand* as Janin, the prince of the tribe.

On April 23, Louis being still unheard from, Berlioz gave his Holy Week concert, *The Infant Christ*. The audience showed its discrimination by liking some of the more hidden beauties of the score. To Berlioz it had seemed the most perfect execution so far. "What pleased me most was that the mystical chorus, 'O my soul, what is yet left . . .' was for the first time sung with the requisite accent and nuance. In that vocal peroration the whole work is summed up, for it seems to me that the feeling of the infinite, of divine love, is in that passage." [27]

Numberless *démarches*, visits, and readings for the sake of *Les Troyens* continued to fill the days. Surprisingly, old Véron, onetime director of the Opera, grew enthusiastic about Dido's funeral pyre and declared that if he were still in charge he would spend 150,000 francs on the show — mostly, one suspects, for faggots. "To be sure, his words cost him nothing . . . Yet they have caused a sensation in the Opera crowd. Will they come, gradually, to the Mountain?" [28] Vain hopes, as Berlioz recognized, because of the lack of fit performers. "There is no *Priameia virgo*, no Cassandra. Dido would be sure to be inadequate and I would rather be stabbed

---

[24] *1386*, Apr. 10, 1859.

[25] Parts of the book have been translated on two occasions. See Bibliography under *Grot.* For further comments on the book, see below, Subchapter 26.

[26] *Grot.*, 20.

[27] *L.I.*, 219.

[28] *Corresp.*, 265. Véron seems to have been roused by the deep-lying appeal of a conflagration, which later made Wagner's *Ring* denouement so quickly popular, and which had of course previously exerted its pull on Virgil and Berlioz — not to speak of Dido.

ten times in the chest with a dirty kitchen knife than to hear anyone mangle the last monologue of the Queen of Carthage." [29]

Berlioz was still giving the score "a good workout with the file" but he declined the Princess's suggestion that he publish the libretto. "It would be to confess a desire for literary fame, to which I do not pretend." [30] When he had had a good day free from gastric pain, he would gather a few musical friends for chamber music as in the past, and now also for an informal sight-reading of this or that scene from his music drama. Only Berlioz could hear it as it should sound, but the others grew to like the great nostalgic melodies unlike anyone else's, and the telling harmonies in which the notes did not seem to account for the shiver that they caused.[31] So much so that in the fall of 1859, at the Beethoven School, Mme. Charton-Demeur and Jules Lefort, with Ritter at the piano, gave two of the duets for twenty or thirty friends of the composer's. The "audience" wishing to hear some of the choral parts, they all sang, Berlioz included. Thus, long before there was any prospect of its production, *Les Troyens* was becoming a public fact; its size and purport were gossiped about in musical, literary, and official circles. Its existence partook of the ghostly, like the shade of Hector, and of the monstrous, like the Trojan horse.

In the interim Berlioz went to Bordeaux where the Saint Cecilia Society had invited him to conduct his own works at its annual concert. Two hundred and fifty musicians gave the *Roman Carnival* overture and excerpts from *Romeo* and *The Infant Christ*. The large theater was full of a cheering multitude who stood to see Berlioz crowned with laurel, and some of them stayed to toast him at an interminable banquet. Other calls came for scores. At Carlsruhe there was talk of *Benvenuto;* in Russia and America his shorter works were beginning to be regularly performed, and news from other German towns led a resentful French critic to accuse Berlioz of causing the same "subversive events" across the Rhine as at home.[32]

Before the Baden season the international situation had become so tense that it was thought impossible to hold a festival. *Romeo and Juliet* had been scheduled, by request, and Berlioz was getting ready for it, but as a result of Napoleon's clear designs upon the South German states, the

[29] *L.I.*, 221.

[30] *S.W.*, 89.

[31] Pauline Viardot found the great female roles of *Les Troyens* "melodious, vocal, clear, soberly accompanied — and in the grand style." (*91*, 154; and again, to Liszt: *207*, II, 242.)

[32] *502*, 429.

Badenese wanted to "eat the French alive." [33] They feared armed invasion, and by a metaphor which has since become the basis of national policy, they feared invasion by foreign talent. They did not think back a month or two — no nationalist does — to Hans von Bülow's "capture" of Paris to the heavy artillery of his tumultuous piano; but he had been a great success and Berlioz had enjoyed his vivacious company and that of his young wife, the former Cosima Liszt.

Although Bénazet's plans were in suspense, he would not release Berlioz from his promise to compose a new opera for two years hence. The libretto, by the popular playwright Edouard Plouvier, was all ready. Based on an episode in the Thirty Years' War, it seemed to hold few attractions for the musician. "In it are to be found a Duke of Saxe-Weimar, a Bohemian girl, a few Francs-Juges, the Devil — and all his train. . . ." [34] Despite Berlioz' repeated begging off, Bénazet wanted the opera "even if his project of building a theatre does not materialize. . . ." Berlioz' heartfelt gratitude, coupled with the memory of his own costly ventures, made him apprehensive: he felt obliged to produce a success. "The risk is his, but there are days when the idea plunges me into despair." [35] At other times it seemed possible. "Perhaps the fire will catch when I once begin. Yet there would be no perhapses if it were a question of dealing with the subject you mention [*Romeo and Juliet*]. *That* fire has been lit a long while; it burns steadily, banked like a buried coal mine which we know exists only through the boiling water it shoots upward. Yes indeed, it is still possible to write a beautiful *Romeo* opera besides the symphony." [36]

The Baden season did take place, and Berlioz was able to add to the program the love duet from *Les Troyens*, sung by Pauline Viardot and Jules Lefort with full orchestra. But Liszt and the Princess, for whom Berlioz had mainly taken the trouble, did not come. Liszt had resigned from Weimar, his post no longer congenial. The death of the Grand-Ducal pair who had appointed him; the younger Duke's interest in plays rather than music; finally the hissing of Cornelius's *Barber of Bagdad* the previous year (for no reason except that the author was a pupil of Liszt's and Liszt was not married to the Princess) drove the pianist to pitch his tent elsewhere. Even in the pianistic world he was losing ground, eclipsed by a new star, Anton Rubinstein. The string of epithets young Cornelius had applied to himself — "Lisztianer, Wagner-Berlioz-Weimarianer" — would no longer carry meaning. The center for the new music was to move about wherever Liszt could get a foothold, and his concentration

[33] *S.W.*, 93.
[34] *S.W.*, 98.
[35] *S.W.*, 98.
[36] *S.W.*, 88.

of effort upon getting the *Ring* produced[37] would ultimately mean a second eclipse, this time as an orchestral composer, at the hands of Wagner.

The Princess was also on her travels. Berlioz heard from her at Baden that she had betrothed her daughter to Prince Constantin Hohenlohe-Schillingsfürst,[38] and that she might be visiting Paris in the autumn. In a different way from Harriet Smithson, she too had played her part in Berlioz' creative life, and this part was over and done with. They remained on the same devoted terms, just as Liszt and Berlioz did, but one by one the vivid threads were fading, the isolation, the twilight, were creeping around Berlioz, leaving clear only that narrow and stony path which leads the predestined to Colonus.

In Paris, articles had appeared about the scene from *Les Troyens* heard at Baden. All were highly complimentary. Ernest Reyer assured his readers that the score was stupendous, and that the book revealed not a librettist but a poet. D'Ortigue hinted that an earlier Napoleon had ordered the production of a comparable masterpiece, *La Vestale*. Berlioz had by now given up as beneath his dignity all attempts to interest the Imperial household. At the Opera a new *Romeo and Juliet*, which was in reality the old one by Bellini, was in production.[39] Berlioz took this opportunity to review all earlier musical Romeos, except his own, and to conclude as he had done in his letter to the Princess, that a worthy operatic score was still to be written.

There are to date five operas whose subjects purport to be that of Shakespeare's immortal drama. The playwrights have all pretended to light their torch at the great love-sun, but all are pale tapers, three of them being hardly little pink candles. . . . Not that it is possible to make a drama into an opera without changing, upsetting, and more or less spoiling the original. But there are so many intelligent ways of committing the desecration which music requires! For example, though it is impossible to keep all of Shakespeare's characters, why has it occurred to none of the arrangers to keep at least some of those they have dropped . . . [and to drop] the entirely new ones they have introduced — these An-

---

[37] This determination had contributed to Liszt's break with Duke Charles Alexander. Since the new incumbent liked plays, Liszt appealed to him to build a special theater and treat himself to the *Nibelungen*. The duke replied by appointing a new director who cut the musical budget.

[38] Younger brother of Prince Chlodwig, who was quoted above (Subchapter 22) and who, before his elevation to the Chancellorship of the German Empire under William II, was to be involved in the politics of Wagner's relation to King Ludwig of Bavaria. See his *Memoirs* (1176, I, 155, 166, 177, 296, 343).

[39] Even Bellini could not be produced without alteration: a last act on the same subject by Vaccai was after a while substituted for the original.

tonio, Alberti, Cebas, Gennaro, Adriani, Nisa, Cécile and so on: what are they for?

Naturally, neither the French nor the Italians — any more than the English on their legitimate stage — have had the courage to keep Romeo's character intact and allow so much as a hint of his first love for Rosaline. How admit that young Montague could love another than the daughter of the Capulets! For shame! It would debase the idea universally held about this model lover; it would take all the poetry out of it: the public is composed of souls that are so constant and so pure! [40]

After the failure of Bellini's *Romeo,* Carvalho at the Théâtre Lyrique announced Gluck's *Orpheus* and put Berlioz in charge of establishing the score, there having been two — an Italian and a French — both corrupt. Inversions, interpolations, "trombonization," and careless *col basso* scoring had long made the work the sport of manhandlers. Carvalho himself, with the powerful drive of the frustrated creator in an artistic profession, wanted Berlioz to use the overture to *Iphigeneia,* insert a chorus from *Armide,* and generally earn his fee. But Berlioz was an old hand at the game and he had vowed that it would be *Orpheus* or nothing, *Orpheus* — as he had said of *Freischütz* — "without *Castilblazade* of any kind." [41] Carvalho he believed to be "full of good intentions"; and he added: "his hell shall be paved with them." [42]

It is because of Carvalho's amiability and this firmness on Berlioz' part that we owe both the preservation of the original Gluck "style" and the existence of a correct edition of the master. For as a sequel to this first task Carvalho and others invited Berlioz to oversee productions of three other Gluck operas; Berlioz coached singers and conductors, and the public responded. He wrote articles on the work of restoration, and these inspired his admirer, Mlle. Fanny Pelletan, to devote her leisure and her fortune to editing Gluck. First with the aid of Berlioz' friend Damcke, whom she chose as theory teacher, then with Berlioz' protégé Saint-Saëns, who tells the story, the work was carried through. [43] No one of

---

[40] *A Trav.,* 331–2.

[41] *L.I.,* 194–5. See above, Chapter 3, Berlioz' first denunciation of Castil-Blaze apropos of Gluck, thirty-four years since.

[42] *502,* 428.

[43] *386,* 125. Confirmed by H. J. Moser who in his book on Gluck says: "*One man deserves to be honored in this connection: Hector Berlioz.*" (P. 348.) Berthold Damcke (1812–1875) a Hanoverian violinist, organist, composer and critic, settled in Paris in 1859, after wide experience in the Germanies. He soon became one of Berlioz' stanch friends and was named as his testamentary executor with Edouard Alexandre.

Fanny Pelletan (1830–1876) was the daughter and granddaughter of distinguished physicians, whose musical talents were cultivated from an early age. The passage in Berlioz that set her on her editorial labors was *Grot.,* 198. In

Berlioz' competence had seen and studied the works of Gluck and his school so thoroughly — as he well knew [44] — and he missed no opportunity to make able proselytes; young Ritter being but one of several. Mme. Pauline Viardot was now entrusted with the role of Orpheus, so Berlioz spent a few days at her house in the country giving her his views on style — equidistant from the trivial and the pompous and (what is even more important) *varied* in successive scenes. She was a pleasure to work with; the merest hint was enough and Berlioz was in the seventh heaven.[45]

He had a bad bout of illness while at the Viardots' and not wishing (as he wrote to Louis) "to burden and alarm this charming family," [46] he returned to Paris. In bed he could read proof on the corrected parts of Gluck that Roquemont was bringing in. "Tonight [September 23, 1859] I finished putting the first act of *Orpheus* in order. Carvalho wants my Trojans for his theatre, but how? He has no tenor for Aeneas. Mme. Viardot suggests that she play both Cassandra and Dido . . . The public might, I believe, accept this anomaly, which is incidentally not without precedent. And so my two roles would be played in the grand style by this great artist." [47]

Princess Carolyne was in Paris as Berlioz worked lovingly at *Orpheus* and *Les Troyens*. They dined together. Face to face she gave him such a liberal dose of the flattery and compassion which served her to express high regard that he could hardly resist living up to her image of him as a stricken lion licking his wounds. He was chronically worn out by pain, it is true, but he still had fortitude, and more than once he rebelled against her emollients.[48] Gently reproved, she measured the strength of his crea-

recognition of her resolve Berlioz presented her with the manuscript of *The Infant Christ*, which she later bequeathed, together with that of Gluck's *Alceste*, to the Bibliothèque Nationale. (Fétis, *Dict.*, Suppl. II, 317.)

[44] In 1839, answering a stranger who was also a Gluckist, Berlioz states that "in the 19 years [*sc.* 18] that I have lived in Paris, I have never missed a single performance . . . I have seen all his works (except *Echo and Narcissus*) fifteen or twenty times each . . . so you see I have not had to 'guess' anything as you thought." (*86*, 579.)

[45] He was so transported that she apparently believed him to be falling in love with her; if she was right, the emotion was very temporary and dependent on musical collaboration. They remained good friends.

[46] *Corresp.*, 266–7.

[47] *Corresp.*, 267.

[48] "Your letter charmed and grieved me at the same time: I was charmed by your goodness of heart and the supreme grace of its expression; I was grieved because its dithyrambic style is carried too far. Yes, you tell me things of such a pitch that you seem to be treating me as a vain and credulous child to whom one promises that the angels in heaven will come down and bring him toys and candy." (*S.W.*, 106–7.)

tive will, and since she truly shared his passion for modern art (she was a great admirer of Delacroix) she urged Berlioz to compose an *Antony and Cleopatra*. "If my strength returns," he replied, "I will try. . . . I do not suppose that any man was ever so unfortunate as that unfortunate wretch after the defeat of Actium and his cowardly flight from his infernal mistress, his serpent of the Nile. I cannot look without shuddering on that ocean of misery. . . . But I see that the Opera is to revive Flotow's *Soul in Pain*.[49] There was an irrepressible need for all of us to hear some Flotow. . . . Farewell; a thousand greetings to Liszt, and to you all my — no, not all, but a great deal. Come, this is foolish. I must take my cup of whatever it is with ten drops of laudanum and forget things until tomorrow. *Forget*. 'Gods of oblivion' — I really wish you could have heard that chorus, but it could not be managed." [50]

Wagner arrived just as the Princess left. Possibly her sudden departure was a tactful move to forestall the need of being loyal both to Berlioz and to Liszt's new companion-in-arms whom she disliked. Not that Berlioz had as yet any proof that a diplomatic revolution had taken place. He knew that Liszt was bestirring himself on Wagner's behalf; he did not know that for two decades to come it would be an exclusive apostolate. At the moment, the Austrian ambassador, urged by his wife, was contriving to secure the adoption of *Tannhäuser* by a Paris theater, preferably the Opera.

For Berlioz, during October and November 1859, *the* opera was *Orpheus*. Restoring the notes was a trifle compared to teaching every one how to sing, act, dress, and even dance — since the ballet had very imperfect notions of the way shades in Hades and the Elysian Fields disport themselves. There were besides a few vocal cadenzas to write, for the traditional ones were either missing or abject. Again, in one of the airs, even though Berlioz did not consider it genuine, he entrusted to Saint-Saëns the task of writing a more manageable accompaniment, saying: "How can you expect me to re-instrument the work of Gluck when I have all my life exterminated people who took such liberties?" [51]

---

[49] "Fantastic Ballet in Two Acts," known in Germany as *Der Förster*.

[50] The allusion is to the final scene of *Les Troyens*. As for the laudanum, it may be remarked that medication for gastric ailments had not improved in fifty years. Dr. Berlioz had taken laudanum; De Quincey's opium eating began as a result of the same prescription (ratified, it seems, by the authority of a Dr. Eatwell!) and Mérimée a little later was only shifted from opium to ether. (See *1204* and *218*.)

[51] *502, 429*.

On the eighteenth of November the work opened and created a furore. It made Carvalho wealthy and renowned; it outlasted current offerings, and it left in the memory of numberless judges an ineffaceable impression. Michelet was transported and Dickens reduced to tears. Flaubert went repeatedly and would go to nothing else.[52] The ordinary public had never seen anything to compare with it, and although some professsional and lay critics still found Gluck detestable,[53] Berlioz was naïvely happy and made hopeful by the fact that when every detail of a production was handled with a craftsman's care and an artist's vision, even the random public responded. He may have suspected that the result of this quest for perfection had struck the beholders chiefly by contrast with their routine fare, but he does not seem to have noticed that at the age of fifty-six he had actually come before the public in a new capacity, that of opera director.

The day after the *première*, still working at his *Troyens*, he was again "intoxicated with harmony" and stirred to musical creation. The Princess's suggestion recurred to him; he reread *Antony*, and assured his correspondent that he would not have the "impertinence to disfigure Shakespeare's creation by fashioning an academic Cleopatra." He imagined a very Shavian creature, part child, part flirt, and part royal lover and sadist, fit only for a "musical fantasia."[54] The upshot was that two weeks later Berlioz definitely made up his mind that he would not compose Bénazet's opera on the Thirty Years' War. His musical faculties were aroused and the dances in *Les Troyens* not having been all composed, the needed music came effortlessly: "*Je fais des airs de danse partout, dans les rues, au café, chez mes amis.*"[55] Other ideas beset him, for which Cleopatra was a temporary peg. "I think I would make an attractive creature out of that torpedo. It would be different from anything I have done."[56] Though Berlioz may not have known it, his next work was begun; naturally it

---

[52] Michelet (to his son, Dec. 25), Flaubert (*192*, III, 177), Dickens (*1163*, 613 *n.*). The latter, a professional judge of acting, reports: "It is worth a journey to Paris to see; for there is no such art to be otherwise looked upon. [M. Viardot] stumbled upon me and took me to her dressing room. Nothing could have happened better as a homage to her performance, for I was disfigured with crying."

[53] "*Orpheus,*" said one kind of dilettante, "is the opera to see when you've just lost your parents — it's like a funeral." And a contemporary maker of opéra-comiques said: "There are not two singing phrases in the whole score. It's all recitative. If we wrote music like that, we would have eggs thrown in our faces." (*86*, 451-2.)

[54] *S.W.*, 108.

[55] *S.W.*, 110

[56] *S.W.*, 116.

would be different — different especially from nearly all that kept sing-songing around him. For while he ruminated novelties, his Institute colleague Halévy was admonishing Bizet about his *envoi de Rome:* "We urge the composer to be on his guard against certain harmonic boldnesses which may sometimes be qualified as roughness." [57] Bizet might have been Berlioz, Berlioz Bizet. Nothing had changed since 1830.

Orpheus continued to sell out for ten days in advance. Besides bringing Berlioz appreciable royalties, this success shook the reputation of the Opera director. There was talk of replacing him with Prince Poniatowski, now more than ever beloved as "that distinguished amateur." The prince, Berlioz told his son, "loudly proclaims — *too* loudly — that he will put on *Les Troyens* if he is appointed. The prince has a work in rehearsal, which the author of *Les Troyens* will have to review: there you are — the familiar game." [58] Meanwhile Berlioz was proofreading the piano score of *Orpheus* and doing his best to get Liszt elected as Corresponding Member of the Institute. "'Is it as a composer or as a virtuoso that you are presenting M. Liszt?' — 'As everything,' I answered, 'does that suit you?'" But Berlioz was kept off the committee, which nominated Conti and Verdi. "Wagner," he reports, "was not even brought up — such are academic bodies." The final vote put in Conti and Verdi.

Flattering for Verdi, isn't it? He had nothing to do with it and must be greatly surprised . . . For I may tell you that Verdi is a true gentleman, very proud and unyielding . . . he is as far from Rossini's railing, buffooning, and joking — sometimes stupid joking — as he is from the snake-like flexibility of Meyerbeer. Many a time he has rescued from the sin of sloth the people in the Opera and the Ministry.[59] You must grant him your esteem at least for that.

We'll do better for Liszt at the next vacancy. Delacroix and a few others have acted rather unworthily.[60] As for Liszt, I am sorry that he attached to this election an importance which it has not for *him.* It was important for *us,* us alone. The Institute should attach to itself . . . the people of stature instead of taking to its bosom with a protecting air so many dwarfs who are not even worth drowning in the irrigations of Gulliver.[61]

[57] *940,* 20.

[58] *86,* 451.

[59] In 1855, when producing his *Sicilian Vespers,* Verdi berated the entire personnel at the dress rehearsal. (*Corresp.,* 229.) It was at that time that Berlioz recommended to him the use of an electric metronome for keeping chorus groups together (*79,* 368), and that Verdi expressed for Berlioz "an affection based upon an elective affinity." (*967,* 140.)

[60] This passing reference may be to the fact that the painter, who had just voted for Verdi and Conti, in whom he had no special interest, kept up seemingly cordial relations with Liszt and the Princess.

[61] *S.W.,* 114.

These activities took time, and took it from the new composition. Hardly "one hour out of forty" could be devoted to music. The rest went, among other things, for new treatments (electrical) which "do me neither good nor harm. . . . What comedians these doctors are!" [62] Louis was also on Berlioz' mind. He was at Dieppe preparing his examinations for a captaincy, but he seemed to his father overexcited about other matters. He expressed frenzied concern over the fate of *Les Troyens* and, as Berlioz failed to see, he worried far too much about his father's health to be able to study calmly. Of the boy's abnormal attachment to him, Berlioz knew something ("We love each other like brothers"), and on his side too, this affection was distressfully passionate: "It seems as if all the tender feelings I bore your mother were now centered on you." [63] Long separations, anxiety and the verbal repetition of frustrated longings were unsettling to both.

Berlioz kept some of his bouts of illness from Louis, and could discuss the boy's future only with his devoted friends, Morel and Lecourt, who had cared for the youth at Marseille. But in his "troubled, anxious" state Berlioz needed something more. He found life at home unsatisfactory, "constantly grating, almost impossible," driving him either to seek calm with friends or even to consider "strong measures." We know no more, for in confiding this to his Brussels friend, Berlioz says "I can tell you no more." [64] Whether Marie grated on him by duplicating in words what he already thought about the present impasse in his career, or whether the irritation came from her comments about Wagner's arrival, we can only surmise. We know that she was ailing too, more seriously than anyone supposed, and that her narrow-gauge spirit was ill attuned to Berlioz' lofty brooding mind in moments of stress.

The fact remained that Wagner was in Paris, had announced a series of concerts, and had gained powerful support for his opera plans. Legitimate curiosity had been aroused by his German reputation and by the novelty of an artist-philosopher. [65] The press republished chapters that Fétis had translated six years before, and "the music of the future" became a fashionable phrase. It was interpreted rightly enough as meaning that Gluck, Mozart, and Beethoven were mere approximations, preparatory

[62] *85*, 709.

[63] *91*, 151; *86*, 452.

[64] *93*, 258.

[65] Looking back on the period, a French critic wrote: "What one discovered was a colossal system, at once musical, literary and philosophic — a magnificent attempt to fuse all the arts — which filled with enthusiasm our poets as much as our musicians." (Mauclair: *469*, 634.)

sketches for Wagner's esthetic fulfillment. And by one of the magic syn-chronizations of the *Zeitgeist*, Darwin's *Origin of Species* had just come out in England and America, and a solemn article expounded evolution in the *Revue des Deux Mondes*,[66] as Wagner stunned Paris with his three con-certs.

Some days before the first of these, Wagner called on Berlioz, and only four days before, sent him the score of his latest work. It was *Tristan* and it bore the inscription: "To the dear and great author of *Roméo et Juliette*, the grateful author of *Tristan und Isolde*." Accom-panying it was a short note: "Dear Berlioz — I am delighted to be able to present you with the first copy of my *Tristan*. Please accept it and keep it out of friendship for: Yours, Richard Wagner. January 21, 1860." [67]

On the evening of January twenty-fifth, Berlioz left his bed to attend the first concert, comprising the *Flying Dutchman* and *Tannhäuser* over-tures, the preludes to *Lohengrin* and *Tristan*, and six other fragments from the two middle works. The audience was divided between raucous en-thusiasm and equally noisy condemnation. At the intermission there were near fist fights in the lobby. Berlioz was seen applauding repeatedly, but unfortunately Marie was present and giving the loose to her tongue.[68] He, suffering from laryngitis, hardly spoke, but in the review which ap-peared before the third concert he mentioned "the prodigious amount of nonsense, absurdities, and even lies which are uttered on such an oc-casion, and which prove that in France at least, when we have to judge a type of music different from that which runs the streets, passion and prejudice hold the floor and keep good sense and judgment from speak-ing up." [69]

---

[66] Nov. 1859 to Apr. 1860. (See *1397*, 1860, I, 647 ff.)

[67] *Bibl. Grenoble.* According to Bülow, Wagner had to wait three weeks for an acknowledgment. This delay — says Bülow, doubtless echoing Wagner — was "like a stab to the heart." (*174*, 170.) Wagner's sensitivity on his own behalf was equaled only by his lack of it where others were concerned. Here it served him to show Bülow that Berlioz was an egotist who refused to drop everything and cure his illness in order to read *Tristan*. Berlioz' messages to Wagner, published half a century later, show that he was unexceptionably attentive. (*Bayreuther Blätter*, 1905, 284–6.)

[68] Ernest Reyer records meeting her and Berlioz on the way home from the concert, and hearing her say, passionately and meaninglessly: "What a triumph for Hector!" She had apparently heard comments about "reminiscences" of Berlioz melodies in Wagner's works and was "claiming" them in a way which Reyer is certain Berlioz would have scorned. (*380*, 309.)

[69] *1386*, Feb. 9, 1860; *A Trav.*, 305. Wagner wisely kept the programs of his three concerts identical, in line with his choice of pieces several of which were quite close in style or form.

Berlioz' review was full of praise. He had come back for the second performance and had been gripped anew by the great power, melodic insistency, and fiery orchestration of the works presented. He analyzed them with care, both technically and poetically. The *Flying Dutchman* overture "takes hold of the listener imperiously and carries him away." The *Tannhäuser* ensemble shows "such vigor and authority" that a certain harshness is "accepted unresistingly." The masterly ease in scoring and the strong characterization of themes elicited Berlioz' strong approval, which his reservations about details did not weaken. And in speaking about the *Lohengrin* prelude he was completely enthusiastic. It seemed to him "a great invention, admirable in all respects . . . a marvel of instrumentation . . . a masterpiece." [70] In the March from Act II, Berlioz found "a period which perhaps has no equal in music for grandiose impetus." [71]

He made, to be sure, a number of general objections, principally to Wagner's harmonic system and to his excessive repetition of certain motives, but the only work of which he declared he could not appreciate the intent was the *Tristan* prelude. Since it was built on the same plan as that of *Lohengrin*, it puzzled him to understand why it had been put on the same program. Besides, his most attentive hearing could make out "no other theme than a sort of chromatic moan, full of dissonant chords, of which the long appogiaturas that replace the real note only increase the cruelty." [72]

In the remaining paragraphs of his review, Berlioz felt called upon to reiterate his pragmatic creed, favoring freedom, innovation, and expressiveness. If this, he said, was the meaning of the slogan "Music of the future," he was willing to be classed among its practitioners. But if it meant something else — which he outlined — he dissociated himself from it wholly, and holding up his hand said "*Non credo*." [73]

Wagner, seizing the opportunity to prolong the public's notice of himself, affected to feel aggrieved and wrote an open letter which Berlioz

[70] *A Trav.*, 307–9.

[71] *A Trav.*, 310.

[72] *A Trav.*, 311. A famous Wagnerian conductor and commentator, Maurice Kufferath, remarks how striking and musically exact this description is: "The motive . . . must be performed just so." (*830*, 180.) As for the intent of the Prelude as a whole, it is generally admitted that lacking a knowledge of the action, which gives significance to the leitmotives, it is impossible to guess the purport of the piece. If it did not please Berlioz as sound, it *could* not move him as drama. (Hadow: *443*, 306–8; Lavignac: *834*, 235, 242; Henderson: *814*, 216.)

[73] *A Trav.*, 315. For greater detail see next Subchapter.

readily published in the *Débats*. According to it, Wagner also repudiated the music of the future. For this term he substituted "the work of art of the future," which was to fuse all the arts, and in which music would be "supplemented and explained by poetry and pantomime." He wound up with a skillful paragraph saying how much he regretted that an intelligent critic who was also a friend, had mistaken him so badly; that he hoped that Berlioz would "let hospitable France give sanctuary to his lyric dramas"; and that he, Wagner, "awaited with impatience the production of *Les Troyens* — for reasons of affection first, of musical importance second, and lastly because of the special relation which that work must bear" to Wagner's own "ideas and principles." [74]

The letter was a master stroke for putting Berlioz in the wrong. The implications — all misleading as to the facts — were that out of jealousy Berlioz had turned against an old friend; that *Les Troyens*, which was the cause of this treachery, really came out of Wagner's "ideas and principles"; and that Berlioz, if he were a man of honor, would out of his good grace and great power "let" *Tannhäuser* be played. The true musical debate was adroitly shifted to "the work of art of the future," which made the "intelligent critic," Berlioz, look ignorant in addition to spiteful [75] — as if the musical analysis of three overtures and two choral ensembles were irrelevant, and as if the praise he had lavished on the bulk of them were a mere trifle.

The germ had been sown. At the moment, Paris lumped the two men together as excessively Germanic musicians, with Wagner having the better right since he could not choose but be a German. But thereafter Wagner's words brought him returns at compound interest. It persuaded the French Wagnerians of Berlioz' mean and ungrateful conduct, so that it seemed right to dismiss and discredit him. Only a few inquiring minds who had looked up Berlioz' review of the three concerts dared to say: "We have reread the article and we frankly admit that we cannot discover in it that preconceived hostility . . . which some have liked to stress so mightily and even to exaggerate." [76]

It would be equally absurd to exaggerate Wagner's craft. Such a perfect barrage of insinuations, confusions, and imputations can scarcely be deliberately contrived; it is a gift of nature, stimulated by the struggle

[74] *1386*, Feb. 22, 1860.

[75] The evidence of Wagner's and Liszt's and the younger Wagnerians' letters shows that "music of the future" was a phrase they used frequently and seriously as a description of the new product.

[76] *442*, 16–17. Scholarship still took it for granted as late as 1934 that Berlioz "detested" Wagner's music and was "desperately jealous." (*1011*, 232.)

for life. That this was so appears most probable when we read the letter which a few weeks later Wagner wrote Berlioz in somewhat imperfect French:

I have just read your article on *Fidelio:* a thousand thanks to you for it. It is a special kind of joy for me to hear your pure and noble accents of the expression of a soul, of an intelligence which understands so perfectly and takes unto itself the most intimate secrets of a creation by another hero of art. There are times when I am almost more transported by seeing this act of appreciation than by the appreciated work itself, because it bears witness to an uninterrupted chain of intimate relationships binding together the great minds which — thanks to this bond alone — will never fall into misunderstanding.

If I express myself badly, I nevertheless like to think that you will not understand me badly.

Your most devoted
RICHARD WAGNER [77]

Paris, on my birthday.
[May 22, 1860.]

Wagner's impulsive recognition that Berlioz understood Beethoven and that there exists a communion of genius, made it all the harder to fathom Berlioz' unwillingness to join in a movement under Wagner's aegis.[78] Pushed by Princess Metternich and a favoring tide of international affairs, Wagner was about to force the doors of the Paris Opera with his *Tannhäuser,* which he would shortly revise on this account. Drawing haughtily on his friends for his personal needs, he could give himself over to the writing and publicizing of his new large-scale works. He felt energetic and buoyant as one who sees a long series of apparently scattered efforts shaping into a public triumph. And in this generous mood he informed Liszt of the presence in the musical world of only three great equals — Wagner, Liszt, and Berlioz. Unfortunately, Wagner always had to seek Berlioz out and he explained the Frenchman's reluctance to be Holy Ghost in this trinity by the fact of Mme. Berlioz' evil tongue. She was "ruining him" according to this somewhat distant observer who had met her twice; she was reducing the "God" to "a poor devil." [79] Despite this puzzling disappointment Wagner in 1860 could complacently measure the progress he had made in twenty years. For in 1840 he had also been

[77] *239*, II, 281–2. Contrary to an opinion again charging Berlioz with ill-will, he replied cordially the next day. (*Bayreuther Blätter*, 1905, 285, and *298*, 321–2.)

[78] Compare Henry James's description of Nash, the artist in *The Tragic Muse,* who inexplicably refuses to enter the "boats" (*i.e.,* doctrines and systems) of his amazed entourage.

[79] *239*, II, 282.

in Paris, but unknown, unprotected, nearly starving, and rich only in the musical revelation afforded him the preceding autumn by Berlioz' *Romeo and Juliet*. And that debt he had just canceled by his inscription in the score of *Tristan*.

Berlioz' essay on *Fidelio* had been prompted by the revival which Carvalho, urged and aided by Berlioz, had produced on May 5, 1860. But the superb critical statement which aroused Wagner to admiration marked Berlioz' own spiritual revival after an almost mortal crisis: shortly after the Wagner concerts, Berlioz had been telegraphed for from Dauphiné where Adèle, suddenly stricken, was dying. Himself in acute pain, he watched by the sickbed of the one woman who had returned his love in equal measure. He could do nothing but wonder why she, ten years younger than he, happy and beloved by husband and daughters, should be the first to die. He waited until the specialist from Lyon came and declared the crisis past, assuring everyone that the patient would recover. Berlioz returned to Paris. A few days later, on March 2, Adèle was dead.

It hardly mattered then that the conductorship of the Opera went to Dietsch, that of the Conservatoire to Tilmant, that of the Imperial Chapel to a protégé of Auber's. In any circumstances these vacancies due to the death of Berlioz' erstwhile friend Girard would have had value only as supplying an orchestra with which to play "real music." To prestige and power the artist was now indifferent. If Carvalho at the *Lyrique* kept following Berlioz' musical direction as he had so far done, that "position" was enough. The enterprise was successful from box office to press seats, and the manager had just announced *Les Troyens*. At this juncture, however, the directorship of the Opéra-Comique fell vacant and Carvalho, eager for an official post, secured it. Under this "normal" blow Berlioz stood resigned but exhausted. Paris was obviously a squirrel cage in which headway was impossible. Ill again, he could only answer inquiry by saying that he was "dying of his life's work." Even the nighttime afforded him no relief. "I desire only sleep while awaiting something more permanent." [80]

It was from this torpor that *Fidelio* had roused him. A bit of good news — Louis's successful passing of his first examination — combined with some excellent chamber music to restore his threatened equilibrium. For the Baden stage he was plotting a new idea, and meanwhile, at the instigation of his friend, the tenor Roger, he had orchestrated Schubert's

[80] *86*, 614.

Erlkönig; [81] it would worthily supply the want of short works for the summer programs. From the finely wrought and polished score no one could suspect anything of the anxiety, illness, or conflicts in his heart and soul. It is delicate, poignant, full of insight into Schubert's master-piece — a compendium of art concealing itself.

When he returned from Baden, where Schubert and parts of the *Damnation of Faust* had been accompanied by thunder and heat lightning, Berlioz had a new work under way.

Berlioz and Wagner, Then and Now

> His great musical powers are sufficiently evi-
> dent . . . He possesses that rare intensity of
> feeling, that inner fire, and strength of will,
> and faith in himself which compel, move,
> and convince. But . . . these qualities would
> be still better set off if they were joined to
> less striving [*recherche*] and more inven-
> tion, as well as to a greater appreciation of
> certain constituent elements of music.
> — BERLIOZ on Wagner in 1860

The relations between Berlioz and Wagner form such an instructive object lesson in the history of art that they should be assigned as a prob-lem to apprentice critics; not indeed as an exercise in finding right answers, but simply to train the power of holding opposite views of a subject in one steady glance. Those who have reviewed the lives of the two artists have tended to think that one or the other should be blamed, and they have sought a verdict by mixing personal and artistic considerations. Some few, wishing well to both masters after their death, have concluded that here was simply another conflict between geniuses, to be forgotten except as a curiosity. This is M. Boschot's view, following Legouvé, and it is so far correct that it removes from both musicians the odium of vulgar envy. But it leaves a good many significant facts in the dark, together with the artistic bearing of the whole relationship. Hence the need to recon-struct, classify, and judge its shifting incidents over a period of twenty-five years.

[81] It is often stated that this score was never published, or has long been out of print. Compilers of reference books simply copy someone's original error. The score was still in print and on sale in Paris before the late war. (*26.*)

Even before we scan the personal contacts between the two men, one important truth invariably overlooked must be learned, quite simply, from the calendar. Berlioz having been born in 1803 and Wagner in 1813, it is assumed that they were contemporaries in the full sense of the term. This is not so. Berlioz' maturity came early and Wagner's late; the resulting gap means that from the start the pair represented two distinct generations. In 1839, the year of *Romeo and Juliet*, when Wagner at twenty-six had scarcely produced any important work, Berlioz had been a publicly produced composer for fifteen years and had written six of his twelve great scores. He held a leading position in the Paris press and was about to carry his music to Europe. Young Wagner "felt like a schoolboy," acknowledged his elder's maturity and resented it without knowing all the reasons why. Like the gifted student everywhere, he was seeking to capture as an equal the attention of the teacher who is only slightly older — a relation which can be neither submissive, nor competitive, nor spontaneously friendly: it is wholly awkward. This is doubtless why Wagner, having received a kind but not effusive welcome from Berlioz and been accepted by him as a contributor to the *Gazette Musicale*, felt the need to show independence by peppering his articles with strong reservations regarding Berlioz, and even by anonymously printing a very sharp critique about his "character" in a German paper. Thus the "friendship" began.

Twenty years later the gap had widened still farther. Wagner, coming to Paris for his first series of concerts, had also in hand his first unquestionable masterpiece, *Tristan*, but he was still an unplayed master so far as his genuinely great work was concerned. He was an exile from his own country, in debt to everyone and wholly without prospects — outwardly a failure. Berlioz meanwhile had virtually completed his career. The work he had in hand for the Baden season was to be a comedy of farewell, not a further musical revolution. The conclusion is inescapable that Berlioz and his music occupy roughly the first half of the nineteenth century; Wagner's the second half. The fact that they kept meeting and corresponding during the overlapping middle decades mattered artistically to Wagner alone, for Berlioz was never a contemporary of Wagner's distinctive work, whereas Wagner learned and fought and hammered out his creations under the constant pressure of Berlioz' art. Given Wagner's character, this meant friction.

After the first meeting of 1840 in Paris, the two men's orbits intersected several times: first at Dresden in 1843, when Wagner was assistant conductor and was reported by Karl Lipinski as secretly maneuvering against his visiting rival, Berlioz.[1] The latter declined to accept the rumor, and publicly thanked Wagner in the *Débats* for his valuable help. After 1848, when Liszt was musical director at Weimar and Wagner was in exile because of his part in the revolution, he undoubtedly sought to undermine Liszt's faith in *Benvenuto Cellini* and the *Damnation of Faust* — two works which Wagner had neither seen nor heard, but which made him ask, "Why not put on *Lohengrin?*" [2] Wagner then published *Opera and Drama*, which purposed to discredit all of Berlioz' work by suggesting that his "enormous musical intelligence" had been misapplied in the creation of "gigantic machines" supposedly lacking in "human feeling." [3]

Although Berlioz had been shown earlier attacks, and heard rumors of new ones, he took no notice but calmly printed in the *Débats* Liszt's eulogy of *Tannhäuser*. When Liszt further tried to establish an entente between his two friends, Berlioz replied that he kept no memory of Wagner's inimical lines and was ready to accept Wagner's friendship if Liszt would "grease the wheels." [4] The "meshing of gears" took place in London during the concert season of 1855 as related above. But Wagner had hardly left when *The Musical World* republished — very likely *without* Wagner's consent — his denunciation of Berlioz' music.[5]

[1] *M.E.*, *54* and *n.*

[2] To recall what was shown above: the exchange of letters begins on April 7, 1852, when Liszt raps Wagner on the knuckles for criticizing the motives behind his own revival of *Benvenuto Cellini* (*239*, I, 116). Wagner apologizes on Apr. 13 but insists that Liszt's liking for Berlioz is a personal and irrational thing which a third party can best appreciate. (158–9.) On Aug. 23, Liszt praises *Benvenuto* "in spite of all the stupid things current about it." (175.) On Sept. 8, Wagner retorts that he is sorry for Berlioz because he has recast an old work. He adds that he could "save him" by offering him the libretto of *Wieland the Smith*, which Liszt has rejected and Wagner is no longer able to work on. (178.) The next month Wagner again apologizes and says he only meant well to Berlioz. (181.) Meanwhile the attack in *Opera and Drama* had been translated by Fétis.

[3] Saint-Saëns has pointed out the irony of Wagner's making the charge of inhumanity and giantism just when he was beginning to fashion the gigantic *Ring* in which there is not a single human being.

[4] Liszt quoted this letter to Wagner (*239*, I, 255) whereupon Wagner, who wanted a passport for a trip to Paris, named Berlioz to the French authorities as sponsor and guarantor of his own good faith. He apparently had not asked permission of Berlioz direct; instead he begs Liszt to straighten things out: "Greet Berlioz for me — he is a funny customer . . . but he is a noble fellow and all will come out right in the end." (264–5.)

[5] After the London meeting, Wagner tells Liszt: "I confess it would interest me very much to study [Berlioz'] symphonies carefully in full score. Do you possess them and will you lend them to me, or will you go so far as to give them to me? I should accept them gratefully, but should like to have them soon." (*239*, II, 97.)

The following February, Berlioz being at Weimar, Liszt repeated his entreaties and arguments for a tripartite alliance, and it was then that a coolness arose between the two old friends, apparently apropos of *Lohengrin*. Since Berlioz sincerely admired much of it, the discussion was exclusively about its significance and that of Wagner in modern music. Liszt admitted as much later on.[6] At this juncture, unfortunately, the women entered the fray. Mme. Berlioz spoke out of turn and to the wrong people, with a total lack of tact or policy. She conveyed a sense of rivalry which existed only in her mind, as she had done earlier in relation to Félicien David. On the other side, the Princess Sayn-Wittgenstein was no neutral. How she steered a course between her feelings for Liszt and Berlioz and her anti-Wagnerian animus — which Liszt did not share and which Berlioz wished to keep clear of — we can only surmise. The fact remains that henceforth Berlioz corresponded with Liszt through the Princess. It was, as Liszt said, no "silly personal quarrel" but disagreement on the new *ism*, which was already the subject of public debate.[7] Even after the "appalling" arguments at Weimar — as Berlioz called them — he and Liszt continued their mutual good offices, personal and musical.

The next phase of the Berlioz-Wagner conflict is that just reviewed in the first section of this chapter. Wagner reappears in several of his previous guises — full of gratitude and respect in the presentation of his *Tristan* autograph, adroitly mischievous, like a sharp subaltern, in the open letter to Berlioz; impulsively friendly in the note of thanks for the *Fidelio* essay; self-pitying in the complaint to Bülow; and downright condescending in the letter to Liszt. Wagner's close friend Praeger assures us that Wagner felt no conscious enmity toward Berlioz, rather the reverse, and this is borne out by such facts as Wagner's boyish desire to play his *Tristan* to Berlioz as soon as possible: Wagner in 1858 still wanted Berlioz' praise.[8]

[6] ". . . without any silly personal quarrel, the burning question of Wagner's art . . . led to coolness between Berlioz and myself. He did not think that Wagner represented the destiny of Germany's musical drama, surpassing Beethoven and Weber." (*235*, II, 387.) This letter was written in 1884 and dates the difference of opinion from 1864, though its roots go back some few years earlier.

[7] By the end of 1854 Joachim Raff had a thick volume on it ready for the press. It is a curious cultural phenomenon that much of this debate occurred in every country before anyone had heard or seen the scores of Wagner which were at issue.

[8] *239*, II, 193–5. Ernest Newman, whose judgment must carry great weight, corroborates Praeger's belief in Wagner's friendly feelings toward Berlioz (*984*,

Had Berlioz on his side felt vindictive about the past, he had in 1860 a fine chance to deal Wagner a crushing blow: he could have let a colleague publish the words of the *Tristan* autograph with the comment that this amiable "bribe" had been sent the critic before the Wagner concerts; and he could have nullified the point of Wagner's open letter by showing that the work of art of the future which it purported to defend was an entirely unknown and unknowable quantity, since the *Tannhäuser* extracts belonged to an earlier, strictly operatic work, which must be judged as such and on musical grounds alone.

Berlioz contented himself with the reasoned and sober creed he had attached to the equally reasoned and quite sympathetic review of the music. But he made a serious mistake in adding to these a light and fanciful *Non Credo* supposedly representing "the music of the future." The grain of sound objection in it was nothing new nor especially anti-Wagnerian: Berlioz had said the same things twenty years earlier in criticizing Hérold and the Parisian school.[9] Here it spoiled his case and gave Wagner his opening. This, added to Mme. Berlioz' indiscreet words and the world's usual misinterpretation of proud reserve, laid the train for an explosion.[10]

It took place a year later, after the first and second performances of *Tannhäuser* in Paris. The opera, as everyone knows, fell before an organized cabal of Jockey Club and other fashionable hoodlums. Before the *première*, the presence of Liszt in Paris, the excitement of the interminable rehearsals — heard or reported — the anger raised by the thought of his *Troyens* so long refused by the Opera — all conspired to make Berlioz lose his self-command. By an astonishing failure of control over will and mind, he allowed himself to interpret the shouting down of Wagner's music as a symbol of good judgment on the part of the public. On the spur of the moment, he wrote in this vein to his musical friends, the Massarts; and on the next day, more coolly to his son, adding, "I am

II, 295). Against these are the opinions of Richard Pohl (*Reminiscences,* quoted in *952,* VI, 289) and Hanslick (*351,* 381) both of whom were contemporaries, Pohl being a Wagnerian disciple favored by the master.

[9] *M.M.,* 136–7: "The abuse of appoggiaturas, which denatures every chord, gives to the harmony a vague coloring . . . weakens the force of certain dissonances or else augments it to the point of discordance . . . seems to me one of the most unbearable affectations of the Parisian school."

[10] Wagner complains to Liszt on May 22, 1860 that it is always he who has to seek Berlioz out (*239,* II, 281–2). He does not seem to have known how ill Berlioz was and attributes the sick man's unsociability to Marie's interference. Later on, in his autobiography, Wagner preposterously attributed Marie's animus to the gift of a bracelet from Meyerbeer — his *bête noire.* (*245, 721.*)

cruelly avenged." [11] No one knew better than Berlioz how cruelly for the hissed author. That word alone makes the phrase a revelation both of Berlioz' worse and of his better self, for he abhorred cruelty. In the *Débats*, he wrote no review but turned his column over to d'Ortigue, who gave a fair account of the work and deplored the outrageous violence of the public.

Berlioz' alleged "offense against Wagner" thus consisted in two private letters — not published until twenty years after the event — and in abstaining from the usual review. For this last, he had the genuine excuse of being ill and on a musical jury at the same time, as well as the conviction that another hand would be fitter than his. But gossipy journalists interpreted Berlioz' silence as concealing a desire to annihilate Wagner, and they went so far as to compare his act to Pontius Pilate's — as if d'Ortigue had crucified the fallen opera. But Berlioz' expiation for his single lapse from grace was not over, since from the moment that Wagner became a recognized genius and a worshiped master, Berlioz has been represented as a faithless and aggressive friend. It was but a few years ago that in a *Wagner Dictionary*, Berlioz was so to speak defined as "a friend and visitor of Wagner in Paris, afterward his enemy." [12]

In the Wagnerite fever of the nineties, it may have been natural to reverse the historical roles in this way. Wagner's success resembled the triumph of a dictator: all must expect to make obeisance or be shot, and Berlioz was retroactively shot many times over. Reviewing the issues today with a fuller knowledge of all the persons in the drama, the balance of good behavior is seen to hang on Berlioz' side. We start with the premise that neither Berlioz nor Wagner was obligated to like the other, nor his music. Wagner could be ten times as great as he is without having in that matter any *rights*. Brahms, Joachim and others formally turned against Wagner and are not on that account held criminal. [13] Berlioz' "crime" therefore is nonexistent, or rather, the one he committed was against his own finer self and superior intelligence, for a brief instant. In

---

[11] To the Massarts: *Corresp.*, 278–9; to Louis Berlioz: *ibid.*, 279–80.

[12] *1363*, 19.

[13] In the "manifesto" of 1860 published in the Berlin *Echo*. Joachim had broken with Liszt in 1857 in a reaction towards the ideals of Schumann, moved in part by his friendship with Clara, the musician's widow. With Brahms, another youngster who was feeling his oats, the signers of the attack on Liszt formed a center of resistance to Wagnerism, which was thus compelled to close ranks: all who were not for them were against. Though Joachim said he had been "incited" by Berlioz' article of 1860, each party thought Berlioz belonged to the opposite camp. Foreseeing this, no doubt, he had declared his independence in his *Non Credo*.

his direct dealings with Wagner he was always irreproachable: he encouraged him as a beginner, overlooked his gadfly skirmishing, opened two newspapers to his uses, reviewed all his music fairly, purchased his scores for the Conservatoire and sent him his own, and did not come to take sides until Liszt forced the "burning issue."[14] For Mme. Berlioz' cackle he was no more responsible than Liszt was for the Princess's.

Wagner's record is not so clear: he asked help of Berlioz and received it, took several opportunities to damn his efforts, adversely criticized music he did not know, tried to undermine Liszt's affection and regard for an old friend, then himself embraced, cajoled, condescended to that friend, only to end by acting toward him the role of injured party. The cry of "Union Now" which Wagner raised in 1860 in the name of modern music, he might have raised ten years before when Berlioz held the fort alone. But at that time Wagner was trying to divide in order to rule. As Mr. William Wallace, who is no friend to Berlioz, says in his book on Liszt, Wagner, and the Princess: "Wagner feared Liszt and Nietzsche, suppressed Liszt on the platform as a composer but upheld him in a pamphlet and in letters which were too effusive to be sincere . . . It would be intolerable were Liszt to transfer his influence and patronage . . . — to Berlioz, for instance." [15]

In Mr. Wallace's history of what he calls this "inscrutable and not altogether scrupulous trio," namely, Liszt, Wagner, and the Princess, Wagner is made out to be consciously scheming. It is more probable that he displayed the natural cunning and alternation of love and ferocity which he showed in his relations generally. Wagner's great charm was his impulsive, unpremeditated self-seeking. He was only intermittently a moral being, and his idolators of the nineties who were overawed by his "mind" should have found this out from the woolly inconsistency of his words on almost any subject.[16]

This looseness and variability were enough in themselves to keep him

[14] According to some of his French friends, Liszt lived to regret his own "enslavement" to Wagner. (*159*, 221.) But this testimony is by no means precise as to time and context though presumably based on a contemporary diary.

[15] *1031*, 97.

[16] Wagner first venerated Weber as a great master, then during an Italian infatuation turned against him, finally reversing himself again. At one time, Beethoven was "a starting point," but later a dead end. In politics, Wagner praised revolution and the folk, only to abjure democracy as *undeutsch* when he became a prince's protégé. Similarly, Liszt's help changed Wagner's view of so-called program music, which he had damned in Berlioz though he himself had written programs to his own Preludes as well as to Beethoven's works. (*241*, V, 123-98.)

from understanding Berlioz, whose lifelong principles were decided and lucidly expressed from his twenty-second year. It is reported that in a conversation between the two men Wagner was expatiating on the process by which a work of art grows, not from within the sensibility, nor from outside circumstances, but from the sensibility absorbing the outer forms to refashion an independent world. "Yes," said Berlioz, "we call that 'digesting.' " [17] The same cloudiness and prolixity appear in Wagner's successive views of Berlioz' music: it was, by turns, inspired but not sufficiently worked out; then it was contrived with tremendous ingenuity but not inspired; in between, Berlioz was a veritable Napoleon and "the savior of our musical world"; and at last, when Berlioz no longer bothered him by his living reality, Berlioz was beyond criticism; more could be learned "from a single bar of his than from all the works of a Meyerbeer"; he was so great that "no one could have been his master," so great that Wagner reprimanded Felix Mottl for carping at some detail.[18] And among Wagner's unfinished essays there was found the beginning of a tribute to Berlioz taken as the prototype of the great, whom survivors must clear from misunderstanding.[19]

So much for the direct dealings between the two men. One can conclude, like Bülow in old age, that Wagner had been unjust to his elder,[20] or one may take the fatalistic view of Eric Blom that Wagner had a constitutional aversion to feeling grateful,[21] which made him attack his benefactors and say, like a Job in reverse: "Though he trusted me, yet will I slay him." If this is true, Wagner had a lifelong reason for attacking Berlioz, for he borrowed more, and more consistently, from Berlioz than from any other composer. It is known how much Wagner took from Weber, Mendelssohn, Marschner, and Liszt. More recently his debt to Meyerbeer has been fully established,[22] and it is no casual suggestion that "few composers have actually invented less than Wagner. . . . He does not so much sum up the work of others, as Bach does, but rather robs them." [23] These strong words are increasingly justified as one comes to know Berlioz' unfamiliar works. It is not only that Wagner

[17] *283*, 390.
[18] Mottl's own statement in *Revue d'art dramatique*, Jan. 1902, quoted in *307*, 370.
[19] *243*, VIII, 376.
[20] *208*, 363. Ernest Reyer, another good Wagnerian, also declared: "I will never forgive Wagner his unjust conduct toward Berlioz." (*998*, 72.)
[21] *768*, 126–7.
[22] *901*, 155 ff.; *719*, 202.
[23] *719*, 206–7.

lifted much-needed melodies, but more important, as Weingartner points out, that he appropriated "atmosphere" entire, that is to say, the intent, the substance, and the suggestive detail. A comparison of *Tristan* with certain parts of the *Romeo and Juliet* symphony shows that Wagner was struck by Berlioz' idea of rendering a love scene orchestrally by means of the gradual amplification of an initial "call" or unsatisfied musical start. He took from Part II the very notes of the call, kept the atmospheric effect of the rising clarinet scales; completed the expression of passion by the turn which occurs in Berlioz' Adagio, and added as well the rhythm and color of Berlioz' later death-scene ("Invocation") and so created his own world-famous Prelude and *Liebestod*.[24]

Undoubtedly the working out of this composite scene is Wagner's own; and its fulness, richness, and solidity are to some listeners undeniable proof that Wagner had the right and even the duty to pick up the materials wherever he chose. Yet the acceptability of the rehandling is no test of its artistic rightness. A more restricted example will make this clear: in the *Symphonie Fantastique* Berlioz opens a pastoral movement with woodwinds in dialogue over a tremolo of strings. The melody, color, and pauses of the music are vividly "characteristic": the passage fulfills a conception of nature and defines a mood of pensive loneliness. In the opening of the third act of *Tristan*, this mood, melody, and dramatic character are reproduced with minor modifications. Now no one questions the complete validity of Berlioz' original. But the damage done to it by Wagner's re-use in another context, which being operatic is for most listeners more explicit, is the damage which results from any confusion. It constitutes in fact a test case of universal import for criticism. Just as we found ourselves needing a Natural History of Tears for judging certain forms of social behavior, so we need here some Principles of Plagiarism.[25] It is granted that the arts live by tradition, borrowing, influence, and rehandling of themes. Swift and Stendhal and Zola lifted

[24] In his perceptive though by no means pro-Berliozian article on "The Influence of Berlioz on Wagner," Mr. Gerald Abraham points out how the score of *Romeo and Juliet* supplied Wagner in these ways. "The more one studies the '*Scène d'Amour*' the more firmly one feels convinced that it exercised a very deep influence on the creation of the Wagnerian masterpiece." (*407, 245.*) And he shows not only that the Wagnerian theme expressing passion was "directly derived" from the Berliozian melody, but that all who have borrowed the same element from Wagner are indebted to that original creation. Wagner himself, we learn from another source, called Berlioz' love-tune "the most beautiful musical theme of the century." (*275, 110.*)

[25] Ambrose Bierce supplied the opening definition: "Plagiarism – a coincidence compounded of a discreditable priority and an honorable subsequence." (Devil's Dictionary.)

technical passages from other writers, Shakespeare versified Plutarch, and Byron confessed to snapping up good ideas everywhere. But Swift, Zola, Stendhal and Byron are not primarily known for the things they took. They worked with originality upon and around what they borrowed. Shakespeare takes legitimate possession of historical or legendary plots by introducing events, characters, and speeches that no one had ever dreamed of, and that dwarf the conceptions he starts from.

In the same way, Berlioz for the most part chose his dramatic occasions, his "plots," from tradition, but he constantly revivified them by treating certain parts in a unique manner or by adding new parts. We remember how he chose elements from the Memoirs of Cellini to lead up to the telling episode of the casting of the statue. Now comes the simple test: when Wagner was attracted to the same general theme, his satisfaction with the first handling made him adapt it to a German historical setting: the chief incidents and ideas of *Die Meistersinger von Nürenberg* are transposed from *Benvenuto Cellini ou les Maîtres-Ciseleurs de Florence.*[26] This could be called a proper rehandling only on condition that no one supposed Wagner was the first to present this artistic allegory in the form and detail that we know.

Wagner's music for *Die Meistersinger* is of course unlike that of *Benvenuto*. But the confusion that exists as to which element belongs to whom is the deeply disturbing thing in the Berlioz-Wagner case. The *Meistersinger* example — like that of the Euphonia-Bayreuth parallel — lies on the intellectual or dramatic side. On the musical, the similar interweaving of pure Berlioz with materials that Wagner borrowed from all sides is even worse, for it blurs the distinctive outline of a music as nearly *sui generis* as it is possible to be. The precision and connotations of the original are spoiled when a fine passage of the *Symphonie Fantastique* comes up as the "Thought Motif" in *Siegfried;* when the rhythm and orchestration of the *Hamlet* March reappear for Siegfried's funeral; when the Prologue of *Romeo and Juliet* is distended into the plan of making *Rheingold* the prologue and thematic catalogue of the *Ring;* when the metrical figure of the *Apothéose* supplies the rhythm of the *Kaisermarsch;* when Dido's death-scene dramatically anticipates Brünnhilde's, though written in a different idiom; when the Sylphs in the *Damnation of Faust* re-enchant us in *Parsifal*, whose Prelude begins like the *Kyrie* of the *Requiem*. It is not only *Tristan* but the revised *Tannhäuser* that reminds

[26] Wagner did not know the *music* of Berlioz' opera when he condemned it, but he knew about the drama from Liszt as well as from the libretto published in 1838 and again in 1852.

us of *Romeo and Juliet;* in the first-named, the love philter music carries echoes of a passage in *Lélio;* and some of the sombre foreboding music in *Die Walküre* recalls most forcibly *Les Troyens.*

The crisscrossing is endless because the normal historical sequence has been exactly reversed: it is a world familiar with Wagner that keeps discovering limbs of him in unfamiliar and "unsatisfactory" Berlioz. Let a good Wagnerian hear Parts II, III, and V of the *Romeo and Juliet* symphony and he will feel as if mystified by double talk. Each frequent suggestion of a familiar phrase leads to unfamiliar and hence vexatious endings; in order to "place" the atmosphere his mind hesitates between *Tannhäuser* and *Tristan,* whose styles he has hitherto felt as distinct; nowhere is the Berliozian texture right. Magical and "quite Wagnerian" moments occur, but passion does not appear to work up any great head of steam; melody, harmony, and dynamics do not sweep him along in the old congenial rhythm, and he is left "unsatisfied."

Thus the good Wagnerian, who is perfectly right as far as his auditory habits take him. But his "habits" beg the question at issue, namely whether the ideas of Berlioz (as well as those of Liszt, Schumann, Weber, or Mendelssohn) were incomplete and mismanaged.[27] Only the answer to this question can decide that of significant priority, for in art what matters is the exploitation of the idea. If *Benvenuto* muffs his great recital in Act II, then Wagner must take the phrase and idea and give us Tannhäuser's Rome narration. The critic will approve and we shall be the gainers — provided two conditions are fulfilled: we must first prove the "if" and not simply equate "later" with "better." And second we must not play fast and loose with the value of originality. We cannot say that priority is trivial when Wagner borrows, and then credit him with "innovations of genius" when we happen not to know whence he took them. A new conception, dramatic or musical, is actually a rare thing, and if it is well executed it casts glory on no one but its maker.

Which brings us back to the major issue, whether Berlioz needed to be "improved." Wagner had something important to say on this subject. He felt that Berlioz needed to be "completed and fulfilled by a poet as a man needs a woman," and he offered himself to be that poet.[28] One may speculate upon the incestuous birth that might have resulted had Berlioz known of this offer and accepted it. But the impulse on Wagner's part

[27] The critic is in no doubt when, being familiar with *The Flying Dutchman,* he hears Weber's infrequent *Oberon;* nor is Mr. Eric Blom in calling Wagner's *Faust* overture "very Schumannesque." The somewhat neglected symphonies of Schumann will repay study as repositories of music that anticipates both Wagner and Liszt. [28] *239,* I, 177–8.

defines the difference between the two artists. On first hearing *Romeo and Juliet,* Wagner felt at once ravished and repelled, wearied and puzzled. It was only much later, he adds, "that I succeeded in clearly grasping and solving this problem." [29] In retrospect the problem seems simple enough: Wagner yielded to the spell of Berlioz' dramatic symphony but wanted more visual or emotional indications to go with it.[30] This is what Wagner the poet would have given Berlioz to "complete" him. Fortunately Wagner completed himself and left Berlioz in his original unity.

This then was the great split between them: Berlioz contended that music should either stand alone, or, in any union with poetry and spectacle, remain supreme; Wagner wanted every art to bring its special quality to an alloy superior to each. As dramatists both were drawn to kindred subjects [31] but Berlioz holding music to be an end in itself, determined to treat only certain chosen situations in a compact, allusive, and self-sufficient manner; Wagner, considering music a means, demanded that poetry and acting establish the continuity and explicitness he expected of drama. The dispute was a recurrence of the earlier difference of views between Gluck and Mozart, clearly stated in Berlioz' objections to Gluck's theories.[32]

In our own day the great Bach authority, Albert Schweitzer, has broadened the debate to cover modern music generally. He distinguishes between "poetic music, which deals more with ideas," and "pictorial

---

[29] *245,* 235.

[30] Hence his famous attempt to programmatize the *Romeo* love-scene: "I now had to hold on to scenic motives not present before my eye, nor even so much as indicated in the program." He goes on seesawing between approval and condemnation: "We have been speaking of one of this gifted musician's happiest inspirations, however, and my opinion of his less happy ones might easily set me dead against this line of work if, on the other hand, it had not brought to light such perfect things as his . . . Scenes in the Country, his Pilgrims' March, etc., which show us to our amazement what may be accomplished in this mode." (*243,* III, 249–50.)

[31] Compare *Tristan und Isolde* and *Romeo and Juliet; Die Meistersinger* and *Benvenuto Cellini; The Nibelungen* and *Les Troyens:* the tragedy of love and death, the drama of artistic integrity, and the epic of duty and supernatural heroism.

[32] *A Trav.,* 157 ff. and see above, Chapter 23. Mozart wrote: "Why do Italian comic operas please everyone in spite of their miserable libretti? — Just because music reigns supreme . . . An opera is sure of success when . . . the words are written solely for the music . . . If we composers were always to stick so faithfully to our rules (which were very good at a time when no one knew better) we should be concocting music as unpalatable as their libretti." (Oct. 13, 1781: *219,* III, 1150–1.)

music, which deals more with pictures, ... Beethoven and Wagner belong more to the poets; Bach, Schubert, and Berlioz more to the painters." [33] We see at once that Schweitzer's labels for the two kinds of musician are dangerously ambiguous, but his further words remove the doubt: "Bach is the most consistent representative of pictorial music . . . , Bach's musical phrase being only the verbal phrase recast in tone . . ." [34] Berlioz had written: "In its union with drama, or with words to be sung, music must always be in direct relation with the feeling expressed, with the character of the singing personage, often even with the accent and the vocal inflexions which one feels to be the most natural to speech." [35] Schweitzer goes on about Bach: "His music is not so much melodic as declamatory. . . . The musical drama is for him a succession of dramatic pictures. . . . Bach is a dramatist . . . [who] . . . seizes upon the pregnant moment that contains the whole event, and depicts it in music. That is why the opera had so little attraction for him." [36] No better words could be found to describe the dramatic theory and practice of Berlioz, and Schweitzer himself draws the parallel: "Even when . . . [Berlioz] is writing for the stage . . . we see the thing simultaneously in a double form — on the stage and in the music. . . . Wagner conceives nature through his emotions, Bach — in this respect like Berlioz — through his imagination . . . the secular cantatas [of Bach] are veritable nature poems." [37]

Here again one feels that Schweitzer's terminology needs revising, for we have got from "poetic music" which is Wagner's way, to "nature poems" by Bach, who is called a "pictorial musician." The truth is that "picture" and "seeing" are the wrong words throughout. In listening to Bach and Berlioz we do not *see* anything, we *realize* through our imagination, which — as was shown in Chapter 14 — is an inward sense accessible through any of the outer senses. Schweitzer gives an illustration by which we may test the truth of this. He is speaking of the second stanza of Bach's great cantata *Wachet auf:* "With this [dance melody] the chorale melody is combined dissonantly, as if it had nothing to do with it: the cry of the watchman strikes into the music of the procession. In order that this may have its proper rural quality, it is written for the strings

[33] *1009*, II, 21.

[34] *1009*, 26.

[35] From the 1860 Credo: *A Trav.*, 312.

[36] *1009*, II, 26, 41. Schweitzer is of course dealing with the choral works, and chiefly the cantatas.

[37] *1009*, II, 42, 43. The same remark about Berlioz' "operas" has independently been made by many observers, as we repeatedly saw above.

unisono with an accompaniment of the contrabasses. The procession arrives, the Gloria is sung, the foolish virgins are left outside. Not until Berlioz shall we meet with any dramatic-pictorial music comparable to this . . ." [38] Perfectly true. Change the subject and the orchestration and you have the union of the students' song with that of the soldiers in the *Damnation of Faust*. But neither in Bach nor in Berlioz is the intention *pictorial* — any more than the result — since evidently a man blind from birth could fully realize for himself the simultaneity, dissonance, and contrast of elements.

What we must say then is that Bach and Berlioz use music for *objectified drama*, whereas Wagner is more usually *subjective and rhapsodical*. He himself says that the thing he calls tone painting *without* a visible counterpart is "the obvious last stage of the evolution of absolute instrumental music," but that "the best and most exalted tone painting addresses itself to the feeling instead of to the imagination, that is, where the external object of the musical picture is simultaneously made visible to the hearer." [39] Allowing for inevitable distortion through words, we conclude that Wagner wanted to put the person or object physically on the stage and utter his feelings about it,[40] whereas Bach and Berlioz were always bent on getting rid of the visual object and seeking to re-create its essence in sound. When they create a number of such essences or "musical objects" and combine them intelligibly, they have made drama out of music alone; the stage fittings can be swept into the discard. This is why, once we know the occasion of Berlioz' dramatic scenes, we want no actors, costumes, or gesticulations. Even in the opera house, the *Benvenuto* finale on Piazza Colonna or the Royal Hunt and Storm in *Les Troyens* are action-in-imagination.

There are limits to the Bach-Berlioz technique; it will not suit any subject taken at random. For one thing, as Schweitzer points out in Bach, "the whole expressiveness lies in the theme," not in circumstantial "effects," hence there is such a thing as "Bach's musical language," which it is the duty of the executant as much as of the critic to learn, for it confines itself to "characterizing . . . a sequence of a few plastic scenes. . . ." [41] In the second place, this dramatic art respects the properties of its medium.

---

[38] *1009*, II, 248.

[39] *243*, II, 332 and *241*, IV, 234.

[40] Wagner's statement of 1851 concerning his later works is clear: "The emotional contents . . . were to be rendered in such a fashion that not the melodic expression *per se*, but the expressed Emotion should rouse the interest of the listener . . . melody [was] only . . . the most expressive vehicle for an emotion already plainly outlined in words." (*243*, I, 372.)

[41] *1009*, II, 43, 52, 39.

As Berlioz said of the *Flying Dutchman* overture: "Here is already manifested the tendency of Wagner and his school to disregard *sensation* and to see only the poetic or dramatic idea to be expressed, without considering whether the expression of this idea compels the composer to go outside the limits of music." Berlioz therefore agrees with Wagner as to the expressive purpose of dramatic music, but he regards as binding the claims of pure sound and musical idea.[42] These must not be sacrificed to message, however noble or passionate. By this criterion alone Wagner's repetition of leitmotives would stand condemned.[43]

Consider now Wagner's preparation for the "common problem" to which he and Berlioz offered opposite solutions. The gap between their years of maturing is here again significant. The century with which Berlioz grew up was, as Romanticism implies, at once lyrical and dramatic, that is, it was strongly individualistic and also enamored of multiplicity and mass movement. It produced many lyricists in verse and in song and it also revived Shakespeare as the dramatist par excellence. Yet except for Shelley's *The Cenci* and Büchner's *Death of Danton*, the period did not produce any great plays. Every other literary form, rather, absorbed the tensions of struggle or conflict as a revivifying tonic, and incorporated dramatic devices into itself. In Romantic art drama is to be found as it were distributed: it occurs as a quality instead of as a genre.

This fact, as was shown above, is most vividly illustrated in music. The lieder of Schubert and Schumann and Beethoven's great songs fulfill the intention already evident in Mozart, of making homogeneity of texture yield to characterization. After Mozart, the next step is the union of contrasts in say, *Der Erlkönig* or *An die ferne Geliebte*. On the same principle Beethoven used soloists, recitatives, and internal reminiscences in his Ninth symphony, enlarging and making more explicit the dramatic elements of the instrumental form. One may find other "lessons" in the Ninth but this is obviously the one that the new generation found when the work was still a mystery and a challenge: it fused the *musical* arts and made possible a new kind of *dramma per musica*, symphonic in texture and in form; vocal (melodic, though not virtuoso) in substance; and dramatic in conception and effect.

The German composers among whom Wagner grew underwent some-

---

[42] *A Trav.*, 307. In the Credo he stated the hierarchy: "sound and sonority rank below the idea; the idea ranks below sentiment or passion" (*Ibid.*, 312); which of course does not eliminate the importance of sound. "Idea" is to be taken here as *musical* idea; "passion" represents the dramatic or psychological element.   [43] See below.

thing of Beethoven's influence and produced works of similar though less concentrated purport. Mendelssohn's overtures and oratorios and Schumann's and Schubert's symphonies exploited Beethoven's dramatic idiom and occasionally added to its vocabulary; Weber profited too, but was most at home in the theater, being also a conscious disciple of eighteenth-century doctrine about the fusion of the arts in a perfected opera. Finally, Meyerbeer adapted with great skill all the gains of modern dramatic music to the demands of the current theater, subordinating music once again to pageantry. The thing seen either "explained" the musical development or the music "underlined" the action: in the *Huguenots* the conspirators of the Saint Bartholomew come on with a sinister brass band at their tail. Though one might think that this "effect" had only to be seen to be disbelieved, its principle of musical labeling, when adapted by a still greater artist, was to have magical consequences.

After half a generation of Meyerbeer and a full generation of Berlioz' influence, Wagner advanced his own solution. He had long recognized the inadequacy of operatic conventions, the emptiness of operatic subjects and the poverty of operatic lyricism. He had pondered the lesson of Beethoven, both at first hand and as expounded by Berlioz. He had heard the latter's four symphonies under the composer's direction, and the decisive shock had been succeeded by the dissatisfaction he felt at not seeing action nor following a poem while the music unfolded its impalpable truths. Wagner was first and foremost a man of the theater and his disquisitional turn of mind was repelled by Berlioz' intense allusiveness. He repudiated him as incomplete, declared Beethoven a terminal point, and took up the opera where Meyerbeer had left it.

The Wagnerian system was not hastily conceived; it came out of much reading and writing. For like all the men of his spiritual generation — the mid-century Realists — Wagner was reacting against Romantic variety and seeking a Rule. Like them too, he found it by skipping the immediate past and harking back to the thought of the later eighteenth century. The *Gesamtkunstwerk* is a rationalist notion which was fully expounded before 1760,[44] and which appeals to common sense in place of the imagination. As Dryden, coming after Shakespeare, had said, "when we hear it, our eyes, the strongest witnesses, are wanting." [45]

[44] *848*, 168.
[45] *Essay on Dramatic Poesy.* He was but repeating one of Ben Jonson's objections to the too-imaginative Shakespeare. In striking parallel, Hebbel begins to veer away from Shakespeare, and to call for a "drama of ideas" in 1843–1844 — the time of Romanticism's "failure," signalized by Hugo's unsuccessful *Burgraves.*

In Wagner's reformed opera, moreover, the librettos would be poems of his own making, written in the spirit that animated Mozart in *The Magic Flute* — the desire to create through legend or allegory a spectacle both popular and religious. Historical subjects such as Meyerbeer and the Italians had used were too limiting, and by the 1850's the charm of local color had begun to fade. In addition, Wagner "rediscovered" thematic recall [46] and cast the short instrumental theme in the double role of musical bond (in the symphonic development) and dramatic signpost (in the development of the play). It was the logical extreme of Realism to weld a common object or idea with a musical phrase, in order that musical discourse might lose its inarticulateness without losing its power.

Music has always depended on "links of reminiscence," and Wagner was working in a tradition like everyone else, but the spirit of system was something new that he and the times found natural and necessary. One properly speaks of Wager*ism*, and its concomitance with Darwinism and Marxism is not fortuitous: the spirit of system and the rhetoric of science carried all before them. Their three greatest prophets proclaimed ultimate syntheses in the name of Solid Reality and patient learning.

Certainly no one had ever had to acquire such an apparatus of information for the enjoyment of any art as was required by Wagner's system, yet within fifteen years of Ludwig II's conversion to it, all educated Europeans were conscientiously cramming. Printed guides, magazines, societies, schools, and lectureships flourished; "leitmotif" was a new word in every language and the habit everywhere accepted of being *led* by motives not only through music but through literature, philosophy, and religion. By the massiveness of his demands and the royal power he drew on to meet them, Wagner seemed to have vindicated the life of art in a business society, and salvaged the unproductive assets of his predecessors in dramatic music. And he did this, as business would expect, by ruthless destruction first, then by reissuing under a new name the shares he had picked up at a discount. Finally he rode on the wave of Germany's success, espousing, like Marx, a nationalism inconsistent with his claim to universality.

Such was the Wagnerian *coup d'état*, inside and outside music. It founded a powerful regime whose pervasive doctrine has proved a stumbling block to many critics — some saying, quite rightly, that without

[46] He relates that the idea struck him while composing *The Flying Dutchman* that similar sentiments should bring back a similar musical phrase. (*243*, I, 367–73.) The idea, used with less absolutism, had already "struck" Weber and Berlioz, whose *idée fixe* in the *Fantastique* plays just such a role.

Berlioz the work of Wagner, Liszt, and Strauss could not have been; others maintaining with equal rightness that Wagner and Berlioz must stop being compared because their works and their philosophies are utterly opposed each to each. The monstrous conclusion from these two truths is that the two artists form a pair of Siamese twins who do not match. When one adds the undoubted fact that Berlioz' music and Wagner's do not sound alike, although Wagner's orchestration, melody, and atmosphere draw heavily on Berlioz, the confusion is complete.

It is this predicament which justifies the backward glance at the position as it stood in 1860, before the issue had become confused, first, through a long period of unopposed Wagnerism, and next, through a purging of that excess, the result of which has been to strip Wagner of his paraphernalia and to leave him a maker of tone poems for the concert hall.[47]

Berlioz' outlook was no less inclusive than Wagner's but it was above all antidoctrinaire, antipedantic, antiparaphernalia: "My musical creed," he had written to Lobe in 1853, "is in what I have done and what I have not done." [48] His declaration of 1860, precipitated by Wagner's theorizing, was pragmatically open to novelty: "Music today is in the strength of youth; it is emancipated and free. . . . Many old rules have been cast aside; they were made either by inattentive observers or by routine minds for other routine minds: new needs of the spirit, heart, and sense of hearing call for new attempts . . . many forms are too worn out to be of further use . . . *Everything*, in effect, *is good*, or *everything is bad*, according to the use made of it and according to the reason that brings about that use." [49]

Such flexibility could obviously not sustain the onslaught of an aggressive system. There was no Berlio*zism*, and none was possible. He rejected systems as fettering and falsifying: he knew that Gluck's theory — that of the Enlightenment — was misleading, and he could foresee that Wagner's would prove similarly delusive. Besides, he found it inadmissible that a man should seek to incarnate the whole future of music with his music of the future. Wagner's quibble about planning an "*artwork* of the future" did not change the implication, which was that after a certain time there would be only one kind of work of art, one artist — Wagner — and therefore one music — his. Social and artistic Darwinism soon made this seem

[47] Condensed at that. See Mr. Stokowski's "syntheses" of whole operas in instrumental form, which are available on records.

[48] See above, Chapter 22.

[49] *A Trav.*, 312.

plausible, but Berlioz was never taken in. He knew there were many musics, many forms surviving concurrently, and we now share his convictions.

In the third place — and this was most important — Berlioz had purely musical objections to Wagner's work, which cut as deep as those Wagner advanced in reverse. Berlioz' criticisms were of long standing and were not the less penetrating for being succinctly expressed. On hearing *The Flying Dutchman* in 1843, he had found "the ideas too far apart and the gaps filled in with too much padding." Intent on "sweating out needless tissue," Berlioz deemed Wagner's repetitions unendurable. In 1860, he felt that they marred the *Tannhäuser* overture: "When the choral theme reappears, this theme being broad and slow, the violin figure which accompanies it to the end is necessarily repeated with a terrible persistence for the hearer. It has already been heard twenty-four times in the andante; it is now heard in the peroration of the allegro one hundred and eighteen times. This *ostinato*, or rather this indefatigable figure thus occurs one hundred and forty-two times in the Overture. Is it not perhaps too much? It reappears often again in the course of the opera, which makes me suppose that an expressive meaning is ascribed to it, which is connected with the action and which I cannot infer." [50]

Berlioz had put his finger on the weak spot in Wagner's solution of the dramatic problem. The day of thematic program books had not dawned, and Berlioz could not guess the great educational effect of such repetitions. But he perceived that the weight laid on these short motives was a threat to melody, since it tended to reduce a piece to a network of "expressive accents." [51] The themes were, to be sure, artfully and solidly woven together but the result, for Berlioz, suggested a willful impoverishment of the resources available to the dramatic composer. Not that Berlioz wanted every piece to make use of every resource. The *Lohengrin* prelude which he thought a masterpiece, had "no real phrase properly so called, but the chord progressions are melodious, enchanting, and interest does not flag for a moment." [52]

In short, from Berlioz' point of view, Wagner's new "artwork" meant the revival of an abandoned heresy; it was giving new life to Gluck's "impious theory" that music must be the handmaiden of the poet, and that poet, actor, and scene designer were needed to bestow power and status

[50] *A Trav.*, 309. Wagner must have anticipated this objection in part, for he wrote programs to introduce three of his preludes.

[51] *S.W.*, 30.

[52] *A Trav.*, 309. See a similar comment on the *Don Giovanni* overture which Berlioz revered: *A Trav.*, 305.

on the art of sound. Berlioz did not know Wagner's later works but we can easily infer what he would have felt about some of the Wagnerian devices for realizing the *Gesamtkunstwerk:* overwhelming voice under an orchestral *continuo;* neglecting rhythm, avoiding choral ensembles and concerted singing for lifelikeness; substituting a steadily speechlike declamation for the three distinct forms of song — melody, *chant récitatif,* and recitative; setting up a repertory of labels to identify inexpressive themes; and repeating these fragments so tirelessly that any character they might acquire by association was chewed out of them as by the reiteration of a common word.[53]

The Wagnerian system, moreover, did not conduce to artistic economy. Had Berlioz known Wagner's later orchestration he would have found it excessive in its proportion of winds to strings.[54] As it was, he considered Wagner intemperate in his use of dissonance and chromatic harmony. On this point Berlioz' ideas were also of long standing, bred on a dislike of appoggiatura and enharmony as well as on knowledge of what would "come through" in performance. It was always the excess, not the thing itself that repelled Berlioz, any effect good or bad being subject to the law of diminishing returns: he praises upper pedals in Gluck and Beethoven, in spite of the resulting double and triple dissonances, because they are sparingly used and well motivated. He himself did not hesitate to write very bold dissonances and modulations in *Les Troyens,* but wished to save up such *grands moyens* in order to give them the grandest effect by contrast. He preferred, so to speak, the war of movement, concentrating all his forces at a given instant, to the Wagnerian war of massive barrage and attrition.

* * *

[53] 717, II, 608. Gurney tersely characterized the central principle of Wagner's *Opera and Drama* as "the prosaic fallacy that the essence of music is vague namable expressiveness, instead of definite unnamable expressiveness." (*812,* 190.) If this seems exaggerated, consider this passage taken at random from a modern handbook to the *Ring,* which explicitly disavows philosophy and stresses the musical side of the drama:

"*Siegfried,* I. iii. med. A difficult allusion. Mime is trying to describe concrete terrors. The motive now under analysis is heard, along with the fire-motives (Nos. 3 and 4). Now, the greatest terror so far known is that afforded by the fire around Brunnhilde. If, then, the music may refer back to that fire, it makes quite good sense, while 'Brunnhilde's sleep' makes nonsense. And the motive *can* easily present the idea of the fire in the first instance, at the end of *Walküre,* but it presents it there from Brunnhilde's side — as a protection; in *Siegfried,* from the outside — as a terrifying thing. (The alternative is to regard the motive as referring generally to Brunnhilde, from whom alone Siegfried *is going to* learn fear. But who on earth could think of this before the third Act?" (*790,* 24.)   [54] See Gevaert (*805,* 246 ff.).

The summing up leaves both artists justified, for the conflict between them is only another form of the irreducible conflict between Heart and Imagination, where Heart means directly induced feeling, the warmth of the orator which communicates itself to the hearer *about* some object of discourse; whereas Imagination means passion aroused by awareness of the expression-as-object. In music this object may be likened to the work not of an orator but of a mime, whose effort has gone into making his ideas and sensations seem as concrete as the stage props which he chooses to do without. Thus to Berlioz the "complete work of art" would err by trying to make one work of several arts all mangled in their juxtaposition, and so failing to stretch the full powers of any one constituent; while to Wagner, Berlioz' very stretching of the powers of music to their utmost appeared as a histrionic conception inimical to beauty. Wagner wanted Berlioz' music to be less intellectual, less "characteristic"; Berlioz on his side disliked Wagner's "musicality," by which he meant the garrulous lyricism which like a rich caressing voice envelops and Wagnerizes every object and idea and induces a general rather than a particular excitement.

The two understood each other to this extent that their objections singled out the distinctive traits which keep them apart. Berlioz versus Wagner means the definite as against the indefinite, the self-aware impulse as against the headlong systematic drive, the compact as against the massive, the sinewy as against the muscular. We can recognize Berlioz' body and soul in his fondness for pizzicato and Wagner's in his love of tremolo; Berlioz in his rhythms, Wagner in his blurring of rhythm. The one builds long steady crescendos and uses repetition in the mood of insistent anguish and self-mortification — as in his monotonies of grief. The other repeats in fulfillment of his system and as if from an inability to tire — like his mounted Valkyries. Nor does he tire of climaxes, which recur and beat down intellectual resistance like the waves of the sea.[55] Berlioz was a melodist and like Bach his "expressiveness was in the theme"; Wagner worked chiefly with motives scarcely expressive in themselves and gave them significance by a one-to-one connection with persons or ideas.

Both tendencies had their dangers. By his overextension of melodic variation and "delay" Berlioz ran the risk of seeming cryptic and disjointed; Wagner with his mottoes ran the risk of becoming mechanical and fulsome. One may admire Berlioz and Wagner equally, as does Maurice Emmanuel in his profound study of the Language of Music, and

[55] Wagner: "the bottomless sea of harmony"; Berlioz: "the wonderful architecture of sounds." (*Soirées* 13th) *Eves.*, 172.)

like him, admit that the Wagnerian leitmotif tends to the diminishing of music's significance.[56] Both products are artistically right in relation to their distinct premises, and what is equally important, in relation to temperamental preferences rooted in our minds and bodies. It is not even necessary to assume a radical incompatibility of tastes corresponding to each esthetic, provided the standards implied by either are not used in adverse judgment of the other's fruits. We can today accept both Berlioz and Wagner, or parts of each, in proportion to our intellectual and emotional self-control in the face of things at once contradictory and overlapping.

Just as there may be born Wagnerites and born Berliozians, there will always be those to whom Liszt's middle course appears the most pleasing of the three. Berlioz' companion of 1830 had been "converted" by the writings of Wagner, yet had not couched his own ideas in the new form. The symphonic poem is like Bach's and Berlioz' music drama in that it relies on music alone to present a "sequence of plastic scenes"; it is Wagnerian in its "grammar and syntax," that is, in its development by the transformation of short themes. But Liszt's themes seek to be expressive as do Berlioz', just as Liszt's dramatic subjects parallel those that Berlioz found appropriate for musical treatment.[57] As to form, Berlioz' orchestral song *La Captive* may have suggested the plan of founding successive sections on alterations of a single musical idea.

Liszt's contribution has not satisfied all critics any more than have the principles of Berlioz or Wagner, and the public has been even cooler than the critics.[58] Yet in the textbooks, Liszt ranks as the creator of a new form, and is sometimes credited with having carried through the structural revolution that Berlioz only hinted at. One detects something paradoxical

[56] Unlike the recall of themes in Bach, Weber, or Berlioz, the Wagnerian motto "has no general or abstract significance. The link which connects it with a person or event is circumstantial and the relation between the sign and the thing signified can only be explained by the will of the composer to have it so. Wagner carried the system to its last consequence, including its overuse. His belief in the need to label his characters and their slightest doing leads him to multiply his themes . . . until they begin to lose part of their meaning." (717, II, 608.)

[57] Besides *Faust*, it is apparent that *Hamlet*, *Tasso*, the *Mountain* Symphony, the *Heroïde Funèbre*, and the *Christus*, parallel the subjects Berlioz chose for himself some two decades earlier. Liszt always acknowledged this inspiration and dedicated his *Faust* symphony to him with an explicit reference to the *Damnation*.

[58] For the best modern view one must go to Mr. Sacheverell Sitwell's *Liszt*, London, 1934. (*1011*.)

in the praise, which shows once again that the study of nineteenth-century dramatic music is still in a rudimentary stage. It appears, for instance, that whereas in Berlioz "the outline of the old form is almost always visible, fettering his music, Liszt wanders away from this form and thus often gives his work the character of improvisation." [59] This seems hardly a recommendation, but the critic goes on: "He starts directly from the poetical subject, from the program, and takes it alone as guide." [60] How such a procedure establishes a new form not fettering to the music, it would be hard to say. When we turn to the musical material itself, we are likely to conclude, with a sympathetic student of the subject that "Liszt's plan — suggested, I fancy, by his improvisatory powers — was to take a short but powerful phrase, and by . . . alteration of the relative length of the notes, convert it into other phrases of widely different character . . . one theme rarely [has] a second to act as a foil to it, but is merely repeated again and again with different embroidery. This inability to make it throw out branches and continue itself is the one serious weakness in all Liszt's original work." [61]

If this is the flaw in Liszt's music, it does not vitiate his dramatic intentions nor the abstract plan of the symphonic poem. This last, as Mr. Gray has remarked, is "as purely musical a form as the fugue, which similarly consists in the development of one single main theme." [62] Wagner too found good arguments, sincere or not, in behalf of his friend's symphonic poems, even though these arguments contradicted those by which he had proved the futility of Berlioz' *genre instrumental expressif*. The three conceptions and their results can now be compared and judgment rendered in the words of the critic who has paid them most attention:

> To Liszt is due the credit for the invention of a new form . . . in which a single theme takes the place of the former duality or multiplicity, and serves as the material out of which the whole work is constructed. . . . In this he was to a certain extent anticipated by Berlioz' employment of . . . a representative theme dominating the entire work. . . . Liszt's choice of name . . . was somewhat unfortunate, for it inevitably suggests the intrusion into music of alien principles derived from literature. . . . There is actually very little illustration in Liszt's symphonic

[59] *754*, 71.
[60] *754*, 71. If the essay on Berlioz' *Harold* symphony can be taken as representing Liszt's best thought, it would seem that his intention was as far from propping up music by program as it was from making poetry and music run in harness *à la* Wagner: Liszt is in fact taking Berlioz' precepts as his own. For a discussion of the essay, see Raabe, *994a*, II, 175–86.
[61] *780*, 136. A theorist of Form in Music confirms this estimate: *1326a*, 255.
[62] *719*, 225.

poems, and if some of them are formally somewhat incoherent it is the fault of the composer, not of the form, and certainly not the outcome of the employment of a literary programme.

Similarly . . . in Berlioz . . . his intention was not, like that of Wagner, to use music as a means to a literary or dramatic end, but, on the contrary, to compel literary ideas to subserve a musical end, which is a very different thing; and so far from allowing foreign elements belonging to the other arts to intrude into the domain of music, he rather extended the boundaries of music in such a way and to such an extent that it was able to express, free and unaided, many conceptions which had hitherto been considered exclusively literary or pictorial, but were, as he conclusively showed, equally suited to musical realization. In a word, the art of Berlioz represents an extension of the frontiers of music. . . .[63]

Liszt's way, it is obvious, was closer to that of Berlioz and farther from Wagner's. The wonder is then that like certain others, he abandoned Berlioz' side to support Wagner's opposite system. The alchemy of human relations cannot be fully analyzed, though certain elements can be enumerated. One lies in the question itself: Wagner had a system, Berlioz refused to make up one. And men feel that a movement, a party, needs a platform. Equally potent was the fact that Berlioz' compositional technique was, compared to Wagner's, a mystery. Berlioz' scores are hard to read aright, as all admit, and it is noteworthy that Liszt was most enthusiastic about those he had professionally worked at.[64] Add to this the greater accessibility of Wagner's spirit — sensual, unaristocratic, prolix, and ready to give the expected dramatic and musical satisfactions — and it is easy to see why Wagner, coming after Berlioz, seemed at once a relief and a culmination.

At first, as we saw, Liszt and his young followers wanted to establish a John-the-Baptist relation between Berlioz and their musical Messiah. When Berlioz refused the role for reasons which he understood better than they but declined to enlarge upon, there was nothing to do but drop him. A letter of Bülow's to Pohl makes this explicit: "With one breath to work for God, Son, and Holy Ghost won't do. No one so far has managed to work for more than one great man at a time . . . it blurs the vision and disturbs the public. Our active enthusiasm for the Trinity cannot be effective all at once. This unity in trinity is the business of posterity to grasp . . . Wagner and Liszt stand at this moment closer to us. I shall play excerpts from Berlioz in my concerts, Bronsart also: that is *quite sufficient*. . . ."[65]

[63] *719*, 224–6.
[64] The piano transcriptions of the first two symphonies, and of one overture, and the conducting of *Benvenuto Cellini*.   [65] October 2, 1861 (*174, 170*.)

Nationalism aiding this shift in party line, the earlier enthusiasm for
Berlioz in Germany tended to cool off, and the vivid sense of his tremendous effort was temporarily obscured.[66] All was laid at the feet of the new
conqueror. Under the spell of the strong man, Bülow was undone and
lived to make everything over to new uses — his wife to Wagner, the
"3 B's" to Brahms, the *Eroica* to Bismarck, the Bach *Chromatic Fantasia
and Fugue* to his own lust for useless ornamentation — even though only
the wife was his to reassign.

At the same time, a predictable turn in the whole cultural kaleidoscope
had helped to eclipse Berlioz — as is shown by the evolution of Nietzsche's
opinions. In the mid-1860's Nietzsche belonged to a small group of
musical amateurs who played the piano scores of *Benvenuto Cellini*
and *L'Enfance du Christ* for their pleasure. Nietzsche went so far as
to compose a *Mystery of Saint Silvester* in imitation of Berlioz' religious
style, and he was twitted by his friends about his passion for the great
Hector. But within ten years Wagner was the living idol whose truth was
marching on. The reason was, he seemed to be liquidating Romanticism
while retaining its technical gains. After another decade, that is, after the
opening of Bayreuth, Nietzsche had been disillusioned and was attacking
Wagner with a fury that has been thought personal and pathological. Yet
stripped of its polemical garb, the critique brings one back, quite simply,
to the initial divergence between Berlioz and Wagner. Nietzsche calls for
a truce to sensuality and a return to a clear, Mediterranean music, filled
with wit and the tragic sense of life. Nietzsche's favorite critic is by now
Stendhal, and Berlioz' music fulfills Stendhal's prescription: energy without wallowing in sense. Nietzsche recognized this at once on the belated
appearance of Bizet: "Hurray, old friend. Again something good to know
— an opera by Georges Bizet (who is he?) *Carmen* . . . a genuine French
talent of the comic opera kind, not at all led astray by Wagner. On the
contrary, a true pupil of Berlioz." [67]

It was now the 1880's and the men of the 1830's seemed far in the past.
The romantic period was "prewar" and Berlioz' legend was dim. While

---

[66] It revived in the decade following Berlioz' death. Bülow himself began
with his *Cellini* performances of 1879. (See his letters from 1877 on.) It was
then Cornelius cried: "*Los von Wagner!*" and that Liszt is said to have experienced his new change of heart. A third crop of enthusiasts — Mottl, Wolf,
Weingartner, Mahler and Nikisch — produced Berlioz with a success which led
directly to the publication in Germany of a "complete" edition of the scores
and writings.

[67] To Peter Gast, Nov. 28, 1881: *221*, II (2) 387. For the supporting views
of a great Nietzsche authority on these personal and artistic relations, see
Andler, *Nietzsche, Sa Vie et Sa Pensée*, vol. II, Paris, 1921, pp. 65, 266 ff., 280 ff.

Nietzsche was leaping ahead into post-Wagnerism, all the Symbolist esthetes were learning music out of Wagner's book. This had begun with Baudelaire and Nerval and it was to continue through Mallarmé and Valéry.[68] A few who knew their Berlioz, and had seen him in the flesh, like the excellent scholar Richard Pohl, remembered their first love and stated it in superlatives, but with the characteristic proviso, "always excepting Richard Wagner." [69]

In one sense, Wagner deserved this priority. Berlioz had taught the creators and had shaped the molds from which all the castings of the century would come, but Wagner had accomplished the greatest educational feat of the age. He had taught an immense number of people to enjoy truly symphonic music at the theater; he had ingrained and made respectable the now universal habit of programmatizing music through a literal ascription of themes to ideas and objects; he had caught and fertilized the imagination of innumerable painters, architects, sculptors, idlers, engineers, and literary men who would otherwise have scorned and neglected music; he had entangled philosophy and social theory so thoroughly with music that the succeeding generation had to say in protest that music was absolutely meaningless and unrelated to life; and he had managed to earn credit for being the first to dramatize the symphony by a miraculous transubstantiation of opera into music drama.

In so doing, it is true, he had thrown not only Berlioz and Weber but Mozart and Gluck into the shade; for he had taken Meyerbeer's public right out of the Paris Opera and magnetically drawn it to Bayreuth, whence they had returned to capture Paris, La Scala, New York, and Covent Garden. People soon learned to pronounce German names and to hum the Siegfried horn call with such conviction that during subse-

---

[68] Not only the leaders, but almost the entire Symbolist generation in France were Wagnerites. Gide is the one notable exception, perhaps because he was independently a musician. In 1908 he wrote: "My passionate aversion has grown steadily since my childhood. This amazing genius does not exalt so much as he *crushes*. He permitted a large number of snobs, of literary people, and of fools to think that they loved music, and a few artists to think that genius can be acquired." (*1249*, I, 225.)

[69] *552*. Saint-Saëns pointed out that in France about the same time "Berlioz is being protected by his worst enemies, who uphold him only on condition of perpetually sacrificing him to the God whose priests they are. Berlioz is never spoken of nowadays without Wagner's being immediately mentioned, and they are invariably compared on the principle that Berlioz may well be right but Wagner cannot ever be wrong." (*1388*, Oct. 5, 1884.)

As for England, Havergal Brian has testified that Franz Hueffer and Edward Dannreuther's "project to belittle Berlioz and then by comparison to belaud Wagner was only too successful." (*324*, 209.)

quent wars they began to imagine the actual notes of music to be politically culpable. More than this, Wagner reinforced by his natural sensuality and by the rhythm and subject of his *Liebestod* the great movement for sexual liberation that began in the sixties. Now that this is an accepted change we need not be so spellbound by a passionate act which requires one hundred and ten men to perform, but in the days when Aubrey Beardsley put its eroticism on paper, Wagner justly ranked with Swinburne and Havelock Ellis as a pioneer in human hygiene.

Finally, Wagner clamped down upon all the arts the demagogic habit of justifying themselves through cosmic doctrines and teachable systems. Since his day, artists have become intolerable and incompetent pedants or — in opposition — ill-natured mutes. In short Wagner, coming after Berlioz, not concurrently with him, summed up an epoch as different from the preceding as it is from ours. He belongs, with Marx and Darwin, as one of the promoters of "Progress," "Realism," and survival by force. Their era, begun in 1859 with the *Origin of Species,* the *Critique of Political Economy* and *Tristan,* could only be an alien world for Berlioz. To him pragmatic flexibility, the plurality of arts, individuals, and styles was the desired norm. He did not want to teach anybody any doctrines, still less to pose as an omnicompetent oracle. Because his first care was music and art, he had fought the Italian monopoly and made room for the diverse merits of Beethoven, Weber, Mozart, and Gluck — and even had room left over for some of the Italians' masterpieces. By his symphonic revolution he had held in check the operatic supremacy of Meyerbeer, and he could reasonably hope to outlive that bourgeois fashion by means of *Les Troyens.* It was then that Wagner, like a Ben Jonson to his Shakespeare, an indefatigable bricklayer to a master goldsmith, came with his cohorts and his genius to inaugurate still another era of musical autocracy.[70]

In that era, Berlioz, aged fifty-seven, lived the last ten years of his life and produced the last and lightest of his great works, the comedy, *Beatrice and Benedict.*

[70] If this seems *le mot injuste,* think of Jonson as the man who wished that Shakespeare "had blotted a thousand lines" and yet was irresistibly compelled to admire his art; as the man who, by demanding that the stage should present life realistically, put Shakespeare somewhat on the defensive and made him say — through the chorus of Henry V — that a history play was not meant to show events but to stimulate the spectator's imagination. (*324, 454.*) And Jonson, too, was the slow, self-made craftsman who became the greatest figure of Shakespeare's age by being "the learned plagiary" of his peers. (Dryden's phrase.)

25. *Prospero's Farewell:* Beatrice and Benedict

September 1860
to August 13, 1862

Beatrice Benedick piques, coquetting.
— THOMAS HARDY

Les Troyens being no nearer rehearsal, Berlioz drew contentment from the understanding he had just reached with Bénazet, to substitute a text of his own for the unarousing work of Plouvier. Berlioz' new subject was his old one of 1833 — *Much Ado About Nothing* — the last shoot on the tree that the Italian skies had first brought to blossom three decades earlier. Berlioz had then made a sketch of the musical situations suggested by Shakespeare's comedy. He had now but to revise, versify, and compose it. His own work, as usual, gave him happiness, health and gaiety. "It looks as if my disease were wearing itself out," he writes to Louis, who had also complained of stomach trouble. "I feel stronger since I no longer take medicines, and I have been working so hard that the occupation itself helps to cure me. I can scarcely keep up with the music of my little opera, so rapidly do the pieces come to me. Each wants precedence and sometimes I begin a fresh one before the previous is done." [1]

As if to reward neglect, *Les Troyens* now seemed to be on the way to production. A friend who remained anonymous guaranteed Carvalho fifty thousand francs to put on the work. The press announced the fact in late October 1860. Commenting upon it, Berlioz told Ferrand: "It's a good deal, but it isn't everything. So much is needed for a musical epic on that scale." [2] Nor was it entirely a question of money. Carvalho was back at the Lyrique, and full of enthusiasm after having obtained official status and the means of building a new theater,[3] but the musical personnel was inadequate. If Berlioz wanted to see his Trojans properly acted and sung

---

[1] *Corresp.*, 270. Scholarship: "During the last twenty years of his life, Berlioz's creative powers were at an ebb. The recognition of this fact, combined with his increasing illness and loneliness, made him an unhappy man." (*1335*, 71.)

[2] *L.I.*, 225.

[3] On the bank of the Seine opposite the Châtelet. The theater subsequently became the Opéra-Comique and later still the Théâtre Sarah Bernhardt.

he must obtain a ukase to have it done at the Opera. But that inevitable and narrow gate was now blocked by *Tannhäuser*, whose endless rehearsals were to cost, together with settings, one hundred and sixty thousand francs. Wagner had entered like a prince, ahead of all other pending claimants and with all his special conditions agreed to in advance. This very expenditure of funds and good will made any repetition of it unlikely in the near future, despite the plausible reasoning that the Wagner precedent should also serve a native composer who was no longer young or unknown.

Yet Berlioz' friends urged him to argue this precedent. The influential Comte de Morny, half brother to the Emperor, had known about the *Trojans* for three years, but in the interim he had become a supporter and indeed a collaborator of Offenbach's: it would be useless to approach a rival poet. The new Minister of Fine Arts, Count Walewsky, might be less partial, so Berlioz gave the minister's secretary yet another copy of his work. "Everything comes to him who waits," he reflected; "if we could only live to be 200, if we could stay young, intelligent, and strong during that couple of centuries, we men of ideas — men of fixed ideas occasionally; and if meanwhile the others died at 30 or 40 no cleverer than they were at birth — then, then, the obstacles in our path would be child's play." [4]

Unfortunately, many of the people in their forties seemed livelier than ever, and stupider. There was a redoubled lust for spiritual messages, not from contemporaries but from the departed. These came through the legs of Empire tables, or rather, Second Empire tables, and therefore not legs but limbs. Berlioz took ironic notice of this in an essay on Beethoven's "fourth manner" — the style of those compositions received through the medium of furniture, that is, the furniture of mediums:

The spirit of Beethoven inhabits Saturn or one of its rings, for Mozart, as everyone knows, occupies Jupiter. . . . Last Monday, a medium who is very familiar with the great man . . . laid hands on his deal table to fetch Beethoven for a chat. . . . These wretched spirits, you must admit, are very obliging. In his earthly life Beethoven would not have bothered to step from Vienna's Carinthian gate to the Palace doors, even if the Austrian Emperor had bidden him; yet now he quits Saturn . . . to join anyone who owns a deal table. What a change death brings about in one's character! . . .

Beethoven comes and says through the legs of the table, "Here I am." The medium asks the composer quite casually to dictate a new sonata. The spirit needs no urging; the table starts romping. The work is taken

[4] *1386*, Nov. 24, 1860.

down . . . Beethoven goes home. The medium and a dozen startled witnesses go to the piano and play the sonata . . . , which is no half-hearted platitude but a complete, full-strength platitude, an absurdity.

After this experience, how can you believe in absolute beauty? I think we are bound to infer that beauty and ugliness not being universal, many productions of the human mind which are admired on earth would be despised in the world of spirits; and I believe (as I suspected before) that many operas which are applauded daily here below might be hissed on Saturn or Jupiter. . . . This view is not calculated to encourage great craftsmen. Several of them, overwhelmed by the discovery, are said to have fallen ill and to be on the verge of passing into the spirit state. Happily that state will last them a good while.[5]

When he wrote this moralistic fantasy, Berlioz was feeling buoyed up by work on his new score, but the New Year 1861 brought harassment. An unexplained inflammation of the left eye and cheek was a mere nuisance, but Marie's ailing condition grew worse, and Louis's perturbations cast a pall on the helpless father's mind. The young man had passed both his examinations; he was now a captain and had at once obtained a berth which would pay him eighteen hundred francs a year. Yet he still needed money, and suddenly he felt a raging impatience to get on faster — doubtless from guilt at being dependent. Berlioz had to rehearse for him his own arduous beginnings and show the young officer that he was relatively fortunate. But sound reasoning, as Berlioz knew, hardly touches feelings like those Louis suffered from. The new-made captain, it appeared, wanted to be married — not to anyone he could name but in general, just like the sad youth in Hamerton who, "without having as yet any particular lady in view, expressed a determination to marry." [6] Berlioz with his two unhappy experiences of matrimony, tried to dissuade his son by sketching the despair, exasperation, and anxieties of marriage under adverse conditions. He was brief and kind on the subject, but Louis felt attacked, or else he misunderstood, and he replied in wounding words which Berlioz begged him to moderate in future. The boy also spoke of nightmares connected with boarding operations and dating back to his service in the Baltic. Clearly, Louis nursed a sense of wrong which from time to time burst through his love for his father, and demanded from him a special pity. All this Berlioz could easily read between the lines: in the paragraph following his "knife thrusts," the wretched boy wanted to know why the newspapers did not more often speak of his father.[7] Berlioz had no re-

[5] *A Trav.*, 88–90.
[6] *The Intellectual Life*, Part VII, Chapter I.
[7] *Corresp.*, 270–4.

source but to be patient and try to soothe the intelligent and affectionate child who had too soon become a flayed spirit.

For a month Berlioz had not been able to touch his score. Besides illness and worry he was swamped with concerts and reviews. Death too was at work and required notice from the survivors. Scribe, Murger, and Guinot in the world of letters; Berlioz' old friend Chélard, the loyal and affectionate Weimar musician;[8] Simon, who had also studied with Lesueur; Mme. Lesueur herself — with each extinction part of Berlioz' known world was disappearing; and for a man who lives not in himself alone, who is therefore especially vulnerable to treading down by the hungry generations, it was needful to have the protection of fame — to become at the right moment a Grand Old Man.

For Berlioz the very reverse was happening. As is clear from the *Tannhäuser* episode, Berlioz' most intimate friends — the Princess, Ferrand, the Massarts and the Damckes — were exacerbating his sense of injury. These last especially, being strongly anti-Wagnerian, aggravated Berlioz' concern over the effect of the new work and deepened his distress at Liszt's apparent desertion. The old friend and fellow warrior who had been unable to go to Baden was coming to Paris to see Wagner through the probable ordeal. Franz and Hector would have to meet: what could they say to each other? They were too intelligent and too well bred not to understand that no one's rights had been violated — Liszt had not taken an oath of eternal allegiance to Berlioz — but the emotional assumptions of a quarter century cannot be forgotten in a twelvemonth. To drown out thoughts of self, Berlioz would ask Mme. Massart to play him Beethoven sonatas. But the return to futilities in speech was upsetting. He felt dizzy: "Never did I have so many windmills to tilt at as this year. I am surrounded by lunatics."[9] For a while Liszt deemed it best not to come after all, thinking perhaps to avoid painful meetings.

Berlioz now faced another stretch of proofreading. He had undertaken to publish the vocal score of *Les Troyens* at his own expense, being determined to hear his Cassandra and Dido and having to be ready for any opportunity. So many times before in his career will power and persistence had breached stone walls, success had so often come against all probability, that there was no point in being reasonable. For the sake of his music drama Berlioz also kept his "armed position" at the *Débats*. "So many rascals would annihilate me if they were not afraid. And yet my

[8] See Chélard's letter of Nov. 15, 1843. (*235*, II, 205–6.)
[9] *Corresp.*, 277.

head is full of ideas and projected works that I cannot undertake because of that slavery." [10] While time dribbled through one's fingers, moreover, one had to wait upon the private secretaries of the great and chat with Emperors and Ministers about the weather or the latest financial suicide. For an artist is expected "to die with a gentle noise under the feet of these pachyderms." [11]

On March thirteenth and eighteenth, 1861, the *Tannhäuser* performances, with attendant riots, took place. It was then Berlioz wrote the two private letters referred to in the previous chapter. Liszt finally came to Paris and dined with d'Ortigue at Berlioz' house. It was a doubly glum and embarrassing occasion. Berlioz spoke in a low voice, looking as if overborne by cheerlessness. "His whole being seems hovering over the grave." Possibly Berlioz was mourning the end of a long and disinterested friendship dedicated to the twin powers of love and music.

The next month, the Conservatoire orchestra played two excerpts from the *Damnation of Faust* to a delighted house. Obviously Berlioz' name could still muster out his concert public; it was even growing, though meagerly fed on scraps. To play fragments cost nothing — "hence they do it," [12] as Berlioz remarked, thinking of what the true presentation of a complete work of art requires in brains and cash. *Les Troyens*, without changing its character, was daily becoming more impossible. At a musicale given by Edouard Bertin, several scenes from the drama were sung with piano accompaniment before a choice and presumably influential gathering. More articles appeared. But the Opera, recovering from *Tannhäuser*, shied away from a new risk. It proposed instead to revive "Berlioz' *Freischütz*," or even better — since Berlioz had shown Carvalho how to make Gluck pay — it would engage Berlioz to help produce *Alceste*. There seems to have been a vague expectation that if Berlioz were allowed to do something at the Opera, he would be "taken care of," he would swallow the score of *Les Troyens* and no one would ever mention it again. *Freischütz* rehearsals actually started, Berlioz giving himself without stint, as usual, like one of his own enthusiasts in the *Evenings with the Orchestra*. But after a month the idea was dropped and *Alceste* reverted to. Berlioz had to withdraw when he found that far from being asked to restore the work as he had done for *Orpheus*, he was expected to arrange it in accord-

[10] *Corresp.*, 274.
[11] *Corresp.*, 281.
[12] *Corresp.*, 275. Orchestra parts, beautifully engraved on fine rag stock, still cost in the neighborhood of six cents apiece, and once bought there was no further expense.

ance with the "desires" of the Opera subscribers. He declined.[13] Walewski, whose word might ordain *Les Troyens*, was annoyed at Berlioz' refusal to tamper with *Alceste*, but Berlioz was adamant.

Meanwhile, Alphonse Royer, director of the Opera had "accepted" *Les Troyens*, reluctantly, under pressure from still other forces. But when it came to the point of setting a date, he seized on every excuse: the work was expensive; the five sets, mid-stage curtain, and processional costumes could not be dug out of the lumber room. Then the novelty of a double tragedy, each part requiring a pair of first-rate singers, was a dreaded obstacle. The first pair would grumble at not coming on again. Besides, the work was long; there would have to be cuts. If only the composer would consent to . . . And to clinch the matter, it was known that Gounod and Gevaert were each at work on something — something which being only rumored, not even written, obviously looked greener than any completed score presenting definite problems. Understandably, Berlioz was becoming nervous about the excess of advance publicity that his work was receiving. The history of *Benvenuto* was repeating itself. Too high expectations might prepare a letdown, and simultaneously too many near-acceptances would brand the work as unmanageable.[14] He decided for the second time to let the matter rest. "I no longer run at Fortune's heels. I stay in bed and await it there." [15]

On August 6, Berlioz arrived in Baden ready to rehearse the *Tuba mirum* and Offertory of his *Requiem* — "to cheer up the gamblers," as he told the Princess [16] — in reality for his own pleasure. Pieces by Verdi, Halévy, and Donizetti, together with *Harold in Italy*, completed the program. The symphony Berlioz "heard for the first time as I want it to be," and after eight rehearsals the *Requiem* numbers went well.[17]

In Paris again by the fall, Berlioz heard a conclave of amateur singing groups perform, among other pieces, his unimportant *Temple Universel*. Earlier in the year it had been sung in London in two languages simultaneously,[18] and Berlioz had been tempted to go and see his many English friends. He decided against it on account of expense. The possibility of a

---

[13] *122.*

[14] Rumor had it that the work called for twenty-two singers (actually nine) and that it required eight hours to play (actually four and a half).

[15] *L.I.*, 227.

[16] *S.W.*, 120.

[17] *L.I.*, 233.

[18] See the letter to C. A. Barry in which, forty years later, August Manns tried to recall the circumstances of that occasion. (*212.*)

year's visit to the "Disunited States" — his own words, for the Civil War had begun — he also put off, foreseeing complications of all sorts, and surmising that the Opera would take his departure as a pretext for canceling its uncomfortable "acceptance" of *Les Troyens*.

Then, still in Paris, where he had made fruitless efforts to help Ferrand publish a book, Berlioz received from Louis the worst blow yet dealt in the boy's fitful correspondence. The father had heard nothing for two months, and what he now heard was reproaches couched in the tone of irony, coupled with the news that Louis was married and had a child — or possibly children: on this point the letter was confused. Berlioz rose to the challenge, not of the boy, but of the situation.

If I did not know what a bad influence sorrow can exert on even the best characters, I should be by way of answering you with home truths. You have wounded me to the heart, most cruelly, and in cold blood — as appears from your careful choice of words. But I excuse you and embrace you. In spite of all, you are not a bad son. If someone who knew nothing about us were to read you, he might believe that I was "without real affection" for you; that people say you are "not my son"; that I "could if I would" find you "a better position" . . . and that I "humiliated you" by comparing you to some hero or other of Béranger's to whom you allude. I must say, frankly and without recrimination, that you have gone too far and made me suffer a pain as yet unknown to me. . . . Ah, my poor dear Louis, it wasn't right.

Don't you worry about your tailor's bill. It will be paid on demand. If you want to have it off your mind sooner, give me the man's address and I will go settle it. It is true that I thought you younger than you actually are, but is this reason enough to impute it to me as a crime that I have no memory for dates? Do I know at what age my father, mother, sisters, and brother died? No. But can you infer from this that I did not love them? Really! And I see that I sound as if I were justifying myself. Once again I tell you that unhappiness has made you speak as in delirium, and that is why I can but love and pity you all the more. . . . Only tell me clearly what I can do and I will do it. . . . Farewell, dear friend, dear son, dear unhappy boy whose misery comes from you and not from me. I kiss you with all my heart and hope for news of you by the next mail.[19]

Berlioz had yielded at last in the matter of *Alceste*. Pauline Viardot was singing the role, which therefore had to be transposed throughout, but she sang it nobly; and by consenting to be involved Berlioz was able to prevent all other alterations. He enjoined the rest of the singers to "keep their embroidering to themselves." Still, the transposition of the soprano part gave Berlioz "shudders of indignation," for although certain airs lost little, "the

[19] *Corresp.*, 284-5.

effect of others was weakened, not to say destroyed; the orchestration became flaccid and dull, and the sequence of modulations was no longer Gluck's." [20] At the same time, Berlioz' study of the score as well as of operas on the same subject by Lulli, Handel, and others, furnished him with the matter for no less than seven articles, published in the fall of 1861.[21]

In effect, "his" *Alceste* was very successful and Count Walewski, mollified, offered Berlioz the royalties usually given only to authors of new works. It was a sardonic comment on the timeliness of Berlioz' musical philosophy that the only exertion that brought him easy and prolonged returns was the work he most abhorred — the "arranging" of Weber and Gluck. On each occasion his consent had been given only in order to forestall worse evils, but this preventive medicine was still bitter. He could contrast with this unhappy compromise the integrity that was his when he acted freely, not *under*, but *above* Carvalho and Bénazet.

The hours left over during these last months of 1861 went into pushing ahead the score of *Beatrice and Benedict*. It had grown (as usual) from one to two acts and was nearly done. The subject and the expected audience both called for light, gay, romanesque, and restful music, which Berlioz miraculously found it in his heart to write despite the plagues of Paris, his constrained home life, and the anguish about Louis. Since the exchange of complaint and expostulation, no news. January 1862 brought none. On March 2, Berlioz wrote to Morel at Marseille, who had so devotedly acted *in loco parentis:* "Could you be good enough to give me some news of Louis? Has he left for India? As I foresaw, he has not dropped me a single line. I cannot tell you anything that you haven't already guessed, but I confess this new grief is among the most poignant I have ever experienced.

"I write to you athwart one of those abominable reviews of the kind which it is impossible to do right. I am trying to hold up our unhappy Gounod who has had a fiasco worse than any yet seen. There is nothing in his score, nothing at all.[22] How can I hold up what has neither bone nor sinew? Still, I have got to find something to praise. . . . And it's his third fiasco at the Opera. Well, he's headed for a fourth. No one can write

---

[20] *A Trav.,* 207.

[21] *1386,* Oct. 12, 15, 20, 24; Nov. 6, 23; Dec. 8. A short account had preceded these on Mar. 26, the whole being revised for *A Travers Chants,* 134–222. Euripides's *Alcestis* also comes into the discussion.

[22] *The Queen of Sheba.* Berlioz' article appeared in the *Débats* for March 8, 1862.

dozens of operas — not great operas. Paisiello wrote 170, but of what sort? And where are they now?" [23]

Come to think of it, where were anybody's operas? Except for the directing activity, from time to time, of a Berlioz, Liszt, or Wagner, no one kept up the cult and tradition of the great dramatic masterpieces.[24] The current output had no connection with either masterpieces or drama, and even Gounod's failure was a bad sign, for obviously the Opera director would be twice as timid as before and poorer still in pocket. The one going concern was Offenbach's *Orpheus in Hell* which still played to full houses after more than four hundred showings. This parody had been given fresh point by Berlioz' revival of Gluck three years before, and thanks to its cynical and sensual mockery of grandeur, it had introduced the henpecked Orpheus and ridiculous Jove to every capital in Europe. While such parasitism flourished, every antique subject — especially antique costume — was ruined for at least ten years. In this state of the public temper a Beethoven program was hissed at the Conservatoire. The *Fidelio* overture, though played with incomparable verve, was barely applauded.[25] Berlioz could almost believe he was dreaming and that the screen of history was unrolling backwards. He philosophized with his characteristic willingness to face facts: "Nothing is sillier than death unless it be life, for what is the use of life? Oh, you will say, don't bore us again with your Shakespearean quotations and sepulchral philosophy: life is for the writing of comic operas." [26]

This sally introduced *The Jeweler of Saint James*, a comic opera and thus a justification of life, though stillborn from natural causes. Fortunately another offspring, better compounded, was in existence and Berlioz had begun to conduct private rehearsals for its *première* the following August: *Beatrice and Benedict* was finished and Baden would have its play. At home, Berlioz was teaching the singers to speak. "It is infuriating to hear lines uttered contrary to sense, but by dint of making the actors parrot after me, I believe I shall succeed in making them talk like men." [27] To Louis meanwhile, Berlioz expressed his firm determination not to undertake any other work.

---

[23] *Corresp.*, 286. The full text of the letter is restored in *85*, 710.

[24] Grout, at the end of his *Short History of Opera:* "The thought of so much buried beauty is saddening, for it is buried for the most part beyond recall, with even less hope of resurrection than old poems or old paintings. . . ." (*722*, II, 536.)

[25] *1386*, Feb. 16, 1862.

[26] *1386*, Feb. 27, 1862.

[27] *L.I.*, 234.

For Louis had at last written from Algeria. He was chastened and well, and Berlioz overlooked the wretchedness his long silence had caused him. "All is well — except me who have again spent 30 hours of agony in bed." [28] In such bad health it was doubly distracting to have to move — and to move twice within a few weeks — but this was made unavoidable by the discovery that the apartment house rue de Calais was on the point of collapsing. Extensive repairs proceeded floor by floor and drove Berlioz out with his papers, manuscripts, proofs, books, and other tools of the man of thought. This contretemps gave added charm to the prospect which arose of being elected Permanent Secretary of the Institute, a post which carries official quarters.[29] Halévy had died at Nice and the committee put Berlioz fourth on their list of nominees. He received fourteen votes but Beulé was chosen by nineteen. Rumor had it that the objectionable Mme. Berlioz precluded her husband's election. Two months later she no longer stood in the way: "I write you just a few lines in my desolation. My wife has just died, in an instant, struck down by cardiac failure. The fearful loneliness I feel at this sudden and violent parting cannot be told. Forgive my not writing at greater length." [30]

Marie Recio Berlioz, who had barely turned forty-eight, had been chronically ill and subject to heart attacks for several years. She and her husband had been spending the day with friends in the country when death occurred without warning on Friday June thirteenth. Berlioz' efforts to be the first to reach her mother failed, and the poor woman, apprehensive at their lateness in returning, arrived to find her daughter dead. Berlioz declined the offers of his nieces and of Louis to come and comfort him. ". . . it is better for me to be left to myself." [31]

After a few days, Berlioz' mother-in-law returned to Paris and he decided to continue living under the same roof. He did hope that Louis would go to Baden in August and meet him there, the young man's "family" not having been mentioned again, and having had, indeed, either a casual or an imaginary existence. "In the intervals of my work," pleaded Berlioz, "you would be my companion; I would introduce you to my friends, in a word you would be with me. . . . Of course I am rather nervous at bringing you into a gambling town, but if you give me your

---

[28] *Corresp.*, 287.

[29] There are other residences open to Members of the Institute, one of which Delacroix made persistent and vain efforts to secure. The present holder of the Secretary's quarters is Adolphe Boschot, which tends to prove that as regards emoluments it is better to write about the great than to be great.

[30] To Ferrand: *L.I.*, 234–5.

[31] *Corresp.*, 288.

word of honor not to risk a single florin, I shall trust you and shall resign myself to the pain of separation when you have to go . . ." [32]

To Berlioz' surprise Louis, disregarding his father's choice of solitude, came at once to Paris and spent an all-too-short week that both enjoyed. After it, Berlioz wrote: "I find it so restful to chat with you. Yes, I agree that it was good, at night, to know that you were here, close by. But don't let the thought upset you. I would rather look on the fact that your new position is going to better your lot. You won't be making those endless trips that take you so far from me . . . We shall see each other oftener. . . .

"I had a letter from Baden this morning, telling me that the choruses now know their parts by heart and are found very effective. The manager is 'sure of a great success' — as if he knew the rest of the score! Everything in this world is ruled by preconceived ideas. Yesterday we began the actual staging in the Opéra-Comique, with every one present, for a change. . . ." [33]

The Princess, by one of her messages of comfort, brought Berlioz' thoughts back to himself: "Your letter made me almost happy for a few hours, but such clearing of the skies is of short duration. . . . Like you I have one of the three theological virtues — charity — but not, as you know, the other two. . . . The insoluble riddle of the world, the existence of evil and pain, the mad fury of the human race, its stupid ferocity, which it vents, everywhere and at all times, upon the most innocent people and often on itself, have reduced me to the state of spiritless and desperate resignation which may be supposed to exist in a scorpion surrounded by live coals. The utmost I can do is not to sting myself to death. . . .

"You wonder how it is that you did not know of the existence of my two-act opera for Baden. It must be that I haven't written to you for a long time. . . . The intervals [of illness] during its composition were so long that on first rehearsing I became acquainted with music which I had lost all memory of. . . . I have my work cut out for me teaching the orchestra, for the thing is a caprice written with the point of a needle and it requires an extremely delicate performance. Farewell, dear Princess, I shall keep you informed." [34]

At the new grave, which he frequently visited, Berlioz meditated on his lost loves from Estelle onwards; on his son whom he too seldom saw, on Liszt now twice remote. The mother of the late Mme. Berlioz had be-

[32] *Corresp.*, 289.   [33] *Corresp.*, 290.   [34] *S.W.*, 121.

come a second mother to her son-in-law — or rather the first real one. He valued her affectionate care and she adored him, yet she could hardly be the domestic companion he had always sought. Blake happy with his unlettered wife, Heine with his grisette Mathilde, seemed to have found gladness and devoted affection at the expense of a communion of minds. Liszt, on the other hand, after his liaison with Mme. d'Agoult, followed by some casual affairs, had allied himself to another woman of intellect whose tastes and activities were not always in tune with his. Berlioz had married an actress and then a singer[35] — the first a finer-grained person than the second, but one who had returned his love too late. His second wife, of greater pretensions than merits, had embittered many a moment and alienated some of his friends. Was Berlioz a poor judge of woman-kind and doomed to the pangs of misprized love? Doubtless, as he made the lovers say in the verses of his Shakespearean comedy —

> Love is a will o' the wisp which cometh none knows whence;
> It flashes then disappears
> That it may lead our souls astray,
> It draws to him the fool and drives him mad.

Yet like them he concluded:

> Tis better, after all, to be fools than clods
> Let us adore, whatever says the world,
> Let us taste folly for a day, let us love.[36]

But Berlioz' management of his feelings could not follow so simple a rule, complicated as they were by his genius for dramatization, that is to say, his desire to objectify his sensations, to see them have shape outside himself, and finally by his tenacious memory. Like the pursuer of the Well-Beloved in Hardy's parable, who finds himself in a similar situation, Berlioz "was wretched for hours. Yet he would not have stood in the ranks of an imaginative profession if he had not been at the mercy of every haunting fancy that can beset man. It was in his weaknesses as a citizen and a national unit that his strength lay as an artist . . . But he was paying dearly enough for his Liliths . . . What had he done to be tormented

[35] Like César Franck and Rossini respectively. Verdi also took an artist into the home — Giuseppina Strepponi (whom Berlioz greatly admired) — and proved in this regard the most fortunate musician of his time.

[36] Act II, Sc. 15, duettino of Beatrice and Benedict. Writing at this time to his niece Josephine Suat about her sister, Berlioz stays consistent, in more prosaic words: "I am much relieved that Nanci turned down the suitor she disliked. One must not in such a serious matter allow oneself to be influenced by anybody or anything." (*91, 170.*)

like this? The Beloved . . . had taken up her abode in the living representative of the dead. . . ." Later on, Hardy's artist-hero has a malignant fever from which he recovers with a very strange result: "He became clearly aware of what this was. The artistic sense had left him, and he could no longer *attach a definite sentiment to images of beauty recalled from the past.*" [Italics added.][37]

In Berlioz as in other artists, it is more than the common accident which makes their "imagination of love" seize upon a fit person or an unfit. The man of imagination may be taking an unfair advantage of the object of his choice, yet the likely mishap is not wholly chargeable to him, for his very faculties exert an attraction often lasting into old age. Berlioz' spiritual energy certainly did so with precisely this result. At the cemetery Berlioz met a young woman of twenty-six, Amélie, whose last name is not known. Sharing kindred sorrows they came to talk, to meet, finally to love each other — though in different ways. Unlike Hardy's protagonist, Berlioz had not lost the power to create nor to idealize fervently, and he loved Amélie in the way that Disraeli at the same age loved the frivolous Lady Bradford;[38] Amélie loved like a Bettina to his Goethe, though without the éclat of a great estate to cast glory on the relation.

The affair could have none but an inward significance. They wrote letters; they were happy in a melancholy way for a space, though having agreed to meet no more. Then the letters stopped. Amélie too had died. After a time, Berlioz experienced other love imaginings, still more distant and chimerical, until the last concentration of his desire to love on the aged and uncomprehending Estelle. But this is to anticipate.

Meanwhile he worked. To coincide with the *première* at Baden, Berlioz had planned to issue another volume of music criticism. This would present the best version of his many reviews of Beethoven's sonatas and symphonies, of his articles on Gluck, Mozart, Weber, and Wagner; and of essays on religious music and other technical subjects, interspersed with shorter and gayer pieces to relieve the intensity. For the collection he had found the poetic play on words *A Travers Chants*, which appropriately suggested the long traverse he had taken through the realms of song: portions of the book dated back to his early *feuilletons* of the thirties. But the brief double motto already referred to expressed in six words

---

[37] *The Well-Beloved*, London, 1922, 101 and 209.
[38] Disraeli wrote her eleven hundred letters in eight years, but she found "embarrassing" the impassioned attentions which her far more intelligent sister, Lady Chesterfield, might have welcomed.

his view of the journey's end — "Love's labor's lost" because (as in the Trojan tragedy) "the enemy holds the walls." [39]

On July 26, 1862 before leaving Paris, he invited the press and the musical world to a private dress rehearsal of *Beatrice and Benedict*. Two weeks later, alone in Baden for the opening, he climbed the podium in such pain that he could hardly hold himself upright.[40] Beautifully staged and played, the exquisite work was greeted with re-echoing applause. The "nocturne" concluding the first act was overpowering, magical. The composer-conductor was called back again and again. And he had besides, in his pocket, a letter from Amélie — a true love letter, as Legouvé testifies.

But the consciousness of his age and exhaustion was for the moment too great — yet not conclusive. He was not moribund enough to be reconciled to life, though the vital energies were at dead center. So for the time being the success of his last score, his last poem, his last reciprocated love, and his last homage in prose to the great dead, seemed disembodied, too far away for him to grasp and call his own.

The Shakespearean Berlioz

> I have now done everything I had to do.
> — BERLIOZ to his son, on completing
> *Beatrice and Benedict*

"Berlioz," said a critic after the Paris revival of *Beatrice*, "worn down by fatigue and worry, and in the grip of one of those *amours de tête* which caused him so much unhappiness . . . Berlioz obviously wanted to divert himself a little and to give proof that noise was not the mainstay of his art. Such proofs he had already put in evidence twenty times, but the world refused to credit it." [1]

The conjecture about Berlioz' desire for diversion is doubtless accurate: the composer himself has told us how one of the most enchanting pages of his score was sketched during a colleague's speech at the Institute. He adds that artists have "a fund of natural impressions, which rearise from

---

[39] See above, Subchapter 22.

[40] Readers of Turgenev's *Smoke* will remember that the novel opens in Baden-Baden, with a description of the promenade in front of the "Conversation." The date given, it so happens, is that of the day after the *première* of *Beatrice and Benedict*, August 10, 1862.

---

[1] *542*, 83.

their souls of their own accord, anywhere." [2] The impressions which came forth as music when he worked at his little comedy he organized around the familiar plot involving the two Shakespearean characters named in the title.[3] From the remainder of *Much Ado* he also borrowed the names of Hero and Claudio, but made them simply sentimental foils to the bickering pair. In addition, for the sake of *musical* humor, Berlioz created the figure of the grotesque *Capellmeister*, Somarone, meaning donkey, beast of burden. The dialogue, spoken throughout, makes frequent use of Shakespeare,[4] and the poem, in Berlioz' purest and simplest vein, is well-nigh faultless.

In adopting the traditional alternation of song and speech it is as if Berlioz had wanted to re-emphasize, besides his kinship with Shakespeare, his undeviating principle that music should express none but musical situations. *Beatrice and Benedict* is once again a discontinuity of occasions brought about by words and allowing symphonic music full sway. Berlioz had shown in *Benvenuto* and *Les Troyens* how he conceived the broadening of the Italian tragicomedy and the antique tragedy. In *Beatrice* he took up French comic opera, seemingly staying within its tradition but by musical inventiveness new-modeling it.[5] With this score, the cycle of innovation begun by Berlioz upon the symphony, opera, oratorio, and cantata, was closed. Under his hand each had acquired flexibility from crossing with elements from the others, and responding to the needs of subject and mood, music was now free.

The mood of *Beatrice and Benedict*, like that of Stevenson's "Young Man with the Cream Tarts," is one of mockery. The well-known overture presents and develops two of the main melodies of the work and establishes the recurring contrast between lively coquetry and gentle melancholy — the melancholy of humor. The instrumentation is filigree work,[6] tonal pointillism which acts upon us like champagne and prepares us for a

[2] *Mem.*, II, 388. Shakespeare: "Our poesy is as a gum which oozes from whence 'tis nourished." (*Timon*, I, i, 21–22.)

[3] Berlioz doubtless did not know that the earliest English references to *Much Ado*, including one in the handwriting of Charles I, call the play *Benedick and Beatrice*. (*1110*, 110–1.)

[4] The recitatives found in some German piano scores were composed by Felix Mottl for his revival of the work in the nineties.

[5] Lostalot: "As for his ideas, no one can reproach him with having borrowed them. . . . Artists of his rank cannot simply let themselves go; they insist on a rationale for their verve and they make it pass the test of an artistry of which they are at once the masters and the slaves." (*542*, 83.)

[6] Hence the unsuitability of the modern arrangement for brass band, which by thickening the texture and slowing the tempo destroys the work. Compare recordings *1410* and *1409*.

drama that occurs in fantasy: its reality is at one remove, like a romance painted on a bright screen.

Shakespeare and Berlioz now collaborate: the people of Messina are singing their liberation from the Moors, and riming "glory" with "victory" — which is more inevitable in French than in English. Beatrice interrupts them with a comment precisely on this literary subject: "Terrible rimes!" says she, "but what can you expect after a war." She goes on to speak of Benedict, whose bullying masculinity she satirizes. But the people break in again to dance a catchy Sicilienne (the native dance) full of delightful Berliozian details.

We next are shown Hero's joy at the return of her lover Claudio, and in further contrast with Beatrice's sharpness of tongue we hear of Benedict's stern celibacy. The three characters are thus quickly established. As Benedict enters, a teasing duet with Beatrice begins, to an orchestral accompaniment which musically combines their ironic give-and-take and the love that hides beneath. At its conclusion Don Pedro and Claudio come to rally Benedict, who protests despite the irresistibly nuptial atmosphere: the court musicians are about to rehearse their parts for the wedding of Claudio and Hero.

For this, Somarone has composed an *Epithalame grotesque* — a fugue which the pedantic maestro explains: "The word 'fugue' means 'flight'; I have made a fugue on a double subject — two themes — so that the two lovers shall think of the flight of time." Being a poor conductor, say the stage directions, he leads "with all sorts of exaggerated gestures." [7] But the fugue manages to be at once charming and smile-provoking. Not at all grotesque in the sense of the *Benvenuto* "King Midas" scene, it belongs, like the later drinking song, to the realm of musical humor, a genre more often spoken of than found, since music lends itself more naturally to wit. The juxtaposition of the two kinds in *Beatrice and Benedict* makes the distinction evident.

After the fugue, Claudio and his prince carry out the Shakespearean plot to make Benedict fall in love. This he does as soon as they have gone, singing a lively rondo to notify himself of the fact.

Twilight has now fallen and Claudio's lovelorn fiancée, Hero, is strolling in the gardens with her maid Ursula. Their dialogue introduces the nocturne-duet which is the richest jewel of the score: *Nuit paisible et sereine.* Hearing its first performance, Gounod was overwhelmed by its perfection: "Here is all that the silence of night and the serenity of nature may do to imbue the soul with tenderness and reverie. The orchestra utters

[7] *Ger. ed.*, XX, 151.

divine murmurings that find a place within this admirable landscape without taking anything away from the delicious cantilena of the voices: it is absolutely beautiful and perfect; it is immortal like the sweetest and deepest things ever written by the great masters." [8] The scene and the act end with a slow "pantomime" between the two women as the "divine murmurings" subside — the long holds on flute and clarinet, the melancholy horn phrases, and above the pizzicato basses, the tight tremolo of upper strings which seems "like the shadowy hum of invisible wings." [9]

A modified reprise of the Sicilienne serves as prelude to the second act, which resumes the preparations for the feast. Soldiers offstage call for Syracusan wine, caterers pass to and fro, and Somarone improvises above their din the verses of a drinking song in which he is joined by the chorus. But he and the rest disappear as Beatrice, still fighting her love, sings a recitative and aria of traditional form and Mozartian insight: Beatrice is haughty from nobleness and formal from excess of self-respect. Hero arrives just as her cousin's heart begins to soften; their song is again a contrast, to which is added that of the distant marriage procession. The rest of the women take up the Bridal Hymn.

Now Benedict too is at hand, and like Beatrice ready to confess his love — if only to take it back the moment after. But the procession has caught up with them: a vocal trio for the women gives us as many views of love and marriage and leads to a Wedding March in steadily increasing animation. On top of this Beatrice and Benedict plight their troth in a fully developed symphonic scherzo-duettino. With the words: "A truce today, tomorrow we shall be foes again," *e finita la commedia*.

For inexplicable reasons, or rather for the good old reason that every new work of Berlioz' surprises by a new style, not to say by more fresh ideas than the mind can assimilate at once, the French critics at Baden were rather baffled by the score. They felt that around the obviously fine blooms lay "a good deal of underbrush." They added that Berlioz' sense of humor in dialogue was often crude, not up to his original, and they quoted as proof passages from the book which turned out to be direct translations from Shakespeare.

The poet-composer took all this quite philosophically. Had he lived thirty years more he would have seen the Paris revival demonstrate again that Time and Repetition are the great music teachers. [10] It was discovered

[8] *991*, II, 45 *n*. 1.
[9] *542*, 84.
[10] "The second performance," wrote a critic in 1890, "won over those who still objected at the first." (*542*, 83.)

at this time that "from the technical point of view, *Beatrice and Benedict*
is an exquisite work. It is rich in graceful melodies . . . and art shines
throughout — an intimate and discreet art, an art of precision and elegance.
. . . Berlioz is in truth the most intellectual of all the masters, and it passes
understanding why he is not defended by all those who attach importance
to refinements of technique. . . . This wire-drawn style is the very essence of Berlioz' genius." [11]

Not long after, Shaw wanted D'Oyly Carte to produce the work [12]
and Mottl actually did so. Since then, though performances have been few,
criticism has caught up with Berlioz' technical originality and mastery of
his theme: "The score is all too short for my taste," writes a judge who is
usually hard to please; "it is bewitching in its variety and full of a fantasy
worthy of Shakespeare . . . a unique combination of laughing verve, wit,
and tenderness." [13]

The name of Shakespeare has occurred more than once throughout
this book, and not solely because Berlioz was reading or quoting him. The
lifelong study of the poet-dramatist by the music-dramatist had, we
know, a philosophic and spiritual significance, and the esthetic likeness
between the two has not escaped certain critics from Jules David in
1834 [14] to the contemporary writer just quoted. Plainly, from the time
of the Eight Scenes from *Faust*, which bear Shakespearean mottoes, to
Beatrice and Benedict and the final page of the *Memoirs* which ends with
"Life's but a walking shadow," Shakespeare's work served Berlioz through
life as a scripture — a book of devotions.[15]

[11] *542*, 83.
[12] *879*, II, 39. He linked Cornelius's *Barber of Bagdad* in the same suggestion,
and had earlier called, in vain, for *Benvenuto Cellini*.
[13] Masson: *289*, 188. "I believe," says Mr. Meyerstein, "or rather *prophesy*,
that we are in the presence of an operatic work of Berlioz that . . . will yet
hold its own triumphantly and survive the mutability of musical fashions."
(1948: *475*, 100.)
[14] "Berlioz has undertaken the glorious task of incorporating into music the
genius and power of Shakespeare." (*Revue du progrès social*, Dec. 1834, quoted
in *299*, 148.)
[15] Though Berlioz' favorite plays were *Romeo and Juliet*, *Hamlet*, *Lear*, *Macbeth* and *Othello*, he had a real fondness for *Henry IV*, *Coriolanus*, *The
Merchant of Venice*, *Midsummer Night's Dream*, *Troilus*, *Much Ado*, and
The Tempest. In his writings he alludes to or quotes some one hundred and
fifty passages drawn from twenty-two out of the thirty-four plays. This does
not include scores or the essays not reprinted. It is most often casually, in
correspondence, that Berlioz uses Shakespeare, like a man who is familiar
with his author. He knew *Hamlet* by heart in French, and much of it in
English.

Part of this reverence expressed the obligation Berlioz felt toward the playwright for his own artistic liberation. It was Shakespeare who woke him from the dogmatic slumbers induced by eighteenth-century French criticism, and who taught him the "versatility of form" that he needed for his musical purposes. The lesson was not merely that one could disregard unity of place and continuity of action in dramatic works, but that every established genre in a given art could find a place within drama provided there was sound reason for the choice. The uneven texture that resulted was a merit, not a flaw: just as in Shakespeare's *Romeo* there are two prologues, two sonnets, prose and poetry, eloquence and catchwords, couplet and blank verse, so in the *Romeo* of Berlioz, which neither illustrates nor resembles the original, we find a transposition answering to the same esthetic principle. This principle Berlioz never abandoned, in spite of his century's return to older models, and his nation's prevailingly opposite tradition.[16] When he inaugurated the "serial idea" in *Les Troyens*, his first remark was that in this regard it followed the scheme of Shakespeare's histories.[17] And it is more than likely that his increasing skill in fashioning librettos and in making lyrical ideas develop into drama grew with his knowledge of the poet.

Berlioz' admiration was an outward going, "objective" act of faith, not a self-identification which hides personal conceit under an attachment to a great name. Shakespeare was a God in the antique sense, like Virgil and Beethoven, and Berlioz continued to think of himself as a mortal.[18] Yet the choice of our idols, if it is conscious and free, defines something in us — a kinship or an opposition; we may seek something we lack or something close to what we possess. In Berlioz' relation to Shakespeare it is safe to say that the link through similarity is the suggestive one;[19] and saying so will not be taken for blasphemy if it is agreed that the Shakespeare who is under discussion is the great but fallible writer of plays, not the fish-eyed figure of the schoolbook whose name is merely a synonym for: "Supreme! and don't let's hear another word about it!"

The question of great power allied to great imperfections occurs at once as significant. From Shakespeare's time to ours — that is, from Ben

---

[16] Neither did Delacroix, who in middle age shifted like Berlioz to antique subjects but retained his devotion to Shakespeare: in 1858, when Berlioz has just revised his *Romeo* score, Delacroix is jotting down subjects from the same source.

[17] *L.I.*, 248.

[18] The inscription of *Les Troyens* is "*Divo Virgilio.*"

[19] Several English writers have advanced the comparison, notably W. J. Turner and Francis Toye. See *309*, 290, and *passim; 1287.*

Jonson to John Crowe Ransom [20] — competent critics of literature have not ceased to point out Shakespeare's singular combination of mastery and ineptitude. He is said to be transcendent and also crude, careless, vulgar, incoherent, rhetorical, exaggerated, naïve, cheap, obscure, unphilosophical, and addicted to bad puns and revolting horrors. Dryden, who admired Shakespeare as Wagner admired Berlioz, found his master's phrases "scarcely intelligible; and of those which we understand, some are ungrammatical, others coarse; and his whole style is so pestered with figurative expressions that it is as affected as it is obscure." [21]

The remarkable fact, of course, is that these faults, any one of which would be enough to sink an ordinary writer into oblivion, did not keep Shakespeare from exacting and receiving the highest praise — often at the hands of the very same critics — and from rising at long last to a position where we simultaneously see his faults and see that they do not matter. Nor is this double vision the result of idolatry; it comes rather from the knowledge that each critic and each age finds Shakespeare's flaws in different places, and that the blemishes seen from one point of view turn into marks of genius when seen from another. This, if anything, is the meaning of the conclusion so often repeated that Shakespeare transcends criticism, baffles judgment, and outtops knowledge.

Perhaps because Shakespeare was a writer — hence more amenable to diverse uses, including that of supreme academic hobbyhorse — criticism has not inquired whether his art is unique in the respects cited above, or whether by those tokens it belongs to a class. An earlier chapter of this book proposed the idea that Gothic and Shakespearean were in this limited sense interchangeable terms and did define a class. If this is true, we can understand why Henry Adams juxtaposed twelfth-century stained glass and Delacroix, and why the parallel between Shakespeare and Berlioz is hard to resist.

Had the objections to Berlioz' taste, judgment and knowledge, no less than to his sense of form, harmony, and counterpoint been artistically founded, they too would long ago have made an end of him. But from Schumann's day the "inevitability" of these presumed errors and the

---

[20] See Jonson's *Timber* (1641). The modern English poet George Barker calls Shakespeare "unsound, turgid, and incomplete" (*1393*, 1942, 500); Mr. Cleanth Brooks compares him unfavorably with Donne as a lyricist (*The Well-Wrought Urn*, 219–20), and Mr. John Crowe Ransom describes him as "the most inaccurate of all the poets," though without attaching blame to the "slashing carelessness of grammatical logic" and failure to develop his multitude of figures. (*American Scholar*, 1942, 60.)

[21] From *The Conquest of Granada*, "Defense of the Epilogue."

power of the music with all its flaws has had to be acknowledged. For
Berlioz too there has been a reversal of opinion on details formerly thought
settled beyond appeal: his crudities have turned into subtleties, his noise
into melody, his harmonic ignorance into bold forecasting of methods
now current. Since from the beginning critics faced the necessity of ac-
counting for Berlioz' baffling power, there grew up the hypothesis (still
in the textbooks) of a volcanic genius, imperfectly educated, in whose
work fine inspirations abound, though always in an aura of sulphur and
brimstone. Thus the eighteenth century was wont to write about Shakespeare's wild untutored genius, regret that he "wanted art," and deplore
his taste for the macabre.[22]

The parallel, let it be said again, does not mean that Shakespeare and
Berlioz are identical or interchangeable, but that their respective works
may be usefully compared as cultural phenomena. We may liken them
as "makers of great imperfect dramas," of "flawed masterpieces" — the
term does not matter so long as we use it to trace indicative consequences.
Can it be simple coincidence, for example, that it was through reiterated
performance, instigated by great actors or great conductors,[23] that both
Shakespeare and Berlioz finally found fit critics? Again, by an involvement
which only strengthens the bond between the pair, it was the men of
Berlioz' own time who forced the last step in Shakespeare's canonization.
Scott, Lamb, Hazlitt, Coleridge, Goethe, Herder, and Berlioz himself had
to combat their fathers' diffidence, and argue much as is done right here.[24]
It was they who destroyed the "clumsy genius" hypothesis and made

[22] Dr. Johnson, who truly admired Shakespeare, thought the tragedies inferior
to the comedies and declared one could not read six lines without stumbling
upon a fault. (Boswell's *Johnson:* Autumn 1769.)
[23] Boswell affirms that Garrick was the real resuscitator of the Shakespeare
repertory as a whole. (*Journal of a Tour to the Hebrides,* N. Y., 1936, 207 *n.*)
For the succession of conductors from Mottl to Harty, Berlioz was similarly
a "vehicle," and an incitement to cut, alter, arrange and edit.
[24] Hazlitt had to prove that not all Shakespeare's effects were achieved by
supernatural means (*1257,* IX, 41) — compare Berlioz the fantastic; Holcroft
had to dispute the generality that Shakespeare excels only in sudden bursts
of passion (*Memoirs,* 267). Wieland who wanted to translate him was met with
a "Why do it?" Herder had to write an essay explaining Shakespeare and explaining the necessity for the essay; while Schiller, aroused, had to study the
works a good while before liking them. In France, Berlioz' generation had to
neutralize the belief derived from Voltaire, that Shakespeare's tragedies were
"monstrous farces" with here and there a redeeming moment of great beauty.
This sacrosanct "taste" Lessing broke down and replaced by one closer to
Shakespeare's own, that is, inferred from his works and presented as tenable.
In short, as Goethe put it, "a great many gifted men labored long to show
him in a good light." (*Poetry and Truth,* II, 40.)

good in its place the assertion that in Shakespeare "the form [is] equally admirable with the matter, and the judgment of the great poet not less deserving of our wonder than his genius." [25]

A good many other critical facts connecting Berlioz with the "Shakespearean mode," and still others corroborating the reality of what has here been called "Gothic" texture, could be adduced, but the reader will prefer to draw them from his own experience.[26] The notion will have justified its use pragmatically if it suggests a way of understanding the artistic life and afterfame of such men as Rabelais, Rembrandt, Bach, or Delacroix.[27] As regards Berlioz, certainly, we need a principle by which to reconcile the many discrepant opinions still found in books. They vary from the view that might be termed the "golden thread" hypothesis — that is, seeing a vein of natural genius but overlaid with rubbish [28] — to the troubled feeling that despite innumerable wonders, Berlioz' art is mysteriously unsatisfying.[29]

When this greater concession is made by a sensitive judge, it is of course not enough to murmur "Shakespearean" and hope to suspend criticism. Rather, "Shakespearean" has to be extended to mean something more than "Gothic," and include the peculiar property of dramatic form. For it can be shown that the combination of a rugged, uneven artistry with objective drama accounts historically for much of the resistance to Berlioz. It accounts for the paradox that he is known at once for his wire-drawn refinements and for being "absolutely devoid of taste." [30] No one can repeat for him the excuse which has served for Shakespeare, that he deliberately composed his works in layers of increasing fineness corresponding to social gradations — puns for the pit and philosophy for the earls. The cliché is almost certainly false for Shakespeare too. What we have in both instances is the state of mind of the dramatist working at an "open" form, which demands fine tooling close by relaxed effort, a will-

---

[25] Coleridge, *Shakespeare*, Ch. 5.

[26] Pope may in fact have been the first to compare Shakespeare with Gothic buildings: see above, Chapter 10. In recent times Hardy used the same analogy to defend his own poetic technique.

[27] See especially Forkel's life of Bach (1803), which started the work of rehabilitation.

[28] *E.g.*, Percy Buck in *A Small History of Music*.

[29] *E.g.*, W. H. Mellers (372).

[30] *Cf.*: "Shakespeare often writes so ill that you hesitate to believe he could ever write supremely well." (Henley: 679, 101.) Yet one keeps reversing one's view of particulars. The lines, for instance, in which Laertes stops his tears with the absurd reflection that the drowned Ophelia has only too much water already, seemed utterly in character as the part was played in Sir Laurence Olivier's screen version.

ingness to let a flat motive do duty side by side with concise harmony or delicate orchestration.[31] Only by abdicating one kind of sophisticated taste does the finished work approximate the reality sought for.

It is this ultimate naturalism which is both Berlioz' strength and his weakness. It is this which makes him arduous or puzzling: one has to seek. And since it is his fundamental outlook on the world which makes him a naturalist of this type, we are not wrong to feel that he is unsatisfying — his naturalism being but the outward expression of his pessimism.[32] Yet "unsatisfying" need not mean unsatisfactory. The beholder seeking for Berlioz' reasons and for Berlioz' order is not in the end disappointed. When close scrutiny has done with these rugged, resistant, and intermittently glowing works, it must confess that the idea of correcting or improving or de-blemishing them is untenable. Somehow (as Schumann said) the whole thing "has an air," an inevitability of its own. Again, when the noble, moving or delicate passages have led us to assimilate the rest, we find everywhere the same passionate desire to achieve exhaustive expression, the same disinclination to linger or repeat, and the same richness of invention and suggestion pressing as it were behind the externally dull or flat design.[33] The four adjectives by which Scott Fitzgerald summed up his judgment of Shakespeare will therefore serve anyone who knows his Berlioz well: "whetting, frustrating, surprising, and gratifying." [34]

The different degrees in which these qualities attract or repel determine the feeling one experiences on hearing Berlioz' several scores. It is a fact that musicians of similar rank have expressed widely different preferences among them. Brahms thought *The Infant Christ* Berlioz' masterpiece;

[31] By inversion it would seem plausible to reconsider the stereotype of Shakespeare as a careless writer, for we know full well how Berlioz polished and revised scores that have been judged careless. Why suppose that Shakespeare alone among writers could reach the sublime as the pen runs? Does not Jonson-of-the-blotter himself speak in his Memorial Verses of Shakespeare's "sweat" and "true-filed lines"?

[32] Need it be said that it is a Shakespearean pessimism, grounded in a similar view of noble-ignoble man? Berlioz writes in 1866 about the Austro-Prussian War: "Yes, let us talk of these hundreds of thousands of idiots who disembowel, knife, and blast one another to bits, and die in mud and blood. . . . How I should like to see a small planet, of only 300 miles' circumference, come and graze our own at the time of a big battle and bring to reason by crushing them all these little monsters who are massacring one another. What a deserved puree! It is then that Nature's indifference would seem sublime — just as it happened to certain antediluvian animals." (*S.W.*, 179–80.)

[33] E.g., the melodic fragment of the opening of the *Corsair* overture, which sets off the fine orchestral harmony and irritates us into anticipation of the tender adagio.

[34] *Note-Books*, printed in *1081*, 176.

Wagner chose the *Funeral* symphony; Liszt adored *Benvenuto;* and Mendelssohn could truly admire only the songs. What is more, the opinions given by capable scholars show that every one of Berlioz' dozen great works appears to some as his greatest, while the rest are unhesitatingly dismissed as inferior. It is clear that if each man's negative vote were accepted, this would make a clean sweep of Berlioz' music, and conversely that if we add together the same men's positive votes, they validate the bulk of the composer's output — which may be another way of saying that Berlioz' range extends on every side beyond the sensibility of his judges.[35]

One perfection at least must be granted the creator of such works — that of being inexhaustible by any single mind.

And this in turn explains the situation which has been erroneously thought peculiar to Berlioz, but which is merely characteristic of his kind, that of not being finally placed. While we wait, it must be set down as a statistical fact that nine tenths of all the music Berlioz wrote has evoked the highest possible praise of those who know. Their consensus is distributive, as for Shakespeare — a con-sensus rather than a unanimity, but it is emphatic and unmistakable.[36]

Shakespeare remains Shakespeare and Berlioz, Berlioz — in spite of all similarities; for the common points define a common type of art and not a reincarnation of souls. But if art has links with both the culture and the self, it is to be expected that kindred species of art and of character will intertwine. In history as in music everything repeats, though in altered form, and the critical question always is: What have we here — the same (essence)? — or difference (accident)? The nineteenth century bears a likeness to the sixteenth, Berlioz' work to Shakespeare's, why not also the man to the man? Any answer involves a risk, but when we consider how Shakespeare seemed to find himself in Montaigne, and how it took a second Romantic period to turn both into great world figures, we are tempted to attach diagnostic importance to Berlioz' feeling of kinship with Shakespeare. "I have to keep consoling myself . . ." he says, "for not having known Virgil, whom I should have so much loved, and

[35] John Morley on Edmund Burke: "It is one of the signs of Burke's singular and varied eminence that hardly any two people agree precisely which of his works to mark as the masterpiece." *Encyclopaedia Britannica*, 14th ed., IV, 416.

[36] An amusing series could be made of articles bearing some form of the title "Berlioz Today," in which every ten years since the composer's death some critic declares him finally done with. For a sketch of Berlioz' afterfame in various countries, see Supplement 1.

Gluck, and Beethoven, and Shakespeare — who might have loved me. (But in truth I am not in the least consoled.)"[37] Berlioz found an uncommon number of his sensations and impulses put into words by Shakespeare. He found the same intensity of feeling, the same "rush of metaphor," and "lucid confusion" answering to his own. He shared also the fierce pleasure in seeing nature dwarf the individual, mixed with great tenderness, humor, and compassion for men. Unwittingly, too — if *The Tempest* is in truth Shakespeare's last word — both men ended on the same note of half-melancholy fantasy. *Beatrice and Benedict* skims lightly over the conflict between sweet purity and Calibanism, and uses grotesque humor, airy figures, and festive pageantry to half-conceal the purblindness of evil. From the composer's artistic serenity we can infer little as to his day-to-day disposition, but we know that after his Shakespearean comedy Berlioz had said farewell to his art, meaning to live on his patrimony and his accumulated earnings from the stage.

[37] *Mem.*, II, 422.

26. *Empire and Industry:* Les Grotesques

August 1862 to
January 1867

Faced with the penny paper, everyone trembled . . . the musician for his opera, the painter for his canvas. . . . The 1830 renaissance had created in France a great public . . . : the penny paper lowered this intellectual level . . . by making the smile of Mr. Worldly Wiseman the arbiter of French taste.

— E. and J. DE GONCOURT
(1860 and 1868)

To SAY THAT AFTER *Beatrice and Benedict* Berlioz retired is true of him as a creator. "I am eager," he wrote Ferrand, "to cut the bonds that attach me to art, so as to be able to say to Death, 'at your service.' "[1] He was weary and ill, but life and will power were not yet spent and he had not abdicated as man, critic, or musician. Indeed he was in these final years to experience his most resplendent defeat and his most gruelling victories. Tragic completeness demanded both, and only after tasting all the joys and miseries of action could it be said of him as of Nelson that "his death is not untimely whose work is done."

By 1862 the Second Empire had been in existence ten years and seemed flourishing in the thick of its special atmosphere. It had won a part of this reward by conscious effort, but the rest had come as a gift — the natural product of a new phase in the onward march of industry and democracy. The Paris that Berlioz returned to after the *première* of *Beatrice* in Baden was spiritually as different from the Paris that had heard the *Symphonie Fantastique* as the streets of that epoch were different from the new boulevards cut by Baron Haussmann. The Baron, also a graduate of the Conservatoire, had ideas on the grand scale like Berlioz, but working as he did in the tangible medium of cobblestones, his plans met more easily with official favor: the new Paris would glorify the regime and facilitate the mowing down of possible insurgents. For now of course the only acceptable revolution was the industrial. The Second Empire

[1] *L.I.*, 238.

bore the emblem of the bee like the original Napoleon, but its motive power was a steam-driven substitute: the very word industry had changed meaning. The imperial tone also was a dubious hybrid, like the operas of Meyerbeer, like the mind of Louis Napoleon.

Canny but not a great diplomat, warlike but not a warrior, jealous of his power but careless in its delegation, ruled by the consort he deceived, frivolous and apprehensive all at once, the Emperor was a living example of what happens to the heirs of genius when underbred and born out of time. It was only during his reign, out of the century following Waterloo, that France resumed the practice of national wars, and neither he nor the nation could manage them. It was only since his reign that it would have been conceivable for the titled leader of fashion — Eugénie — to give her favorite shade of red the name of a pointless and un-Napoleonic victory: it was peace and dishonorable bargaining that had added Nice and Savoy to the territory of France.

The decadence of mind which had begun after 1848 became oppressive after 1852 and well-nigh unbearable in the sixties. Machine industry fostered its characteristic social revolution, by which the lower middle class is perpetually extended yet never wholly acclimated, consisting as it does of those who know enough to want more but do not know enough to want the right things — "the generation born and bred in the back-shop, reared on small tricks and frauds . . . on bad atmosphere and bad blood." [2] These were the potential mass men whom Flaubert insulted generically and vocally from the terrace of his house on the Seine as boat-loads of them plied up and down in Sunday excursions. They were the indestructible butt of his anger in *Madame Bovary*, published and censured at law in 1857; they were the multitudinous sitters for the portrait of the druggist in the novel, which has made Homais the name of a cultural phenomenon.

In the arts, this new class had its counterpart in Bohemia — "a new race of intellects without ancestry, without mental luggage, without homeland in the past, free from any tradition . . . Bohemia brought the sharp demands of practical life into the pursuit of its aims: its appetites held its principles by the throat." [3] The outlet for these nipping, eager talents was the penny paper, offspring of Girardin's *La Presse* [4] and

[2] Goncourt: *1251*, 163.

[3] *1251*, 140. On a higher plane, Sainte-Beuve observed that the generation of Taine, who was just leaving the Ecole Normale in 1851, seemed unpleasantly "bookish, absolutist, hurrying forward its raw intellect and tracking down ideas in the fashion of science." (*1212*, VIII, 79.)

[4] See above, Chapter 15.

progenitor of yellow journalism. By the time that Berlioz retired as critic on the *Journal des Débats* in 1864, the intellectual press he had been bred to and had helped make famous was already an anachronism. Not that newspapers as yet enjoyed the huge circulations we now expect — the London *Times's* 51,600 in 1860 was considered a record — but the style and contents of the new sheets were showing the effect of vulgarization. Invective itself became coarser and duller, and the careers of a Berlioz or a Delacroix ended in volleys of personal insults.

In the realm of physical things, rapid expansion was setting new standards of judgment by touch and quantity. The evidence of things unseen paled before those yearly tables showing always more mileage, more tons of coal, more bales of cotton. Between Berlioz' first and second visit to Russia, twenty years apart, European railroads had extended their network fivefold, and the mode of travel which had proved a wonderful conquest of mind as far as the Russian frontier was now a common carrier all the way to St. Petersburg. Comfort subtly usurped the place of pleasure — a passive for an active thing.

As the scale of success rose in these goods, so did the scale of required success in things of the spirit — a play or opera had to run hundreds instead of dozens of nights to be even noticed; it had to be played in six European capitals instead of one. Mankind had entered the age of numbers in which unity is necessarily the least, and as a consequence, while the channels of communication become clogged with things, the power of attention dwindles under an excess of stimuli. Repetition ranks as the chief intellectual force. Delacroix, also reading Taine in 1858, feels that here is "another of those who want to say everything, after which he says it all over again." [5]

In a word, the aristocratic ideal was dead, and what replaced it was not so much the reign of democratic equality as the pressure of all to reach and to enforce identity. "There are epochs," wrote Baudelaire with some irony, "when the techniques of art are sufficiently numerous, perfected, and cheap for everyone to acquire them in roughly equal amounts." [6] At first the tendency had seemed like a new wave of enlightenment, fulfilling the humanitarianism shared by Lamennais, Carrel, or Louis Blanc — clerical, liberal, and socialist alike. But there came a period of glut and apathy, as of the boa constrictor after an indigestible meal, and by the mid-sixties we find the men of three generations (Zola, Doudan, Sainte-Beuve) noting "a kind of general intimidation of the human spirit. . . . As time goes on, Mind becomes more cotton-woolly and insipid.

[5] *182*, III, 207–8.   [6] *1049*, 202.

Berlioz imagined by Daumier (*c.* 1856)

"He had the beak of an eagle and the mane of a lion
and the strange aspect of an heraldic animal."

— BARBEY D'AUREVILLY

This can be seen in things both large and small.[7] Only the abnormal has any life in it." [8]

This last remark helps to explain why *Les Fleurs du Mal* and *Salammbô*, Hugo's *Les Misérables* and Renan's *Life of Jesus* caused such perturbations. Nothing less than shock could distract the public of the sixties from the color of Eugénie's crinoline or the equally factitious bustle of the stock exchange. Even the expedition to Mexico and the World's Fair of 1867 fell upon dulled senses.

In this Empire, quite unworthy of any Tacitus, would Berlioz and his Trojans produce the kind of explosion, of vengeful satisfaction which the separately oppressed master spirits required? Baudelaire, who was not so sure a critic of music as he was of poetry and painting, preached Wagner, quite understandably, side by side with Delacroix and Hugo: *l'art romantique* was for him the repository of true glory, of protest and assertion by genius. But the one romantic composer who by chronological and intrinsic right should have occupied the open place in this French triad was obscured by the uniqueness of his own art and the evolution of his mind. The subject of *Les Troyens* falsely suggested a neoclassicism in the style of Ponsard or of the painter Cabanel. Besides, who had heard the music? *Tout Paris* thought it knew all about it and fashioned a queer reputation for it *in absentia*. So dark is the day for spiritually kindred contemporaries when the national circulation of ideas is stopped by a repressive government riding high upon a giddily prosperous public.

Flaubert could at least write and swear in peace, at home; he could publish and be read without his detractors' making it an auto-da-fé. Nor did he need the intelligent aid of a hundred men and the expenditure of a quarter million francs to exist as an artist. But without that prodigal prince, Bénazet, Berlioz' musical life would have been limited to occasional fragments at the Conservatoire or at Pasdeloup's Cirque d'Hiver.[9] Bénazet's faith was such a tonic that when Berlioz returned to Paris in the fall of 1862, he expanded *Beatrice and Benedict*, adding the trio and chorus now found in the second act. This once done, he wanted like his

[7] Sainte-Beuve may have been thinking of the ridiculous outcry made in 1860 in Passy, a wealthy suburb, when the district was assigned the number 13. The offending digits were transferred to the Gobelins, where the population was too poor to object.

[8] *1212*, XI, 214 and 224 *n.* For Zola see *La Tribune*, Nov. 29, 1868, and for Doudan, *188*, III, 411 and IV, 30 ff.

[9] Even so this amounted to rather more than has been done for most twentieth-century innovators in music: *e.g.*, Van Dieren, Carl Ruggles, Edgard Varèse.

own Dido to mark by words the termination of his career. He wrote to the Princess toward the end of September: "Yesterday I set down the last orchestral note with which I shall ever blot a sheet of paper. *No more of that. Othello's occupation's gone.* [In English.]" [10]

From this resignation a great artistic experience roused him: the reading of Flaubert's new novel, *Salammbô.* The book pleased Berlioz by its mixture of elevation and irony, by its antique setting and plastic prose. He thought for a moment of making it into music; [11] but he stuck to his resolve, urging Reyer to try his hand instead.[12] Besides *Salammbô*'s superficial similarity of setting with *Les Troyens,* which might be dangerous in the eyes of a skittish public, Berlioz feared that any new undertaking would seem quixotic in view of his unplayed score. He contented himself with writing Flaubert an enthusiastic letter and helping out the sale of the book with notices in the *Débats.*[13]

At the Opera another *coup d'état* had taken place. Emile Perrin was the new director and his predecessor's promises were so much wind. True, the Opéra-Comique was toying with the idea of producing *Beatrice and Benedict;* foreign orchestras were playing Berlioz' symphonies of thirty years before; and in Paris, the first thought of a new but ephemeral society was to ask Berlioz to conduct two concerts, mainly of his own works. In March, moreover, the Conservatoire gave the nocturne of *Beatrice* and its cool impressionism stirred the audience to a vociferous *da capo.* But these were "victories without sequels, which exhaust an artist and discourage him as much as a defeat." [14]

[10] *S.W.,* 126–7. At that very time, Liszt was writing to Brendel: "Berlioz was so good as to send me the printed piano score of his opera *Les Troyens.* Although for Berlioz' works piano editions are plainly a deception, yet a cursory reading through *Les Troyens* has made an uncommonly powerful impression on me. One cannot deny that there is enormous power in it, and it certainly is not wanting in delicacy — I might also say subtlety — of feeling." (*204,* II, 7.)

[11] The "symphonic" passage in which the roar of the lions is heard above the human cries and confusion has since been called "analogous" to the close of the *Lacrymosa* of Berlioz' *Requiem.* (*611.*)

[12] Reyer's *Salammbô* was produced in Brussels in 1890 and in Paris in 1892. The subject also attracted Moussorgsky, who in 1867 began a setting of which ten numbers in piano-vocal score were published in 1939.

[13] *1386,* Dec. 23, 1862. He said among other things that so far he had read the book "only twice." Parisian opinion found the novel difficult and strange, on the principle that whatever could not happen on the Boulevards must lack reality. So good a judge as Mérimée said: ". . . it is perfectly crazy . . . but after all there is talent in it." (*218,* II, 211.) Flaubert had his fingers rapped by authoritative pedants, but he knew his subject and crushed their knuckles with the finality of a sledge hammer. See the correspondence — including, alas, a foolish note from Sainte-Beuve — which is reprinted at the end of any good edition of *Salammbô.*   [14] *542,* 82.

Not for vanity, which Berlioz had outgrown long since as one outgrows the thrill of seeing oneself in print, but for the sake of rounding out his musical life, it was imperative that he should make every effort to see his Virgilian score produced on home ground. *Beatrice* could not supply that sizable effect, that variety of means, and that serious public test which Berlioz' sense of form about his career made him desire. Accordingly, as he wrote to Davison on February 5, 1863, "if within a week the Minister does not put *Les Troyens* in rehearsal, I'll give in to Carvalho's urging and start getting ready for production at the Théâtre-Lyrique, risking fate in December. For three years I have been kept dangling at the Opera, and I want to hear and see my great musical affair before I die. . . . I live like a man who will die any minute, who no longer believes in anything, and yet who acts as if he believed in everything." [15]

Earlier, Berlioz had accepted a call to direct *The Infant Christ* for the Strasbourg festival in June,[16] and meanwhile he was apprised that the Grand Duchess of Weimar would like to commission *Beatrice* for her birthday.[17] He accepted again, and on March 30 set out for the old city where he had experienced so many artistic emotions. Physical pain beset him but as he told Ferrand, he "had no time for it." [18] Seven years had gone by since Weimar's last "Berlioz Week"; Liszt and the Princess were no longer there to greet him, and the crowd of intelligent youth, now staider and less free, had also scattered.

From Rome, where his friends no longer sought marriage but surcease from care and the consolations of faith, Liszt would soon send a copy of the *Faust* symphony, just published and dedicated to Berlioz.[19] After a first reading the recipient wrote to the Princess: "It is a great work." [20] But in Weimar Berlioz had also heard a fine performance of *Tannhäuser* and had

---

[15] *83*, 173. For form's sake, Berlioz had written on January 10 to the new director of the Opera, Emile Perrin, to remind him of *Les Troyens'* existence. (*140*, printed in *91*, 163–4.)

[16] The "tradition" thus established has lasted to this day. Like Manchester, Munich, Carlsruhe, and Glasgow, Strasbourg is a "Berlioz city." To this fact we owe the critical and directorial work of such eminent Berliozians as Albert Schweitzer, Abbé Hoch, and Charles Münch.

[17] As Liszt's correspondence with Grand Duke Charles Alexander shows, the Duchess — and the town of Weimar — remained devotees of Berlioz until long after his death. As late as 1883, there is discussion of the sum to be sent for Berlioz' statue in Paris. (*208a*, 200 ff.)

[18] *L.I.*, 244.

[19] Liszt's pupil and early biographer, Lina Ramann, ascribes the inspiration of Liszt's masterpiece to the influence of Berlioz' technique and principles. (*995*, I, Ch. 8.) It is certainly true that in the sixties Liszt was scanning again Berlioz' *Fantastique* and *Faust* and making fresh piano transcriptions of parts of those works. (*994a*, II, 271–2.)   [20] *S.W.*, 126.

at once written: "It contains some truly beautiful things, in the last act especially. It is profoundly melancholy in tone and in the grand style, but why then is it necessary — no, there would be too much to say. Farewell." [21]

His own little work pleased the distinguished audience. No applause was allowed because of the presence of the Ducal Highnesses, but they bade the composer to their box and fed him the most delicate flattery. Later, the artists and other celebrities from nearby centers gave Berlioz a banquet at which his praises were sung. A second performance brought enthusiasm to a peak and Berlioz was asked to give a reading (*faute de mieux*) of his *Troyens* poem before the sovereigns and their guests.

Housed by his faithful admirer and translator Richard Pohl, Berlioz was resting agreeably on his laurels when an invitation came from Prince Hohenzollern-Hechingen, now moved to Löwenberg in Silesia, who desired an all-Berlioz concert under the master's hand. The Prince had himself arranged the program and begun rehearsing. Neither man had forgotten the time twenty years earlier when at Hechingen proper, Berlioz had arranged without fee and for a minute orchestra a concert of his then unknown works. Now the Prince could put sixty men at Berlioz' disposal and, matching the artist's earlier care and thoughtfulness, he prepared for the composer the most exquisite pleasure in his career. When Berlioz arrived he found a small concert room of excellent acoustics, which connected with greenrooms, a musical library and an apartment for the visiting artist.

At four each day they come into my study to tell me the orchestra is assembled. I open a double door and find half a hundred players seated and *already in tune*. They rise as I step to the podium. I lift my baton, give the first beat, and we're on our way . . . If you can believe it, at the first rehearsal they went through the finale of *Harold* without a mistake, the adagio from *Romeo and Juliet* without missing an accent. . . . Seifriz, the capellmeister, told me after this [in French]: "Sir, when we listen this piece we ever in tears."

Do you know, dear friends, what touches me most in these marks of affection? It is the discovery that I must be dead. So much has happened in 20 years which I have the impudence to call progress: I am played almost everywhere [in Germany]. . . . My *Corsair* Overture is widely played though I myself have heard it only once. The others, *Lear* and *Benvenuto Cellini*, are often given and they are just the ones least known in Paris. Day before yesterday (laugh or smile if you like) I found myself unable to hold back a tear in conducting the *King Lear* . . . I was thinking that perhaps Father Shakespeare would not curse me for having made his old

[21] To Morel, Aug. 7, 1863. (Bibl. Conserv., partly quoted in *298*, 325.)

British King and his sweet Cordelia speak in those strains. I had forgotten the work since writing it at Nice in 1831. . . .

There being no harpist here, one was bidden to come 300 miles from Weimar. . . . The Prince is kept in bed by the gout . . . so during meals he writes me pencilled notes which are brought to me and which I must answer between fruit and dessert (for there is no cheese here)[22] . . . He knows everything I have written in prose and music. This morning he said, "Come and let me embrace you: I have just read your analysis of the Pastoral Symphony. . . ."[23] But I am exhausted. This is because a theatre orchestra is a slave stuck in a cave, whereas a concert orchestra is a king on his throne; and then these great symphonic passions upset me a good deal more than the make-believe sentiments of *Beatrice*.[24]

The events and emotions of this Löwenberg visit bear the stamp of a valedictory. After the last concert on April 20, the Prince awarded Berlioz the Hohenzollern Cross as to a captain commanding troops; an officer climbed the stage and affixed the medal in military fashion. The next day, the Prince being still bedridden, Berlioz read *Les Troyens* before a small company gathered near the patient, who at the end called Berlioz to him, kissed him and said: "You are going back to France: to those who love you, say I love them."[25]

Not long after, the Prince died, his orchestra scattered, and the name Hohenzollern attached to other deeds. But one of the visitors to Löwenberg during Berlioz' concerts had been Dr. Leopold Damrosch, who had moreover played under the composer at Weimar and who, on emigrating to the United States in the seventies, brought with him an orchestral tradition that contributed not a little to America's musical awakening. Somewhat prematurely, no doubt, the elder Damrosch gave Berlioz' great concert works in this country.[26] On a lesser scale his sons maintained Berlioz on the programs through the world's Wagnerian period, down to the present when others were ready to enlarge the repertory.

On April 24, Berlioz was in Strasbourg to start chorus and orchestra on their studies of *The Infant Christ*, and four days later he was back in Paris. The first news he heard was that difficulties were brewing with regard to *Les Troyens*. "When I turn my back, nothing goes right."[27]

[22] As regrettable a lack, for a Dauphinois, as the absence of mountains in Paris.
[23] Obviously in *A Travers Chants*, which Berlioz must have just given him.
[24] *Corresp.*, 297–9.
[25] *L.I.*, 248.
[26] See Supplement 1.
[27] *L.I.*, 246; Wellington agreed: "Our generals are really heroes when I am on the spot to direct them, but when I am obliged to quit them they are children." (*1143*, 200.)

The previous half year had not been without disquiet of the familiar kind. Louis had impulsively thrown up his land post in the merchant marine and come to Paris without means or purpose. His father's pleasure in seeing him was naturally mixed with the worst apprehensions. Slowly, Berlioz persuaded the "boy" of twenty-eight to resume his career. By March Louis was in Mexico, having signed on a ship with the promise of being master of his own vessel at the first opportunity.

By sympathetic identification Berlioz had also been shocked by the sudden death of Liszt's daughter, Mme. Emile Ollivier. And his own romance with Amélie was over, though he did not yet know of her death — "a love which came to me smiling, which I did not seek, and which I even resisted for a time. But the isolation I live in, and the imperious, destroying desire for affection overcame me. I let myself be loved, and then loved in return, far more than I should. A voluntary break became necessary, compulsory, complete, without compensation — absolute as death. That's all. I recover little by little. . . ." [28]

Humbert Ferrand to whom he wrote these words was himself in wretched health and spirits. After a long period of intermittent correspondence, the two men had resumed their steady exchange, commenting upon one another's works and days, and matching philosophies like the aged Jefferson and John Adams. Ferrand's letters must have been still more confiding than Berlioz' for we find the latter excusing himself in case he seemed too reserved. Berlioz repeats that Humbert's letter has done him good, but that its praise is excessive; the sight of Ferrand's handwriting has made him happy the whole day, but "I can not so well as you express certain feelings we share in common; yet I feel them, too, do believe it. Moreover, I dare not yield myself too much. . . ." [29] Without any break in friendship, there had been a contrary motion in their development as characters, Ferrand growing more direct about the simplicities of life as Berlioz came to cover them with stoicism.

The erstwhile poet was at this time half-paralyzed and greatly impoverished. He was easily distraught, and Berlioz expressed regret at causing him needless anxiety by reporting the musical goings-on in Paris. "Do not be at the pains to send me extended comments. . . . Writing must be for you as my feuilletons are to me . . . *Miseris sucurrere disco.* It is enough if I have drawn your mind for a few moments away from your sufferings.

"At last Carvalho and I are harnessed to this huge affair of the Trojans.

---

[28] *L.I.,* 241–2.
[29] *L.I.,* 219 and *passim.*

Three days ago I read the piece to the assembled personnel of the Théâtre-Lyrique and the chorus rehearsals are about to begin. The negotiations with Mme. Charton-Demeur are concluded; she is engaged to sing Dido. . . . But I had to consent to letting the work be cut down to the last three acts only; they will be re-divided into five and preceded by a prologue which I have just written, the theatre being neither large enough nor rich enough to put on *The Taking of Troy. . . .*"[30]

Five months from the date of this letter, five years after the completion of the work, which is to say in December 1863, the mutilated *Troyens* was to have its *première*. But the half year's preparation for it was neither easy nor pleasant. Carvalho had banked on a subsidy of one hundred thousand francs from the Ministry of Fine Arts, which had been promised but not paid. Berlioz had to join in the campaign to get it. Then the contralto playing Dido's sister Anna turned out to be "non-music incarnate."[31] She had a superb voice and face but Berlioz had to teach her the part one note at a time. Dido, on the other hand, was enamored of her role but terrified by its scope and power. She had bouts of weeping and the composer had to reassure her.

There was agitation backstage as well. To damp the extravagance of meddlers, Berlioz applied to Flaubert for an opinion on the Carthaginian costumes.[32] This was a pleasure to both men, but since the capital on hand was barely enough, recourse was finally had to the ready-made. The publisher Choudens, speculating on the chances of success, bought the score outright for fifteen thousand francs. This was exactly twenty times the amount paid for the *Damnation of Faust*, but there was in this liberality a hidden joker which the composer could not foresee and which his admirers have not been able to circumvent.[33]

---

[30] *L.I.*, 250–1.

[31] *L.I.*, 254.

[32] *91*, 166. Flaubert insisted on being the one who should call on the other, and henceforth referred in letters to his "great friend Berlioz."

[33] The fact is that despite the contract Choudens never published the full score. After Berlioz' death, suit was brought by the heirs against the publisher, who managed to make a scapegoat of the Conservatoire as depositary of the autograph. The court enjoined publication (see full report in *157*) but this was carried out in a peculiarly French fashion: the score was engraved and printed but not put on sale, except to opera houses who agree to buy or rent parts. The rights have long since fallen into the public domain, but by the comity of publishers no one else has brought out a rival edition. (This is true of other operatic scores by French composers, which are monopolized beyond all legal terms.) If one goes into Choudens's shop and so much as inquires about the full score one is treated with suspicion amounting to rudeness. It is only fair to add that by 1923 the firm did issue their *Fantaisie pour orchestre* on *Les Troyens*, for

Meantime Berlioz had been at Strasbourg for the Rhineland Festival and returned. "I am back . . ., ground to powder, deeply moved.[34] *L'Enfance du Christ*, performed before a veritable *people* made a profound impression. The hall had been built *ad hoc* on Place Kléber and held 8500 persons, yet everyone could hear. They wept and applauded, to the point of interrupting several numbers . . . You cannot imagine the effect of the final mystic chorus: it was the religious ecstasy which I had dreamed of and felt in composing it. An *a cappella* group of 200 men and 250 young women had rehearsed it for three months and they did not drop an eighth of a tone. . . . Carvalho's enthusiasm for *Les Troyens* is growing. The year began well: will it end the same way? Make a wish!" [35]

The following month, when Berlioz had begun to expect a rather lonely three weeks in Baden (*Beatrice* to be played twice) Louis arrived from Mexico. They decided to go together and even planned Louis's return after a forthcoming cruise so that he might hear *Les Troyens*. While at Marseille Louis had gone to concerts and operas and now his interest in music, amateur though he was, partook of the intense ambivalent love he

---

which potpourri they were willing to make all arrangements with "cinemas, casinos, music halls, concerts and beer gardens." (Plate No. 2674, Bibl. Nat. Fol. Vm² 1150(2).)

[34] At the international festivities following the concert, Berlioz made a brief speech — the only one whose text has been preserved of the many he made in thirty years of public life:
Sir:
My colleagues and I were happy to accept the invitation of the City of Strasbourg, and we regret only that we could not do more to second your noble enterprise. You have rightly said, Sir, that under the influence of music, the soul is uplifted, the mind broadens, civilization progresses, and national hatreds dwindle. See how France and Germany mingle on this day: the love of art brings them together and this worthy love will do more for their complete union than the wonderful Rhine bridge and other modes of rapid transport in use between the two countries.
The great poet has told us that
> The man that hath no music in himself,
> Nor is not moved with concord of sweet sounds
> Is fit for treasons, stratagems, and spoils.
> . . . Let no such man be trusted.
No doubt Shakespeare has used here of the freedom to exaggerate which is granted to poets. Yet observation shows that even if his assertion is excessive when applied to individuals, it is much less so as regards nations; one must acknowledge today that where music stops there barbarism begins.
I give you the great civilized city of Strasbourg, the great civilized cities of France and Germany — which have joined together for the accomplishment of this magnificent festival. (72.) [These remarks were repeated the next day, and translated into German, for the inauguration of the bridge at Kehll.]
[35] *L.I.*, 251-3.

bore his father. The sight of Baden, its fashions, women, and wealth, and above all the response of an audience of habitués to his father's work, acted upon the son as glory does upon a possessive mistress.

The Paris season at the Lyrique began very poorly on September 1 with the *Marriage of Figaro*. Money grew scarcer, which pinched still more the staging of Berlioz' work, but it was too late to cry halt. Rehearsals of innumerable "sections" went on daily, in a milieu Berlioz grew to dislike more and more.[36] The creaky machinery for which his work had in fact not been conceived, irritated him in every fiber. "What a collection of tricks and traps! Benches that collapse amid supposititious flames; cupboards in which handsome youths are folded up once each way and then turn out to be empty; thunder that rolls deliberately, like a mayor in his scarf of office walking down the town hall steps; Albanian pirates, old Turks who can't walk, and old choristers who can't sing. Alas! concerts are a thing of the past; the theatre has swallowed up everything."[37]

These autumn months also swallowed up friends, artists, notables. In September, Delacroix died, shrouded in that semi-neglect, semi-recognition characteristic of the epoch.[38] Similarly misknown, Vigny, the affectionate friend and admired poet, who had been godfather, so to speak, of *Benvenuto Cellini*, also died obscurely in his retreat. Then one of the two librettists of the same work, Léon de Wailly, a friend to both Vigny and Berlioz, also died. And lastly, the ever warm and cheerful Horace Vernet, who ended as he began, painting Napoleons and helping artists greater than he.

Carvalho's next productions, meant to recoup the losses incurred over Mozart, were Weber's *Oberon* and Bizet's first opera, *The Pearl Fishers* — both failures. Berlioz, who could tell a real musician by ear, tried to minimize Bizet's fiasco in the eyes of the public by a review in which he not only praised the young musician's merits but gave a prescient indication of his characteristic genius.[39]

[36] Bruneau's description of the way Carvalho directed, without plan, by sudden inspiration mixed with back chat, shows what must have profoundly repelled Berlioz, whose notion of art was not improvisation but order. (*936, 29.*)

[37] *269, 585.*

[38] The historian of Impressionism, Mr. John Rewald, writes: "Delacroix's isolation had increased during the last years of his life . . . The old and lonely painter closed his eyes at the very moment when many of those who . . . had benefited from his liberating influence were beginning to rally around Manet, a man of their own time." (*1115, 77.*)

[39] Excerpts from the article are in *M.M.*, 343–5, and see below next Subchapter.

After this third bad investment, Carvalho's bank balance was seriously nicked and he became intransigent with Berlioz. The composer could not have the quite reasonable orchestra originally called for. He who thought he had "set down his last orchestral note" now had to reinstrument parts of his work. He had moreover composed a Prelude to replace the first "day" of his epic action: *Les Troyens* was being whittled down to the size of a stock-company budget. And not only whittled down, but puttied up. The know-it-all office staff led by Carvalho wanted words removed, measures added or cut to help an exit, not to mention other details to be altered for strong but incommunicable reasons. Berlioz changed none of the parts but granted the cuts and patiently argued the existence and attributes of the Roman gods.[40] Carvalho's last imposition was to set the opening date a month ahead — avowedly to start the intake of cash as soon as possible.

At the dress rehearsal on November 2 the preparation was visibly inadequate. Though some passages were magnificently sung — which stirred not Berlioz alone to deep feeling — many others required constant aid from the prompter. Nor had unity of presentation been achieved. The clumsy scenery on which the producer counted so heavily made the show last from eight o'clock to half past twelve. On the opening night, one of the intermissions lasted fifty-five minutes though nothing in the way of effect justified such a wait. Again, the actors forgot their parts, lost their place, floundered about; their costumes (it is said) made them self-conscious. The fact was that the music was as new to them as that of *Benvenuto* and the *Damnation* had been two and three decades before.[41] Thirteen years later at Bayreuth, the *Ring* made a similar impression of disorder and incompetence, but here in 1863 there was no backing to sustain the piece through a bad start: it must make its own way.

The public was bewildered too, except at three or four places where the feeling expressed was so simple and the music so well performed that it carried immediately. The septet was encored. But the "Royal Hunt and Storm" was taken as an affront: it was symphonic music, no action goes

[40] Carvalho is speaking: "Do you want to do me another favor?"
Berlioz: "What now?"
"Let us omit Mercury; his wings at head and foot will cause laughter. No one has ever seen wings except at the shoulders."
"So, human figures have been seen wearing wings at the shoulders? I never knew it, but no matter. . . . Since Mercury is not often seen in the streets of Paris, let us suppress Mercury." (*Mem.*, II, 378.)
This was the critique of Flaubert's *Salammbô* in a new guise.
[41] See above the tenors Duprez (Chapter 11) and Roger (Subchapter 17).

with it on the stage, therefore it was too long (it lasts under six minutes).[42] The sailor's melancholy song was also too novel to be understood. Debussy had only been born the year before and the Russian school would not be heard in Paris for half a century. As for the sentries' dialogue, its imputation that quartered troops enjoy idleness, women, and good food shocked the pure taste of Paris. For opera, such naturalism was only a shade less objectionable than the statement in *Benvenuto* that at dawn in the country roosters crow.

In spite of these grave blemishes, when the curtain fell Berlioz' name was acclaimed, with one loud hiss to keep him from becoming conceited. The press the next day — barring a half dozen free lances — was respectful and even laudatory. Some had been deeply moved; others were beginning to understand; and as a group they felt the futility of further battle. Even the acrimonious Scudo was hushed, recognizing Berlioz' artistic power, misdirected though he felt it to be.[43] At bottom everyone knew that the Romanticist generation was depleted enough to give no more trouble, and that Berlioz as its musical representative could safely be paid the next-to-last honors.

It was the funny papers and the pamphleteers who made the most of the occasion. They were bidding for that cynical laughter of which the Goncourts speak, and they descended to the coarsest personalities. One journalist described the burial of the Trojans at Père Lachaise; others combined their recollections of Wagner with the popular idea of Berlioz to caricature them as Beethoven's sons now spawning further abortions, *Tannhäuser* and *Les Troyens*. Even Offenbach, for all his admiration of Berlioz, could not resist composing a parody, *Il signor fagotto*.[44]

The curious fact was that *Les Troyens* rescued Carvalho from his risky ventures in Mozart, Weber, and Bizet. The public came to hear Berlioz only twenty-two times, but it paid the boosted prices so readily that the

[42] In the *Revue Germanique*, Bertrand defended this and other parts of the work like a loyal member of the opposition: "One whole act is pure symphonic music; I do not like this symphony, but I find that people mock the author's very conception; I should rather thank him for it, so highly do I esteem the free invention of forms." Earlier, the critic spoke of Berlioz' having "long and bitterly expiated the crime of starting a musical revolution alone," and then made him out to be "a good deal responsible for Wagner." (*655*, 5–8.)

[43] *1397*, Nov. 15, 1863.

[44] His excuse must be that like Carvalho he had to keep a theater going, whose public he had accustomed to this sort of fare. Out of one hundred and one operettas produced at the Bouffes in six and a half years, thirty-five were by Offenbach. But in other ways Offenbach had long been a champion of Berlioz: he had among other things ridiculed the idea that any other French musician could be his rival.

composer's share, amounting to fifty thousand francs, freed him from his drudgery at the *Débats*. He signified his intention in December 1863, his last word having been written in support of one who was to continue a part of his own work, Georges Bizet.

To be sure, the last twenty-one performances gave the public no adequate idea of Berlioz' *Troyens* — hardly of the contents of the *première*, let alone of the entire work. For Carvalho's single thought was cut, cut, cut. The sailor's song, Dido's imprecations in the last act, the Hunt and Storm, the Nubian dance, the sentries' dialogue, the workmen's processional and four other vocal numbers — in all ten large omissions were made in three fifths of the "gigantic and [otherwise] convincing music drama." Even so, the run did not end because of slackening demand. The singers gave out first, for business reasons. Mme. Charton-Demeur had accepted a reduced salary for Berlioz' sake,[45] and was booked for other engagements. Others followed and were replaced by poor understudies whom Berlioz rehearsed in vain. The orchestra relaxed its tempi, and the chorus, preoccupied with a new piece, could be heard in this one only intermittently — like the voices in Shakespeare's magic isle.[46]

Still, most of the younger musicians came and Meyerbeer was present night after night, "for my pleasure," said he, "and my instruction." [47] One evening quite early, Berlioz was in the pit with a friend who observed the seats filling up and said: "They are coming." To which the composer dryly replied, "Yes, but I am going." He had, happily, moments of musical satisfaction. "It is beautiful, beautiful," he murmured at certain passages, and sometimes he wept silently.

At other times, disgust at the old practices which he knew so well got the better of him. What Choudens was publishing was not the full score mentioned in the agreement, but a hacked-up vocal score matching the current production.[48] A few pieces were issued separately. "You can buy

[45] He had helped her at the beginning of her career around 1851. (See Chapter 18 above.)

[46] This effect of overwork motivated the original tradition of the Paris Opera, which has always been to play only three nights a week and rehearse only four days. But the musical result is no better and the "majestic slowness" of the establishment is a byword.

[47] *269, 593.* There were other touching results Berlioz did not know, such as that Corot had become a devotee; he knew the score by heart, and sang it at his easel when he could not have his neighbor, Mme. Charton-Demeur, singing the airs for him. (*285, 299 n.*)

[48] There are at least three states of the published vocal score, all except that which bears Berlioz' notes for producers being extremely imperfect. Even the order of scenes and acts is chaotic and absurd. The version that Berlioz himself

bits of me for ten cents, as you do at a butcher's stall . . . Ah! Trade and Art are mortal enemies." Besides, as he candidly told the Princess, the continuing stream of insults and mean-spirited jokes pierced his revivified sensibility: "Hard as I try, I am wounded by them, and ashamed of being wounded." [49] He was moreover distressed that some of his old friends had not come, notably Pauline Viardot, who may have been piqued at not being given the role of Dido. He had not had a free hand, naturally, and could not satisfy everyone. Roger, who had gradually come to appreciate Berlioz' melody, was hurt at not being asked to sing Aeneas — though he had lost one arm and his singing voice — but he did attend and he wrote a warm letter to the composer.

The finest testimonial, however, came from abroad — a sober, subtle, competent and reassuring message from the musician Daussoigne-Méhul, formerly professor at the Paris Conservatoire, then living in Liège and speaking with the accents of posterity:

From the depths of my lair, whence I occasionally cast a glance on the men and things of our age, I have glanced at everything that the Paris press, big and little, has had to say about your *Troyens.* For my part — and I can only speak on the strength of the glorious precedents you have set — I put little faith in the praises of most reviewers and even less in their censure. . . . We Parisians, who pretend to lead the world in all things, actually rise up in arms against every innovation in the fine arts. Let an artist's eagle eye gaze steadily at the sun and seek to deflect one of its rays for the benefit of all — directly you see the inhabitants of the new Athens hide their heads like owls and curse the light that makes them blink.

. . . We must deplore the evil result of so damnable a habit, for it might well be (such cases are not unknown) that a devout artist who should aspire to modify the conditions of his art would grow discouraged and give up his effort on the verge of its fulfillment. Of course *you,* my dear Berlioz, you who have fought victoriously for a quarter century, you will make light of all these stupidities. . . . With the help of routine and imitation we should still today be writing the music of Lully, Rameau, or Philidor! . . . All honor, then, to the men of genius who have enlarged our horizons. So forge ahead, Berlioz, and do for our nephews

---

supervised having had a very limited printing, he knew it would soon be unprocurable. Hence his complaint here and in the *Memoirs* at Choudens's breach of contract.

[49] *S.W.,* 129. One Albert Wolff called on the French to kill Berlioz by ridicule and urged the composer to busy himself about ordering his tombstone: such were the witticisms published in Paris and reported to Berlioz by sadistic friends. Incredible as it may seem, this same Wolff later blamed his contemporaries for having "vilified Berlioz' genius." (*285,* 288.)

what others did for us. Music was born yesterday and art is boundless.
. . . Courage! Germany awaits you and France will perhaps honor your
fame in 1964. Does this not suffice for a man of spirit? [50]

The last word on the partial staging of his music drama must be left
to Berlioz himself, speaking in gratitude to his chief encourager, the
Princess: "You were not there, nor Liszt either . . . But let me now put
myself at your feet, take both your hands in mine, and thank you with
all my heart . . . for your sympathetic words, your unforgetting friendship, your flights of soul, and your harmonic vibrating to the distant
echoes of *our* work. Again my thanks, dear intelligence, believe in the
deep and grateful feelings of your devoted Berlioz." [51]

On December 20 all was over in Paris, but an English manager was
interested, an English edition of the score had been arranged for, and
Berlioz' ducal patrons at Weimar, besides sending congratulations, had
ordered one of the scenes from the omitted Part I to be played at their
theater. From St. Petersburg, Alexis Lvov also wrote, telling the sad news
that he had lost his hearing and urging Berlioz to compose a new work
for the stage.[52] A Polish lady, unknown to the composer, sent him a bronze
vase filled with flowers; and Auguste Barbier, the friend of Roman days,
colibrettist of *Benvenuto* and now an extinct poet, dashed off a warm
note beginning "Well-roared, lion!" [53]

Berlioz was far from cold to so much personal good will, but he was
once more alone. Louis, who had gone to every performance and measured the applause, had sailed again. Without the hurly-burly of public
and private attentions Berlioz would have felt even more deserted. For
the truth was that despite his resolve, music still held him thrall. It stopped
his physical pain and restored his zest for life, his oneness of being. When
Ferrand chose to write words for the processional in Gluck's *Alceste*,
Berlioz sought out the original score and would not let the poet change
a single note: "On such perfectly pure and beautiful music the words
must fit like a drapery by Phidias on his nude statue. Try again patiently
and you will find the right thing." [54]

[50] *97*, 16–17.
[51] *S.W.*, 132. This acknowledgment may possibly account for the amazing
assertion of one scholar, that the Princess was the author of Berlioz' poem.
(Eckart's *Cosima Wagner: 947*, 112–3.)
[52] *L.I.*, 264. Berlioz thanks his Weimar patrons and gives an account of the
Paris performances in a letter the following year. (*103*.)
[53] *235*, II, 212.
[54] *L.I.*, 264.

These passionate accents show us a Berlioz who might have called himself, like Hokusai in another art, "an old man crazy about music." Here lay the wonder and the tragedy. When Berlioz was busied with music he felt his expenditure of will to be self-justifying, soothing in its very tussle with the plastic material. But the work once finished, he was impelled not so much to exhibit it as to bring it conclusively to life by performance. In so doing his will struck other wills; his expense of energy was no longer selfless; it became ignoble, nauseating — and pain and pessimism returned. The conditions afforded by Prince Hohenzollern should have been his to command, for like the poet's imagined hero

> His thoughts are so much higher than his state
> That like a mountain hanging o'er a hut
> They chill and darken it.[55]

Thus when the post of conductor fell vacant at the Conservatoire, Berlioz, though turned sixty, put his name down among the candidates. In a sense the place was due him: for experience, reputation, and mastery he ranked first in the world. But he was considered too old — and too new — a possible danger to the gently ossifying tradition. Seeing this, Berlioz supported George Hainl, who was appointed and immediately called for excerpts of *Romeo and Juliet*. Lack of time postponed the concert, but Berlioz turned over all his musical scores and parts to the Society, knowing it and them in good hands.

In the spring of 1864, Pasdeloup played without permission the *Trojans* septet; and shortly afterwards, with greater courtesy, the Conservatoire obtained a warm reception for the *Flight into Egypt*. Berlioz' "indefinite leave" from the *Débats* being now a definite retirement [56] he had time to rest and contemplate — or so it seemed. But first he had to undergo in real life one of those Shakespearean scenes apparently reserved for the supremely conscious. A notice from the burial ground where Harriet lay informed him that either a transfer of her remains or a new lease would have to be made. Not imagining what it implied, he chose the transfer to the plot where Marie was buried, and where he expected to lie also. At the St. Vincent cemetery, Yorick's men opened not only the grave but the coffin as well, to convey the ashes in a different container. Berlioz, required by law to be present, had to endure the sight, noise, and other horrors of the operation, arriving shattered at the vault in Montmartre. He did not even yet know that Amélie whom he had met here lay buried, perhaps nearby.

[55] Thomas Lovell Beddoes: "A Lofty Mind, fragment" (*1238, 318*).
[56] D'Ortigue and later Ernest Reyer succeeded him.

Toward the end of April, Berlioz was to dine with Meyerbeer — a late beginning of the social relations that the German composer had been circuitously seeking for thirty-five years. The meeting was put off. On May 2 Meyerbeer died. Symbolic as it may have seemed to Berlioz, it was for the musical world the greatest commotion of the year. Rossini is said to have burst into tears. The funeral was that of a prince — indeed finer than that of some princes, for although, like Don John of Austria, Meyerbeer was borne slowly across France, it was not done in secret, the corpse carried piecemeal by mules: Meyerbeer's return to Berlin was a public procession punctuated by speeches and performances of the master's own works. The common feeling was that the realm of music had lost its sovereign. Berlioz, Liszt, and Wagner were not to be mentioned in the same breath.

Berlioz could deem it a private compensation that his protégé Theodore Ritter was playing in a fortnightly series the five concertos of Beethoven, accompanied by "a delightful orchestra . . . I go and hear those marvels. Our *Harold* has again been given with success in New York . . . what can be the matter with those Americans?" [57] Hearing music, however, had to be paid for by enduring the increased ugliness and noise of the city. Berlioz longed at times to be with Ferrand. "Voice and look have a certain power that paper lacks. Have you at least some flowers and new shoots outside your window? I have nothing but walls opposite mine. . . . Fortunately I also have close neighbors who are literate musicians and full of kindness toward me. I often spend the evening there. They allow me to lie on a couch and listen to conversation without taking part in it. Rarely do any bores come. When this occurs it is understood that I may leave without a word." [58]

Through the summer, there was blessed calm. The only news was that Scudo of the *Revue des Deux Mondes* had gone insane. In August, when Louis came back from Mexico, he, his father and Stephen Heller took an excursion into the country outside Paris. At the close of day, finding a moonlit sky, they decided to return on foot. The sights of nature opened the sluices of the two musicians' hearts; they sang and wept, to the uneasy surprise of the young sailor. Yet Louis was beginning to give his father more unmixed satisfaction. "He is a good young fellow, whose heart and mind have developed late but abundantly." [59] His visits were nec-

[57] *L.I.*, 268. It was first performed by Theodore Thomas's orchestra the previous year, on May 9, 1863. The Philharmonic Society, then in its 39th season, did not play *Harold in Italy* until 1880, but the overtures and symphonies occasionally figured in its programs. (*1333*, Appendix.)

[58] *L.I.*, 269.   [59] *L.I.*, 269.

essarily short and the moment of separation never grew easier for Berlioz.

He varied his evening visits to the Damckes with longer ones to Spontini's widow and sister-in-law who resided in the Château de la Muette in Passy. On other days he went to the cemetery ("I know people there") or reread his favorite works — Virgil, Cervantes, Shakespeare, Molière, La Fontaine, Bernardin St. Pierre. He even took walks "into the vicinity of lyric theatres, so as to have the pleasure of not going in." [60] After Louis's departure of mid-August 1864 Berlioz yielded to a longing for the Dauphiné: Paris was in bloom and this made all the more enticing a sight of real country and of his sweet young nieces. Just before he left, he found he had been raised in rank within the Legion of Honor, twenty-five years after his first decoration. Legouvé had shared in the promotion, and they exchanged congratulations together with news of their respective ailments. At the official dinner, Mérimée shook Berlioz' hand, and with his usual cryptic raillery said: "This delay proves that I have never been Prime Minister." [61]

The stay in Dauphiné had a soothing effect, though it began with the shock of seeing Adèle's portrait and the discovery that her daughters were inevitably and healthily beginning to forget her loss. Being the stranger and unoccupied, Berlioz could only live by recollecting. Just as his impulse to art had been remembered emotion, his life was now wholly memory, for there was nothing to drain off the reservoir. It overflowed and covered everything — place, persons, ideas — obliterating time. It reached farther and farther back, mirroring the vision, the name, the valley home of Estelle, to whom — as Boschot curiously notes — Berlioz returned in a regular cycle of sixteen years.[62] Berlioz decided to make a pilgrimage.

Meylan revisited was like a balm. Those mountains "composed" in the same sense that his feelings constituted his life. Not to act on the renewed impulse was impossible. He drafted a letter to his *Stella Montis,* more formal than the one which had been left unanswered in 1848, and having ascertained her address in Lyon, called. She received him, an aged lady of nearly seventy. The interview narrated in the Epilogue to the *Memoirs* was outwardly calm and of significance (at first) only to Berlioz. Mme.

[60] *Corresp.,* 308.
[61] *Corresp.,* 307. The meaning is, "or else you would have had the honor sooner" — an example of true raillery, by the way, which consists in hiding a delicate compliment under what seems an insult or a piece of egotism.
[62] 1816, 1832, 1848, 1864. Since childhood Berlioz had actually seen her only for an instant in 1832.

Fornier was a simple good woman who was naturally amazed that an old gentleman, member of the Institute and wearing the rosette of the Legion of Honor, should be moved to such a visit by a childhood memory that she hardly shared. No doubt she had vaguely heard of Dante and of the poetic tradition, born in that same South, from which the *Vita Nuova* and the *Paradiso* sprang. But she could not be expected to feel the unspoken parallel. Besides, the modern world cast its black-coated literalism over the scene, since which even wiser heads than hers have failed to see that Berlioz' pragmatic testing of his love-illusion was an act of supreme faith comparable to the realization of his creative dreams.

His understanding of the position, long before Freud, was perfectly clear and open: "She has no active recollections; she thinks . . . that my imagination is at work . . . and she never questions the conviction that what is imagined is *false*. But perhaps, unknown to herself, she is coming to feel that *the other one* [Berlioz as a child in love with her] is in control, and will remain master until the end, for he is not false but real. . . . And perhaps some day she will secretly admit to herself that it would be a pity not to have been loved so well." [63]

She had indeed the grace to speak of him and her as "two children who had long known each other" (unless this should be Berlioz unconsciously supplying the fit phrase) and she accorded him permission to write. The remainder of the idyll is well known: she would not at first reply to his quite controlled effusions, then she tried to persuade "the other one" that they were really strangers, whom age and retirement from active life must keep from being anything else. This, said Berlioz, was a "masterpiece of grim reasonableness." [64] But he quietly pressed his claims and she did not rebuff him.

Toward the end of the year he received from her newly married son and daughter-in-law a delightful visit in which he was affectionately scolded. He charmed them in return, and insensibly was established as part of their family circle. The next spring, he obtained Estelle's photograph; after this their regular correspondence was interrupted by only one rebuke on her part. He next visited her in Geneva, where she had removed, and again a second time — in answer to a confidence that she was in financial difficulties. Being still anxious about Louis, he was unable to help her immediately. Six months after this she lost one of her sons, and Berlioz went to condole with her. It was the last visit; when he went again to Dauphiné in August 1868 for a celebration in his honor, he was

[63] *S.W.*, 151.
[64] *Mem.*, II, 411.

virtually dying and lacked the strength to make the side trip. In his will he left her an annuity.[65]

We return from our anticipatory glance to the fall of 1864 and find Berlioz again in Paris, where news awaited him that *Beatrice* was being produced at Stuttgart. At Passy on November 4, a surprise party was given him to commemorate the *première* of *Les Troyens*. Gounod sang the love duet with Mme. Banderali, and by himself Hylas's reverie. The next month the Viennese celebrated Berlioz' sixty-first birthday with a concert of excerpts from the *Damnation*.

Between times Liszt had come to Paris, and by avoiding the subject of music the two friends recaptured their old intimacy. The elder was moreover surrounded by affectionate friends who did their best to busy his mind and fill his heart. At the Château de la Muette, where he had read *Les Troyens*, the Spontini-Erard family asked him to read *Othello*. "I gave myself to it as if I had been all alone. There were only six people present and they all wept splendidly. Heavens! what a shattering revelation of the human heart! . . . And to think that a creature of our own species wrote it." [66]

Through the winter, Berlioz read proof on his *Memoirs*, which he had definitely ended on January 1, 1865. At the printshop his pale face, "carved as in marble, but reflecting every shade of thought" [67] and surmounted still by abundant hair, all white, arrested every glance. His nervous accurate step and firm voice had the imposing air and aloof dignity that Balzac assigns, through the person of Marshal Hulot, to the survivors of the great age.[68] Like the Marshal, Berlioz expected to die at any moment. He supervised the printing of Ferrand's words for Gluck's March from *Alceste;* he gave up for the second time the Baden conductorship; he sorted his papers. But spring came and Louis returned. This was revigorating and Berlioz went to St. Nazaire to meet him.

As master-on-probation, Louis had saved his ship in a severe storm and had been congratulated upon his making port at Martinique. His promo-

---

[65] Twenty years later, Estelle's niece testified that this legacy "lightened the last days of a woman who had suffered grievous misfortune." (*308*, Dec. 13, 1903.)

[66] *L.I.*, 274 and *S.W.*, 154. It is very likely that the walls which echoed Berlioz' voice in these readings are now in the Boston Museum of Fine Arts. The paneling of two apartments from the Château de la Muette were acquired in 1924.

[67] *689*, 185. The author of this verbal portrait used to meet Berlioz at the press as well as at the house of friends. His estimate of Berlioz' character and music alike is very searching and has been undeservedly overlooked.

[68] *La Cousine Bette*, Chapter 31.

tion to full rank was now a mere formality. Yet all was not well. Dissatisfied with life at sea, oddly lacking in self-confidence despite his ability and experience, wishing to marry (again? or for the first time?) the thirty-year-old captain needed fatherly help in money and advice. He had to be reasoned with, too, being in one of his shamefaced obstinate moods. When he sailed again, Berlioz was at once saddened and relieved.

In August, Berlioz revisited his nieces as well as Grenoble and La Côte — three weeks of restful coddling. He was only occasionally ill by day, yet could sleep only with the aid of laudanum and this he dare not use too frequently.[69] In the autumn at the Institute, the customary eulogy was delivered upon the departed Meyerbeer by Berlioz' successful rival for the post of Secretary. The assemblage was informed that Meyerbeer was a supreme artist whose influence on the age surpassed that of either Byron or Chateaubriand. This, said the speaker, was because eclecticism was the mark of nineteenth-century art. He mentioned as a sign of virtue the fact that Meyerbeer never hesitated to make large outlays of money to insure his fame. Berlioz, who had attended the rehearsals of the posthumous *L'Africaine* — a financial success despite its unfinished and incoherent state — could be glad that he had neither to review the work nor to eulogize the great eclectic.

Though Berlioz himself was no longer a threat to Parisian music makers, he continued to be mocked and attacked, usually when news came of his being played in Russia, Denmark, Germany or the United States. At a Pasdeloup performance of the *Francs-Juges* overture, four thousand people cheered, but the hissing contingent was there too. Outside, indignant young men stopped him on the street and begged to shake his hand: "A strange experience — and it's you, my dear fellow, who caused me to write that thing 37 years ago!"[70] The rest kept saying that such music ought to be prohibited.[71] But Berlioz saw to this himself: when

[69] *S.W.*, 166.

[70] This recalls Redon and other young painters who in Delacroix's last years used to go and watch him paint from outside his window. Among the musicians of the same generation, Henri Maréchal tells how Berlioz seemed to him and his fellow students "mysterious, enigmatic . . . a Sphinx awaiting Oedipus. If we read his scores, they were so much at variance with our teachers' views that the most openminded were disconcerted. . . . To find out his true meaning we attended Pasdeloup's concerts . . . and there we put on a counter-demonstration against those who hissed . . ." (*367*, 294.)

[71] Jan Gordon, the English painter, recalls that on seeing his first Cézanne he said to himself: "One *cannot* compose pictures like that! I do not remember how many years it needed to awaken my appreciation . . . Now I cannot imagine how I ever found it dull, for in spite of the fact that it is hardly a masterpiece, there is magic in it." (*1083*, 28.)

the creator of Dido's role was approached for a revival of *Les Troyens*, Berlioz begged her to refuse. He did not want to undergo "a new assassination" — an allusion not to the insults of the press but to the shabby means at Carvalho's disposal. "Why, for heaven's sake, mayn't I be left alone?" [72]

It was asking too much. Even the Sultan of Egypt was after him, to know the reason why the *Treatise on Instrumentation* could not be made the official plan for reorganizing that country's military bands. A stubborn secretary had to be shown that the work taught the use but not the playing of instruments. The New Year (1866) brought a proposal from the Opera that Berlioz direct a production of Gluck's *Armide*. Berlioz' triumph of seven years ago when he had directed *Orpheus* had not been forgotten. He accepted the new task, counting on the help of Saint-Saëns and feeling rejuvenated at the thought of real music. At the same time his stipend as Librarian of the Conservatoire, which had been reduced at the *coup d'état*, was now doubled. "Quite so!" exclaimed Berlioz to the Princess, "if one could only live to be 200, one would ultimately grow rich, learned, famous, and — who knows? — young besides." [73]

This Shavian hypothesis was offset by the fact that death was still busy. Scudo was dead, and, closer to Berlioz, Vincent Wallace and Ferrand's brother. Berlioz became, if possible, more of a Shakespearean pessimist than ever; he quoted from *Hamlet* so often that his friends, the Massarts, urged him to give a reading of it to their circle: the wife knew the play but to the rest it was simply a name before which one gravely and ignorantly bowed. Berlioz could hardly credit it: "Not to know *Hamlet* at the age of 45 or 50 — it is like having lived all one's years in a coal mine!" [74]

The reading took nearly five hours, for he would make no cuts. On another occasion he read *Coriolanus*, yet these tasks did not fatigue him, rather the reverse. About this time also, he met again in Paris the English composer Balfe, whose *Maid of Honor* Berlioz had directed for Jullien, and who had meantime "discovered" Shakespeare and become an enthusiast. [75] Equally exciting was the fact that Joachim was in Paris and playing Beethoven's chamber music. Berlioz heard the "Archduke" trio, the Quartet, Op. 59 No. 2, and a number of the violin sonatas.

Besides these pleasures there were interesting chores. For one thing the *Memoirs* took a long time to produce because of a printers' strike. [76] For

[72] *Est.*, 27.   [73] *S.W.*, 176.   [74] *L.I.*, 286.   [75] *Corresp.*, 319.
[76] Berlioz refers to the need of overseeing all details himself. (*S.W.*, 156.) His care in the organization of his book is shown in the erratum referring to the place of the *Macbeth* epigraph, which occurs in French (with an English title) at the head of the *Memoirs*, and in English (with a French title) at the end.

another, Ernest Reyer, who had replaced Berlioz at Baden and wanted to continue the Berlioz tradition, would call on him for help in program making. And finally the house of Choudens, who had bought *Les Troyens*, had begun their delaying tactics and Berlioz tried to bring them to book. He had several reasons for wanting the work published: the artist wants his *latest* great work to make its way; he was rightly suspicious of arrangers, and he wanted to supplement the inscription to Virgil with a dedicatory epistle to the Princess.[77]

His correspondence with that lady continued fairly active for a man whose waking hours were subject to paralyzing pain. She kept badgering him affectionately and inquisitively, and he remained warm while sidestepping her traps.[78] Like others of his friends, she did not wholly understand him, but knowing perhaps that she was thoroughly understood, she felt something akin to fear. When Liszt took holy orders in April 1865, she begged Berlioz not to make fun — as if his response to this foreseeable step could have been other than one of respectful regret. Had not Berlioz lived in long intimacy with the devout d'Ortigue? Apropos of Liszt again, she finally went too far. He had come to Paris in March to oversee the performance of his *Graner* Mass at St. Eustache — a work which Berlioz found antithetical to all his own principles, the "negation of art." Indeed, the work was designed to signalize Liszt's conversion by a change of heart with regard to expressiveness. Though Berlioz may have been blind to its musical merits, he was at least consistent with himself.[79] By temperament, we know, he was repelled by a certain kind of religious mood which to others is the only one they recognize. Liszt, with the ardor of a neophyte, attempted to justify his work to Berlioz by a demonstration at the piano before a group of their friends. Berlioz remained unconvinced. Rather than argue against his old companion, he left,[80] and some time

[77] None of the scores in print carries this dedication, which must be read in *S.W.*, 162–5. Berlioz rewrote the text several times; each time he speaks of the work, he refers to it not as an opera but as either *Les Troyens*, or "a large lyrical composition." The final subtitle is *Poème Lyrique*, *i.e.* to be sung.

[78] The Princess had received an advance copy of the posthumous *Memoirs* containing a few of Berlioz' letters to Estelle. He had asked the latter's permission before sending the book, as well as before printing the letters. Whereupon the Princess wrote a letter to Estelle, asking Berlioz to deliver it. This he tactfully declined to do. (*S.W.*, 174.)

[79] At a commemorative concert at St. Eustache in 1936 both Berlioz' *Te Deum* and Liszt's *Graner* Mass were given in one afternoon.

[80] Scholarship: "Berlioz turned over his column in the *Débats* to d'Ortigue who shared his adverse opinion." (Editor of the *S.W.* collection, 177 *n.*) Berlioz, it will be remembered, had resigned more than two years before, and d'Ortigue had been the regular music critic of the *Débats* since then.

later the Princess chided him in terms that elicited a forthright reply:

"You propound in regard to music a paradoxical theory of 'ancestors' and 'descendants' which, if you will allow me to say so, is at once palpably absurd and a libel against me. It is as if you accused me with philosophic calm of being a liar and a thief. This made me indignant. I admire with passion many works by the descendants and I heartily detest many illustrious ancestors given over to what is false or ugly. . . . Times, periods, nationalities are all one to me, and nothing would be easier for me than to prove it. But let us drop these arbitrary systems designed to forward a special cause — one might as well dispute about theology.

"You have the kindness to wonder what I am doing, thinking, reading . . ." [81]

This was the only time that Berlioz asserted, indirectly but unmistakably, his priority in the musical leadership of the century, and he did this not because his claim was being challenged — he had made no claim — but because the doctrine of "ancestors and descendants" was being used to dispose cavalierly of the one claim he did make about his music, the claim implicit in any work of art that it shall be judged for what it brings of new joy. The Princess, who had prodded Berlioz on the subject even earlier, can hardly have appreciated at its true worth the reticence he assured her of: "*Not one word* in my Memoirs' account of the last ten years has to do with Wagner, Liszt, or the Music of the Future." [82]

Berlioz was determined to let the future take care of itself — and of him. Though the two younger men were flushed with the hope of belated success — *Tristan* had just been produced — and their forgetfulness was therefore understandable, they could not expect Berlioz to blot his perfectly good memory of the chronology. We may be sure that he grasped the relation between his thirty years of singlehanded innovation and their relatively recent burst of "futurist" music.[83] If modern musicologists find

[81] *S.W.*, 178–9.
[82] *S.W.*, 161; May 11, 1865. The two references to Wagner go back to the 1840's and are altogether friendly: *Mem.*, II, 66–7 and 312.
[83] Consider the chronology:

	Berlioz	Liszt	Wagner
1830 —	*Symphonie Fantastique*	Works for Piano	*The Fairies*, an opera (1833)
1840 —	{*Romeo and Juliet* / *Funeral Symphony*	Bonn Cantata (1845)	*Rienzi* (finished in Paris, 1840)
1850 —	*Te Deum*	1st Symphonic Poem (*Berg-symphonie*)	*Lohengrin* (finished 1848)
1860 —	*Les Troyens*	12th Symphonic Poem (*Die Ideale*)	*Tristan* (finished 1859)

that Berlioz' works were an "inexhaustible quarry" from which these two and others were to draw their materials,[84] it may be supposed that Berlioz' ear detected the exploitation too. He said nothing until the roles began to be depicted in reverse, and then only because the allegation made him out "a liar and a thief."

The rehearsals of *Armide* showed how long it takes for posterity to get a clear notion of anything into its collective head. Gluck had been dead some eighty years, yet nearly everywhere his masterpiece was "blasphemed, insulted, disembowelled, resisted, and libeled — and by everybody: singers, managers, conductors and publishers."[85] With music, aural tradition is everything: no one reads or heeds. "It is amazing to see the prima donna [Mme. Charton-Demeur] fumble around in these sublimities, the light of her understanding brightening up gradually."[86]

In the midst of this conquest over darkness, the Opera decided to halt production. No one came to the rescue of Berlioz and Saint-Saëns, neither of them having the kind of position which exerts the force of an "It isn't done." The musical world seemed in fact singularly uncouth. When in April 1866 Pasdeloup again played the septet from *Les Troyens* to a cheering multitude, no one thought of sending Berlioz a seat. Hearing of the concert by chance he bought his own, and once there was forced to rise and take repeated bows. The next day, he received from a group of musicians a letter identical in wording with a passage he had written in the *Evening with the Orchestra* to praise Spontini's *Cortez*.[87] That same month, *The Flight into Egypt* was given at the Conservatoire. The process of excerpting and serving up a "chef's special" had begun. It was touching and willful and amounted also to a "negation of art." Why create "one work" only to have it broken up again and the fragments worn thin by repetition out of context?[88] The answer was always the same one of cultural incapacity, not to say contrariness.

After this relatively quiet period ending with the spring of 1866, Berlioz' musical concerns upsurged again. First he became Curator of the Instrument Collection at the Conservatoire, replacing Clapisson, though without stipend. In the two years of his tenure, Berlioz was to acquire ten

[84] P. G. Clapp (*421*, Dec. 12, 1944).

[85] *L.I.*, 292.

[86] *Ibid.*

[87] *Soirées* (13th) *Eves.*, 160.

[88] Wagner experienced the same discomfiture when his purposely operatic movements were boiled down to concert form and size.

pieces for the collection, and equally important, to reorganize both the Library and the Collection so as to make them actually serve the needs of students.[89] Then in midsummer, the Opera drew forth *Alceste* from its cache and again Berlioz agreed to direct it. On top of this a Belgian competition for religious music took him to Louvain, where he helped choose one of sixty masses. After a trip to Dauphiné and a few pleasant hours with Estelle, he came back for the opening of *Alceste*. It was a gala occasion. Fétis wrote to Berlioz: "You have fully entered into the mind of the great composer . . . In such an interpretation as yours, one discerns not only great musicianship but the skill of the poet and the philosopher." [90]

Berlioz replied: "Your letter made me very glad . . . If anything could restore to me a courage which I no longer need, it would be your approval. I defend our gods." The gossamer irony of this message duly answered Fétis's variable attitude during four decades. He had generally considered Berlioz' musicianship finer than his soul; others felt the reverse and a few saw the balance of skill and soul. Now he came round too: in the end they all seemed to come round — after Berlioz had worn them down by avalanches of proof. From Vienna, where twenty years before the *Damnation of Faust* had been called a travesty, there now came an invitation to hear it entire. It would be rehearsed before his arrival, would he direct the *Generalprobe* and the performances?

As Berlioz was rejoicing at the prospect, a sudden stroke carried off Joseph d'Ortigue. It was a bitter blow: his most faithful, understanding, and competent critic, who had always praised and blamed him with perfect freedom, with whom he could disagree about sacred music and yet treat as an equal in criticism, was gone — and gone in the same breath the companion of forty years whom he loved like a brother. Only a short while before, d'Ortigue had urged that Berlioz be commissioned to compose a symphony for the opening of the Exhibition in 1867. "Berlioz would give us a companion piece to his [Triumphal] symphony

[89] From Berlioz' reports to the Minister of Fine Arts, Prodhomme concludes that "Berlioz' conception of a music Library was very modern and practical . . . his views have not even now [1913] fully prevailed. His good sense saw the dangers to which valuable documents are liable in show cases, and the distinction to be drawn between a Library and a Museum. . . . He had always in mind the double duty of the Librarian as Keeper of documents and servant of readers." (*379, 805.*) One may compare this with the inaccurate estimate of Berlioz' librarianship by his enemy and late successor J. B. Weckerlin (*909,* xxiii).

[90] *269, 636.*

of 1840, that is to say, another masterpiece." [91] It was d'Ortigue's last effort in behalf of art.[92]

The rehearsals in Vienna proved almost too much for Berlioz. The strain of thirty hours by railway, the barrier of language and the excitement at rehearsing for the first time in thirteen years the whole of a work which the Parisians had doomed to extinction and which was returning to life of itself, made Berlioz irritable and even inadequate on the podium. He knew it and gave up the idea of conducting, saying "I am sick unto death." The performance, he felt, brought him the greatest triumph of his career. He was recalled eleven times, banqueted and toasted: "Glory to the man who has opened new ways to our art . . . who has fought dullness since the very morrow of Beethoven's death . . . I drink to the genius of Hector Berlioz." [93] This was Herbeck, Master of the Imperial Chapel. Cornelius also was there, his faith undimmed: "To thee, knightly singer, great and daring artist, blessed with the spirit's fire, all German hearts must bring a tribute of adoration. . . ." [94]

This validation of Berlioz' lifework was most welcome, most necessary to his peace of mind, for his diminishing strength let him sink into abysses of discouragement. Despite the tributes from younger men, even in France, he felt cut off and would say to himself: "It is somehow not right: I did not do what ought to have been done." [95] Seeing his creation and feeling in every fiber how much he had put of himself into it, how much he had sacrificed for it, even to the sacrifice of his home and health and his son's happiness, he was wracked by the agony of self-doubting which is the traditional lot of martyrs, philosophers, and saints.

Yet as soon as Berlioz heard his music again it spoke to his spirit — as it does to ours — of precisely the vibrant life he buried within it. He knew his work was both beautiful and solid, blemishes included. He should have steadily remembered that, as Maclean puts it, "the works were indubitably *there*." [96] But Berlioz had not the good fortune of being a thorough monomaniac. His obsessional dream, necessary for all creation, ceased when that function was accomplished, leaving in charge the critical intellect. This told him plainly that despite an enormous deal of launching his music caught on, as we say, only in fragments. True, he knew that

[91] *186.*
[92] Berlioz was represented at the concert of the Exposition by his *Hymne à la France* of 1844. (See below, Chapter 27.)
[93] *1406,* Jan. 1867, 16.
[94] The original is in verse, reprinted in *354, 371.*
[95] *367,* 294.
[96] *394,* 127.

Gluck and Weber survived mainly because he and a few others kept pushing hard, but this comparison brought no comfort; it told rather against a whole species of music to which his own belonged. With his quick insight into public psychology, he could tell that the growth of a Wagnerian cult did not so much raise a rival as confound a tradition.[97]

Berlioz had faced rivals all his life — Rossini, Meyerbeer, Mendelssohn, Schumann, even Félicien David, had certainly competed with him for public attention. But none of these could destroy him: the contrast was always clear cut and even Berlioz' exclusion or dismissal was undamaging. But with the rise of Lisztian Wagnerism, which was widely supposed to be the consequence of Berlioz' own handiwork, he was as it were kid-naped and made away with, the clinching fact being that the music of the future — evolutionary and prophetic — set Wagner atop a pyramid of musical dinosaurs whom it declared extinct: Gluck, Mozart, Beethoven, Weber — and Berlioz.

Only a godlike conceit could have ignored the evil omen. Berlioz had discouraged all advances to form a "school" around him; he hated coteries and slogans. Once he had given up his posts of critic and conductor to Reyer, he had no favors to dispense nor power to share. He wanted admiration to come from independent minds — as it did from Saint-Saëns, Gounod, Cornelius, Reyer, Bizet, Pohl, Massenet, Moussorgsky, and others. But critics would not have it so. He was regimented against his will. When Hanslick turned against the new music, he repudiated Berlioz and Wagner in one breath, as one tendency. Other wise heads described the pair as the offspring of Beethoven's demented latter years. An artificial neoclassicism was in the making which felt compelled to lump all the recent past in one reprobation.

This could not down Wagner, who was new, operatic, and buoyed up by system. But Berlioz' music was exposed bare and defenseless. How could its maker know that within fifty or sixty years, the succession of artistic "isms" pushing one another into limbo would become so common-place and dull that uncankered minds would begin again to approach music and the other arts without apparatus or jargon, preferring to draw their own inferences in freedom?

Meantime it was 1867. Gluck was succumbing at the Opera under the productive pressure of Ambroise Thomas, just as the Wagnerians were sapping the reputation of Meyerbeer. This would leave, a decade hence,

[97] This was evident in the Parisian caricature showing *Les Troyens* as a grown boy asking his nurse to let him see his little brother *Tannhäuser*. (*Charivari*, Nov. 25, 1863.)

two admissible styles — the light French and the heavy German; for Verdi had not yet rearisen from the ashes of his Italian output and revivified the native school. Given Berlioz' position in art and in history, there was only one thing for him to do: undertake a new campaign, preferably in Germany, with his finest and least-known music. To this resolution, momentarily blurred by the death of the great painter and Gluck worshiper, Ingres, Berlioz gave his mind as the new year began.

Berlioz the Critic

> The voice of the critic has but a feeble
> echo. The reverberation of a beautiful score
> is more powerful than all our phraseology.
> — BERLIOZ in 1846

When Berlioz acknowledged the toasts of his Viennese friends at the banquet of 1866, he had every reason to think this would be the last occasion of its kind, and he took the opportunity to speak to his fellow musicians of his career as critic. He told of having recently given up journalism and of the long drudgery he had endured in its service. He said that only necessity had made him a regular reviewer and that it had always gone against his grain to cast blame on others' work. He felt he had no critical "felonies" on his conscience and trusted that his occasional severity had been of the sort that does not crush talent but spurs it to follow a better road.[1]

Later comers have sometimes doubted Berlioz' statements that he hated his job of reviewing; his criticism is so full of zest that they feel he must have enjoyed writing what gives so much pleasure in the reading. Hence, they argue, his distaste was affected.[2] But to those who know his character,

[1] Report in *Signale*, Jan. 1867, 16.
[2] 67, 8. In his introduction to the English version of the *Evenings with the Orchestra*, Mr. Newman makes much of an apparent contradiction in Berlioz' report on the beginnings of his career in letters. "He would have us believe," says Mr. Newman, "that he was *forced* to become a writer for the press. 'Fatality!' he cries in his *Memoirs;* 'I became a critic; I had to write feuilletons.' And he proceeds to tell us how his friend Humbert Ferrand suggested that he should undertake the musical criticism of *Le Correspondant*. The truth is that it was he himself who in 1828 asked Ferrand for a letter of introduction . . . with a view to becoming the musical critic of that journal." (P. xi.) There is

methods of work, and musical mission, it is clear that this imputation is gratuitous: once again Berlioz' self-knowledge and sincerity withstand the closest scrutiny. It is true that like all great wits he delighted in his own quips and epigrams, that as a literary artist he enjoyed telling good stories in good prose, and that as a musician the publication of his ideas gave him strength and satisfaction. But there is every difference (as his too-ready disbelievers should know) between writing for self-expression under an inner necessity and writing for a livelihood under the pressure of a deadline.[3] It is surely to Berlioz' credit that he made his innumerable columns on routine subjects so readable and so meaty, whence it becomes something of an outrage to make this conscientiousness the ground for doubting the author's feelings about doing journeyman work.

From the beginning to the end of his life the burden of a *feuilleton* never grew lighter, rather the reverse: "It sometimes takes me four days now," he wrote in 1861 to Ferrand;[4] and his account of staring at a piece of paper, writing and crossing out and rewriting, is borne out by surviving manuscripts.[5] It would obviously have been much pleasanter for him to keep his witticisms and stories for friends at his fireside, instead of attending piano recitals and operettas; and if in leafing through the tremendous bulk of his uncollected reviews we come upon pieces of wisdom or gaiety that we think he must have been glad to set down, all we have a right to infer is that being a man of thought, Berlioz could link his stored-up reflections to the doings of the latest prima donna or teacher of harmony.

He himself indicated the varied substance of his writings when he chose as the subtitle of his last collected volume: "Etudes Musicales, Adorations, Boutades et Critiques."[6] This was the *A Travers Chants* of 1862. It contains the final version of the great essays on Beethoven, Gluck, and Weber — the "studies" which were also "adorations." The

---

of course no inconsistency in Berlioz' saying that Ferrand made the first suggestion and that he himself asked this same friend for a letter of introduction to an editor. As for the first point, it is inexact to say that Berlioz "would have us believe" that in taking up journalism he was somehow coerced or browbeaten. He did it willingly, of course, and at first cheerfully, but the task became a drudgery. Mr. Newman himself tells us why in the next paragraph: music did not pay and "Berlioz could make both ends meet only by writing for a number of papers."

[3] Meredith: "No slavery is comparable to the chains of hired journalism." (*1214*, 65.)

[4] *L.I.*, 225; see also pp. 250, 253, *S.W.*, 20, 67, 176, and *Corresp.*, 274.

[5] See 70. "Composing music," he says in the *Memoirs* (I, 117) "is for me a natural function; writing prose is toil."

[6] *Boutades* = sallies.

rest comprises reviews of concerts by Wagner, Reber, and Heller; the essay on Euripides's *Alcestis;* two or three brilliant fantasias on musical manners and practices; the superb report on Concert Pitch, an article on Religious Music and some half dozen "sallies," of which the last, entitled "The Lapdog School of Singing," is curiously placed at the very end, as if perversely meant to be an anticlimax. Contrariwise, the *Grotesques,* published in 1859, begin with some hundred pages of anecdotes and trivia that hardly prepare us for the sustained and moving writing of the latter half. One might therefore say of the three volumes fashioned by Berlioz' own hand that *A Travers Chants* could stand a little pruning, or at least rearrangement; that the unevenness of the *Grotesques* could be repaired by simple division; and that the *Evenings with the Orchestra* is perfect.[7]

Berlioz had planned to bring out two other collections under the respective titles *Les Musiciens et la Musique* and *Historiettes et Scènes Musicales.*[8] This last remained a project, but the first came out posthumously, though with no likelihood that the contents were Berlioz' choice. If his entire journalistic output were to be reprinted, there would be matter for some twenty-five volumes French size — ten of our usual octavos, out of which possibly half would possess intrinsic or historic value. The discourse on "Imitation in Music," for example, belongs to the first category; the Biography of Beethoven, to the second.[9] Much of this sound prose, as we saw above, would consist of asides upon art, social conditions, cultural history, as well as upon criticism itself, for like a Sainte-Beuve or a Hazlitt, Berlioz saw art as continuous with life and human character. Had he been free of the need to write for money he might have kept these reflections for Note Books, Table Talk, or a Journal. One would then have read more indulgently after his death what he put into his columns fresh from the mint.[10]

Barring a modicum of human error, his treatment of whatever he touched follows and illustrates the three great principles of the true critic: intellectual integrity, technical competence, and exact expression. A critic

---

[7] Berlioz had an exact notion of their relative importance. He knew that the *Evenings* was "one work" — "which I took infinite pains to write *in French:* what an infernally difficult tongue!" (*M.C.,* 30.) Of the *Grotesques* he says, perhaps too modestly: "They comprise the groans and growls hitherto scattered in a host of feuilletons, nothing more." (*S.W.,* 92.)

[8] *1314,* I, 234.

[9] *1398,* Jan. 1 and 8, 1837; *1377* (1829) Nos. 22, 23, and 31.

[10] If one imagines the forthright criticism and unconventional philosophy of Delacroix's *Journal* being published bit by bit over 40 years, one may form some idea both of Berlioz' audacity and of the antagonism it was bound to arouse. See Monselet: *373, 348* ff.

born, Berlioz could not brook any interference with the act of judgment; every other emotion must yield to the esthetic: "You find it quite natural," he exclaims, "that one should not admire those who do not admire us, and conversely. But that is dreadful! It amounts to the utter denial of art. I can no more prevent myself from admiring a sublime work by my greatest enemy than from loathing the nonsense of my most intimate friend." [11] And practice followed precept: he praised Mendelssohn whom he knew to dislike his own works. This might be thought the effect of an exceptional friendship contracted in youth. But about the same time Berlioz was certainly no friend of Cherubini's, yet his praise of that master's dramatic works is steadily intelligent and sincere. The same relation obtains with regard to Italian music, and notably about Rossini, whom Berlioz censured for explicit reasons while praising *William Tell*, *Comte Ory*, and *The Barber of Seville*. Heller testifies that on hearing this last-named score, Berlioz could not restrain his tears of joy, despite all the malicious nonsense that the "gay fat man" (Rossini) continued to circulate about his admirer.[12] It is also proper to recall that none of Wagner's teasing or attacks made Berlioz deviate in his public judgment, which was consistent not only with itself from 1841 to 1863, but with Berlioz' other expressed opinions regarding the elements of dramatic music.

One test of a critic's powers is of course his capacity to discover new talents, and this duty becomes even more exacting when the critic is himself a creator, since the production of strong original work presupposes a certain blindness to other possible modes of creation. Of the new musicians who came to Berlioz' attention, he seems not to have missed a single one: in France — David, Gounod, Saint-Saëns, Reyer, Bizet and Massenet;[13] in Germany — besides Mendelssohn and Wagner, Berlioz saw at once the merits of Cornelius, Joachim, and Brahms; among the Russians, he discerned Glinka first and later, as we shall see, The Five. His judgment of performance, whether vocal or instrumental, was equally prophetic,

---

[11] *S.W.*, 141. Shaw, also speaking of himself, defines the critic in virtually identical terms, and elsewhere adds: "When my critical mood is at its height, personal feeling is not the word: it is passion: the passion for artistic perfection. . . . Let all young artists look to it, and pay no heed to the idiots who declare that criticism should be free from personal feeling. The true critic, I repeat is the man who becomes your personal enemy on the sole provocation of a bad performance, and will only be appeased by good performances." (*1207*, 107–8.)

[12] Letter to Hanslick, reprinted in *502*, 424.

[13] He owed his Rome Prize in large part to Berlioz — and on hearing of this embraced him. (*977*, 35.) As for César Franck, he made his debut as composer while Berlioz was out of the country (1846) but received Berlioz' high praise as a pianist. (*1398*, Mar. 31, 1839.)

and a long list could be made of the men and women who had their superior ability first signalized in the *Débats*.[14]

Long after his death, a letter of Berlioz' came to light which shows how and why in his last days as reviewer, far from assuming the infallibility of an old judge, he continued to regard his critical functions critically. The letter, dated March 28, 1863, is addressed to Marmontel, Professor at the Conservatoire, and concerns Bizet's *Pearl Fishers:*

I have had until now neither time nor strength to open the manuscript that you entrusted to me, and I should apologize for this if you did not already know that the facts are so. But I promise you to get at it soon and to deal with your friend otherwise than cavalierly. Just think of it! I have his work by me; I will have read it — read it by reading it — and for once I shall be writing with a full knowledge of the case. If composers only knew with what casualness, or in what somnolent states we licensed critics listen to their works, they would call us b——ds and it would be perfectly fair.

But suppose I dislike this score. You will then take pity on my predicament since it will involve a young artist who is dear to your kindly heart. Why come to me, who am *a musician* — not any old musician, but one whose preferences have warped his judgment? Do you think it quite honest on the part of a combatant to present the work of a colleague? The critic may so easily be dense and the work good. I entertain a vigorous hate against certain kinds of music which are none the less healthy, and I have had to reverse many a decision in which I proved a foolish judge. I hope for love of you that these three acts will please me. But don't go hanging yourself, nor let the author do the same, if they bore me: it won't prove a thing. Weber said Beethoven was mad.

The art of music changes, and that too is a necessity.[15]

The allusion to Beethoven reminds us that there was critical genius in Berlioz' proclaiming his greatness in the Paris of 1827, particularly when this admiration included the Ninth Symphony and the late quartets. Neither Schubert, Weber, nor Wagner went so far so soon. But Berlioz' prescience is made all the more remarkable by his anticipation of the twentieth-century judgment that among Beethoven's works the late piano sonatas and quartets hold perhaps a higher rank than the symphonies.[16] Berlioz' fondness for chamber music has been justly recognized by the

[14] To cite at random: Parish-Alvars, Ernst, Laub, Lübeck, Reichardt and Stockhausen, besides Zani de Ferranti, Louis Moreau Gottschalk and Saint-Saëns as pianists, Pauline Viardot, Charton (-Demeur), and others we have met on previous pages.   [15] *123*, 140–1.

[16] Berlioz said this on numerous occasions: "The great sonatas of Beethoven will serve as a yardstick to measure the development of our musical intelligence." (*A Trav.*, 67.)

well-known British authority on the genre [17] — a genre which the composer, despite his supposed mania for huge ensembles, did his best to acclimate and encourage in France.[18]

These many impeccable judgments certainly owed much to Berlioz' pragmatic relativism, which was but the intellectual counterpart of his dramatic sense. He could see how the artistic object looked from various points of view, he liked this variety (short of flat contradiction) and he had a range of discernment which kept him from the critic's worst fault — that of believing perfection marred by unacceptable detail. Thus in his analysis of Beethoven's symphonies, Berlioz points out chords or progressions that strike him as flaws or whims. But his lifelong conviction about Beethoven was that "the man had everything and we — have nothing." [19] The reader will also have noted how accurately Berlioz places Gluck far below Beethoven as a musician, while at the same time maintaining that Gluck's creations are perfect in their kind.[20]

A final test of acumen in the creator-critic is his opinion of his own work: we have already seen what a balanced judgment Berlioz rendered upon himself in the *Memoirs*. It remains, after a century of scribbling by others, "immeasurably the finest criticism" of Berlioz' music ever written; [21] to which one might add that the composer's choice among his own scores never mistakes trifles for masterpieces, and that he keeps a nice balance between liking movements of his that glow with inspiration and those that shine by virtue of technical imagination.

If only because they have given rise to many misstatements, Berlioz' lacks and limitations as a critic deserve a separate summary. He had, it is said, no historical sense and thus failed to appreciate the older masters. He is similarly supposed to have rejected all Italian music because he hated that of his own day. The facts are otherwise. Berlioz was one of Mozart's

[17] W. W. Cobbett. After testifying to Berlioz' enthusiasm for the (British) Beethoven Quartet Society, Cobbett goes on: "He wrote so admirably about music that I am tempted to quote once more, etc. . . . ." (*1297*, I, 123.)

[18] To Morel in 1855: "I hear you're writing a quintet. Good! May that difficult genre flourish in France!" (*Corresp.*, 224.) From the thirties to his death, Berlioz had frequent sessions of chamber music at his own house. See his letters, *passim*.

[19] *502*, 424.

[20] *E.g.*, the comment to Ferrand about the March from *Alceste:* "You must know that in spots the tenor part is very badly written . . . hardly any pupil would dare show his teacher such an awkward harmony exercise. . . . But the bass, the harmony, and the melody sublimise everything." (*L.I.*, 266.)

[21] W. H. Mellers: *372*, 122.

most clear-sighted and fervent admirers, as is proved not only by his praise of *Don Giovanni, Idomeneo, The Magic Flute*, and the three great symphonies, but by the fact that upon such a work as *Die Entführung* Berlioz' criticism and Mozart's own judgment independently concur.[22]

As for Berlioz' total rejection of Italian opera, it too is a myth: we have just seen his attitude toward Cherubini and Rossini; his mature opinion of Bellini is full of warmth and would be endorsed by any fair judge; and his respect for Verdi as a great craftsman speaks for itself.[23] Of the earlier Italian masters, he knew more than is generally supposed, having a special fondness for Marcello and having arrived by himself at the modern view that Piccinni's "system" did not differ so greatly from Gluck's as the eighteenth-century polemic about the rivals would suggest. With regard to Palestrina, Berlioz' objections to the *Improperia* need not be shared to be understood and justly represented.[24] Berlioz felt that the absence of rhythm — and therefore of melody in the modern sense — combined with a steadily consonant harmony, made them something less than works of art. This did not keep Berlioz from putting Palestrina's madrigals on his programs.

Of the "ancients" this leaves Bach, Handel, and Haydn. Of Bach, Berlioz heard but little in Paris. In Berlin, the *Saint Matthew Passion* impressed him by its dramatic power and harmonic richness, though its esthetic principles — the necessarily limited vocal "orchestration" and the continuo (played on a piano) — struck him as monotonous.[25] Late in Berlioz' life, Saint-Saëns played him some of the clavier works, which moved Berlioz deeply and completely won him over to Bach.[26] Handel, again, Berlioz knew only through bad and dull performances, the kind Shaw was to call "in-churchy," and the music struck him as for the most part pedestrian. Now and then an air or chorus elicited his praise. If one adds to this Berlioz' view of Purcell and his choice among the works of Lully and Rameau, one can see that the dramatic composers of the seventeenth and early eighteenth centuries spoke least vividly to their nineteenth-century descendant. It is a clear deficiency, all the more note-

[22] *A Trav.*, pp. 250–4, and Mozart's *Letters* (*219*, III, 1145–6). For Berlioz' judgments of Mozart's lesser works, see *867*.

[23] *S.W.*, 114.

[24] It may be relevant to add that the correct text of these works was not available until 1919. Nor, of course, did Berlioz know the then buried music of the fifteenth- and sixteenth-century French masters, with whom he had certain points in common.

[25] *Mem.*, II, 120–1.

[26] *502, 425*.

worthy that certain modern critics have found Berlioz' harmony akin to Purcell's and his dramatic sense related to Handel's![27]

We may regret as students of cultural change that Berlioz did not investigate his temperamental indifference to these composers. But it was not his business, and from the point of view of ethical criticism we can only commend him for not wasting his time in spinning rationalizations in the void. True criticism, regardless of its conclusions, must spring from love — passion for the object presented or, in censure, passion for the object aimed at and missed. The critical relation does not obtain when the artist's very purpose seems to the critic futile, or remains a mystery — which incidentally explains much of the foolish writing about Berlioz' own music. As his treatment of Haydn shows, competence in the juridical sense requires something more than familiarity. Berlioz knew Haydn's oratorios and some of the symphonies, but he disliked the descriptive element in the former,[28] and what he took to be the affected naïveté of the latter. Hence he refrained from elaborate analysis and used as a safety valve occasional sallies in private letters:

". . . Haydn's *Creation* is a work that has always been deeply antipathetic to me — I make this confession to you regardless — . His lowing herds, his buzzing flies, his light in C major which dazzles like a patent lamp, and then his Adam, Uriel, and Gabriel, the flute solos and all the goody-goodiness of it exasperate me and make me want to commit mayhem. The English love their pudding well covered with a layer of fat: I loathe it, and it is just this sort of fat which envelops the musical pudding of old man Haydn. Naïveté is a fine thing, but it ought not to be overdone. . . . Don't scold me, beat me, or hush me up: I desist of my own accord . . . But see the influence of good health: I utter blasphemies: I must be well."[29]

Having let off steam and been "pardoned" by his correspondent, Berlioz' natural sobriety regains the upper hand and gives us a clue to his considered (historical) belief: "May I say 'the good Haydn,' seeing that Horace said 'sometimes good Homer nods'? Well, the good burgher style of treating great poetic subjects prevailed almost everywhere in Europe when Haydn wrote, and his temperament moreover led in the

---

[27] Romain Rolland, *1003*, 109; Ernest Walker, *604*, 104.
[28] When dealing with musical imitation, Berlioz opposed Beethoven to Haydn's "system" (see above Chapter 7), though he did not know that Beethoven would have agreed with his opinion of these two works of Haydn's. (*1021*, II, 120.)
[29] S.W., 85–6.

same direction. He was a great simple musician and simply a great musician . . . It is said that after the taking of Vienna by the French, he made
a delightful remark to some officers who came to see him: 'And so, gentlemen, you have deigned to call upon a poor man of genius like me?' Yet I
prefer . . . Mozart's reply to the Archduke who greeted him after *The
Marriage of Figaro* with the silly comment: 'There are certainly a great
many notes in your score, my dear Mozart.' — 'Not one too many, my
lord.' " [30]

This preference not only attests Berlioz' feeling that quiet self-assurance is more modest than proclaimed humility; it also acknowledges limits
to the mind's powers of assimilation and thus lessens the harm of any
deficiency by making it explicit. He says elsewhere: "If I weren't myself
guilty of the same fault as regards other masters, . . . I should say that
Wagner is wrong not to see in our puritanical Mendelssohn a fine and
rich personality. When a master is a master, and when this master has always and in all ways honored and respected art, one must honor and respect him too, whatever be the divergence between the path we follow
and that which he has elected . . . But no one is perfect." [31]

This conscientious relativism, as we shall see, does end by yielding
a view of "the object as it really is." But the music critic faces a special
difficulty in that he deals with an elusive object and he therefore requires
a special art, of which it was said on an earlier page that only a scant half
dozen men besides Berlioz have attained mastery. Berlioz' disciple Ernest
Reyer points out wherein the difficulty and the art reside, when he asks:
"Why write from Cairo to Paris that the romance of Rhadames [in *Aïda*]
is in B-flat and that the song of Termuthis . . . returns in G-flat minor?
Isn't it to dip a dull pen into the inkpot and say nothing with it?" [32] How
then can Reyer say that Berlioz "wrote some admirable essays in this
[technical] genre upon the art of Spontini, Gluck, and Beethoven?" [33]
The answer is that technical detail can achieve significance. Analysing,
for example, the transition from the Scherzo to the Finale in Beethoven's
Fifth Symphony, Berlioz writes:

The motive of the scherzo reappears in pizzicato; silence gains little by
little; one hears only a few notes plucked on the violins and the strange
little cluckings of the bassoons playing their high A flat, closely brushed
by the G, which is the octave of the ground note in the chord of the
dominant ninth. Then, breaking the cadence, the strings gently take up
with the bow the chord of A flat and doze off on that held note. The

[30] *S.W.*, 89–90.   [32] *997*, 194–5.
[31] *207*, II, 32.   [33] *997*, 194.

timpani alone maintain the rhythm by light strokes with sponge-headed sticks — a dim pattern above the general stagnation of the rest of the orchestra. These drum notes are C's; the key of the piece is C minor, although the long-sustained chord of A flat in the other instruments seems to introduce a new tonality; yet the isolated C's of the timpani tend to preserve the feeling of the original key. The ear is still uncertain, not knowing the outcome of this harmonic mystery, when the dull pulsations on the drums, increasing in intensity, join with the violins (which have now re-entered and changed the harmony) to give the chord of the dominant seventh — G, B, D, F — in the midst of which the drums roll their stubborn tonic C. Thereupon the whole orchestra, aided by the trombones which have not yet been heard, bursts in the major mode on the theme of a triumphal march and the finale begins.[34]

Commenting on this passage, a modern theorist bids us "notice how exactly the above lines describe what takes place and how truly they convey the effect produced. The description is a model of soberness. It does not contain a single epithet, allusion, or simile introduced for the deliberate purpose of suggesting ideas or emotions. Strip it of technicalities or suppose it read by someone who does not know what such terms as C, G, pizzicato or ground note or dominant ninth mean and its significance will remain." [35] As Mr. Calvocoressi implies, technical words are just as extraneous to the music as a list of metaphors, synecdoches, or chiasmuses would be to a poem. But the one or the other, if properly set in simple prose description, may so to speak lead us into the neighborhood of the real object and induce a state of mind favorable for beholding it. This it does by singling out features and relations that we should attend to, hasty conclusions we should avoid, and possible ones we may wish to attain in emulation of him who has pondered their premises.

Knowing that not everyone's imagination can be reached through the same set of words, Berlioz blended in his analyses the technical, the poetical, the abstract, and the humorous, never overindulging in any one rhetoric. The result is that his essays hardly date, even though music criticism — at least in newspapers — now avoids technicalities, and though epithets and metaphors have changed many times since Berlioz. One element in his work that makes it perennially effective is that pace and form follow contents in such a way that our instinctive responses aid our understanding. "His literary articles are built almost like symphonic movements, with changes of rhythm, repetitions, and cadences. One could often put at the top of a page: *allegro* or *andante* or even *scherzo*." [36]

[34] *A Trav.*, 35–6.   [35] Calvocoressi: 776, 127–8.
[36] A. Hallays, Preface to *M.M.*, viii–ix. A good example of such an article is *Grot.*, 237–46 on the death of Sontag.

In his short biographies, Berlioz naturally uses a purely literary form — as old as Plutarch and as difficult as a lyric — and in still other pieces, reportorial or fictional, he shows again that he natively possessed the dramatist's eye and ear. This is unusual enough in criticism to warrant the reader's being cautioned. For example, in the often-quoted review of *William Tell*, Berlioz says of the trio in the second act that he refuses to do a piece of dissection; "I can only shout with the crowd: 'Beautiful! Superb! Admirable! Heartrending!' " [37] He is acting as spokesman for "the crowd" as much as for himself, but from the choice, precisely, of *their* words we may infer a hair's breadth of reserve in his judgment; so that it is a serious error to take the review as "an expression not so much of admiration as of wild enthusiasm." [38] Berlioz' enthusiasm was often intense but, as regards music, never wild. In this very essay, after quoting the crowd's exclamations he coolly advises us to keep a few superlatives in store for the finale. This he describes vividly and exclaims again "Ah! it is sublime!" but follows it with: "Now to catch our breath!" The subtle shift in tone, twice repeated, is possibly more evident in French, but it is enough to invalidate any estimate of the review as "hyperbole." [39] The four articles of which it is composed form on the contrary a self-possessed effort to correct an earlier, quite partial statement, while maintaining and developing certain technical arguments against Rossini's method. One has only to read Berlioz on Gluck or Beethoven to see that when he actually felt hyperbolic he was not in the habit of dramatizing the crowd or stage-managing his epithets.

Like most writers, Berlioz reached lucidity only at the end of laborious effort, and he was never satisfied with his handling of words: "As for my style, if I may be said to have one, it is that of a writer who seeks the word capable of rendering what he feels without ever being able to find it. I am too eager; I have tried to calm my violent efforts and have not succeeded, which gives to my prose the air of a limping, drunken walk." [40] The reason Berlioz judged so harshly the result of his tussle with words was that ideas came to him in abundance and with great speed — just as they did when he composed music. But the technique of sorting and ordering them gave him much less pleasure when he was fashioning prose, because the product was in a sense not a new creation. It merely stated what he knew and what he felt everybody ought to know.

[37] *1398* (1834) 343.
[38] *1025*, 147–8.
[39] *Ibid.*
[40] S.W., 144. This was written in 1864, after he had left the *Débats*.

Still, his writings in all genres show what Pascal sought in every book — a man, not an author. And put side by side, his art in both kinds of composition reveals one and the same spirit. The unflagging motion, multiplicity of ideas, rapid transitions, lightness, and transparency of the music are found again in the prose. Take as an example a casual sentence at the tail end of a scribbled note relating a professional disappointment (the French is needed to show the lightning turn of mind): "*Nous restons* [*ceux*]. . . . *qui n'ont ni places, ni argent, ni honneur, ni cordon, excepté le cordon de leur portier — qu'ils seront même obligés de voler le jour où ils voudront se pendre.*"[41] The pivotal word is *cordon*, meaning both the scarf of a medal and the bell pull in a porter's lodge — a double meaning which, stumbled on at the end of an ordinary enumeration, sets up a series of flashes — the bell pull, the use to which a rope can be put, eventual suicide, and the need of the destitute to steal even the means of ending their distress — five ideas fused in nineteen words. The vision is overcharged, if you like, dramatic certainly, but in any case glowing with the potency of the perceiver.

Flaubert, who had treasured his few interviews with Berlioz in 1863, was struck again by the force of the artist's personality when ten years after his death the first collection of his letters was issued.[42] "There was a man!" Flaubert tells Maupassant, and he repeats his enthusiasm to Edmond de Goncourt, Mme. Régnier and other correspondents.[43] Flaubert kept marveling at the completeness of Berlioz' presentment of his mind and fate in this day-to-day spontaneous record: "It beats Balzac!"[44] Undoubtedly, if one sign of genius is the free and abundant association of ideas, then these letters afford a daily proof of genius. Berlioz' mind does not run in grooves: it cuts its own; though as a stylist Berlioz does not coin phrases in the obvious sense, but rather reshapes the known to fix the unnamed. For example, to describe the mixed noises of a large audience roused to a frenzy of mixed delight and abhorrence, he takes the phrase for earthquake (*tremblement de terre*) and turns it into the perfectly clear and useful *tremblement de salle*.

The same power of analogy accounts for the love of puns — in him and others. It is surely no accident that electrical intellects such as Shake-

---

[41] To Fiorentino, his fellow music critic: *86*, 424.

[42] This was the inaccurate and bowdlerized *Correspondance Inédite* of 1879. Of this same volume, Zola wrote: "I have just read a book which has moved me deeply . . . [As a critic] Berlioz might keep saying, 'white,' people read 'black.' This is the astonishing thing . . . which always happens when a thorough artist addresses himself to the stupid multitude." (*691*, 320–1.)

[43] *192*, V, 363–6.   [44] *192*, V, 364.

speare, Rabelais, and Swift reveled in the juxtaposition of the remote through sound. The practice may seem subversive of order and decency, but in its higher reaches the verbal modulation becomes wit and poetry. Notice how economically, in the article on *Fidelio* which so rejoiced Wagner, Berlioz gives us together with his judgment an insight into the psychology of musical hearing: "The public, charmed though it be by this graceful *andante*, is left agape as a result of not getting with it their final *allegro*, their cadence, their lash of the whip — come to think of it, why not give them a lash of the whip?" [45] And still more epigrammatically, in defense of one of Bellini's "most touching inspirations — *on danse là-dessus. Mais quoi! On danse sur tout. On fait tout sur tout.*" [46]

Clear marks of temperament as these sallies are, it would be wrong to take them for principles and to derive from them Berlioz' philosophy of criticism — much more to infer either a systematic scorn for the public or a character of scratchy malignity.[47] These cullings merely illustrate a verbal technique appropriate to a flashing vision. Taken as wholes, Berlioz' essays and letters show an unforced tendency to balance opposite considerations, and a care for precise wording that seems even more indispensable to the critic than to the scholar. Berlioz may have thought he was overeager in his search for the right word, but his readers can only feel grateful for the success of his quest. Nowhere in his writings does one stumble upon contradiction between the evidence and the verdict, or suddenly lose view of the object in the critic's murkiness of mind or speech. To put the same virtue affirmatively, Berlioz understood and observed the laws of criticism and was that rare thing, an ethical critic.[48]

At a time, for example, when doctrines of race were being elaborated with a great show of scientific approval, Berlioz could quickly disentangle the fact from the fiction, while holding the scales equal between two friends, one recently dead: Wilhelm von Lenz, the living, had argued

[45] *A Trav.*, 76.

[46] *A Trav.*, 340.

[47] As late as 1866, that is after all his personal disappointments, he writes to a young musician: "I regret to see you preoccupied, like the Paris managers, with fears as to the public's tastes. It is from perpetually trembling at the thought of its habits and lack of education that one gives eternal lease to prejudice and routine. I think it would be better to break once for all with cowardice and not even seem to believe in the reality of *imprudence*. But then you must let the public hear only things of beauty irresistibly performed." (*93, 258.*)

[48] Aware of the usual malpractice, he imagined a "Penal Code for Art," applicable to both performers and critics. (*Grot.*, 275–6.)

that Mendelssohn's music "could not become the property of the whole world" because of the "Hebraic element discernible in his thought." Berlioz "begs leave to dispute this opinion, which other critics have previously uttered. . . . Is there not a certain prejudice in this manner of judging a great composer, and would M. de Lenz have written those words had he been ignorant of the fact that the composer of *St. Paul* and *Elijah* was a descendant of the celebrated Israelite, Moses Mendelssohn? I can with difficulty believe it. 'The psalmodies of the synagogue,' he goes on to say, 'are elements one finds again in Mendelssohn's music.' Now, it is hard to see how these psalmodies can have influenced the musical style of Felix Mendelssohn since he never professed the Jewish religion. Everyone knows that he was a Lutheran, and an earnest, fervent Lutheran at that. Moreover, what music is there which can ever become 'the property of the whole world without distinction of time or place?' None, assuredly. The works of the great German masters such as Gluck, Haydn, Mozart, and Beethoven, who all belonged to the Catholic, that is 'universal' religion, will no more attain to this status than the music of others, however beautiful, living, solid or powerful it may be." [49]

It was not merely because Berlioz was free from the common prejudices of race and nation that he was able to reduce Lenz's plausibility to naught, but because he invariably asked himself, "What must one know in order to make this particular statement?" Nine tenths of all published criticism is worthless just because of the fatal gap between data and conclusion, or conversely, the hopeless amalgam of incompatible ideas. Berlioz was a great critic because he had the power to *dis*sociate the ready-made as freely as he associated the remote — the power which makes the difference, between, say, a telephone exchange and a clothesline. The critics of any art could in effect study their craft in the pages where Berlioz conducts not a technical but an intellectual analysis. Platitudinous as it may seem, the true critic must respect the facts, imply nothing absurd, and say just what he intends. If this is so, what do we make of the many statements that Berlioz being French, we can hardly expect important music from him? [50] Or that since he wrote chiefly for full orchestra, he "cannot have felt the beauty of chamber music"; and because he disliked vocal fugues in quick time, he had "a rooted objection to contrapuntal treatment?" [51] Yet these are the calm utterances of leading critics — misleading, rather —

[49] *Soirées* (2nd Epilogue) *Eves.*, 305–6.
[50] *850*, 163; and again, *360*, 291.
[51] Respectively *775*, 56 and *776*, 38.

who not infrequently assume towards Berlioz a superior moral tone in proportion to the gravity not of his, but of *their* offenses.[52]

Judging from the results, apparently few critics of Berlioz can read, and many are dazzled out of their sober senses by the strong personality they are tackling. The problem is not simply one of factual error. All men are fallible and the most conscientious work is pitted with mistakes. But there is a way for doing everything, including the committing of errors, and the critical way safeguards both critic and reader by disclosing what is assumed and separating this from what is known. That is the true meaning of "seeing the object as it really is." In so defining criticism, Matthew Arnold did not imagine that the critic could usurp the place of Divinity and furnish an absolute description of the work of art. He meant that the true critic would be free from conventional attitudes and would escape vulgar pitfalls. He would judge with his eye on the object and, allowing for his personal equation, take open risks — as when Berlioz suggested that the allegro of the Seventh Symphony was a kind of peasant dance. The academic Grove, thinking conventionally, berated Berlioz for this "outrageous proposal" which for him was incompatible with the august image he had formed of Beethoven. But a modern scholar has vindicated Berlioz by showing the thematic connection with Celtic folk tunes.[53]

[52] None has been more frequently culpable, and with less excuse, than the late Sir Donald Tovey — in spite of his great competence and great gifts. Almost all his articles on Berlioz reveal, side by side with a just appreciation, a critical license which should rather be called licentiousness. Writing of the *Romeo and Juliet* symphony, for instance, Tovey says that Berlioz did not make it an opera because he was too impatient to set the words. Evidence for this? — none. Evidence for Berlioz' lack of industry in general? — none. But the impression given of Berlioz the Headlong is clear.

Tovey goes on to assert that at the joining of the fast and slow tunes in the Ball scene, Berlioz *proudly* writes "*réunion des deux thèmes*" and that in the preceding section the slow tune "depicts Romeo's growing love for Juliet." Then harking back to the imputation of impatience, he retracts it in a footnote saying *Les Troyens* is a genuine, monumental, and convincing music drama, and he condones his own error with the words "You never know where you are with Berlioz." (*590*, 89 and *n.*) This was the chance to be decently egotistical and to say: "*I* never know where *I* am." Of what use is the critic to his readers if he does not know or does not say that (a) the slow tune does not depict "growing love" nor anything else — the movement as a whole being marked *Tristesse;* and (b) the note in the score on the reunion of themes was no source of pride to Berlioz, who was as familiar with the device as with the five lines of the staff; it was a necessary indication for inept conductors. Tovey's "criticism" simply throws back upon his subject in the form of a vague odium the uncertainty of a judgment couched in irresponsible words.

[53] *897*, 255.

The lesson is plain, even though not every object of critical study is as many-faceted, subtle, and startling as Berlioz. To see the object as it really is requires, in addition to a gift for the material medium of the art, a passion for correct identification. This in turn calls for minute, searching, artistic documenting of one's impressions,[54] and (since these are multitudinous) long meditation about their net effect. This is far from the procedure of ordinary judges who are struck by a fact and who let fly a plausible broadside almost in one instant. Consider by way of contrast, how much quiet thought, following upon enjoyment, went into this portrait of a favorite author by which Berlioz introduces a musical subject:

There once was a man of great wit, very good natured and very gay, but whose sensibility was so fine that by dint of having his heart chilled and bruised by the world around him, he became at last melancholy. A great defect spoiled all his extraordinary qualities: he was a jester, indeed such a jester as no one ever was after or before him. He made fun of everyone if not of everything — of philosophers and lovers and scientists and ignoramuses; of pious people and impious; of old men and young men and sick men; of doctors (especially of doctors), of fathers, children, and innocent virgins; of guilty women; of lords and burghers and actors and poets; of his enemies, of his friends, and finally of himself. Musicians only seem to have escaped — do not ask me how — his indefatigable raillery. It is inconceivable that after castigating so many people, the excellent fellow I speak of was never once assassinated. After his death, it is true, the people would have liked nothing better than to drag his body through the mud, but his wife somehow managed to appease them by throwing money from the window of the mortuary chamber.

Though he was but the son of an upholsterer, he had had a good classical education and he wrote in verse and prose in remarkable fashion. So steadily was this remarked that after 150 years of deep thought the Parisians decided to erect in his honor a bronze statue bearing the titles of his works. An excellent idea, but those in charge of glorifying the man of letters proved somewhat lacking in knowledge of their own letters and engraved the name of one of the masterpieces as *L'Avarre*. . . .[55] The superintendent of works had to have the inscription scraped down during the night. This was a just return of fate; for you, illustrious scoffer, once made fun of a man who begged to be employed as Corrector of Signs and Inscriptions in Paris, and now in the nineteenth century you are put down, in Paris, as the author of *L'Avarre*.

[54] Berlioz regretted even an incautious word, written after thirty years' absence, concerning the gardens of the Vatican: "You were right to make fun of me: it will teach me to speak only of what I know thoroughly." (*S.W.*, 118.)

[55] *The Miser*, which should read: *L'Avare*.

This misanthrope — who would have guessed it? — was named Poquelin de Molière, and here is my excuse for speaking of him now. The lash of this incorrigible lasher of foibles never fell (as I said) on the shoulders of musicians. Yet by an ironic turn of fate, many musicians have seemed bent on, I will not say, defacing, but dressing up, prettifying, his creations. . . . One of these ungrateful men went to work at Molière's expense with such energy and success as have not, fortunately, been equalled since. His name was Mozart . . . and thus came into being the *Don Giovanni* whose counterglory has for many years cast a kind of shade on the glory of *Don Juan.*[56]

[56] *Grot.,* 190-2.

27. Holy Russia and
Giddy France: 33 Melodies

January 15, 1867
to February 14, 1868

Berlioz . . . pointed the way for untold
generations.

— BUSONI

WHEN EARLY IN 1867 Berlioz was planning a final mission to Germany,
it was to combat with music the darkness he felt closing in. From his
point of view, the music of the future was retrograde, the music of
Ambroise Thomas stationary, the tomfooleries of Offenbach decadent.
For the past half dozen years he had felt that art had taken refuge among
the "new peoples" — in the United States and Russia.[1] In Europe, it lay
in hiding (in the realms of Bohemia and little coteries) or it wore a
disguise. Saint-Saëns, the most gifted of younger musicians was making
his way with difficulty. Gounod, born to be a hyphen, was working on
a Romeo and Juliet opera as he had worked on *Faust* — diluting and
sugaring up the master's inspirations and spoiling the taste for the stronger
originals.

In the outer world, science excepted, everything seemed to stifle the
forms of life that Berlioz stood for.[2] The strong men, Bismarck, Napoleon III, Francis Joseph — drew to themselves the attention which for
half a century had been monopolized by men of thought. Napoleon's
Mexican expedition (in which Louis Berlioz as captain of a transport was
now involved) excited more public interest than Cyrus Field's laying an
ocean cable. Scientific achievements were fast becoming a drug on the
market. You could see a whole buildingful for one franc at the Great
Exhibition in Paris that very summer; and even if the new Paris Guide
had been composed by literary masters, the crowds behaved childishly,

[1] *93, 258.*
[2] Berlioz was not nostalgic about olden times, on the contrary: "I admire our
civilization more and more, with its post, telegraph, steam, and electricity —
slaves to the human will, which permit the more rapid transmission of thought."
(*L.I., 277.*) But he wished that a way were also found for keeping the thought
from being so generally dull and unhappy. (*Ibid.*)

possessively, destructively. A wave of primitivism, senseless and aggressive, seemed to sweep over France.[3]

Berlioz left. At Cologne, where he arrived by the end of February, his stout old friend Ferdinand Hiller had made everything ready. A room was reserved near the hall so that Berlioz could spend as many hours as possible reclining ("for I am one of the most horizontal men alive") and the rehearsals were so far advanced that Berlioz found the conducting easy and pleasant. The audience warmly applauded, from *Beatrice*, Hero's nocturne and the whole of *Harold in Italy*. The excellence of this execution, together with the revival of the *Damnation* at Vienna and the demand for a new edition of the *Requiem* by his Milan publisher, made Berlioz "almost quite happy."[4]

He came back to find Paris turning itself inside out for the Exhibition, in which, as a member of the Institute he was tediously involved.[5] One hundred and four cantatas had been written for the competition which he and his confreres were to judge. They sat and listened. Berlioz made a successful plea for choosing the work of Saint-Saëns, and he ran to the young man's house to be the first with the news. "At last our musical world has done a sensible thing! It has given me fresh strength. I could not have written you [Ferrand] such a long letter without this joy."[6]

Berlioz had other, remoter pleasures through hearsay: Cosima Liszt wrote to him that *Romeo and Juliet*, conducted by her husband Bülow, had been well received in Basel. From Copenhagen he had warm reports on *The Infant Christ*. And Louis from Mexico expressed passionate interest in the echoes of his father's success. Meanwhile Gounod's *Roméo et Juliette* had met with fair response, and the composer, who had discreetly failed to invite Berlioz to either rehearsals or *première*, took the first chance to seek him out at the Institute and give him a filial embrace.

---

[3] It was only two years before that the whole country had taken up the meaningless cry "*Hey! Lambert!*" to which the answer ran "Yes, it's Lambert!"

[4] *86, 615.*

[5] The arts at this Exhibition were chiefly in the hands of Berlioz' old enemies. That is why in the famous *Paris-Guide* issued for the occasion, there is no mention of him. Roqueplan wrote on the theater (I, 803 ff.), giving most of his article to Meyerbeer and Gounod. The essay "Bals et Concerts" in the second volume is by Champfleury, who systematically scorned the older generation (including Flaubert) in the name of Realism. Oddly enough, the great exile Hugo had been reinstated by the censorship in an effort of the Government to prove itself more liberal: *Hernani* was revived in June, Hugo wrote the introduction to the *Paris-Guide* — and politics once again decided what artists might and might not exist.

[6] *L.I.*, 305.

"I cannot imagine why," remarked Berlioz with his magnanimous candor.[7]

By the late spring Berlioz was deeply worried at the lack of news from Louis. He lived torn between recollections of his son's childhood and anxieties as to his future. As he had written some months before, "My dear Louis — if I did not have you! Just remember that I loved you even when you were little. And it was so difficult for me to love little children! There was something about you that drew me. Afterwards it grew less, in your middling years when you did not know what you were about. But it has since come back, enhanced, and I love you as you know that I do, and it will only increase more and more."[8]

This was the truth mingled with the thin self-deception of guilt about those middle years, for which Berlioz was about to pay a greater price than even the Lord's vengeance is said to exact. Towards the end of June a few intimates invited Berlioz to a morning reception in the studio of the Marquis Visconti. On the richly hung wall of the room they had put Berlioz' portrait, decorated with leaves and flowers. On the other walls placards bore the names of his great works. Theodore Ritter, Stephen Heller, Ernest Reyer, the Massarts and the Damckes, who were the prime movers, would greet the master with music, and in front of other guests present him with personal tokens and remembrances.

The appointed hour came for the surprise party but Berlioz did not appear. Ritter was sent to find him. Berlioz, sensing something strange in his household — with good reason, as events proved — had decided to stay at home. With Ritter's arrival at the house there began a series of rash though well-meant attempts to continue hiding the truth in hopes of salvaging the party. First, Berlioz' mother-in-law admitted that something was wrong, saying that their neighbor Damcke had suffered a grievous personal loss. Berlioz at once left with Ritter to seek Damcke. He, knowing the real facts, played up to the deception by promising Berlioz a full account later. The three men now left for the Marquis's studio, but the conspiracy was doomed: a few steps away from the door an acquaintance came up to Berlioz offering condolences on the death of Louis, news of which was in the papers. Louis had died of yellow fever in Havana on June 5, aged thirty-three.[9] Berlioz reached home and collapsed. Reyer

[7] Berlioz' *Romeo and Juliet* had made on the young Gounod an undying impression which he later recorded in an autobiographical fragment (see *L.I.*, viii-ix). His first work in Rome was an opera on that subject, to which he returned after twenty years.

[8] *Corresp.*, 327.

[9] The last of one Berlioz line unbroken for three centuries.

who stayed with him tells of his ceaselessly repeating: "It was for me to die." Callers found him lying mute, his head turned to the wall.

A week afterwards, he went to his office in the Library of the Conservatoire, drew out all the letters, notices, diplomas, decorations, batons, wreaths and other memorials of his career and, aided by his clerk, watched them burn.

He could not sleep; even large doses of laudanum brought no relief. He walked in a daze which his friends hardly knew whether to ascribe to grief or to the half-effective narcotic. His *Hymne à la France*, sung at the Exhibition, made a deep impression which they wished to tell him of.[10] He no longer cared. Business slowly drew him out, for Louis's affairs had to be wound up with his employers, and just then Ferrand, who had no son but a protégé of doubtful character, applied for help in an emergency. Berlioz ran at once to the Emperor's favorite legal counsel, who held the composer in high esteem, received advice and transmitted it. But Ferrand as was his custom made no reply, which compelled Berlioz to write twice more.

By this time Berlioz was in bad shape, and his doctor sent him to take the waters of Néris. He took five baths before the local physician decided that they were contraindicated. He predicted laryngitis, which duly ensued, and bundled Berlioz into a train bound for Dauphiné where his nieces nursed him back to health. He recovered his voice, though when the throat affection left, the intestinal returned. He went several times to see Estelle, who had just lost a son also. On the ninth of September they met for the last time.

Two days later the elder of his nieces was married and insisted on her uncle's being a witness. The groom was "charming in every way, otherwise I would not have witnessed the least little bit" wrote Berlioz with a momentary flash of gaiety.[11] From all over the county the Berlioz family, numbering thirty-two, had gathered. "We were all there but *one*, alas! It was the oldest whom I most enjoyed seeing again – my uncle the colonel, aged 84."[12] The Marmion uncle who had dazzled young Hector with firsthand accounts of Napoleon, who had sung and fiddled for him, who had flirted with Estelle, who had initiated the young medical-musical student into Parisian fashions, who had tried to find the famous conductor-composer amid the crowds of the Crystal Palace – he and these multiple selves were face to face again. "We wept. . . . He seemed as if ashamed to be still alive: I am much more ashamed."[13]

* * *

[10] 702, 4.   [11] *Corresp.*, 338.   [12] *Corresp.*, 339.   [13] *Ibid.*

Berlioz playing the guitar
(drawn from life, no date)

Louis Berlioz, aged about thirty

"The thread of my life is but the continuation of his. When it is cut, both lives are at an end."

— LOUIS BERLIOZ

Hardly had Berlioz returned to Paris, his German mission lost, when the Grand Duchess Helen of Russia began a campaign of her own to have him come and direct five concerts in St. Petersburg. "I have done a reckless thing . . . she coaxed and flattered me so, herself and through her officers, that after consulting several of my friends I accepted." The terms were as flattering as the insistence: Berlioz was to receive fifteen thousand francs and his expenses. He was to lodge at her palace and have the use of a carriage, to make his own programs and receive help at rehearsals. "At least if I die of it, I shall know it was worth it." [14]

At the same moment Steinway, on his own account or in partnership with other impresarios, wanted Berlioz to come to New York at a fee of twenty thousand dollars.[15] When he met with steadfast refusal, "this good man was so angry that he had a bronze bust made of me . . . to put in a hall which he has just built . . . You see that everything comes to him who waits — who waits long enough to be practically good for nothing." [16]

Musical visitors from everywhere — the American, Theodore Thomas, was cordially received and given a mint copy of the *Requiem* — hardly made life sweeter; the very endearments which the young and pretty singer, Adelina Patti, lavished on Berlioz in public emphasized his weariness, though he retorted with puns sufficiently potent.

News of a brilliant concert of his works at Meiningen roused him but little. The paradox of eternal youth wearing out its bodily shell struck him afresh when he saw the Princess's daughter: "I found her so changed — there's Life for you!" [17] And its purpose? "Absurdity now seems to me man's natural element, and death the noble goal of his mission." [18] When

[14] *Corresp.*, 339.

[15] This mention of Steinway is made on the strength of high probability. The records of the firm, kindly consulted by the present Theodore Steinway, show no direct offer to Berlioz. Yet the original Steinweg had heard and seen the composer in Brunswick, was a manufacturer of pianos, as Berlioz says (*Est.*, 47), had just finished building a new concert hall in New York (1866), and in other ways fits the circumstantial account given by Berlioz.

[16] *L.I.*, 311. Berlioz' bust (by Perraud) is still in Steinway Hall, New York, and in the concert advertisements of Steinway pianos the interesting letter he wrote on September 25, 1867: "Messrs. Steinway and Sons: I have heard the magnificent pianos which you manufacture. Allow me to compliment you on their excellence. . . . Their tone is splendid and truly noble. Moreover you have found the secret of reducing to an imperceptible point the disagreeable harmony of the minor seventh, which hitherto was audible on the eighth and ninth vibration of the longer strings, thus making their sounds cacophonous. Like so many of your other improvements, this marks a great step forward in piano making, and one for which every artist and amateur of delicate ear will owe you a debt of gratitude. Please believe, etc." (*141*.)

[17] *S.W.*, 183–4.   [18] *S.W.*, 183.

those who have done much are reduced by time to the vegetating which the great majority are content to deem synonymous with life, the contrast of past and present is itself a death blow. For every man sets the standard of intensity for his own existence, and as Samuel Butler showed, each of us dies when his organism becomes too puzzled to go on.

Nature herself seemed throughout 1867 to have lost her equanimity. From March to August the world was shaken by cyclones, tidal waves, and earthquakes. Vesuvius and Aetna shook the land as far as the British Isles, Mauna Loa erupted, and Hawaii, Mauritius, Ecuador, Peru, and San Francisco suffered from the tremors. In October the earth was showered with five thousand meteors and the ensuing winter was so severe that many rivers froze: one could walk across the Seine. Berlioz who only a year before had been greatly interested in the Bad Lands and their paleontology now seemed indifferent to the upheavings of *Nature immense*. In the *Memoirs* he had ironically remarked that no sign had told his mother she was bearing a dedicated child; he was now free to think that the earth mother was presaging his death. But his mind dwelt rather on the Russian cold and the long hours on the train.

It was an arduous trip. At Berlin he stopped for three days, which he mostly spent in bed. In St. Petersburg he rested three days more. He declined all social invitations, saving his strength for work.[19] When music was in the air, the old Berlioz "came back to life" like Lélio. The orchestra was superb and the *Symphonie Fantastique* sounded as young as its composer for the moment felt. The work had been included by request, for the Grand Duchess considered that in his proposed programs his own works were far too modestly represented.[20] To the first three he therefore added the *Benvenuto Cellini* and *Roman Carnival* overtures and the *Symphonie Fantastique*. There was music for soloists by Bach and Haydn, Paganini and Wienawski. But the main courses were the Pastoral, the Eroica, the Fifth and the Ninth (three movements only, for lack of fit singers), choral fragments from Mozart, Weber, and Gluck, including the second act of *Orpheus* with one hundred and thirty choristers.[21] "The

[19] Rimsky-Korsakov does not seem to have understood how ill the composer was and imputes to self-importance the fact that Berlioz on this visit was hard to approach. Of the crowd of young musicians he saw chiefly Balakirev and Stassov. (*1000*, 74–5.)

[20] Compare the programs Berlioz submitted — in which he hardly figures until the sixth — with those actually played. (*345*, 239–40 and 243–4.)

[21] To Kologrivov, who had suggested a larger hall for the final concert of Berlioz' own works, the composer had replied: "It must not be. I cannot acquiesce in the idea that the public will be more eager to hear my compositions than those of the great masters." (Oct. 10, 1867, 258, 237.)

Russians, who knew Gluck only through frightful hashes committed by incompetent people . . . could hardly stop applauding. Oh, it is bliss for me to reveal to them the masterpieces of that great man . . . In two weeks we shall give the first act of *Alceste*. The duchess gave orders that I was to be obeyed in everything. I don't abuse her authority, but I use it.

"She asked me to come and read *Hamlet* to her one of these evenings. . . . Here they love what is beautiful, they lead a literate and musical existence; they have in their bosoms something that makes one forget the snow and the cold. Why am I so old and tired?" [22]

Berlioz' birthday (December 11) had been celebrated with gifts, banquets, and public tributes. He was allowed to recover, for he felt "as sick as eighteen horses," then was taken to Moscow for two more concerts. The local directors had commandeered the largest hall and engaged five hundred performers. "This idea, which had struck me as mad, produced the liveliest success." [23] Twelve thousand four hundred listeners heard *Romeo and Juliet* and the Offertory of the *Requiem*. "I went through agonies when this last piece, which had been requested because of reports from Saint Petersburg, got under way. Listening to the 300 voices repeating their two notes, I suddenly feared the crowd might be bored and not let us finish. But they understood my idea; their attention grew, rather; and in fact they were gripped by this expression of resigned humility. At the last measure, acclamations broke out. I was brought out four times, the orchestra and chorus joined in, I did not know where to hide my head. It was the deepest impression I ever produced." [24]

Back in St. Petersburg after the New Year 1868, Berlioz had two more concerts to give — the last in every sense. "What joy for me when I have beaten the final measure of the *finale* in *Harold!* . . . I shall go to Saint-Symphorien [to see Estelle, who had written to him in Russia] and thence to Monaco, to lie down among the violets and sleep in the sun." [25]

The ultimate program had been ordered by the Duchess to be all Berlioz. Just as after *Beatrice and Benedict* he could feel his creation done, so after this sixth concert he could feel his mission accomplished. For he had met and played for the newest force in European music — the Russian Five. Balakirev, Cui, and Stassov were his special friends and admirers; Rimsky had attended rehearsals; Moussorgsky was deep in the *Treatise* and ebullient with enthusiasm. At their request and to show his apprecia-

[22] *Corresp.*, 343–4. He did not seem tired during performance. "Berlioz' beat," says Rimsky, "was simple, clear, and beautiful." (*1000, 75.*)
[23] *Corresp.*, 346.
[24] *Corresp.*, 347.
[25] *Corresp.*, 348–9.

tion for their regard, Berlioz had left them the autograph score of his *Te Deum*. The gift was doubly symbolic: thanks to it, one of the most moving sections of the work was later saved from destruction; thanks to the genuine entente he had established, the continuity of Berlioz' fame was assured. As in 1847 he had blessed "Holy Russia, that hast saved me," so twenty years later he could have repeated the grateful cry, for he had now forged the firmest link binding to him the next generation of creators.

Berlioz' Legacy of Song

A Thousand Greetings to Balakirev!
— From Berlioz' last letter,
August 21, 1868

The affinity which nineteenth-century Russia felt for the music of Berlioz is quite understandable. That country's new school of composers was inspired by a revival of folk melodies, coinciding with a flowering of legend, lyric poetry, and sacred music — the Romanticism of Glinka and Pushkin coming immediately after the great religious composer Bortniansky (1751–1825) had concluded his work of codifying and embellishing the native liturgy. Berlioz' tradition and first awakening were, as we know, remarkably similar, whence his lifelong sympathy with Russia's musical life is not surprising. We have seen his early sympathy with Glinka and noted its results.[1] Even before this, he had been interested in Russian religious music and had arranged for the Tzar a number of sixteen-part chorales which have unfortunately been lost.[2] On his first Russian visit in 1847 he made the acquaintance of Alexis Lvov, to whom he owed the knowledge of Bortniansky so admiringly recorded in his *feuilletons*.[3]

But in 1847 there was as yet no modern Russian school. Tchaikovsky and the later Five were still children, whose true vocation was dormant for nearly two decades more. When in the sixties Balakirev, Rimsky, Cui, Borodin, Moussorgsky (and Stassov, who was the critic of this "Mighty

[1] See above, Chapter 15.
[2] In 1843 (*285*, 380). This commission and its remuneration undoubtedly account for the dedication of his next printed score (which happens, oddly, to be the *Symphonie Fantastique*) to Nicholas I.
[3] *Soirées* (21st) Eves., 231–2, and again: *1386*, Oct. 19, 1850, Jan. 17, 1851, Dec. 13, 1851, Nov. 6, 1862. (This last is a review of Lvov's History of sacred music in Russia.)

Heap")[4] heard and studied Berlioz, they felt the presence of a master whose lessons were at once congenial and free from any constrictive system. He was sufficiently removed in years not to be a rival and he brought them as he had brought his colleagues in other lands the first modern orchestral style; they even more than others could respond to the dramatic technique which served a Romanticism in the genuine tradition. Thus Moussorgsky's first important orchestral score, *St. John's Night on Bald Mountain* (1867) was a new working of the Faustian elements in the *Fantastique*.[5]

What is more, Berlioz' melodies and developments fell gratefully on the ears of young men bred on Russian folk songs, for these, like Berlioz' tunes, tend to be modal, to consist of uneven groupings of phrases, and to combine in free rather than scholastic polyphony.[6] The stars in their courses seemed to make Berlioz the predestined mentor of these ultimate creators of the century; and conversely it was through them that he who had fought to a standstill on Western ground might have seen his musical principles sweep the world: Russian ballets, suites, monodramas, and symphonic poems were the offspring of the dramatic symphony; their light, transparent orchestration was his;[7] and *Boris Godunov* — a *Cellini*-like conception — came forth in 1869, the very year of Berlioz' death. Three years later, Moussorgsky, its author, was convinced that "in music there are two giants: the thinker Beethoven, and the super-thinker Berlioz. When around these . . . we gather all their generals and *aides-de-camp*, we have a pleasant company; but what has this company of subalterns achieved? Skipping and dancing along in the paths marked out by the giants . . ."[8]

[4] This is the meaning of *Mogrichaya Kuchka*, the name by which the Five were known. (*882*, 428.)

[5] The composer describes its parts as follows: "(1) assembly of the witches, their chatter and gossip; (2) cortege of Satan; (3) unholy glorification of Satan; and (4) Witches' Sabbath . . . The form of interspersed variations and calls is, I think, the most suitable for such a commotion . . . the transitions are full, without any German approach, which is remarkably refreshing." (*220*, 85-7.)

[6] See Mr. Slonimsky's useful résumé of Sokalski's authoritative book in *882*, 422.

[7] They admired Wagner's too, but explicitly preferred that of Berlioz. Among Moussorgsky's half-dozen bedside books in the room where he died was the *Treatise*. (*220*, 415.) As for Tchaikovsky's relation to the French master, though it was variable in words, it seems to certain critics to have also been that of an unconscious beneficiary. (*305*, 6 and 136.) The published correspondence between Tchaikovsky and Balakirev offers striking confirmation of these judgments. (*936a*.)

[8] *220*, 199.

We may argue the fitness of these terms but not the significance of the connection in the minds of these interpreters and successors of Berlioz who actually produced new music. The linkage moreover strengthens the general truth that the Impressionism and Naturalism of the end of the century are in any art the direct heirs of Romanticism.[9] And since the young Russians were to find kinship in late as well as early Berlioz, in the *Te Deum* and *Troyens* as well as in the *Fantastique* and the songs, this fact alone is enough to refute the foolish notion that Berlioz' career is that of a lost Romantic who returned to an "essentially French" classicism in old age[10] or — as others would have it — to a sterile reaction against true modernity.

This interpretation rests on a confusion between life and art, between biography and criticism. Though Berlioz received from his young friends warm testimonials of their admiration, he could naturally not gauge the full extent of his success as a culture hero, for his success like that of the germinating grain must first take the form of failure through apparent disintegration.[11] It signifies as a marvel of right instinct that Berlioz worked to the end for both success and failure. He rejected every expedient that might have tied his works to the musics that seemed to be winning the future; and instead embraced martyrdom with the passion of the elect. Yet he took excellent care that his musical affairs should be left in order and that his career should seem a completed cycle — should show a musical

[9] A twentieth-century critic finds a good deal of Stravinsky in the *Requiem;* another hearing Borodin's *Prince Igor* and Berlioz' *Te Deum* at one concert acknowledged that Berlioz was "the true father of the Russian School" (*444*); the connection resting of course on the last two movements of the *Te Deum* which — and this is another confirmation — were the only ones to cause Tchaikovsky "great enjoyment." (*1020*, 311.)

[10] It was in that very year 1867 that Berlioz revised his *Requiem* for a third Italian edition, saying "If I were threatened with the destruction of my whole output save one score, I should beg grace for the *Requiem*." (*L.I.*, 303.) This score of 1837 which Berlioz was so far from repudiating thirty years later is "Romantic" enough; it even contains ideas dating back to his twenty-first year. Again in *Les Troyens*, many passages — notably "The Royal Hunt and Storm" — are as "Romantic" as anything in *Romeo* or the *Funeral* symphony. What critics have miscalled a return to classicism is the effect of perspective first — the *Damnation of Faust* seems "classical" in 1934 — and second, of the natural shift in an artist's powers as he grows older: he has a suppler technique and a surer hand in exploiting ideas to the full; but less exuberance does not mean less fire.

[11] In his perceptive essay on Berlioz, W. H. Mellers admirably contrasts Wagner's success with Berlioz' failure, seeing each as appropriate but asking for an analysis of the failure. I should like to think that certain parts of this book had supplied a beginning of explanation.

shape. It was no accident that together with works of his own which belonged to the first half of his life, he brought the Russians Gluck, Weber and Beethoven — his well-loved Pastoral and the Ninth, which was his fighting standard of 1828. His own later works he left in shadow, supplying only the scores, so that formally his end was in his beginning. There is a beautiful fitness in the fact that the titles of his first and last publications likewise echo each other — *Nine Melodies* in 1830, *Thirty-Three Melodies* in 1865.[12]

The *Thirty-Three Melodies* gathered in one volume the works for one or more voices which he wished to preserve alongside the bigger scores. In the thirty-five years of his productive life he had composed twelve full-size dramatic works, nine overtures, and these songs, chiefly orchestral.[13] Another dozen or more cantatas, occasional pieces, arrangements, album sketches, or discarded first drafts, fell from his pen, by no means all negligible, though he attached to them but little importance.[14] With this output Berlioz had filled exactly that great gap of one third of a century when European music was at a low ebb. From 1820 to 1830, the years of his preparation, the output had been extremely rich. Beethoven, Weber and Schubert, Rossini and Bellini, were pouring forth masterpieces for stage, voice, and instrumental ensemble. The next three decades, apart from Berlioz' scores, were to be notable for the piano works of Chopin, Liszt, and Schumann. Vocal and orchestral music was less richly represented by Mendelssohn and Schumann, whose sway was also limited and local. As for Liszt and Wagner, their masterpieces in various degrees of gestation saw the light of day only at the close of the Berliozian age, as did also the great music dramas of the twice-born Verdi. And from that time forward the musical output has not only been abundant but infinitely varied and generally regarded as one of the dominant forms of man's spiritual expression.

[12] This terminal date is approximate to within a year, because of the publisher's practice. It will be remembered that the *Eight Scenes of Faust,* which antedate the first melodies, was at once withdrawn.

[13] This count takes the *Symphonie Fantastique* and *Lélio* to be two works, but numbers the *Tempest* as an overture-fantasia and excludes the overture of the *Flight into Egypt* which is not really separable from the chorus that follows it. If the bulk of *Lélio* were reclassified, the total number of "melodies" would be raised to thirty-eight.

[14] In sending Reyer a pile of works for the summing up which the young critic projected, Berlioz wrote: "Here is more than enough; there may be things in the lot which should not even be shown, but I have destroyed so many manuscripts — oratorios, overtures, operas, cantatas — that I may be pardoned for this. . . ." (*91*, 764.)

The more this artistic treasury is examined, the more clearly its relation to the thought of Berlioz is discerned. Are we, for example, interested in the revival of the modes, which has extended the moderns'
sense of tonality? Crediting the Russians or Mr. Vaughan Williams is
just, provided we remember their antecedents as did Debussy at Bayreuth.[15] If we study French music and record the influence of the
Schola Cantorum with its manifesto in behalf of a free and inventive
music, Romain Rolland reminds us that this was the burden of Berlioz'
teaching. Dalcroze's crusade for founding musical education on rhythm
is nothing but the carrying out of Berlioz' wish for "20 classes in rhythm"
in every conservatoire.[16] The historians of jazz are led back to Berlioz'
syncopations and use of drums for a starting point in the development
of their popular art; [17] and the modern Viennese hope to deliver melody
from the bar line — a hope which goes back as far as Reicha, and which
was successfully realized in our own day by Koechlin and Van Dieren —
is the extension of Berlioz' actual creation of an unshackled melody.

It is in fact his devotion to draftsmanship, his fertility in the invention
of lines of every kind, which makes Berlioz impregnable to criticism and
perpetually rich in suggestion; so that if it is true to say with Mr. Sollertinski that "Berlioz was the dominant influence in music up to the First
World War," it is also true to say with Mr. Cecil Gray that "the composer of the recent past [who is] of particular significance in respect of
the music of the future as here conceived is Berlioz." And Mr. Gray speci-
fies that his "melodic writing, alone among the great masters provides an
anticipation" of the new classicism based on linear beauty.[18]

It should therefore be less and less difficult to state the measure of
Berlioz' contribution without seeking for his "school," and without taking
away from the merit of the many geniuses whose minds or ears he
tuned to his own note: Berlioz' orchestra, his dramatic conceptions,
rhythms, chords, and melodies formed the living literature upon which
was bred the second international age of music after Mozart and Gluck.
Berlioz enforced no manner, gave no formula to exploit, but left his
mark everywhere, differently on different men, in accordance with his
own pluralistic art; so that by noticing the varied usages to which he gave

[15] Conversing with his teacher Guiraud in 1889, Debussy found Wagner
"less of an innovator" than was commonly thought and pointed out especially
that Berlioz was "less strictly tonal" than Wagner. (*975*, 44.)

[16] *Grot.*, 244.

[17] See — or rather hear — the recorded jazz version of the "Pilgrims' March"
from *Harold.* (*1437.*)

[18] Sollertinski: *305*, 5–8; Gray: *721*, 230–2.

rise and putting their principles together again, one could reconstruct the great original.[19]

This is a type of influence, not the most common, and hence open to question until many men are dead and many books fumigated. But if we take the free testimony of those most closely concerned, it is clear that no important musician since his day has been outside Berlioz' musical field of force. The same statement may be made about Wagner, and it is also true, but it means something different, something more literal and vivid, and hence more quickly perceived: which is what led Busoni to say of a critic who missed this distinction: "Was he so blind as not to see that it was Berlioz who had pointed the way for untold generations?"[20]

To sum up these historic relations is to describe simply Berlioz' public or ecumenical import. It is far less easy to describe his intrinsic and intimate effect. As an earlier chapter made clear, Berlioz' admirers choose different works as his characteristic or supreme masterpiece, which really means the one congenial to their idiosyncrasy. This might lead us to infer that diversity is his special effect if the term did not suggest a scattering, a diffuseness, which is in fact the opposite of his (no less special) concentration. Taken together in ever varying guises, this pair of hallmarks is likely to disorient even a capable and sympathetic listener on hearing an unfamiliar score; on which account one group of interpreters feels that Berlioz applied his powerful mind to make music legitimately serve novel uses;[21] whereas another group asserts that "he is not a musician: he is music itself."[22] The implication here is that Berlioz spoke music's tongue with the freedom of the native born and the exuberance of a creator. But in truth the two interpretations are not so far apart as they seem. They differ only in their initial assumption about the goal of art — decoration or expression; repose or energy — which irresistibly brings us back to the Shakespearean parallel: in the work of Berlioz it is the esthetic and not the technique or the raw material, which divides friend from foe.

To come under Berlioz' intimate spell one must accept his esthetic, for good or for the time being, and then treat it as an accepted thing, which is to say, more than half forget it — as we do with all our working assumptions. The result almost invariably is that one begins to make out his melody and to find pleasure in it. This is the great step to take,

---

[19] Philip Greeley Clapp: "Many composers' eyes have gleamed over Berlioz' original ideas, which remain characteristically his own after more than a century of exploitation by nearly everybody else." (*421*, Apr. 14, 1943.)

[20] *944*, 280.

[21] *692*.

[22] *504*, 25.

for it is in melodies — melodies that are at once complete statements and independent objects of art — that Berlioz thinks and delivers himself.[23]

One need only lend an ear to the exquisite collection of *Summer Nights* to feel the power, the variety, the precision of what he called Expression — neither depiction nor labeling, but the embodiment in sound of intimations lying deeper than articulate thought. Conventional in words and subject, these six songs or variations on the theme of longing achieve the utmost originality, and with the simplest means — a human voice and a few strings and woodwinds. The first, *Villanelle*, is a spring ditty, whose modulations impart freshness to the familiar in rhythm while strengthening the delicacy of line. The *Spectre de la Rose* is by contrast a dramatic scene — that of the well-known ballet danced to Weber's music — which in Berlioz' hands has the added quality of sentimental dalliance suddenly raised to passion. *On the Lagoon* is a *chant récitatif* broken by a refrain — a monotony movingly rendering Berlioz' recurrent "evil of isolation." The next song (the gem of the collection) is, as the title *Absence* implies, another expression of the same feeling of void, but the tremendous call to the departed lover springs from a loneliness that has once been shared and is now twice bitter. *Au Cimetière* takes us with gruesome immediacy to the realm of the dead fearing oblivion, and *L'Ile Inconnue* sings mankind's nostalgic hope of a lotus land of eternal love and perpetual delight of life.

The myriad nuances of these inner realities transcribed by Berlioz do not come from words nor do they submit to identification in words. The magic is tangible, imperishable, yet defies analysis. So precise in Berlioz' *melos* are the modifications of pitch and time that paradoxically the virtue may not fully strike us if we merely hear; we must heed. This is no doubt why Schumann long ago recommended that one sing out Berlioz' melodies, as it were to feel in the body and reproduce by vocal effort the motions of Berlioz' spirit. For it is an active and subtle spirit, who is likely to escape us if we sit passive and wait to be moved.

Once we are attuned to this governing element, the rest becomes naturalized in relation to it: harmony, rhythm, counterpoint, orchestration and form. It is then and then only that one may be said to *hear* Berlioz, that is, to enjoy as he did the sensations he chose and to perceive as he did

---

[23] An otherwise useful guide to *Music for the Voice* (1949) states rather incautiously that "the very few songs of Berlioz are perhaps among his least representative compositions," and lists but four, not counting excerpts from two of the major scores. (*1328*, 256 and 441 ff.) It is apparent that until Berlioz' whole output is seen as dramatic vocal music — "melodies" in his own broad sense — every part will seem "unrepresentative" of his thought.

the relations he contrived. Having done so we can see that our former bewilderment or sense of alienating coldness was based on an "understanding" which took illicit priority over concrete experience. We knew, or thought we knew, more than we heard.

Only beyond this point does a comparison of Berlioz with other composers become just: one must first learn to live reflectively with passages, movements, or "moments" from his music as one does with recollections of other great utterances. Within Berlioz himself groupings and comparisons suggest themselves: the love music in the *Harold* and *Romeo* symphonies or the Faustian and Trojan dramas; the prayers and invocations, from the *Francs-Juges* overture to the death of Dido; the fugues — diabolic and rousing as in the *Fantastique*, gentle and quaint as in *The Infant Christ;* the great funeral "monotonies" in *Romeo*, the *Requiem*, the *Te Deum, Hamlet* and the *Funeral* symphony; the roistering or mass scenes in *Harold, Benvenuto*, the *Damnation* and *Beatrice;* the twelve superb marches — the most varied collection, perhaps, in modern music; the tender nocturnes or pastorales that recur from the *Fantastique* to *Beatrice*, taking in nearly all the overtures and dramatic works in between; and finally the haunting "calls" uttered by flute or oboe, French or English horn, in the mysterious movements such as the *Queen Mab* Scherzo, the Ride to the Abyss or the "Royal Hunt and Storm."

Once we have been drawn in, literally by the ears, to explore this rich world, acquired momentum propels us ever closer to the reality of Berlioz as musician. More intent on undergoing, let us say, the third movement of the *Fantastique* than on knowing whence it came or how it is tied to the rest of the score by words or notes, we ask of Berlioz neither what he felt nor what he knew, but what he *sounds*. And there, at the close of this ample hymn to natural beauty, we find delight and excitement in a remarkable detail: the plaintive English horn melody of the beginning returns, but its answer is not as before on the oboe; instead we hear softly pulsating chords on the kettledrums. This musical pleasure is *sui generis* and indescribable. The habit of words may make us exclaim "how dramatic!" or "what realism!" — which is correct enough — but these notions only single out aspects of something which justifies itself to the ear and the imagination long before it is motivated or classified by reason.

This is again true of another and yet a different surprise, whose material means is still less obvious — the sharpening of the D in the *idée fixe* melody at the end of its exposition in the first movement. Here we cannot apply any adjective of conventional criticism, we cannot explain why this modification by a half step is so powerful and right, why it produces a total illumination of its surroundings like a subtly colored flare bringing a landscape out of darkness.

Berlioz' music is full of such moments, which is to say full of creation, unceasingly expressive. And it is this quality, hidden at first, which makes his admirers call him "simply one of the greatest composers who have ever lived." Compared to this power, which he shares with very few, the art of fashioning clear, strong and satisfying movements appears, for all its importance, ancillary and almost mechanical.

Nor is this the end of our discoveries in Berlioz' music. At many points in his work we encounter passages of which the effect seems more than masterly, for it is visibly out of proportion to the notes. These would be normally transitional or quite commonplace, or at times perversely crude, yet they affect us as would a discharge of energy directly into our nerve endings. This disparity between cause and effect is by no means unknown in the other arts, but in music it is specially remarkable because it seems to act in defiance of the very skill to which the artist usually owes his power. The fact has been noted with particular reference to Berlioz by Mr. John Foulds in his book *Music Today*, where he explains it by what he calls "devic influences" — from Hindu "devas," the Bright Ones.[24] There is no need to believe in the action of a transcendental force in order to see that the critic has aptly named an element of mundane artistic reality which others have independently noticed and tried to describe. Mr. Foulds gives as an example of what he means the persistent A flat in the opening of the *Fantastic* symphony, a passage long deemed a typical Berliozian *gaucherie*, although it is the very passage that Koechlin, who probably knows nothing of devas, instances as a proof of harmonic genius.[25]

We may connect with this "radioactive" property of a few simple notes the experiences noted by Saint-Saëns and others on hearing parts of the *Requiem*,[26] as well as Rachmaninoff's report of a performance of the *Fantastique* under Mahler,[27] or Ernst's remark about the concluding chorus of *Les Troyens*, Part I, that "the music seems charged with electricity." [28] Berlioz himself was apparently aware of a like quality in Beetho-

[24] ". . . lacking some understanding of the deva impacts which he so frequently transcribes in his works . . . it is impossible fairly to evaluate Berlioz' work." (*802*, 285.)

[25] *452*, 124.

[26] *502*, 431.

[27] "He conducted it magnificently, especially the March . . . the windows shook, the very walls seemed to vibrate." (*994*, 160.)

[28] *428*, 305.

ven. He says, speaking of the Scherzo of the Fifth, "It is a strange piece, the first measures of which, although there is nothing fearful about them, cause that inexplicable emotion one feels under the magnetic gaze of certain persons." [29] And he likens the mood to that of Goethe's "Blocksberg" scene in *Faust*, that is, he instinctively thinks of the unseen powers at the very root of Being.

When Berlioz found it appropriate in his own scores to call up such emanations from the depths, he was generally able to do so, and it is this rather than any conscious devices of timbre or dynamics which makes so many of his passages glitter, tingle, throb or — to use his special word — "vibrate." [30] In analyzing our intimate response to Berlioz, it is therefore not enough to remember that all music is a trembling and that the inevitable physical by-product of making any music at all is to set up sympathetic vibrations in our nerves, bones and skin. The further technical question arises whether Berlioz' rationale for blending rhythm, melody, harmony and timbre precisely as he did, "in despite of common sense," [31] was not dictated by an intuition of what is needed to detonate unsuspected charges of primal energy stored up or concealed within us. If this were so, it would afford another clue to the understanding of Berlioz' public triumphs without sequels. To this day one may observe listeners deeply moved by a brilliant Berlioz performance and yet soon objecting to his art: the audience has been aroused to an uncommon pitch of enthusiasm, but shortly a feeling akin to shame mixed with resentment overlays the first impression. It is as if a too secret fiber had been acted on by a thaumaturgist who is henceforth feared and disliked, or else simply not remembered as having shaken the soul.

For the composer who wields this power and administers it in concentrated form instead of diffusing it thinly through his works, our genteel responses create a cruel dilemma: if his music is dully played, he makes no impression; [32] if he is brilliantly played, he runs the risk, by overstimulating his hearers, of giving them grounds for grievance. Yet this is a disadvantage which may in time turn out to be his salvation with the fearless, for the primitive, devic, or magnetic force is simply the principle of life imparted by the creator to his clay. If Berlioz' music has survived, not disfigurement merely, and neglect but also anger and organized attack, it is largely due to the fact that whenever played he has always struck

[29] *A Trav.*, 35.
[30] See *A Trav.*, 95.
[31] *502*, 431.
[32] This holds especially for light orchestrators, witness not only Berlioz but Mozart.

some men as possessing the Promethean fire.[33] "The reason," said the late James Agate, "why I would rather hear the worst Berlioz in preference to the best of anybody else, is that he is the only composer who can be (a) noble (b) voluptuous and (c) exciting all at the same time." [34]

This testimony from an amateur of music is most important, for it is the devoted laity who in the end discover an artist's meaning to the world and so decide his fate. The professionals pave the way (or block it) with arguments and adjectives, but the affectionate minority have the last word, both because they represent numbers and because they are the only group disinterested enough to acknowledge what they inwardly recognize. And what they respond to, given enough good chances, is the quality of funded life. All our critical slang — Realism, dramatic truth, form, beauty, variety, tension, devic force, structure or conception — all this is imagery to catch the manifestation of life as it finds its mysterious equivalent in art: the very terms are derived from our attempt to dissect or describe life, which is also — real, dramatic, structural, multiple, and the fruit of conception. Hence it is no verbalism to relate, as Freud and others have done, the artistic impulse to the magnetic core of life which is love. In defining music as the imagination of love in sound, the critic is proceeding as soberly as the religious thinker who puts love at the center of the world of spirit, or as the mathematician Laplace who, on his deathbed, set love higher than the knowledge of physical laws.

To his enlightened hearers, Berlioz' art speaks intimately of the mystery of this trinity of Art, Love, and Life, upon which his own existence was a commentary. Though capable of rendering the many motions of the vital energy, from the dark and diabolical to the bright and heedless, his predominant coloring, as Kufferath rightly pointed out is the "tragic sadness." [35] In striking this note, Berlioz convinces us that the love which possessed him was no unanchored eroticism seeking Nirvana but a strong tenderness alive to the Virgilian *lacrymae rerum*. It was out of this love that his melodies were born first and last, and it was the same loving self

[33] The image itself was used by Rubinstein on hearing *Cellini* (*171*, Feb. 3, 1879). One may compare the magnetic effect of the living Berlioz on many of his contemporaries with what a critic of the graphic arts felt on meeting George Eliot: "She has singular power, which is a thing found only in extraordinary genius. She put so much will . . . in trying to convince me that it took a certain effort on my part to keep my own ideas clear." (*1088*, 324.) Could this account for the inability of some of Berlioz' readers to retain more than a fragment of what he clearly says?

[34] Quoted in *1374* (1945) 191.

[35] *830*, 265.

that he gave unsparingly to art and to love, in the faith that they were "the two wings of the soul." The phrase, it so happens, is the next-to-last dictum in his *Memoirs*, the burden of which — insofar as they relate to his person — was a demonstration of the law that

> We are not free to choose
> What we are free to love.

Having, in art and life, fulfilled the law, Berlioz could say, with valedictory truthfulness: "I shall now be able to die without bitterness and without anger." [36]

[36] *Mem.*, II, 423.

28. Memory's End

February 15, 1868
to March 8, 1869

I have known when there was no music
with him but the drum and fife.
— *Much Ado*

ON FEBRUARY 15, 1868, Berlioz had left the Russian capital, his musical life completed. As if he knew it was his only life, his handwriting shows the sudden disintegration within. At the sight of it his friends could feel what M. Boschot, usually so harsh, expresses with true feeling: "His hitherto admirable script — so decorative, artistic, imperious, and which had not changed in fifty years — is now painful to see. From [1819 to 1868] his hand stayed firm, tracing on paper without any faltering the visible and spontaneous symbols of a body and soul endowed with prodigious stamina, and giving proof of a character truly cast in bronze. . . . One shudders, one weeps at the sight of these autographs of 1868." [1]

There was no need of Dr. Nélaton's verdict, given in Paris, to tell Berlioz that he was doomed. His handwriting alone recovered. On March first he left for the South. Nice drew him, as before, with its life-giving air, its memories of earlier healings, and its old ruined tower where *King Lear* and *The Corsair* had been conceived. He paced the shingle and enjoyed the sea. He drove to Monte Carlo and clambered over the rocks. It was so magnificent that for a few moments he no longer wished to die. [2] But without even the warning of dizziness he fell head first. Passing workmen picked him up, bruised and bled, and brought him to his carriage. He returned to his hotel in Nice, slept, and next day felt well enough to go out. This time, in going from one terrace bench to another, he fell again. Two young men escorted him to his room where he lay for a week.

When his mother-in-law saw his battle-scarred face, she had hysterics, for he had returned to Paris alone, having told no one of his two accidents, probably because he hoped that he would not recover from the second. Death was striking all around him — his old associate, Edouard Monnais, editor of the *Gazette Musicale*, then Pillet and Duponchel, one-

[1] *269, 652.*   [2] *Corresp., 349.*

Death bust, by S. Lami

"Thus passed away a Stoic."
— HAVERGAL BRIAN

time directors of the Opera, who must seemingly die as they have lived, in pairs. Worst of all, disaster struck again at Ferrand. This oldest of friends, crippled and impoverished, lived with his wife in a remote mountain hamlet, where they had adopted a child named Blanc Gounet.[3] This was the protégé on whose behalf Berlioz had run errands to a Paris solicitor, for despite his foster parents' kindness the youth had grown into a vicious drunkard and a thief. In 1868 he was on parole under a sentence of ten years' imprisonment and living with the Ferrands. During the night of May twenty-fifth, he strangled Mme. Ferrand and disappeared with her few trinkets. Ferrand, equally devoted to his wife and to the boy, was shattered. Berlioz, who refused the consolations of glib philosophies for himself, could tender none to his friend. He became ever more silent and abstracted, pondering life and the blindness of those who call Shakespeare "morbid" or "exaggerated." On his way south Berlioz had avoided seeing his other dear friends, Lecourt and Morel, because they had known Louis so well. "I should have been broken up by your society more than by any other. Few of my friends loved Louis as you did. And I cannot forget — forgive me both." [4]

In July, a little more than six months before Berlioz' death, Dauphiné woke up to the fact that the province had given birth to a great man. The town of Grenoble invited him to preside at a competition of local singing clubs, and to witness the dedication — also a bit tardy — of a statue to the first Napoleon. It was an excuse to fete the composer. In Grenoble, Nanci's husband, Judge Pal, took Berlioz in charge. "There were banquets and toasts to which I hardly knew what to reply. The Mayor gave me a crown of laurels made of gold. . . ." [5] Though he was not far from Estelle and Ferrand, he could not summon the further strength to visit them. Poor Ferrand, whose foster son had been caught and condemned to death, was working to obtain a reprieve.

In his Paris apartment, rue de Calais, Berlioz was still badgered by the living, incorrigible as of yore; "They ask me for impossible things. They want me to say something favorable about a German musician — in which indeed I concur — but only on condition that I shall also say something unfavorable about a Russian, whom they want the German to supplant, although the Russian is actually deserving. . . . What the devil of a world is that?" [6]

The last months laid low other companions or enemies of early days. The murderer Gounet having been guillotined in September, Ferrand

---

[3] Not related to Berlioz' early friend, Thomas Gounet.
[4] *Corresp.*, 353.   [5] *Corresp.*, 354.   [6] *Ibid.*

died a few days later. The next month, death took Stephen de la Madelaine, forty years a colleague in musical affairs; then Léon Kreutzer, a fellow student at the Conservatoire; and in November Rossini, who was buried in a mood of carnival gaiety, to refresh the jaded Parisians. Twelve days later, Berlioz went out for the last time. Charles Blanc, who had helped him keep the Librarianship during the troubles of 1848, was a candidate for the Institute and called in the regular way to solicit Berlioz' vote. Seeing him so ill, Blanc withdrew his request and was about to leave in some confusion but Berlioz bade him stay. "My days are numbered — the doctor has even stated the number. I can and will vote for you." [7] On the appointed day, Berlioz had himself carried across Paris by his manservant (aptly named Schumann) and cast his vote for Blanc, who was elected.[8]

In the last note we have from his pen, he told Stassov: "I feel I am dying; I no longer believe in anything." But he added: "I should like to see you; you might act as a tonic, you and Cui. . . . A thousand greetings to Balakirev." [9] Through the winter he lingered on, silent but not losing his faculties, receiving his friends — the faithful Massarts and Damckes, Saint-Saëns and Reyer, his Dido, Mme. Charton-Demeur. Toward the beginning of March he fell into a partial coma. His tongue seemed to be paralyzed; he could only smile. At half past twelve in the afternoon of March 8, Berlioz died in the arms of his mother-in-law. A friend of hers and Mme. Charton-Demeur were also present. Reyer watched the night through.

The funeral on March 11 was of the conventional sort for a member of the Institute, Librarian of the Conservatoire, and Officer of the Legion of Honor.[10] A company of the National Guard, to which Berlioz had once belonged, stood at attention rue de Calais. Trumpets blew for the raising of the coffin. The pallbearers included Gounod, Reyer, Ambroise Thomas, and Baron Taylor. At Trinity Church, Pasdeloup's orchestra and singers from the Opera played excerpts from Gluck, Beethoven,

---

[7] Reported by Legouvé, *362*, 139.

[8] The date is ascertainable from Charles Blanc's election: Nov. 25, 1868. Since the Revolution Blanc had made his name as a productive historian and critic of art; he had founded the *Gazette des Beaux-Arts* (1859) still in existence; and his election in replacement of Comte Walewski was fully deserved.

[9] *Corresp.*, 354–5. The note to Estelle, printed in *125*, seems to be the next-to-last autograph extant.

[10] Berlioz, who had foreseen so many things, had long ago chaffed Elwart, of the Conservatoire, "If you are going to be there and make a speech, then I'd just as soon not die." (*269, 661*.)

Mozart, and Cherubini; also the *Hostias* from Berlioz' *Requiem*, the septet from *Les Troyens*, and the religious march from *Harold*.

To the sounds of his own Funeral Triumph, the procession moved through the heedless streets toward the cemetery where Harriet and Marie already lay. The Institute delegation in uniform and a considerable following marched behind the hearse. Four speeches were to be made, the last of which, by Elwart as predicted, infuriated Georges Bizet by its absurd reference to the great dead as "our colleague." But before the body had reached the grave, a final Berliozian incident — never to be believed had it been recorded by a Romantic of 1830 — took place. Not far from the goal, the pair of mourning-coach steeds, black and tame as Paris undertakers themselves, suddenly seized the bit in their teeth, plowed through the brass band in front of them, and brought Berlioz alone within the gates.

SUPPLEMENTS

1. Berlioz' Afterfame: 1869–1949

> Once dead he will live for a long time.
> — STEPHEN HELLER on Berlioz (1844)

The history of a man's posthumous reputation is the most uncertain of subjects: depending on what one takes to be a sign of renown, almost any account may be given. The fact of Shakespeare's neglect for two hundred years has been disputed because in the century following his death a few dozen Englishmen wrote verses about him, after which he received increasing attention from actors and critics. All this is true, but it is also true that the Shakespeare we know, the "supreme dramatist" and "world poet" did not emerge until the early nineteenth century, as is proved by the controversies that went on between Hazlitt and Gifford, and the things that Coleridge, Goethe, and Berlioz had to keep repeating until the trade-mark "Shakespeare" became a byword for excellence.

With regard to Berlioz himself, one cannot simply correlate estimates of his fame and decades of time: one must also speak of countries, for when he is considered with others as a world figure it is usually as a standard-bearer of Romanticism, which in some quarters means not renown but disgrace. In the eyes of the French he has not become a representative of the nation's art, and he is thus deprived of the respect that peoples pay one another formally and diplomatically, in the spirit of log-rolling.

1. France

Immediately after his death in the spring of 1869, he was virtually forgotten. Sainte-Beuve (who himself did not survive the year), and a few others paid him honor in print.[1] The appearance of the *Memoirs* early in 1870 reminded the journalists of Berlioz and brought forth lukewarm comments, of which the tenor was that Berlioz the writer had been a bitter critic and Berlioz the musician a man of great purposes rather than of great achievements. No one could pin a label on him, few could cite

[1] *1212*, XII, 152. See also *408, 412, 498, 997*.

correctly half a dozen titles of his scores, and operagoers could only argue whether *Les Troyens* had or had not failed.[2] For the anniversary of Berlioz' death, a commemorative concert was given, under Reyer's direction, at the Opera. But for most of those concerned it was a perfunctory affair, which had been put through only with the greatest difficulty. The performance could not even be got ready for the scheduled date.[3]

Then came the war with Prussia, which engulfed everything. Regime, dynasty, art, reputations, and national pride went under. When the horrors of invasion, siege and civil war — which Berlioz had been mercifully spared — receded into the distance, the feelings of the period just previous seemed like those of a prehistoric age. Germany was the new fact, perceived in humiliation, and from it grew two divergent attitudes — one the reassertion of ancient national glories; the other, the thirst for new and foreign things.

It thus came about that in the mid-seventies, Wagner and Berlioz were again pitted against each other. But although most Berlioz admirers were also Wagnerites, the bulk of the Wagnerites were anti-Berlioz. The latter accused the others of harboring narrow views and of resurrecting an old fogey purely on nationalistic grounds. Wagner was the new coming man, still living, princelike at Bayreuth or Triebschen, a pilgrimage to which stamped you as a superior intellect. He redeemed Germany's might by the right of great art.[4]

As against this the Berliozians could do little; they were at odds among themselves; no Berlioz tradition existed, and they had too much integrity to turn Wagner into a common enemy.[5] The vacillations of Carvalho in 1878–1879 show what choices offered: whether to revive *Les Troyens* or put on *Lohengrin*. It proved a deadlock. Yet Berlioz was not altogether defeated. For the young conductor Edouard Colonne had meanwhile begun to study the *Damnation of Faust*, and repenting of some earlier misdeeds committed by him on Berlioz' music, he devoted the whole season of 1876–1877 to rehearsing a work of which only fragments were

[2] Edmond About's opinion prevailed, that music was healthy except for the two monstrosities, *Tannhäuser* and *Les Troyens*. (*1141*, 324–5.)

[3] See Ernest Reyer's account in *1386*, reproduced in *997*.

[4] It was not generally known then that at the time of the siege of Paris, Wagner had written a sneering skit about the fallen city, ridiculing Victor Hugo and other notables, in revenge for his humiliations of 1839 and 1861.

[5] The absence of tradition and even of common sense was shown in the inadequate performance and absurd alteration of *The Infant Christ* in 1875; the lack of unity was emphasized by the lawsuit of the following year about the publication of *Les Troyens*. Judgment was rendered as against the heirs and the Conservatoire in favor of publishers who refused to publish. (*157*.)

known to the public. His older rival, Pasdeloup, was stung into emulation and the two conductors played the score on the same day.

When it burst forth on February 18, 1877, after thirty years of obscurity, the public shared Colonne's contrition and the *Damnation of Faust* was launched. Colonne had to repeat it on six consecutive Sundays. The public went wild and Flaubert, rejoicing for Berlioz, damned the bourgeois once again.[6] Gounod's *Faust* had helped them to understand what Berlioz' "dramatic legend" took for granted, and from that moment on, the work has been the mainstay of the Berlioz repertoire in France. It was staged at Monte Carlo in 1893 and regularly at the Paris Opera since 1920. By 1908, the total of concert performances at Colonne's alone had reached one hundred and sixty. Berlioz had not only made the reputation of this *Association Artistique*, but his music filled its coffers.

Meantime between 1880 and 1890 the great Wagnerian battle was fought and won. A "new art" possessed the minds of the Symbolist-Impressionist generation. Berlioz looked Romantic and remote. Except for the *Damnation*, he could be heard only in fragments, badly played by Pasdeloup in the uninviting Cirque d'Hiver. That is no doubt where Huysmans, Van Gogh, and Odilon Redon went to hear and applaud him, for better opportunities did not come until 1890. In that year, largely owing to the great vogue of Berlioz in Germany, *Les Troyens* was revived, with an extraordinary young woman of sixteen named Delna in the double role of Cassandra and Dido.[7] The work caused a stir, particularly among young composers and critics, and from then on until the centenary celebration of 1903, the tone of reviewing and the knowledge of the scores notably improved. The substance was still fragmentary. Two new schools — the pupils of César Franck and his prophet Vincent d'Indy, and the numerous songwriters clustering about Debussy, Fauré and Ravel — were still resistant to Berlioz. Neither at the *Schola Cantorum* nor at the Conservatoire was it considered proper to like or to study him.

The centenary was in effect more bookish and statuarian than musical.

[6] "Three times now the *Damnation of Faust* has been played, which in the lifetime of my friend Berlioz achieved no success, and today the public — that eternal imbecile called 'They' — recognize, proclaim, bawl that he was a man of genius. But this won't make the bourgeois any more diffident the next time it happens." (*284,* 149.)

[7] Her real name was Marie Ledan, made into Delna by anagram. She sang at a *café* in Meudon near Paris and an intelligent patron brought her to a gathering of musicians including Chabrier, who completed her launching. Her understanding of the role of Dido was, according to everyone, a miracle of intuition.

Berlioz was praised, patronized, compared, and criticized anew, with a perhaps increasing sense among his French observers that he transcended their measure and remained baffling. The enthusiasm of the Germans, Russians, and a few English disconcerted the rest. Some began to discover a wild charm in the remote Romantic, but others were moved to wildness themselves — like the British critic John Runciman, upon whom Berlioz seemed to have exactly the effect that he had had upon the undertaker's horses.[8] To be sure, the announcement that a German publishing firm was bringing out Berlioz' scores in full impressed the French public, and so did the proselytizing of Felix Weingartner, who conducted at the Grenoble concerts and thereafter came to Paris frequently, always with a Berlioz work in hand. Romain Rolland, whom all acknowledged as artist and musicologist, demonstrated in a short biographical essay how profoundly musical Berlioz' genius was and how clearly this was recognized beyond the Rhine. Concurrently, the *Fondation Berlioz* (established 1908) sought to unite the efforts of all those who wanted to hear something more in the regular repertory than the *Roman Carnival* overture and the Rákóczy March. These efforts culminated in the Weingartner performances of the *Requiem* and *Benvenuto Cellini* in 1912 and 1913.

Meantime, Adolphe Boschot's biography (1906–1913) had appeared and by its tone of steady denigration had created a second legend quite damaging to Berlioz' music, since listeners, whatever they may say, tend to read character into art and to demand "depth" and sincerity, which they associate with solemnity. Instead, the Boschot biography gave them a flighty poseur. The outbreak of war in August 1914 extinguished the *Fondation Berlioz* and with it the chief influence counteracting the anti-Romanticist crusade of Boschot and his supporters.[9]

By 1919, France had once more had cause to take stock of its past. A retrospective view of the century could not fail to show how great Berlioz' role had been in shaping modern music. Recognized authorities like Koechlin, Emmanuel, and P. M. Masson wrote articles and books

---

[8] See above Chapter 28. Runciman's first article begins: "Berlioz me no Berlioz festivals." (*506, 635.* See also *474.*)

[9] Part of the archives of the *Fondation*, now in my possession, show how eager its foreign members — *e.g.*, Richard Strauss — were to further its aims. Yet such a valuable undertaking as Prodhomme's *Le Cycle Berlioz*, consisting of studies of the great works, did not reach No. 3, and the admirable essays composing Tiersot's *Berlioziana* were never gathered in book form. The project of issuing the Complete Writings in France has also remained a dead letter since 1912. The French public wanted — and had — a "fantastic" Berlioz, a "genius" in the abstract, with music merely an accidental characteristic.

which for the first time sustained the tone of respect from beginning to end. Boschot himself had receded from his truculent position, and when with his aid *Les Troyens* was staged at the Opera, he wrote about the work very differently from ten years before.[10] Shortly after this revival, Berlioz' music drama ranked fourth in a subscribers' poll, but lack of adequate personnel drove it anew from the repertory.

More important still, a postwar patriotic occasion had led to the rediscovery of the "monumental" works. Berlioz wrote a *Te Deum* for ceremonies both religious and military; so the French government chose the *Requiem* and with it honored the memory of the generals fallen in the First World War. The work made a profound impression and has since been performed a dozen times. The *Te Deum* was played only in 1936, to commemorate at once its first Paris performance some eighty years before, and that of Liszt's *Graner* Mass in 1866.

In the concert hall, however, the situation had not improved. Unless Weingartner, Furtwaengler, or Kleiber came over from Germany, Berlioz was scarcely represented on the programs, or badly played.[11] By 1939, the veteran musical biographer, Guy de Pourtalès, having written about Liszt, Chopin, Wagner, and others, came round to Berlioz and devoted to him his broadest and most thoughtful study. But he reports in the preface that very little interest is shown by the French in the composer's work, and that the orchestral fragments continue to be "shabbily played." [12]

Pourtalès's book made its appearance in the sultry atmosphere preceding the storm. A second world war, opening just seventy years after Berlioz' death, led to the grim *rappel de thème* which he had not lived to witness the first time — the occupation of Paris. A third stock-taking by the French showed them again that Berlioz was of the great lineage. As they rediscovered Victor Hugo through equivalent experience, they rediscovered Berlioz through direct sight of tragedy. Tokens of this awareness were soon forthcoming. The Chorale Passani recorded the *Requiem* and the *Damnation of Faust;* and a little later, the biographical film en-

[10] His essay about the work bore the title "A masterpiece awaiting revival." (770, I, 74 ff.)

[11] Henry Prunières wrote in 1932: "In his first program, Furtwaengler presented . . . selections from *Romeo and Juliet* and the overture to the *Carnaval Romain* of Berlioz. It was a revelation to those Frenchmen who have turned away from Berlioz (for all that he is the father of the modern French school, analogous to Delacroix in painting). These pieces . . . sounded as if they had been composed last winter." *N. Y. Times,* May 15, 1932.

[12] *298,* 1. Half a dozen years earlier, Léon Constantin had complained of a kind of official boycott exercised against Berlioz in high places. (*274,* 15 ff.)

titled "Symphonie Fantastique" was put together with evident good intentions. In it, despite arrant nonsense, two things stand out as new: the film is interlarded with extracts from the master's music — his life is a musical life; and second, the life ends on a note of national recognition. At the supposititious scene of his burial service, Victor Hugo turns to another member of the Academy and says, "He was the greatest of us all." It is only a movie, to be sure, but the conclusion is sound.

2. Germany and Central Europe

While he was entering the shadows in his own country and lifetime, Berlioz had the satisfaction of knowing that foreign musicians were still reading and playing him. From Geneva, Lausanne, New York, Boston, Copenhagen, Brussels, Vienna, Leipzig, Hamburg, and Dresden came notices of concerts and messages of cheer and congratulation.[13] But a posthumous falling away from his influence was inevitable, almost in proportion to the impact he had made, and the coincidence of his death with the deterioration of Franco-German relations was the signal for the change. Besides, from 1865 on, Wagner had risen in his native land and remained in the ascendant until near the time of his own death. The seesaw which raised up Berlioz once more can be dated from 1879, when Bülow revived *Benvenuto Cellini* in Hanover and introduced the composer to a new generation of conductors and musicians. He taught Mottl how to conduct the *Requiem*, "discovered" *Harold* and *Romeo* for himself, and urged the overtures upon Vienna.[14] The intense excitement of this resurrection can be read in Bülow's letters — the picture of Berlioz appeared on his notepaper — and in his polemic on Berlioz' behalf against a new batch of hostile critics.[15] Liszt was still alive to share in this renewed enthusiasm, and find his earliest judgments confirmed.

From 1879 to 1914, the second Berlioz boom continued: Mottl and Nikisch, Mahler and Weingartner carried his music wherever they played. *Benvenuto* was staged in twenty cities.[16] Mottl in 1890 inaugurated a "Berlioz Cycle" in Carlsruhe, giving *Les Troyens* entire, arranging *Beatrice and Benedict*, and stimulating choral societies to risk the *Requiem* and

[13] *Est., passim.*

[14] See, in various collections, Bülow's letters from Aug. 28, 1877 to Oct. 2, 1884. (*E.g., 174*, 319 ff.)

[15] *174*, 405–6. "I have, if you will, become an esthetic reactionary, but my glowing enthusiasm for Berlioz contradicts this, or seems to. You will at least grant me the fact that is significant here, namely the non-trumpery quality of all [Berlioz'] barbarisms." (*Ibid., 515.*)

[16] The list is given in *504*, 18 *n.*

Te Deum. He then carried *Les Troyens* and *Benvenuto* to Vienna and Munich,[17] by which time Weingartner in Berlin and Mahler in Vienna had reinstated the symphonies and overtures into the repertory. Criticism kept pace with musical production, this being the period when scholars and artists joined forces to establish Berlioz in Germany: Hugo Wolf, Strauss, and Busoni made definitive statements that were matched by the writings of Smolian, Scholtze, Rudolf Louis, and others in works of erudition.

The First World War, despite its occasional bursts of artistic nationalism, did not destroy the Germans' feeling for Berlioz. Halm republished his essays in 1916; the *régisseur* of the Dessau opera told the Viennese of his experiences in staging *Benvenuto Cellini;* [18] and immediately after the peace, Kapp issued his study of the "Triple Star," Berlioz-Liszt-Wagner, followed shortly by his biography of the first-named. Berlioz' symphonies continued to be played at concerts, but economic conditions made the larger works inaccessible. It was in the next decade that blood-ideology displaced him and other French composers from the programs, despite valiant attempts to prove that the soul of Berlioz, at any rate, was Germanic.[19] The Second World War and the disturbed occupation of Central Europe by rival powers have made the present cultural situation in most respects unassessable, though there are signs of a return to the cultural internationalism that made Berlioz find his truest interpreters east of the Rhine.

As a postscript to the Central European situation it may be said that in Switzerland, Scandinavia, Italy, Spain, Portugal, and the Low Countries, the reputation of Berlioz has tended merely to echo current opinion among their larger neighbors. None the less, all six of these accidental satellites have made important contributions to both performance and study of Berlioz' works.[20] It is a noteworthy fact in itself that Weingartner spent his last years teaching conducting at Basel, where he imposed a good dose of Berlioz on his pupils.[21] Lately, publications on Berlioz in Denmark, Belgium, Holland, and Italy have increased in both number and quality.

[17] See Annette Kolb, *665.*

[18] Franz Mikorey, *550.*

[19] *478,* 333 and *411.* The Hungarians, however, honored him by a statue next to that of Liszt in Budapest, and their scholarship cleared him of having "plagiarized" the Rákóczy March. (*572.*)

[20] For which see Bibliography Secs. 3 and 4. A special word should be said in honor of the Belgian conductor Maquet who reintroduced Berlioz to Lille, and whose wife after his death continued to perform the great works.

[21] See a report by one of them, *1391,* Feb. 1931, 125.

3. England

Next to Germany, Great Britain has given the works of Berlioz the most painstaking study and wholehearted response. This too came in waves. When Berlioz left England for the last time in 1855, he was regretted most deeply by the young men who had heard or played under him, such as August Manns and Wilhelm Ganz, but it was not until twenty years later, when they had "arrived," that a Berlioz revival got under way. Ganz signalized his accession to the conductorship of the New Philharmonic in 1874 by featuring the *Symphonie Fantastique*, which had never before been played entire in England. It created a sensation which he followed up with other works, but pleased though the audience were, the critics were hostile.[22] The public wondered, as *Punch* said, who this new Russian and his strange music might be — and whether he was alive or dead.[23]

Those who knew the answers kept on. Manns gave many "firsts" of Berlioz scores at his Crystal Palace concerts, and Hallé — Berlioz' former colleague, now in Manchester — made musical history by bringing his admirable orchestra to London in 1880, offering as a test of its powers the *Damnation of Faust*. Newspaper notices began to be more appreciative as the music grew familiar and as echoes of German successes showed that the works were "serious," technically and artistically.

But this, according to English students of the period, brought a counteroffensive by the Wagnerians. "Hueffer and Dannreuther's project to belittle Berlioz and then by comparison to belaud Wagner, was only too successful. . . . The influence of their antagonism exists today."[24] A little later, Shaw became a discriminating admirer of Berlioz, but he too felt that socio-political strategy required him to concentrate on forcing Wagner's entry. By 1900, the Perfect Wagnerites were triumphant and though the Berlioz centenary brought out a new crop of *premières*, revivals, and fresh devotees, the position was still confused: other French masters occupied the scene, and Wagnerian revelation was still being distilled[25] — not to speak of the simultaneous discovery of Russia, her ballets and operas.

It was left for the period between the twentieth-century wars to pro-

[22] *955*, 63, 138, 144–5.

[23] *955*, 145–6.

[24] Havergal Brian (1934): *324*, 209.

[25] *Mein Leben* did not appear until 1911, and to this day the Bayreuth archives retain the many secrets carefully guarded by Cosima until her death in 1933.

duce the steady hearing and understanding of Berlioz which now obtains in England. Sir Hamilton Harty led the way by his great performances at Manchester; Sir Thomas Beecham, Sir Adrian Boult, Mr. Erik Chisholm, and Mr. Constant Lambert have continued. Several of these men have written elucidations of the works, and gradually a public opinion deserving the name of critical has been formed. In this movement, it is but fair to say, the leading Wagner scholar Mr. Ernest Newman was a pioneer,[26] ably seconded by younger musicologists and composers such as Cecil Gray, Laurence Powell, Peter Warlock, and W. H. Mellers. In 1934 the late W. J. Turner — poet, critic, and musician — published his excellent biography after a dozen years of skirmishing in the press; and a year later, Tom S. Wotton, who had studied Berlioz for half a century, produced his masterly volume. Since then, radio and records aiding, Berlioz has held his place in English ether and English minds. One can hear his operas in concert performance by the B.B.C. or witness the realization of one of his unacted plans — an evening of Shakespearean music from his pen. Meanwhile, magazine articles keep on appearing at close intervals, and the greatest enterprise of Berlioz scholarship — Mr. Hopkinson's bibliography of the musical and literary works — is in press.

4. Russia

The history of Berlioz performances in Russia since his second trip of 1867–1868 also shows ups and downs, following the rise and fall of *other* momentary fashions. His young disciples — Rimsky excepted — remained faithful to his memory and kept him before the public. Up to 1917, if we except again the judgment of Rimsky's pupil Stravinsky, it was an accepted generality that Berlioz was the strongest influence in European music, and conductors such as Emil Cooper produced his works enthusiastically and with great success.[27] Others, like Leopold Auer, had to follow suit whether they liked to or not and the young expressed their admiration.[28]

Since the Revolution, the story is more difficult to trace. In the first rejection of western and bourgeois ideas, Berlioz suffered like other nineteenth-century artists; but this phase was relatively short and perform-

---

[26] It is instructive to note how Newman's opinions have evolved between 1901 and the present. Full of reservations at first, he has come to see in half a century how Berlioz' melody, harmony, form and personality are justified by a purpose which transcends routine criticism.

[27] *155.*

[28] *925, 52–6* and *253.*

ances of the usual scores, with even an occasional hearing of the *Requiem*, were reported in the thirties. After the outbreak of war, news became inaccessible to the student equipped with only the ordinary instruments of research.[29]

5. United States

Although Berlioz believed that "the originality and subtle refinement of a special talent could only be appreciated in very old societies," [30] he always responded to the free and open judgments of younger cultures and on this account felt especially grateful to Russia and the United States for their acceptance of his work.[31] Whenever an American musician sought out Berlioz in Paris, he was cordially received, with the result that as early as the 1840's notices of works by Berlioz appeared in New York newspapers — notably in the critiques of William Henry Fry.[32]

In the fifties Jullien came over and is said to have played, if not works by his former associate, at least variations upon some of his themes. By then the New York Philharmonic Society was under way, and Berlioz overtures were occasionally to be heard under its conductors, Eisfield and Bergmann.[33] Only fragments of the larger works could be heard at these concerts, for Bergmann inclined to Liszt — and later Wagner — rather than to Berlioz.

In the sixties, Theodore Thomas, who competed with the Philharmonic, prided himself on bringing new works, and of these four were by Berlioz.[34] But it was in the next decade that his fame reached its first flowering on these shores. Leopold Damrosch, who had played under him, challenged Thomas's supremacy as a bold adventurer and produced the *Requiem* and *Damnation* in successive seasons.[35] From then on to about 1890, various choral and orchestral societies tackled Berlioz, with only temporary effect. The great educator was Wagner, and by the time that the echo of the Berlioz centenary came to this country — bringing with it a revival of

[29] Inquiries addressed to respectable agencies for the exchange of cultural information proved futile. Asking for sources about Berlioz performances within the last two decades met with the suggestion that Stassov's letters be consulted: Stassov was a contemporary of Berlioz and died in 1906.

[30] To Louis Moreau Gottschalk: *956*, 250.

[31] *93*, 258.

[32] *725*, 132. William Henry Fry, said to be the composer of the first American opera, had also composed a *Childe Harold* symphony.

[33] Full list in *1333*.

[34] Listed in *1022*, II, 359, and see *749*.

[35] *942*, 27, 33–4, 337. See the interesting account of the rehearsals of the second by the tenor who sang Faust. (*970*, 41, 43, 119 and 144.)

the *Damnation* — the critics found Berlioz "lacking in true eloquence" or alternatively "having nothing to say and saying it wonderfully." [36]

Little change occurred in America's public taste until the advent of Monteux and Koussevitzky after the First World War, and the development of the gramophone and radio which permit rehearing at close intervals. Still, as was said at the beginning of this book, during the twenties the Berlioz repertory continued to be extremely meager, and Debussy was the "modern" who had yet to be assimilated.[37] Boston was then the best place to hear Berlioz, but visits by Harty and Beecham in the thirties, reinforced by Toscanini's emergence as an orchestra conductor (as against opera) opened up new reaches of the music, and criticism followed suit, Mr. B. H. Haggin taking up the tradition which Paul Rosenfeld had inaugurated amid general indifference in the previous decade. By now, American opinion, lay and professional, may be said to have attained the stage of eager inquiry, which the present work was designed in some degree to satisfy.

If one had to generalize about the bearing of these several series of musical events since 1870, one could not do better, perhaps, than to quote Weingartner's conclusion made from his vantage point at the midway mark: "As for Berlioz, one need not fear that he will ever fall out of fashion, for he possesses the most certain sign of immortality — he has never had anything in common with fashion." [38]

[36] Respectively: Lawrence Gilman (*569*) and James Huneker (*Old Fogy*).
[37] I may bear witness to the fact that at a concert in Philadelphia *The Afternoon of a Faun* was not exactly hissed but murmured against.
[38] *394, 202.*

SUPPLEMENT 2. *Biographer's Fallacy: Boschot's* Berlioz

> . . . What we oft do best
> By sick interpreters is not ours
> Or not allow'd.
> — SHAKESPEARE

Chesterton wittily remarks that the biographers' great sin and snare is to consider everything characteristic — "characteristic carelessness when their hero drops his pipe, and characteristic carefulness if he picks it up again." [1] The implication is that in order to write a particular life one must first have a fair idea of what human life, life at large, is like. The chances are that even a careful man will sometimes drop his pipe, and the incident is not worth pouncing on with gleaming eyes. The sense of likelihood, the calm acceptance of what may be stranger than fiction, measures the biographer's scope just as it distinguishes the philosopher from the provincial.

Reading the first accounts of himself in his latter years, Berlioz concluded that the life of a man could not be written down with exactitude. [2] He perceived that his multifarious doings strained the mental categories of Paris journalists, academic Englishmen, and stay-at-home German critics. It was his misfortune that thirty years after his death, his career should have attracted the painstaking attention of a biographer at once sedentary, academic, and Parisian. M. Adolphe Boschot, onetime music critic of *L'Echo de Paris* and now Permanent Secretary of the Institute of France, was trained as a pianist in the classical way, but early showed ambition as a poet and journalist. He founded the Mozart Society and, despite a strong anti-Romantic bias, ultimately chose Berlioz as the subject of his life's work. He devoted several years to study and research and one cannot overestimate the patience and resourcefulness he displayed in hunting down documents, verifying dates, or seeking in contemporary

[1] *1154, 5.*
[2] *93, 242.*

events now forgotten the elements of the atmosphere in which Berlioz lived and worked.

All this is so worthy of admiration that his three-volume work, obviously detailed and seemingly accurate, has discouraged other attempts on the same scale. It has been held definitive by default, and until the present review his text has received no thoroughgoing examination. Because he brought to light many new facts, it was not seen how much he darkened that was becoming clear. The length of his book concealed its frequent contradictions, and the newness — when first published — of his novelistic effects disguised the lack of a firm conception in his portraiture. The author was perpetually guilty of Chesterton's fallacy, but he had done a meritorious amount of spadework which entitled his results to be called indispensable. Hence anyone who also calls them unreliable must in fairness specify the shortcomings.

Moreover, not content with being Berlioz' most elaborate biographer, Boschot became as it were his champion in reverse: he continued to write dozens of articles about him, and issued a popular, one-volume abridgment of the Life which was widely translated and of which the latest reissue appeared in 1939. He also published books of commentary on the musical works, the latest in this category being dated 1945. Hence — again — anyone who disputes Boschot's findings is not attacking a negligible error and he must quote chapter and verse for the grounds of his objections.

Perhaps the most direct proof of Boschot's inadequacy is to be found in the description of Berlioz near the end of the third volume, when after the final trip to Russia, the composer's shattered health is reflected in his handwriting — a handwriting, says Boschot, which had been "hitherto admirable . . . decorative, artistic, imperious . . . the spontaneous evidence of a body and soul of prodigious stamina, of a character truly cast in bronze." [3] The reader who up to this point has taken in some eighteen hundred pages of small print can only be thunderstruck on discovering that such is the character he has been reading about. For except in rare moments presently to be noted, Berlioz has been steadily shown as an ineffectual man and a half-conscious, wayward, incoherent artist. Boschot's tone, style, method, and opinions have throughout been those of the systematic debunker. No doubt his was a reaction against the genteel conventions of a certain type of biography, where the rule of *De mortuis* engenders an incurable dullness, or *tedium vitae*. But Berlioz had

[3] III, 651. Quoted more fully above, Chapter 28.

never been subjected to an excess of eulogy requiring exposure, and in the course of Boschot's opposite excess almost every department of the biographical art suffered harm.

Boschot's first false premise is that fact is the same thing as truth. Accordingly, the biographer set out as much to correct the names and dates in Berlioz' *Memoirs* as to tell the story of their author's life. Pride of discovery and pleasure in putting Berlioz in his place are displayed without shame — and without awareness that these feelings argue a misunderstanding of what autobiographies, letters, and documents signify.[4] For the second form of Biographer's Fallacy is to adopt an invariably lawyerlike attitude to all written texts — whether business contracts, love letters, or day-to-day by-products of an artistic career — and with their aid pursue the hero as if he were a malefactor.[5] The biographer himself has many times declined invitations on the pretext of an imaginary engagement; has given an intimate correspondent a rough instead of strict idea of his opinion on a subject, knowing he could explain or amplify later; has mistaken names and dates; and has shifted his point of view with age and circumstance. In the course of an industrious life, traces of these variations survive in abundance, and hearsay complicates what letters record. The true biographer, therefore, must not merely juxtapose his conflicting data but interpret them.

If he is bent on debunking, however, it is easy for him to destroy character and cast doubt on sanity by a literal transcript which shows up discrepancies. He argues from texts as if they were Euclidian theorems and his Q.E.D. certifies his subject as liar or lunatic. He believes moreover that by ascertaining a multitude of details — Boschot boasts of having unearthed for the duration of Berlioz' active years an average of "one document a week" — he has exhausted reality and re-created the sense of life. What he has done rather is to create a pettifogging atmosphere, at once exasperated and exasperating, which exhausts only the patience of the judicious reader.

This "scientific" illusion corresponds to the atomistic psychology which was considered critical simply because it destroyed the *Gestalt* of events. But this kind of analysis also appeals to the modern leveling

---

[4] I, 524–6 and with gloating, II, 562 *n.*

[5] This "positivism" goes back to the scientific pretensions of historians in the seventies and eighties. It is no accident that Boschot's predecessor in the war against Berlioz' *Memoirs* was the diplomatic historian, Edmond Hippeau, whose *Berlioz Intime* (1883) was put forth as a work of science (Pref., 4). Hippeau follows Taine's "rigorous method" which Boschot amends by adding the "artistry" of Renan, but the naïve faith in facts is the same (I, 513–26).

instinct: we take apart the great man and, seeing him less great in his dismemberment, are much comforted. Hence the continued vogue of the Derisive School of biography, which has only recently been challenged, at the same time as the scientific historian's illusion was exposed. The complexity of life is being respected anew. Indeed, Mr. Harold Nicolson, whom no one could suspect of misplaced sentiment, has even been impelled to advocate the omission of facts for the sake of truth: "If a biographer discovers material which is so sensational and shocking that it will disturb, not only the average reader, but the whole proportions of his own work, then he is justified in suppressing the actual facts. He is not justified, however, in suppressing the conclusions which he himself draws from those facts, and he must alter his portrait so that it conforms to those facts." [6]

Adolphe Boschot obviously did not practice Mr. Nicolson's art of selection. He seems to lack the imaginative experience of life, like those "average readers" who must be protected by a suppression which is at best arrogant and might easily become illiberal. Like them too, Boschot has the curiosity of the gossip without the judicial temper which asks: "What is the evidence for this?" And "What else could such a man do in such a position?" The consequence is that his surfeit of details turns out as misleading as the shocking fact, and as illiberal as the censored text. The reader is swamped under so many trivia that no character remains, certainly no artist, and life itself is vaporized. We do not see Berlioz armoring his soul with bronze and describing a clear curve of accomplishment; we do not see him leading and inspiring the musical world, nor revolving in his mind the great riddles of time and eternity. We do not even get a glimpse of his friendships or active devotion to a large circle who were devoted to him. We see only a harassed self-seeker humiliated by clever contemporaries; it is hard to resist the thought that had Boschot been alive at the same time he would have been among the sniggerers.

There is, at any rate, inverted sentimentality in Boschot's failure to take the shocks and battles of the artist's career in the proper militant spirit. He keeps repeating that "Berlioz had no public" and won only a "false success" [7] — making this a grievance just like a skeptical parent. At

[6] *1108*, 109. He gives an instance from his own work: "I gave no illustration of the extent to which [Curzon's] acquisitive instincts were manifested in his daily life . . . It was not that I desired to whitewash Curzon . . . I knew that this eccentric failing would . . . convey an actually false impression." (*Ibid.*, 110.)

[7] *E.g.*, II, 390. But two pages later this "false success" is forgotten and Berlioz is shown as a "spoiled child" by reason of his early fame.

bottom he takes the comic papers' view of those thirty years crowded with results; invariably suggesting — contrary to eyewitness reports — that Berlioz was not really acclaimed or influential abroad. The artist's iron determination, funded experience, and organizing powers do not emerge from the mass of quoted snippets out of which Boschot spins his web of doubts. He mistakes generalship for improvisation, and cannot discern the fruitful respites in what he calls the "breathless" pace — meaning, of course, that he himself would have been out of breath long before the end. Scarcely does the supposition enter his mind that Berlioz' plan of existence was vaster than his own, nor that despite vicissitudes, the composer produced works whose balance and serenity quite outshine his reprover's. In short, the biographer is blind to order and continuity because he takes "quiet" and "orderly" for synonyms — as might a maiden aunt writing the life of Napoleon.

2

All these errors in Boschot's presentment derive from faulty conception. The remaining ones are due to faulty method. To the end of the work one is puzzled by the biographer's principles of criticism. At times, the author suggests that Berlioz' tradition, differing as it did from the German, disqualified him for music.[8] At other times, the biographer shows unexpected wisdom — as when he tells us that the grandeur of the *Kyrie* of the *Requiem* comes from an original technique subdued to an artistic intent;[9] or when he suddenly perceives the great significance of *Romeo and Juliet* for the entire future of music.[10] But these glimmerings are of short duration. He contradicts himself from chapter to chapter and volume to volume. He writes egregious nonsense such as: "Unable to play either the violin or the piano, Berlioz could not grasp chamber music"[11] — this in the teeth of Berlioz' penetrating remarks on the genre. In one place Boschot makes fun of Romanticist music criticism for its imagery, and in another he wisely explains that the critics' metaphors change with each generation and are equally valid when rightly understood.[12] And again, though Boschot is ever ready to accuse Berlioz of

[8] I, 280–3; II, *passim;* III, 29; and wherever Bach, Mozart or Beethoven is mentioned.

[9] II, 359–60. But see p. 373.

[10] II, 509. In later essays, Boschot reiterated this point. Another true insight can be found in III, 136, but again at variance with other passages.

[11] II, 652.

[12] II, 296.

literary intentions, he himself analyzes Berlioz' great works in language that is unwarrantably "poetical" and melodramatic to a degree.

This brings us to the ultimate class of Boschot's biographical failings: misstatements of fact, through ignorance or through verbal irresponsibility. It is not too much to charge him with liberties bordering on fabrication and suspiciousness amounting to obsession.[13] Moreover the debunker loves to jest; thus when he finds Berlioz briefing Scribe on their projected libretto and saying he is willing to treat "scenes of terror laid in the Middle Ages or in the last century," Boschot puts down: "And so our Romantic wants to dally with Louis XV!"[14] It was surely obvious that the scenes of terror in the last century could only refer to *the* Terror of the French Revolution — hence the futility of the biographical caper. But Boschot can seldom resist the temptation to make a *mot*. *Les Troyens*, he declares, is "more Spontinian than spontaneous."[15] This obscure judgment was, on emission, widely quoted in a knowing way. Within ten years Boschot recanted; the score was then a great work, unjustly neglected.[16] Who did he suppose had had a hand in giving it a bad name?

Turning to persons, one is astonished to see a writer who sets out to attack the veracity of Berlioz' *Memoirs* and who pads his own volumes with undocumented and often unprovable statements. Page after page of the narrative is sheer embroidery or pure conjecture, couched in the language of fact.[17] In addition, one finds phrases and epithets which, being documented at one point, are served up again and again like Wagnerian leitmotives whenever the context permits. Often Boschot joins these bits together with bad imitations of Berlioz' least mature style, and since the parodist gives no footnote references for any quotations, the reader is at his mercy: he cannot know whose words he is reading — much less appreciate the spectacle of Adolphe Boschot mimicking Berlioz for posterity.[18]

[13] See above, Chapter 8, his admission that Berlioz accurately described the Vatican choir. Soon after, Boschot "discredits" Berlioz' enthusiasm for Subiaco, denying that it was picturesque. Yet Gounod, who followed in Berlioz' footsteps eight years later, derived the same impressions. M. Boschot's perpetual distrust may be due to a lack of the seeing eye.

[14] II, 475.

[15] III, 482.

[16] 770, I, 74 ff.

[17] *E.g.*, I, 65 and 445; II, 116. The signal instance is the final paragraph of III, 243 where Berlioz' clothing, health, and deportment are gratuitously described as going to pieces. The letters and portraits of the period (1850) give the lie to this fiction, which is mere "background" for the musical hard times.

[18] If these and the novel-like passages were eliminated, the substance of one volume out of three might be disposed of. See the romancing in III, 100–3, including a misquotation.

The upshot of these practices is that the would-be objective narrator of Berlioz' life does without excuse what he condemns in the *Memoirs:* he distorts the truth. Up to a point no narrative can avoid this; the selection of terms and linking of ideas alters the reality; but Boschot carries rhetorical freedom to obscene lengths. The adjective is used advisedly, as any candid reader will admit who recalls the nauseating variations in Volume Two on the subject of Harriet Smithson's "blond and fleshy" person.[19] Boschot harps on her shoulders and throat, evincing a pruriency which culminates in his speculations about her sexual life in marriage — all of it presented as fact. Again, when Berlioz wrote to Liszt and Ferrand in order to still the slander he had unknowingly spread, Boschot's words subtly multiply the two brief notes into a general communiqué on Harriet's innocence.[20] The system is clear: whatever Berlioz does or leaves undone, he is in the wrong; and the condemnation, seldom forthright, is never argued: it is implied and insinuated.

But the biographer's animus does not pursue Berlioz alone; as regards nearly everyone in his story, Boschot adopts an attitude of preconceived hostility.[21] When, in 1822, an elderly academician pays a kindly call on the young musician, a mean motive is imputed for the visit.[22] And usually, when another object of derision is at hand, the pressure on the protagonist is relaxed. Thus a mention of Berlioz' parents, sisters, and brothers makes them out weak, stupid, or sickly, while Hector is momentarily exempt

[19] Ch. III and following. She is unremittingly "apathetic" as well.
[20] II, 197; see also I, 106–7 and 472.
[21] Much should be said about the forgotten art of dealing justly with the people who in any given biography are for the time being secondary actors. It is impossible to study them as fully as the main subject, and yet the result of depicting them by means of conventional half truths or untruths is to create a general opinion which is actually unexamined hearsay — *e.g.,* the treatment of Berlioz in books on Wagner, Mendelssohn, or Liszt.
To assist the ethical biographer on this point, we need a kind of who's who which would define by actual examples the commonest adjectives that are so blandly misused — "impatient," "undisciplined," "morbid," "self-centered." By making them comparative and illustrating their application, such a lexicon would show — to take only composers — that the headlong, inaccurate and violent musician is not Berlioz, but Gluck, perhaps, or Wagner; that the ungrateful and self-centered one was Debussy, or that the lover of the macabre was Bruckner, who attended executions and took trips to view the charred remains of fire casualties. In a word, the biographer should have present to his mind the series of like cases, just as if he were a physician making a diagnosis. Naturally, the infirmities so tabulated should not be imputed as crimes darkening the memory of their sufferers; but being no guilt in those to whom these traits are justly ascribed, how much less of a blemish in those to whom they do not apply!
[22] I, 115.

from flaws.[23] After Harriet, Marie is the chief victim of Boschot's extrapolations; once she has left the scene, the cuffs fall on Berlioz' devoted mother-in-law.[24] At any earlier point, when the substitute target has been hit, the hounding of Berlioz is resumed: he is accused of not loving his brother, of forgetting Lesueur, of condescending to Nanci, of "not knowing how to suffer," of not being amiable, of being diseased too early in life, and of missing the consolations of a true faith. We are meant to gather that this and other faults justify our feeling superior and our being reconciled to the artist's buffetings.[25] Noting this lack of equity — to put it no worse — an early reviewer justly characterized Boschot's work as having "a flavour of acridity, a nagging censoriousness, which is intensely irritating and not a little contemptible." [26]

To sustain his *parti-pris*, Boschot is led to twist his sources — often unwittingly — and sometimes to overlook what is plainly before his eyes. Thus in discrediting the *Memoirs*, he exclaims that if Berlioz' story is true the parts of the Rákóczy March must have been miraculously copied in a twinkling: the fact is that Berlioz tells us how and when they were copied, quite normally and in ample time.[27] Elsewhere, to prove that a surviving notebook of airs in Berlioz' hand were not by him, Boschot quotes the composer's remark that his youthful melodies were "all in the minor mode." Berlioz' statement reads: "almost all in the minor." [28] Misrepresentation goes still farther: in a letter to Hiller dating from their student days, Berlioz affectionately calls his friend a "big scoundrel." [29] In Boschot's hands this becomes a recurrent description of Hiller, and it is quoted as if Berlioz had uttered it behind his friend's back. This done, it is in keeping for Boschot to suppress what Hiller himself tells us, namely that it was Camille Moke who pursued Hector and told him she loved him. The reader, after these two strokes, will naturally believe anything of Berlioz' unworthiness in love and friendship.

[23] II, 97–8. Prosper, who presumably had typhoid, died prematurely, according to Boschot, because he was born of "tired parents." (II, 466–7.)

[24] III, 100, and *passim*.

[25] II, 466 and 664; III, 90; III, 69 and 193.

[26] *314.*

[27] Boschot, III, 97 and *Mem.*, II, 211. The mood of suspecting the criminal hero may be a catching disease: that earlier critic of the *Memoirs*, Hippeau, elaborately thanks a colleague for having hunted up the verses to which Berlioz wrote his first melody, those verses being all the while available in the fourth chapter of the *Memoirs*. Again, an English critic scoffed at Berlioz' recital of composing Moore's *Elegy* — "When Hector knew not a word of English!" Hector states in the account itself that he was using a French translation.

[28] I, 68 and *Mem.*, I, 17.

[29] *Corresp.*, 91.

More neutral errors of fact also abound in Boschot's work, which are not worth detailing. No sizable history can help being marred by such specks. Only, the knowledge of this should have made Boschot more indulgent toward Berlioz' lapses of memory. In an appendix, the biographer shows how Berlioz wrote down the name of one actor of the 1820's instead of another, the report dating from twenty-five years after the event. For this Boschot deserves that someone in an appendix should call him to task for saying that the third act of *Les Francs-Juges* had hardly more than one piece of music composed for it; when it is actually the fullest;[30] for saying that at the *première* of the *Symphonie Fantastique* Berlioz also gave his *Chant Guerrier*, although no chorus was present; and for being taken in by the forged program of *Rêverie et Caprice*. M. Boschot has less excuse than his victim in such errors and confusions, for after all he worked not from memory, like Berlioz at bay in London, but from data patiently collected.[31]

Boschot did not, it must be added, collect much outside France: he ignores or misquotes the English and German sources despite their accessibility when he wrote. He also overlooks the glaring faults of the German edition of the scores, which his colleague Malherbe assured him was soundly critical. In short, Boschot did an estimable amount of digging and dating; he had to belittle his subject in order to bring it within his grasp; and he was impelled by a mistaken but not unworthy ambition to make "literature" out of his subject. One can only regret that despite its pedestrian virtues the result must be held — in the judicial phrase — "incomplete, contradictory, suspicious, and unworthy of belief."

[30] I, 251 and Bibl. Nat. Ms.

[31] Memory plays tricks even on anti-Romantic scholars: Boschot in 1906 speaks of having unearthed an average of one document for each week of Berlioz' active life (I, 519); by 1939 this has turned into "one document a day" (*Une Vie Romantique*, pref. of 1939, p. v).

SUPPLEMENT *3. Desiderata; Present State of Berlioz Studies*

It need not run to a Berlioz Society. . . .
— W. R. ANDERSON in 1932

1. Records

The first thing needful is more records. Although small bits of the less well-known major works have at one time or another been recorded, these fragments are usually no longer "in print," and conductors and companies continue to bring out new "interpretations" of the *Symphonie Fantastique* and the Rákóczy March. The latest important recordings are of the *Damnation of Faust* and the *Requiem* (*1414* and *1448*) but the taste for these might be prepared by the issuing of some of the shorter works complete. In his book on Berlioz, T. S. Wotton suggested that the collection of songs, *Summer Nights,* should be recorded as a representative sample of the composer's fine work on a small scale — and also as an inexpensive undertaking. Since then Miss Maggie Teyte has included two of these *Nuits d'Eté* in her splendid album of French songs (*1444-1445*), but this not being generally available, she should be encouraged to record the six songs in an independent Berlioz collection for sale on the open market at standard prices.

Likewise, the Toscanini excerpts from the *Romeo and Juliet* symphony should lead to the recording of the full score, before, during, or after one of the maestro's admirable performances, but preferably with soloists of more equal merit than he has yet been able to muster. In giving us two of the orchestral fragments, Toscanini was compelled to omit the choral introduction to the *Adagio*. This is a great pity, both in itself and as a sample of the too frequent misrepresentation of the composer: the editorial passion, we know, is to cut. But in fairness to the artist, the cuts or rearrangements should be indicated. In the available list of Berlioz records, excision is too frequent: the latest *Damnation of Faust* is sold as *intégrale* but it is cut; the Aeneas scene from *Les Troyens* is cut; the Herod scene from *L'Enfance du Christ* is cut; the *Repos de la Sainte*

Famille omits the choral "hallelujah" at the end; in several other records the orchestration — though in no way special — is shamefully reduced or unbalanced.[1] All this has been thought a safe risk because so few listeners had any basis for comparison and so few critics seemed willing to consult the scores. But this attitude is visibly changing, and commercial enterprises would be well advised to furnish faithful renditions of Berlioz or hold their hand altogether.

Of the moderate-sized major works, *The Infant Christ* suggests itself as combining very modest means with very wide appeal, through both subject matter and style. To the overtures now available it would be good to add the youthful *Waverley* and *Rob Roy* [2] and to do afresh the *Hamlet* March, with the drums and obligato vocalizing as scored. Indeed, a collection of a dozen Berlioz marches would form an impressive album of astonishing range, just as a selection of dramatic arias, beginning with *Benvenuto Cellini* and ending with *Beatrice and Benedict* would yield many pleasant surprises. In general it is futile or harmful to make orchestral excerpts from Berlioz' dramatic works: the three from the *Damnation of Faust* and the "Royal Hunt" from *Les Troyens* only bewilder by their lack of context, or make hearers suppose that they know the whole from a minute part. But the situation is different as regards songs if these are wisely chosen. A well-contrived "anthology" in album form, sold with a booklet of words and accurate comment would fall within an established form of issue.

When, nearly twenty years ago, Mr. Anderson deprecated a Berlioz society, he was hoping to obtain in due course more records like the *Beatrice and Benedict* overture, without the trouble and solemnity of grouping Berlioz admirers into a "market." But the commercial output since then has been distressingly repetitive, and experience has shown that even with better-known composers an organized demand is the only effective demand. We should still be without the Beethoven piano sonatas had it not been for a subscription scheme. If record collectors do not want next year's catalogues to offer them the fifty-first Hungarian March and the seventeenth *Symphonie Fantastique*, they had better pool their purchasing power, approach the companies, and direct the directors.

---

[1] *The American Record Guide* noted: "English Decca taught us something we previously had not really appreciated — Berlioz' remarkable uses in the [*Roman Carnival* overture] of the triangle, the tambourine and the cymbals. . . ." (May 1949, 266. The ref. is to *1453*.)

[2] Tovey: "A presentable and engaging work." (*590*, 75.)

2. Books

In English, what is urgently needed is a well-edited volume of selected essays and another of selected letters.

In French, the undertaking is more vast. It amounts to nothing less than a critical edition of Berlioz' literary works. This would include not a few of the critical essays still buried in newspaper files, as well as a comprehensive, correct and complete edition of the letters available to date. Many of these have been printed in periodicals since the six extant volumes appeared. In those volumes, dates and names are frequently untrustworthy, and the editors have often omitted musical details. A paragraph about a waistcoat that Berlioz left by mistake somewhere on his travels is given full space, whereas remarks upon music and musicians have been excluded as "less interesting." Such childishness is no longer tolerable: the French government owes it to the nation to subsidize a complete Berlioz — prose works and scores — in clear type and correct form. The present printing of the *Memoirs* in French is full of misprints, completely unedited, and offered in a format which if employed for dime novels would damn the civilization that produced it.

3. Scores

The scores, as is evident from Supplement 5 to the present book, need thorough re-editing. Not one, but several French scholars, working as a team on *both* the musical works and the prose documents, are required to accomplish the task. The autograph scores in the Bibliothèque Nationale and the Conservatoire; the first editions corrected in Berlioz' hand in the former repository and at his birthplace; the two piano scores by Liszt, as well as numerous other arrangements, not to speak of the critical works of Tiersot, Wotton, Montaux, Pohl, and Bartenstein, must be consulted before an accurate variorum edition can be produced. The score of the *Te Deum*, left by Berlioz as a gift to Russia, must be consulted, even if it takes a war to obtain permission. For the *Freischütz* recitatives, the *Benvenuto*, and the *Troyens* scores, the libraries of the Paris, Weimar, and Berlin Operas must be ransacked.

Moreover, for the instruction of scholars and concert annotators everywhere, the long series of articles published by Julien Tiersot under the title "Berlioziana" in *Le Ménestrel* from January 3, 1904 to December 1, 1906 should be reprinted in book form. These essays are not only informative, they are lively and inspired, and together with Wotton's *Hector*

Berlioz (London and New York, 1935) they form the core of any technical literature worth keeping in print.

The miniature scores of the first three symphonies and seven of the overtures (Eulenburg) must be put back into circulation just as soon as practicable under the conditions of German decay and European paralysis. The same applies to the miniature scores of the *Damnation of Faust* and *L'Enfance du Christ* (Costallat). But these must be supplemented: *Benvenuto Cellini* and *Les Troyens* constitute an underground literature in Choudens's subbasement and must be brought out into the light of day in cheap handy editions. The *Requiem* (Ricordi) and the (unavailable) *Te Deum* likewise; while the American edition of the *Funeral and Triumphal* Symphony by R. F. Goldman (all done but one third published by the Mercury Music Corporation) should be completed. With a very few corrections, a photographic reduction of the *Beatrice and Benedict* score from the Breitkopf and Härtel edition might be made available. Given the five handy scores previously published and the six here proposed, the orchestral and choral works would lie open to the needs of students and listeners. There would remain to be produced a comparable edition of twenty to twenty-five songs, *in the original keys*, for amateur and professional singers.

4. Musicology

The studies to be undertaken henceforth about Berlioz suggest themselves upon examining the lacunae of the present book: nearly every "second section" of the narrative chapters presents a subject for further investigation. Each of Berlioz' main works deserves re-analysis and replacement in the tradition (narrowly considered) to which it belongs. And each of the "constituents of music" (as he called them) must — with the possible exception of orchestration — be studied from the ground up. Berlioz' harmony especially should engage the attention of a mature theorist and practical orchestrator. Berlioz' rhythm is entitled to a monograph, and his melody to something as yet unattempted — a critical thematic catalogue. His form and counterpoint could then be dealt with, leaving dramatic and esthetic principles as the proper objects of attention for critics capable of synthesis.

If it is felt that such a treatment has never been accorded any composer, the answer must be: "Begin now." Musicology has many mansions, some of which only seem to be inhabited: the rest are haunted houses in which the rustling of paper gives an unnatural illusion of life. Putting thought and effort into the work proposed would animate not merely the place where Berlioz dwells, but might by contagion enliven neighboring houses.

5. Biography

The chief desideratum — the reader will perhaps agree — is that the dropsical bulk of the present work be reduced to humane proportions. This can be done as soon as technical discussions on the one hand, and factual narrative on the other can be handled without reference to the superstitions with which they have hitherto been mixed. Certain points in the life of Berlioz may be cleared up by evidence still to come, and aspects of his character will continue to evoke opposite opinions; but the task of later scholars should be to understand still better and re-create still more vividly the life of a subject assumed worthy of their efforts. Whatever controversy may continue should be pursued on the plane of High Contracting Powers. This will raise many problems, infinitely more subtle, engrossing, and rewarding in their solution than those offered by faulty tradition to all previous biographers without exception.

6. Honors and Celebrations

It is idle to summon a bankrupt continent to establish for Berlioz, his predecessors and followers, the Euphonia he envisioned. Unlike the kings and noblemen that Berlioz and Wagner dealt with, the present crop of rulers do not number any who are crazy about music and so willing to found a new, less exclusive Bayreuth; rather, they seem uniformly mad without preference as to object.

Still, from time to time they spend public moneys in commemoration of the extinct race of great men, and it is possible that if by 1969 airborne evil has not extinguished our species, there may be musical and other festivities to mark the hundredth anniversary of Berlioz' death. This is most likely to happen in England and France. The English, having started the modern revival by playing the works, may be trusted to continue. To the French, the recommendation should be to temporarily forget the *Damnation of Faust,* which is all they know, and put on *Benvenuto Cellini* and *Les Troyens* at the Opera; to publish or republish a few useful books by or about Berlioz; and to keep down to a minimum the making of busts and statues. If a real desire exists to celebrate Berlioz' memory otherwise than by playing his music, there is in Paris a roomy public building on the pediment of which is written *Aux grands hommes, la patrie reconnaissante.* Exhume Berlioz and place him in the Pantheon with his peers. He now lies in the Cimetière Montmartre, section 7, row 2, No. 32. As his ashes enter the domed mausoleum for which he planned his *Fête musicale funèbre à la mémoire des hommes illustres de la France,* there should resound the *Funeral and Triumphal* symphony which is but a fragment of the former projected work. The four unwritten movements having remained unwanted, like much else that he had to give, are among those secrets of musical expression which Saint-Saëns said Berlioz had carried with him to the grave. *Requiescant in pace.*

MAHLER   ROMAIN ROLLAND   VAN DIEREN

BUSONI   PETER WARLOCK   ALBERT SCHWEITZER

ROBERT PITNEY   W. J. TURNER   G. B. SHAW

Eminent Berliozians: 1890–1950

"It is my lot to hear a good deal of music . . . and
everywhere I find the trail of the Berlioz serpent."
— JOHN RUNCIMAN (1903)

SUPPLEMENT *4. Euphonia and Bayreuth: Musical Cities*

> As to old music, reverence is carried so far
> that we often do not perform it at all . . .
> — FREDERIC HARRISON

When Berlioz in 1852 returned from the first "Weimar Week" in his honor, he inscribed his volume of *Evenings* simply: "To my good friends, the artists of the orchestra of X . . . , a civilized town." Seven years later, in the preface to his next book, he explained this to his Paris players, saying how deeply touched he had been by the devoted attentiveness of his performers in German cities. He went on to compliment his French colleagues for their merits and their patience, but he inscribed that second volume, "To my good friends, the choristers and players of the Opera in Paris, a barbaric town." [1]

Long before making either of these comparisons, Berlioz had formed a definite view of the role that music should play in modern civilization and had expressed his convictions at every opportunity. As early as 1829, he had invoked the example of the ancients for musical festivals in the service of religion. [2] In 1834, while preaching Beethoven to the Parisians, he had written that just as Homer had been made an object of worship in Greece, so Beethoven should have a shrine in modern Europe: until it was established, no one could call the age civilized. [3] This notion of a dedicated place for the performance of great music as a religious rite is Berlioz' calculated *idée fixe*. In a later essay he dreams of sailing for the site of Troy and after erecting "a Temple of Sound at the foot of Mount Ida," commissioning the best orchestra in the world play the *Eroica*. [4] Such music must be heard by an audience familiar with antique lore and

---

[1] *Grot.*, 15. See, one year earlier, his sober and discouraging survey of the musical resources in Paris, "that great capital of the civilized world." (*M.M.*, 307–11.)
[2] *1377*, Apr. 11, 1829 and see above, Subchapters 13 and 22.
[3] *A.R.*, 254.
[4] *1398*, Jan. 28, 1841.

imbued with the religion of the City. Wagner read and quoted from this article in his Paris days, and according to his biographer it was this vision which suggested to him the conception of the *Bühnenfestspiel* and its home — eventually Bayreuth.[5]

The example of Greek lyric drama was certainly vivid in the minds of both composers. Berlioz speaks of an arena like the ancient theater, and Wagner had the Bayreuth edifice built on the plan of the theater of Bacchus at Segesta. But it is not necessary that Wagner should have developed the notion on his own. All he had to do was to read a later essay on the same theme; for Berlioz himself amplified the statement of his root idea and made his point again and again to the end of his days.[6] The preamble to his plan, so to speak, occurs in the widely reproduced open letter which he wrote to solace Spontini in his troubles of 1841. After praising the master, Berlioz says: "If music were not abandoned to public charity, there would be somewhere in Europe a theatre, a lyric Pantheon, exclusively devoted to the presentation of the monumental masterpieces. These would be produced at wide intervals *by artists*, with the care and grandeur that they deserve, and they would be listened to on the solemn festal days of art by audiences at once receptive and intelligent." [7]

Two years later, Berlioz reprinted this letter in his *Voyage Musical*, and later again in his biographical sketch of Spontini.[8] The stipulation of long intervals between performances of the same work is grounded in the knowledge that music can be worn threadbare by heedless repetition. Both audience and performers end by coming to the most sublime works as to their Sunday dinner, and this perfunctoriness is the antithesis of the religious attitude towards art.[9] Again and again Berlioz complains that

[5] W. A. Ellis: *952*, VII, 139 *n*. He and other Wagnerians like Arthur Symons naturally took Berlioz' words as representing "merely a rhetorical flourish." (*890*, 175–6.)

[6] *E.g.*, "The Musical Customs of China" in *A Trav.*, 264–70.

[7] *A.R.*, 427 — anticipating Shaw's dictum that music taken immoderately can become "the brandy of the damned."

[8] *V.M.*, I, 404 (1844) and *Soirées* (13th) *Eves.*, 164–5 (1852).

[9] In writing to Schumann in 1837, Berlioz had already dwelt on the need to preserve a work from vulgarization. (*Corresp.*, 120.) This does not of course invalidate the equal need for a new and difficult work to be heard often — learned, in fact, before being truly heard "at wide intervals": "Eisfield, first conductor of the New York Philharmonic Society, shared his duties with Carl Bergmann, a vigorous apostle of Wagner's music, and once while administering a generous dose of Wagner, someone ventured to expostulate. 'But Mr. Bergmann, the people don't like Wagner!' — 'Don't like Wagner!' replied Bergmann, 'Den dey must hear him till dey do!' " (*697*, 78.)

music is cheapened not by being too abundant but by being slackly lavished on the inattentive.[10] And while fashion prescribes the tireless repetition of certain works for a few decades, the great achievements of the past fall into unmerited oblivion. Berlioz analyzes the causes which produce this glut and scarcity, causes which can be summed up as the commercialization of art. The point is not that artists should work for nothing, nor that the public should be given their highest pleasures free, but that the dumping methods and adulterating practices of ordinary trade reduce art to the shoddiest of commodities.[11]

It was these reasons and observations that led Berlioz to draw up a plan for a truly musical city, which he named Euphonia and placed significantly in the Germany that had welcomed him. He first described this Utopia in the *Gazette Musicale* for April 28, 1844, near the end of a semi-autobiographical novelette which happens to be also a "science fiction" fantasy.[12] The description of Euphonia, it will be seen, anticipates not only Bayreuth [13] but also such recent offshoots of the idea of providing high art with a proper setting and a working discipline as Glyndebourne in England and Tanglewood in America.[14] Berlioz' insistence on putting his Musical City under Spartan rule grows out of his experience of bad musicians and their perversions of masterpieces. He did not live to see the ultimate effect of "too much music," which is the public and the conductor's search for "new readings" in hopes of making Beethoven's Fifth seem fresh. In Berlioz' day, conductors were likely to be tepid rather than eccentric, and Euphonia's martial law, like all its other provisions, has but one goal, which is to train everyone in the morality of musicianship. A product of that training, Berlioz' fictional hero gives the Academy of Palermo a report entitled:

[10] On his complaint of too much music, see *Grot.*, 121, 214.
[11] *V.M.*, I, 219; *Grot.*, 244 ff. His arguments, often rising to eloquence make one think of Yeats's lines:

> How but in custom and in ceremony
> Are innocence and beauty born?

[12] Reprinted in *Soirées* (25th), with slight changes in the fiction.
[13] The concealed orchestra does not feature in the plan, but neither is it original with Wagner: the idea goes back to Grétry; it was repeated by Choron, used by Berlioz in *Lélio*, and proposed again by Adolphe Sax in 1867.
[14] Berlioz applied the principle to other arts as well: "I am in the habit of going every year into a *poetry retreat*. I lock myself up at home and read Shakespeare or Virgil, sometimes both. This makes me a trifle unwell at first, but I sleep it off and recover wonderfully, though I am left unconquerably sad." The description is of course ironic. *Soirées* (5th) *Eves.*, 55.

A Description of Euphonia

Euphonia is a small town of twelve thousand souls, situated on the slopes of the Harz, in Germany. The whole town may be looked upon as a great Conservatory of music, since the exercise of this art is the sole purpose of its inhabitants' activity.

All Euphonians, men, women, and children, are exclusively occupied with singing and playing instruments, and with everything else that has a direct connection with music. Most of them are both instrumentists and singers. A few who do not perform devote themselves to the manufacture of instruments or to the engraving and printing of music. Others give their time to acoustic research and to the study of whatever in physics bears on the production of sound.

The singers and players of instruments are grouped by categories in the several quarters of the town. Each type of voice and instrument has a street bearing its name, which is inhabited only by the part of the population which practices that particular voice or instrument. There are streets of sopranos, basses, tenors, contraltos; of violins, horns, flutes, harps, and so on.

Needless to say, Euphonia is governed in military fashion and subjected to a despotic regime. Hence the perfect order which obtains in study and the marvelous results that ensue for art.

Moreover, the Emperor of Germany does all he can to make the Euphonians' life a happy one. All he asks in return is that they send him, two or three times a year, a few thousand musicians for the festivals which he organizes at different places within the Empire. Seldom is the whole population required to leave its home for that purpose. On the contrary, at the time of the solemn festivals whose sole object is art, it is the listeners who migrate in order to come and hear the Euphonians.

An amphitheater, somewhat similar to the amphitheaters of Greek and Roman antiquity, but constructed under far better acoustic conditions, is consecrated to monumental performances. It can accommodate an audience of twenty thousand, and performers to the number of ten thousand.

The Minister of Fine Arts selects from the population of the several cities of Germany the twenty thousand privileged listeners who are permitted to attend these festivals. The choice is always determined by the greater or lesser intelligence or musical culture of the individuals. In spite of the extraordinary interest that these gatherings excite throughout the

Empire, on no account would a listener known to be unworthy be granted admittance.

The education of the Euphonians is carried out in the following manner: the children are trained from an early age in all kinds of rhythmics; within a few years they reach the point where the dividing of any beat in the bar, the syncopated forms, the blending of irreconcilable rhythms, and so on, hold no difficulty for them; next comes the simultaneous study of solfeggio and instruments, and later on, of singing and harmony. At the time of puberty, that moment of life's flowering when the passions begin to make themselves felt, it is sought to develop in them a true sense of expression, and, as a consequence, of good style.

The rare faculty of appreciating truth of expression, whether in the work of a composer or in its performance by interpreters, ranks above all others in the mind of the Euphonians. Whoever is shown to be absolutely destitute of it, or who takes pleasure in works that are false as to expression, is inexorably banished from the city, however eminent his talent or exceptional his voice, unless he consents to descend to some inferior employment, such as the making of catgut or the preparation of skins for kettledrums.

The teachers of singing and of the various instruments have under them a number of assistant masters whose duty it is to teach certain specialties in which they are known to excel. Thus, as regards the classes for violin, cello, and double bass, in addition to the principal master who directs the main study of the instrument, there is one who teaches exclusively the pizzicato, another the use of harmonics, another the staccato, and so on. Prizes have been established for agility, precision, beauty, and even tenuity of tone. Hence the admirable *piano* nuances which, in Europe, the Euphonians alone know how to produce.[15]

The signal for working-hours, meals, and meetings by streets and wards, as well as for rehearsals by small or large masses, is given by a gigantic organ placed at the top of a tower rising above all the buildings of the town. This organ is worked by steam, and so great is its sonority that its tones can easily be heard four leagues away. Five centuries ago, when the ingenious manufacturer Adolphe Sax, to whom we owe the precious group of brass-reed instruments bearing his name, put forward his idea of a similar organ designed to perform in more musical fashion the function of bells, he was looked upon as a madman, like the unfortunate man who in former days had talked of the application of steam to navigation and rail-

---

[15] For other details of Berlioz' demands in musical education, see *Mem.*, II, 238–46; *Grot.*, 244; *M.M.*, 307.

ways, and like those who, two hundred years ago, steadfastly worked at devices for directing aerial navigation, which has changed the face of the world.

The language of the tower organ, this aural telegraphy, is hardly comprehensible by any but Euphonians; they alone understand telephony, an invention the importance of which was foreseen by one Sudre in the nineteenth century, and which one of the prefects of harmony in Euphonia has developed and brought to the degree of perfection it has reached today. They also possess television, so that the rehearsal leaders have only to make a simple sign with either or both hands and the conductor's baton, to indicate to the performers that they are to give out, loud or soft, such and such a chord followed by such and such a cadence or modulation, to perform a given classical work all together, or in a small body, or in crescendo, by having the divers groups enter in succession.

When it is a question of performing some important new composition, each part is studied separately for three or four days; next, the organ announces the rehearsal in the amphitheater of all the voices first. There, under the direction of the singing-masters, they sing by "centuries," each hundred constituting a complete chorus. At this rehearsal, all the breathing-points are indicated, and so disposed that there is never more than a quarter of the singers breathing at the same point; whereby the voice production of the entire mass never suffers any appreciable interruption.

The first rehearsals are aimed at literal exactitude; then come the broad nuances; lastly style and EXPRESSION. Any marking of the rhythm by bodily movements during the singing is strictly forbidden to the choristers. They are also trained to silence, a silence so absolute and profound that if three thousand Euphonian choristers were assembled in the amphitheater or in any other resonant place, one could still hear the buzzing of an insect, and a blind man in their midst would think he was quite alone. They are so highly practiced that even after a long silence of this sort, which means the counting of hundreds of pauses, they have been known to attack a chord *en masse* without a single singer missing his entrance.

A similar system is employed for orchestra rehearsals; no section is allowed to take part in the ensemble before it has been heard and severely examined separately by the prefects. The entire orchestra then rehearses by itself; the vocal and instrumental masses are brought together only when the prefects have declared themselves satisfied that each group has been sufficiently rehearsed.

The grand ensemble is next subjected to the criticism of the composer, who listens from the upper part of the amphitheater which the public will occupy; and when he finds himself the absolute master of this huge intelligent instrument, when he is sure that nothing remains but to communicate to it the vital nuances that he feels and can impart better than anyone else, the moment comes for him to become a performer himself. He climbs the podium to conduct. A tuning fork attached to every desk enables the instrumentists to tune noiselessly before and during the performance; trial runs or any the slightest noise in the orchestra are rigorously forbidden. An ingenious mechanism, which might have been invented five or six centuries earlier had pains been taken to design it, and which is actuated by the conductor without being visible to the public, indicates, *to the eye* of each performer and quite close to him, the beats of each measure. It also denotes precisely the several degrees of piano or forte. In this way the performers are immediately and instantaneously put in touch with the intention of the conductor, and they respond to it as promptly as do the hammers of a piano under the hand pressing the keys. The master can then say with perfect truth that he is *playing the orchestra.*

Chairs of musical philosophy are held by the most learned men of the time and serve to spread among the Euphonians sound ideas as to the importance and purposes of art. They learn the laws on which it rests, and acquire accurate historical notions of the revolutions it has undergone. It is to one of these professors that we owe the singular institution of *concerts of bad music,* which the Euphonians attend at certain periods of the year in order to hear the monstrosities admired for centuries throughout Europe, the rules for producing them having been taught in the conservatoires of Germany, France, and Italy. The Euphonians come to study these works in order to get a clear idea of what to avoid — for instance, the majority of the cavatinas and finales of the Italian school at the beginning of the nineteenth century, and the vocal fugues of the more or less religious compositions of epochs preceding the twentieth.

The first experiments thus made on a population whose musical sense is today extraordinarily fine and well-nigh impeccable led to rather strange results. Some of the masterpieces of *bad music,* false in expression and ridiculous in style, which nevertheless produce an effect that is if not agreeable, at least bearable to the ear, aroused in the Euphonians a feeling of pity; it seemed to them that they were listening to the productions of children lisping a language that they do not understand. Other works made them burst out laughing, so that it became impossible to continue the performance. But when it came to singing the fugue on *Kyrie eleison* from the most celebrated work of one of the greatest masters of our ancient German school, and they were assured that this had been written, not by a madman, but by a very great musician, who in doing so was merely imitating other masters, and who was in turn imitated for a very long time, their consternation cannot be portrayed. They were seriously grieved at the thought of this humiliating malady to which, they realized, even human genius was not immune; and their religious sense joining their musical sense in revolt against these ignoble and incredible blasphemies, they sang with one accord the celebrated prayer *Parce Deus*, the expression of which is so true, as if they might thereby apologize publicly to God in the name of music and musicians.

Since every person possesses some kind of voice, every Euphonian is bound to exercise his and to have some idea of the art of singing. The result is that the orchestral players of string instruments who can at once sing and play form a second reserve choir, which the composer draws upon in certain circumstances, and whose unexpected entrance occasionally produces remarkable effects.

On their side, singers are compelled to master the mechanism of certain string and percussion instruments so as to be able, if need be, to play them while singing. Thus all of them are also harpists, pianists, and guitarists. A great number of them can play the violin, the viola, the viola d'amore, and the cello. The children play the modern sistrum and the harmonic cymbals, a new instrument, each stroke upon which produces a chord.

The parts in works for the stage and the vocal and instrumental solos are entrusted only to Euphonians whose native gifts and special talents fit them best for right performance. They are selected at a competition held publicly (and patiently) in the presence of the entire population. All the necessary time is given over to it. When it was required not long ago to celebrate the decennial anniversary of Gluck, an eight months' search was made among the women singers for the one most capable of playing and singing Alcestis, and nearly a thousand women were successively heard for the purpose.

In Euphonia no privileges are granted any artists to the detriment of art. There are no leading singers, no property rights in the title roles — even when such roles are clearly unsuited to someone's special talent and physique. The composer, the minister, and his prefects determine the essential qualities required to fill appropriately such and such a part, to represent this or that character; a search is then made for the person best endowed with these qualities, and were he the most lowly in Euphonia, he is elected as soon as discovered. Occasionally the search and the labor of our musical government are in vain. Thus in the year 2320, after having sought a Eurydice for fifteen months, we were compelled to give up the idea of staging Gluck's *Orpheus*, for lack of a young woman beautiful enough to represent that poetic figure and intelligent enough to understand the part.

To the literary education of the Euphonians much attention is given; they are able, at least up to a certain point, to appreciate the beauties of the great ancient and modern poets. Those among them whose ignorance and lack of culture in this respect are incurable can never aspire to a part in any of the higher musical functions. And so it is that thanks to the intelligent will of our Emperor and to his untiring solicitude for the most powerful of the arts, Euphonia has become a wonderful Conservatory of Monumental Music.

The academicians of Palermo thought they were dreaming as they listened to the reading of these notes drawn up by the friend of Xilef, and asked themselves whether the young Euphonian prefect had not been trying to impose on their credulity. Accordingly it was decided then and there that a delegation from the Academy should visit the musical town, so as to judge for itself of the truth of the extraordinary facts just laid before them.[16]

[16] In contrast with this European center for music, in which the discipline is that of a religious order dedicated to art and giving the fruits of its austere labors for the pleasure and edification of mankind, we may compare Wagner's plan — its subsequent modification in practice is too well known to need comment.

Although in speaking of Bayreuth, Wagner sought to assign its first conception to the year 1851, there is no word of a special theater or shrine in the *Communication to My Friends* which he wrote in that year; merely a mention of the "Festival Play" in four evenings. Two years before, in pleading for a national theater in Germany, Wagner wanted to keep sacred music in the church and deny it any instrumental accompaniment save that of the organ; and it was again the *national* idea, stimulated by the victories of 1870–1, that brought forth the Bayreuth proposal in the form of two pamphlets, reissued in 1873. In these, Wagner calls for a "national theater in which should be given works of true German spirit." The first performance should be that of the Ninth Symphony, in order to "sound the triumph of the German spirit against decadent modernism." Even the architecture of the *Festspielhaus*, based on the central idea of a concealed orchestra, should be "unborrowed from abroad"; and the remainder of the discussion expresses little more than Wagner's xenophobia, combined with his continuing acrimony against Meyerbeer. (See *243*, I, 391; III, 414; VII, 343–4; V, 303 and 328–40.)

The more relaxed and religious interpretation of the establishment as it came to be in the late seventies is due to the writings of Wagner, Wolzogen, and other members of the several *Wagnervereine* in the pages of the *Bayreuther Blätter* (1878–1927).

SUPPLEMENT *5. Errors in the "Complete" Edition of the Scores*

> Thus we have the remarkable spectacle of an edition of a man's works in which his own music is in small type while the ideas of his editors are in unblushing large characters.
>
> — T. S. WOTTON

The scores of Berlioz which are most commonly found in libraries for readers, as well as for concert and opera performance, belong to the so-called German edition, edited by Charles Malherbe and Felix Weingartner for Breitkopf and Härtel. The edition began to appear in 1900 and comprises twenty volumes, beautifully engraved and printed. Its handsome format and its well-publicized coincidence with the Centenary celebration have made most twentieth-century critics take it for granted that the edition is faithful, monumental, and complete — "as advertised."[1]

It is in fact none of these things, since the monumental quality could only arise from the other two. After collating the greater part of the edition, T. S. Wotton pointed out in the *Musical Times* for November, 1915, how frequent and serious were the errors in this supposedly definitive version of Berlioz' works. He continued his research, which I began to second under his guidance in 1930. The corrections listed below embody the result of this collaboration in which he had the leading and the larger part. Although with this list of errata we are brought closer to Berlioz' thought, much remains to be done. Until all Berlioz' letters are printed in full (*i.e.*, with his musical comments included instead of removed) and until his memoranda in the several autograph and printed scores in libraries from Paris to Leningrad have been collated by a scholar of Wotton's stature, we shall not have an edition worthy of the name.

[1] *E.g., Die Musik* (1902), 453. Mr. Nicolas Slonimsky signalizes the event in his valuable chronology, *Music Since 1900:* "January 1st, 1900 — The first volume of the complete edition of the works of Hector Berlioz, precursor of modern developments in music, is issued by Breitkopf and Härtel." (*1360, 3.*)

Meanwhile, a knowledge of the defects in the current version should be of help to both critic and performer. For example, the article on Orchestration in the latest edition of Grove's Dictionary (vol. III, p. 730) is vitiated by the fact that the author followed the German scores in drafting his remarks about the "new" instrumentation of the *Damnation of Faust*. And the author's further remarks about Berlioz' use of multiple crooks for his horn parts will certainly mislead anyone who refers to that same edition in which they have been changed from the original without notice.

As for the performer, he is repeatedly handicapped by the altered disposition of forces. The number of strings which Berlioz often specified and which varied from work to work are omitted. Worse than this, Berlioz' usual four bassoons are reduced to two, which may lead a conscientious conductor to reduce his forces accordingly and thus nullify the composer's wish. Finally, certain important directions as to tempo or expression are falsified or rendered meaningless by bad editing.

What seems to have happened to the well-meant undertaking of the German firm is this: Weingartner was asked — or took it upon himself — to rearrange the works so as to fit the usual resources of German orchestras at the turn of the century. Malherbe, then archivist of the Paris Opera, was to supply the historical and documentary background and collate the editions. This, in spite of his large collection of Berlioziana, he was not equipped to do.[2] His lack of sympathy with the composer and ignorance of his methods stood in his way at every step. Lacking these prerequisites he could not even date accurately the composition and publication of certain works although the evidence was at hand.

The result is that this German edition is a true counterpart of Boschot's French biography — indispensable but untrustworthy. When the veteran

[2] See below, note to page 5 of *Symphonie Fantastique*. On January 12/24, 1900, Balakirev, who had been consulted by the editors with regard to the autograph score of the *Te Deum*, wrote to Charles Malherbe: ". . . the second part of your letter upset me a good deal. It seems that instead of taking up arms to preserve intact Berlioz' instrumentation, you are completely in agreement with the projected changes . . . But if one allowed editors to change instrumentation in accordance with the current state of the orchestra, one would need new editions every fifteen or twenty years. . . .

"You thanked me in your kind letter for the trouble I took in raising objections to the changes made by M. Weingartner in the score of the *Te Deum*. For the glory of Berlioz, I am ready to work twice and thrice as hard, provided it be in an undertaking I find congenial. If you really wish to be grateful, the most handsome and indeed the only possible honorarium would be the *complete restoration of Berlioz' instrumentation* in the edition you are preparing. . . . Hasten while it is yet time to retrieve a step of which the whole moral guilt will fall back on you. . . ." (*80*, 17–19.)

teacher and theorist Ebenezer Prout thought of the mutilations he wept with anger and chagrin.[3] Wotton's protest at the time did compel the publishers to strike off some eight new plates in replacement of their original falsifications. But by a characteristic publishers' decision, the Prefaces to each score, in which the editors sometimes reveal their alterations, were made available only to subscribers who took the whole set. Throughout, the translations into German and English — both of the score markings and of the prefatory remarks — were done by incompetent hacks. Moreover, Berlioz' nomenclature in perfectly clear French was turned into less accurate Italian. To render the indication *sons bouchés* by *con sordini*, or *sans timbre* (for drums) by *coperti* adds further confusion to the unfaithful reproduction of scores which were quite satisfactory in their original editions. Why it should be precisely the "creator of the modern orchestra" (Weingartner's phrase) who is singled out for a treatment which stultifies the study of his orchestration, defies conjecture. And why a composer who took the greatest pains to make his intentions pellucid and his scoring practicable should be misrepresented in regard to both features by errors in the text and innuendo in prefaces, can only be ascribed to the animus of one of the editors, M. Boschot's close friend and collaborator Charles Malherbe.

Lastly, the German edition lacks the two indispensable scores of *Benvenuto Cellini* and *Les Troyens*.[4] Here was a splendid opportunity to serve musicology and the memory of the composer by publishing them as soon as they fell into the public domain. Regard for the inexistent "rights" of French publishers prevented. But no such regard was paid to Berlioz' order and classification of his works, though he signified it in a plan for a collected edition in 1852. The German grouping is in some ways arbitrary and far less significant; it prevents, for example, the ready comparison of succeeding versions of the songs. In short, the editing of Berlioz has yet to be done.

---

[3] *154*, 13.

[4] It also lacks the fragments of *Les Francs-Juges, Erigone, La Nonne Sanglante*, the first version of the *Incendie de Sardanapale* and the subsequently discovered score of *La Mort d'Orphée*. Compare what had happened to Mozart a century before: ". . . when preparing their *édition de luxe* [Breitkopf and Härtel] should have obtained definite information . . . it is most revolting to hear these gentlemen talking of the great expense they have not shrunk from incurring to honor Mozart in his grave . . . [when] they did not even trouble to inquire into . . . authenticity." (March 1800, *219*, 1471.) The *Edition Complette des Oeuvres de W. A. Mozart* was no more complete than the Berlioz of 1900.

VOLUME I

General Preface

p. viii: Note lack of sympathy with Berlioz' mind or outlook. The editors speak of the "eccentricity" (*bizarrerie*) of his literary tastes, which caused him to "hold in equal adoration Virgil and Goethe, Shakespeare and Bernardin de Saint Pierre, and which is found again in his musical preferences, for his idols were simultaneously Gluck and Spontini, Beethoven and Weber." This is inaccurate as to the "equality" of admirations, and even more as to the "eccentricity" of such catholic taste.

p. ix: Quotes a "still unpublished letter . . . to his friend Morel," in which Berlioz is supposed to have written: "I dream of a carefully executed German edition, done in Leipzig, comprising the whole of my works." They go on to state that the present edition, done in Leipzig by Breitkopf und Härtel is the fulfillment of Berlioz' hope. Berlioz' actual words in the letter are: "done *by Kistner* of Leipzig" [5] a publisher with whom Berlioz had had dealings and from whom he appears to have obtained an estimate of cost. Berlioz also wrote to Liszt, asking him to approach Härtel, but the editors of the present edition do not quote that inquiry, preferring to suppress a phrase of Berlioz' letter to Morel and suggest what is contrary to fact.

List of Works

(See below for arrangement intended by Berlioz.)

p. xxii item 13: *Hymne Vocal* arranged for six Sax instruments (1843) is the same as the *Chant Sacré*.

Symphonie Fantastique

Pref. p. xxvi: Ref. to p. 39 bar 8 — "the flutes are given a chord of *c-a* which is doubtless mere carelessness on the composer's part. We have replaced it by a chord of *e-c*." Turning to page 39, bar 8, one finds that the editors have done the opposite of what they promise, leaving the *c-a*.

Pref. p. xxxvii: The "memorandum" stating that the B-flat ophicleide "could be replaced by an E-flat Tuba" does not occur in the first impressions of the score.

First Movement

p. 3:2 Fagotti — four in 1st edition.

    2 Cornetti in B (B flat) orig. in G.

[5] *M.C.*, 214.

p. 5: *poco rallent, et riten. al tempo I* makes nonsense, asking as it does that conductor slow down and maintain a tempo at the same time. The note in the Preface p. xiv shows that the editors are trying to improve without understanding. The original marks are: over bar 2: *poco rallent.;* over bar 3: *retenu jusqu'au premier mouvement;* over bar 6: *un poco ritard.*

Fourth Movement

p. 76: Corni: add to part: *faites les sons bouchés avec la main sans employer les cylindres,* i.e., use the hand, not the valve.

p. 81 bar 3: Corni: *avec les cylindres* (both parts).

p. 90 bar 5: in 1st ed. only one ophicleide plays the passage here marked *a 2.*

p. 96 bar 4: in 1st ed. the G given here to the 2nd bassoon does not occur. Bassoons I and II play in unison the upper part of the line.

Fifth Movement

p. 99 bar 3: Corni: add *bouché avec les cylindres.*
p. 101 bar 4:   ”   ”   ”   ”   ”   ”
p. 132 bar 9:   ”   ”   ”   ”   ”   ”
p. 133 bar 2:   ”   ”   ”   ”   ”   ”

Symphonie Funèbre et Triomphale

Pref. p. xlvii: The editors say they have changed Berlioz' instrumentation in order to bring it in line with the resources of symphonic orchestras, *e.g.,* ophicleides have been replaced by tubas. They do not state, however, that they have written the 2nd ophicleide-tuba part for the lower octave throughout, nor do they explain how they square their remark about symphonic orchestras with an earlier and more correct remark to the effect that the work was not intended for such an orchestra.

First Movement

p. 151: Composed 1840 — *Published 1847.*

Flauti piccoli: read: *petites flutes en ré.*

Flauti: read: *flutes tierces en mi.*

Corni III and IV orig. in A flat and add: *Cors à pistons ou cors ordinaires.*

Cornetti I and II orig. in A flat.

Tube I and II should be: Ophicleide in C, Ophicleide in B flat.

Tamburi I and II should be *sans timbres ou voilés,* not *coperti.*

Cinelli and Gran Cassa. (*A l'autre extremité de l'orchestre, loin des tambours*) should read: away from the side drums, *not* kettledrums.

Trombone basso *ad lib*. throughout the score: should be printed in same size type as other instruments, since Berlioz wrote the part, not the editors.

p 167: Tromb. bassi: read bass*o*.

p. 183 bar 7: In 1st ed. cello part *ad lib* has no mf and the second half note has > without the tremolo; the next two bars, without ff and in whole notes with tremolo.

Second Movement

p. 184: Corni III and IV orig. in G.

   Tamburi I and II add: *sans timbres ou voilés*.

Third Movement

p. 192: Corni III and IV orig. in G.

   Tamburi I: *avec timbres* NOT *non coperti*.

NOTE on disposition:

Louise Pohl's book *Hector Berlioz' Leben und Werke*, based on mss. left by her father Richard Pohl, gives list of instruments (before the strings were added to the score) amounting to 190, as follows: 6 piccolos, 6 flutes, 10 small clarinets, 18 clarinets, 8 oboes, 8 horns in E, 8 in G, 8 in D, 10 trumpets in F, 9 in B, 10 cornets in G, 12 trombones (alto and tenor), 6 trombones (basso), 1 trombone (solo), 16 bassoons, 6 ophicleides in B, 8 in C, 6 drums without snares (caisses roulantes), 12 side drums, 6 bass drums, 10 pair cymbals, 4 Chinese crescents, 2 tam-tams.

Boschot gives the number of original performers as 207, which suggests that the 17 additional instruments may have been second clarinets in B flat, since the Pohl list usually gives double, or nearly double, the number of instruments in the engraved score, *except* for the second clarinets.

VOLUME II

Harold en Italie

Pref. xvi: Here as elsewhere, the English translator guesses at the meaning of *contretemps* (syncopation): he calls it in this instance "contrary motion." Just above, the editor refers to this syncopation as given by the trumpets, trombones and tubas. For Trumpets read Horns.

First Movement

p. 1: The 1st trombone should alone be written in viola clef, the 2nd and 3rd in bass.

p. 2: The oboe and clarinet parts should be marked *solo*. [The editors remove this frequent marking of Berlioz' on the ground that it is obsolete, although many modern composers use it or its equivalents.]

The bassoons marked *a 2* in bar 10, should be marked *unis*, which means the *four* bassoons intended by Berlioz.

p. 4 bar 8: bassoon part: *solo*.

p. 33 bar 8: bassoons: ff.

p. 43 bar 3: here only 2 bassoons play.

p. 51: According to the ms., Berlioz struck out the repeat, which would mean going from bar 6 on this page to bar 3 on p. 56.

p. 56: The English translation of the note should read: "Here the tempo should gradually have reached about double that of the opening of the Allegro."

p. 58 bar 9: only two bassoons.

Second Movement

p. 83: The last note of the harp marked *solo* and *son harmonique*, pppp.

Third Movement

p. 84: *One* 1st bassoon and *one* 2nd. (The editors' reduction of the bassoon tone without notice in the earlier movements works its further evil here, where a conscientious conductor, wishing to restore Berlioz' balance, will put in four in this movement as well.)

Fourth Movement

p. 160: "To the instruments playing the recall of the March theme in the wings, add 2 oboes to the 1st and 2nd violins and a bassoon to the cello, altering the notes of the 2nd violin which are too low for the oboe. The oboes are silent during the bars of the psalmody." These were Berlioz' instructions to Liszt in a letter of June 7, 1852. Consequently on

p. 161 bar 2: the second violins should have *e* flat twice and *c* instead of going down to *b* flat and *a*.

VOLUME III

Roméo et Juliette

Pref. p. x: The editions quoted give 20 tenors and 20 basses, not 30 each; as for the Englishing of *clef* into "key," with the added error of "contralto key" for tenor clef, it may be unnecessary to draw attention to it, except as another instance of poor editing. More serious nonsense occurs on

Pref. p. xi: where the conductor is asked to "divide each quarter note by two, not by three"; the *beat*, not the note, is intended.

Pref. p. xiv: The mixup about the mutes is referred to below, in the comment on p. 105 of the score.

Pref. p. xvii: The similar confusion about the bowing of the double basses, p. 126, will be dealt with at that page also.

The second variant of the musical quotation, lower line of second violins, bar 3, should have two *b* natural.

Pref. p. xxii: The autograph ref. to p. 199 of the score gave different vocal and wind parts, as well as strings, and the original 10 bars grew to 16.

Pref. p. xxiii: Berlioz did not "transpose the trumpet part to B" but "changed the part of the trumpets in B."

Part I

p. 1: second Cornets orig. in E flat, 3 trombones all tenor.

Prologue

p. 17: sung by a *contralto* solo and *contralti*, not as marked by editors.

Part II Allegro

p. 74 bar 5: 1st bassoon solo, not I and II.
    bar 8: top line: bassoons I and III, second line: bassoon II.

p. 75 bar 1: second line: bassoons I and II.

Part II Adagio

p. 105 bar 12: beginning here, the arrangement of the mutes is confused by the editors in their effort to correct an obvious engraver's error in the 2nd French edition. For the 1st part of the Adagio (pp. 99–104) the viola and cello parts, which carry the melody, have mutes. In the second part of the Adagio as far as p. 113, the 2nd violins and violas carrying the arpeggio accompaniment. Therefore

p. 107 bar 3: the *con sordini* should not appear over the viola and cello parts but should appear over the 2nd violins at bar 6. Further,

p. 113 bar 2: the *senza sordini* over the cellos should be struck out (see also Subchapter 12, *n.* 11 of the present work).

Part II Scherzo

p. 122: The third horn orig. marked in A flat also.

p. 135: The notation of the harp harmonics is misleading: Berlioz states in his *Treatise* that the written note gives the actual sound, the o above it showing that the note an octave below is to be plucked. The diamond-shaped notes given in the edition properly signify the note plucked, which consequently sounds an octave higher. In his later works, Berlioz employed the modern notation which gives the plucked notes.

Part III Andante

p. 155: Distribution of voices should read: Soprani I and II; Tenori, al meno 20; Bassi, al meno 20.

Part III Allegro agitato

p. 165: second horn orig. in A flat.

VOLUME IV

Pref. p. ix: Where the English translator writes "*legato* signs," read "slurs."

Pref. p. xi line 8: read "flutes and violins," not cellos.

Ouverture de Waverley

p. 1: The orchestration should read: violins I, at least 15; violins II, 15; violas, 10; cellos, 12; basses, 9.

p. 4 bar 5: Berlioz' mark for the woodwinds is pp not p; similarly for the timpani in bar 7.

p. 5 bar 6: Berlioz' mark for the woodwinds is f not ff, and the same is true again in

p. 6 bar 2.

Ouverture des Francs-Juges

p. 39: See the disposition of strings under *Waverley*. The orig. time for *Les Francs-Juges* is *alla breve*.

p. 46: The metronome time for the *Allegro assai* should make the whole note equal 80, for in the Adagio prayer beginning on p. 52, the quarter note equals a whole note, which would be absurd if the quarter note equaled 40, as the editors make it.

Ouverture du "Roi Lear"

p. 87: number of bassoons not specified; the editors have put in the 2. The strings, on the contrary, should follow the distribution of the previous two overtures: 15–15–10–12–9.

p. 109 bar 7: It is likely that here and on p. 110 bar 1, the double basses would play the low *e* with the cellos, but for the fact that Berlioz could not be sure of having 4-stringed instruments. See below note vol. X, p. 116.

Ouverture de "Rob Roy"

p. 143: 4 bassoons very likely; in any case *not* 2 as marked.

VOLUME V

Pref. p. xiii: Mistranslation of "bass clef" and "timpani" — kettledrums, *not* cymbals.

Pref. p. xviii: The editors' solution of the problem presented by the metronome mark for the Andante of the *Béatrice et Bénédict* Overture is imbecile. They omit metronome time entirely because they find that the vocal score has quarter note equal to 25, which is clearly wrong. Had they turned to the same andante air in the opera, either in the vocal score *or in their own orchestral score*, they would have found the marking 52, which supplies the needed time and explains the 25 as an engraver's error.

Ouverture de Benvenuto Cellini

p. 1: 4 bassoons: strike out *ossia* 2. Trombone I on tenor clef; II and III on bass. Strings: 15–15–10–12–9.

p. 5 bar 1: bassoons: *unis*, not *a* 2.

The slurs over the woodwind accompaniment are without authority from the original and since Berlioz wrote them alike in the 3 parts there is no pretext of "standardizing" to justify their alteration. As they stand they nullify the editors' remark that slurs over woodwinds are generally to be taken in one breath.

p. 28 bar 2: bassoons: *unis*, not *a* 2.

Ouverture du Carnaval Romain

p. 45: 4 bassoons not 2; Trombones arranged in Berlioz' usual way.

Ouverture de la Fuite en Egypte

No corrections, except that Berlioz did not consider this piece separable from its choral sequel.

Ouverture Le Corsaire

p. 97: 4 bassoons, not 2; strings 15–15–10–10–9.

p. 109 bar 1: bassoons *unis*, not *a* 2. Moreover, for the whole passage from bar 1 to bar 17 the four bassoons in the orig. are marked ff. The decrescendo marks f to p under each pair of bars are a gratuitous effect contributed by the editors.

p. 115 bar 1: The orig. ed. has *b* natural for the ophicleide or tuba on the second beat.

p. 116 bar 11: the *c* is doubled in the 2nd horn part and all four instruments have f instead of ff.

p. 119 bars 11–12: should read ff > p for all the strings. Bar 12 has p for all nine parts and bar 15 also has *cresc.* for all parts. The same phrase occurring earlier kept Berlioz' sforzando markings. As marked here the ff passage would end on

p. 120 bar 1: with a *forte*.

Ouverture de "Béatrice et Bénédict"

p. 137: Cornets I and II in D orig. marked *à pistons*.

p. 142: Andante un poco sostenuto: add: quarter note equals 52.

Prélude des Troyens à Carthage

p. 175: Cornets I and II in F orig. marked *à pistons*.

VOLUME VI

Rêverie et Caprice

p. 13: The "program" reprinted here is not by Berlioz, but was added to a reprint of the score in 1880.

p. 27: As the editors note in the preface, some of the bowings in the violin part are due to J. Armingaud.

Marche Funèbre pour la Dernière Scène d'Hamlet

p. 41: 4 bassoons: strike out *ossia 2*.
      Trombones: add: tenor.
      Vocal parts: Femmes, Hommes, not *Soprani*, etc.
      6 Tamburi: add: *voilés ou sans timbres*.
      String parts: 15–15–12–12–10.

Marche Troyenne

p. 78 bar 4: omitted mark: *cymbales seules*.

VOLUME VII

Pref. p. vi: The vocal passages changed by the editors in the *Resurrexit* on the ground of unsingability were not written for *contralti* (women's low voices) but for *hautes contres* (high tenors). Since this score has only an historical value among Berlioz' works, there was no call to alter it in any way or for any reason.

Pref. p. ix: The reference to the *Requiem* scoring should read "four gongs," not three.

Pref. p. xiii: The note referred to at the bottom of the page was not in the first edition but was added between the first and second.

Pref. p. xiv: The editors report a change they have supposedly made in substituting tubas for ophicleides in the *Lacrymosa*. They have in fact made no change.

Resurrexit

p. 1: Instead of tubas, the scoring should read: *Serpent d'harmonie et ophicléide.* Berlioz' letter to Ferrand (*L.I.*, pp. 5–6) should have been quoted by the editors as throwing an interesting light on the orchestration used by Berlioz when the Mass was performed a second time on Nov. 22, 1827. The present arrangement lacks all documentary value — the vocal parts being "unsingable" besides — as they would not be if Berlioz' terminology (*Dessus, Hautes-Contre, Tailles* and *Basses-tailles*) were retained.

Grande Messe des Morts (Requiem)

p. 65: Soprani I and II (not *ed alti*).

p. 83: The 2 tubas of Orchestra no. 1 for the *Tuba mirum* were originally: *1 ophicléide monstre à pistons.* Other variants of the first edition would be worth noting from an historical point of view.

p. 117: Tam-tam: in the 3rd ed: tam-tams.

p. 146: subtitle of *Offertorium* is omitted here: *choeur des âmes du purgatoire.*

pp. 105–110: The tuba part being written in lower octave affects nine bars out of 58.

VOLUME VIII

Pref. p. iv: Two remarks by the editors show how they damaged their edition by failing to understand and to quote their author correctly. Berlioz marked Trombones II and III *tenor* so that they could play the pedal notes called for in the *Judex crederis*. He also marked the organ passage in question *Ped.*, knowing perfectly well that the low notes were not on the keyboard. But the *idée fixe* that Berlioz has to be helped out led the editors to overlook this marking and to suggest that they are supplying it for the first time.

Pref. p. v: A similar misrepresentation of Berlioz' score: he wrote the bassoons on *two* staves and in his arrangement the first pair could not play with the oboes — as marked here — since they are playing already.

Pref. p. vi: The editors point out a choral progression written in a manner usual in Berlioz' day but which brings about hidden octaves. They suggest a change proposed originally by Balakirev but decide to leave the passage as written by Berlioz. *In spite of their own decision,* they made the change in the score, thereby avoiding the octave between top line and inner part in a 5-part passage.

Te Deum

p. 1: 6 Tromboni: add: *tenori.*

2 Tube: 1 ophicleide and 1 tuba.

Vocal parts: 1st chorus: 40 soprani, 30 tenori, 30 bassi;
2nd chorus: the same;
3rd chorus: 600 soprani ed alti.

String parts: 25–24–18–18–16.

p. 11 bar 6: Questionable distribution of trombones. French ed. makes it possible that all six are in two parts.

p. 44 (*Prélude*): 6 Tamburi militari: add: *sans timbres* and strike out *senza tuono preciso.*

p. 53 bar 9 to p. 54 bar 2: Bassoons I and II should be given the part here given to bassoons III and IV, who count pauses. The doubling of the oboes in the overlapping measure is the editors' idea.

p. 67: Under *Soprani* II, strike out (*Alti*).

p. 105 bar 7: Here occurs the change which the editors announced they would not make. Read *b* in the tenor part despite the *b* of the sopranos.

p. 107 (*Judex crederis*): The trombones should be written on three staves and in three clefs. As to tubas and drums see note above: *Prelude* p. 44.

Organo: add: *Jeu de trompettes.*

p. 109 bar 2: add: *ophicléide seul.*

p. 123 bar 8: The editors go against both the ms. and the French edition by delaying the entry of the horns, double basses, and basses until the next bar, simply because this entry does not balance the first three measures of the same page. But this may be intended by the composer, for *his* version preserves the rhythm and sounds more impressive. Whatever one's preference in the matter, it is not likely that Berlioz' manuscript should carry a detail of this magnitude as a mere oversight.

p. 143 (March): Tamburi: add: *Avec les timbres;* strike out: *non coperti.*[6]

p. 158 bar 4: upper line of cellos: add: *six 1ers violoncelles: tous les autres violoncelles en double corde.*

p. 160 bar 2: organ part: add: *Grand jeu.*

VOLUME IX

Pref. p. iv: The editors add mutes to the double basses, thinking Berlioz had forgotten them. In the *Treatise* he had written: "Mutes are sometimes used on double basses as on other stringed instruments, but the effect they produce is not so clearly characterized. They merely lessen the sonority of the basses, making it darker and duller."

L'Enfance du Christ

p. 4 bar 3: As indicated above, the mutes should not appear on the double bass part.

p. 75: Organ: add: *Céleste et tremblant doux.*

p. 78 bar 1: omitted mark: *sourdine vocale,* which is explained in the note.

p. 100 bar 6: The *con sordini* on the double bass part is correct here.

VOLUME X

Pref. p. iii: The comment on Berlioz' note to p. 8 of the score argues ignorance of its history. Berlioz wrote the work while still a pupil of Lesueur's and it was his master's habit to give such dramatic directions. Moreover, the note *says* precisely what the editors explain it might mean. Their interpretation is at once condescending and needless, and the translation of the note is garbled as usual.

Pref. p. iv: The "correction" of the *a* for kettledrums is doubtless necessary but it has not been carried out by the editors who mention it.

[6] On the representation of T. S. Wotton, the publishers corrected and issued new pages for the orchestral disposition and terminology of the *Prelude, Judex crederis* and *March.* There are thus some copies of the edition which carry the proper indication as to the snares for drums. But none of the other changes were incorporated.

Scène Héroïque

p. 1: 4 bassoons (strike out *ossia 2*); ophicleide instead of tuba.

p. 8: footnote: the last word of the English translation should be *pity*, not *tenderness*.

pp. 9 and 17: Vocal parts should read *Hautes-contre*, *Tailles* and *Basses-tailles*.

p. 52: All the *ossia 2* opposite the woodwinds should be struck out, and the *Alti* should read either *Soprani* III, or even better *Dessus*, as the editors suggest but fail to write.

p. 67: 4 bassoons and vocal parts as corrected above. The time sig. should be *alla breve*, because of a serious error committed on

p. 78: where the editors add (and sign) a note instructing the conductor to *battre à deux temps*, which is laconically rendered in English as Two Beats. The cause of this interpolation is that the copyist's manuscript bore incompatible indications of tempo at the beginning and at the middle of this section (pp. 67 and 78). These *should* read: p. 67: half note equals 80 and p. 78: *Doppio Movimento*. Whole note equals 80. The clearest fact is that Berlioz intended his *doppio movimento*. The editorial note assumes that this mark came from the copyist's own brain and overlooks the possibility that his contribution was simply the tail added to the whole note. At any rate, editorial handling alters the tempo of 216 bars for the sake of clearing up an obvious error in the first eight. Knowledge of Berlioz' letter to Ferrand, where he describes this finale as a *"marche précipitée,"* would have conclusively settled the difficulty and prevented the incoherent guesses recorded in the Preface.

Huit Scènes de Faust

p. 107: *Componirt zu Paris 1829:* read: 1828.

The nomenclature of the vocal parts has been altered as usual (see above *Scène Héroïque*).

bars 1–4: In the cello part, the *d*'s on open strings are noted in the first (and only) edition.

p. 111 bars 1 and 2: The English horn and Clarinet have *solo* over their entries.

p. 111 bar 6: Clarinet has p; cellos and double basses: $>$ $<$.

p. 114 bar 4: strings have B double flat in original.

p. 116: Berlioz' note about writing a low F for double basses in the hope that the 4-stringed instruments would soon be available in France should have been retained as historically significant. Before bar 2, the original has: *Choeur beaucoup plus nombreux qu'au commencement.*"

p. 119 bar 1 et seq.: 1st Cellos written an octave higher in orig.

p. 121 bars 2 et seq.: *Vocalisation* (in original and no doubt needless, but important as biographical detail).

p. 122 bar 1: pp. in all instrumental parts — a first instance of Berlioz' preparation for the coming diminuendo of all the parts, p. 17 bar 2.

p. 126 bar 3: both harp parts: > ; cellos have their *g*'s marked open string till the end.

p. 132: For Basse I and II read *Bariton* and *Basse;* Bassoons *unis*, not *a 2* throughout.

p. 133 bar 3: violins and violas have *cresc.*

p. 137 bar 4: Altos and tenors marked *solo;* cellos marked *soli.*

p. 157 bar 5: All vocal parts: *cresc. poco a poco.*

p. 161 bar 6: Harp part: *solo.* NOTE: throughout this first published score, Berlioz wrote *sons harmoniques* next to the notes in the harp part. Since, in the cello part, he clearly indicated that the notes meant the real sounds, it is likely that he meant the same arrangement for the harp part. The diamond-shaped notes of the present edition are therefore ambiguous.

p. 178: Under Brander add: (*Ivre*), and over his part: *A pleine voix.* Over the string parts: *A un tems* (sic).

p. 182: Clarinet I and Bassoons have *solo*, and of course the tuba is an ophicleide.

p. 188 bars 2 and 4: add ff's.

p. 194: The English horn is *solo*, which is marked again at the various re-entries.

p. 201: The *Lento appassionato assai* is marked: quarter note equals 58.

p. 203 bar 1: marked *Allegretto*, half note equals 58.

p. 212: The accompanying instrument is marked *Guitare* by Berlioz. Giving the Italian name and omitting the vertical notation opposite the staves — *Effronterie* — is a needless distortion.

VOLUMES XI–XII

La Damnation de Faust

Pref. pp. vi–ix: The editors' reasoning about the use of ophicleides and/ or tubas is neither clear nor correct, as these notes on the score will show.

This is a pity, here being the first work for which Berlioz indicated a tuba part. Moreover, when they state that the second ophicleide part has been given by them to the 3rd trombone they misread their own arrangement: it is given to trombone I. And they altogether omit mention of the part in the Fugue.

Pref. p. xi: line 3: "bar" should be "beat."

Pref. p. xiv: In the comment referring to p. 288, the editors misstate the facts about the piccolo part in the French edition and fail to mention what the autograph indicates.

Pref. p. xviii: The variant quoted, and omitted by the editors from the score itself, is certainly "practicable" and had every reason to be included.

Pref. p. xix: The further reference to the tuba part is absolutely contrary to fact; both the arrangement imputed to Berlioz and the editors' own alterations are here misrepresented — from carelessness, not design.

p. 8: though the orchestration on p. 5 bears the correct number of bassoons, *i.e.*, four, the indication here that only 2 bassoons are playing has no basis in the original.

p. 13: *con sordini* for violins I not in Fr. ed.

p. 14: *Tutti* for violins I and II occurs eight bars later in Fr. ed.

p. 26: The indication of only 2 bassoons in this scene (No. 2) is gratuitous.

p. 52 (Hungarian March): should have: *ophicleide and* tuba, which on

p. 63 bar 1: are marked *unis.* Later, on

p. 69 bar 8: the ophicleide plays in the upper octave continuing

p. 70 bars 1 and 2, and being *unis* again to the end.

p. 78 (Easter Hymn): Corni III and IV orig. in A.

p. 79 bar 5–8: Bassoons *unis* throughout, not *a 4, a 2.*

p. 110 (Drinkers' Chorus): Bassoons should be I and II, III and IV, not as shown and Tromb. I, Tuba should read: 2 ophicleides.

p. 134 (Fugue): Tromb. I and III should be Ophicl. I, and Tuba: Ophicl. II. The entire tone color of these last two scenes is altered by having the ophicleide part played by a trombone with thumb attachment.

p. 142 bar 1 and

p. 143 bar 4 have *sons bouchés* for the horns: *con sordini* is wrong.

p. 168 bar 1: bassoons should have *I and II unis.*

p. 172 bar 1 et seq.: All four bassoons play.

p. 241 bars 1 and 2: The orig. has the entry of the double basses marked ppp, the English horn pp, and the rest of the wood p. Here everything has been made uniform at pp.

p. 242 (Scene X): The editors add a part for cymbals (in small type) to punctuate Mephisto's entrance. But the chord when used earlier joined cymbals and piccolo. Since Berlioz uses no piccolo here, he needed no cymbals, and he merely reminds us of Mephisto by sounding the rhythm of his appearance on strings and brass — a change which exemplifies the difference between an allusive and a mechanical mind.

p. 249 (King of Thule): The metronome mark is doubtful and probably too slow.

p. 303 (Scene XIII): The 2 bassoons is gratuitous; doubtless the usual four play until

p. 312 bar 3, where the orig. ed. has: *un seul basson.*

p. 317 bar 2: should have: *1ᵉʳ et 2ᵉ bassons unis.*

p. 371 (Scene XVIII): The 4th horn with pistons.

p. 378 (Scene XVIII): *ophicleide and* tuba.

VOLUME XIII

Pref. p. v: The commentary on *Le Pêcheur* which they promise "elsewhere" is not to be found.

Pref. p. vi: The editors do not seem aware of the fact that the *Choeur d'Ombres* they are discussing came, with a few changes, from the prize cantata *Cléopâtre* which they reprint in vol. XV. A comparison of the two would have cleared up some of the difficulties.

Pref. p. viii: The doubt about the proper place for the sf is settled by consulting the 1st French edition.

Pref. p. xi: To omit *suivez le chant* as "superfluous" and then to put in *ed canto* seems pure whimsy.

Pref. p. xii last line: The question about the harp part is settled by a look at the *Treatise* where the passage is reproduced, with an *e*. Likewise, on

Pref. p. xiii: the questions about the Vlns. Div., and the "*2 pianos à 4 mains*" for the *Tempest* fantasia.

Pref. p. xxxvi: The substitution of tubas does cause a change in the notes, as the editors themselves admit on p. xxxviii.

Lélio ou le Retour à la Vie

p. 2: Throughout, the English text is full of mistranslations and absurdities.

p. 9 (*Choeur d'Ombres*): The *con sord.* on violas, cellos, and basses are neither in the first ed. nor in the autograph. They are added here because the violins I and II have them — for two beats, Berlioz' obvious desire being to mix the timbres in the arpeggio series.

p. 22 bar 3 et seq.: Instead of *con sord.* for the Horn in F, read: Solo: *sons bouchés avec les cylindres* over bars 3 and 4; *sans cylindres* over bar 5; and *sons bouchés avec*, etc. over bars 6 and 7.

p. 89 bars 6 and 7 (*La Tempête*): In Fr. ed. the 8 violins soli do not play, to give them time to put on mutes.

p. 150 bar 7 (*Le Cinq Mai*): add: *Moderato* (quarter tone equals 92).
Tromboni: add: tenori.

p. 169 bar 4: Instead of *con sordini: faites les sons bouchés avec la main, sans employer les cylindres.*

p. 176 (*L'Impériale*): Corni III and IV orig. in A.
Instead of Tube (5) read: *2 tubas et 3 ophicleides.*

p. 209 bars 4 et seq.: Tubas and ophicleides in upper octave, as far as
p. 212 bar 3 inclusive.

VOLUME XIV

Pref. p. iv: The condensed score quoted here is inaccurate.

Pref. p. ix: The Bibl. Conservatoire has a fully orchestrated 5th stanza of the *Hymne à la France* in Berlioz' own hand, and therefore to be consulted in any edition of the work.

p. 1 (*Méditation Religieuse*): The metronome time of the piano version (quarter note equals 66) should be noted.
Woodwinds are in pairs, strings: 10–10–8–8–8.

p. 7 (*Chant sacré*): Woodwinds in pairs except for horns. Soprani I and II not *alti*. The editors might have noted the use of this same work rescored for a tryout of Sax's new instruments, including the saxophone, in February 1844.

p. 24 bar 2 (*Chant des Chemins de Fer*): In the piano version bar 2 is repeated.

p. 75 (*La Mort d'Ophélie*): 2 flutes, English horn, 2 clarinets in B flat.
Strings: 15–10–10–8–8.

p. 89 (*Sara la Baigneuse*): Piccolo, 2 flutes, oboe, 2 clarinets in A, 2 bassoons. Contralti (after Soprani II) Strings: 12–12–10–10–8.

p. 105 bar 4: Horns marked *soli*.

p. 115 bar 3: Tenor part of chorus I marked *solo*, as somewhat more prominent than the rest, p against pp. Marked *solo* again on

p. 119 bar 1 over the mf of the other tenors.

p. 127 (*Hymne à la France*): "Instrumentiert 1851" is wrong: the work was composed, orchestrated, and performed in the same year, 1844.
Bassoons *unis*, not *a 2*, no number being specified.
Ophicleide instead of tuba and soprani I and II, contralti.
Metronome time of the piano version is quarter note equals 48.

p. 130 bar 1 upper line: Soprani I; second line: Soprani II and Contralti.

p. 130 bar 5 upper line: Soprani I and II.

p. 133 bar 5: Tempo in piano version: Moderato (quarter note equals 84).

p. 140 bar 1: Bassoons: *unis*, not *a 2*.

p. 149 (*La Menace des Francs*): same remarks as previous *Hymne* regarding disposition.

p. 152–p. 157: Indications for trombones *a 2* and *a 3* without warrant.

VOLUME XV

Pref. p. vii: In the collection of "33 Mélodies" published in 1863[?] the slurs and notes differ from the 2 examples here quoted.

p. 99 bar 4 (*Cléopâtre*): the English note to the singer should read: "with weakened voice" *not* "with great excitement," and similarly for the German. On

p. 100 bar 4: it should read "still weaker," etc.

p. 110 (*La Belle Voyageuse*) bar 16: the dotted quarter should be marked pppp.

p. 121 (*Absence*): The date of composition is without warrant. "Before 1841" is all that can be said. Strings indicated on facsimile in Kapp's *Berlioz*: 4–4–3 and 5 basses.

p. 126 (*La Captive*): 2 bassoons should be noted; 1st string orch.: 10–10–8–8–6; second string orch. should be marked: *Tous les autres 1ers violons*, etc. down to *Toutes les autres contrebasses à 4 cordes*.

p. 135 top: the direction is to beat six quavers, not crotchets, to each bar, *i.e.*, six eighth notes.

p. 160 (*Le Chasseur Danois*): Strings: 5–5–3–2–3.

p. 184 (*Sur les Lagunes*): Woodwinds in pairs, the second horn in F being *à cylindres*.

VOLUME XVI

Pref. p. x last lines: The "few nuances" referred to by the editors come from their own unaided imagination since there is no orchestral score of *Irlande* to which they can "conform."

p. 1 (*Ballet des Ombres*): Berlioz' note is mistranslated: he wishes the voice to *drag* between the marked notes; that it should be "carried on" went without saying.

p. 47 (*La Mort d'Ophélie*): The first version for single voice was undoubtedly composed before 1848 — the date here given — and in Paris, not London, since it originally appeared in a New Year's album offered by the *Gazette Musicale* in 1848.

p. 59 (*Apothéose*): This rearrangement of the last movement of the *Symphonie Funèbre et Triomphale* should not be dated merely London 1848, since the symphony was completed in 1840.

p. 101 (*Prière du Matin*): Soprani I and II in place of Soprani and Alti.

VOLUME XVII

Pref. p. xi: The *Chant de Bonheur* was drawn from *La Mort d'Orphée*, the ms. of which had not been found when the editors wrote their preface.

Pref. p. xiv: *Je crois en vous* was originally for *mezzo soprano*, which is worth noting.

p. 48 (*Elégie*): The French translation of Moore's poem is not by Berlioz but by Thomas Gounet, and the date of composition is 1829 not 1830. (See *L.I.*, 39 and 58.)

p. 49 bar 9: The ". . . poco rit." should go as far as Tempo I.

p. 56 (*Le Pêcheur*): Tiersot maintains that this is the first version, not the second as stated here, and the likelihood is all in Tiersot's favor, since *Lélio* is a *rifaccimento* of previous parts and therefore constitutes the second version of those parts.

p. 66: The same holds true of the *Chant de Bonheur*, for which the evidence is conclusive.

p. 131 et seq. (*Nuits d'Eté*): The dates given here for this collection of six songs are worthless. They were composed before 1841, hence it is absurd to mark these first versions as having been "reworked" in that year. The later versions of Nos. 2 and 5 belong to the year 1856.

p. 212 (*La Mort d'Ophélie*): This version for single voice being in all probability the first should not bear the date 1848 nor the place London (see note to vol. XVI p. 47); nor does it, in this form, have anything to do with *Tristia*, Oeuvre 18.

VOLUME XVIII

p. 2 (*Marseillaise*): Trumpets I and II are *à pistons*, the rest *ordinaires*. The 2 *tube* are, of course, *ophicleides*.

p. 6 end of bar 2 has double bar and repeat sign.

p. 8: The voice parts are divided into: *1ᵉʳ choeur d'hommes* and *2ᵉ choeur d'hommes, femmes, et enfants*.

p. 10 5th stanza, should be marked: *un peu moins vite*.

p. 12 end of bar 1: double bar and sign.

p. 16 6th stanza: *Religioso plus lent*.

p. 17 bar 3: 1° tempo.

bar 4: double bar and sign, plus note: *Les basses tailles à l'octave des ténors jusqu'à l'entrée du 2ᵉ choeur*.

p. 32 (*Der Erlkönig* — arr.): Oboe (single), Corni III: add: *à pistons*. The French translation by M. Chassang is not the one set by Berlioz, who used the far superior version of Edouard Bouscatel. Restoring Schubert's vocal part could have been done without falling into verbal bathos.

p. 36 bar 1: *Fag. I* is gratuitous.

p. 46 bar 7: strings are fff.

p. 50 bar 5 and p. 51 bar 1: fp not sfp.

Extracts from the *Treatise*

p. 19: Since a note refers the reader to the full score of *Roméo et Juliette* in vol. III of this edition, some notice should have been taken of the absence of mutes on the strings in the present excerpt.

pp. 80, 117, and 124 (Meyerbeer), 89 and 197 (Berlioz): the substitution of tubas for ophicleides stultifies the value of the examples, since they presumably reproduce a treatise on orchestral practice at a certain date while misrepresenting that practice.

VOLUMES XIX–XX

Béatrice et Bénédict

Pref. p. ix: The note referring to the *b* flat given the violins on p. 214 bars 5 and 6 indicates that the substitution of an *a* goes against the autograph score. It also goes against the vocal score, in which Berlioz had a hand.

p. 39: Corni III and IV: add: *à pistons*.

p. 74: 2 trombe in D: add: *à pistons*.

p. 105 bar 7: Vocal score has: half note equals 112; the time sig. should be *alla breve*.

p. 108 bar 8: Vocal score has: *Allegretto* (quarter note equals 132).

p. 117: Corni I and II: *à pistons*.

p. 184: Vocal score has *Allegretto;* Corni III and IV: *à pistons*.

p. 191 (Act II): Guitare should be in the singular.
2 Trombe in E: *à pistons*.

p. 206: 2 Corni in Es: *à pistons*.

p. 214: See note above: Pref. p. ix.

p. 244: Again *Guitare* in the singular.

p. 249: Corni I and II: *à pistons*.

p. 265: same as p. 249.

p. 267: Corni III and IV: *à pistons*.

Berlioz' Own Arrangement of His Works up to 1852

OEUVRE 1. *Ouverture de Waverley*
OEUVRE 2. *Irlande*
OEUVRE 3. *Ouverture des Francs-Juges*
OEUVRE 4. *Ouverture du Roi Lear*
OEUVRE 5. *Messe des Morts (Requiem)*
OEUVRE 6. *Le Cinq Mai*
OEUVRE 7. *Les Nuits d'Eté*
OEUVRE 8. *Rêverie et Caprice*
OEUVRE 9. *Ouverture du Carnaval Romain*
OEUVRE 10. *Traité d'Instrumentation*
OEUVRE 11. *Sara la Baigneuse*
OEUVRE 12. *La Captive*
OEUVRE 13. *Fleurs des Landes*

OEUVRE 14. *Episode de la vie d'un artiste*
OEUVRE 14b. *Le Retour à la vie*
OEUVRE 15. *Symphonie Funèbre et Triomphale*
OEUVRE 16. *Harold en Italie*
OEUVRE 17. *Roméo et Juliette*
OEUVRE 18. *Tristia*
OEUVRE 19. *Feuillets d'album*
OEUVRE 20. *Vox Populi*
OEUVRE 21. *Ouverture du Corsaire*
OEUVRE 22. *Te Deum*
OEUVRE 23. *Benvenuto Cellini*
OEUVRE 24. *La Damnation de Faust*
OEUVRE 25. *La Fuite en Egypte*
[OEUVRE 26. *L'Impériale*] [7]

[7] Not included in the original prospectus, but added in advertisement sheets of *Grot.* in 1859. See Bibliography under *Grot.*

> How can anyone deny to M. Berlioz the
> gift of formal clarity?
> — MAURICE BOURGES in 1842

More real harm has been done to art in recent years by indiscriminate talk about Form than has been due to any other type of Philistinism. The habit belongs, to be sure, to the Higher Philistinism — it marks those whom Nietzsche called Culture-Philistines — but it is none the less anti-artistic, for the emotion behind it is almost always a false and ignorant superiority. As for the damage done, it could be demonstrated by simply pointing to the artists who have either been hindered by critics' objections to their form or — worse still — who have suppressed their true instincts in deference to this vague but menacing criterion.

Form is necessarily, inevitably, the creator's chief concern in any art: the artist does nothing but shape material things, even when as a dancer, singer, or actor he uses his own body as a plastic substance. Hence the artist is alert to opinions about his forms — which are his works — and by extension he responds to criticism about what has come to be called his Sense of Form, as if it were a separate faculty used in only one department of his work. To the choosy connoisseur, it may seem very knowing to say in a depreciatory tone: "Ah, yes but formally — " or: "Very moving, I admit, but I find the architectonic somehow not — "; the truth is that such judgments betoken little more than airs and graces mixed with current critical cant.

Even in more serious discussions, the dangerous assumption is made that a classified object belongs to its class by an act of God, not of man, and that consequently a moral obligation compels everyone to discountenance objects that lack some feature defining the class: they seem as if rejected of the Lord. Thus earnest young men taught by certain pundits go about wondering whether *Pickwick Papers* is or is not a novel, and persons culturally proud will declare that jazz is not music. They do not see that the only hope of true culture is to make classifications broad and criticism particular. For by their mode of definition one must in the end conclude that only one school, age, or artist truly practiced the given art; all others must be deemed heretical, and more or less tolerable only as they approach the Norm, the Form. The trouble is that in so narrowing his experience for emotional comfort, the Culture-Philistine meets rival sovereignties of the same kind, and culture becomes even more broken up and sectarian than it regrettably is.

The history of art makes short shrift of these white-livered tastes, and does it in two ways that illuminate the discussion of Form. In the first place, almost all the great works that have been persistently admired fall outside the classifications based on points of form. What De Quincey called the literature of power consists of apparently lopsided, incomplete, and faulty works. One must say *apparently*, for it can be shown that the *Odyssey*, *King Lear*, and the *Brothers Karamazov* are not formless, and that their authors were anything but "deficient in the sense of form." Rather, they strove to create forms suited to unusually massive materials, in the full knowledge that they were giving up symmetry and smooth surface. To dismiss the works as unformed or ill-formed is to show lack of perception in the very category where one claims superior knowledge — which proves again the deplorable effect of teaching the sanctity of set forms instead of teaching their function. A *caveat* must accordingly be addressed to the beholder: don't talk about Form until you have yourself tackled the problems of craftsmanship in some art; until you have met in a piece of work the particular difficulties which its unique form is supposed to master while revealing the intent that gave them rise.

For the artist, the principle is different. He is at liberty to restrict himself like, let us say, Henry James in the novel, to any formal limits he chooses — the "point of view," the giving up of omniscience, the adoption of one or all of the unities. He does this in the light of his temperament and of his purpose too: if Hardy had elected to treat the subject of *The Dynasts* on the plan of the three unities he would have been mad. We see in what he did why large subjects (which is not the same thing as great works) [1] require the "open" forms in order to exist at all. One

---

[1] There is, of course, a relation between size and greatness. The modern distaste for magnitude involves the illicit assumption that because a work is large its substance will be shoddy. But given equally fine substance, the larger the work the greater it will be. This does not diminish the worth of small works; it only determines their rank: the poems of the Greek Anthology are wonderful but they are not great as Homer is.

Is the *Iliad* then greater than *Hamlet*? Do we, after ascertaining power or quality, merely count pages? The mind rebels at the thought. Yet the imagined procedure, which no one would dream of carrying out, has something to

then judges the creator's formal power not by reference to some classified plan suitable to another subject, but by measuring the degree to which massive materials have been grasped and held in place by the organizing mind.[2] When the centripetal force of the substance has been overcome, we have Form.

To this general rule of tension in large works, there is an important corollary which explains the apparent faults of surface workmanship. For a long time the mind of man in its naïveté desired the planets to move in round orbits and at regular speeds. But the splendid equilibrium of the solar system is based on a not-quite-elliptical plan, which involves irregularities, compensations, and — to the hasty observer — absurdities, such as the retrograde motion of Mars. Just so in art. The half-educated or semithoughtful observer has no conception of the degree to which successful form is a matter of compromise and compensation — the greater the art the more frequently so. Indeed, the artist might borrow from mathematics the symbol *P.E.* and make it stand for his own principle of *Preferable Error*, which is the rule in all material creation, from shipbuilding to fresco painting, for the highest goals are not all attainable simultaneously. Hence, "the critic would discover, if he came to know more of the matter, that the artist had been hampered by difficulties which nobody but an artist could fully appreciate, and that he had made some compromise or sacrifice, intentionally, so as to preserve as much of one quality as was compatible with the existence of another. . . . There is no such thing as *absolute* technical perfection . . . sacrifices have always to be made somewhere, and . . . it is grievous injustice in a critic to pounce upon the sacrificed parts, and exhibit their purposeful slightness or dullness as an imperfection which a better workman could have avoided."[3]

This is no more than what Dr. Johnson meant when he warned the readers of *Paradise Lost* — a work to which incidentally he did not instinctively respond — that "he who can put the faults of that wonderful performance . . . in balance with its beauties must be considered not as

---

suggest: it tells us, notably, that we can no longer read *Hamlet* as a work by itself. If Shakespeare had written only this one, or if it were the only grand design among his works, we should certainly not compare his greatness with Homer's. As it is, we read into *Hamlet*, and quite properly, the greatness of all the other plays. Quantity, or as we say more genteelly, "scope," "range," has us thrall. Its parts cast mutual reflections like the parts of a planetary system, and like mass in physics, massiveness in art exerts an irresistible gravitational pull.

[2] I am indebted here to conversations with my colleague James Gutmann, and to his article *1084*.

[3] Hamerton: *1087*, 259–60.

nice but as dull." [4] It is the part of pedantry — the prevailing vice of modern criticism — to haggle over faults, supposed or real, as if they stood by themselves, or as if it were the sole aim of the artist to avoid them. The truth is that the artist's desire for perfection goes with a kind of carelessness which has the effect upon the whole work that magnanimity has upon the human character. This carelessness is not inattention or ignorance, it is the attending to superior things by ignoring the lesser; it is the "sacrifice" which will preserve the greatest number of qualities, however inconsistent in their natures: it is Preferable Error.

How this applies to Berlioz has been shown several times before — in connection with his aims as a dramatic musician and with his interest in more than the common number of musical elements. "The composer's business," said Berlioz more than once, "is to write true and beautiful music, music remarkable by its expression, by its melody, by its harmony, by its rhythm, and by its instrumentation . . . But if you try to establish a doctrine of absolute beauty, I give up." [5]

Berlioz reminds us here that there is a link between the critic's failure to understand the motives that lead an artist to choose the preferable error and the casual imputation of ignorance based on inability to distinguish different goals or types of beauty. The history of styles — and this is the second lesson of history — shows that artists do not always seek the same effects, and that equally valid results are often mutually exclusive. The poet cannot at the same time be honey-tongued like Tennyson and rugged like Donne. What is tried for in one esthetic is avoided like the plague in another, whence it follows that criticism is worthless when it counts as blunders the very merits striven for. Dickens, we are told by certain moderns, did not know how to write. The fact is that Dickens handled words like a virtuoso even though he never attempted the limpidity of Addison and Steele.

Now, numerous as are the possible literary and pictorial styles, the conceivable variety in music is infinitely greater because neither spoken language nor visual conventions restrict it. Sound is moreover so plastic as to require the imposition of arbitrary patterns, which again makes for diversity. The "logic" of music is by no means inherent, but rather acquired — as is shown by the different kinds of melody, harmony, counterpoint, and so on, whose extension is still open to genius. Even if we exclude oriental musics, which are music whether we "recognize" them or not, the course of western history from the Gregorian chant to Schoenberg, Cowell,[6] and Partch [7] shows what can be done in less than a millennium. One may prefer what for the moment looks "central," namely the stretch from Bach to Beethoven, but the abundance of masterpieces in these closely allied styles no more constitutes a standard of musical right and wrong than the technique of Vermeer stands as a reproach to Goya.

The charge that after Beethoven music becomes formless; that the Romantic period stressed contents at the expense of form; that "the school of Berlioz, Liszt, and Wagner" was revolutionary in the sense of anarchical — all these clichés of secondhand scholarship rest on the unspoken premise that form in music must be based on the usages of major-minor harmony developed in the eighteenth century and on nothing else. By an historical illusion it has come to be believed that from eternity everything has worked toward that high point, from which by definition there can be nothing but decline.

> Through formalism her progress lay,
> Arrived at form there let her stay,
> For if she still must onward press,
> 'Tis but few steps to formlessness.

These words by William Watson about music are those of a man in unfamiliar territory, expressing the fears that come from confusing Form with formulas. "Arrived at form" is nonsense. The earliest attempts in all the arts are always the most "formal" in the sense of symmetrical, regular, ritualistic — especially so in music. What the poet really means is that he enjoys and hopes to eternalize the complex forms of his time, and principally the sonata form which was then about a century old. But sonata form or any other is only an empty mold into which certain musical ideas may be cast. The actual form of a given sonata — the form that is artistically valuable — does not lie in mere concordance with the textbook pattern. It is found, rather, in every detail of the work, down to the indications of tempo and dynamics; so that one really ought to say that the form of a musical piece varies with each performance: if the pianist misuses the pedal, the form is in part destroyed.[8]

[6] For his conception of "tone clusters," see his *New Musical Resources* (*781*).

[7] For his 42-tone scale and the instruments that play it, see his recent book, *Genesis of a Music*, Wisconsin University Press, Madison, 1949.

[8] This is the reason why calling music "pure form" is absurd. If music were valued exclusively for the abstract and *fixed* relations within the work, then one sonata would suffice — why write another? And equally intricate relations could be fashioned with matches on a tablecloth — why instruments and the grueling effort of perfect performance?

For brevity, of course, the word "form" may stand for "type of form" but this obvious ambiguity should not impose on anyone. In one usage, Form is a specified cut of the cloth; in the other it is a property of the texture and the fit. Only by playing on words can theorists raise the bugbear of predicting formlessness from the modification of forms. The new patterns may be good or bad or hard to schematize on first hearing, but they have form — just as what we call a shapeless lump has a shape. It is only Mr. Mantalini in Dickens who confounds reality with geometry and refers to his wife's "beautiful outline."

Neither musical patterns nor the arts of tailoring follow immutable laws. They follow habit and history, which may be why our judgments are always in danger of becoming provincial. Generally speaking, modern European music is descended from two sources: the repertory of dances and the vocal polyphony of the fifteenth and sixteenth centuries. From the former, which follows an external "program" insofar as it is foot music and thus has to be repetitious for social use, instrumental music derived its unhappy passion for symmetry, squareness, and shortness of phrase.[9] When someone lengthened the minuet phrases it was truly scandalous, for the dancers were caught off base. From vocal polyphony — programmatic again because made to suit words or religious rites — modern music derived its happy passion for expressiveness and multiplicity. It also derived from a third sort of program — the riddles, messages, and ciphered puzzles of the decadent period — a possibly unhealthy interest in "difficulty overcome." By the eighteenth century this last tendency was strengthened as a result of the new convention of the tempered scale and the arbitrary rationalism of a "classical" harmony.[10] The false analogy between musical art and the dominant science of mathematics, which had reduced "invention" to "problems," was also inherited; so that to this day one finds among the many contradictory types of formal analysis such bland definitions of musical form as "solving the problem of establishing a key, leaving it, and returning to it" — "without," one is tempted to add, "being seen."

[9] Mr. Werner Wolff: "Incidentally, in spite of the efforts of Berlioz, of occasional attempts by Schumann, and of the onslaughts of the younger Stravinsky, musical creation is not yet rid of the hampering chains of symmetry." (1942) *1038*, 122.

[10] The belief in the wickedness of consecutive fifths, the dissonance of the fourth, the folly of certain inversions and resolutions, regardless of the ear's experience, equaled the fanaticism of religious dogma. Until well into the nineteenth century, harmony was deemed a science and its laws held mandatory — by another play on the word "law." Genuine science, that of Helmholtz, refuted Rameau just as Rousseau and Berlioz had done on empirical grounds.

What this narrow definition takes for a fundamental principle is simply a temporary goal of the enharmonic system, which relied on key relations to outline the sections of a piece: "It can hardly be doubted that the . . . practically new discovery of the element of positive harmonic or tonal form . . . must have acted like many other fresh discoveries in the realms of art, and tended to swamp the other elements of effect; making composers look to form rather as ultimate and preeminent than as inevitable but subsidiary. It seems not improbable that the meaningless commonplace which often offends the sensitive musician in the works of Haydn and Mozart, and appears like just so much rubbish shot in to fill up a hole, was the result of this strong new feeling. . . . In [them], it is common to find very sweet tunes in each of the primary sections, and then a lot of scurrying about — "brilliant passages" as they are often called — the only purpose of which is to . . . point out that the tune just finished is in such and such a key." [11]

In the light of recurrent excesses of this sort, it would be easy as well as gratifying to show that, as a class, musicians tend to have a rather blunted sense of form, precisely because they rely on formulas, none of which (since they change with the times) necessarily correspond to that "inner logic" invoked by critics. When one considers how childishly obvious are some of the august commands of tradition — the alternation of slow and fast, of melody and refrain, of A and B in order to reach A once more; when one knows how long it took for music to develop sizable movements that were not made so by repeats; how great the innovation seemed when the melodies of an opera began to be used in its overture; and how ready musicians have been to patch together original ideas with inherited commonplaces — one is driven to admit that the constructive imagination is as rare in composers as the melodic. The great majority work with others' tunes on others' plans and content themselves with deft spinning. But it must be pointed out at the same time that many works are sublime in spite of formalistic excess and ungainly shape. Schubert's chamber music supplies many examples, of which perhaps the clearest and greatest is the first movement of the *Death and the Maiden* quartet.

To call a movement ungainly brings us back to the criterion by which to judge Form, old or new, and more particularly, *the* form of a given sample — what has here been called Form as against formula. Most errors come from supposing that one and the same mental operation will suffice

[11] H. C. Colles in *Grove's Dictionary*, art. "Form." (*1315*, II, 276.)

for all musics. Yet it should be clear that in certain instances our "sense of form" legitimately relies on an *expectation* derived from a knowledge of the models, whereas in others it effects a *discovery* guided by the piece itself. Until that exploration has been fully charted, it cannot in the nature of things give the hearer the same pleasure that he feels in expectation fulfilled. And this in turn explains why the modern music of any age undergoes a twenty-year period of probation during which it is called formless.

To analyze new music by first principles one must at the outset recognize that all successful musical forms, large or small, answer to a simple pattern which might be called the oratorical plan: exposition, development, and summing up.[12] In groups of movements the same goal is still more broadly understood: one wants kinship with a difference, which is symbolized in the formula ABA, the second A being desired heavier or faster — more conclusive.[13] The classical symphony in four movements is just as plainly reducible to the satisfaction of these fundamental artistic needs. Derived from the French or Italian overture (fast — slow — fast or the converse) into which dance movements were inserted toward the close (which in turn called for a slow introduction to prop up the structure from in front) the symphony grew by successive distortions and reformations. The last phase of rapid change took place between 1750, when the *sinfonie* or opera overtures began to be copied as pieces independent of the play, and the time when Haydn (after the Mannheimers) expanded the three-movement form to introduce the minuet, altered in tempo. Beethoven substituted the scherzo for the minuet, amplified each division, added a fifth movement (in the Pastoral) writing titles for each, and finally (in the Ninth) introduced soloists and chorus, recitatives, and dramatic ensembles. At that point, the greater architectonic of "one work" using voice and instruments came into play. Its design was different for each work in order to organize the various unrestricted means and subforms.

These expanded creations still bear some relation to the "oratorical plan," though its application on this scale may become too abstract to be useful. Instead, a definition may be hazarded which will aid in the judg-

---

[12] In so-called binary form, this is reduced to its simplest expression — question and answer.

[13] In the extended forms, repetitions and digressions are allowed (*e.g.*, episodes in the fugue), and the space required for one or more developments is fixed. But as each user's deviations show, the rigor of the rule is solely for the maintenance of the ABA prime effect.

ment of forms on any scale; it is at the same time a summary of what history and observation show: *Organic, or better, intrinsic musical form resembles form in all the other arts; it consists in achieving the richest compromise among the claims of the constituent elements of the art, in such a manner that bare sensations, their interrelations, and their retinue of associations shall present the appearance of unity and coherence among themselves.*

Two subdefinitions are obviously called for. Unity has been immortally defined by Mr. Curdle as "a sort of a general oneness," and it would be rash to try to do better; still it can also be defined by its effects: unity satisfies the sense of economy by persuading us that ornament has grown out of main subjects. Coherence, on the other hand, satisfies the desire to follow without stumbling, by making one moment lead easily to the next.[14] In music, the traditional forms differ greatly with respect to these two qualities. If theme and variation is the most unified, it may also be the least coherent; the late-Beethoven sonata form is thoroughly coherent but less unified than a fugue or a "regular" sonata. As for balance and proportion, apart from obvious measurements of space or time, they are clearly a function of the unequal attention given to unity and coherence in a particular work.

A final caution is necessary lest the groundwork of this definition be used to the detriment of certain styles. What has been said about "formulas" does not disqualify them for use in music, any more than the facilities of the sonnet should keep a poet from using the pattern, or the warning about clichés should prevent their occurrence in good prose: it is a matter of which formulas are used, when, and how. The critic may condemn Haydn and Mozart for repeating their cadences and making "mere business" of stressing the divisions of the form; and he may praise Beethoven for turning form from an absolute, overt feature into "a hidden presence."[15] But there is no need to follow the critic as far as the edge of superiority which he would accord Beethoven's conception of form. It is but another ideal, which leaves intact the ideal of Haydn and Mozart in their best works, and which must not be erected into another absolute. Every type of form has its advantages and its defects, and every type engenders its special fatigue in the listener who does not vary the diet — which is why historic forms become exhausted and are replaced. The critic who cannot play fair with the past but must praise each period

[14] The musician, therefore, may be said to ask himself at any point, "Do I repeat or do I vary?"
[15] *1315*, II, 276.

or person at the expense of the others is unfit to exercise his craft.[16]

It follows that in order to deal justly with Berlioz' sense of form, one must consider him as coming after Beethoven in the expanded realm of dramatic music. Yet since he was not an imitator but a continuator, he must be judged as a disciple who held to the point of the lesson rather than to the terms of it. The place where one finds his models is Beethoven's latest works — not so much the instrumental symphonies as the Ninth and the late piano sonatas and quartets. It is there that we discern the prototypes of Berlioz' melodic variation, the development by altered restatement, the harmonic concision, and the construction by interweaving rather than juxtaposing sections within a movement.

In making form a hidden presence by these devices, the composer is forced to consider his entire pattern at every point instead of at stated intervals, and this in turn multiplies the occasions when he must choose the Preferable Error. This preoccupation being further complicated in Berlioz by his special concerns enumerated earlier — from distinctive melody and dramatic intent to rhythm and timbre — the resultant shapes were bound to differ in striking ways from familiar ones.[17] We may well believe him when he intimates that he bent the whole force of his intellect on fashioning the right form for each piece.[18] This is not to say that he invariably succeeded, but that his endeavor was never perfunctory; so that those who undertake to analyze his works must bring to bear a comparable degree of intelligence before they can reconstruct his reasoning. Sir Donald Tovey who, despite his automatic levity and weak historical sense, can be depended on in matters of technique, has validated Berlioz' forms in a truly suggestive statement:

[16] James Agate: "The worst of dramatic critics is that they will not make up their minds about a thing and stick to it. Lewes has quite settled, has he not, that Rachel had no pathos? Now take his description of her Phèdre: 'Nothing I have ever seen surpassed this picture of a soul torn by . . . conflicts . . . The remorseful lines *were charged with pathos.*' " (*1142*, 87–8.)

[17] On a small scale, this is well illustrated by Stewart Macpherson's comments on the English horn melody in the *Roman Carnival* overture: "Unity is preserved [because] . . . we are made to feel that the various 'limbs' are in keeping one with another although varied in outline . . . the accompaniment figure is continuous and there is a certain relevancy of character throughout the whole strain of the melody." (*1326a*, p. 28 and ex. 47.) This is another, and an excellent way of describing intrinsic form.

[18] Berlioz never published a word about his formal prowess. On two occasions he regretted being the author of some of his music because it kept him from discussing its technical interest. (*207*, II, 20 and *M.C.*, 81.) Manners have changed and now our leading artists inform us unblushingly about their profound workmanship.

From the two typical defects of bad highbrow music, Berlioz is absolutely free: he never writes a piece consisting of introductions to introductions; and he never writes a piece consisting . . . entirely of impassioned ends. His hollowness . . . may be said to lie on the surface; inwardly all is as true as if Mr. Gulliver had spoken it . . . His forms are totally different from (and infinitely better than) anything they profess to be.

Tovey being on the whole a purist, one would expect him to recognize that a piece of music cannot profess to be anything other than it is, and he does add that Berlioz had "a genius for composition and not merely for orchestration.[19] In a word, Berlioz fulfills the Aristotelian requirement of Beginning, Middle, and End, and is moreover steadily inventive. For Tovey's modifier about forms "infinitely better than what they profess to be" can only mean Tovey's expectation of (let us say) a traditional first movement when a work is entitled symphony.[19] In this left-handed way of putting his approval and in his surprise at meeting intrinsic form, we have the clearest demonstration of the thesis here presented, namely, that until critics are emancipated from fetishism and misleading formulas they will scarcely be able to enlighten the rest of mankind. Nor indeed will they be able to pay the serious attention to form which they pretend to give, and which the subject deserves in all considerations of Art.

[19] 590, 76.

Chronology

1803	Dec. 11: Berlioz born	Beethoven's first sketches of *Fidelio*. Birth of Adolphe Adam, Mérimée
1815	Berlioz' uncle at Waterloo Hector studies flute and guitar	Schubert's *Erlkönig*. Béranger's first collection of songs
1816	Berlioz' first "musical event" Earliest compositions	Rossini's *Barber of Seville*. Byron's *Childe Harold*, Canto III
1817	Love for Estelle. Emotions caused by Virgil and Florian	Byron's *Manfred*. Death of Méhul, Mme. de Stael
1820	Prosper Berlioz born	Donizetti's *Nozze in Villa*
1821	November: Berlioz in Paris. Discovery of Gluck and the French masters of opera	Beethoven's Piano Sonata Op. 110. Weber's *Freischütz*. Birth of Pauline Viardot, Flaubert. Death of Napoleon
1822	Berlioz' first cantata, *The Arab and His Horse*	Beethoven's Piano Sonata Op. 111. Liszt's debut in Vienna. Birth of César Franck
1823	Berlioz a pupil of Lesueur. Publishes first essay on music	Diabelli asks 51 musicians (incl. Beethoven, Schubert and Liszt — aged 11) for variations on his waltz theme
1824	Berlioz' second musical article. B.S. degree. First return home	Beethoven's Quartet Op. 127. Stendhal's *Life of Rossini*. Death of Louis XVIII, Byron. Birth of Bruckner
1825	Berlioz' *Mass of 1825* finished and performed (July 10). Defense of Gluck and Weber against Castil-Blaze	Weber's *Freischütz* and *Euryanthe* produced in Paris. Schubert's *Songs from Walter Scott*. The Mendelssohns in Paris
1826	Berlioz seeks out Weber, in vain. Completes cantata "The Greek Revolution." Admitted to Conservatoire. Composing *Francs-Juges*	Beethoven Quartets Op. 131 and 135 and new finale to Op. 130 (last composition) Mendelssohn's Overture to *Midsummer Night's Dream*

1827	Berlioz' *Mort d'Orphée* and first sight of Harriet Smithson in Shakespeare. Discovers Goethe and Beethoven	Rossini's *Moïse* in Paris. Hugo's *Cromwell* (with Preface). Nerval's *Faust*. Delacroix's *Sardanapalus*. Death of Beethoven
1828	First Concert of his own works (May 26): *Waverley* and *Francs-Juges* Overtures, Second Prize in Rome contest. Composes *Roi de Thulé*	Establishment of Concerts du Conservatoire: Beethoven symphonies played for first time in Paris. Death of Schubert
1829	Berlioz' *Mort de Cléopâtre*, eight scenes from *Faust* and biography of Beethoven. Reads De Quincey, Hoffmann and Thomas Moore	Rossini's *William Tell*. Chopin's debut. First performance of Bach's *St. Matthew Passion* in Berlin. Birth of Gottschalk
1830	Berlioz' *Irish Melodies*, *Tempest* Fantasia, *Symphonie Fantastique*, and Rome Prize. Love affair with Camille Moke	Hugo's *Hernani*. Delacroix's "Liberty Leading the People." Gautier's first poems. Death of Hazlitt. Birth of H. von Bülow
1831 to 1832	Berlioz in Rome. Engagement to Camille broken. Revision of *Fantastique* and preparation of *Lélio*. Projects of a lifetime. Paris concert. Hector meets Harriet	Bellini's *Sonnambula* and *Norma*. Lamennais's break with the Church. Death of Scott, Cuvier, Goethe, Bentham. Birth of L. Damrosch, Joachim. Mendelssohn's *Hebrides* Overture. Donizetti's *Elisir d'Amore*
1833	*Rob Roy* Overture played. Concerts and benefits. Married to Harriet Smithson (Oct. 3)	Donizetti's *Lucrezia Borgia*. Birth of Brahms. Death of Hérold
1834	Berlioz' *Harold in Italy*. Sketches libretto of *Benvenuto*. *Gazette Musicale* founded. Louis Berlioz born (Aug. 14)	Schumann's Symphonic *Etudes*. Delacroix's "Algerian Women." Balzac's *Père Goriot*. Death of Choron, Boieldieu. Birth of Borodin
1835 to	Berlioz takes up career of conductor (December). Aids Louise Bertin put on her opera	Donizetti's *Lucia*, Vigny's *Chatterton*. Birth of Moussorgsky, Saint-Saëns, Cui. Meyerbeer's *Les Huguenots*
1837	Berlioz' *Requiem*. Full reconciliation with family at La Côte. Encyclopedia article on Music	Wagner's *Liebesverbot*. Schumann's *David*. Birth of Balakirev. Death of Lesueur, Leopardi, Pushkin
1838	Completion of *Benvenuto Cellini*, *première* and fall of opera. Death of Berlioz' mother. Gift of Paganini. D'Ortigue's book on Berlioz' dramatic music	Schumann's *Kinderscenen* and *Kreisleriana*. Jenny Lind's debut. Birth of Bizet, Bruch, Edouard Colonne, La Mara

1839   *Romeo and Juliet* Symphony. Death of Prosper. Berlioz receives Legion of Honor. Wagner in Paris

Donizetti's *Favorita*. Turner's "Fighting Temeraire." Invention of photography. Death of Nourrit. Stendhal's *Charterhouse of Parma*

1840   *Funeral and Triumphal* Symphony. Biography of Paganini

Schumann's *Frauenliebe und Leben*. Birth of Tchaikovsky, Zola. Death of Paganini

1841 to 1843   Berlioz' adaptation of *Freischütz*. Publication of *Nuits d'Eté*. Affair with Marie Recio. Musical mission in Germany

Schumann's First Symphony. Birth of Chabrier. Death of Cherubini. Mendelssohn's Scotch Symphony. Hugo's *Les Burgraves*

1844 to   *Roman Carnival* Overture. *Treatise on Modern Instrumentation and Orchestration*. *Euphonia; Voyage Musical*. Friendly separation from Harriet. Visit from and concerts with Glinka

Schumann's *Faust* (Epilogue). Verdi's *Ernani*. Birth of Nietzsche, Verlaine. Dumas's *Count of Monte Cristo*. Death of Dalton, Thorwaldsen. Birth of Rimsky-Korsakov

1846   Trip to Austria, Hungary, and Bohemia. *Damnation of Faust* (in Paris). *Requiem* (second time in Paris) to commemorate Gluck

Wagner's *Tannhäuser* (1st version). Rossini's *Robert Bruce*. Mendelssohn's *Elijah*. Meyerbeer's *Le Prophète* (ms). Saint-Saëns's debut, aged 10

1847 to 1848   Berlioz' first trip to Russia sees *Hamlet* in Riga and composes two "scenes." First trip to England. Begins *Memoirs*. Death of Dr. Berlioz

Flotow's *Martha*. Verdi's *Macbeth*. Marx and Engels's *Communist Manifesto*. Death of Mendelssohn. Birth of Duparc. Death of Chateaubriand, Bielinski. Wagner's *Lohengrin* (ms)

1849   *Te Deum*. Berlioz publishes Liszt's article on *Tannhäuser*. Founds Philharmonic Society

Liszt's *Prometheus*. Verdi's *Luisa Miller*. Death of Chopin, Habeneck, Nicolai

1850 to 1851   Berlioz begins *Enfance du Christ*. Death of Nanci. Biography of Spontini. Final version of *Corsair* Overture

Liszt's *Berg-symphonie*. Schumann's *Julius Caesar* Ov. Verdi's *Rigoletto*. Birth of Vincent d'Indy. Death of Balzac, Spontini, Turner, J. F. Cooper

1852   *Benvenuto* a success at Weimar, *Requiem* in Paris. Berlioz conducts Ninth in London. Publishes *Soirées*

Lenz's *Beethoven and His Three Styles*. Cornelius in Weimar. Schumann's *Requiem*. Death of Gogol, Wellington, Thomas Moore

1853   Third trip to London. *Benvenuto's* second fall. Trip to Germany. Success of *Fuite en Egypte* in Paris. Suit about *Freischütz*

Schumann's *Faust* Overture. Verdi's *Traviata*. Steinway begins manufacture of pianos. Death of Onslow

1854 Completion of *Infant Christ.* Death of Harriet. Trip to Germany. Marriage with Marie Recio. Ms. *Memoirs* continued. *Emperor* cantata

Meyerbeer's *Stella del Nord.* Dickens's *Hard Times.* Delacroix's "Lion Hunt." Liszt's *Orpheus.* Death of Lamennais. Birth of Rimbaud

1855 Visit to Liszt at Weimar. *Les Troyens* begun. *Te Deum* at St. Eustache. Trip to London, cordial meeting with Wagner. *The Art of Conducting*

Verdi's *Sicilian Vespers.* Manns musical director at Crystal Palace. Birth of Chausson. Death of Kierkegaard, Rude, Nerval

1856 Trip to Germany: success of *Benvenuto* and *Damnation of Faust.* Orchestration of Songs. *Les Troyens* under way. First Baden concert

Liszt's *Tasso* and *Dante.* Rubinstein's debut. Birth of G. B. Shaw. Death of Schumann, Heine, Ad. Adam

1857 Berlioz' illness diagnosed, henceforth severe. Concert with Th. Ritter. Poem of *Troyens* finished, read in public; music four-fifths done

Liszt's *Heroïde Funèbre* and *Bergsymph.* (rev.) Verdi's *Simone Boccanegra.* Bizet wins Rome Prize. Birth of Bruneau; death of Musset

1858 *Les Troyens* completed. Visit from Wagner. P.S. added to *Memoirs. Romeo* at Baden. Illness increasing

Cornelius's *Barber of Bagdad.* Gounod's *Médecin malgré lui.* Offenbach's *Orpheus in Hell.* Death of Rachel

1859 *Grotesques de la Musique. Les Troyens* sung (with piano) at private hearing. Directs *Orpheus* and inspires editing of Gluck

Wagner's *Tristan* (ms). Gounod's *Faust.* Meyerbeer's *Dinorah.* Darwin's *Origin of Species.* Death of Spohr, A. v. Humboldt, De Quincey

1860 Berlioz' article on Wagner. Death of Adèle. Orchestration of *Erlkönig. Beatrice and Benedict* begun

Wagner's concerts and propaganda. Autographed copy of *Tristan* to Berlioz. Revival of *Fidelio.* Offenbach's *Barkouf.* Birth of Fanelli, Mahler, H. Wolf

1861 Second private hearing of *Troyens.* Berlioz directs revival of *Alceste*

Tannhäuser riot in Paris. Liszt's *Faust* Symphony, dedicated to Berlioz. Death of Lipinski

1862 *Beatrice and Benedict* completed. Death of Berlioz' second wife. Publication of *A Travers Chants.* Praise of *Salammbô*

Verdi's *Forza del Destino.* Beethoven hissed in Paris Conservatoire. Birth of Debussy. Death of Halévy

1863 Trip to Weimar. Celebration in Berlioz' honor at Loewenberg. *Enfance* and Speeches at Strasbourg. *Les Troyens* cut and performed in Paris

Bizet's *Pearl-Fishers.* Birth of Felix Weingartner. Death of Vigny, Delacroix, Vernet, Hebbel, Thackeray

1864 Resigns from *Débats*. Visit to Estelle. Visit from Liszt. *Memoirs* sent to printer

Offenbach's *La Belle Hélène*. Death of Meyerbeer, Hawthorne, Walter Savage Landor

1865 Trip to Geneva to see Estelle and stay with nieces in Dauphiné. Proofreading and dating of *Memoirs*

Verdi's *Macbeth* (revised). *Tristan* first performed. Paul Dukas born. Liszt takes orders in Rome

1866 Directs revival of *Armide* (with Saint-Saëns) and *Alceste*. Readings of Shakespeare. *Damnation of Faust* in Vienna

Erik Satie born. Death of d'Ortigue. Thomas's *Mignon* a great success

1867 Death of Louis (June 5). Second trip to Russia (St. Petersburg and Moscow) *Requiem*, rev. ed.

Strauss's *Blue Danube* waltz. Charles Koechlin born. Death of Ingres

1868 Trip to Monaco and Nice, fall on the rocks. Illness. Last visit to Institute for Charles Blanc (Nov. 25)

Wagner's *Meistersinger*. Boïto's *Mefistofele*. Death of Ferrand, Léon Kreutzer, Rossini. Baudelaire's *L'art romantique*

1869 March 8: Berlioz dies. March 11: Funeral

Flaubert's *Education Sentimentale*. Death of Sainte-Beuve, Lamartine

Bibliography

> You have read 1500 books in order to write *one*. It does you no good — as long as you write well, you are not a serious scholar and your friends treat you like a schoolboy.
> — FLAUBERT in the last months of his life

For convenience, the bibliography has been subdivided into the categories below. It may thus serve as a guide to the Berlioz literature in addition to indicating the authorities used in this book. Critical or explanatory remarks have been added after titles wherever it seemed advisable.

1. *Berlioz' Works*
   - A. Music Printed and Manuscript
   - B. Librettos and Dramatic Poems
   - C. Prose Writings (1) Books and Articles
     - (2) Prefaces and Notes to Scores
   - D. Letters (1) Collected (2) In Books or Periodicals
     - (3) Autographs (4) Facsimiles
2. *Other Primary Sources, Printed and Manuscript*
   - A. Private Collections
   - B. Letters and Contemporary Works
   - C. Handbills, Programs, and Other Fugitives
   - D. Iconography: Paintings, Lithographs, Busts, and Photographs of
     - (1) Berlioz (2) Associated Persons and Places
3. *Biographies of Berlioz*
   - A. Books
   - B. Essays
4. *Criticism of Berlioz and His Works*
   - A. General Estimates
   - B. Particular Works
5. *Histories of Music*
   - A. General Works
   - B. Special Studies
   - C. Memoirs and Lives
6. *Works on Esthetics and Other Arts than Music*
7. *Biographies and Works on Political and Social History*
8. *Works of Literature*
9. *Works of Reference and Periodicals*
10. *Gramophone Records*

NOTE ON ABBREVIATIONS:

P = Paris; L = London; B = Berlin; N. Y. = New York. *Min. Sc.* = Miniature Score: consult Sec. 1A for editions used in the text. Similarly, other abbreviations, such as *A.R.*, *Corresp.*, and so on, will be found in place of numbers opposite the work intended. See below, Sections 1C and 1D.

1. *BERLIOZ' WORKS*

A — MUSIC PRINTED AND MANUSCRIPT

A complete list of Berlioz' published scores, original and transcribed, would fill a volume and require years of bibliographical work. The items below represent all the works extant in various forms that either are of special interest or have been referred to in the text.

[As this book goes to press, the publication of a true bibliography is announced in England. Its author, Mr. Cecil Hopkinson, has been collecting Berlioziana for fifteen years, and his work, scheduled to appear within the same fortnight as this biography, clearly deserves to head the present imperfect list. Would that it had preceded it in time as well as space!]

A Bibliography of the Musical and Literary Works of Hector Berlioz, by Cecil Hopkinson, Edinburgh Bibliographical Society, 1950.

Bibl. Conserv. Bibliothèque du Conservatoire

Owns all the autograph scores except the *Te Deum* (in Leningrad), *L'Enfance du Christ* (Bibl. Nat.) and the fragments *12, 21,* and *22.*

Also the originals of many letters and other documents, as well as the famous guitar bearing the signatures of Paganini and Berlioz. [Photograph in *Musique,* 1928, No. 4, p. 159.]

Bibl. Nat. Bibliothèque Nationale

Owns, in addition to *L'Enfance du Christ* and the autographs listed in *12, 21* and *22,* the printed scores, with annotations by Berlioz, of:

Huit Scènes de Faust; Symphonie Fantastique; Harold en Italie; Roméo et Juliette; Symphonie Funèbre; Damnation de Faust; Te Deum; L'Enfance du Christ; Tristia; L'Invitation à la Valse; Waverley, Francs-Juges, and *Roi Lear* overtures; and three songs.

Bibl. Opera Bibliothèque de l'Opéra (Paris)

Owns miscellaneous duplicates of scores above, portraits, playbills, etc.

Musée Musée Hector Berlioz, La Côte St. André (Isère)

Collection of notebooks, scores, portraits, passports, maps, musical instruments, etc. Some 130 items, including Berlioz' guitar and umbrella as well as annotated music and books, are listed in *259.*

1.   *Beatrice und Benedict, Oper in 2 Akten;* German tr. R. Pohl; Die Recitative von G. zu Putzlitz und Felix Mottl. Berlin (E. Bote und G. Bock) 1888

2.   *Benvenuto Cellini* [copy of score in Berlioz' hand, with notes taken by him, see *Musée*]

3.   *Benvenuto Cellini, Opera in 3 Acts* (piano score) P. (Choudens) AC 989 [*c.* 1865]

4.   *Benvenuto Cellini, Oper in Drei Akten von de Vailly und Barbier.* Deutsch von Peter Cornelius, Musik von Hector Berlioz; (piano score) Braunschweig, Henry Litolff (12173) n.d.

5.   *La Damnation de Faust,* P. (Richault) 1854

6.   ————; [adapted by Raoul Gunsbourg as an opera in 5 acts and 10 scenes] P. (Costallat) 1903 [Contains verses and stage directions added by adapter without notice]

7.   ————; Piano score with German text after Goethe. N. Y. (Schirmer) 1880

8.   *Erigone* [fragments of text and music, *c.* 1840] Ms. in Bibl. Conserv.

9.   *Huit Scènes de Faust.* P. (Schlesinger) 1829 [also represented in the Goetheana Collection of the Yale University Library]

10.   *Le Faust de Goethe,* tr. Emile Vedel, music by Berlioz, Schumann, Liszt, Gluck, and Florent Schmitt; produced at the Odéon, Paris, 1912–1913

11.   Berlioz-Liszt, *Episode de la Vie d'un Artiste, Grande Symphonie Fantastique; Partition de Piano par François Liszt.* 2nd ed. Leipzig (FECL 2893)
       [Does not follow Berlioz' last revisions of his orchestral score]

12.   *Lenor ou Les Francs-Juges,* Opera [Remains of Ms. score without the overture] Bibl. Nat. Rés. Vm² 177

13.   *Ouverture des Francs-Juges, Oeuv. 3. arrangée pour le Pianoforte à quatre mains par C. Czerny.* Brunswick (G. M. Meyer, Jr.) No. 431 n.d.

14.   *Grand Symphony for Band* (Funeral and Triumphal) Revised and edited by Richard Franko Goldman: III. Apotheosis. N. Y. (Mercury Music Corporation) 1947

15.   *Apothéose* [from the *Funeral and Triumphal* symphony] transcribed for voices and instruments by J. Tiersot. P. (Rouart Lerolle) 1923

16.   *L'apothéose, Chant héroïque extrait du final de la Symphonie funèbre et triomphale avec accomp. de piano.* L. (Cramer, Beale & Co.) 1848
       [The only extant copy is in the Boston Public Library, bound with other Berlioz scores, with interesting annotations by him]

17.   Thalberg, S., *Grand Caprice pour piano sur la marche de l'Apothéose de H. Berlioz.* P. (Schlesinger) Leipzig (Breitkopf und Härtel) 184?

18. [Weber, C. M.], *Le Freyschütz, Opéra en 3 actes . . . avec récitatifs de Hector Berlioz. Partition chant et piano.* P. (J. Thierry) 1873

19. Berlioz-Liszt, *Harold en Italie, Symphonie en Quatre Parties avec alto principal. Partition de Piano par F. Liszt.* P. (Brandus) 12533
    [Does not follow Berlioz' last revisions of his orchestral score]

20. *L'Incendie de Sardanapale, Fragment symphonique transcrit pour piano à quatre mains par Joseph Boulnois. Publications du Monde Musical.* P. *Supplément du 15 décembre 1907.* No. MM 197

21. *La Mort d'Orphée, Monologue et Bacchanale à grands choeurs et à grand orchestre.* Ms. Bibl. Nat. Facsimile by Editions de la Réunion des Bibliothèques Nationales. P. 1930

22. *La Nonne Sanglante* [fragments] and *Sardanapale* [part of first draft] Bibl. Nationale

23. [*Nuits d'Eté*] *Die Sommernächte, ins Deutsche übertragen von P. Cornelius.* Winterthur (Rieter-Biedermann) 1856
    [No. 2 differs from both the French and the German scores; for details of this publication during Berlioz' lifetime, see *95*]

24. *Summer Nights.* English version by Francis Hueffer. L. (Novello) 1881

25. *Rêverie et Caprice.* P. (Richault) No. 6297R n.d.
    [Later reissues carry, on a new title page, the supposititious "program" which was written at Pasdeloup's instigation. See *308*, Nov. 5, 1905, *356*]

26. *Le Roi des Aulnes, Der Erlkönig; Ballade de Goethe. Musique par François Schubert, orchestrée par Hector Berlioz.* P. (Legouix) No. O.L.G. 450

27. *Roméo et Juliette* (piano score) Winterthur (Rieter-Biedermann) 1857
    [Transcription by Theodore Ritter; copy with Berlioz' autograph inscription to him — in the possession of Jacques Barzun]

28. *Romeo and Juliet,* Dramatic Symphony composed from the Tragedy of Shakespeare; [tr. by J. H. Cornell] is the property of Theodore Thomas, published by John Church for the Cincinnati Music Festival Association, 1878
    [A very fair translation, with the minimum of poeticizing; should be used instead of the English in the German edition]

29. *33 Mélodies pour chant et piano.* P. (Richault) [*post 1863*] 1887 No. 13,682R

30. *Les Troyens; Partition Chant et Piano.* P. (Choudens) A.C. 987, 1863, 2 vols.
    [Contains Berlioz' printed notes and is the only genuine piano score]

31. *Les Troyens à Carthage,* arranged as a dramatic cantata by H. E. Krehbiehl for performance in English. N. Y., Feb. 26, 1887

[A poor patchwork but has a useful essay by the arranger on the history of the work]

Ger. ed.   *Werke, herausgegeben von Charles Malherbe und Felix Weingartner.* Leipzig (Breitkopf und Härtel) 1900–1907, 20 vols.

[See Supplement 5]

Min. Sc.   *La Damnation de Faust.* P. (Costallat) [No plate no.]

Min. Sc.   *L'Enfance du Christ.* P. (Costallat) 11277

Min. Sc.   *Harold en Italie,* Pref. A. Smolian, Ernst Eulenburg (23) Leipzig 1899 (3623)

Min. Sc.   *Sieben Ouvertüren von Hector Berlioz; Waverley* (17) *Francs-Juges* (18) *Roi Lear* (19) *Carnaval Romain* (20) *Le Corsaire* (21) *Benvenuto Cellini* (22) *Beatrice et Benedict* (23) Pref. A. Smolian, Ernst Eulenburg, Leipzig 1899 (Nos. 3717 to 3723)

Min. Sc.   *Roméo et Juliette,* Pref. A. Smolian, Ernst Eulenburg (24) Leipzig 1900 (3624)

Min. Sc.   *Symphonie Fantastique,* Pref. A. Smolian, Ernst Eulenburg (22) Leipzig 1899 (3622)

IB — LIBRETTOS AND DRAMATIC POEMS

32.   *Lenor, ou les Francs-Juges* [in collaboration with Ferrand] Ms. only, Bibl. Nat., but see *1196a* and *308,* July 1 and 15, Aug. 5 and 12, 1906

33.   *Lélio, ou le Retour à la Vie;* see *Ger. ed.,* vol. XIII; *308;* and *1278*

34.   *Benvenuto Cellini* [in collaboration with Vigny, Wailly, and Barbier]

Several versions, of which the original is entitled: *Benvenuto Cellini, Opéra en deux actes, Paroles de MM. Léon de Wailly et Auguste Barbier, Musique de M. Hector Berlioz . . . Paris, D. Jonas, éditeur, à l'Opéra . . . 1838, 32 pp.*

It bears the initial date of the opening (Sept. 3) one week ahead of the actual date.

The text as recast by Berlioz fourteen years later may be found in the full score at the Liszt archives in Weimar, but should be collated with still later revisions in Berlioz' own copy, now at the Birthplace Museum. See also *1190.* A German text by Peter Cornelius was published by Breitkopf und Härtel, Leipzig, v.d.

35.   *Roméo et Juliette* [in collaboration with Emile Deschamps] printed in its original form in Deschamps's translations from Shakespeare (see *1248*). Revised form in *Min. Sc.*

[For the second Prologue, see *308,* July 24, 1904 and *1385,* Feb. 28 and Mar. 7, 1909]

36.   *La Damnation de Faust* [in collaboration with Gérard de Nerval and Almire Gandonnière]

Final text in *Min. Sc., Ger. ed.,* as well as several vocal scores. The autograph bears a note in Berlioz' hand: "The words of Mephisto's recitative in Auerbach's Tavern, of the students' Latin song, of the recitative preceding the Minuet, of the Finale of Part 3, and of the whole of Part 4 and the Epilogue — except for Gretchen's romance — are by Mr. H. Berlioz."

37. *L'Enfance du Christ;* final text in *Min. Sc.*

38. *Les Troyens;* final text in Berlioz' own piano-vocal score in two parts, though division into three and five acts is a compromise with his true intention. This is to be found only in the full score, privately printed, and available only in the libraries of opera houses. The word-books issued by Michel Lévy (1863) and Choudens and Calmann-Lévy (1891) represent gross distortions of the poem.

39. *Béatrice et Bénédict;* final text in *Ger. ed.*

1C — PROSE WRITINGS

(1) Books and Articles

40. Berlioz, Hector, *Grand traité d'instrumentation et d'orchestration;* P. (Schonenberger) S. 996, 1844

41. ————— *Le chef d'orchestre, théorie de son art;* P. (Schonenberger) 1856

42. ————— *The Orchestral Conductor, Theory of his Art;* N. Y. 1902

43. ————— "Monograph on Conducting — Republished by Request"; *Etude* (1927) pp. 825 ff. and 911 ff.
[Editor's note states that "owing to the rarity" of the *Treatise on Orchestration* this essay is "seldom seen today." P. 825]

Tr. ————— *Traité d'instrumentation et d'orchestration. Nouvelle édition suivie de "L'art du chef d'orchestre";* Henry Lemoine No. 14518 (S. 996) n.p. n.d.
[A reprint from the original plates of the first revised edition. The references in the present book are to this edition]

44. ————— *Die moderne Instrumentation und Orchestration;* tr. J. C. Grünbaum, Berlin n.d.
[An earlier German version of Berlioz' *Articles* on Instrumentation had been given by J. A. Leibrock: *Die Kunst der Instrumentirung,* Leipzig, 1843, 112 pp.]

45. ————— *A Treatise upon Modern Instrumentation and Orchestration;* tr. Mary Cowden Clarke, L. 1856
[Other editions 1858 . . . down to the present, which retain some of the errors of the original translation: see *127* and *154*]

46. ————— *A Treatise on Modern Instrumentation and Orchestration, to which is appended "The Chef d'Orchestre";* tr. Mary Cowden Clarke, new ed. revised and ed. Joseph Bennett, L. and N. Y. (Novello) (Theoretical Series No. 7) n.d.

47. ————— *Gran tratado de instrumentación y orquestación de M. E. Berlioz . . . para uso de los compositores españoles;* por Oscar Campo y Soler; Madrid 1860

48. —— *Instrumentationslehre. Ein vollständiges Lehrbuch zur Erlangung, nebst einer Anleitung zur Behandlung und Direction des Orchesters;* autorisiete deutsche Ausgabe von Alfred Dörffel, Leipzig 1864
[Contains special preface by Berlioz, in German]

49. —— *An Abridged Treatise on Modern Instrumentation and Orchestration;* tr. and ed. Johann Bernhard (?), N. Y. 1888, reissued 194?

50. —— *Grosse Instrumentationslehre, mit Anhang: "Der Dirigent";* ed. Felix Weingartner, Leipzig 1904

51. —— *Instrumentationslehre;* ed. Richard Strauss, Leipzig 1905, 2 vols.
[Tr. into French by M. Closson, P. Fischbacher, n.d.]
[Tr. into English by Theodore Front, N. Y. (Edwin Kalmus) 1948]

52. —— *Grande trattato di instrumentazione e d'orchestrazione moderne di Ettore Berlioz con appendice di Ettore Panizza;* Milan (Ricordi) 1912, 3 vols.

Soirées *Les soirées de l'orchestre;* P. 1852, and many times since. Refs. are to 1927 printing (by *Soirée*) and (by page) to:

Eves. *Evenings in the Orchestra;* tr. Charles E. Roche, introd. Ernest Newman, N. Y. 1929
[Many mistranslations; the Newman Introduction on Berlioz as critic marred by misplaced skepticism]

Grot. *Les grotesques de la musique;* P. 1859 (Later ed. reprinted P. 1927)
[Original edition includes advertising pages which carry forward the Catalogue of works (*251*) to Oeuvre XXVI — *L'Impériale;* add *Les Troyens* without numbering; and mention 2 vols. of unpublished Memoirs among the Writings]
"Curiosities of Music" extracts from *Les grotesques de la musique,* tr. Francis Harling-Comyns (*Musical Times,* 1937, pp. 599–601, 693–5, 791–4). Other extracts: "Musical Freaks" (*Monthly Musical Record,* 1941, pp. 108–9 and 124–7)

A Trav. *A travers chants: études musicales, adorations, boutades, et critiques;* P. 1862
[Critical essays] tr. Edwin Evans, Sr.:
1. *Beethoven's Nine Symphonies;* N. Y. 1913
2. *Gluck and his Operas;* N. Y. 1915
3. *Mozart, Weber and Wagner, with various essays on musical subjects;* L. 1918

53. "Voyage musical en Italie" and "Académie de France à Rome"; *L'Italie pittoresque,* May 22, 1835 and ff.
[The first draft of the "Italian Journey" chapters in the later Memoirs]

V.M. *Voyage musical en Allemagne et en Italie, Etudes sur Beethoven, Gluck, et Weber. Mélanges et nouvelles;* P. 1844, 2 vols.
German tr. J. C. Lobe, Leipzig, n.d., 2 vols.

54. *Musikalische Wanderung durch Deutschland;* tr. Aug. Gathy, Hamburg 1844 [A brief extract]

55. Notes written for d'Ortigue to use in his biographical sketch of the composer, published in *Revue de Paris,* Dec. 1832. Bibl. Conservatoire

56. Reprinted with comments by Charles Malherbe, *Rivista Musica Italiana,* 1906, pp. 506–21

57. Comments by A. Pougin on the above, *Ménestrel,* Sept. 21, 1906 [misleading as to contents of Berlioz *Notes*]

58. Correction by Julien Tiersot printed in *Musical Times,* Nov. 1, 1906

59. Autobiographic note written for use in the Russian press, 1847; printed in *345,* pp. 192–4

60. Notes on biographic article in a "Who's Who" of 1858; in "Un document berliozien"; *Revue Musicale de Lyon,* 1911, pp. 612–6

61. *Mémoires de Hector Berlioz;* P. 1870
[The first edition in one volume, from the type set up during his lifetime; tr. R. Pohl, Leipzig 1865, 2 vols.]

Mem. ―――― 2nd ed., 2 vols. P. 1878 and many times since.
[See also the extracts: *Souvenirs de Voyage,* ed. J. G. Prodhomme, P. 1932]

62. *Memoirs;* tr. Rachel and Eleanor Holmes. Ernest Newman ed., N. Y. 1932
[Reprinted by Tudor Publishing Co., 1948; the full text, in fairly good English, but requiring further editing]

63. *The Life of Hector Berlioz as Written by Himself in his Letters and Memoirs;* ed. Katharine F. Boult, Everyman's Library No. 602, L. 1912, reprinted 1923
[A florid and sometimes inaccurate translation, redeemed by a perceptive Introduction]

64. *Memorie;* tr. Mario Giordano, Rome 1945

M.M. *Les musiciens et la musique;* P. n.d. [1903] Pref. by André Hallays [on Berlioz as critic]
[The volume, originally advertised in 1872, contains fragments of Berlioz' articles in the *Débats* (1835–63)]

64a. *Beethoven;* ed. J. G. Prodhomme, P. 1941
[Articles by Berlioz, repr. with introd. and notes by the editor]

65. *Gesammelte Schriften;* ed. R. Pohl [Authorized German edition] Leipzig, 1864, 4 vols.
4 vols. in 1, 1877

66. *Literarische Werke;* Leipzig 1903–4, 10 vols. in 5
[Neither this nor preceding tr. is complete or correct]

67. *The Critical Composer: the musical writings of Berlioz, Wagner, Schumann, Tchaikovsky, and others;* ed. Irving Kolodin, N. Y. 1940

68. *Michael Glinka;* Milan, 1874
[A reprint of the article of 1845 in *M.M.*]

69.   *"Instruments de Musique," Exposition Universelle de 1851,* P. 1855, vol. III, Part 2, pp. 1–8
            [Report by Berlioz for the Tenth Jury, Sec. 1]

70.   Autograph: "Chants avec accompagnement de piano de M. Meyer-Beer" British Museum Add. Ms. 33,965 fol. 232–6
            [Wrongly attributed to Liszt]

71.   Autograph: Note on the Organization of the Imperial Chapel; Bibl. Conservatoire
            [Memorandum for Napoleon III, whom it probably never reached]

Bibl. Grenoble   Autograph fragments, portraits, letters, and association items; Library of The City of Grenoble

72.   Draft of toast spoken by Berlioz in Strasbourg, June 22, 1863; Bibl. Conservatoire; printed in *Monde Musical,* Mar. 1919

IC (2) — PREFACES AND NOTES TO SCORES

73.   *Symphonie Fantastique: Programme* (5 versions) see *308*

74.   *Freischütz:* Preface [prob. in collaboration with Pacini] see *308* and *18*

Min. Sc.   *Roméo et Juliette:* Preface to second edition (1857); see *Min. Sc.*

Min. Sc.   *Damnation de Faust:* Preface; see *Min. Sc.*

Bibl. Conserv.   *Te Deum:* Autograph Note of 1855; see *308*

75.   *Les Troyens:* Foreword and extended notes on performance; Berlioz' own piano-vocal score, *30*
            [Reprod. in part in *479* and *385*]

76.   Special Preface to *Treatise* in German translation of 1864; see *48*

ID — LETTERS

(*1*) *Collected*

The originals of many letters listed below are in the Bibl. Conservatoire, Grenoble or the Museum in Berlioz' birthplace; but many others are in private collections, the archives of public bodies, or the hands of dealers in autographs. The catalogues of these firms suggest that many items are still unsorted and unknown, so that the following list is only a first approximation, designed to shorten the labors of future editors.

Corresp.   *Correspondance Inédite* (1819–1868); ed. Daniel Bernard, P. 1879
            [With a biographical sketch by the editor. Text full of errors and suppressions, see *85*]

L.I.   *Lettres Intimes;* Pref. Charles Gounod, P. 1882
            Life and Letters; tr. H. M. Dunstan, L. 1882 2 vols. [Vol. 1 gives the *Correspondance Inédite,* vol. 2 the *Lettres Intimes*]
            Letters; selected and tr. W. F. Apthorp, see *317*
            Letters 1819–1855; ed. Julien Tiersot in 3 vols. P. 1904–30:

A.R.   *Les Années Romantiques* (1819–1842)

| M.E. | *Le Musicien Errant* (1842–1852) |
| M.C. | *Au Milieu du Chemin* (1852–1855) |

[Invaluable but incomplete and uncompleted; see:

77. "Errata to the printed letters"; J. G. P[rodhomme], *Zeitschrift der Internationalen Musikgesellschaft*, 1907, p. 433]

S.W. *Briefe an die Fürstin Carolyne Sayn-Wittgenstein;* ed. La Mara, Leipzig 1903
Letters to Liszt; see *207*

78. *Lettres Inédites de Hector Berlioz à Thomas Gounet;* ed. L. Michoud, Grenoble, 1903

Est. *Une Page d'Amour Romantique. Lettres à Mme. Estelle F.;* Editions de la Revue Bleue, P. 1903

ID (2) — LETTERS IN BOOKS OR PERIODICALS

79. "Nouvelles Lettres d'Hector Berlioz"; ed. J. G. Prodhomme, *Rivista Musicale Italiana*, XII, No. 2, 1905
[Chiefly 1830–1848; some have been reprinted in various collections]

80. "Lettres de musiciens, etc. . . . à Berlioz ou sur Berlioz"; ed. J. Tiersot, *Rivista Musicale Italiana*, XXXVII, No. 1, 1930
[An important adjunct to Berlioz' own letters; reproduced in *235*]

81. "Unpublished Berlioziana"; ed. J. G. Prodhomme, *Musical Quarterly*, 1919, pp. 398 ff.
[Two letters to Berlioz' uncle Victor: (1825 and 1826 but misdated by editor) relating to difficulties with his family about becoming a musician]

82. Letters and notes to Alfred de Vigny from 1833 to 1854: see *339*

83. Letters of Berlioz and J. W. Davison; *Guide Musical*, Feb. 16 and 23, Mar. 2, 1913; Postscript to the series, Mar. 16, 1913
[See also *94*]

84. Letters relating to the Librarianship of the Conservatoire; *Guide Musical*, Dec. 14 and 21, 1913

85. Letters to Auguste Morel; *Guide Musical*, Oct. 27, Nov. 3, 10, 17, 24, and Dec. 1, 1912
[These give the original text cut or bowdlerized in *Corresp.*]

86. Letters to Scribe, Horace Vernet, Léon Pillet, Jules Janin, Lipinski, Desmarest, d'Ortigue and others; *Revue Bleue*, May and Oct. 1912

87. Further Letters to Auguste Morel
[See *86* and *94*]

88. Letters to Sainton and others, from London in 1853; reproduced in English, *Daily Telegraph*, Aug. 10, 1935
[Three letters in English tr., not otherwise available in full. See *115*]

89. Letters to George Hainl; *Revue d'Auvergne*, 1918, pp. 1–11

90. Letters to Edouard Monnais; *Revue Musicale*, Apr. 1, 1923

91. "Lettres de Berlioz sur *Les Troyens*"; *Revue de Paris*, 1921, pp. 449–73, 749–70, 146–71

[By no means complete for this period. Missing parts and missing letters can be found in *502*]

92. Letter to the government, on his project of a *fête funèbre; Guide Musical*, Aug. 4 and 11, 1912

93. Twenty Letters to Adolphe Samuel (1853–1866); *Ménestrel*, Jun. 8, 15, 22, 29, and Jul. 6 and 13, 1879. One Letter to Heinrich Ernst; *ibid.* Jul. 13, 1879

94. Nine Letters to his sister, Davison, Griepenkerl, and A. Samuel on his activities in 1852–1854; *Monde Musical*, Mar. 1930, pp. 93–5
[Tr. Gerta Brücher, *Die Musik*, Jun. 1930]

95. Eighteen Letters of Berlioz to his publisher (Rieter-Biedermann) in Winterthur (1856–1859); *Schweizerisches Jahrbuch für Musikwissenschaft*, 2, 1927, pp. 90–106

96. Three Letters (1854 and 1864–1867) from the collection of Marc Pincherle
[See *226*]

97. Four Letters to Daussoigne-Méhul (1854–1855); ed. Sylvain Dupuis: *Académie des Sciences de Belgique, Bulletin de la Classe des Beaux Arts*, No. 1–2, 1927, pp. 10–17
[Show how Berlioz prepared a concert in outlying centers]

98. Letter to Prince V. P. Odojewsky; undated but clearly written a few days before March 14, 1847; *Music* (Chicago) Sept. 1899, pp. 479–81
[Deals with advance publicity for Berlioz' concerts and the *Damnation* in particular]

99. Letter to Stassov; Sept. 10, 1862 in *345* p. 231
[Acknowledging the attentions paid by the young Russians and offering the Ms. of the *Te Deum* to comply with their request]

100. Letters to Basil Kologrivov; Oct. 10, 1867, *ibid.* (pp. 236–7), Oct. 22, 1867 (pp. 241–2), Nov. 12, 1867 (p. 242)

101. Letter to César Cui; Aug. 7, 1867 (p. 247)

102. Letter to the Russian Music Society (pp. 248–9)

103. Letter to Grand Duke Karl Alexander of Weimar (May 12, 1864); Eng. tr. in *Monthly Musical Record*, May 1939, pp. 108–10
[States his situation in Paris and thanks the duke for his intercession about *Les Troyens*]

104. Two Letters to Seghers (1831 and 1861?); *The Chesterian*, May 1924

105. Three Letters to Dessauer (1832 ff.); listed in catalogue of Gilhoffer and Rauschburg, Nov. 1933, items 183–5

106. Letters relating to first performance of *Requiem;* Oct.–Nov. 1837, *Guide Musical*, Jun. 11 and 18, 1911

107. Open Letter in *Revue du 19ème siècle;* Sept. 29, 1838
[Exonerates singers from blame in ill-success of *Benvenuto Cellini*]

108. Letter of Jan. 1843, no correspondent named; listed in Parke-Bernet catalogue, Apr. 4, 1939, item 37

109.   Letter to the Préfet de la Seine (Aug. 1845) complaining of double taxation as result of change of address; *Comoedia*, May 3, 1913

110.   Letter to Ambros dated Pesth, Feb. 16 [1846]. See *572*, p. 219
[In German, reprinted from *Der Spiegel*, No. 17, the original not having been found. English version in footnote, *ibid.*]

110a.   Extract: To Belloni dated London Dec. 19, 1847 about altering *Faust* for the stage; in Stargardt (Berlin) catalogue No. 2, July 1936

111.   "Letters of Mr. Hector Berlioz" [on the London Exhibition of 1851] see *1194*, pp. 594–623

112.   Open Letter to J. C. Lobe on the state of music (Leipzig, Nov. 28, 1853); first published in French and German in *534*, V, 296–300; original ms. printed in *Ménestrel*, Feb. 22, 1885 and reprinted in *M.C.*, 130 ff.
[With Lobe's first initial incorrect, and *douce* for *longue* three lines from bottom of p. 133]

113.   Letter to Th. Ritter from London, June 1855; *Le Temps*, Dec. 20, 1894
[About his visits with Wagner]

114.   Two Letters to Richard Wagner; Sept. 10, 1855 (*Musikalisches Wochenblatt*, Nov. 26, 1903) and May 23, 1860 (*Bayreuther Blätter*, 1905), pp. 279–80 and 285–6; the former reprinted in *Corresp.*, 225; the latter in *298*, pp. 321–2

115.   Three Letters in English translation not otherwise available in full. *Monthly Musical Record*, May 1, 1885

116.   Letter to his London publishers; Jan. 30, 1856
[Extract in M. Bridel (Lausanne) catalogue No. 20, Oct. 1948, item 82]

117.   Letter to G. A. Osborne; Feb. 23, 1859, about a projected performance of the *Fantastique* in London
[See *224*, p. 104; original in full in *79*, 370–1]

118.   Letter to Pauline Viardot; Jan. 25, 1860, about work on *Troyens* and Wagner concerts, *Guide Musical*, Nov. 29, 1903
[Omitted from series in *91* where it belongs]

119.   Letter to Franz Erkel; dated Paris 1860, about the pirating of the Rákóczy March
[In *574*, p. 9 *n.*]

120.   Four small notes to Wagner, written during his Paris visit, Jan.–Feb. 1860; *Bayreuther Blätter*, 1905, pp. 284–5

121.   Letter (of 1861?) to one of the directors of the Orphéon; about the engraving of *Le Temple Universel*
[*308*, Jan. 28, 1906, p. 27]

122.   Letter to Reyer; May 31 [1861?]: about *Alceste*. Bibl. Grenoble. Published with wrong date in *Nouvelle Revue*, 1903, 23, p. 553

123.   Letter to Marmontel; Mar. 28, 1863, about Bizet's *Pêcheurs de Perles*, *Revue de Musicologie*, Nov. 1938
[Authenticated by Maurice Emmanuel, tr. in present book, Subch. 26]

124.   Letter to Edward Silas; Jan. 6, 1864, about the latter's oratorio *Joash, Musical Times,* Dec. 1938, pp. 893–5
     [With comments by Edward Lockspeiser]

125.   Letter to Mme. Fornier; July 1868, *Courrier Musical,* Dec. 15, 1933
     [Tr. in *Musical Times,* Feb. 1, 1934, pp. 130–1]

ID (3) — AUTOGRAPHS

126.   Autograph notes, various dates; New York Philharmonic Society and Boston Symphony Orchestra

127.   Thirty-six A.L.S. and one autograph program covering the years 1829–1863; Sibley Musical Library, University of Rochester

128.   A.L.S. to Charles Duveyrier; Rome, July 28, 1831, Drouot Catalog, May 9, 1934, p. 11
     [Expresses sympathy with Saint-Simonian reform of society]

129.   A.L.S. to Spontini; Rome, Mar. 29, 1832, Drouot Catalog, Apr. 27, 1934, p. 4
     [Refers to his broken engagement, the state of music in Italy, and plans to go to Berlin]

130.   Twenty A.L.S. (1835 to 1854) listed in Otto Haas Catalog No. 7; Karl Henrici Catalog No. 79, and Drouot Catalog of May 9, 1934

131.   Eleven A.L.S. to Mme. Lemoine (the publisher), Fétis, Leroy, and others about musical matters; in Pierre Bérès Catalogs, N. Y., 1948–49

132.   A.L.S. to Busset; Oct. 9, 1836, New York Public Library
     [Together with A.L.S. to Dietsch about stoppage of *Requiem,* printed in *A.R.* and original of note to Chopin, given *ibid.,* 262 with different wording]

133.   Three autograph notes in the collection of Jacques Barzun. C.1850
     [Added to *153*]

134.   Two autograph notes (1839 and 1861) in the collection of Professor Henry K. Dick, N. Y.

134a   Four A.L.S. (1836? to 1846) about Kastner, Weil, and other musical affairs; plus one *feuillet d'album;* in collection or catalogues of Carnegie Bookshop, N. Y., 1949

135.   A.L.S. to Louis Schlösser; Jan. 28, 1844, with postscript by Marie Recio, in the collection of Mr. Arnold Whitridge, N. Y.

135a   A.L.S. to Belloni, London, Dec. 19, 1847, about Liszt, Drury Lane, and reworking of *Damnation.* Extract in J. A. Stargardt Catalog No. 369, July 1936

136.   Letter signed (with others) as member of committee of Société Philharmonique de Paris, Feb. 20, 1850, Library of Congress

137.   A.L.S. [to Peter Cornelius?] dated Leipzig, Dec. 6, 1850, in Hermann Scholtz collection at Dresden
     [Facsimile available in New York Public Library]

138. Autograph copy of verses (*Nature immense*) from a German album (1853) in Goetheana of Yale University Library

139. A.L.S. to Roquemont; Hanover, April 1, 1854, Drouot Catalog, May 9, 1934, p. 11

140. Ten A.L.S. and one musical manuscript from the Gentili di Giuseppe Collection, deposited in the Houghton Library of Harvard University
[Chiefly from the period 1854–1863, though one letter – to Janin – dates from 1838 and is the acknowledgment of the journalist's article about Paganini's gift]

141. Two A.L.S. to Theodore Steinway; Aug. 28, 1856 and Sept 25, 1867, Steinway Collection, N. Y.
[Thanks for congratulations; comment on new pianos]

141a. A.L.S. to Edward Silas accepting the dedication of his oratorio [*Joash*], Mar. 3, 1860; in collection of Mr. Cecil Hopkinson

142. A.L.S. to Isidor Lotto; June 17, 1862, Library of Congress

143. A.L.S. to Escudier; Aug. 4 or 5, 1862, on flyleaf of copy of *Mémoires*, 1870, in Boston Public Library

143a. Three A.L.S. in the collection of Mr. Edwin Franko Goldman; the chief item dealing with the Russian tour of 1867.

ID (4) — FACSIMILES

144. Berlioz' first letter to music publishers, etc. See *178*

145. Letter to [Busset?] about Schlesinger's refusal to publish the addressee's comments on Fétis. See *821*
[If this refers to the controversy in *Gazette Musicale* it should be dated Oct. or Nov. 1836. The street address and the acknowledgment of a gift of wine support the hypothesis]

146. Two letters, to Richard Pohl (Aug. 17, 1859) and B. Cossmann (Nov. 1852?)
[In *286*; the first apropos of *Troyens*, the other about a Weimar concert]

147. Letter to the Leipzig Singakademie; Dec. 3, 1853, reproduced from its archives in *Neue Zeitschrift für Musik*, Dec. 9, 1903

148. Letter answering a request for autobiographical facts; in *Allgemeine Musikzeitung*, Dec. 11, 1903
[Contains a list of works each briefly described, the last of which dates the letter as *c*. Dec. 1855]

149. Letter to Toussaint Bennet [*c*. 1860] inviting him and his son [Theodore Ritter] to the Italian Opera. See *820*

150. Letter of Dec. 24, 1862, disclaiming credit for the Historical Concerts given by Fétis. *Neue Zeitschrift für Musik*, Dec. 9, 1903

151. Letter to B. Jullien; Apr. 20, 1867, *285, 349*
[On the pronunciation of Latin verse]

152. Letter to G. de Massougnes; Feb. 25, 1868
[Frontispiece of *290*]

2. OTHER PRIMARY SOURCES, PRINTED AND MANUSCRIPT

A — PRIVATE COLLECTIONS

153. Archives of the *Fondation Berlioz,* consisting of letters from composers and conductors, programs and reviews of performances, and other memorabilia of the period 1908–1914.
To this collection have been added:

154. T. S. Wotton, Correspondence with Jacques Barzun (1929–1938), and

155. Letters to Jacques Barzun by musicians (1929 to date)
[All three collections will be deposited in due course in the Library of Columbia University]

B — LETTERS AND CONTEMPORARY WORKS

156. Anon., "Er ist nicht mehr"; in *Didaskalia,* Frankfort a.M., May 9, 1844
[Signed X, but presumably by Franz Xaver Schnyder, this letter compares Berlioz to Napoleon invading Germany]

157. ———— "Les Troyens au Palais"; *Journal de Musique,* July 1, 1876
[Report of the suit regarding the score of *Les Troyens* between Berlioz' executors and the firm of Choudens]

158. ———— Letter from niece of Mme. Estelle Fornier regarding Berlioz' kindness in her old age (Unsigned by request); *Ménestrel,* Dec. 13, 1903

159. Adam, Juliette Lamber, *Mes premières armes littéraires et politiques;* P. 1904

160. Balakirev, Mili, Letter to Charles Malherbe; Jan. 1900, *Musical Times,* Apr. 1, 1930, p. 322
[About the German ed. of Berlioz' works]

161. Balakirev, Bülow, Liszt, Pohl, Stassov and others, Letters to Berlioz; *Revue Musicale,* May 1930

162. Balzac, H., *Letters to His Family;* ed. W. S. Hastings, Princeton 1934

163. ———— *Correspondance Inédite avec Mme Zulma Carraud;* ed. M. Bouteron, P. 1935

164. Barbier, Auguste, *Souvenirs Personnels et Silhouettes Contemporaines;* P. 1883

165. Beethoven, L. van, *Letters;* ed. A. C. Kalischer, tr. J. S. Shedlock, L. 1909, 2 vols.

166. Berlioz, Louis Victor Joseph, *Dissertation sur les phénomènes et les maladies que produit la première apparition des règles;* P. 1802
[Doctoral thesis of Berlioz' father]

167. Berlioz, Louis Victor Joseph, *Mémoire sur les maladies chroniques, les évacuations sanguines et l'acupuncture;* P. 1816

168. Beyle, H. [Stendhal], *Correspondance* (1808–1811); ed. Le Divan, P. 1933, vol. III (vol. 56 of *Oeuvres Complètes* 1927 ff.)

169. ———— *Mélanges Intimes et Marginalia; ibid.,* P. 1936, vol. II

170. Boutarel, Amédée, "Une lettre de Berlioz à Goethe"; *Ménestrel,* Feb. 15 and 22, 1902

171. Bülow, Hans von, *Briefe;* ed. Marie von Bülow, Leipzig 1899, 2 vols.

172. ———— *Letters to Richard Wagner, Cosima Wagner, Carl Bechstein* [and others]; ed. Du Moulin Eckart, tr. H. Waller, N. Y. 1931

173. Bülow, Hans von, *Early Correspondence;* ed. by his widow, tr. C. Bache, N. Y. 1896

174. —— *Hans von Bülows Leben dargestellt aus seinen Briefen;* ed. Marie von Bülow, 2nd ed. Leipzig 1921

175. Busoni, Ferrucio, *Letters to His Wife;* tr. Rosamond Ley, L. 1938

176. Chabrier, Emmanuel, *Lettres; Mercure Musical* (S.I.M.) Jan. and Feb. 1909
[See also *183*]

177. Chopin, Frédéric, *Letters*
[See *223*]

178. Comettant, Oscar, *Un Nid d'Autographes;* P. 1885

179. Cuvillier-Fleury, A. A., Letter about Berlioz' Concert in the Palais de l'Industrie (1844); in *1158*, I, 328-9

180. Davison, Henry, ed., *Music during the Victorian Era: From Mendelssohn to Wagner;* L. 1912
[Many Berlioz letters in translation and accounts of his musical activity in London; but confused in chronology and incomplete. See *83*]

181. Delacroix, Eugène, *Correspondance Générale d'Eugène Delacroix;* ed. A. Joubin, P. 1935-7, 5 vols.

182. —— *Journal,* ed. André Joubin, P. 1932, 3 vols.

183. Desaymard, J., "Les Lettres d'Emmanuel Chabrier"; *La Veillée d'Auvergne,* Apr. 1, 1909, 165-74

184. Diehl, A. M., "A Visit to Berlioz"; *The Musician,* Sept. 1909, p. 417

185. d'Ortigue, J., *Le Balcon de l'Opéra;* P. 1833
[Chapter on Berlioz' life and work to date]

186. —— Letter to Mme. Moet de Crèvecoeur; June 25, 1866, about Berlioz and reply to her by Mme. d'Agoult; *Ménestrel,* Dec. 20, 1903
[Concerns Paris Exposition of 1867 and Berlioz]

187. —— *De l'école musicale italienne et de l'administration de l'Académie royale de musique à l'occasion de l'opéra de M. H. Berlioz;* P. 1839
[Preface, in form of a letter to Léon Kreutzer is about *Cellini,* as is also Ch. 4. With a new Preface and minor changes, the book was reissued as *Du Théâtre Italien;* P. 1840. Same pagination]

188. Doudan, Ximenes, *Mélanges et Lettres;* 4 vols. P. 1876-1877

189. Escudier, Léon, *Mes Souvenirs;* P. 1863

190. Etex, Antoine, *Les Souvenirs d'un artiste;* P. 1877

191. Ferrand, Humbert, *Compte-rendu* [de] *Voyage en Sardaigne par le Comte Albert de la Mamora;* P. 1840

192. Flaubert, Gustave, *Correspondance* in *Oeuvres Complètes;* ed. Louis Conard, P. 1910, 6 vols.

192a. Fouque, O., *Michel Ivanovitch Glinka d'après ses Mémoires et sa Correspondance;* P. 1880

193. Fournier, A., and Rivière, J., *Correspondance;* P. 1926, 4 vols.
[Vol. I, pp. 199-204 on Rivière's opinion of Berlioz' *Damnation of Faust*]

194. Goethe, J. W. von, *Correspondence with Zelter;* ed. A. D. Coleridge, L. 1887

194a. Guizot, François, *Lettres à sa Famille,* ed. Mme. de Witt, 2nd ed. P. 1884

195. Hawkins, R. L., ed., *Newly Discovered French Letters;* Cambridge, Mass. 1933

196. Heller, Stephen, Open letter in reply to Hanslick's article of 1879 [*351*]; *Neue Freie Presse,* Jan. 1879; then *Guide Musical,* Feb.; *Gazette Musicale,* Mar. 2 and 9, 1879; again reprod. in *502*

197. Joachim, Joseph, *Letters* [from and to]; selected and tr. by Nora Bickley, Introd. J. A. Fuller-Maitland, L. 1914

198. Keats, John, *Letters;* ed. Maurice Buxton Forman, L. 1935

199. Keller, Gottfried, *Briefe* [in *Werke,* 10 vols.]; ed. Emil Ermatinger, Zürich 1943–1944

200. Lalo, Edouard, "Quelques Lettres Inédites"; ed. A. Jullien, *Revue Musicale* 1923, pp. 108–18

201. Lesueur, J.-F., Letter to Comte de Martignac in support of Berlioz' application for grant-in-aid; facsimile in *476, 355*
    [Reprinted *A.R.,* 52–3]

202. Liszt, Fr., *Correspondance de Liszt avec Mme d'Agoult* (1833–1840); ed. Daniel Ollivier, P. 1933

203. —— *Correspondance de Liszt et de Mme Ollivier* [his daughter Blandine]; ed. Daniel Ollivier, P. 1936

204. —— *Letters of;* ed. La Mara, tr. C. Bache, L. 1894, 2 vols.
    [See also *239*]

205. —— Letter to F. Denis (Sept. [?] 1838) about Berlioz' *Benvenuto Cellini;* Otto Haas Catalogue, 1938
    [Reprinted in *298,* 168–9]

206. —— Letter to Edmond Hippeau (May 15, 1882) about Berlioz; *Rivista Musicale Italiana,* Oct.–Dec. 1932

207. —— Letters to ——; La Mara (Marie Lipsius) ed., *Briefe hervorragender Zeitgenossen an Franz Liszt;* Leipzig 1895–1904, 3 vols.

207a. —— *Briefe au die Fürstin Sayn-Wittgenstein,* ed. La Mara; Leipzig, 1899–1903, 4 vols.
    [The last four vols. of the *Briefe;* Leipzig, 1893–1902, 8 vols., which do not include:

208. —— *Briefwechsel zwischen Fr. Liszt und H. von Bülow;* ed. La Mara, Leipzig 1898, nor:

208a. Franz Liszt und Carl Alexander, Grossherzog von Sachsen; ed. La Mara, Leipzig, 1909
    [The previous four items contain a great many references to Berlioz]

209. —— "De la situation des artistes et de leur condition dans la société"; Ms. British Museum, Add. 33965 Fol. 237–242
    [Reprinted in *210*]

210. —— *Pages Romantiques;* ed. J. Chantavoine, P. 1912
    [A collection of Liszt's articles in French]

211. Mainzer, Joseph, *Chronique Musicale de Paris;* P. 1838·
    [An attack on *Benvenuto Cellini*]

212. Manns, August, Letter to C. A. Barry (Dec. 19, 1903) relating to Berlioz' *Le Temple Universel*
    [Copy found in papers of T. S. Wotton and added to *155*]

213. Maretzek, M., "Sharps and Flats"; *The American Musician,* Mar. 8, 1890
    [A contemporary's view of Berlioz in London (1847–1848) by his chorus-master. See also:

213a. Martezek, M., *Crotchets and Quavers, or Revelations of an Opera Manager in America;* N. Y. 1855
[Opening Chapter, addressed to Berlioz, harks back to London music in 1848]

214. Mendelssohn, Felix, *Letters;* ed. G. Selden-Goth, N. Y., 1945

215. —— *Reisebriefe;* ed. Paul Mendelssohn-Bartholdy, 4th ed., Leipzig 1862, 2 vols.

216. —— *Letters from Italy and Switzerland;* tr. Lady Wallace, L. 1862

217. —— *Letters to Ignaz and Charlotte Moscheles;* Boston 1888

218. Mérimée, Prosper, *Lettres à une Inconnue;* ed. H. Taine, P. 1874, 2 vols.

219. Mozart, W. A., *The Letters of Mozart and His Family;* ed. Emily Anderson, L. 1938, 3 vols.

220. Musorgsky Reader, The [Biographical Letters and Documents], ed. and tr. Jay Leyda and Sergei Bertenson, N. Y. 1947

221. Nietzsche, Elizabeth Förster-, *Das Leben Friedrich Nietzsches;* 2 vols. in 3, Leipzig 1895–1904

222. Olivier, Juste, MS. *Journal*
[Extract concerning Harriet Smithson communicated by Professor André Delattre of the University of Pennsylvania]

223. Opienski, Henryk, *Chopin's Letters;* tr. E. L. Voynich, N. Y. 1931

224. Osborne, George A., *Musical Coincidences and Reminiscences, Proceedings of the Musical Association;* April 2, 1883, pp. 95–113

225. Paganini, Nicolo, A.L.S. to Luigi Guglielmo Germi (Nice, Mar. 2, 1840); tr. into English, Maggi Bros. Catalogue (1906)51
[Recommends Berlioz as trustworthy friend and great artist]

226. Pincherle, Marc, *Musiciens peints par eux-mêmes; Lettres de Compositeurs écrites en Français* (1771–1910); P. 1939

227. Pougin, A., "Berlioz et l'Exposition Universelle de 1867"; *Ménestrel,* Dec. 20, 1903
[Includes letters by d'Ortigue and Mme. d'Agoult]

228. Quinet, Edgar, *Lettres d'Exil à Michelet et à divers amis;* P. 1885–1886, 4 vols.

229. *Rapport et Arretés pour l'établissement en France d'un diapason musical uniforme;* P. (Imprimerie Impériale) 1859
[Berlioz was of the committee which drafted this report, subsequently made into law]

229a. Sainte-Beuve, *Correspondance Générale,* ed. J. Bonnerot; P. 1935–47, 5 vols.

230. Savigné, E. J., *Hector Berlioz: Historique des comités dauphinois et parisien;* Vienne 1903

231. Schumann, Clara, and Brahms, Johannes, *Letters of,* 1853–1896; ed. Berthold Litzmann, N. Y. 1927, 2 vols.

232. Schumann, Robert, *The Life of Schumann in His Letters;* tr. May Herbert, L. 1890, 2 vols.

233. Smithson, Harriet, Letters. [See *235,* II, pp. 200–1; *A.R.,* 259; *M.E.,* 154–5]

234. —— "Unpublished Letters of Harriet Smithson"; ed. E. Lockspeiser, *Musical Times,* Dec. 1938, 893 ff.
[See also British Museum, Add. Ms. 33965 fol. 89 ff.]

235. Tiersot, J., *Lettres de musiciens écrites en français du 15ème au 20ème siècle;* Turin 1924–1936, 2 vols.
[Both volumes contain letters relevant to Berlioz]

236. Van Gogh, Vincent, *Lettres de Van Gogh à Emile Bernard;* ed. E. Bernard, P. 1911

237. Verdi, G., A.L.S. dated Milan [Jan.?] 12, 1847; British Museum, Add. Ms. 33965 fol. 399
     [Refers to Berlioz' views on opera]

238. Vernet, Joseph, Carle, and Horace, *Correspondance et Biographies;* ed. A. Durande, P. 1864

239. Wagner, R., *Briefwechsel zwischen Wagner und Liszt;* ed. Erich Kloss, 3rd ed. Leipzig 1910, 2 vols.
     [The English tr. by Franz Hueffer, L. 1888, 2 vols., is incomplete and somewhat bowdlerized]

240. —— A.L.S. (Jan. 21, 1860) accompanying his gift of the *Tristan* score to Berlioz; Bibl. Grenoble

241. —— *Gesammelte Schriften und Dichtungen;* 2nd ed. Leipzig (1887–1888) 10 vols.

242. —— *Oeuvres en Prose;* tr. J.-G. Prod'homme, F. Holl, Fr. Caillé, and L. van Vassenhove, P. 1908–1925, 13 vols.

243. *Prose Works;* tr. W. Ashton Ellis, L. 1902, 8 vols.

244. —— *Mein Leben;* Munich, 1911, 2 vols.

245. —— *My Life;* N. Y. 1911, reprinted (Tudor Publishers) 1936
     [Not a satisfactory translation]

246. —— *Ma Vie;* tr. R. Valentin and A. Schenk, P. 1912, 3 vols.
     [An accurate but awkward translation]

247. *Wagner: Musiciens, Poètes, et Philosophes;* ed. C. Benoit, P. 1887
     [The volume of selections from Wagner's writings which introduced Wagner the theorist to the French public]

248. Werfel, Franz, *Verdi through His Letters;* N. Y. 1942

2C — FUGITIVES

Berlioz has been the subject of numerous commendatory verses, including some by Saint-Saëns [see *394, 254, 256*]. The most recent as well as impressive set is

249. "Berlioz: an Ode" by E. H. W. Meyerstein (*Music Review*, Nov. 1943, pp. 214–5) which presents the composer as redeeming conquered France.
     Other fictional treatments are: Meré's 4-act play [*291*] the short story involving Scudo by G. de Massougnes [*466*]; an imaginary dialogue by Charles F. Kenyon [*423*] and

250. Feydeau, J. P. and Legrand, H. A., *Symphonie Fantastique:* An A. F. Films, Inc. release, N. Y. Dec. 1947
     [Musical fragments from Berlioz' works; incidents from his life turned upside down; chronology chaotic]

251. Prospectus: *Oeuvres Complètes de Hector Berlioz. 1852*
     [On pink paper, 2 pp., found in various libraries including the Bibliothèque Nationale, British Museum, and Boston Public Library; Reprinted in Berlioz' lifetime in *Soirées, Grotesques,* and *1382,* II, 190–2]

252. Playbill: Franz Lachner's *Benvenuto Cellini* "frei nach dem Französichen" München, Königl. Hof- und National Theater, Oct. 12, 1849

253. Program of the first performance of *Romeo and Juliet* Symphony, arranged in 7 parts and including Second Prologue
     [Reprinted in *308*, Dec. 13, 1903, p. 396]

254. *Festival Berlioz;* Grenoble, Dec. 29, 1890
    [Contains essays and commendatory verses]
255. Catalogue of the Berlioz Exhibition; Frankfort, 1901
256. Copy of a sonnet found on Berlioz' tomb in June 1896; *Ménestrel,* Sept. 13, 1903
257. Fondation Hector Berlioz; *Programme du 24 juin 1909; Statuts et Mission de l'oeuvre.* Paris and Grenoble, 1909
258. *Le Théâtre des Champs-Elysées: Le Monument, le Programme, l'Abonnement;* P. 1912
    [Descriptive catalogue of the new theater designed to help revive the French operatic school, beginning with Berlioz' *Cellini,* and to feature the Ballets-Russes]
259. Association des Amis de Berlioz; *Souvenirs de l'Inauguration de la Maison Natale de Berlioz;* La Côte St. André July 7, 1935
    [Lists memorabilia in each room]
260. Announcement of the publication of Wagner's Memoirs by the booksellers Röder und Schunke, Leipzig "middle of January 1911"

2D — ICONOGRAPHY

For this first survey of a scattered field, which his book will not cover, Mr. Cecil Hopkinson has kindly pooled his information with mine. The starred items are originals in his possession. The student should consult, in addition:

261. Rénier, F., "Les caricatures sur Berlioz et Wagner"; *Le Livre,* 1889, p. 98
262. Riat, G. "Berlioz dans l'art et la caricature"; *Monde Moderne,* vol. XVIII, pp. 671–80
263. *Richard Wagner en Caricatures;* ed. J. Grand-Carteret, P. 1891
264. *Steinway Collection, The* [Catalogue of] *Paintings by American Artists, together with Prose Portraits of the Great Composers by James Huneker;* N. Y. 1919
    See also: *394,* 113–21; *235,* II, 217–8; and *Guide Musical,* June 24–July 1, 1900 [For the history of the Daumier portrait]

NUMBERS IN BIBLIOGRAPHY RESUME ON P. 403

(1) *Portraits and Caricatures*

For ready reference, these abbreviations have been used:

Jull. = *285;* Kapp = *286;* Livre = *394;* Newman = *62;* Bosch. = *271*

*Anon., Pencil drawing: Berlioz seated playing the guitar
Formerly in Heyer Collection, Cologne
    [Listed in Henrici Catalogue, Sept. 12–13, 1927]
—— Lithograph: Berlioz standing with crossed arms and baton (*c.* 1838)
V.M., I, frontispiece; Bosch., 179
Manskopf Museum, Frankfort; *Neue Musik Zeitung,* Dec. 1903
    [See also Hüssener below]
—— Caricature: 1847
Livre; Kapp, 33
—— Photograph of painting by V. Baur: *c.* 1847
Bruckmann's Portrait Collection, B.
—— Woodcut: Head and shoulders, facing right, P. 1848
Bibl. Nat.

—— Photograph: Berlioz standing, *c.* 1850
Charles Picardy Collection, Grenoble
—— Oil: Berlioz standing, facing straight, P. *c.* 1855, Musée Masséna, Nice
[Apparently done from Pierson photograph, see below and *Musical Courier*, Sept. 16, 1903 p. 8]
—— Photograph: Head and shoulders, head turned, facing straight, P., *c.* 1856
Engraved by Dochy, Jull., 225; Kapp, 23
—— Photograph: Berlioz seated in armchair, hands in pocket, *Symp. Fant.* largo autograph beneath, dated Apr. 1865
Monde Musical, Nov. 30, 1903; *Neue Zeitschrift,* Dec. 9, 1903; Kapp; Newman (cut)
—— Photograph: Berlioz seated, clasped hands on back of chair, n.p., n.d.
Bosch., 293
—— Photograph: Berlioz seated, facing left, hands clasped in front of him, P., 1866
Kapp, 42
—— Photograph: White hair, medals on lapel (two poses, facing left and right) St. Petersburg, 1867
Jull., 305; Kapp, 43; Newman; Bosch., 424
—— Stamps of the Third French Republic: "For the Intellectual Unemployed"; 1936 (40c.: green; 55c.: purple)
Also: "Les Amis de Berlioz" [for the benefit of the Musée] sepia
Basset, Bronze statue: Grenoble, Aug. 1903
[Melted for bronze during German occupation, 1940 ff.]
Guide Musical, Aug. 23 and 30, 1903; Nov. 29, 1903; *Musica,* March 1908; Kapp, 45
Baugniet, Lithograph: L., 1851
Manskopf Museum, Frankfort; Jull., 209; *Musical Times,* July, 1903
Bernstamm, Marble bust: Monte Carlo, 1903
Supplement to *Musica,* May 1903; *Revue Musicale,* Aug. 15, 1903; Plaster replica at Menton Museum
Blatez, Bronze statue: Nice, 1948
Boulenaz, Etching: Head and shoulders, facing right, P. n.d.
Bibl. Nat.
Brunswick, Drawing (posthumous) Grenoble, 1890
Program of *Festival Berlioz,* Grenoble, Dec. 29, 1890
Carey, Etching: Berlioz in armchair, n.p., n.d.
Kapp, 40
Carjat, Lithograph caricature, full-length facing right: P., 1857
Le Diogène, Feb. 12, 1857; Jull., 232
—— Caricature with titles of works in background: P., 1863
Le Boulevard, 1863; Jull., 261; *Musica,* May 1903; Kapp; Bosch., 339
—— Engraving: Berlioz standing, 1862
Jull. 257; Kapp, 41
[From the Pierson photograph, *c.* 1855]
Carlier, Bust: P., 1885
Bibl. Opera; replica at birthplace; *Musica,* 1903, p. 320
Cham, Caricature: Berlioz conducting in all parts of the world at once by means of an electrical baton, P., 1855
Charivari, Dec. 2, 1855; Jull., 242

Cham, Caricature: "Tannhäuser asking to see his little brother," P., 1863
Charivari, Nov. 1863; *Musica*, Mar. 1908; Bosch., 377
*Charpentier, Lithograph: 1847 P.
Jull., 193 (Based on Prinzhofer's drawing)
Courbet, Oil: P. 1850
Louvre; Engraved by Gilbert, *Gazette des Beaux Arts*, 1878 (18) 22; Jull.,
325; Kapp; Newman. Exists in two states, Metropolitan Museum of Art,
N. Y.
[In the critique by Paul Mantz (*Gaz. Beaux Arts*, 1878, 17, p. 574) it is
said that there are two versions of the oil]
Dantan (the elder), Medallion: Rome, 1831
Tiersot, *Les Années Romantiques*, frontispiece; (original ed. only, P. 1904)
Dantan (the younger), Bust-caricature and rebus: "Ber-lit-haut," lithographed
in *Charivari*, May 5, 1836, Jull., 101; *Musical Times*, Aug. 1903; Kapp;
Bosch., 168; included in *Le Musée Dantan: Galerie des charges et Croquis
des Célébrités de l'Epoque*, P. 1839
[Plaster original or copy in Musée Carnavalet, Paris]
Daumier, Caricature: "Les Saltimbanques," P., 1843
Charivari, Apr. 5, 1843; Jull., 161; *Musica*, Mar. 1908; Bosch., 225
[Jules Janin, David d'Angers, Hugo, Berlioz, and Paul Delaroche]
————— Caricature in oil: P. c. 1860
Versailles Museum; Eulenburg *Min. Sc.* (bound vols. only)
[The authenticity of this portrait was questioned by an anonymous critic
in Paris in 1911. (See *153*.) Recently the work was ascribed by Mr. Hein-
rich Schwarz to André Gill (Gosset de Guins, 1840–1885). See *Magazine
of Art*, Nov. 1949, p. 255]
Guide Musical, Nov. 29, 1903; Kapp; Newman; Bosch.
Doré, Caricature: Berlioz conducting the *Société Philharmonique*, P. 1850
Journal pour Rire, 1850; Jull., 213; Livre; Kapp
Dubufe, Oil: P. 1830
Bibl. Conserv.; Kapp, 6
[Probably not a portrait of Berlioz; for grounds of attribution, see *Méne-
strel*, Apr. 3, 1909, with reprod.]
Dunn, Oil: Berlioz and the *Fantastic Symphony*, N. Y., n.d.
Steinway Hall, N. Y.; Catalogue, *The Steinway Collection* (*264*)
Dupré, Engraved Centenary Plaque: P., 1903
Guide Musical, Aug. 23 and 30, 1903; *Monde Musical*, Nov. 30, 1903
[Duplicates obtainable at Hôtel des Monnaies, P.]
Fantin-Latour, Oil: *Hommage à Berlioz*, P. 1876
Grenoble Museum; Livre
————— Fourteen lithographs on Berlioz' Works
Originally for Jull.: Frontispiece, xvi, 50, 82, 104, 122, 142, 186, 206, 230, 250,
274, 290, and 366
Four in G. Kahn, *Fantin-Latour*, tr. W. Jackson, N. Y. 1927; two in Kapp;
two in Bosch
————— Four additional lithographs (chiefly on *Les Troyens*)
Monde Musical, Nov. 30, 1903
Feinberg, Bust: n.p., n.d.
At birthplace
Fuhr, Lithograph after a photograph by Pierre Petit: P. 1863
Jull., 281; Newman; Bosch., 363
[The "familiar" pose]

Godebski, Medallion on Berlioz' Monument (by A. Jouvin) P. 1884
    Montmartre Cemetery; Jull., 329; *Monde Musical*, Nov. 30, 1903; Kapp
Grandville, Caricature: "Concert à Mitraille" P. 1846
    Reybaud's *Jérôme Paturot* (2nd ed., 1846); *Musica*, Mar. 1908; Kapp; Bosch., 242
        [Berlioz in profile, conducting artillery; imitated by Andreas Geiger, see *Die Bastei*, 1946, No. 5, p. 10; Bosch. 316]
———— Caricature: Two hands on one arm
Jérôme Paturot; Jull., 131; Bosch., 215
        [Pen and baton allude to Berlioz' double role as composer and critic]
Granges, Bronze bust: n.p., n.d.
    Birthplace Museum
Guiguet, Lithograph: "Scenes in the Country" from the *Symphonie Fantastique*, n.p., n.d.
    Livre
Heim, Drawing? Berlioz seated, in academician's uniform, P. 1861
    Bosch., 335; *Illustration*, Feb. 25, 1928
Hensel, Drawing: Leipzig 1843 (?)
        [By Mendelssohn's brother-in-law: not found in reprod. but mentioned in Bossert, *Etudes de littérature allemande*, 284]
Hüssener, Auguste (Frau), Copperplate: P. *c.* 1838
    Bibl. Nat.; *Revue Musicale*, Aug. 15, 1903; *Guide Musical*, Nov. 29, 1903; *Neue Musik Zeitschrift*, Dec. 3, 1903
        [See also *V.M.*, I, frontispiece, and variants of pose – by same artist? – in: Jull., 157 and 193; Kapp, 9]
Huvos, Marble statue: Budapest 1939. Bronze duplicate purchased for birthplace; since melted (?)
        [Intended as companion piece to statue of Liszt in City Park; temporarily in Karolyi Palace]
Itasse, Jeanne, Bust, P. *c.* 1885
    Paris Conservatoire
*Kriehuber, Lithograph: Half length, facing right, holding glove, Vienna 1845
    Jull., 179; Kapp, 19
———— Lithograph: A Morning Session at Liszt's, Vienna 1845
    Städtische Sammlungen of Vienna; Jull., 129; *Musica*, 1903, p. 230; Bosch.
        [Liszt at piano, Ernst holding violin, Kriehuber with pencil, Berlioz and Czerny behind piano]
Lahaye, Oil: P. 1886
    Bibl. Conserv.
Lami, S., Bronze bust resembling a death mask: P. n.d.
    Bibl. Opera
    Program of Paris Opera, Jul. 6, 1937
Lauchert, Oil: Weimar 1855
        [Mentioned by Cornelius as having been done during last "Berlioz Week"; not otherwise traceable]
*Legros, Etching: Head and shoulders, facing left, P. n.d.
    Metropolitan Museum of Art, N. Y.
Lenoir, Bronze statue, P. Square Vintimille, 1886
        [Melted for bronze during German occupation, 1940 ff.]
    Duplicate at La Côte St. André 1890
    Jull., 345; Kapp; *Monde Musical*, Nov. 30, 1903

Leverd, Medallion: P. *c.* 1830

Tiersot, *Histoire de la Marseillaise,* 109

Lieure, Etching: Head and shoulders, facing left
Offered as premium by *Monde Musical c.* 1910

*Lucroy, Etching: Head and shoulders, facing left, P. n.d.

Marais, Cartoon: Berlioz — Yesterday and Today, P. 1881
Figaro, Mar., 1881; Jull., 340–1; *Musical Times,* Nov. 1903; Kapp
["Yesterday" Berlioz is being stoned; "Today," a pedestal is made of the stones and his statue put up. Based on a casual remark of Berlioz himself]

Masson, Etching: full face, P. n.d.
Bibl. Nat.

Mauron; Lithograph: head and shoulders, facing right, in oval frame, P. 1877
Bibl. Nat. (2 states); *Monde Moderne,* vol. 18, p. 671

Mollard, Caricature: 1855
Bibl. Nat.; Livre; Kapp, 33 (lower right)

*Nadar [pseud. of Félix Tournachon], Photograph: three-quarter length, facing right, arm on table, P. *c.* 1865
Hopkinson, *Bibliography,* frontispiece

—— Photograph: Berlioz standing, in a greatcoat, arms tucked in opposite sleeves, P. 1856
Engraved by Metzmacher, Jull., 245; Metropolitan Museum of Art, N. Y.
[Obvious source of Daumier portrait]

—— Caricature: "Les compositeurs au Panthéon-Nadar," P. 1858
Jull., 237
[Rossini on top; then Berlioz, Reyer, Auber, David, Halévy, Meyerbeer, and Offenbach]

Perraud, Marble bust: P. 1867
Institut. Replicas: Paris Conservatoire; Birthplace; N. Y. Steinway Hall; Jull., 313

*Petit, Pierre, Photograph; P. 1863
Monde Musical, Nov. 30, 1903; Kapp (misdated); Bosch., 363
[The original of the "familiar" pose. See Fuhr above]

Pierson, Photograph: Berlioz standing, facing right, left hand in pocket, P. *c.* 1855
Pl. no. 77 in *Les Premiers Temps de la Photographie* (P. 1930); *Musical Courier,* Sept. 16, 1903, p. 8

Pommaurne, Miniature: P. *c.* 1839
Jull., 133; *Musica,* Mar. 1908; Kapp

Prinzhofer, Drawing: Half length, facing left, Vienna 1845
Jull., 177; Kapp; Newman; *Westerman's Monatshefte,* Jan., 1904; Bosch., 253
["The best of me so far," writes Berlioz, *M.E.,* 297]

Rambaud, Statue: "The Dying Berlioz"
Grenoble Museum (reserve); plaster replica at Rambaud Museum, Allevard (Isère)

*Reutlinger, Photograph: Head and shoulders facing left. B. 1867
Berlin Photographische Gesellschaft; *Guide Mus.* Nov. 29, 1903; engraved by Guillaumot, Metropolitan Museum of Art, N. Y.

Salomon, Bas-relief in plaster: P. 1852
Jull., 211; Kapp, 23

Signol, Oil: Rome 1832
Villa Medici; copy by Syeffert (misdated) *Musica,* Mar. 1908; Bosch., frontispiece. Engraved by Dochy, Kapp; Newman

—— Another copy at Birthplace Museum
—— A modified copy, non-caricature, by Syeffert ? *Ibid.*
Traviès, Lithograph: Panthéon Musical, P. 1843
　Jull., 166
　　[Leading French composers, each with a caption. Berlioz shown in a car-
　riage, with the words: "While crossing the forests which he stirs with the
　noise of his symphonies, Berlioz sends to the *Journal des Débats* his impres-
　sions of travel."]
*Trumpf, Etching: Head and shoulders, facing right, hand in waistcoat, n.p.,
　n.d.
Valloton, Woodcut: Head facing right
　Winterthur, Kunstverein, reprod. in *L'Oeuvre gravé de Félix Valloton,*
　P. 1932, No. 82
Vernet, H., Pen and ink caricature: Rome 1831
　Livre; Kapp, 33; Bosch., 93
Viardot, E., Medal in relief: P. n.d.
　Musica, Mar. 1908
Viardot, Pauline, Pencil sketch: n.p., n.d.
　Ibid.
*Weger, Etching: Head and shoulders, facing right, n.p., n.d.
　Frontispiece, *Nuits d'Eté,* Augener ed.
Winkler, Oil: Zurich n.d. (posthumous) Various postcard reprod.
Yvon, Sketch in oils: "Paganini and Berlioz in 1838," P. 1884
　Jull., 137

2D — ICONOGRAPHY

(2) *Associated Persons and Places*

Anon., Lithograph: Birthplace at La Côte St. André n.d.
　Manskopf Museum, Frankfort; *Musical Times,* July 1903; *Neue Musik
　Zeitung,* Dec. 3, 1903; *Neue Zeitschrift,* Dec. 9, 1903; *Musica,* 1903, p. 232;
　Kapp; Newman; *Illustration,* July 20, 1935
Anon., Drawing: Berlioz' house at Montmartre, L. 1924
　London *Times,* Dec. 29, 1924
　　[The plaque affixed by the *Fondation Berlioz* on Dec. 11, 1908 was re-
　moved and replaced on a tall new building on same site in 1926. See *Dépêche
　Dauphinoise,* Aug. 31, 1934]
De la Ficre (?), E., Drawing: Berlioz' house at Montmartre, n.p., n.d.
　Bosch. 157
Son, Johannes, Drawing: Berlioz' house at Montmartre, n.d.
　235, II, 179
Tiret-Bonnet, Watercolor: Berlioz' house at Montmartre, n.d.
　At birthplace; *Dépêche Dauphinoise,* Aug. 31, 1934
*Tournell, Colored etching: Berlioz' house at Montmartre, n.d.
Utrillo, *Oil: Berlioz' house at Montmartre, n.d. Oblique view looking east
　　[Utrillo may have lived in house]
—— Oil: same subject, looking southwest, n.d.
　Tabarant, *Utrillo,* P. 1926, p. 49; also Courthion, *Utrillo,* Berne, 1947
—— Oil: same subject, facing east, 1914
　Formerly in collection of Duc de Trévise
—— Oil: same subject, snow scene, looking north
　Tabarant, *op. cit.,* 75

Utrillo, Oil: same subject, snow scene, facing south
Ibid., 81
—— Oil: same subject, same position, but with one more downstairs window, 1914
Pallucchini, *Utrillo*, Milan 1945, Plate 17
Van Gogh, ?: Berlioz' House at Montmartre
Reference in *280*, not otherwise traceable
Barberi, Lithograph: "La Tour Bellanda [Nice] where Berlioz lodged in 1844"
Musée Masséna, Nice; reprod. in their catalogue of Feb.-Apr., 1935, p. 19.
See also, *Illustration*, Nov. 26, 1932

Various hands, Berlioz family portraits: father, mother, grandfathers, uncle, two sisters and their husbands
At birthplace; a few in Catalogue (1935) as well as *Monde Musical*, Nov. 30, 1903 and *Musica*, Mar. 1908; Bosch., *passim*
Anon., Louis Berlioz (son of Hector)
Bosch., 419
Baugniet, Lithograph: Harriet Smithson, n.p., n.d.
Manskopf Museum, Frankfort; *Musical Times*, July 1903
*Clint, Oil: Harriet Smithson, prob. L. *c.* 1820
Engraved by R. Cooper and publ. July 30, 1822; *Musical Quarterly*, Oct. 1949
D'Apvril, Miniature: Dr. Louis Berlioz, n.p., n.d.
Program of *Festival Berlioz*, Grenoble Dec. 29, 1890
Deveria, Drawing: Harriet Smithson, P. *c.* 1828
Bibl. Nat.; *Revue Musicale*, Aug. 15, 1903; Bosch. 50
Dubufe, Oil: Harriet Smithson, n.p., n.d.
Frederick Whyte, *Actors of the Century*, L. 1898, p. 98; Hadow, *Studies in Modern Music*, p. 86
*Francis, Lithograph: Harriet Smithson, P. 1827
Jull., 73; Kapp; Newman; Bosch., 34 and 140
—— Lithograph: Kemble and Smithson in *Hamlet*, P. 1827
Jull., 53
—— Two lithographs: Kemble and Smithson in *Romeo and Juliet*, P. 1827
Jull., 29 and 33; *Monde Musical*, Supplement, Apr. 15, 1911
Guys, Watercolor: Pauline Viardot in *Orpheus*, P. Nov. 1859 (showing Delacroix in side box) *Corresp. Eugène Delacroix*, V, p. 192
Lami, E., Oil: The Lobby of the Opera, P. 1843
[Halévy, Hiller, Fanny Elssler, Dr. Véron, and others]
Alophe, Drawing: Camille Moke, P. *c.* 1830
Bosch., 51
Prinzhofer, Camille (Moke) Pleyel, Vienna 1845
Mueller Collection, N. Y. Public Library
Anon., Photograph: Marie Recio, P. *c.* 1860
Jull., 252; Kapp; Newman; Bosch., 213
[The only extant portrait]
Hébert, Princess Sayn-Wittgenstein, n.p., n.d.
Bosch. 331
Anon. Photograph: Princess Sayn-Wittgenstein, n.p., n.d.
Kapp, 18; for other portraits, see La Mara, *Aus der Glanzzeit der Weimarer Altenburg*. (*972a*.)
—— Photograph: Estelle Fornier, n.p., n.d.
Monde Musical, Nov. 30, 1903; Kapp; Newman

Baugniet, Pantheon of Sixteen Musicians, L. 1853
   Guide Musical, Nov. 29, 1903
      [Besides Berlioz: Spohr, Hiller, Vieuxtemps, Ella]
Fantin-Latour, Oil: "Emmanuel Chabrier (at the piano) with d'Indy, Ad. Jullien, and other admirers of Berlioz and Wagner" P. 1870
   Kahn, *Fantin-Latour,* Plate 11
Anon., Photograph: Massine and Baronova in ballet, "Symphonie Fantastique," L. and N. Y. 1937
Brook, *Five Great French Composers,* opp. p. 53

3. BIOGRAPHIES OF BERLIOZ

A — BOOKS

265. Allix, G., *Sur les éléments dont s'est formée la personnalité artistique de Berlioz;* Grenoble 1903
266. Bennett, J., *Berlioz;* L. 1883 [No. 1 of Novello's Primers]
267. Boschot, Adolphe, *La Jeunesse d'un romantique;* P. 1906
268. —— *Un romantique sous Louis-Philippe;* P. 1908
269. —— *Le crépuscule d'un romantique;* P. 1913
270. —— *Une vie romantique: Hector Berlioz;* P. 1919
271. —— The same, illustrated: *Les editions musicales de la Librairie de France,* P. 1927; rev., with a new Preface, P. 1939; transl. into several languages
272. Bouillat, J. M. J., *Berlioz;* n.d., n.p.
273. Brenet, Michel [pseud. of Marie Bobillier], *Deux Pages de la Vie de Berlioz;* P. 1889
      [On *Benvenuto Cellini* in Paris and Berlioz in Germany down to 1887]
274. Constantin, Léon, *Berlioz;* P. 1934
275. Coquard, Arthur, *Berlioz (Les Musiciens Célèbres);* P. n.d.
276. Daniskas, J., *Hector Berlioz;* Stockholm 1947
      [A short biography in the *Symphonia* series: quite advanced as to facts and judgments]
277. Degeorge, L., *Berlioz: sa vie et ses oeuvres;* Bruxelles 1879
278. Elliot, J. H., *Berlioz (Master Musicians);* L. 1938
279. Farga, Franz, *Der späte Ruhm: Hector Berlioz und seine Zeit;* Zurich 1939
280. Fink, G., *Hector Berlioz . . . suivi d'une notice comparative sur Wagner et Berlioz;* Angoulême 1898
281. Galibert, P., *Berlioz compositeur et écrivain;* Bordeaux 1890
282. Hippeau, Edmond, *Berlioz Intime;* P. 1883
283. —— *Berlioz et son temps;* P. 1890
284. Jullien, Adolphe, *Hector Berlioz: La Vie et le Combat; Les Oeuvres;* P. 1882
285. —— *Hector Berlioz: sa vie et ses Oeuvres;* P. 1888
286. Kapp, Julius, *Berlioz: eine Biographie;* Berlin and Leipzig 1917
      [Contains valuable facsimiles from autograph scores and a bibliography which professes to correct and supplement Prod'homme (See *1349*) though it is still incomplete]
287. Lockspeiser, Edw., *Berlioz;* L. 1939
      [A 16-page biography]

288. Louis, Rudolf, *Hector Berlioz;* Leipzig 1904

289. Masson, P. M., *Berlioz (Les Maîtres de la Musique);* P. 1923

290. Massougnes, G. de, *Hector Berlioz; son oeuvre;* P. 1919
[Reprint of the brochures of 1868 and 1870]

291. Méré, Charles, *Berlioz,* a play in 4 acts and 19 scenes, first acted at the Théâtre de la Porte St. Martin, Jan. 22, 1927; P. (La Petite Illustration) May 7, 1927
[A reasonably sentimental version of Berlioz' life; 18 excerpts from Berlioz' music were played during or between the acts]

292. Mirecourt, Eugène de [pseud. of C. J. B. Jacquot], *Berlioz;* P. 1856
[A very inaccurate short biography, reprinted with many others in the author's *Histoire Contemporaine,* P. 1867, 1869 ff. in several vols. each]

293. Mouthier, P., *Hector Berlioz;* Dilbeck (Belgium) 1944

294. Muñoz Escamez, J., *Hector Berlioz: su vida y sus obras;* P. 1929

295. Neumann, Wilhelm, *Berlioz, eine Biographie;* Cassel 1855
[A short contemporary essay quite accurate but drawing much on Schumann for critical opinions]

296. Pohl, Louise, *Hector Berlioz' Leben und Werke;* Leipzig 1900
[Based on materials left by her father, Berlioz' friend and translator, Richard Pohl]

297. ――― Richard, *Hector Berlioz: Studien und Erinnerungen;* Leipzig 1884

298. Pourtalès, Guy de, *Berlioz et l'Europe Romantique;* P. 1939

299. Prod'homme, J. G., *Hector Berlioz;* 1st ed. P. 1904

300. ――― The same, 2nd and 3rd eds. P. 1927

301. Ratez, E., *Une visite de Berlioz à Lille;* Lille 1926

302. Rey, Etienne, *La vie amoureuse de Berlioz;* P. 1929

303. Robert, Paul Louis, *Etude sur Hector Berlioz;* Rouen 1914

304. Schrader, Bruno, *Berlioz;* Leipzig 1907
[Reclams-Universal Bibliothek, No. 5043]

305. Sollertinski, Ivan Ivanovich, *Hector Berlioz* (Leningrad Philharmonic Association) Leningrad 1935
[In Russian]

306. Thompson, S. R., *Hector Berlioz: a critical monograph;* 1894

307. Tiersot, J., *Berlioz et la Société de son temps;* P. 1904

308. ――― *Berlioziana*
[A source book in article form, published weekly in *Le Ménestrel* from Jan. 3, 1904 to Dec. 1, 1906]

309. Turner, W. J., *Berlioz: the Man and his Work;* L. 1934

310. Wotton, T. S., *Hector Berlioz;* L. 1935

3B — BIOGRAPHICAL ESSAYS

311. Anon. [prob. C. L. Gruneisen], "Berlioz"; *Illustrated London News,* Feb. 12, 1848, pp. 88 and 90. [Short biography and review of his first concert in London]

312. Anon., "Berlioz"; *Temple Bar,* Oct. 1883, 204-25
[Inaccurate but friendly testimony by "L. E." prob. Louis Engel]

313. ――― "The Centenary of Berlioz"; *Athenaeum,* Aug. 29, 1903, pp. 295 ff.

314. ――― Review of Boschot's *Un Romantique sous Louis-Philippe; Academy,* Sept. 5, 1908

315. ———— "Hector Berlioz"; *Atlantic Monthly*, 1880, pp. 699–702
[Review of Apthorp's *Selections*. See 317]

316. Aldrich, Richard, "Berlioz Today"; *Musical Discourse from the N. Y. Times*, N. Y. 1928

317. Apthorp, Wm., Introductory Sketch in *Selections* from the Works of Berlioz; N. Y. 1879

318. Beaunier, A., "Une vie romantique: Hector Berlioz"; *Revue des Deux Mondes*, Apr. 1, 1920, pp. 687–98

319. Blackburn, Vernon, "Berlioz at Cologne"; *The Dome*, N.S. (1898), pp. 128–31

320. Blondel, Raoul, "La jeunesse médicale de Berlioz"; in *Propos variés de musique et de médecine*, P. 1934

321. Bottenheim, S., "Berlioz vereering in Amsterdam"; *Caecilia*, 1919, pp. 149–51

322. Bordeaux, H., *Vies Intimes;* P. 1919
[A somewhat sentimental essay on Berlioz and his native landscape, pp. 279–87]

323. Brenet, Michel [pseud. of Marie Bobillier], "L'Amitié de Berlioz et de Liszt"; *Guide Musical* Aug. 14–Sept. 25, 1904

324. Brian, Havergal, "Hector Berlioz"; *Musical Opinion*, Dec. 1934, pp. 209–10

325. Brent-Smith, A. E., "Hector Berlioz"; *Music and Letters*, Oct. 1926

326. Brook, Donald, *Five Great French Composers*, L. 1946

327. Bruneau, Alfred, "Berlioz"; *Monde Musical*, Nov. 30, 1903

327a. Brussel, R., "Hector Berlioz"; *Le Manuscrit Autographe, Jan.–Feb.*, 1931, pp. 63 ff.

328. Bücken, Ernst, "Berlioz"; Musikalische Charakterköpfe; Leipzig 1925

329. Calvocoressi, M. D., "Berlioz in 1936"; *Musical America*, Oct. 10, 1936

330. Celle, J., "Berlioz à l'Institut"; *Revue Bleue*, 1906, pp. 219–22

331. Clément, Felix, "Berlioz"; *Musiciens Célèbres;* P. 1868
[Admires love duet from *Les Troyens* almost to the exclusion of everything else in Berlioz]

332. Comettant, Oscar, "Hector Berlioz"; *Ménestrel*, Oct. 10, 1886
[Comments by an acquaintance of Berlioz, who stresses the preponderance in Berlioz of the imagination over the "heart"]

333. Cook, D., "Berlioz and Jullien"; *Belgravia*, May 1880, pp. 285–96
[Excellent]

334. Creighton, Ursula, *Music;* With a Preface by Edward J. Dent, N. Y. 1928
[The brief and simple chapter on Berlioz, pp. 171–79, is almost the only acceptable treatment to be found in pedagogical works of this sort]

335. David, Jules, "Berlioz: Souvenirs intimes et personnels," *Revue de la Société des Etudes Historiques*. Amiens Nov. 1887

336. Debuchy, Albert, *Concert of French Theatrical and Romantic Music;* Cambridge, Mass. 1907
[Contains a poorly translated and frequently inaccurate short biography of Berlioz (pp. 56–123), which is nevertheless of some value. The author was an orchestral player in the *Troyens* revivals of the nineties and became director of the Opéra-Comique. As an admirer of Berlioz he collected reviews and articles from which he quotes very fully here]

337. De Railles, X., "Hector Berlioz"; in *Biographies du 19ème siècle;* P. n.d.
[Uneven but with insight into Berlioz' situation]

338. D'Estrées, Paul, "L'art musical et ses interprètes depuis deux siècles";
Ménestrel, May 25, 1902
[Brief account of personal enmities at work against Berlioz' music in Paris]

339. Dupuy, Ernest, "Alfred de Vigny et Hector Berlioz"; *Revue des Deux Mondes,* 1911, pp. 837–65
[Sympathetic account of a great friendship; quotes letters]

340. E.[dwards], F. G., "Berlioz in England"; *Musical Times,* July–Nov. 1903, and "Berlioziana"; *ibid.,* Dec. 1903
[Gives letters, extracts from reviews, and list of first performances]

341. Elliot, J. H., "Berlioz in our Time"; *Hallé* [bi-monthly bulletin] Manchester Jan. 1948, pp. 1–4

342. Evans, Edwin, Sr., "Berlioz"; in *Lives of the Great Composers;* ed. A. L. Bacharach, L. 1935

343. Feis, Oswald, "Hector Berlioz, eine Pathographische Studie"; *Grenzfragen des Nerven- und Seelenlebens;* vol. 12, No. 81, Wiesbaden 1911

344. Fétis, F. J., *Biographie universelle des musiciens;* 2nd rev. ed., P. 1861–6, 8 vols. in 4
[The article on Berlioz written by April 1855, after Fétis had once more become friendly]

345. Fouque, O., *Les révolutionnaires de la musique;* P. 1882
[Contains a long account of Berlioz, especially useful for his Russian sojourns]

346. Goehler, G., "Hector Berlioz"; *Zukunft,* 1905, pp. 433–9
[An example of the use of biographical fact to read unfavorable qualities into the work of art]

347. Gonse, Louis, "Hector Berlioz"; *Gazette des Beaux-Arts;* 1880, pp. 501–5
[Ostensibly a review of Jullien's book; actually a penetrating summary of Berlioz' work]

348. Grenier, Felix, "Cherubini et Berlioz"; *Guide Musical,* Nov. 23, 1903

349. Guillemot, J., "Berlioz"; *Notices Biographiques,* P. 1919

350. Hadow, Sir Wm., *Studies in Modern Music,* vol. II, 12th ed., n.d.
[Devoted to Schumann, Berlioz, and Wagner]

351. Hanslick, Eduard, "Hector Berlioz in seinen Memoiren"; *Deutsche Rundschau,* 1882, pp. 369–85

352. Hiller, Ferdinand, "Hector Berlioz"; *Westermann's Monatshefte,* 1879, 45, pp. 554–93
[Reprinted in *Künstlerleben,* Cologne, 1880]

353. Istel, Edgar, "Peter Cornelius' 'Hector Berlioz in Weimar' "; *Die Musik,* Feb., 1905, pp. 159–68
[Tr. from *Gazette Musicale,* 1855]

354. ——— "Berlioz und Cornelius"; see *478*

355. Jullien, Adolphe, "Hector Berlioz en Russie"; *Revue d'Art Dramatique,* 1888, pp. 159–65

356. ——— "Berlioz"; in *Famous Composers and their Works,* Boston 1891, 3 vols. [Vol. II, pp. 675–90]

357. Kapp, Julius, *Das Dreigestirn Berlioz-Liszt-Wagner;* B. 1920

358. Keeton, A. E., "Hector Berlioz 1803–1869"; *Fortnightly Review,* Dec. 1903, pp. 928–40

359. Klein, Herman, "Rediscovering Berlioz"; *Monthly Mus. Record*, Feb. and Mar.–Apr. 1934
    [By a witness of the period since 1880]

359a. Kling, H., "Goethe et Berlioz"; *Rivista Musicale Italiana*, 1905, pp. 714–33

360. La Mara (Marie Lipsius), "Berlioz"; in *Musikalische Studienköpfe*, vol. 2, Leipzig: 1881
    [See also *207*]

361. Landormy, Paul, "Berlioz auf Reisen"; *Die Musik*, Dec. 1932

362. Legouvé, E., Extracts from *Soixante Ans de Souvenirs* relating to Berlioz, *Monde Musical;* Apr. 15 and 30, May 15 and 30, 1903
    [Tr. Suzanne Bräutigam, Breitkopf und Härtel, Leipzig, 1898]

363. Lüning, Otto, "Hector Berlioz, ein Pionier der Tonkunst"; *Neujahrsblatt der Allgemeinen Musik-Gesellschaft* in Zürich, LXXXI–LXXXII, 1893 and 1894
    [Full of small errors, yet useful as criticism]

364. Maclean, Charles, "The Country of Berlioz"; *Musical Times*, Sept. 1903
    [Report on the Centenary Celebration by a thorough Berlioz scholar]

365. —— "Berlioz and England"; *Sammelbande der Internationalen Musik-Gesellschaft*, 1903–1904, pp. 314–28.
    [Admirable survey, followed by an English bibliography to date]

366. Malherbe, Charles, "Une Autobiographie de Berlioz"; *Rivista Mus. Italiana*, 1906, pp. 506–21
    [Unintelligent editing]

367. Maréchal, Henri, "Souvenirs d'un Musicien"; *Ménestrel*, Sept. 23, 30, 1907
    [Reprinted as part of *Paris-Souvenirs d'un Musicien;* P. 1907]

368. Marteaux, J., "Sainte-Beuve et Berlioz étudiants en médecine"; *Mercure de France*, Jul. 1, 1934, Jan. 1, 1936

369. Mason, D. G., *The Romantic Composers;* N. Y., 1930
    [A curious discrepancy of tone between the treatment of Berlioz and that of the other Romantics; see the author's more detailed essay, *464*]

370. Mathieu, Paul, "Berlioz"; *Conférence faite au lycée de Chaumont*, n.p. 1891

371. Maury, L., "Critique d'*Une vie romantique: Hector Berlioz* par A. Boschot"; *Revue Bleue*, July 16, 1921, pp. 461–3

372. Mellers, W. H., "A Prophetic Romantic"; *Scrutiny*, June 1938, pp. 119–28
    [An excellent review of J. H. Elliot's biography, replacing its platitudes and errors with a masterly sketch of Berlioz' significance]

373. Monselet, Charles, *Petits Mémoires Littéraires;* P. 1892
    [Full of personalities and portraits of which the details are often more accurate than the bearing. Partly just about Berlioz]

374. Newman, Ernest, "Berlioz: Romantic and Classic"; in *Musical Studies*, L. 1905; 2nd ed. 1908.
    [A pioneering essay]

375. Newmarch, Rosa, "Berlioz in Russia"; *Monthly Musical Record*, July 1, 1903

376. Pissin, R., "Hector Berlioz der Mensch"; see *478*

377. Powell, L., "Berlioz and the Stiff Room"; *Disques;* June 1931, pp. 155 ff.

378. Prod'homme, J.-G., "Berlioz, Musset, and Thomas DeQuincey"; *Musical Quarterly*, Jan. 1946, pp. 98 ff.
[Originally in *Le Ménestrel*, Oct. 17 to 31, 1930]

379. ——— "Hector Berlioz Bibliothécaire au Conservatoire"; *Guide Musical*, Dec. 14, 21, 1913

380. Reyer, Ernest, "Hector Berlioz: Biographical Notes and Personal Reminiscences"; *Century;* Dec. 1893, pp. 304–10

381. Rolland, Romain, "Berlioz"; *Revue de Paris*, Mar. 1 and 15, 1904, pp. 65–88, 331–52
[The original of the chapter in *Musiciens d'aujourd'hui*, which has been translated in *Great Short Biographies*, ed. Barrett H. Clark, N. Y. 1928 and repr. in *859* (1948)]

382. Royall, Emily, "Hector Berlioz," *Harper's Magazine*, 1880, pp. 411–7

383. Royer, Louis, "Stendhal et Berlioz"; *Le Divan*, Jan.–Feb. 1935, 365–9

384. Saint-Saëns, C., "Hector Berlioz"; *Guide Musical*, Sept. 6 and 13, 1903, 626–7

385. ——— "Berlioz"; *Le Ménestrel*, Oct. 21, 1921
[The last article Saint-Saëns wrote, two months before his death]

386. ——— *Portraits et Souvenirs;* P. 1903
[Contains an essay and many references to Berlioz]

387. Schenk, Erich, "Berlioz in Wien"; *Bastei* (Vienna) 1946, pp. 9–13

388. Schloesser, Adolph, "Personal Recollections of Franz Liszt and Hector Berlioz"; *The R*[oyal] *A*[cademy] of *M*[usic] *Club Magazine*, Feb. 1911

389. Schloesser, Louis, "Gedenkblätter an Hektor Berlioz"; *Allgemeine Deutsche Musik Zeitung*, Apr. 21 and 28, 1882

390. Stassov, Vladimir V., *Liszt, Schumann and Berlioz in Russia* [in Russian] [St. Petersburg] 1896

391. Stowe, G. W., "Fading Fame of Once-Famous Berlioz"; *Musician*, Dec. 1946, pp. 164–5
[The wish being father to the thought]

392. Valetta, Franchi-Verney, Count della, "Berlioz"; *Nuova Antologia*, Dec. 16, 1903, pp. 680–93
[A fair résumé giving details about Berlioz' reputation in Italy by the biographer of Chopin]

393. Van Scheuerleer, D. F., *Twe Titanen der negentiende Eeuw: Hector Berlioz en A. Wiertz;* Haarlem 1878

394. Various Hands, *Livre d'Or du Centenaire d'Hector Berlioz;* Grenoble and P. 1906

395. Viotta, H., "Louise Pohl's Hector Berlioz"; *De Gids*, 1900, pp. 563–80

396. Williams, Becket, "The First Mrs. Berlioz"; *Musical Opinion*, Sept. 1946, pp. 359–60

397. Wotton, T. S., "Hector Berlioz"; *Proceedings of the Musical Association* (England) Thirtieth Session, Dec. 8, 1903, pp. 15–36

398. ——— "Hector Berlioz, 1803–1869"; in *The Heritage of Music*, vol. II, ed. Hubert J. Foss, L. 1934

399. Young, Filson, *Mastersingers . . . with an Essay on Hector Berlioz;* L. 1902
[The type of incoherent scorn]

4. CRITICISM OF BERLIOZ AND HIS WORKS

A — GENERAL ESTIMATES

400. Anon., *Saturday Review*, Jan. 29, 1927, pp. 154–5
401. —— *Musical World*, June 28, 1879
402. —— "Who's Who in the Orchestra"; in *Fundamentals of Musical Art*, vol. II
403. —— Letter from a Conductor; *Musical Times*, 1929, p. 739
404. —— "Wanted a Modern Berlioz"; *Etude* (44) 428
405. —— Editorial in *The Musician;* Apr. 1900, p. 114
406. —— [Gauthier-Villars, H., and Ernst, Alfred], *Lettres de l'Ouvreuse.* 2ème série; P. 1890
   [See also *917*]
407. Abraham, Gerald E. H., "The Influence of Berlioz on Richard Wagner"; *Music and Letters*, 1924, pp. 239–46
   [One aspect of that influence detailed by one whose sympathies go more naturally to Wagner's music]
408. Ambros, A. W., *Bunte Blätter: Skizzen und Studien;* Leipzig 1872–1874, 2 vols.
   [Obituary of Berlioz in vol. I, pp. 93–106]
409. Baldès, P., "Hector Berlioz"; *Revue Internationale*, 1888 (20) pp. 478 ff.
410. Barzun, J., "Berlioz and Biography"; *University Review* (Kansas City) Summer 1939; pp. 275–80
411. Baser, Friedrich, "Hector Berlioz und die germanische Seele"; *Die Musik*, XXVI, No. 4, Jan. 1934
412. Blaze, Henri, "Hector Berlioz"; *Revue des Deux Mondes* (80) 1869, pp. 1006–22
   [A magnanimous obituary by an opponent of his style]
413. Boschot, A., "Berlioz" in *Le Romantisme et l'Art;* P. 1928, pp. 275–88
414. Bouyer, Raymond, "Petites Notes sans Portée"; *Ménestrel*, Sept. 6, 13, 20, 27; Oct. 4, Dec. 7, 1903
415. —— "Pour le Centenaire d'un Maître Français"; *Ménestrel*, Feb. 8, 1903
416. —— "Un portrait d'Hector Berlioz"; *Ménestrel*, Mar. 22 to Apr. 12, 1903
417. —— "Berlioz et Wagner en 1903"; *Nouvelle Revue*, 1903, 24, pp. 417–23
418. Browne, W. Denis, "Modern Harmonic Tendencies"; *Music Association Proceedings*, 1914, pp. 141 ff.
   [On Berlioz and the guitar]
419. Calvocoressi, M. D., "Berlioz Reconsidered"; *Christian Science Monitor*, Mar. 2, 1929
   [On Berlioz' harmony]
420. —— "From My Notebook"; *Musical Opinion*, Apr. 1935
   [A comparison of this article with *419* and *329* will show how the ablest of critics may vacillate]
421. Clapp, Philip Greeley, *Program Notes for the Concerts of the Iowa State University Orchestra;* 1941 to date
   [Excellent notes on Berlioz scores; see also letter in *155*]
422. Cumberland, Gerald [pseud. of Chas. F. Kenyon], "The Psychology of Berlioz"; *Musical Times*, 1911, pp. 95–96

423. Cumberland, Gerald, *With the Great Composers;* L. 1925
[Imaginary dialogues in one of which Berlioz takes part]

424. Dukas, Paul, *Écrits de Paul Dukas;* P. 1948
[Many of Berlioz' works reviewed]

425. Ehlert, Ludwig, *Lettres sur la musique à une amie (Briefe über Musik an eine Freundin)* B. 1859; tr. F. Grenier, P. 1889; F. R. Ritter, Boston, 1879

426. Elliot, J. H., "Berlioz"; *Musical Times,* July 1, 1929, pp. 602 ff.

427. Emmanuel, Maurice, "Berlioz"; *Le Correspondant,* 1920, pp. 327–61
[Indispensable to the modern student; by a master musicologist]

428. Ernst, Alfred, *L'oeuvre dramatique de Hector Berlioz;* P. 1884

429. Escholier, Raymond, "Pour sauver la maison de Berlioz"; *Revue des Deux Mondes,* Nov. 1, 1931, pp. 220 ff.

430. Evans, Raymond Leslie, "Berlioz: musicien du romantisme français"; in *Les Romantiques français et la musique,* P. 1934, Part II, ch. 4

431. Ferreira, Julio, "Berlioz"; *Amphion* (Lisbon) 1890; Nos. 17–20

432. Feuillet, G., *L'Oeuvre intense de Hector Berlioz;* P. 1903

433. Flat, Paul, "Le cas Berlioz"; *Revue Bleue,* 1913, 719–22

434. Gautier, Théophile, *La Musique* [Collected musical articles]; P. 1911

435. Gillet, L., *Les Arts* in *Histoire de la Nation Française;* ed. G. Hanotaux, vol. 13
[Good on Berlioz and nineteenth-century music]

436. Goetschius, Percy, *Masters of the Symphony;* Boston, 1929

437. Gray, Cecil, "Notes on Music"; *The Calendar of Modern Letters,* Sept. 1925 to Feb. 1926, pp. 55, 126, 198, 275, 362, 434

438. —— (London) *Nation,* May 28, 1927, and Mar. 23, 1929

439. —— "Letter on Berlioz in Reply to Feste"; *Musical Times,* July 1929, p. 635
[Important comments on several aspects of Berlioz]

440. Griepenkerl, Wolfgang Robert, *Ritter Berlioz in Braunschweig;* Brunswick 1843
[The opening gun in the "German Campaign"]

441. *Guide Musical,* Berlioz centenary numbers (3 issues); Aug. 23 and 30, 1903; Sept. 6 and 13; and Nov. 22, 1903

442. —— Berlioz number; Nov. 29, 1903

443. Hadow, Wm., *Studies in Modern Music;* L. 1898, 9th ed. 1911
[Long essay on Berlioz]

444. Harty, Sir Hamilton, "Berlioz"; *Music Teacher,* Oct. 1926, pp. 521–23

445. —— "Berlioz"; *Music and Letters,* Jan., Apr. and Dec. 1926
[Comments by an outstanding producer of Berlioz' works in England]

446. Howard, J. M., "Discovering Berlioz"; *The American Music Lover,* VIII, No. 7, March 1942, pp. 235–8

447. Hughes, Herbert, "Notes from a Musical Diary"; *Saturday Review,* Apr. 28, 1934, p. 485

448. Hussey, Dyneley, "Berlioz the Fantastic"; *Saturday Review,* Oct. 18, 1924, pp. 390–1

449. Imbert, H., "Berlioz initiateur de la haute culture musicale"; see *442*

450. Jahn, Otto, *Gesammelte Aufsätze;* 2nd printing, Leipzig 1867
[Contemporary attack on Berlioz]

451. Jong, J. de, "Berlioz"; *De Gids,* 1879, pp. 138–73

452. Koechlin, Charles, "Le Cas Berlioz"; *Revue Musicale*, Feb. 1922
453. ———— "Berlioz" in *Traité de l'Harmonie*, P. 1925, vol. II, pp. 176–9 and *passim*.
454. La Laurencie, L. de, "Hector Berlioz et le public de son temps"; *Courrier Musical*, Jan. 1, 1904
455. Lambert, Constant, "The Isolation of Berlioz: Academic Criticism"; *Daily Telegraph*, Apr. 27, 1929
     [On his harmony and melody]
456. Lancelotti, Arturo, "Ettore Berlioz"; in *Musica d'Oggi*, Milan 1931, pp. 302–10
457. Lawrence, Robert, "Beecham, Berlioz, Borodin"; *Saturday Review of Literature*, Sept. 27, 1947
     [Review of a set of records by a judicious admirer of Berlioz]
458. Lobe, Johann Chr., *Consonanzen und Dissonanzen;* Leipzig, 1869
     [Excellent remarks on Berlioz (pp. 55–68 and 313–8) by a contemporary and eyewitness of his musical activities]
459. Locke, G. W., *Music and the Romantic Movement in France;* L. 1920
     ["Standard" but inadequate on Berlioz]
460. Marnold, Jean, "Hector Berlioz, Musicien"; *Mercure de France*, Jan. 15, 1905, pp. 205–20 and Feb. 15, 1905, pp. 362–78
     [A relentless attack]
461. Marteaux, J., "Un festival Berlioz à la Côte St. André"; *Journal des Débats*, July 17, 1931
462. ———— "Réalité du génie de Berlioz"; *ibid.*, May 18, 1934
463. Marx, A. B., *Die Musik des 19ten Jahrhunderts;* Leipzig 1855
     [An early admirer reviewing a quarter century's achievement]
464. Mason, D. G., "Hector Berlioz and Realism in Music"; *Outlook*, Nov. 10, 1906, pp. 621–5
465. Masson, P.–M., "Berlioz"; *Revue Musicale*, Mar. 1, 1923
466. Massougnes, G. de, "La Revanche de Berlioz"; *Ménestrel*, Oct. 10, 1886
     [A fictional account of the relations between Berlioz and Scudo]
467. ———— "Le Cycle Berlioz à Carlsruhe"; *Gazette des Beaux-Arts*, 1893, p. 500; *Revue Bleue*, 1893, p. 659
468. ———— "Berlioz et Wagner"; *Revue d'Art Dramatique*, N.S. V. 9 pp. 5–22
469. Mauclair, C., "La musique française depuis Berlioz"; *English Review*, 1910 (6) pp. 629–50
     [An excellent account of Berlioz' influence]
470. Maury, L., "Hector Berlioz"; *Revue Bleue*, 1908, pp. 92–4
471. ———— "Reflexions sur Berlioz"; *Revue Bleue*, 1920, 186–8
472. Mendès, Catulle, "Hector Berlioz"; *Le Courrier Musical*, May 15, 1903
     [A sample of appreciation by a poet and critic under the sway of Wagnerism. Berlioz is given very high rank except for the fact that he did not produce works like Wagner's]
473. Mesnard, L., *Essais de critique musicale: Hector Berlioz; Johannes Brahms;* P. 1888
474. Messager, André, "Le centenaire de Berlioz"; *Grande Revue*, Jan. 15, 1904
475. Meyerstein, E. H. W., "An approach to Berlioz"; *Music Review*, May, 1948, pp. 97–101

476. *Monde Musical*, Berlioz Centenary number; Nov. 30, 1903
  [Contains letters, portraits, lithographs by Fantin-Latour, as well as articles of which the most important is A. Mangeot's study of the Berlioz-Wagner relations]

477. *Musica* (Paris), Berlioz number; March 1908
  [Valuable for its reproductions of Fantin-Latour's lithographs, and articles by Colonne and Bruneau on the posthumous career of Berlioz and his works]

478. *Musik, Die*, Berlioz number; No. 5, 1903–1904
  [Articles by various hands on all aspects of Berlioz' works. Dedicated to Weingartner]

479. *Neue Musik-Zeitung* (Stuttgart-Leipzig), Berlioz Number; Dec. 3, 1903
  [Useful articles by Rudolf Louis on Berlioz' relation to Wagner and by Kurt Mey on Berlioz as Writer]

480. *Neue Zeitschrift für Musik*, Berlioz Number, Dec. 9, 1903

481. Newman, Ernest, "The Work of Berlioz"; *Contemporary Review*, Feb. 1901, pp. 212–20

482. ———— "The Case of Berlioz"; *Sunday Times*, May 22, 1921

483. ———— "A Berlioz Revival"; *Sunday Times*, Mar. 11, 1923, reprinted in *Living Age*, Apr. 28, 1923

484. Newman, Ernest, "Freedom in Music"; *Sunday Times*, Sept. 18, 1921
  [On Berlioz' form and method of development]

485. ———— "The B.B.C. Concert"; *Sunday Times*, Jan. 23, 1927
  [A definitive statement about the character of Berlioz criticism]

486. ———— "Eye and Ear in Music"; *Sunday Times*, Jan. 21 and 28, 1934
  [On Berlioz as melodist]

487. ———— "The potency of Berlioz in modern music"; *Century Library of Music*, Vol. I, 18–22, N. Y. 1900

488. Niecks, Fr., "The Influence of Berlioz as an Orchestrator"; *Monthly Musical Record*, May 1, 1911, pp. 111–3
  [Superseded by new evidence]

489. Noufflard, Georges, *Hector Berlioz et le mouvement de l'art contemporain;* P. 1885
  [On the influence of the Dramatic Symphony]

490. Offenbach, J., Notes on Berlioz in *L'Artiste* (1855) reprinted in *Ménestrel*, Dec. 6, 1903

491. Ogdon, J. A. H., "Berlioz: The Earlier Phase"; *Life and Letters*, May 1931
  [Full of insight but thesis-ridden]

492. Passy, Jacques, "Berlioz et Wagner"; *Correspondant*, June 10, 1888

493. Photiadès, Constantin, "Hector Berlioz et Andromède"; *Revue de Paris*, Feb. 15, 1931
  [Excellent on the staging of *Les Troyens* since 1863 and indicative of modern views on Berlioz' "romanticism"]

494. Pitrou, R., "Le Romantisme de Berlioz"; *Correspondant*, 1931, 322, pp. 510–28

495. Pizzetti, Ildebrando, "L'arte di Hector Berlioz"; in *Musica e dramma*, Rome 1945

496. Pohl, R., "Hector Berlioz"; *Zukunft*, 1897 (18) pp. 75–9

497. Pontmartin, A. de, *Souvenirs d'un Vieux Critique, 2ème série;* P. 1882

498. ———— *Nouveaux Samedis, 7ème série;* P. 1878
      [A fair sample of the Parisian critic and polygraph]
499. Prod'homme, J. G., "Hector Berlioz jugé par Adolphe Adam"; *Zeit-schrift der Internationalen Musikgesellschaft,* 5th year, 1903–1904, pp. 475–82
500. Puttmann, Max, "Hector Berlioz"; *Allgemeine Musik-Zeitung* (Berlin) Dec. 11, 18 and 25, 1903
501. ———— "Hector Berlioz und sein Orchester"; *Neue Musik Zeitung,* Dec. 3, 1903
502. *Revue Musicale,* Berlioz number, Aug. 15, 1903
      [Letters, reminiscences, foreign opinions, and important documents, notably birth, marriage and death certificates]
503. Ritter, H., *Einiges zum Verständnis von Berlioz;* Oppeln 1899
504. Rolland, Romain, *Musiciens d'Aujourd'hui;* P. 1908
      [Leading essay on Berlioz; tr. with a Preface by Claude Landi, N. Y., 1914]
505. Rosenfeld, Paul, *Musical Portraits;* N. Y., 1920
      [Sound essay on Berlioz]
506. Runciman, John, "Berlioz"; *Saturday Review,* Nov. 21 and 28, 1903, pp. 635–6; 667–8; 729–30
      [Excellent samples of anti-Berliozian fury]
507. ———— "After Berlioz"; *Saturday Review,* Dec. 12, 1903, pp. 729–31
      [Continued denunciation for having laid "a serpent's trail" through all modern music]
508. Schumann, Robert, *On Music and Musicians;* ed. Konrad Wolff; tr. Paul Rosenfeld; N. Y. 1946
      [Contains the essays on Berlioz]
509. ———— *Hector Berlioz et Robert Schumann;* ed. Maurice Kufferath, Brussels 1879
      [A French translation of the writings on Berlioz]
510. ———— *Hector Berlioz et Robert Schumann;* P. n.d.
      [Another French translation, anonymously published]
510a. Schuré, E., "Beethoven, Berlioz, Wagner"; *Revue des Deux Mondes,* Apr. 15, 1884, pp. 789–916
511. Sear, H. G., "Delacroix and Berlioz"; *Music Review,* Nov. 1943, pp. 216–23
      [An admirable essay, exact and concise]
512. Seidl, Anton, "On Conducting"; in Finck, Henry T., *Anton Seidl: a Memorial;* N. Y. 1899
      [Describes Berlioz' style from Cosima Wagner's recollections]
513. ————, Arthur, "Vier Erzwagnerianer der Musik"; in *Wagneriana;* n.p. 1901–1903, pp. 283–323
      [Berlioz among them]
514. Shawe-Taylor, D., "The Operas of Berlioz" (London); *Spectator,* Apr. 3, 1936
515. Smith, Fanny Morris, "Berlioz and the Romantic School"; in *Music of the Modern World,* N. Y., 1905, vol. I, pp. 167 ff.
516. Smolian, Arthur, "Berlioz"; *Kunstwart,* Dec. 1903
517. Squires, Paul C., "The creative psychology of Berlioz"; *Journal of Musicology,* Sept. 1940, pp. 76–87
      [Assumes "mental disorder" in Berlioz and shows its "concurrence with musical genius"]

518. Stebbins, R. P. (pseud. "Cherubini"), "Shakespeare and Hector Berlioz"; MS. submitted at Harvard University for a Bowdoin Prize, 1933 (Communicated by Mr. Stebbins)
[A most thorough and able study, though marred by acceptance of the conventional view of Berlioz' mind]

519. Stoll, Dennis, "Hector Berlioz"; *London Philharmonic Post*, I, No. 12, pp. 4–5
[This periodical, besides using a musical quotation from the *Roman Carnival* Overture as part of its cover design, often prints interesting comments on British performances of Berlioz]

520. Storer, H. J., "The Student Struggle of Berlioz"; *Musician*, 1917, 22, p. 712

521. Thomson, Virgil, "The Berlioz Case"; *N. Y. Herald Tribune*, Oct. 11, 1942

522. Tiersot, J., "Berlioz Compositeur de musique religieuse"; *Revue Bleue*, 1895, pp. 500–3

522a. "Berlioz à l'Aube du Romantisme"; *Musicale*, Nov. and Dec. 1927; Jan. 1928, pp. 53–67; 119–23; 167–78

523. Toye, Francis, "The Cult of Berlioz"; *Morning Post*, Oct. 31, 1934

524. Turner, W. J., "Problem of Berlioz"; *New Statesman*, Oct. 25 and Nov. 8, 1924

525. ———— "Homage to Berlioz"; *New Statesman*, Mar. 21, 1936

526. Various Hands, *Berlioz, being the report of a discussion held on Dec. 17, 1928* [under the auspices of *The Dominant*]; L. (Oxford University Press) 1929. See also

527. "A Postscript to a Discussion"; *Musical Times*, Apr. 1, 1929, pp. 304 ff., by M. D. Calvocoressi; and

528. "A Berlioz Conference"; by T. S. Wotton, *Musical Times*, Apr. 1, 1929, pp. 318 ff.

529. Verne, D. B., "Berlioz *versus* the Organ"; *The Organ*, Jan. 1927, pp. 171 ff.
[A good example of ranting, religious animus, and anecdotal incoherence]

530. Villars, Henri Gauthier, "Berlioz et Wagner"; *Renaissance Latine*, May 15, 1903, pp. 410 ff
[See also *406* and *917;* Villars' pseudonym for other occasions was Willy]

531. Wolf, Hugo, Essays on Berlioz in *Hugo Wolfs musikalische Kritiken, im Auftrage des Wiener akademischen Wagnervereins, herausg. von Richard Batka und Heinrich Werner;* Leipzig, 1911

532. Wood, Ralph H., "Berlioz?"; *Musical Opinion*, Dec. 1942, pp. 77–78

533. Wotton, T. S., *Berlioz: Four Works* (Musical Pilgrim Series); L. 1929
[The *Symphonie Fantastique*, Overture to *Benvenuto Cellini, The Corsair, La Captive*]

534. ———— "Berlioz the Blood-Curdler"; *Musical Mirror*, Nov. 1930, p. 319

535. ———— "Berlioz as Melodist"; *Musical Times*, Sept. 1, 1929

536. ———— Introduction to Breitkopf und Härtel British Catalogue of Centenary Edition; L. 1904
[English version of the same article in *Mitteilungen von Breitkopf und Härtel in Leipzig*, No. 73, Mar. 1903, pp. 2814–8]

537. ———— "The Scores of Berlioz and Some Modern Editing"; *Musical Times*, Nov. 1, 1915, pp. 651–6

538. —— "Stray Notes on Berlioz"; *Zeitschrift der Internationalen Musik Gesellschaft,* 5th year, Leipzig 1903–1904, pp. 395–9

539. Zuth, Joseph, "Die Gitarre des Berlioz"; *Zeitschrift für die Gitarre,* Apr. 1, 1922, pp. 8–11
[See also *827*]

4B — CRITICISM: PARTICULAR WORKS

(in alphabetical order; not including chapters from works listed elsewhere)

Beatrice and Benedict

540. Hanslick, Eduard, "Beatrice and Benedict"; in *Studies in Music by Various Authors,* ed. Robin Grey, L. 1901, pp. 324–32
[Mainly disapproval with some just insights]

541. Imbert, H., "Béatrice et Bénédict"; in *Symphonie: Mélanges de Critique Littéraire Musicale;* P. 1891
[A Wagnerian's view]

542. Lostalot, Alfred de, "Revue Musicale"; *Gazette des Beaux Arts,* 3ème Période, vol. 4, pp. 82 ff.
[One of the best statements about Berlioz' art, apropos of *Béatrice et Bénédict*]

543. Rostand, Claude, "Béatrice et Bénédict" [P.] *Radio 48,* Sept. 9, 1948
[Note on the broadcast version]

Benvenuto Cellini

544. Anon., *Notice sur Benvenuto Cellini;* Théâtre des Champs Elysées, P. Apr. 1913

545. Blaze, H., "De l'Ecole fantastique et de M. Berlioz"; *Revue des Deux Mondes,* Oct. 1, 1838

546. Bornoff, J., "Some Notes on Berlioz' Benvenuto Cellini"; *Nineteenth Century,* Mar. 1940, pp. 341 ff.

547. Brecher, G., "Le Carnaval Romain" (*Musikführer* No. 175); Leipzig n.d.

548. Bülow, Hans von, "Hector Berlioz: *Benvenuto Cellini*"; *Neue Zeitschrift für Musik,* Apr. 2 and 30, 1852; repr. in *Ausgewählte Schriften,* Leipzig, 1911, 2 vols., I, 190 ff.

549. Lalo, P., "*Benvenuto Cellini*"; feuilletons du *Temps,* Oct. 11, Nov. 8 and 22, 1910 and Apr. 8, 1913
[Best essay in French]

550. Mikorey, Franz, "*Benvenuto Cellini:* einiges über die Aufgaben des Regisseurs"; *Merker* (Vienna) 1915, pp. 269–72

551. Pohl, R., "Berlioz' *Benvenuto Cellini*"; in *Franz Liszt,* Leipzig 1883, pp. 146–60

552. —— "Berlioz' *Benvenuto Cellini* in Carlsruhe"; *Musical World,* May 22 and 29, 1886
[Sound criticism by a contemporary of the earlier revival under Liszt at Weimar]

552a. Prodhomme, J. G., "Les deux *Benvenuto Cellini* de Berlioz"; *Zeitschrift der Internationalen Musikgesellschaft,* Apr.–June 1913, pp. 449–60
[Comparison of texts of 1838 and 1852 with comments on performances of 1911]

553. Smolian, Arthur, *Benvenuto Cellini* (Opernführer No. 31) Leipzig n.d.

554. Turner, W. J., "Glasgow's Great Enterprise"; *New Statesman*, Apr. 4, 1936
  [On *Benvenuto Cellini* and *Beatrice and Benedict*]
555. Würz, Anton, *Franz Lachner als dramatischer Komponist*; Munich 1927
  [Indicates relation of Lachner's *Benvenuto* to that of Berlioz]

Damnation of Faust

556. Anon., "Berlioz' Faust"; *Saturday Review*, Nov. 29, 1885
  [An admirable critique]
557. Anon., "Production of Berlioz' *Faust* as an Opera by the Carl Rosa Opera Company," *Athenaeum*, Feb. 10, 1894, p. 187
558. ———[McN.(aught, W.)] "*La Damnation de Faust* as an Opera"; *Musical Times*, July 1933, pp. 645–6
559. Bellaigue, Camille, "*La Damnation de Faust*"; *Revue des Deux Mondes*, 1903, 16, pp. 220–9
560. Bonnefon, P., "Les avatars du Faust"; *Revue Bleue*, May 12, 1917, pp. 292–5
  [Relates the dealings of Berlioz and Scribe and confirms the justness of Berlioz' remarks on Gounod's opera]
561. Boschot, Adolphe, *Le Faust de Berlioz*; P. 1910
  [Later eds. revised and augmented]
562. Capell, Richard, "*The Damnation of Faust*"; *Daily Telegraph*, May 27, 1933
563. Carraud, Gaston, "Les Marionettes du Docteur Faust"; *Revue des Deux Mondes*, Mar. 1, 1909, pp. 85–115
564. Champeaux, G., *La Damnation de Faust*; booklet accompanying the French Columbia recording; P. n.d. [1945?]
565. Cooper, Martin, "Music"; *London Mercury*, Apr. 1936, p. 628
566. Debussy, Claude, "Berlioz et M. Gunzbourg"; *Gil Blas*, May 19, 1903
567. de la Rosa, Rodrigo [On Berlioz and the Rákóczy March], *Györi Közlöny* [Gyor (Raab)] Jan. 15, 1860
568. D'Udine, Jean (pseud. Albert Cozanet), "*La Damnation de Faust*"; *Courrier Musical*, Jan. 1, 1904
  [The best essay in French]
569. Gilman, Lawrence, "Berlioz' *Damnation of Faust*"; Harper's Weekly, Dec. 22, 1906
570. Halm, August, *Von Grenzen und Ländern der Musik* (*Ges. Aufsätze*); 2nd ed. Munich, 1916
  [Excellent essays on *Damnation of Faust* and *Les Troyens*]
571. Hanslick, Eduard, *Aus dem Concertsaal*; Vienna 1869
  [Contains a long essay on the *Damnation of Faust* from the point of view of a convert to neoclassicism]
571a. Henderson, W. J., "*The Damnation of Faust* at the Metropolitan"; Review in the *N. Y. Sun*, repr. in *Metropolitan Opera Annals*, ed. W. H. Seltsam, N. Y. 1947, p. 172
572. Harazsti, Emile, "Berlioz, Liszt and Rákóczy"; *Musical Quarterly*, April 1940
  [The completest essay, with only one or two slips about matters extraneous to the main subject]
573. Hoechst, C. R., "*Faust*" in *Music*; Gettysburg, 1916
  [Sensible treatment of Berlioz' *Damnation*]

574. Isoz, Kalmán, "Le manuscript original de 'Rákóczy' de Berlioz"; *Revue des études hongroises,* 1924, 5–17
[Plausible until one consults 572]
575. Landormy, Paul, Introduction to Recording of *La Damnation de Faust* (French H.M.V.); P. 1931
575a. Lawrence, Robert, "The Greater Berlioz"; *N. Y. Herald Tribune,* Apr. 28, 1940
[Review of a Cleveland performance, by a perceptive student of Berlioz]
576. Lefèvre, Maurice, "*La Damnation de Faust*"; *Musica,* May 1903
[A history of the work after Berlioz' death]
577. Newman, Ernest, "*La Damnation de Faust*"; *Sunday Times,* May 28, 1933
578. Prod'homme, J. G., *La Damnation de Faust* (Le Cycle Berlioz) 2ème ed., P. 1896
579. Rougier, Elzéard, *Hector Berlioz: La Damnation de Faust à Marseille,* P. 1884
580. Sternfeld, R., "Hector Berlioz und seine Faustmusik"; *Westermanns Monatshefte;* Jan. 1904, pp. 485–92
581. Tiersot, Julien, *La Damnation de Faust;* P. 1924
582. Winterbottom, R., "Music"; *The Choir,* Jan. and July 1932, pp. 32 and 144
[A good criticism of the Hallé Orchestra performances of the *Damnation of Faust,* written from the point of view of a choral conductor]

Funeral and Triumphal Symphony
583. Bonavia, F., "Stravinsky and Berlioz in London"; *New York Times,* Mar. 22, 1936
[On the *Funeral* symphony and *Requiem*]
584. Boutarel, Amédée, "Berlioz und seine architecturale Musik" (see 478)
585. Goldman, Richard Franko, "Grand Symphony for Band"; Mercury Music Corp., N. Y. 1947
[Preface to his edition of Berlioz' *Funeral and Triumphal* symphony]
586. Hughes, Patrick, "Two Works of Berlioz"; *Daily Telegraph,* March 5, 1934
[*Funeral* symphony and *Requiem*]
586a. Wotton, T. S., "Berlioz' 'Funeral and Triumphal' Symphony"; *Musical Opinion,* July 1936, pp. 841–2

Harold in Italy
587. Liszt, Franz, *Hector Berlioz und seine Harold-Symphonie;* Deutsch bearbeitet von L. Ramann; Leipzig 1881
588. Montaux, A., "Berlioz: son génie, sa technique, son caractère; à propos d'un manuscrit autographe d'*Harold en Italie*"; *Ménestrel,* July 27 – Sept. 7, 1890
[Deals chiefly with the second movement of the symphony, and makes useful remarks, though occasionally extends inference beyond reasonable limits]
589. Ritter, Herman, *Einiges zum Verständnis von Berlioz' Haroldsinfonie und künstlerischer Bedeutung,* Oppeln 1899

590. Tovey, Sir Donald, *Essays in Musical Analysis;* L. 1936, Vol. IV
      [On *Harold in Italy, Romeo and Juliet,* etc.]

The Infant Christ

591. Anon., Review of *L'Enfance du Christ, London Times,* Jan. 1885
592. ―――― "L'Enfance du Christ"; *Guide Musical,* Mar. 19 and Apr. 3, 1911
      [Report on the staging of the oratorio]
593. Bonavia, F., "London Hears a Berlioz Oratorio"; *N. Y. Times,* Jan. 28,
      1945
594. Brunet, J., "L'Enfance du Christ"; *Guide Musical,* Apr. 3, 1911
595. Prod'homme, J. G., *L'Enfance du Christ (Le Cycle Berlioz);* P. 1898

Overtures, Songs and Cantatas

596. Anon., Program Notes to Maggie Teyte, "An Album of French Songs";
      The Gramophone Shop, N. Y. 1938
597. Anon., Review of anniversary performance of Berlioz' *Cléopatre* and
      Méditation Religieuse, Pall Mall Gazette, Nov. 13, 1903
597a. Casembroot, J. L. de, "L'Ouverture des Francs-Juges: opinions de Men-
      delssohn, Schumann, et Moschelès"; *Revue Internationale de Musique,*
      1899 (21) pp. 1327–33
598. Cooper, Martin, "Berlioz' song cycle: *Nuits d'Eté*"; *Radio Times,*
      Mar. 21, 1936
      [Analysis coupled with reluctant admiration]
599. Louis, Rudolf, Review of Berlioz "Heroic Scene: the Greek Revolu-
      tion" and "Religious Meditation" in *478;* see also *479*
600. Pitt, P., and Kalisch, A., *Analytical Notes of Berlioz Centenary Program;*
      Queen's Hall, Dec. 11, 1903
601. Puttmann, Max, "Hector Berlioz als Gesangkomponist"; *Neue Zeit-
      schrift für Musik* (Leipzig) Dec. 9, 1903
602. Smolian, Arthur, Preface to *Sieben Ouverturen;* Eulenburg *Min. Sc.,*
      Leipzig 1899
      [As well as Prefaces to Eulenburg *Min. Sc.* of *Phantastische Sym-
      phonie, Harold in Italien, Romeo und Julia*]
603. Spills, Helen, "French Art Song Composers before Fauré and Debussy";
      Etude Jan. 1944
      [Excellent on Berlioz' role as pathfinder]
604. Walker, Ernest, "The Songs of Berlioz"; *Monthly Musical Record,*
      June 1932, pp. 103 ff.
      [A sample of choosy but fair appraisal]
605. Wotton, T. S., "A Berlioz Caprice and its 'Programme' "; *Musical Times,*
      Aug. 1, 1927
      [Points out that the program printed with Berlioz' *Reverie et
      Caprice* was written some eleven years after Berlioz' death]
606. ―――― "An Unknown Score of Berlioz"; *Music Review,* November
      1943, pp. 224–8
      [A posthumous article about *Sardanapale* made up of fragments
      found in Wotton's copy of the incomplete score]

Requiem

607. Anon., "Berlioz' *Requiem*"; *Athenaeum,* June 2, 1883
608. Barry, C. A., "Berlioz' *Requiem*"; *Musical Review,* May 26, 1883
      [On the day of the first English performance]

609. Barzun, J., "The Requiem: Program Notes"
[For the performance at Columbia University, April 25, 1941]

609a. Berrsche, Alex., "Berlioz: Totenmesse" in *Trösterin Musika* (*Ges. Aufsätzen*) Munich, 1942, pp. 555 ff.

610. Boughton, Rutland, "The Requiem of Berlioz"; *Vocalist*, Dec. 1902
[A "Symbolist" view written at the age of 24]

611. Boutarel, A., "Le Requiem de Berlioz"; *Ménestrel*, Jan. 31, 1904

612. Champeaux, G., *"La Grande Messe des Morts* de Berlioz"; (Columbia-Pathé-Marconi) 1944

613. Darrell, R. D., "Requiem Mass"; *Review of Recorded Music,* Oct. 1948, p. 12

614. Dukas, Paul, "Le Requiem de Berlioz"; *Revue Hebdomadaire,* 1894; 22; pp. 466–71

615. Hallynck, P., "Comment fut exécuté pour la première fois le *Requiem* de Berlioz"; *Annales Politiques et Littéraires,* Nov. 22, 1925, pp. 537 ff.

616. Imbert, H., "Le *Requiem*"; *Guide Musical,* Jan. 24, 1904

617. Lawrence, Robert, "Berlioz and the Four Brass Bands"; *Saturday Review of Literature,* Oct. 30, 1948, pp. 55–60

618. Ochs, Siegfried, *Der deutsche Gesangverein für Gemischten Chor;* 4ter Teil; Berlin 1928
[A manual for performers arranged by periods and authors, valuable for Berlioz' *Requiem*]

619. Schlitzer, Franco, *Il Grande Requiem di Ettore Berlioz;* Naples 1939

620. Toulmon, Bottée de, "Du Requiem de M. Berlioz"; *Gazette Musicale,* Dec. 10, 1837

621. Turner, W. J., "A Musical Cataclysm" [The *Requiem*]; in *Musical Meanderings;* N. Y. n.d.

Romeo and Juliet

622. Bagar, R., and Biancolli, L., *Program Notes for N. Y. Philharmonic Society Concert of Oct 7, 1942*

623. Barzun, Jacques, "A Note on Berlioz' 'Romeo' Setting"; *N. Y. Times,* Oct. 4, 1942

624. Bayliss, Stanley, *"Romeo and Juliet* by Hector Berlioz"; *Choir,* Feb. 1940
[A negligible patchwork of quotations]

625. Capell, R., "Berlioz' Rare *Romeo*"; *Daily Telegraph,* Jan. 18, 1934

626. Dukas, Paul, *"Romeo et Juliette* de Berlioz"; *Revue Hebdomadaire,* 1894, 31, pp. 464–72

Symphonie Fantastique (and *Lélio*)

627. Anon., "The Richter Concerts"; *Saturday Review,* June 21, 1884
[Explains how unsympathetic conducting and niggardly means ruined the *Symphonie Fantastique*]

628. ———— "The Bristol Festival"; *Daily Telegraph,* Oct. 12 and 13, 1905
[Accounts of the performance of the "Episode in an Artist's Life" (*S. Fantastique* and *Lélio*)]

629. ———— "Bristol Musical Festival"; *Times* (London) Oct. 12, 1905
[Reports a performance of *Lélio* with Lawrence Irving in the title role]

630. Bonavia, F., "Berlioz"; *Monthly Musical Record,* Aug. 1929, pp. 231 ff.
[One of the best short statements concerning the *Symphonie Fantastique* and Romanticism in Berlioz]

631. Bourges, Maurice, "Examen de quelques compositions de M. Berlioz sous le rapport du plan"; *Gazette Musicale*, Mar. 27, 1842
    [Notably the *Symphonie Fantastique*]

632. Capell, Richard, Review of the *Symphonie Fantastique; Daily Telegraph*, Feb. 24, 1933

633. Gilbert, Richard, "Symphonie Fantastique"; *Victor Record Review*, June 1940, pp. 4 ff.

634. Hahn, Arthur, "Berlioz: Episode aus dem Leben eines Künstlers. Phantastische Symphonie in fünf Sätzen"; in *Musiker und Ihre Werke*, Frankfurt a.M. n.d.

635. Hale, Philip, *Great Concert Music;* ed. John N. Burk, Garden City, 1939
    [Essay on *Symphonie Fantastique* and references to other works]

636. Magnette, Paul, *Les Grandes Etapes dans l'Oeuvre de Berlioz;* I: *Symphonie Fantastique;* Liège 1908

637. Sternfeld, Richard, "Ist der *Lélio* Aufführbar?" in *478*

638. Turner, W. J., "Massine's Berlioz Ballet"; *New Statesman*, Aug. 1, 1936
    [A choreographic rendering of the *Symphonie Fantastique*]

639. Whittaker, W. G., "*Lélio* at Strasbourg"; *Musical Times*, Sept. 1, 1929, p. 814

Te Deum

640. Anon., "Berlioz' *Te Deum*"; *Athenaeum*, Apr. 25, 1885
    [A good review of the first English performance]

641. Capell, Richard, "Beecham and Berlioz: Thrilling *Te Deum*"; *Daily Telegraph*, Apr. 20, 1934

642. Newman, Ernest, "Berlioz' *Te Deum*"; *Sunday Times*, Apr. 22, 1934

643. Pohl, Richard, "Berlioz' *Te Deum*"; *Musical Review*, May 1, 1885
    [Account of the first complete performance of the score in Germany]

644. Rankin, Nancy, and Falle, George, *Festival Montréal* [featuring Berlioz' *Te Deum*] Program of Oct. 12, 1945

645. Smolian, Arthur, *Berlioz' Te Deum (Musikführer* No. 193/194); Leipzig n.d.

646. Tiersot, J., "Le *Te Deum* d'Hector Berlioz"; notice written for the performance of May 14, 1936 in Paris
    [The last comments by this indefatigable Berlioz scholar]

647. Turner, W. J., "A Berlioz Masterpiece"; *Listener*, July 8, 1943
    [On a performance of the *Te Deum*]

Les Troyens

648. Anon., " 'Les Troyens' at Brussels"; *London Times*, Jan. 1, 1907
    [A good review which details the mistakes so commonly made by managers of revivals, to the detriment of the work revived]

649. —— "Die Trojaner"; in *Münchener Zeitung*, June 9, 1908

650. —— "Die Trojaner"; in *Münchener Neueste Nachrichten*, June 7, 1908

651. —— "*The Trojans at Carthage* in Manchester"; *Manchester Guardian*, Nov. 2, 1928

652. —— "The Trojans at Manchester"; *Musical Times*, Dec. 1, 1928, Jan. and Feb. 1929

653. Bellaigue, Camille, "Les Troyens à Carlsruhe"; *Revue des Deux Mondes*, 1892, 112, p. 459

654. ————— "Les Troyens de Berlioz"; *Revue des Deux Mondes,* 1921, 4, pp. 223–9

655. Bertrand, G., "La Crise musicale. A propos des *Troyens*"; *Revue Germanique,* Dec. 1, 1863
    [A superb essay by an opponent who understands despite his objections]

656. Boschot, A., "*Les Troyens* de Berlioz"; *Revue Politique et Littéraire,* July 16, 1921, pp. 461–3

657. Bouyer, R., "*Les Troyens* de Berlioz à l'Opéra"; *Revue Politique et Littéraire,* Nov. 15, 1919, pp. 700–3

658. Capell, Richard, "Berlioz' Trojans"; *Musical Times,* Jan. 1, 1929

659. Cooper, Martin, "Berlioz' Trojan Operas"; *New Statesman and Nation,* May 29, 1947, p. 848

660. Destranges, E., *Les Troyens de Berlioz;* P. 1897
    [A good brief critical analysis]

661. Gilson, Paul, "Les Troyens"; *Le Soir* (Brussels) Dec. 28 and 29, 1906

662. Halm, August, "Die Trojaner" in 570

663. Joly, A., "A propos des *Troyens* de Berlioz"; *Guide Musical,* Dec. 16, 1906

664. Jullien, A., "Les Troyens à Carlsruhe"; *Revue d'art Dramatique,* 1891 21, pp. 65 ff.

665. Kolb, Annette, "Berlioz à Munich"; *Mercure de France,* 1908, 71, p. 373

666. Newman, Ernest, "Berlioz and 'The Trojans,'" *Sunday Times,* June 19 and Sept. 4, 1921

667. ————— "The Trojans"; *Sunday Times,* Mar. 24, 1935

667a. Peyser, Herbert F., "Revival of Berlioz Opera Heard in Paris" [*La Prise de Troie*], *N. Y. Times,* Jan. 1, 1939

668. Robert, Paul-Louis, *Hector Berlioz: Les Troyens;* Rouen 1920
    [Fine essay by a lifelong student of Berlioz]

669. Scudo, P., "*Les Troyens* de M. Berlioz"; *Revue des Deux Mondes,* 1863, 48, pp. 503–6

670. Smolian, Arthur, *Die Trojaner* (Opernführer No. 4) Leipzig n.d.

671. Thoinan, E. (pseud. "Feu Nantho"), *L'Opera Les Troyens au Père Lachaise;* P. 1863
    [The scurrilous author, using a double pseudonym, is now known to be Ernest Roquet, on whom see anonymous article in *Guide Musical,* May 5, 1907]

672. Turner, W. J., "The *Trojans* at Glasgow"; *New Statesman,* Mar. 30, 1935

Writings

673. Bartenstein, Hans, *Hector Berlioz' Instrumentationskunst und ihre geschichtlichen Grundlagen;* Leipzig 1939 (Vol. 28 of Karl Nef's *Sammlung Musikwissenschaftlicher Abhandlungen*)
    [The completest and closest study to date]

674. Bernoulli, Ed., *Hector Berlioz als Æsthetiker der Klangfarben;* Zürich 1909

675. Boschot, A., *Hector Berlioz, critique musical;* Bruxelles 1938

676. Cuvillier-Fleury, A. A., "M. Hector Berlioz en Italie"; in *Dernières études historiques et littéraires;* P. 1859, vol. II

677. Hallays, André, "Hector Berlioz, critique musical"; *Revue de Paris,* 1903. pp. 560–95
    [The best single study on the subject]

678. Helms, F., "Berlioz' Musikalische Wanderungen durch Deutschland"; *Kleine Musikzeitung*, Hamburg 1848. Pp. 142–4 and 150–2
     [A nationalist critique]
679. Henley, W. E., *Views and Reviews*
     Vol. I: *Literature;* L. 1892
     [Essay on Berlioz' Memoirs]
680. Jong, J. De, "Berlioz als Criticus"; *Onze Eeuw*, 1904, pp. 41–67
681. Kenyon, C. F., "The Autobiography of Berlioz"; *Musical Standard*, Oct. 26, 1901
682. Lanctot, E. C. N., "Berlioz' Picturesque Memoirs"; *Etude*, Feb. 1946, pp. 83 ff.
683. Mey, Kurt, "Hector Berlioz als Dramatiker"; in *478*
684. Morillot, Paul, *Berlioz Ecrivain;* Grenoble 1903
     [Brief but just]
685. Strauss, Richard, "Sur l'Orchestration"; tr. E. Closson of Strauss's remarks on Berlioz' *Treatise. Bulletin S.I.M.*, Mar. 1909
     [Originally for volume of Strauss's comments (Peters) Leipzig 1909]
686. ———— Reviewed by Pierre Lalo, *Le Temps*, Oct. 2, 1909
687. ———— Reviewed by Ernest Closson, *Guide Musical*, Sept. 26, and Oct. 3, 1909
688. Thompson, Francis, *Literary Criticism. Newly Discovered and Collected* by T. L. Connolly; N. Y. 1948
     [Refers to Berlioz' *Memoirs*, pp. 23–4]
689. Villemer, Marquis de (pseud. of Charles Emile Yriarte), *Les Portraits Cosmopolites;* P. 1870
     [Eyewitness of Berlioz' latter days and reviewer of the *Memoirs* in the year of their appearance, having read them at the printing press where both authors came to read proof]
690. Wotton, T. S., " 'Infernal Language': a Berlioz Hoax"; *Musical Times*, Oct. 1936
691. Zola, Emile, "Hector Berlioz"; in *Le Roman Experimental;* P. 1893, pp. 320–7

5. HISTORIES OF MUSIC

A — GENERAL WORKS

692. Abraham, Gerald, *A Hundred Years of Music;* L. 1938
693. Allen, W. D., *Philosophies of Music History;* N. Y. 1939
694. Apel, Willi, *Masters of the Keyboard;* Cambridge (U.S.A.) 1947
695. Apthorp, W. F., *The Opera, Past and Present;* N. Y. 1901
696. Bekker, Paul, *The Story of the Orchestra,* N. Y. 1936
697. Berg, D. E., *Early and Classic Symphonies and the Functions of the Conductor;* N. Y. 1927
698. Bernstein, Martin, *An Introduction to Music;* N. Y. 1946
699. Blom, Eric, *Music in England;* L. 1947
700. Botstiber, Hugo, *Geschichte der Ouvertüre und der freien Orchesterformen;* Leipzig 1913
701. Brendel, F., *Geschichte der Musik;* Leipzig 1852; 7th ed., 1887
702. Bruneau, Alfred, *La Musique Française;* P. 1901
703. ———— *Musiques d'hier et de demain;* P. 1900
704. Burney, Charles, *A General History of Music;* L. 1935, 2 vols.

705. Carse, Adam, *The History of Orchestration;* L. 1925
706. —— *The Orchestra from Beethoven to Berlioz;* Cambridge (Eng.) 1948
707. Chantavoine, Jean, *De Couperin à Debussy;* P. 1913
708. Coeuroy, André, *La Musique Française Moderne;* P. 1924
709. Colles, H. C., *The Growth of Music;* vol. III: *Ideals of the 19th Century;* L. 1920
710. Comettant, O., *La musique, les musiciens, et les instruments de musique chez les différents peuples du monde . . .;* Archives de . . . l'Exposition internationale de 1867, P. 1869
711. Coquard, Arthur, *De la musique en France depuis Rameau;* P. 1891
712. Cui, Cesar, *La musique en Russie;* P. 1881
713. Dorian, Frederick, *History of Music in Performance;* N. Y. 1942
714. —— *The Musical Workshop;* N. Y. 1947
715. Dumesnil, René, *La Musique romantique française;* P. 1944
716. Einstein, Alfred, *Music in the Romantic Era;* N. Y. 1947
717. Emmanuel, M., *Histoire de la langue musicale;* P. 1911, 2 vols
718. Ferguson, Donald N., *A History of Musical Thought;* N. Y. 1936
719. Gray, Cecil, *A History of Music;* 2nd rev. ed. (*The History of Civilization*), N. Y. 1835
720. —— *A Survey of Contemporary Music;* L. 1927
721. —— *Predicaments, or Music and the Future;* L. 1936
        [These three volumes form a trilogy in which the author develops the most comprehensive body of critical ideas in modern musicology]
722. Grout, Donald J., *A Short History of Opera;* N. Y. 1947, 2 vols.
        [Throughout a very useful work; perceptive as to *Les Troyens* though conventionally mistaken as to *Benvenuto Cellini*]
723. Hervey, Arthur, *French Music in the 19th century;* L. 1903
724. Hill, Edward B., *Modern French Music;* N. Y. 1924
725. Hipsher, E. E., *American Opera and its Composers;* Philadelphia, 1927
726. Howard, J. T., *Our American Music;* N. Y. 1929
727. Hueffer, Francis, *Half a Century of Music in England;* L. 1889
        [Rev. ed., Boston, 1931]
728. Klauwell, Otto, *Geschichte der Programmusik;* Leipzig 1910
729. Koechlin, Charles, "Evolution de l'harmonie"; *Encyclopédie de la Musique,* vol. I
730. —— "French Music"; *Encyclopedia Americana,* 1918–1947 ed., vol. XI, pp. 680–8
731. Lalo, Pierre, *De Rameau à Ravel;* P. 1947
732. Lambert, Constant, *Music Ho!;* L. 1934
        [Brilliant treatment of modern music]
733. Landormy, Paul, *La musique française de la Marseillaise à la mort de Berlioz;* P. 1944
734. Lang, Paul H., *Music in Western Civilization;* N. Y. 1941
735. Lavignac, Albert, *Music and Musicians;* N. Y. 1901
736. Lavoix fils, H., *Histoire de la musique;* P. n.d.
737. —— *La musique française;* P. 1891
738. Malliot, A.-L., *La musique au Théâtre;* P. 1863
        [A study of Paris institutions by a colleague of Berlioz]
739. Mason, D. G., *From Grieg to Brahms;* N. Y. 1903
740. Moos, Paul, *Die Philosophie der Musik von Kant bis Eduard von Hartmann;* 2nd ed., Leipzig 1922

741. Naumann, Emil, *The History of Music;* tr. F. Praeger, L. n.d., 2 vols.
742. Nettel, Reginald, *The Orchestra in England. A Social History;* L. 1946
743. Newmarch, Rosa, *The Music of Czechoslovakia;* L. 1942
 [Useful on Berlioz' teacher Reicha]
744. Niecks, Frederick, *Programme Music in the Last Four Centuries: A Contribution to the History of Musical Expression;* L. 1907
745. *Oxford History of Music,* ed. W. H. Hadow; vol. VI: *The Romantic Period* by Edward Dannreuther; L. 1905
 [Long considered "standard," the account of Berlioz is both prejudiced and inaccurate]
746. Pannain, Guido, *Modern Composers (Musicisti dei Tempi Nuovi,* 1932); L. 1932
747. Prunières, Henry, *A New History of Music: The Middle Ages to Mozart;* Introd. Romain Rolland; tr. Edw. Lockspeiser, N. Y. 1943
748. Rockstro, W. S., *A General History of Music;* 3rd ed., L. 1888
749. Russell, C. E., *The American Orchestra and Theodore Thomas;* N. Y. 1927
750. Sachs, Curt, *Our Musical Heritage: a Short History of World Music;* N. Y. 1948
751. Scholes, Percy A., *The Listener's History of Music;* L. 1930
752. Streatfeild, R. A., *The Opera;* L. 1934
753. Various Hands, *English Music. Lectures at the Music Loan Exhibition;* L. 1911
 [Especially useful on the history of instruments]
754. Weingartner, Felix, *The Symphony since Beethoven;* L. 1904
755. Weinstock, Herbert, and Brockway, Wallace, *The Opera: a History of its Creation and Performance: 1600–1941;* N. Y. 1941
756. White, William Carter, *A History of Military Music in America;* N. Y. 1944

5B — MUSIC: SPECIAL STUDIES

757. Abraham, Gerald, ed., *The Music of Schubert;* N. Y. 1947
758. Aldrich, R., "Beethoven and George Thomson"; *Music and Letters,* April 1927, pp. 234–42
759. Ambros, A. W., *Die Grenzen der Musik;* Prague, 1856
760. Amster, Leonard, Review of Alban Berg's Violin Concerto; *Decision;* Oct. 1941
761. Apthorp, W. F., *By the Way . . . Essays on Music . . . from the Program-Books of the Boston Symphony Orchestra;* Boston 1898, 2 vols.
762. Bairstow, E. C., *Handel's Oratorio "Messiah";* L. 1928 (Musical Pilgrim Series)
763. Berteval, W., "Wagner et la hantise de Beethoven"; *Grande Revue,* Oct. 1933, pp. 597–617
764. Bertrand, G., *Les nationalités musicales étudiées dans le drame lyrique;* P. 1873
 [Close and sympathetic attention to Berlioz, mixed with biographical guesswork]
765. Biggs, E. Power, "The Organ Revival: Music Old and New"; *Modern Music,* June 1944
 [The casual type of error about Berlioz]

766. Blaze, Henri, "Meyerbeer"; *Revue des Deux Mondes*, Jan.–Feb. 1836, pp. 678 ff.
767. —— *Musiciens du passé*; P. 1880
768. Blom, Eric, *Stepchildren of Music*; L. n.d.
       [For Wagner's songs, relations to Schumann, etc.]
769. Boschot, Adolphe, *Carnet d'Art*; P. 1911
770. —— *Chez les Musiciens*; P. 1922–1926, 3 vols.
771. Boys, Henry, "Stravinsky"; *Monthly Musical Record*, Dec. 1934, pp. 227 ff.
772. Bruneau, A., "La musique en Russie"; *Revue de Paris*, 1902
773. Busoni, Ferruccio, *Scritti e Pensieri sulla Musica*; ed. Luigi Dallapiccola and Guido M. Gatti; Florence 1919
774. —— *Sketch of a New Esthetic of Music*; tr. Th. Baker, N. Y. 1911
775. Calvocoressi, M. D., *Musical Taste*; L. 1925
776. —— *Principles and Methods of Musical Criticism*; new ed. enlarged, L. 1931
777. Chantavoine, Jean, "Le Centenaire de Gounod"; *Revue Hebdomadaire*, Aug. 1918
778. —— "Wagner peint par lui-mème"; *Revue Hebdomadaire*, 1912, vol. 43, pp. 542–55
       [A sympathetic but thorough account of the unreliability of *Mein Leben*]
779. Combarieu, J., *Les rapports de la musique et de la poésie considérés au point de vue de l'expression*; P. 1893
780. Corder, F., "Franz Liszt"; *Bulletin Mensuel de la Société Internationale de Musique*; Jan. 1912, 131–6
781. Cowell, Henry, *New Musical Resources*; N. Y. 1931
782. Crosten, William L., *French Grand Opera, an Art and a Business*; N. Y. 1948
       [Admirably compact]
783. Cucuel, G., *Etudes sur un orchestre au 18ème siècle*; P. 1913
784. Curzon, H. de, "Les contrefaçons et parodies du *Freischütz*," *Guide Musical*, May 6, 1906
785. Dalcroze, Emile Jaques-, *Rhythm, Music, and Education*; tr. H. F. Rubinstein, L. 1921
786. d'Anglas, Boissy, *Essai sur les fêtes nationales, suivi de quelques idées sur les arts*; P. 1794
787. Daubresse, M., "Quelques compositrices françaises"; *Guide Musical*, Nov. 17, 1907, pp. 695–9
       [Section on Louise Bertin]
788. Davies, Sir W., *The Pursuit of Music*; L. 1944
789. Debussy, Claude, *Monsieur Croche, antidilettante*; 7th ed., P. 1926
       [References are to: tr. B. N. Langdon Davies; N. Y. 1928; reprinted (Lear Publishers) N. Y. 1948]
790. Dickinson, A. E. F., *The Musical Design of the Ring* (Musical Pilgrim Series); L. 1926
791. d'Olonne, Max, "Mélodie et harmonie"; *Ménestrel*, Jul. 14, 1933
       [Expresses succinctly the traditional French view that all good melodies imply a single and "correct" harmony]
792. Duhamel, Raoul, *Eugène Delacroix et la musique*; Milan 1939
793. Dumesnil, René, "La musique"; *Mercure de France*, Nov. 1, 1939, p. 202
794. Dyson, George, *The New Music*; L. 1933

795. Einstein, Alfred, *Greatness in Music;* N. Y. 1941
796. Epstein, Peter, "Opera Oratorio: zur Gegenwartslage der Oper"; *Die Musik,* Sept. 1928, pp. 866–72
797. Ergo, Em., *Dans les Propylées de l'instrumentation;* P. 1908
798. Finkelstein, Sidney, *Jazz: a People's Music;* N. Y. 1948
799. Fitzgibbon, H. M., *The Story of the Flute (Music-Story Series)* L. 1914
800. Flesch, J., *Maladies professionnelles et hygiène du musicien;* tr. Pierre Hoff, P. n.d.
 [Deals with Berlioz' health and physique]
801. Forest, Paul, "La musique française contemporaine d'après M. Romain Rolland"; *Revue Musicale de Lyon,* Jan. and Feb. 1909, pp. 393–403 and 466–71
 [A compilation of Rolland's views derived from both the musical essays and the novel *Jean-Christophe*]
802. Foulds, John, *Music Today;* L. 1934
803. Gassner, F. S., *Traité de la partition;* tr. F. Hofer, P. 1851, 2 vols.
804. ———— *Dirigent und Repienist;* Karlsruhe 1844
805. Gevaert, F.-A., *Cours Méthodique d'Orchestration;* P. and Bruxelles 1890
806. ———— *Nouveau traité d'instrumentation;* P. and Bruxelles 1885
807. Goldman, Richard [H. M.], Franko, "The Symphony Band"; *Columbia* [University] *Varsity,* Oct. 1927
808. ———— *The Band's Music;* N. Y. 1938
809. ———— *The Concert Band;* N. Y. 1946
810. Gray, Cecil, *Contingencies;* L. 1947
811. Grétry, C., *Mémoires, ou Essais sur la musique;* P. 1797, 3 vols.
812. Gurney, Edmund, "Wagner and Wagnerism"; *Topics of the Times;* N. Y. 1883
813. ———— *The Power of Sound;* L. 1880
814. Henderson, W. J., *Preludes and Studies;* N. Y. 1892
815. Howe, M. A. deW., *The Boston Symphony Orchestra;* rev. ed. Boston 1931
816. Iacuzzi, Alfred, *The Vogue of Favart;* N. Y. 1932
817. Istel, Edgar, *Die Blüthezeit der musikalischen Romantik in Deutschland;* Leipzig 1909
818. ———— "Die Entstehung des deutschen Melodramas"; *Die Musik,* Feb. and Mar., 1905–1906, pp. 143 ff.
818a. ———— *Studien zur Geschichte des Melodramas: I. Jean-Jacques Rousseau, Etc.;* Leipzig, 1901
819. Jentsch, Ernst, "Musik und Nerven"; *Grenzfragen des Nerven- und Seelen-lebens;* vol. 12, No. 78, Wiesbaden, 1911
 [Deals with Berlioz psycho-physiologically]
820. Jullien, Adolphe, *Musiciens d'hier et d'aujourd'hui;* P. 1891
821. ———— *Musiciens d'aujourd'hui; 2ème série;* P. 1894
822. Kastner, Georges, *Cours d'instrumentation considérée sous les rapports poétiques et philosophiques de l'art;* P. 1837
823. ———— *Traité général d'instrumentation;* 2ème ed., P. 1836; *Supplement;* P. 1844 [?]
824. ———— *Manuel général de musique militaire;* P. 1848
825. Kirby, P. R., *The Kettledrums;* L. 1930
826. Kolodin, Irving, "Music"; *Arts Weekly,* May 7, 1932, p. 196

827. Kolon, Victor, "Die Pariser Gitarre von Paganini-Berlioz"; *Zeitschrift für die Gitarre*, Apr. 15, 1926, pp. 50–3
828. Korngold, Julius, *Die romanische Oper der Gegenwart;* Vienna 1922
829. Kufferath, M., "Weber et Wagner"; *Société Nouvelle*, VII (1) 1891, pp. 322–30
830. —— *L'art de diriger;* P. 1909
831. Kurth, Ernst, *Romantische Harmonik und ihre Krise in Wagner's Tristan;* Berne and Leipzig 1920
832. Lang, Paul H., "Background Music for *Mein Kampf*," and "Easter and Richard Wagner"; *Saturday Review of Literature*, Jan. 20 and Mar. 31, 1945
833. —— "Hearing Things"; *Saturday Review of Literature*, Dec. 14, 1946
834. Lavignac, Albert, *The Music Dramas of Richard Wagner;* tr. Esther Singleton, N. Y., 1905
835. Lavoix fils, H., *Les traducteurs de Goethe en musique;* P. 1869 (Orig. articles in *Revue et Gazette Musicale*)
    [Pedestrian review of both serious and frivolous scores]
836. Maril, Konrad, "Ferruccio Busoni: 1866–1924"; *The American Music Lover*, July 1939, pp. 78–81
837. McKinney, H. D., and Anderson, W. R., *The Challenge of Listening;* New Brunswick, 1943
838. Mellers, W. H., "The textual criticism of Music"; *Scrutiny*, Mar. 1939, pp. 480–5
839. Müller, Heinrich, *Das Verhältnis Cornelius-Wagner;* Rostock, 1933
    [A careful review of the literature on a significant question involving art and biography]
840. Myers, C. S., "Listening to music"; *British Journal of Psychology*, vol. XIII, pp. 52 ff.
841. Myers, Robert M., *Handel's "Messiah"*; N. Y. 1948
842. Newlin, Dika, *Bruckner, Mahler, Schoenberg;* N. Y. 1947.
843. Newman, Ernest, "Music and Race" in *Studies in Music*, ed. Robin Grey, L. 1901, pp. 302–10.
    [A thorough blasting of Parry's fallacies on the subject, especially as regards Berlioz]
844. —— *A Musical Motley;* N. Y. 1925
845. —— *The Great Operas;* N. Y. 1928–1930, 3 vols. in one
846. Nohl, Herman, *Typische Kunststile in Dichtung und Musik;* Jena 1915
    [Erroneously assigns Berlioz to Group I – the realists and positivists who explain by matter]
847. Noli, Bishop Fan S., *Beethoven and the French Revolution;* N. Y. 1947
848. Oliver, A. R., *The Encyclopedists as Critics of Music;* N. Y. 1947
849. Panzer, Fr., *Richard Wagner und das Deutschtum;* Frankfort 1933
850. Parry, Sir Hubert, *Style in Musical Art;* L. 1924
850a. Partch, Harry, *Genesis of a Music: Monophony;* Pref. Otto Luening, Madison (Wis.) 1949
851. Pole, William, *The Philosophy of Music* (*International Library of Psychology, Philosophy, and Scientific Method*); N. Y. 1924
852. Potts, Joseph E., "Jullien and the Popularisation of Orchestral Music"; *Musical Opinion*, Apr. 1949, pp. 344 ff.
853. Prod'homme, J. G., *Les Symphonies de Beethoven;* P. 1906
854. Redfield, John, *Music: A Science and an Art;* N. Y. 1930

855. Rimsky-Korsakov, N., *Principes d'orchestration;* tr. M. D. Calvocoressi, P. 1914, 2 vols.
856. Robinson, Franklin W., *Aural Harmony;* N. Y. 1936
857. Rogers, Cornwell B., "Songs – Colorful Propaganda of the French Revolution"; *Public Opinion Quarterly,* Fall 1947, pp. 436–44
858. Rolland, R., *Some Musicians of Former Days;* N. Y. 1915
859. ——— *Essays on Music;* N. Y. 1948
     [Reprints the essays on Berlioz, pp. 284–319, but not in full: see *504*]
860. Rood, Louise, "A Plea for Serious Viola Study"; *Proceedings of Music Teachers National Association,* 1944, pp. 399 ff.
     [An excellent review of current neglect of the instrument, exactly 100 years after Berlioz' similar complaint]
861. Rosenkaimer, Eugen, "Das Saxophon in seinen Frühzeiten und im Urteil berühmter Musiker"; *Die Musik,* Sept. 1928, pp. 896–900
862. Rothe, Frieda R., "Russian Music"; *Kenyon Review,* Winter 1942, pp. 48 ff.
863. Rousseau, J.–J., *Dictionnaire de Musique* in *Oeuvres Complètes,* P. 1832, vols. IX and X
864. ——— *Lettre sur la musique française* in *Oeuvres Complètes,* P. 1832, vol. X
865. Runciman, John, *Old Scores and New Readings;* L. 1898
866. Sabaneev, Leonid, "Mussorgsky"; *Musical Times;* April 1931, p. 311 f.
867. Saint-Foix, G. de, *The Symphonies of Mozart;* N. Y. 1949
868. Schoenberg, Arnold, "The Musician" in *The Works of the Mind;* ed. R. B. Heywood, Chicago, 1947, pp. 68–89
869. ——— *Harmonielehre;* Vienna 1911
870. ——— *Theory of Harmony;* tr. R. D. W. Adams (abridged) N. Y. 1948
871. Scholes, Percy A., *The Puritans and Music;* L. 1934
872. Schrade, Leo, *Beethoven in France;* New Haven 1942
873. Schuman, William, "Unconventional Case History"; *Modern Music,* May 1938
874. Schumann, Robert, *Gesammelte Schriften über Musik und Musiker;* Leipzig 1854, 4 vols.
     [See *508* and *509*]
874a. Schünemann, Georg, *Geschichte des Dirigirens;* Leipzig 1913
875. Schweitzer, Albert, "Le symbolisme de Bach"; *Revue Germanique,* 1905, pp. 69 ff.
876. Scudo, P., *L'année musicale;* P. 1861
     [Chapter V contains review of Wagner concerts of 1860]
877. Séré, O., *Musiciens français d'aujourd'hui;* P. 1911
878. Sessions, Roger, "The Composer and His Message" in *The Intent of the Artist;* ed. Augusto Centeno, Princeton 1941
879. Shaw, G. B., *Music in London: 1890–1894;* L. 1932, 3 vols.
880. ——— *London Music in 1888–9;* L. 1937
881. Singer, Kurt, *Diseases of the Musical Profession;* tr. Wladimir Lakond, N. Y. 1932
882. Slonimsky, Nicolas, "Music and Composers" in *U.S.S.R. A Concise Handbook;* ed. Ernest J. Simmons, Ithaca (N. Y.) 1947, pp. 422–38
883. Smith, Charles T., *Music and Reason;* L. 1947
884. Sorabji, K., *Around Music;* L. 1932
885. Spalding, W. R., *Music, an Art and a Language;* N. Y. 1920

886. Squire, W. B., "Purcell's Dramatic Music"; *Sammelbände der Internationalen Musikgesellschaft*, 1904, pp. 551 ff.
    [See also (on other *Tempest* music) *Musical Quarterly*, 1921, 565 ff.]
887. Stoll, Dennis, "The Orchestra Looks Back"; *London Philharmonic Post*, Mar. 1941
888. Stravinsky, Igor, "Avertissement"; *The Dominant*, Dec. 1927
889. —— *Poétique musicale sous forme de six leçons;* Cambridge (U.S.A.) 1942
    [Tr. Arthur Knodel and Ingolf Dahl: *Poetics of Music;* Cambridge 1947]
890. Symons, Arthur, "The Ideas of Richard Wagner" in *Studies in Seven Arts*, N. Y. 1906
    [Wagner worship at its height]
891. Terry, C. S., *Bach's Orchestra;* L. 1932
892. Thompson, Randall, *College Music;* N. Y. 1935
893. Tiersot, Julien, *La chanson populaire et les écrivains romantiques;* P. 1931
894. —— "Rousseau Musicien"; *Les Annales*, June 30, 1912
895. —— "Vingt Ans de la Vie de Wagner: Madame Cosima"; *Ménestrel*, Aug. 25, 1933, pp. 337–40
896. Tovey, Sir Donald, *A Musician Talks:*
    1. *The Integrity of Music*
    2. *Musical Texture;* L. 1941, 2 vols.
897. Travis, James, "Celtic Elements in Beethoven's Seventh Symphony"; *Musical Quarterly*, 1935, p. 255 ff.
898. Turner, W. J., *Music and Life;* N. Y. n.d.
    [Eng. ed. appeared L. 1921]
899. —— *Orpheus, or the Music of the Future;* L. n.d.
900. —— "A French Musician" [Ravel], *New Statesman*, Jan. 1, 1938
901. Van Dieren, Bernard, *Down Among the Dead Men;* L. 1935
    [Remarkable essays on music and musicians]
902. Various Hands, *First New England Music Critics' Symposium;* sponsored by the Hartford *Times;* Hartford (Conn.) 1948
903. —— *Music and Criticism: A Symposium;* ed. Richard F. French, Cambridge 1948
904. Veinus, A., *The Concerto;* N. Y. 1944
905. Vernon, P. E., "Non-Musical Factors in the Appreciation of Music"; *Musical Times*, Feb.–Apr. 1929, pp. 123–5, 227–8, 320–2
    [A classic study]
906. Volbach, Fritz, *Das moderne Orchester;* Leipzig 1910
    [References are to 2nd ed. Leipzig and B. 1918, 2 vols.]
907. Waltershausen, Hermann W. von, *Der Freischütz: ein Versuch über die musikalische Romantik;* Munich 1920
908. Weber, Johannes, *Les Illusions Musicales;* P. 1883
909. Weckerlin, J. B., *La bibliothèque du Conservatoire National;* P. 1885
910. —— *Musiciana;* P. 1877 ff.
    [3 series; numerous hostile references to Berlioz]
911. Weingartner, Felix, *Akkorde;* Leipzig 1912
912. —— *On Conducting;* tr. Ernest Newman, 2nd ed. Leipzig 1925
913. Wellesz, Egon, *Die Neue Instrumentation;* Vienna 1928

914. Whittaker, W. G., *Collected Essays;* L. 1940
    [Excellent treatment of varied musical subjects, notably Purcell and Berlioz]
915. Widor, Ch.-M., *Initiation musicale;* P. 1923
916. Willeby, Charles, "The Composer of Carmen"; *Yellow Book* II, July 1894, pp. 63–84
    [An excellent essay, more perceptive than the usual short biographies even though entirely untechnical]
917. Willy [pseud. H. Gauthier-Villars], *Propos d'ouvreuse;* P. 1925
    [A compilation from earlier series]
918. Winnington-Ingram, R. P., *Mode in Ancient Greek Music;* Cambridge (Eng.) 1936
919. Wotton, T. S., Correspondence in *Musical Opinion*, Feb., Apr., and May 1902
    [Concerns Berlioz' chapter on drums in *Treatise*]
920. ——— "The Future of the Orchestra"; *Musical News*, July 29, 1905
921. ——— "Orchestral Balance"; *Musical Times*, Feb. and Mar. 1929
922. Zimmerman, Pierre, "Bernard Sarrette, Fondateur du Conservatoire"; *France Musicale*, Nov. 21, 1841, pp. 404 ff.

5c — MUSICAL MEMOIRS AND LIVES

923. Adam, Adolphe, *Souvenirs d'un musicien;* P. n.d. [1857]
924. ——— *Derniers souvenirs d'un musicien;* P. n.d. [1859]
925. Auer, Leopold, *My Long Life in Music;* N. Y., 1923
926. Auer, Max, *Anton Bruckner: sein Leben und Werk;* 5th ed., Vienna 1947
927. Bauer, Harold, *His Book;* N. Y. 1948
928. *Beethoven the Man and Artist, in His Own Words;* ed. Fr. Kerst and H. E. Krehbiel, N. Y. 1905
929. Bekker, Paul, *Beethoven;* L. 1932
930. Bennett, Joseph, *Forty Years of Music;* L. 1908
931. Beyle, Henri, *Vie de Rossini; suivie des notes d'un dilettante;* ed. Henri Prunières; P. 1922
932. ——— [L. A. C. Bombet, pseud.], *Haydn, Mozart, Metastasio;* tr. Wm. Gardiner; Boston 1839
    [An interesting feature of this version is the translator's notes, which he says amplify his own *Music of Nature*]
933. Blom, Eric, *Mozart (Master Musicians);* L. 1935
934. Bowen, Catherine Drinker, *Free Artist: the Story of Anton and Nicholas Rubinstein;* N. Y. 1939
935. ———, and Meck, Barbara von, *Beloved Friend: The Story of Tchaikowsky and Nadedja von Meck;* N. Y. 1937
936. Bruneau, Alfred, *A l'ombre d'un grand coeur;* P. 1932
    [Autobiography mixed with memoir of Zola as librettist]
936a. Calvocoressi, M. D., "The Correspondence between Balakirev and Tchaikovsky"; *Musical Times*, Nov. 1912, pp. 712–5
937. Cannon, B. C., *Johann Mattheson;* New Haven, 1947
938. Chorley, Henry F., *Thirty Years' Musical Recollections;* L. 1862, 2 vols.
939. Comettant, O., *Histoire d'un Inventeur au XIXème Siècle;* P. 1860
    [On Adolphe Sax, with portrait]
940. Cooper, Martin, *Bizet;* L. and N. Y. 1938

941. Crowest, F. J., *Cherubini;* N. Y. 1890
942. Damrosch, Walter, *My Musical Life;* N. Y. 1926
943. David, Ernest, *Vie et Oeuvres de J. S. Bach;* P. 1882
944. Dent, Edward J., *Ferruccio Busoni;* L. 1933
945. d'Indy, Vincent, *César Franck;* P. 1912
       [Translated with an Introduction by Rosa Newmarch; L. 1909]
946. Drumont, E., *Richard Wagner, l'homme et le musicien;* P. 1869
947. Du Moulin-Eckart, Richard, Count, *Cosima Wagner;* tr. Catherine Alison Phillips, N. Y., 1930, 2 vols.
948. Dupré, Henri, *Purcell;* tr. Catherine Alison Phillips and Agnes Bedford; N. Y. 1928
949. Duprez, Gilbert Louis, *Souvenirs d'un Chanteur;* P. 1880
950. Einstein, Alfred, *Gluck* (Master Musicians); L. n.d. [1936]
951. ———— *Mozart;* tr. Arthur Mendel and Nathan Broder; N. Y. 1945
952. Ellis, William Ashton, *Life of Richard Wagner;* tr. with notes from Glasenapp's *Leben Richard Wagner's;* L. 1900–1908, 6 vols.
952a. Emmanuel, M., *Antonin Reicha;* P. 1937
953. Engel, Louis, *From Mozart to Mario;* 2 vols. L. 1886
       [Entertaining and useful comments by Shaw's predecessor on the *World*]
954. Eymieu, Henry, *L'oeuvre de Meyerbeer;* P. 1910
955. Ganz, Wilhelm, *Memories of a Musician;* L. 1913
956. Gottschalk, Louis Moreau, *Notes of a Pianist;* Philadelphia, 1881
957. Gounod, Charles, *Mémoires d'un artiste;* P. 1896; refs. are to *Autobiographical Reminiscences*, tr. W. H. Hutchinson, L. 1896
958. Gray, Cecil, *Peter Warlock: a Memoir of Philip Heseltine;* L. 1936
059. Harvey, H. B., *Claude of France: The Story of Debussy;* N. Y. 1948
960. Hellouin, P., and Picard, I., *Un Musicien Oublié: Catel;* Pref. J. Tiersot, P. 1910
961. Henderson, W. J., *Richard Wagner;* 2nd ed., N. Y. 1923
962. Hensel, S., *Die Familie Mendelssohn;* 2nd ed., B. 1891, 2 vols.
963. Hervey, A., *Alfred Bruneau* (Living Masters); L. 1907
964. Hévesy, André de, *Beethoven;* P. 1927
965. Hill, Ralph, *Johannes Brahms* (Great Musicians); N. Y. n.d. [1949]
966. Hughes, Patrick, *Opening Bars: Beginning an Autobiography;* L. 1946
       [Views on Berlioz of a young composer and critic; see also *586*]
967. Hussey, Dyneley, *Verdi* (Master Musicians); L. 1940
968. Jahn, Otto, *Mozart;* tr. Pauline D. Townsend; L. 1882, 3 vols.
969. Jansen, Albert, *Rousseau als Musiker;* B. 1884
970. Jordan, Jules, *The Happenings of a Musical Life;* Providence 1922
971. Kapp, Julius, *C. M. von Weber;* B. 1931
972. Kaufman, Schima, *Mendelssohn;* N. Y. 1934
972a. La Mara (Marie Lipsius), *Aus der Glanzzeit der Weimarer Altenburg;* Leipzig, 1906
973. Lamy, F., *Jean-François Lesueur* (1760–1837); P. 1912
973a. Landormy, Paul, *Bizet (Les Maîtres de la Musique),* P. 1929
974. Liszt, Fr., *Life of Chopin;* tr. Martha Walker Cook, 4th ed. revised, Boston 1882
975. Lockspeiser, Edward, *Debussy;* L. 1936
976. Lombard, Louis, *Observations of a Musician;* tr. R. de Lagenardière, P. 1905
977. Massenet, Jules, *Mes Souvenirs;* P. 1912

432   *Bibliography*   [*978–1011*]

978. Moscheles, Ignaz, *Aus Moscheles' Leben;* Leipzig, n.d. [1872–3] 2 vols.
        [Letters and diaries ed. by his wife and tr. in part as
979. —— *Life of Ignaz Moscheles;* ed. A. D. Coleridge, L. 1873, 2 vols.]
980. —— *Recent Music and Musicians;* ed. by his wife and adapted from
        the German by A. D. Coleridge; N. Y. 1874
981. Murdoch, William David, *Chopin, His Life;* N. Y. 1935
982. Newman, Ernest, *Hugo Wolf;* L. 1907
983. —— *Wagner As Man and Artist;* N. Y. 1924
984. —— *The Life of Richard Wagner;* N. Y. 4 vols., 1933–1946
984a. Newmarch, R., *Tchaikovsky: His Life and Works;* ed. E. Evans, Sr.,
        L. 1908
985. Panzacchi, Enrico, *Nel mondo della musica;* Florence 1895
986. Pougin, Arthur, *Jean-Jacques Rousseau Musicien;* P. 1901
987. —— *Monsigny et son Temps;* P. 1908
988. Pourtalès, Guy de, *La Vie de Franz Liszt;* P. 1925
989. —— *Chopin ou le Poète;* P. 1927
990. Praeger, F., *Wagner as I Knew Him;* N. Y., 1892
991. Prod'homme, J. G., and Dandelot, A., *Gounod: Sa Vie et ses Oeuvres;*
        P. 1911, 2 vols.
992. Pulver, J., *Paganini;* L. 1936
993. Quicherat, L., *Adolphe Nourrit: sa vie, son talent, son caractère;* P. 1867,
        3 vols.
994. Rachmaninoff, S., *Recollections;* N. Y. 1934
994a. Raabe, Peter, *Liszt's Leben und Schaffen;* Stuttgart, 1931, 2 vols.
995. Ramann, Lina, *Franz Liszt;* L. 1882, 4 vols.
        [By a friend and pupil; full but untrustworthy as to details]
996. Reissmann, August, *Life and Work of Schumann;* A. L. Alger, tr.,
        L. 1886
997. Reyer, Ernest, *Notes de Musique;* P. 1875
998. —— *Quarante Ans de Musique;* P. 1909
999. Riesemann, Oskar von, *Moussorgsky;* N. Y. 1926
1000. Rimsky-Korsakov, N., *My Musical Life;* tr. J. A. Joffe, ed. Carl Van
        Vechten; N. Y. 1924
1001. Roger, G., *Le carnet d'un ténor;* P. 1880
1002. Rolland, Romain, *Beethoven;* tr. B. C. Hull, N. Y. 1917
1003. —— *Handel;* tr. A. E. Hull, L. 1916
1004. Safránek, Milos, *Bohuslav Martinu: The Man and His Music;* N. Y.
        1944
1005. Saint-Saëns, C., *Harmonie et Mélodie;* P. 1885
1006. —— *Ecole Buissonnière;* P. 1913. Tr. E. G. Rich, *Musical Memories,*
        Boston 1919
        [Serious mistranslations in Berlioz chapter]
1007. Schauffler, Robert Haven, *The Unknown Brahms;* N. Y. 1936
1008. Schubert, Franz, *Letters and Other Writings;* E. D. Deutsch, ed., tr.
        Venetia Savile, with a Foreword by Ernest Newman; N. Y. 1928
1009. Schweitzer, Albert, *Bach;* L. 1923, 2 vols.
        [First published in French in 1905]
1010. Shostakovich, Dmitri, and others, *Russian Symphony: Thoughts about
        Tchaikovsky;* N. Y. 1947
1011. Sitwell, Sacheverell, *Liszt;* L. 1934
        [Admirable about Berlioz' music; untrustworthy about his char-
        acter]

1012. Smith, Moses, *Koussevitzky;* N. Y. 1947
1013. Specht, R., *Brahms;* tr. Eric Blom, L. 1930
1014. Spohr, Louis, *Autobiography;* L. 1878, 2 vols.
1015. Spoll, E. A., *Madame Carvalho;* P. 1885
1016. Stanford, Sir Charles Villiers, *Pages from an Unwritten Diary;* N. Y. 1914
1017. Stebbins, L. P. and R. P., *Enchanted Wanderer: C. M. von Weber;* N. Y. 1940
1018. —— *Frank Damrosch;* N. Y. 1945
1019. Stefan, Paul, *Anton Dvořák;* tr. Y. W. Vance, N. Y. 1941
1020. Tchaikovsky, P. I., *The Diaries;* tr. with notes by W. Lakond, N. Y. 1945
1021. Thayer, A. W., *The Life of Ludwig von Beethoven;* tr. and ed. Henry E. Krehbiel, 3 vols. N. Y. 1934
1022. Thomas, Theodore, *A Musical Autobiography;* ed. Geo. P. Upton, Chicago 1905, 2 vols.
1023. Törne, Bengt de, *Sibelius: a Close-up;* L. 1937
1024. Tovey, Sir Donald, *Beethoven;* L. 1945
1025. Toye, Francis, *Rossini;* N. Y. 1934
1025a. —— *Giuseppe Verdi: His Life and Works;* L. 1931
1026. Turner, W. J., *Mozart, The Man and His Works;* N. Y. 1938
1027. —— *Wagner* (Great Musicians) L. and N. Y., n.d.
    [A good character sketch, useful for comparisons of Wagner and Berlioz]
1028. Vallas, Léon, *Claude Debussy;* tr. by M. and G. O'Brien, L. 1933
1029. Viardot, Paul, *Souvenirs d'un Artiste;* P. 1910
    [By the son of Berlioz' friend and "pupil," Pauline Viardot. Interesting but untrustworthy]
1030. Vuillermoz, E., *La vie amoureuse de Chopin;* P. 1927
1031. Wallace, Wm., *Liszt, Wagner, and the Princess;* L. 1927
1032. Walter, Bruno, *Gustav Mahler;* tr. James Galston, with a biographical essay by Ernst Krenek, N. Y. 1941
1033. —— *Theme and Variations;* N. Y. 1946
1034. Weinstock; Herbert, *Chopin: the Man and His Music;* N. Y. 1949
1035. —— *Tchaikovsky;* N. Y. 1943
1036. Wellesz, Egon, *Arnold Schoenberg;* tr. W. H. Kerridge, L. n.d.
1037. White, Eric Walter, *Stravinsky: His Life and Work;* N. Y. 1948
1038. Wolff, Werner, *Anton Bruckner;* N. Y. 1942
1039. Wolkonsky, Prince Pierre, "L'Opera de St. Pétersbourg; Souvenirs personnels"; *Revue Musicale,* 1923, pp. 148–60
    [The former Director of the Imperial Theaters tells of his difficulties in imposing the new Russian composers at the turn of the century]
1039a. Young, Percy M., *Handel* (Master Musicians), L. 1947

6. WORKS ON ESTHETICS AND OTHER ARTS THAN MUSIC

1040. Abraham, Pierre, "On the Fantastic"; tr. from the *Revue des Vivants, Living Age* Oct. 1934, pp. 138–42
1041. Adams, Henry, *Mont Saint Michel and Chartres;* Boston 1936
1042. —— *The Education of Henry Adams;* Boston 1918

1043. Amiguet, Philippe, *Technique et poésie de la montagne;* P. 1936
1044. Archer, William, "Hugo and Wagner" in *About the Theatre;* L. 1886, pp. 321–8
1045. Aurevilly, Jules Barbey d', *Les Oeuvres et les Hommes: 19ème siècle;* P. 1891–1912, 24 vols.
1046. —— *Les Quarante Médaillons de l'Académie Française;* P. 1864
1047. —— *L'Esprit de Barbey;* ed. Octave Uzanne, P. 1908
1048. Barzun, Jacques, "The 'New' Biography"; *The Lion and Crown: A Quarterly;* Fall 1932, pp. 3–14
1049. Baudelaire, Charles, *L'Art Romantique;* P. 1929
1050. Beach, Joseph Warren, *A Romantic View of Poetry;* Minneapolis 1944
1051. Bentley, Eric Russell, "The Theatres of Wagner and Ibsen"; *Kenyon Review*, Autumn 1944, pp. 542–69
1052. —— *The Playwright As Thinker;* N. Y. 1946
1053. Bernard, Emile, ed., *Lettres de Van Gogh à Emile Bernard;* P. 1911
1054. Beyle, Henri, *Racine et Shakespeare* in *Oeuvres Complètes de Stendhal,* ed. P. Martino, P. 1925, 2 vols. (not numbered in series)
1055. Blanche, Jacques-Emile, *Les Arts Plastiques;* P. 1931
1056. —— *Passy;* P. 1928
1057. Borgerhoff, J. L., *Le Théâtre anglais à Paris sous la restauration;* P. 1912
1058. Bourget, Paul, *Essais de Psychologie Contemporaine* (1883–1885); rev. ed. P. 1901, 2 vols.
1059. Bozzi, José, *Balzac et les médecins dans la Comédie Humaine;* Lille 1932
1060. Burr, Anna Robeson, *The Autobiography;* Boston 1909 [Inadequate on Berlioz]
1061. Chamberlain, Houston Stewart, *Le Drame Wagnérien;* P. n.d.
1062. Chambers, Frank P., *Cycles of Taste;* Cambridge 1928
1063. —— *The History of Taste;* N. Y. 1932
1064. Chapman, John Jay, "A Study of Romeo"; in *Emerson and Other Essays,* N. Y. 1909
1065. —— *Dante;* Boston 1927
1066. Chesterton, G. K., *Generally Speaking;* N. Y. 1929
1067. Clarke, Charles Cowden and Mary, *The Shakespeare Key;* L. 1879 [An exhaustive study of Shakespeare's verbal and dramatic arts by means of classified devices and peculiarities in his works]
1068. Clutton-Brock, A., *An Introduction to French Painting;* L. 1932
1069. Connolly, Cyril, *The Unquiet Grave;* N. Y. 1945
1070. Courteline, Georges, *La philosophie de* —— in Oeuvres Complètes; P. 1930, vol. VIII
1071. Craven, Thomas, *Men of Art;* N. Y. 1931
1072. Croy, R. de, *Etudes et Croquis;* P. 1877 [Contains a characteristic attack on Delacroix as man and artist]
1073. Duckworth, George E., "Virgil and War in the *Aeneid*"; *Classical Journal,* Dec. 1945
1074. Duhamel, Georges, Letterpress in *Album de France,* Association Française d'Expansion Touristique; P. 1934, no pagination.
1075. Dwiggins, W. A., *Mss.;* ed. Watson Gordon, The Typophiles, N. Y. 1947 [A collection of essays]
1076. [Eckermann's] *Gespräche mit Goethe;* ed. Gustav Moldenhauer, Leipzig 1884, 3 vols.

1077. Elliot, George, *The Impressions of Theophrastus Such;* Chicago 1886
1078. Escholier, Raymond, *Delacroix: Peintre, Graveur, Ecrivain;* P. 1929, 3 vols.
1079. Eyma, X. and De Lucy, A., *Ecrivains et artistes vivants;* P. 1840
1080. Fineshriber, William, Jr., *Stendhal: The Romantic Rationalist;* Princeton 1932
1081. Fitzgerald, F. Scott, "Note-books" in *The Crack-up;* ed. Edmund Wilson, Norfolk (Conn.) 1946
1082. Fosca, François, *Delacroix,* ed. G. Jedlicka, Lausanne (Alfred Scherz) 1948
1083. Gordon, Jan, *Modern French Painters;* L. 1923
    [A lucid account of the facts, problems, and purposes which motivate the arist]
1084. Gutmann, James, "Integrity As a Standard of Valuation"; *Journal of Philosophy,* Apr. 1945, pp. 210–6
1085. Hamerton, P. G., *Thoughts About Art;* new ed. L. 1873
1086. ——— *The Life of J. M. W. Turner;* Boston 1882
1087. ——— *Portfolio Papers;* Boston 1889
1088. ——— *An Autobiography and a Memoir . . . ;* L. 1897
1089. Hapgood, Norman, "Henri Beyle"; *Yellow Book,* Jan. 1895, pp. 207–33
    [An excellent essay on Stendhal when he was still virtually unknown to English readers; contains a fine passage on Stendhal and Berlioz in relation to Shakespeare]
1090. Henley, W. E., *Views and Reviews;* vol. II; *Art,* N. Y. 1902
1091. Hildebrandt, K., *Wagner und Nietzsche: ihr Kampf gegen das 19te Jahrhundert;* Breslau 1924
1092. Hofmannsthal, Hugo von, *Die Berührung der Sphären;* B. 1931
    [Excellent on Balzac]
1093. Holme, Ch., ed., *The Genius of J. M. W. Turner;* L. 1903
1094. James, Henry, *The Question of Our Speech; The Lesson of Balzac: Two Lectures;* Boston and N. Y. 1905
1094a. Kirstein, Lincoln, *Dance;* N. Y. 1930
1095. Korff, H. A., *Geist der Goethezeit;* Leipzig 1923–1940, 3 vols.
1096. ——— *Humanismus und Romantik;* Leipzig 1924
1097. Körner, Christian Gottfried, *Gesammelte Schriften;* Berlin 1881
1098. Lafarge, John, *Great Masters;* N. Y. 1903
1099. Langer, Susanne K., *Philosophy in a New Key;* Cambridge 1942
    [Contains an excellent chapter on significance in music by one who both plays it and knows its import]
1100. Lanier, Sidney, *Music and Poetry. Essays upon some Aspects and Interrelations of the two arts;* N. Y. 1898
    [A remarkable study of program music and kindred questions by a musician, poet, and thinker]
1101. Le Breton, André, *Le Théâtre romantique;* P. 1923
1102. Levin, Harry, *Toward Stendhal;* N. Y. 1946
1103. Lewes, G. H., *Principles of Success in Literature;* Introd. T. S. Knowlson, P. n.d.
1104. Lothar-Mohrenwitz, S., *Delacroix und die Romantik in Frankreich;* Frankfurt 1913
1105. Maurras, Charles, ed., *Cahiers d'Occident,* II; P. 1928
1106. McGrath, Earl J., and others, *Toward General Education;* N. Y. 1948
1107. Moreau, A., *Delacroix;* P. 1878

1108. Nicolson, Harold, "How I Write Biography" in *What is a Book? Thoughts on writing;* L. 1936

1109. Nostrand, Howard Lee, *Le Théâtre antique et à l'antique en France: 1840–1900;* P. 1934
  [Valuable on the period, inadequate on *Les Troyens*]

1110. Palmer, John, *Comic Characters of Shakespeare;* L. 1946

1111. Peyre, Henri, *Writers and their Critics: A Study of Misunderstanding;* Ithaca (N. Y.) 1944

1112. Proust, Marcel, *Chroniques;* P. 1927

1112a. Prévost, Jean, *Eiffel* (Maîtres de l'Art Moderne) P. 1929

1113. Reid, Louis Arnaud, *A Study in Aesthetics;* N. Y. 1931
  [The fullest and best philosophical treatment of the arts]

1114. Renouvier, Charles, *Victor Hugo: le Poète;* P. 1893

1115. Rewald, John, *History of Impressionism;* N. Y. 1946

1116. Reynaud, Louis, *Le romantisme: ses origines anglo-germaniques;* P. 1926
  [Typical French nationalist attack on Romanticism in scholarly style but full of misstatements]

1117. Richardson, E. P., "Allston and the Development of Romantic Color"; *Art Quarterly,* Winter 1944, pp. 33–57
  [An excellent analysis based on a self-aware artist and showing the unity of the Romantic arts]

1118. Rivière, Jacques, *Etudes;* P. 1911

1119. Rothenstein, Wm., *Goya;* N. Y. 1901

1120. Ruskin, John, *Stones of Venice* (Everyman); L. 1907, 3 vols.

1121. Santayana, George, *Reason in Art* (vol. IV of *The Life of Reason*); N. Y. 1917

1122. Sarrailh, Jean, *Enquêtes Romantiques: France-Espagne;* P. 1933

1123. Schweitzer, Albert, *Goethe;* N. Y. 1948

1124. Séché, L., *Le Cénacle de la Muse française;* P. 1908

1125. Shaw, G. B., Preface to *The Dark Lady of the Sonnets* in *Misalliance, The Dark Lady of the Sonnets,* and *Fanny's First Play;* N. Y. 1914

1126. ―――― Preface to *Great Expectations* in *A Book of Prefaces* (Limited Editions Club); N. Y. 1941

1127. Silvestre, Théophile, *Les Artistes Français;* P. 1926, 2 vols.
  [Contains fine studies of Delacroix, Vernet, and Rude]

1128. Simon, Charles, ed., *Stendhal, par Gobineau;* P. 1926

1129. Smith, D. Nicol, ed., *Shakespeare Criticism: a Selection* (World's Classics); N. Y. 1916, 1942

1130. Solvay, L., *L'Evolution Théâtrale;* P. 1922
  [On Berlioz, pp. 49–61]

1131. Spencer, Hazelton, *Shakespeare Improved;* Cambridge 1927

1132. Symons, Arthur, *The Symbolist Movement in Literature;* rev. and enlarged ed. N. Y. 1919

1133. Tourneux, Maurice, *Eugène Delacroix devant ses contemporains;* P. 1886

1134. Valéry, Paul, *Variété II;* P. 1930

1135. Wackenroder, Wilhelm Heinrich, *Werke und Briefe;* Berlin 1938

1136. Wilde, Oscar, *A Critic in Pall Mall* (ed. E. V. Lucas); N. Y. (Putnam) n.d.

1137. ―――― "The Critic as Artist" in *The Prose of Oscar Wilde;* N. Y. 1916

7. BIOGRAPHIES AND WORKS ON POLITICAL AND SOCIAL HISTORY

1138. Anon., *Observations sur les moeurs et les usages français au commencement du XIXème siècle;* P. 1825

1139. —— *An Englishman in Paris;* vol. I. *The Reign of Louis Philippe*
[A literary hoax ascribed to Philip Vandam, published *c.* 1885, and purporting to be memoirs of the period by an eyewitness. Excellent on the lawsuit about "Berlioz' *Freischütz*"]

1140. —— *François Rude: sa vie, ses oeuvres, son enseignement;* Dijon 1856

1141. About, Edmond, *Le Progrès;* 4th ed., P. 1867
[Chapter 13, on the arts, besides special references to Berlioz and Wagner gives a fair idea of contemporary "educated" opinion]

1142. Agate, James, *Rachel (1821–1858);* N. Y. 1928

1143. Aldington, Richard, *The Duke;* N. Y. 1943
[Life of Wellington]

1144. Altick, Richard D., *The Cowden Clarkes;* L. 1948

1145. Andler, Charles, *Nietzsche, sa vie et sa pensée;* P. 1920–1931, 6 vols.

1146. Beyle, Henri, *Life of Henri Brulard;* tr. C. A. Phillips, London n.d.

1147. Birrell, Augustine, *Obiter Dicta;* 2nd series, L. 1887

1148. —— "Byron's Letters" in *More Obiter Dicta,* L. 1924

1149. Bled, Victor du, *La Société française depuis cent ans;* P. 1923

1150. Butler, Samuel, ed., *Life of Dr. Samuel Butler* in *Butler's Works,* Shrewsbury ed., vols. X and XI

1151. Chambrier, James de, *La cour et la société du Second Empire;* P. 1902, 2 vols.

1152. Charléty, S., *Histoire du Saint-Simonisme;* P. 1931

1153. Chasles, Philarète, *Mémoires;* P. 1876–1877, 2 vols.

1154. Chesterton, G. K., *Robert Browning* (English Men of Letters); L. 1905

1155. —— *Charles Dickens* (L. 1906); N. Y. 1942

1156. Ciano, Count Galeazzo, *The Ciano Diaries;* ed. Hugh Gibson, N. Y. 1946

1157. Daudet, A., *Trente Ans de Paris;* P. 1888

1158. d'Aumale, Henri d'Orléans, duc (1822–1897), *Correspondance du duc d'Aumale et de Cuvillier-Fleury;* ed. R. Vallery-Radot, P. 1910–1914, 4 vols.

1159. Démy, A., *Essai historique sur les Expositions Universelles de Paris;* P. 1907

1160. De Vane, William C., *A Browning Handbook;* N. Y. 1935

1161. Ducamp, Maxime, *Paris . . . dans la seconde moitié du XIXème siècle;* P. 1879, 6 vols.

1162. Duncan, Isadora, *My Life;* N. Y. 1927
[Reports a curious conversation with Cosima upon Wagner's error in seeking to unite verbal with lyrical drama, pp. 151 ff.]

1163. Forster, John, *The Life of Charles Dickens;* ed. J. W. T. Ley, L. 1928

1164. Fouillée, Alfred, *Tempérament et Caractère selon les individus, les sexes et les races;* P. 1895

1165. —— *Psychologie du Peuple Français;* P. 1898

1166. Frederix, G., *Trente ans de critique;* P. n.d.

1167. Freud, S., *On War, Sex, and Neurosis;* N. Y. 1947

1168. Friedell, Egon, *A Cultural History of the Modern Age;* tr. Charles F. Atkinson, N. Y. 1930, 3 vols.

1169. Gozlan, Leon, *Balzac en pantoufles;* P. 1890
1170. Gurian, Waldemar, "Lamennais"; *Review of Politics;* April 1947, pp. 205–29
1171. Gutzkow, K., *Paris und Frankreich: 1834–74* in *Gesammelte Werke,* Jena, 1873–1875, vol. VII
1172. Hardy, F. E., ed., *The Early Life of Thomas Hardy;* N. Y. 1928
1173. —— *The Later Years of Thomas Hardy;* N. Y. 1930
1174. Harris, Frank, *Bernard Shaw;* L. 1931
1174a. Herzen, Alex., *Lettres de France et d'Italie* in *Pages Choisies;* ed. M. Delines, P. 1912, pp. 232–349
1175. Hewett-Thayer, Harvey, *Hoffmann: Author of the Tales;* Princeton 1948
1176. Hohenlohe-Schillingsfürst, Prince Chlodwig, *Memoirs;* ed. Fr. Curtius, English ed. supervised by G. W. Chrystal; N. Y. 1906, 2 vols.
1177. Houssaye, A., *Souvenirs de Jeunesse: 1830–50;* P. 1896
1178. —— *Les Confessions: 1830–90;* P. 1885–1891, 6 vols.
1179. Howe, M. A. de Wolfe, *Holmes of the Breakfast Table;* L. 1939
1180. Hugo, V., *Choses Vues;* Nelson ed., P. n.d. [1887]
1181. Infeld, Leopold, *Whom the Gods Love: The Story of Evariste Galois;* N. Y. 1948
1182. Jasinski, René, *Les années romantiques de Théophile Gautier;* P. 1929
1183. Johnson, Samuel, *Lives of the Poets;* N. Y. 1857, 2 vols.
1184. Jones, H. F., *Samuel Butler: A Memoir;* London 1920, 2 vols.
1185. Jones, Howard Mumford, *The Harp That Once . . .;* N. Y. 1937
    [A biography of Thomas Moore; makes no mention of Berlioz]
1186. Josephson, Matthew, *Victor Hugo;* N. Y. 1942
1187. Jullien, Adolphe, *Le romantisme et l'éditeur Renduel;* P. 1897
1188. Karénine, Wladimir, *George Sand: sa vie et ses Oeuvres;* P. 1899–1926, 4 vols.
1189. King, Helen M., *Les doctrines littéraires de la Quotidienne: 1814–1830;* (Smith College Studies) Northampton 1920
    [An admirable monograph dealing with the Romantic movement in journalism]
1190. Labaste, H., "Alfred de Vigny, Collaborateur de Berlioz"; *Revue Universitaire,* 1920, II, pp. 369–74
    [Refers to *Benvenuto Cellini*]
1191. Labussière, P., *Louis Véron;* P. 1930
1192. Lan, Jules, *Mémoires d'un chef de claque;* P. 1883
1193. Landreth, Helen, *The Pursuit of Robert Emmet;* N. Y. 1948
1194. Lardner, Dionysius, *The Great Exhibition and London in 1841;* L. 1852
    [Contains a translation of Berlioz' three letters on the subject, originally published in the *Débats*]
1195. Lefebvre, Georges, *Napoléon* (*Peuples et Civilisations* series); P. 1935
1196. Lockhart, J. G., *Memoirs of Sir Walter Scott;* London 1914, 5 vols.
1196a. Loève-Veimars, François-Adolphe, Baron, *Précis de l'histoire des tribunaux secrets dans le Nord de l'Allemagne;* P. 1824
    [Source of Berlioz' *Francs-Juges* libretto]
1197. Loliée, F., *Le Duc de Morny et la Société du Second Empire;* P. 1909
1198. Lovenjoul, Spoelberch de, *Histoire des Oeuvres de Balzac;* P. 1886
1199. Maclean, Catherine M., *Born under Saturn; A Biography of Hazlitt;* N. Y. 1944
    [An excellent, full and perceptive study]

1200.   Maigron, Louis, *Le romantisme et les moeurs;* P. 1910

1201.   Marsan, Jules, *Autour du Romantisme;* Toulouse 1937
         [Deals with Emile Deschamps among others]

1202.   Maurois, A., *Chateaubriand;* P. 1938

1203.   Overmeyer, Grace, *Government and the Arts;* N. Y. 1939

1204.   Page, H. A., *Thomas De Quincey: His Life and Writings;* N. Y. 1877, 2 vols.

1205.   Pailleron, Edouard, *Discours Académiques,* P. 1886
         [On Charles Blanc]

1205a. Palfrey, Thomas, *L'Europe Littéraire (1833–4) Un Essai de Périodique Cosmopolite;* P. 1927

1206.   Paul, Elliot, *The Last Time I Saw Paris;* N. Y. 1943

1207.   Pearson, Hesketh, *G. B. S. A Full-length Portrait;* N. Y. 1942

1208.   Picavet, François; *Les Idéologues;* P. 1891

1209.   Potiquet, Alfred, *L'Institut National de France 1795–1869;* P. 1871

1210.   Rocker, Rudolf, *Nationalism and Culture;* tr. Ray E. Chase, Los Angeles 1937

1211.   Rumbold, Sir Horace, *Recollections of a Diplomatist;* L. 1903, 2 vols.
         [Covers the period between 1840 and 1878 when most of text appears to have been written]

1212.   Sainte-Beuve, Charles A., *Nouveaux Lundis;* P. 1870–1894, 13 vols.

1213.   ――― *Chateaubriand et son Groupe Littéraire sous l'Empire;* P. 1878, 2 vols.

1214.   Sassoon, Siegfried, *Meredith;* N. Y. 1948

1215.   Séché, Léon, *La jeunesse dorée sous Louis-Philippe;* P. 1910

1216.   Seyd, Felizia, *George Sand;* N. Y. 1940

1217.   Shaw, G. B., *What I Really Wrote about the War;* N. Y. 1931

1218.   Simond, Charles, *Paris de 1800 à 1900;* P. 1900–1901, 3 vols.

1219.   Strong, L. A. G., *The Minstrel Boy;* L. 1937
         [A biography of Thomas Moore; no mention of Berlioz among those who set Moore to music]

1220.   Tennyson, Hallam, *Alfred, Lord Tennyson: a Memoir;* N. Y. 1897, 2 vols.

1221.   Thackeray, W. M., "The Second Funeral of Napoleon" in *Roundabout Papers, Complete Works;* ed. W. P. Trent and J. B. Henneman, N. Y. n.d., vol. 22

1222.   ――― "Jerome Paturot"; in *Literary Essays, ibid.,* vol. 25

1223.   Tocqueville, A. de, *Souvenirs;* ed. Luc Monnier, P. 1942
         [References are to: *Recollections;* tr. A. T. de Mattos and J. P. Mayer, L. 1947]

1224.   Toksvig, Signe, *Emmanuel Swedenborg: Scientist and Mystic;* New Haven 1948

1225.   Trahard, Pierre, *Le romantisme défini par le Globe;* P. 1924

1226.   Valetta, Franchi-Verney, Count della, *L'Académie de France à Rome (1666–1903);* Turin 1903

1227.   Various Hands, *Paris-Guide* [à l'Exposition de 1867] Introd. Victor Hugo, P. 1867, 2 vols.

1228.   Véron, Louis, *Mémoires d'un bourgeois de Paris;* P. 1856–1857, 5 vols.
         [The chapter on music and painting contains details given by Delacroix, who was Véron's boyhood friend]

1229.   Visan, Tancrède de, *Ballanche;* Lyon 1926

1230. Wellington, Arthur Wellesley, Duke of, *The Words of Wellington;* ed. E. Walford, L. 1881

1231. Whitridge, Arnold, *Vigny;* L. 1933

1232. Williams, Blanche Colton, *George Eliot;* N. Y. 1936

1233. Wirth, Moritz, *Bismarck, Wagner, Rodbertus: Drei Deutsche Meister;* Leipzig 1883

1233a. Wyzewa, Isabelle de, *La Revue Wagnérienne,* P. 1934

8. WORKS OF LITERATURE

1234. Amiel, Henri-Frédéric, *Journal;* tr. Mrs. Humphry Ward, N. Y. 1906, 2 vols. in 1

1235. Balzac, H., *Oeuvres Complètes;* P. (Ollendorff) 1901, 50 vols.

1236. —— *Les Illusions Perdues; ibid.,* 3 vols.

1237. Baudelaire, Charles, *Oeuvres Posthumes;* P. 1908

1238. Beddoes, Thomas Lovell, *The Works of* ——; ed. H. W. Donner, L. 1935

1239. Beyle, Henri, *Lamiel;* Pref. Jacques Leclercq, N. Y. 1929

1240. —— *Mémoires sur Napoléon;* vol. II of *Napoléon* in *Oeuvres Complètes,* ed. L. Royer, P. 1929

1241. —— *Napoléon* in *Oeuvres Posthumes;* ed. Jean de Mitty, P. 1897

1242. —— *On Love,* tr. H. B. V. rev. C. K. Scott-Moncrieff, N. Y. 1927

1243. Chateaubriand, François-René de, *Le Génie du Christianisme;* ed. Calmann, P. 1885, 2 vols.

1244. Chesterfield, Lord, *Letters, Sentences and Maxims;* N. Y. (A. L. Burt) n.d.

1245. Crispin, Edmund (pseud. of Bruce Montgomery, Oxford scholar and musician), *Dead and Dumb;* N. Y. 1947

1246. Crofts, Freeman Wills, *The Cask;* L. n.d.
[Uses a performance of *Les Troyens* at the *Théâtre de la Monnaie* as a principal alibi in a story of crime. The author is a well-known English chorus master]

1247. d'Azeglio, Massimo Tapparelli, Marchese, *Ettore Fieramosca, ossia La disfida di Barletta;* P. 1834

1248. Deschamps, Emile, *Oeuvres Complètes;* P. 1874, 6 vols.
[Vol. V: *Théâtre, 1ère partie* contains the famous translation of *Romeo and Juliet*]

1249. Gide, André, *Journals;* tr. Justin O'Brien, N. Y. 1947–1949, 3 vols.

1250. Goethe, J. W. von, *Faust, Part I;* ed. Calvin Thomas, N. Y. 1892

1251. Goncourt, E. and J., *Selections;* ed A. G. Cameron, N. Y. 1898

1252. —— *Journal;* P. n.d., 4 vols.

1253. —— *Journal;* tr. (in part) by Lewis Galantière, Garden City 1937
[Contains a typically erroneous account of Berlioz in the Glossary of names]

1254. Hazlitt, William, "My First Acquaintance with Poets"; *Winterslow* (World's Classics), L. n.d., pp. 1–23

1255. —— "Coriolanus" in *Characters of Shakespeare's Plays;* L. 1869, pp. 49–59

1256. —— *Table Talk;* ed. W. C. Hazlitt, L. 1870

1257. —— *Complete Works;* ed. P. P. Howe, L. 1930–1934

1258. —— *Lectures on the English Comic Writers* (World's Classics), L. 1907

1259. Hebbel, *Sämtliche Werke;* ed. R. M. Werner, Berlin, 1901–7, 24 vols.
1260. Heine, Heinrich, *The Poetry and Prose of* ——; ed. Frederic Ewen, tr. various hands, N. Y. 1948
1261. —— *Sämmtliche Werke;* Philadelphia 1870, 7 vols.
1262. Hugo, Victor, *Cromwell;* P. (Nelson) 1939
1263. Huysmans, J. K., *Against the Grain;* tr. Havelock Ellis, N. Y. 1931
1264. Loève-Veimars, François-Adolphe, Baron, "Le chat d'Hoffmann" "Le Blocksberg" "L'ancien et le nouvel opéra" in *Le Nepenthès, contes, nouvelles, et critiques;* 2 vols. P. 1832
1265. Melville, Herman, *Journal of a Visit to London and the Continent: 1849–50;* ed. Eleanor Melville Metcalf, Cambridge 1948
1266. Musset, A. de, *La Confession d'un enfant du siècle;* P. 1865
1267. Montaigne, Michel Eyquem de, *Journal de Voyage en Italie* in *Oeuvres Complètes;* P. 1928, vol. VII
1268. —— *Essais;* ed. J.–V. Leclerc; P. 1925, 4 vols.
1269. Moore, Thomas, *Poetical Works;* N. Y. (Crowell) n.d.
1270. Parrott, T. M., and Telfer, R. S., eds., *[Four Plays of] Shakespeare;* vol. II, N. Y. 1931
Péguy, Charles, *Oeuvres Complètes,* 1916–1944; P. 15 vols.
1271.   Vol. II: *Notre Patrie*
1272.   Vol. IV: *Notre Jeunesse*
1273. Rabelais, François, *Oeuvres;* ed. Louis Moland P. (Garnier) n.d.
1274. [Reybaud, Louis] *Jérôme Paturot à la recherche d'une position sociale,* Brussels 1843, 3 vols. [refs. are to 1 vol. ed., P. 1879]
1275. Redon, Odilon, *To Oneself* [extracts from a diary] tr. from the original in *The Chesterian,* May 1924, pp. 211–5
    [Refers twice to Berlioz]
1276. Rolland, Romain, *Jean Christophe,* vol. V: *"La Foire sur la Place;* P. 1908
    [A vivid and amusing account of French musical life at the turn of the century]
1277. Rousseau, J. J., *Confessions* in *Oeuvres Complètes,* P. 1832, vol. XI.
1278. Sand, Georges, "La marquise" in *Simon, etc.;* P. 1857
    [The novelette which supplied the name Lélio for Berlioz' melologue]
1279. Scott, Sir Walter, *Waverley;* in Centenary ed., Edinburgh 1871, 25 vols.
1280. Thoreau, H. D., *Essays and Other Writings;* ed. Will H. Dircks (Scott Library), L. and N. Y., n.d. [1907]
1281. —— *The Writings;* Boston 1906, 20 vols.
1282. Vigny, A. de, *Servitude et Grandeur Militaires;* P. (Nelson) 1936
1283. —— *Chatterton;* ed. E. Lauvrière, Oxford 1908
1284. —— *Journal d'un Poète;* ed. Louis Ratisbonne; P. 1882
1285. Yeats, W. B., *Dramatis Personae;* Dublin 1935

9A. WORKS USED FOR REFERENCE

1286. A. L. A. *Portrait Index,* ed. W. C. Lane and Nina E. Browne, Library of Congress, Washington, 1906
1287. Affelder, Paul, *How to Build a Record Library;* N. Y. 1947
1288. Apel, Willi, *Harvard Dictionary of Music;* Cambridge 1945
1289. Bacharach, A. L., ed., *The Musical Companion;* L. 1936
1290. Bagar, Robt., and Biancolli, Louis, *The Concert Companion;* N. Y. 1947

1291. Baggers, Joseph, *Méthode de Timbales et Instruments à Percussion;* P. n.d.

1292. Benedictine of Stanbrook, A, *A Grammar of Plainsong;* Worcester (England) [1905] 1926

1293. Benezit, ed., *Dictionnaire des Peintres, Sculpteurs, Dessinateurs et Graveurs;* P. 1924 (1913) 3 vols.

1294. *Boston Symphony Orchestra, Program Notes;* by W. F. Apthorp in 1892–1893 [See *761*] and until 1901; then by Philip Hale until 1934–1935, when John N. Burk was adjoined; by Mr. Burk since 1935–1936

1295. Burk, John N., *Boston Symphony Program Notes,* Berkshire Festival, August 1, 1946

1296. Carse, Adam, *Musical Wind Instruments;* L. 1939

1297. Cobbett, Walter Willson, *Cyclopedic Survey of Chamber Music;* L. 1929, 2 vols.

1298. Corder, F., *The Orchestra and How to Write for It;* L. 1895

1299. Culver, Charles A., *Musical Acoustics;* 2nd ed., Philadelphia 1947

1300. Curzon, H. de, *L'Evolution Lyrique au Théâtre: Tableau Chronologique;* P. 1908

1301. Davison, Archibald, *The Technique of Choral Composition;* Cambridge 1945
Encyclopédie de la Musique et Dictionnaire du Conservatoire; eds. Albert Lavignac and Lionel de la Laurencie,
Part I.   Histoire de la Musique

1302.   Vol. II   *Italie, Allemagne*
1303.   Vol. III   *France, Belgique, Angleterre*
Part II.   Technique, Esthétique, Pédagogie
1304.   Vol. I   *Tendances; Technique Générale*
1305.   Vol. IV   *Orchestration; Musique Liturgique*
1306.   Vol. V   *Esthétique*

1307. *Encyclopedia of Recorded Music;* ed. R. D. Darrell, N. Y. 1936

1308. ———; rev. ed. [biog. ed. Herbert Weinstock] N. Y. 1942

1309. ———; 3rd ed. [ed. Robert H. Reid], N. Y. 1948

1310. Forsyth, Cecil, *Orchestration;* L. 1914, rev. ed. N. Y. 1946

1311. Frank, Paul, *Tonkünstler Lexikon;* ed. Wilhelm Altmann; 12th ed., Leipzig 1926

1312. Glasenapp, C. F., and Stein, H. v., *Wagner Lexikon;* Stuttgart 1883

1313. Goetschius, P., *Theory and Practice of Tone Relations;* 6th ed., N. Y. 1900

1314. Grove, Sir George, ed., *A Dictionary of Music and Musicians;* L. 1890, 4 vols. and Index vol.

1315. ——— 3rd ed. revised; ed. H. C. Colles, L. 1935, 6 vols.

1316. *Guide de l'amateur d'ouvrages sur la Musique;* Pref. Michel Brenet; P. 1909

1317. Haggin, B. H., *A Book of the Symphony;* N. Y. 1937

1318. ——— *Music on Records;* N. Y. 1938

1319. ——— *Music on Records* (A new guide); N. Y. 1941

1320. Halm, August, *Harmonielehre;* B. 1920

1321. Hatin, Eugène, *Histoire politique et littéraire de la presse en France;* P. 1859–1861, 8 vols.

1322. ——— *Bibliographie historique et critique de la presse périodique française;* P. 1866

1323. Helmholtz, H. von, *The Student's Helmholtz;* ed. John Broadhouse, 3rd ed. L. 1892

1324. Hines, John; Hyams, Ben; and Ripperger, Helmut, *Record Collector's Guide;* N. Y. 1947
[Contains an excellent essay on Jazz]

1325. *Hinrichsen's Musical Yearbook: 1944;* 1945–1946

1326. Howard, John Tasker, *The World's Great Operas;* N. Y. 1948

1327. Hofmann, R., *Katechismus der Musikinstrumente;* Leipzig 1890

1328. Kagen, Sergius, *Music for the Voice: a Descriptive List* (vol. III: *The Field of Music,* ed. Ernest Hutcheson) N. Y. 1949
[Inadequate about Berlioz]

1329. *Key's Yearbook of Music;* N. Y. 1926

1330. Kinsky, Georg, *History of Music in Pictures;* Introd. Eric Blom, L. 1930

1331. Koechlin, Charles, *Traité de l'Harmonie,* P. 1925, 3 vols.

1332. Kolodin, Irving, *Guide to Recorded Music;* Garden City, 1941

1333. Krehbiel, H. E., *The Philharmonic Society of New York: A Memorial* [fiftieth anniversary]; N. Y. 1892

1334. —— *A Book of Operas;* N. Y. 1917

1335. Lieberson, Goddard, ed., *The Columbia Book of Musical Masterworks;* N. Y. 1947

1336. *Livre du Centenaire du Journal des Débats;* P. 1889

1336a. Macpherson, Stewart, *Form in Music;* London 1915

1337. Mahillon, V.-C., *Catalogue du Musée Instrumental du Conservatoire de Bruxelles;* 1893–1912, 4 vols.

1338. Mason, D. G., *The Orchestral Instruments and What They Do;* N. Y. 1908

1339. Moore, Elizabeth C., *An Almanac for Music Lovers;* N. Y. 1940

1340. Mooser, R. Aloys, *Opéras, intermezzos, ballets, cantatas, oratorios, joués en Russie durant le 18ème siècle;* Geneva 1945

1341. Moser, H. J., *Musik-Lexikon;* B. 1932

1342. Nettement, Alfred, *Histoire Politique et Littéraire du Journal des Débats;* P. 1842

1343. *Neues Musiklexikon nach dem Dictionary of Modern Music and Musicians* von Eaglefield Hull; ed. Alfred Einstein, B. 1926

1344. *New Encyclopedia of Music and Musicians;* ed. W. S. Pratt, N. Y. 1924

1345. *New International Encyclopedia;* N. Y. 1914
[Vol. III, pp. 178–9 art. Berlioz fairly represents state of opinion before the First World War]

1346. ——; rev. ed., N. Y. 1949–1950
[Art. Berlioz by Jacques Barzun; art. French Music by Ch. Koechlin, Virgil Thomson, and Jacques Barzun]

1347. Piston, Walter, *Counterpoint;* N. Y. 1947

1348. —— *Principles of Harmonic Analysis;* Boston 1933

1349. Prod'homme, J. G., "Bibliographie berliozienne"; *Zeitschrift der Internationalen Musikgesellschaft,* 1903–1904, pp. 622–59
[A useful guide, arranged by years, itemized and annotated, but not free from errors and limited to French periodical publications. See *286*]

1350. Prout, E., *A Course of Lectures on Orchestration* (At the Royal College of Organists); L. 1905

1351. —— *The Orchestra;* L. 1897–1899, 2 vols.

1352. Prout, E., and Ricci, V., *Strumentazione;* Milan 1901, 2nd ed.

1353. Riemann, H., *Dictionnaire de Musique;* tr. G. Humbert, P. 1931, 3rd ed.
1354. ———— *Dictionary of Music;* tr. J. S. Shedlock, L. n.d.
1355. Sachs, Curt, *Handbuch der Musikinstrumentenkunde;* Leipzig 1920
1356. Sandi, Francesco, *Trattato di Strumentazione Pratica;* Milan 1864
1357. Scholtze, J., *Opernführer;* B. 1925, 6th ed.
1358. *Shakespeare Allusion Book, The;* ed. John Munro (1909)
       Reissued with Pref. by Sir Edmund Chambers, L. 1932, 2 vols.
1359. Shillgart, Hermann Albert ed., *Illustriertes Musik Lexicon;* B. 1927
1360. Slonimsky, Nicolas, *Music Since 1900;* N. Y. 1937
       [Invaluable chronological guide and source book]
1361. Spalding, W. R., *Tonal Counterpoint;* Boston and N. Y. 1904
1362. Stanford, Sir Charles, *Musical Composition;* N. Y. 1922
1363. Terry, Edward M., *A Richard Wagner Dictionary;* N. Y. 1939
1364. Teuchert, Emil, and Haupt, Walter, *Musik-Instrumentenkunde in Wort und Bild;* Leipzig 1910–1911, 3 vols.
1365. Thompson, Oscar, ed., *The International Cyclopedia of Music and Musicians;* N. Y. 1943
       [Art. Berlioz (by Gilbert Chase) a fair appraisal, given the sources at hand]
1366. Upton, Geo. P., *The Standard Oratorios;* Chicago 1888
1367. ———— *The Standard Operas;* Chicago 1896
1368. ———— *The Standard Cantatas;* Chicago 1899
1369. ———— *The Standard Symphonies;* Chicago 1899
1370. Vodarsky-Shiraeff, Alexandria, *Russian Composers and Musicians: a biographical dictionary;* N. Y. 1940
1371. Wotton, T. S., *Dictionary of Foreign Musical Terms and Handbook of Orchestral Instruments;* Leipzig 1907
       [The only work of its kind for completeness, accuracy, and philosophical grasp of its subject]
1372. Zahm, J. A., *Sound and Music;* Chicago 1892

9B. PERIODICALS

1373. *Allegro;* Official Journal, Local 802 AFL (New York City) American Federation of Musicians
1374. *American Record Guide, The* (formerly *The American Music Lover*)
       [A most useful periodical, ed. P. H. Reed]
1375. *Annales Politiques et Littéraires, Les* [Weekly]
       Berlioz number: July 5, 1910
       [Articles by Saint-Saëns, Bordeaux, Boschot, and L. de Fourcaud]
1376. *Artiste, L'*
       [Founded 1831; Berlioz and other great Romantics contributed and were frequently reviewed; intermittent publication until 1901]
1377. *Correspondant, Le* (1)
       [Weekly, founded March 1829; became *Revue Européenne* in 1831]
1378. *Correspondant, Le* (2)
       [Founded October 1855]
1379. *Corsaire, Le*
       [Daily, founded 1822, to which Berlioz contributed his first articles]
1380. *Daily Telegraph, The*
       [London newspaper; music critic: Mr. Richard Capell]

1381.   *Figaro, Le*
> [Daily, founded Jan. 1826; bought by Bohain in 1827 as a weapon against the régime, which it helped destroy]

1382.   *Fliegende Blätter für Musik*
> [Irregular, ed. at Leipzig by J. C. Lobe, 1855–1857, 3 vols.]

1383.   *France Musicale, La*
> [Founded by Escudier brothers, 1841. At first inimical to Berlioz; Adolphe Adam one of their chief contributors]

1384.   *Gramophone, The*
> [Monthly devoted to discs, ed. Compton Mackenzie and Christopher Stone]

1385.   *Guide Musical, Le*
> [Brussels fortnightly, ed. at one time by Maurice Kufferath; the issues often carry two dates a week apart on a single number]

1386.   *Journal des Débats Politiques et Littéraires*
> [Founded 1789, bought by Bertin in 1800, who inaugurated *feuilleton;* present title since 1805; Berlioz music critic, 1835 to 1863]
> [See also *1342* and *1336*]

1387.   *L'intermédiaire des chercheurs et curieux*
> [Fortnightly, founded 1864]

1388.   *Ménestrel, Le, Journal du Monde Musical*
> [Founded 1880 under a title dating back to 1833]

1389.   *Monde Illustré, Le*
> [Weekly founded 1857 as rival to l'*Illustration;* published parts of Berlioz' *Memoirs*]

1390.   *Music Review, The*
> [Cambridge (Eng.) monthly founded 1940; ed. Geoffrey Sharp]

1391.   *Musical Times and Singing-Class Circular, The*
> [London semi-monthly, later monthly, founded 1844, published by firm of Novello]

1392.   *Musical World, The*
> [London monthly founded by J. W. Davison, critic of *The Times*]

1393.   *Nation, The*
> [New York weekly; music critic: B. H. Haggin]

1394.   *Notes and Queries: a Medium of Intercommunication*
> [Founded Nov. 1849; weekly, later fortnightly]

1395.   *Quotidienne, La*
> [Founded 1792, interrupted 1797, resumed 1814 as leading Royalist daily. Berlioz' friend d'Ortigue wrote music criticism for it beginning in the thirties]

1396.   *Revue Bleue* [See *1402*]

1397.   *Revue des Deux Mondes, La*
> [Founded 1829, hospitable to the Romantics except in music; critic: Henri Blaze, a devotee of Meyerbeer]

1398.   *Revue et Gazette Musicale de Paris*
> [Originally *Gazette Musicale de Paris,* founded 1834 by Maurice Schlesinger, acquired double title by merging with Fétis's *Revue Musicale,* 1835; edited by Berlioz, 1836–1837]

1399.   *Revue Européenne*
> [Title of *Le Correspondant* (*1377*) 1831–1835]

1400. Revue Musicale
    [Founded 1827 F. J. Fétis; merged 1835 with Schlesinger's *Gazette Musicale* (*1398*)]
1401. Revue Musicale, La
    [Founded 1900; re-established by Henry Prunières, 1920; interrupted May 1940–Jan. 1946; continuing thereafter]
1402. Revue Politique et Littéraire — Revue Bleue
    [Weekly founded 1863]
    Revue Wagnérienne: Fondateur-Directeur: Edouard Dujardin
1403.   Vol. I: Feb. 1885–Jan. 1886
1404.   Vol. II: Feb. 1886–Jan. 1887
1405.   Vol. III: Feb. 1887–Jan. 1888
1406. Signale für die Musikalische Welt
    [Irregular weekly, founded 1843; published by Senff, Leipzig and Berlin]
1407. Sunday Times (London)
    [Weekly newspaper unconnected with the daily (London) *Times*; music critic: Ernest Newman]

10. GRAMOPHONE RECORDS

This list is believed to be complete as far as the works of Berlioz available by December 31, 1949 are concerned. It is not complete with respect to *duplicate recordings* of these same pieces. When several versions are mentioned below, it is in the belief that each supplies some quality of performance, completeness, or reproduction missing from its competitors, or else that one is more readily available than the rest. Some of these records have in fact been withdrawn, but given the brisk trade in second-hand discs that has sprung up in the wake of the manufacturers' capricious policies, the following are at least potentially purchasable.

BEATRICE AND BENEDICT

1408. Overture: Sir Hamilton Harty and the London Philharmonic Orchestra
    English Columbia: LX–371; U. S.: 68342–D
1409. ————: Julius Kopsch and Berlin Philharmonic Orchestra
    Polydor 27163 (identical with Decca LY 6006)
1409a. ————: Basil Cameron and Liverpool Philharmonic Orchestra
    English Columbia DX–1145
1410. ————: Transcribed for band by Franz Hennig; played by Edwin Franko Goldman and his band Victor 25757

BENVENUTO CELLINI

1411. Overture: Pierre Monteux and Paris Symphony Orchestra
    Victor: 11140–1

CORSAIR OVERTURE

1412.   Sir Hamilton Harty and London Philharmonic Orchestra
    Columbia 68287D English Columbia DX–664
1413.   Sir Thomas Beecham and Royal Philharmonic Orchestra
    Victor 11–9955
1413a.   Charles Münch and Conservatoire Orch. London T.5364

LA DAMNATION DE FAUST

1414. ———— (with recitatives and only two portions cut)
Jean Fournet and Chorale Emile Passani
Orchestre de Radio-Paris Columbia LFX 614–628

1415. ———— (without recitatives and much cut)
Piero Coppola, Concerts Pasdeloup and Chorale St. Gervais
HMV L–886 – L–895

1416. Three Orchestral Excerpts
Sir Thomas Beecham and London Philharmonic Orchestra
Columbia set X–94

1417. Vocal Excerpts: Mephisto's aria, Serenade and Song of the Flea
Martial Singher and Metropolitan Opera Orchestra cond. by Breisach
Columbia 71679D

1418. Serenade de Mephisto [wrongly labeled with words from Gounod's
Faust]
Marcel Journet and Orchestra   Victor 1123–A

1419. Merci, doux crépuscule
René Maison and Orchestra   Odéon 123501

1420. Air du Roi de Thulé
Mireille Berthon and Orchestra HMV P–806

1421. ———— Germaine Martinelli and Orchestra   Polydor 66969

1422. D'amour l'ardente flamme
Rose Bampton and RCA Victor Orchestra cond. by Wilfred Pelle-
tier   Victor 12–0015 [Marked on the label as taken from "Act IV"]

1423. ———— Yvonne Gall and Orchestra   Columbia LFX5

1424. Invocation to Nature
Georges Thill and Orchestra   Columbia L 2064

1425. ———— Georges Jouatte and Orchestra   Odéon 123783

1426. ———— Raoul Jobin and Metropolitan Opera Orchestra
In Columbia set MM 696

L'ENFANCE DU CHRIST

1427. (La Fuite en Egypt: Overture to Part II)
Francis Cébron and Orchestra   Lumen 30082

1428. Songe d'Hérode (cut)
Louis Morturier and Orchestra HMV W–1137

1429. ———— Narçon and Orchestra   Columbia RFX 8

1430. Adieu des Bergers
Abbé Hoch and Strasbourg Cathedral Choir and Orchestra
Columbia 69693–D

1431. ———— Paris Teachers' Chorus (piano accomp. only)
Columbia DF 1184

1432. Le repos de la Sainte Famille
Jean Planel and Orchestra cond. by F. Ruhlmann   Pathé X 93102

1433. Trio des jeunes Ishmaélites
Lily Laskine, Marcel Moyse, Albert Manouvrier   Decca TF 139

LES FRANCS–JUGES OVERTURE

1434. Sir Adrian Boult and BBC Symphony Orchestra   HMV DB3131–2
U. S. Victor set DM 803

FUNERAL MARCH FOR THE LAST SCENE OF HAMLET

1435.   (Arranged by Sir Hamilton Harty for Hallé Orchestra)
Columbia 68429D

HAROLD IN ITALY

1436.   Serge Koussevitsky and Boston Symphony Orchestra
Victor DM-989
1437.   Lost Love (based on Berlioz' Pilgrims Chorus [*sic*] from *Harold in Italy*) arranged by Henri René with his Orchestra and Chorus
RCA–Victor International Series 38–2010
1438.   As a curiosity: in the mid-1930's before the full work had been recorded anywhere, a Victor ten-inch record (24755) illustrating the march form played a few bars from the Pilgrims' March of this symphony, the excerpt being listed as: "Prob. abbreviated."

INVITATION TO THE [WALTZ] DANCE   Weber-Berlioz

1439.   Dr. Weissmann and Philharmonic Orchestra   Decca-Odéon 25055–B
1440.   Toscanini and the BBC Orchestra   Victor 15192

KING LEAR OVERTURE

1441.   Sir Hamilton Harty and London Symphony Orchestra
English Decca K792
1442.   Sir Adrian Boult and BBC Symphony Orchestra   HMV DB 3093–4
Also in U. S. Victor set DM 803

LA MARSEILLAISE   Orchestrated by Berlioz (cut)

1443.   Peters Rosset and Chorale Populaire de Paris   Decca G–20613A

NUITS D'ETE

1444.   1. Absence
1445.   2. Le Spectre de la Rose
Maggie Teyte and London Philharmonic Orchestra
HMV JG 177 (CTPX 11583–4)
1446.   3. Villanelle (piano accomp. only)
Ninon Vallin   Pathé PG 62

REVERIE ET CAPRICE

1447.   Joseph Szigeti and Philharmonia Orchestra cond. by Constant Lambert   Columbia LX 946

[REQUIEM] GRANDE MESSE DES MORTS (slightly cut)

1448.   Jean Fournet and Chorale Passani with Orchestra
Columbia LFX 659–669; U. S. MM 769 [Now on 2 LP records, SL 159]

ROMAN CARNIVAL OVERTURE

1449.   Gabriel Pierné and Colonne Orchestra
Columbia G 67744–5/D
1450.   Leo Blech and Berlin Philharmonic Orchestra
Victor 9207   HMV D–1365
1451.   Erich Kleiber and Berlin State Opera
Decca CA–8197

1452.   Sir Thomas Beecham and London Philharmonic Orchestra
      Columbia 68921–D
1453.   Victor de Sabata and London Symphony Orchestra
      English Decca K1552

ROMEO ET JULIETTE

1454. Romeo seul; Tristesse; Concert et Bal; Grand Fête chez Capulet
      Gabriel Pierné and Concerts Colonne
      Decca-Odéon 25029A & B; 25550A & B
1455.   Sir Hamilton Harty and London Philharmonic Orchestra
      Columbia DB 1230–31 in Columbia History of Music, vol. IV
1456. Romeo seul; Tristesse; Concert et Bal; Grand Fête chez Capulet; Scène
      d'Amour (choral introduction omitted)
      Arturo Toscanini and NBC Symphony Orchestra Victor DM–1160
1457. Queen Mab Scherzo
      Sir Hamilton Harty and Hallé Orchestra Columbia 67422D
1458. ——— Piero Coppola and Conservatoire Orchestra HMV–DB 4827
      [see also *1474*]

SYMPHONIE FANTASTIQUE

1459.   Felix Weingartner and London Symphony Orchestra
      Columbia 67174D–67179D (AX–1112 – AX–1118)
1460.   Pierre Monteux and Paris Symphony Orchestra
      Victor 11093–11098 (69247–69258)
1461.   Pierre Monteux and San Francisco Symphony Orchestra
      Victor 119027A–119032B
1462.   Artur Rodzinski and Cleveland Symphony Orchestra
      Columbia set MM–488
1463.   E. Van Beinum and Concertgebouw Orchestra of Amsterdam
      English Decca EDA–56

LES TROYENS A CARTHAGE

1464. Overture [Prelude]
      Pierre Monteux and Paris Symphony Orchestra Victor 11141B
1465. Royal Hunt and Storm
      Sir Hamilton Harty and Hallé Orchestra
      Columbia DX 291
1466. ——— Sir Thomas Beecham and London Philharmonic Orchestra
      DB–6241 in Victor set DM 1141 [see also *1474*]
1467. Inutiles regrets (cut)
      Georges Thill, Orchestra and Chorus
      Columbia 9098 M [Reissued as LFX 358]
1468. 1. Adieu fière cité
1469. 2. Chers Tyriens
      Mme. Frozier-Marrot and Orchestra (Paris)
      HMV W–1032
1470. Marche Troyenne
      Felix Weingartner and Conservatoire Orchestra
      Columbia 70089–D in set X–169
1471. ——— Sir Hamilton Harty and London Symphony Orchestra
      English Decca K792

1472. ―――― Sir Thomas Beecham and London Philharmonic Orchestra
Victor 11–9669 B in set DM–1141 HMV–DB 6238
1473. ―――― E. Van Beinum and Concertgebouw Orchestra
Decca FFRR AK 1649

1474. "A Berlioz Program" [1949]
Charles Münch and Conservatoire Orchestra
London [formerly English Decca] LLP3 (long-playing discs); com-
prises: *Romeo and Juliet,* Rêverie, Fête, Love Scene, and Scherzo;
Les Troyens, Royal Hunt and Storm

ADDENDA (December 1949)

Two important publications relating to Berlioz have just been issued as this
volume goes to press:
1. Kochnitzley, Léon, *Adolphe Sax and His Saxophone* (Art, Life, and Science in Belgium, No. 13) N. Y. (Belgian Government Information Center)
1949
2. Ganz, A. W., *Berlioz in London.* [Announced in England, without publisher's name, as "Biography and unpublished letters of the great composer,
Illustrated." The author is the son of Wilhelm Ganz, referred to in these pages.]

Acknowledgments

The long task of following Berlioz' footsteps and guessing at his mind was made possible only by the help of many persons, known and unknown, to whom collectively I here tender my thanks. At their head I would inscribe the name of the late T. S. Wotton (1862–1939), foremost Berlioz scholar of his generation,[1] whose wisdom, warnings, and encouragement sustained me in my beginnings; and whose great collection of documents — now mine by his wish — enabled me to carry on when European archives were cut off or destroyed.

In telling of my deep gratitude to Tom Wotton, I cannot help thinking regretfully of my book as it would have been had he lived to lend his hand to its improvement. Fortunately, I have received compensation in the form of advice generously given by friends in the American musical world: I owe much to conversation and correspondence with Randall Thompson, Otto Luening, William Schuman, Richard Franko Goldman, Philip Greeley Clapp, Paul H. Lang, and Roger Sessions.

Moreover, in the twenty years that my pursuit of Berlioziana has been known to my friends and colleagues, I have been repeatedly indebted to them for gifts of books, scores, autographs, and records, as well as for information leading to the apprehension and arrest of these fugitives. I take pleasure in acknowledging my obligations to my excellent friend Wendell Taylor, in the first instance; as well as to Mrs. F. E. Lowell, Mrs. James Hardy Ropes, Mrs. Haven Emerson, Mrs. Ropes Cabot, Miss Orrea Pernel, Mrs. Douglas C. Macintosh, Dr. Hildegard von Barloewen, Mrs. Gabrielle Clarke, the late Joseph L. Seligman, Mr. Richard G. Appel, Mr. Harry K. Dick, Mr. Henry Morton Robinson, Mr. Herbert Jacobson, Mr. Richard Poate Stebbins, Mr. Arnold Whitridge, Mr. Joseph Schaaf, Dr. Paul Beik, Mr. Henry Allen Moe, and Mr. Theodore Steinway.

For the use in the foregoing pages of much copyright material (indicated above in due form) I thank the authors and publishers of the books listed in the Bibliography. I need hardly add that librarians and booksellers here and abroad have again and again put their knowledge and good will at my service in making this bibliographical task manageable. The firm of Pierre Berès was particularly helpful in the person of M. Lucien Goldschmidt.

It is obvious, moreover, that an undertaking of this sort cannot be brought to completion without the loyal aid of close associates and the forbearance mingled with advice of one's own family. To my father, who began my musical education in the manner that Montaigne reports of his own infancy,

[1] "Mr. Tom Wotton, who is the greatest authority on Berlioz . . ." (*Sunday Times*, Nov. 3, 1929.) By an odd coincidence, his last letter to me, a few weeks before his death, is dated on Berlioz' birthday, December 11, 1938.

I owe whatever intuition of the art I may possess. Subsequent teaching and discourse — which includes my father's vivid memories of Paris music before the First World War — supplied me with innumerable insights and perspectives not otherwise obtainable.

I have similarly drawn on my wife's extensive knowledge of the musical repertory and on her professional experience as a performer. All the while, she and the rest of the household magnanimously endured at once the encumbrance and the preoccupation incident to the work. In the same spirit, my friend Lionel Trilling steadily gave aid and comfort over and above the practical service of reading a bulky and illegible manuscript. This, in turn, only reached publishable shape because of the intelligent efforts of (successively) the Misses Carolyn Robinson, Emiliana Pasca, Lillian Beresnack, Dora Bierer, Violet Serwin; after whose labors Mrs. Rush E. Welter and Mr. Wolf Franck went over the text most carefully and saved me from many grievous errors. I am moreover deeply indebted to Mr. Franck for many suggestions drawn from his great stock of knowledge about European culture.

Further aid was given me by the musical directors of broadcasting companies, particularly Mr. Samuel Chotzinoff at NBC and the officials of CBS, ABC, and the Canadian Broadcasting Company, who allowed me to hear or obtain transcripts of Berlioz programs. I owe similar help to Mr. Mirko Paneyko of M.P. concert installations, Erich Kleiber of the Berlin State Opera, and Mr. J. B. Comstock of The Gramophone Shop, New York. From another quarter of the globe, members of the United States Foreign Service in Vienna, Prague, and Budapest supplied me with details about the present state of archives relating to Berlioz' travels in those parts.

Even when I add that in mid-passage I was honored by the award of a Guggenheim Fellowship, I am bound to feel that I have given but a hint of the many energies that propelled the enterprise. My publishers have helped at all points, and notably Mr. Stanley Salmen, who provided friendly interest and displayed an editorial skill that I cannot overpraise. I can only hope that so much kindness may find in the work itself a justification transcending any expression of my heartfelt gratitude.

J. B.

INDICES

Index to Misconceptions about Berlioz and to Their Corrections

Index of Names and Subjects

A

Mattheson, J. I, 454 and *n.* on music for the ear I, 460
Maupassant, G. de. II, 269
Mayer, Wilhelm. I, 449*n.*
Mazzini, G. Roman Republic I, 552
McGrath, Earl. Editor of educational essays I, 423*n.*
McKinney, Laurence. On violins gregarious I, 82*n.*
Medea (Delacroix's). I, 562*n.*
Medea (Corneille's). II, 119
Méhul, E. H. Cited I, 60, 288, 371 *Stratonice* I, 50, 53 *Joseph* I, 225 *Chant National* I, 287*n. Chasse du Jeune Henri* I, 455 B.'s essay on II, 55
Meistersinger, Die. And *Benvenuto Cellini* I, 300, 304, 307–8 and *n.;* II, 68*n.* significance 307*n.*, 378–9, 427*n.* Weingartner on Prelude I, 502*n.*, 568*n.*
Mellers, W. H. Cited I, 12; II, 309 on "pure" music I, 186*n.* on B.'s art II, 224 and *n.* on B. and Wagner II, 284*n.*
Melody. Gray on B.'s I, 13; II, 286 B.'s characteristic style I, 39–41, 145, 161, 198; II, 196, 287–8 Lambert on I, 106*n.* MAIN TREATMENT I, 106–18 dramatic role I, 182; II, 188–9, 196, 288 and contrapuntal richness I, 248, 502 and *n.;* II, 20 psychological truth I, 118, 181, 182*n.*, 196, 426; II, 190, 288 and development I, 499ff. relation to form I, 501 Hadow on B.'s I, 501 Weingartner on B.'s combining I, 502*n.*, 567–8 in Bach II, 188–9, 196 in early Romantics II, 190 in Beethoven I, 40, 112; II, 35, 190 in Wagner I, 499*n.;* II, 194 in Liszt I, 499*n.;* II, 197–9 *See also:* Leitmotif *and* Thematic Index
Melville, Herman. English journey I, 514*n.* postwar isolation II, 156
Mendelssohn, Abraham. I, 208*n.*
Mendelssohn, Felix. Cited I, 97, 138, 413, 500, 520; II, 226, 285 meets B. in Rome I, 207–8 in Leipzig 432ff. B.'s opinion of I, 207–8, 479, 515, 518; II, 21*n.*, 261, 266 *Italian* symphony I, 518, *Scotch* I, 518 B. plays I, 556; II, 26*n.*, 44, 87 describes B. I, 208, 567 divergences from B. I, 209; II, 99*n.*, 226, 257 his father meets B. in Paris 208*n.* personal relations with B. I, 228, 434–5, 518, 559; II, 21*n.*, 99*n.* "symphony cantata" I, 326 and *n.;* II, 191 *Walpurgisnacht* I, 326*n.* "Hymn of Praise" 326*n. Midsummer Night's Dream* 332 B. on 479 overture 479*n.*

Athalie (March) I, 353 exchange of batons I, 374, 435 and *n.* and Wagner I, 394; II, 183, 185 Koechlin on I, 569*n.* a "modern" I, 421; II, 27, 191 death I, 515, 557; as conductor II, 57, 60, 111 *Antigone* I, 515 *Elijah* I, 515 piety II, 99*n.*, 104, 270–1
Mendelssohn, Moses. II, 271
Mendelssohn, Paul. I, 226*n.*
Mendès, C. I, 390*n.*
Menotti, Ciro. I, 201, 523
Merchant of Venice. H. Smithson in I, 94 B. borrows lines II, 117 and *n.*, 141, 220*n.* B. quotes II, 238*n.*
Méreaux, J. A. de. I, 420*n.* identified 514*n.* befriends Louis B. 514 transcribes *Infant Christ* 514*n.*
Meredith, George. Cited I, 17*n.* on brigands I, 254*n. Modern Love* I, 497*n.* religious views II, 99 on journalism II, 259*n.*
Mérimée, Prosper. Cited I, 87 *Charles IX* 104 takes ether pearls II, 120*n.*, 167*n.* tutor to Empress II, 123 on Flaubert II, 232*n.* to B. on Legion of Honor II, 247 and *n.*
Merrill, Stuart. I, 390*n.*
Metternich, Prince Klemens von. Chats with B. I, 475 and *n.*–476*n.*
Metternich, Princess Pauline. Aids Wagner II, 174
Mey, Kurt. On *Cellini* I, 307 on *Troyens* II, 149*n.*
Meyer, Leopold von. *Moroccan March* I, 446 B. orchestrates I, 446*n.* at B. concert II, 39
Meyerbeer, G. Cited I, 97; II, 151, 154 on B.'s *Eight Scenes* I, 98 imitative effects in 198 *Robert le Diable* 199 and *n.*, 214 and *n.*, 265, 406, 408 Balzac on 262 his eclecticism I, 232, 262, 295, 364, 417, 550; II, 151, 160, 228, 250 expert in public relations I, 239 master at the Opera 260, 262, 265, 267, 317, 344, 420, 550–1 and *n.;* II, 85, 126, 202 B. conducts I, 268, 546; II, 109, 113 cash intake I, 295, 407 attends works of B. I, 295*n.*, 437; II, 242
Artistic significance I, 301; II, 191, 192 *L'Africaine* (in ms.) I, 344 *Les Huguenots* I, 408; II, 38, 191 in Berlin I, 432, (resigns) 512 personal relations with B. I, 437, 548–9 and *n.*, 550–1 on Sax instruments I, 442 B. cites in *Treatise* I, 456*n.* plays piano at Bruhl I, 472 *Le Prophète* I, 548–9 and *n.*, B. reviews 551 and *n.;* II, 38, 109